Jimi Hendrix

musician

Jimi Hendrix
musician

KEITH SHADWICK

JIMI HENDRIX MUSICIAN

by Keith Shadwick

A BACKBEAT BOOK
First edition 2003
Published by Backbeat Books
600 Harrison Street,
San Francisco, CA94107, US
www.backbeatbooks.com

An imprint of The Music Player Network
United Entertainment Media Inc.

Published for Backbeat Books by Outline Press Ltd,
Unit 2a Union Court, 20-22 Union Road, London, SW4 6JP, England.
www.backbeatuk.com

ISBN 0-87930-764-1

Consultant: Joel J. Brattin
Art Director: Nigel Osborne
Editor: Tony Bacon
Design: Paul Cooper
Picture Research: Peter Symes, Andy Neill

Printed in Canada

03 04 05 06 07 5 4 3 2 1

contents

introduction

To paraphrase Newton: of necessity, all biographers stand on the shoulders of giants. No matter how much original research is done, even the most common assumptions about a subject originated somewhere other than the biographer's own experience of his subject. Sometimes it is also true that his interviewees are unwittingly relaying media memories rather than personal experience, so we have to be both vigilant and lucky to identify such things. This book is no exception.

I grew up within a family of music enthusiasts and lived in a house well stocked in the relevant records and books. My introduction to the music of Jimi Hendrix came in 1967. At the time I was a teenaged avant-garde jazz enthusiast with an interest in rock and classical music and a curiosity about music from other cultures. Our local library had an uncommonly good LP section. At the shop where I and my family bought most of our records (imports, of course) there worked a young drummer, Tim Purcell, who was usually abreast of everything out there. He'd always phone me when a new batch of ESP-Disk albums came in, or a fresh consignment of Impulse! releases – Coltrane, Shepp and so on.

One day in spring 1967 Tim showed me the cover of a factory-fresh copy of Track's *Are You Experienced*. Urging me to buy it, he said, "He's the only one in rock who's doing it." He didn't mean that literally – he meant in relation to the avant-garders with whom we were both obsessed. In those days record shops still had listening booths. He played me 'Third Stone From The Sun'. I bought the album. Soon after, I'd traced and bought the three singles Hendrix had previously issued – 'Hey Joe', 'Purple Haze' and 'The Wind Cries Mary'. My brother also became a fan.

From that time on I kept abreast of Hendrix's progress on records, eventually purchasing all the official releases (although I cheated with the Lonnie Youngblood and Curtis Knight material, borrowing the LPs from friends and returning them with a sigh of relief that I hadn't actually paid good money for them). I continued with this interest after Hendrix's death, and I picked up a good assortment from among the proliferation of bootleg vinyl in the early 1970s as well. Like every other sucker, when CDs came along I duplicated everything, often discovering like every other sucker that the CDs sounded no better, and often worse, than the vinyl originals. By the early 1990s I was keen to write a book about Hendrix's music, and in my naiveté I wrote a sample chapter in order to fish out a publishing deal. No one home, and the idea went away. I continued my career in other genres of music.

But I kept alive my interest in Jimi's music, buying any book I came

Hendrix taking part in one of his beloved jams: it's the music that counts.

across just to keep up with current thinking on the subject. I missed a lot. I wasn't an anorak. I'm still not an anorak. I can't pretend to the depth of knowledge about Hendrix arcana that the real Hendrix experts have acquired over decades. But I kept listening and kept thinking about his music. Then one day my publisher asked me if I'd like to take a rest from writing about jazz, blues and classical music and write a book about Jimi Hendrix. They didn't know. I'm sure they didn't. Of course I said yes, then told them that it was a book I'd been contemplating for a decade. So the coincidence was a happy one.

This book was conceived as a long look at Hendrix's music, his musical career and the events in his life that had a direct bearing on the type of musician he became in his short but earthshaking maturity. What surprised me when I read most books written about Hendrix was that few concentrated primarily on the music. Perhaps that was because Hendrix became such an icon, and all icons have a cultural significance that can obscure the very things that made them special to begin with. There were other things about his short life to examine, and they do seem to have been thoroughly examined. Often, when people wrote about his music away from specialist music and instrument magazines and journals, they concentrated on the song lyrics rather than the music that brought them to life. Well, that's fine, but I wanted to look closely at the music, and if that meant sacrificing some of the detail about Hendrix's life, his loves and other personal and professional issues, then there were other books that covered those things very well. I didn't need to duplicate all that.

Whether I have succeeded in writing convincingly about Hendrix's music is for the individual reader to decide, but I would have written an infinitely poorer study were it not for the generous help of a number of key people. First and foremost must come my editor, Tony Bacon, whose prescience and balance, as well as his unfailing courtesy and probity, has been a rock I have fallen back upon many times during the course of this book's creation. The people with whom I have come into contact, either for the first time or through renewing old friendships, and who have proved unusually and unfailingly generous, reliable and helpful from the word go, are of equal importance in the qualities they have lent this book, so I mention them alphabetically in order to avoid an order. Niko Bauer has been of inestimable help, not only because of his own authoritative research into the post-Army, pre-fame Hendrix career, and his generous willingness to discuss everything, from the smallest points to the larger picture, but also because his example gave me a positive thirst for solving the problems of authentication and cross-referencing that plague those early years. Johnny Black gave me great encouragement and complete freedom to use all of his previous research as I wished. Joel J. Brattin proved an astonishingly exacting and authoritative authenticator and a man who was repeatedly able to bring his analytic intelligence to bear on particular points of contention in a constructive and courteous way. Steve Rodham, the éminence grise behind *Jimpress* and all the good works associated with that fount of Hendrix knowledge, has time and again shown generosity and good humour in dealing with my not always well-timed or particularly lucid cries for assistance. Through her own book and others she suggested and sourced for me, Mary Willix helped me become familiar not only with Hendrix's early years in Seattle, but with the much wider picture of the ongoing Seattle cultural and musical story, from the early 1900s up to the present day. She also introduced me to Joel Brattin. I am grateful to her for permission to quote from her own fine book on Hendrix's Seattle years.

Next come some people who gave me tremendous help and often unsought encouragement when I was in need of it and who deserve special mention – but who through no fault of their own (usually down to time constrictions or my own juggling of research and writing timetables, and sometimes due to the very precise nature of the help they could offer) had a less pervasive personal impact on the book. They deserve no less praise. Animals expert Joe McMichael and I spent many a pleasant exchange of emails plotting and uncovering the full extent of the last Animals US tour of 1966, before the original band broke up, thus helping to chart more accurately Chas Chandler's chronology in the months of his first contact with Hendrix. Photographer Jan Persson was generous in his help and in the sharing of his knowledge of Hendrix in Denmark. Old friends Barry and Jane McCann shared their beautiful house and Barry's extensive collection with me in my hunt for first-hand Hendrix sources. Old friends abroad who were able to give me fantastic back-up and telling logistical support include Jenny Bloomfield and Mike Wollenberg. They were also able to offer me that invaluable aid to a mid-project author – continuing good humour and a sense of fun. My brother Ian Shadwick helped out with copies of hard-to-find discs and articles. Much closer to geographical home, Sara Nathan offered invaluable help in landing important texts and documents when I most needed them. I thank Kathy Etchingham for permission to quote at will from her fine autobiography. I am also happily indebted to the great Joseph Jarman for freely giving permission to reproduce his poem, *Ericka*, at the end of this introduction.

Erika

BY JOSEPH JARMAN

ERIKA
child of our uncharted microtones
thrown through the dawn
the maze of longing
     as she matures in Black America
the Panther, paying homage to the people
torn with gun. television hero
    gone to madness –
seeking the answer
      can we.........endure

MOTHER
once freaked with acid
product of the "new frontier"
becoming the maiden lonely,
Hiroshima's crime, the horror,
insane visions for her child/locked forever
in her womb,
seeking the answer
      can we.........endure

FATHER
paints his nightmare
a black sore of fear
      in technicolor
coated sorrow coated "i" forgive
a silver cup again – his youth,
the bare facts of existence –
image, the black saint whom Leroi calls
"the heaviest spirit"

ERIKA
  after this America
where humans wonder wandering – do peace movements care
her eyes, tender smile
      a flower garden,
all gentle being
    must she endure   visionless   alone –
"rise up" 'hari om' alone "rise up" 'hari om' alone "rise up" 'hari om'
     "rise up"

COPYRIGHT JOSEPH JARMAN. Reproduced by permission of the author.

At Backbeat, the telling contributions to the photographic and design content from Nigel Osborne, Paul Cooper, Peter Symes, Andy Neill and Phil Richardson were greatly appreciated, as were their sheer enthusiasm for the project and levels of input throughout its life, while Mark Brend and John Ryall were instrumental in getting to the project the essential oxygen of publicity, home and abroad. In this context I must also extend grateful thanks to Corinne Honan and my wife, Alison Cole, both of whom gave generously of their time and expertise in order to help things along. Sandra Russell I thank for her unquenchable enthusiasm and her shared love of Jimi Hendrix's music. Others within the larger music community who were of help at the right time were Ira Gitler, Dave Gelly, Caesar Glebbeek, Douglas Hinman, Karsten Laybourn, Francis Mansell, Barry McRae, Andy Neill, Jon Newey, Claus Rasmussen, Adam Sieff and Valerie Wilmer. I would also like to thank sincerely those people who graciously gave of their time to be interviewed: Kevin Ayers, Chris Barber, Alan Bates, Alan Douglas, Jon Hiseman, Roger McGuinn, Jan Persson and David Redfern. There are many people from within the music industry to whom I owe a debt of thanks. These are (alphabetically): Julie Allison at Universal (thanks for trying!); Jennifer Auh at Rhino; Marc Connor at Air; John Cronin at BMG; Florence Halfon at Warners; Emma Kelley and Wendy Day at EMI; Sharon Kelly at Sony; Neil Scaplehorn at Ace; Lee Simmonds at Sanctuary; Mike Siniscalchi at Delmark; and Pat Tynan at Koch. All of the above gave unfailing and courteous support through a long project and the book would have been infinitely poorer without their help. Pat was especially generous in landing me some key interviews which he knew were of no direct or immediate benefit to himself or the artists concerned.

No book of mine would be complete without a round of thanks to all the staff at the Mole Jazz shop in London's King's Cross for their unflappable good humour, help and advice in tracing obscure objects of the biographer's desire, from out-of-print magazines to discographies and hard-to-find records. Similarly, without the support of my immediate family – Alison, Jay and Louis – I would never have got this far.

This book is dedicated to Gary Norwell, a fine drummer who was the first person I knew to buy *Electric Ladyland*, who played on-stage with me half a world away the night Hendrix died, and who has never forgotten the music.

KEITH SHADWICK LONDON, SEPTEMBER 2003

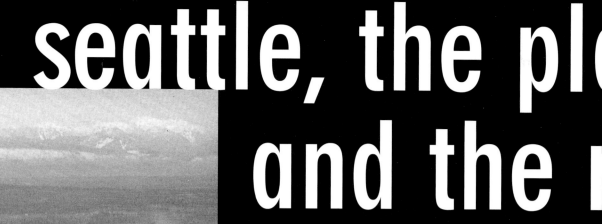

seattle, the pla
and the n

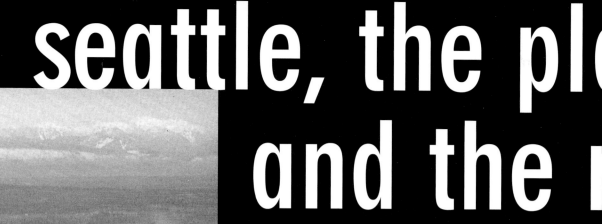

It's a simple fact, but it's centra
Jimi Hendrix was born and raise
Washington state. He wasn't bor
New Jersey, or New York City, or T
other Southern states. He was bo
family of mostly second-generat
This would have a significant be
that Jimi Hendrix became and w
because Seattle is a city with its
political and social ambience.

T he city was founded in the 18th century by fur tra
to the area. In time, Seattle became an importar
United States and Canada was settled about 100
Seven years later, some 150 miles south of the
Oregon. At that time Seattle's entire population could be ex

Washington state remained a backwater until the last de
including farming, became economically important. Alon
rivalled established trades. World War I saw the creation
beginning of plans to develop hydroelectric power through
Columbia River to the east, which in turn fed the rapid gro
exploded by the Second World War, growing from some 81,0

Washington, mountainous and naturally wooded, is bo
Oregon, the north by Canada, and to the west by the Pacific
harbour, Puget Sound, reached by the Strait of Juan de Fuca
south and Vancouver Island to the north. The city sits or
beyond the straits. Vancouver is on the same shore, son
Washington state is separated from the rest of the US: to
Midwest plains, and to the south by the largely mountainou
and northern California. Oregon's capital, Portland, is 200 c

Washington's late development and relative isolation ab

Seattle (left), 1947, looking east across the harbour towards Lake Washington.

problems that afflicted many of the older American population centres. Of course, the early traders did what all other European settlers and expansionists did, expropriating the land from the American Indian tribes in the area. Seattle is named after an early 19th century chief whose Suquamish tribe lived in and around the area now covered by the city named after him. The territory had little in common socially with the rest of the eastern seaboard and the southern states. The region was instead characterised by what many Washingtonians regard as a political radicalism that sprang from their rugged independence and a sense of idealism that grew among the urban and rural workforce.

From the beginning the predominantly Scandinavian settlers had stressed such principles as social harmony and understanding of the environment. In part this was simple common sense as they depended so much on the environment for sustenance, but it was something they brought with them from their own isolated part of the Old World.

Washingtonians have been markedly liberal during most of the state's organised existence. One of the most notable examples was Centralia, a 640-acre site developed into a town by black ex-slave George Washington. He was given his freedom by the white Virginian couple who adopted and educated him, and attempted to found a city for poor blacks in six different states

Jackson Street, the centre of Seattle's musical nightlife, in the 1940s.

before having his wishes granted in Washington. In 1852, his adopted parents bought the necessary land for him at a time when blacks were barred by state law from doing so, and in 1857, with the repeal of the repressive land-ownership laws, he began planning his utopia. By 1889 the town had a settled population of 1,000, and although the economic slump of the 1890s pushed it into crisis, Centralia survived into the 20th century.

Seattle's immigrant ethnic mix had three important streams: white; black; and Pacific Asian, from the islands and Japan as well as the mainland. Jimi's father Al Hendrix, reminiscing about his childhood and early adult life in the 1930s and '40s, specifically recalled little or no racial disharmony between blacks and whites – although there were petty incidents, like swimming-pool owners insisting on segregation. Instead, Al noted a distinct economic divide, with more racial tension and distrust between the white and Asian communities. This came to a head after the bombing of Pearl Harbor by Japan in December 1941. Al saw racial prejudice as the authorities reacted to the bombing. "Not long after … they started talking about rounding up Japanese people in the United States to send them to relocation centres. I thought it was terrible. I said, 'Damn! If Japanese people were born and raised here, hell, they should leave them alone.' … I ran around with a lot of Japanese kids … and I knew it was nothing but racism. It had to be. They didn't do it to the Germans or the Italians."[1]

The city's inhabitants were forced by Seattle's geographic isolation to develop their own nightlife, starting in the 1890s and in full flow by the time the young Hendrix was working his first gigs as a teenage novice in the late 1950s. Seattle's situation echoed those in Chicago, Kansas City and New Orleans, which all tacitly encouraged the corruption, graft, vice and gambling that were essential in creating conditions amenable to any musician's daily living in those pre-television days.

By 1910, according to Seattle historian and author Paul de Barros, the city was the centre of the largest vaudeville circuit in the US, with a network of theatres owned by Alexander Pantages.[2] Early acts brought to Seattle by Pantages included jazzmen W.C. Handy and Freddie Keppard; a little later Duke Ellington and Lester Young were regular visitors. During the Swing Era virtually every leader of note regularly brought their big-band to the city, including Gene Krupa, Benny Goodman, Woody Herman. It was this Seattle circuit that attracted Al's parents, Ross and Nora Hendrix, both of whom worked in the city's flourishing vaudeville industry, Ross as a stage-hand, Nora a dancer.

Lower even than the vaudeville venues on the social and entertainment ladder were the honky-tonks and low-life hangouts where local musicians and visiting hustlers and professionals could make a living. Jelly Roll Morton, as adept at pool-sharking, pimping, card-sharping and bent gambling as any music-making, spent time doing all these things in Seattle in 1920 – and wrote a song about it, 'Seattle Hunch'.

All this activity took place in Seattle's own "tenderloin" district – a semi-official red-light area – originally to the south of Yesler Way and later up in the International District. It was run along similar lines to the tenderloin areas of many US cities, the most famous of which in New Orleans had been shut down in 1917. Like Kansas City in the 1930s, Seattle was a "wide open" town. As historian de Barros explains, "Running a wide open town was a profitable tradition that involved everyone from the cop on the beat to the mayor and the chief of police. By the early part of the century, corruption was so embedded in local politics that candidates often ran for office on the 'wide open' platform, arguing that Seattle's vice industry generated income and a healthy economy for its more prudent citizenry."[3]

Black people had begun to arrive in Washington in significant numbers during the 1890s, and by 1910 there were 800 in Seattle, largely in the Central District. This contained Jackson Street, which emerged in the following decades as the centre for music and nightlife. Employment for

Jimi's grandparents, Ross and Nora Hendrix, worked in Seattle's flourishing vaudeville industry, Ross as a stage-hand, Nora a dancer.

musicians in the tenderloin area down by the docks had become plentiful enough for a Negro Musicians' Union to be formed in 1913, running parallel to the established Musicians' Union for whites. This was normal practise in the United States at the time, and reflected the geographical segregation of the work available to the two racial groups, north and south of Yesler Way. Seattle's two unions would not be integrated until 1956 – still a good time before some other cities, including Los Angeles. By the 1920s, a split between middle-class blacks and the inhabitants of the 'wide open' parts of town had also opened up as the town and its economy expanded and diversified.

Despite its isolated position, Seattle remained an important part of the West Coast music scene before World War II. The city was a regular stop-off for any moderately successful Los Angeles or San Francisco band as well as nationally established acts. The local fraternity yielded many jazz musicians and singers. Some never left Seattle; others became international celebrities. Vocalist Mildred Bailey, from Spokane near the Idaho border, spent years in Seattle before joining the Paul Whiteman band and finding fame. Saxophonist Floyd Turner Jr stayed within reach of the city, and was briefly a member of Duke Ellington's Orchestra in 1951, leaving once they completed their obligations on the West Coast. Tenor saxophonist Dick Wilson, who died at the age of 30 in 1941, toured and recorded with Andy Kirk's Clouds Of Joy and was described by Dizzy Gillespie as "right up there with Lester Young and Herschel Evans".[4] Both remain little known outside Seattle.

By the Depression years Jackson Street was ethnically diverse, the largest groups being Jews and Italians, with blacks, Japanese and Chinese following on. There was also a sizeable population from the various Pacific and South East Asian islands, and as a consequence there were a number of Asian dance bands and small combos. Alto saxophonist Marshall Royal recalled to de Barros, "They were a different type of people up in Seattle. You had a lot of fun. They were nice, they were cordial. I'm not just speaking of black people. I'm talking about the Chinese guys that owned the cab companies and things. They were our buddies."[5] Some of the venues weren't so congenial. The Trianon Ballroom had a strict segregation policy that applied to bands and dancers alike. The only black bands that played there were from out of town, like Seattle regulars Lionel Hampton & His Orchestra. Segregation in Seattle was never backed by any legislation, but was routinely enforced. "Despite numerous obstacles to the realisation of their full capacities as useful human beings here," said historian Esther Mumford, "Seattle and Washington state offered considerable improvements over the places most blacks had left."[6]

Segregation plagued labour relations through the war years and the later 1940s when the black population trebled and finally became larger than the Japanese community. Boeing retained a whites-only hiring policy, blaming the local unions for not casting the net more widely. The Housing Authority in Seattle ran 'separate but parallel' housing for whites and other ethnic groups. Pressures of war production and the fight for equal rights and opportunities finally led Boeing to change its recruitment policy, while other restrictive customs throughout Seattle were slowly relaxed. De Barros records that by summer 1944 Boeing had 1,600 black workers.[7]

After America's entry into World War II there was an influx of workers needed by heavy industries earmarked for essential war production. A similar wave of young musicians arrived with the touring bands, and some of them stayed and put down roots. Pianist Jimmy Rowles was one of these. The segregated musicians' unions in Seattle were consequently pressured by whites as well as blacks to integrate, although some white musicians were happy with the existing guarantee of the best local work. By 1956 the momentum proved irresistible and a major stumbling block to freedom of employment was removed when the two unions merged. By then, Jackson Street and its music had changed, and would never revert to the old days.

The shift in popular taste – detailed in chapter 3 – that occurred when the troops came home after the war was felt as much in Seattle as elsewhere. Small groups playing shuffles and R&B attracted dancers and clubgoers; singers dominated the radio and the big theatres. Seattle also had its version of bebop in the after-hours hang-outs. Trumpeter Leon Vaughn remembered 34 clubs of all kinds on Jackson Street's main beat in 1948.[8] The venues ranged from high-class establishments to clip joints and dives. White and black musicians played music that was stylistically closer than in many other urban centres. Jackson Street historian Paul De Barros observed: "Barriers

between black and white traditions were never as clear-cut as they were in other western cities, such as Los Angeles, where a 'cool' white school evolved in contradistinction to the 'hard bop' played by blacks. In Seattle, the music of both blacks and whites tended to merge toward an agreeable middle."[9] This sort of amalgam was underlined from around 1946 by visits from Norman Granz's famous Jazz At The Philharmonic tours, which from the start were integrated both musically and racially as a point of policy.

Into the melting pot of Seattle came younger players who would eventually use this unusual blend to their advantage, the most famous before Jimi Hendrix being Quincy Jones and Ray Charles. Both men came to Seattle from elsewhere – Jones from Chicago at the age of ten, Charles from Tampa, Florida, as an adult – and both went through the Seattle hothouse. Jones finally left with Lionel Hampton; Charles went out on his own. Beginning as keen young beboppers, they developed and maintained a wide open attitude to music-making; before the 1950s were out, both would cross stylistic barriers that many had thought uncrossable.

At the R&B and nightclub end of Jackson Street there were major shifts of emphasis as the 1950s began. In the decade after the war ended in 1945 there was a continued migration of poorer black families and individuals from the Southern and Southwestern states. These newcomers made ripples, good and bad, in the established black community. Their musical tastes prompted

Teenagers soon picked up cheap guitars, forming their own groups and looking for places to play.

a change of direction for some musicians, who were quite happy to deliver a new, simpler type of music: a shuffle, maybe, or some country-style blues. Some of the new arrivals felt distinctly unwelcome; others from the older community were resentful of the newcomers with their Southern habits and lack of sophistication.

Musician Buddy Catlett recalled, "You don't want to see so-called ignorant people coming [into] your domain, because that means the whites you have to deal with are going to look at you in the same manner. When you get halfway cool, you don't want nobody to come around and rock the boat."[10] On the other hand, Catlett agreed, this influx of new ideas and attitudes meant a virtual transfusion of musical culture that enlivened the Seattle scene. He felt that it was "the people in the fields" that created the culture, but that more established blacks resented the "harshness" of the blues and saw it is an intrusion on their values. Catlett saw the local US military base, Fort Lewis, with its requirement for entertainment, as the main catalyst for the development of local music.[11]

During the early 1950s, music in Seattle began to diversify away from Jackson Street. Washington state had begun to liberalise its liquor-consumption laws in the late 1940s, while the city police put pressure on after-hours clubs in an effort to close them down. It was simple economics: legitimate liquor was just as profitable as the illicit variety, and the Seattle establishment had no intention of allowing the fast-runners to make huge profits under their noses.

The nightclub and lounge scene began to clean up and move to other areas, notably the Italian district and Downtown. Bands playing the newly dominant R&B styles were taking regular spots and the audience began its slow metamorphosis from purely black to white teenage middle-class kids looking for kicks. Full-fledged rock'n'roll was just around the corner. Teenagers would soon be picking up cheap guitars and learning riffs from records, forming their own groups, and looking for places to play. One of them would be the Seattle-born son of Al Hendrix.

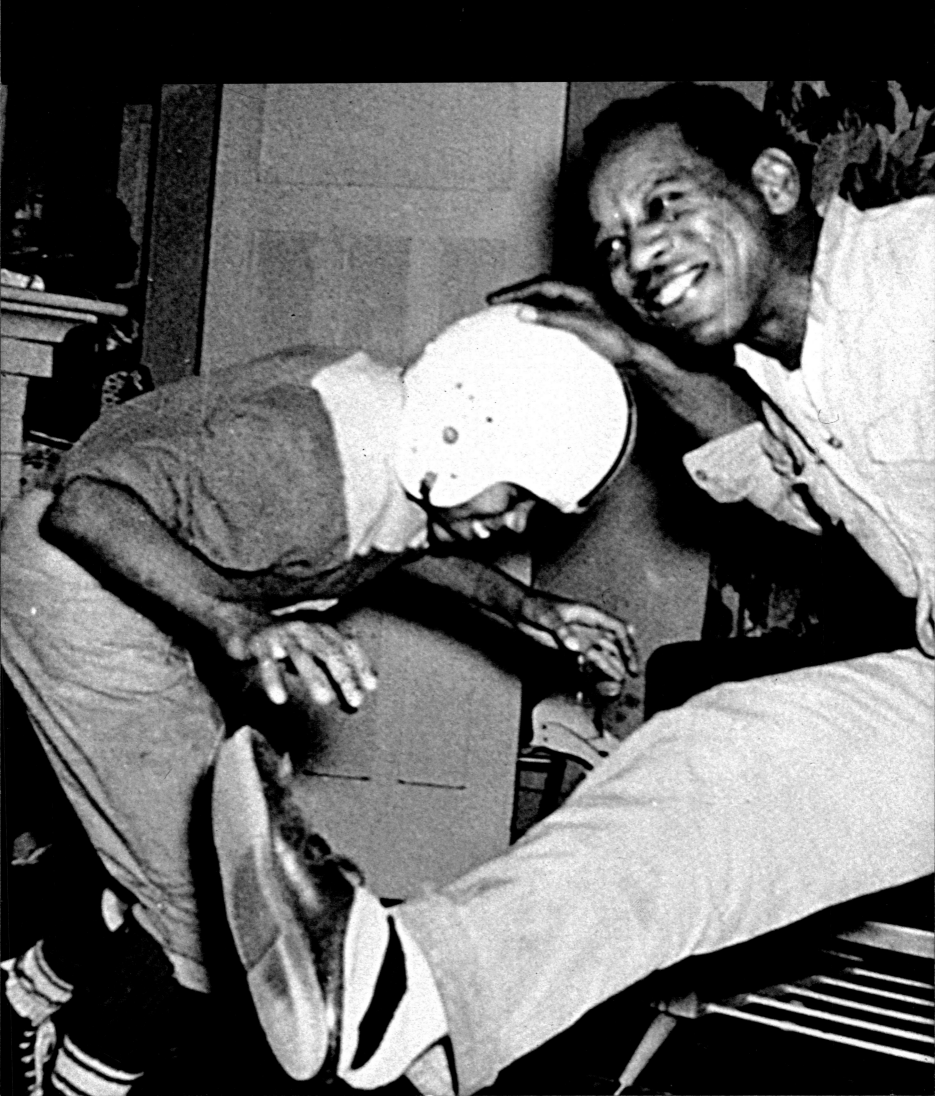

a seattle boy

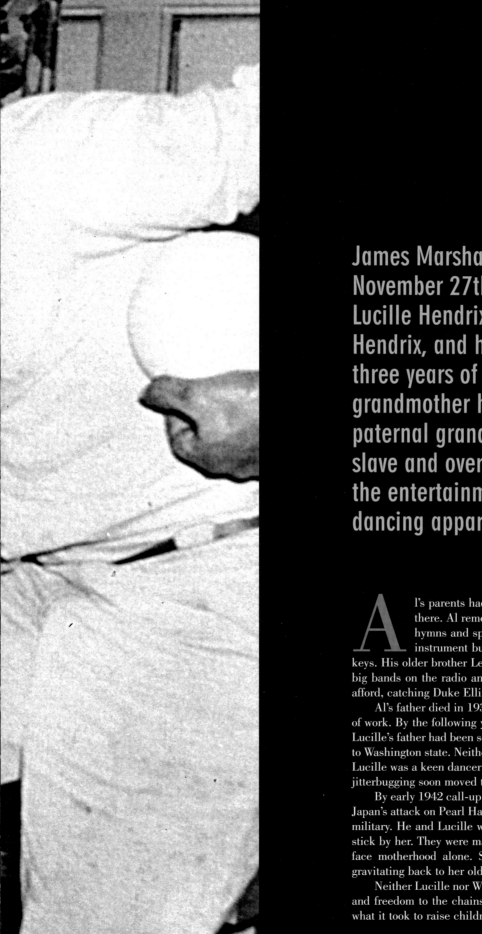

James Marshall (Jimi) Hendrix was born in S[...] November 27th 1942, the first child born to A[...] Lucille Hendrix. At first Lucille called him Joh[...] Hendrix, and he was known by that name for [...] three years of his life. Johnny's paternal grea[...] grandmother had been a full-blood Cherokee[...] paternal grandfather was born from the unio[...] slave and overseer. The family had some expe[...] the entertainment business, and Al's talent f[...] dancing apparently came from his mother.

A l's parents had settled in Vancouver, where there was regular work, an[...] there. Al remembers music in the house "all the time"[1] when he was a [...] hymns and spirituals sung by the family or music heard on the radio. [...] instrument but took enough basic music lessons to be able to read si[...] keys. His older brother Leon, who died young with peritonitis, played violin and p[...] big bands on the radio and attended as many dances and concerts in his teenage[...] afford, catching Duke Ellington's band at Vancouver's Arena in 1936.

Al's father died in 1934 and hard times followed before 21-year-old Al moved [...] of work. By the following year he'd met Lucille Jeter, then 17 years old. The Jeters[...] Lucille's father had been schooled in Boston during a colourful life that traversed th[...] to Washington state. Neither he nor his wife Clarice were noted for musical abilities[...] Lucille was a keen dancer and music fan. That was the main reason she hit it off wi[...] jitterbugging soon moved to other shared passions.

By early 1942 call-up papers were arriving at millions of homes across the Unit[...] Japan's attack on Pearl Harbor, and Al was waiting for his posting thousands of mile[...] military. He and Lucille were especially worried, for Lucille was pregnant and Al [...] stick by her. They were married just three days before Al was drafted. Lucille, stil[...] face motherhood alone. She was definitely not the homebuilding type, soon a[...] gravitating back to her old friends and taking lovers, principal among them John W[...]

Neither Lucille nor Williams showed any interest in putting down roots. They p[...] and freedom to the chains of work, pay and respectability. Young and wild, Lucil[...] what it took to raise children and had little inclination to find out. Her child was o[...]

Hendrix (left) at age 13 with his father Al in Seattle, 1956. At the time he was known as Jimmy.

Members of Jimmy Hendrix's extended family pictured in Seattle during the summer of 1943. The woman on the right holding six-month-old Jimmy is his maternal grandmother, Clarice Jeter.

of her mother, or with her sister Dolores, or with the Gautier family in whose house Lucille's mother occasionally worked as a cleaner. This temporary arrangement was too fragile to last, and through contacts at Mrs Jeter's Pentecostal church a friend, Mrs Walls, took in Johnny. When Walls died soon after, her sister – a Mrs Champ from Berkeley, California – came and took Johnny back to her home. He stayed in Berkeley for the duration of the war.

It was Al who pulled it all back together on his return from the services in September 1945. After a brief stop in Vancouver to see his mother, he travelled to Berkeley and collected the boy from Mrs Champ. "It was a strange union," Al wrote later. "Johnny didn't seem scared or anything. He was just bashful, and I felt the same way. I knew I was going to feel that way the first time I saw my son, especially seeing him so big. A new warm baby would have been different. Here he was, three years old, and he was able to look and judge for himself."[2] Soon after arriving in Seattle, Al had the child's name legally changed to James Marshall Hendrix, and most people now called him Jimmy (his dad also nicknamed him Buster). Al and Lucille were quickly

reconciled and they made a stab at family life, moving into a one-bedroom unit in an area known as Rainier Vista, a housing project in Seattle's Rainier Valley. For a time they shared something approaching normal family life.

Although Al and Lucille's marriage lasted barely four more years, two more sons were delivered: Leon in 1948, and Joseph ("Joey") the following year. Lucille flew the coop for good that same summer. According to Al in his autobiography, neither Leon nor Joey were his. Even so, he sued for divorce and went for the custody of all three. With Lucille uninterested in such matters, custody was granted to him under the settlement in late 1951.

Life proved tough for Al and the boys. Joey was fostered out while still an infant, and Leon eventually shared the same fate. Only Jimmy stayed with Al all the way through. Two girls, Cathleen and Pam, and a further boy, Alfred, were born to Lucille – all to different fathers – after the marriage broke down. All were put up for adoption. Jimmy and Leon continued to see their mother from time to time, but she faded from their day-to-day lives as she pursued her own wayward interests. According to Al, she spent what would be her

"Jimmy would do his schoolwork, but I didn't bother him too much about it. Jimmy was just an average student."

Al Hendrix, father of Jimi (known then as Jimmy)

final years mostly on liquor and lowlife men. It is not difficult to describe Jimmy's early years as hard.

The young Jimmy started at Seattle's Rainier Vista School in September 1948,. Throughout most of his childhood, he often spent part of the summer holidays in Vancouver with Al's brother Frank and his wife Pearl and, later, Al's sister Pat Hendrix. He even attended primary school in Vancouver for two months in the autumn of 1949, and then rejoined Rainier Vista School in early 1950, beginning a bewildering sequence of school swapping that would see him at three elementary schools (some of them twice) before eventually moving up to Junior High in September 1955. His last primary years – between April 1953 and June 1955 – were at Leschi Elementary School. The adolescent Jimmy was an unremarkable but reasonably diligent student, occasionally playing truant and generally showing a moderate interest in the standard curriculum. "It wasn't hard to get Jimmy to do his homework," remembered Al later. "I'd just notice Jimmy in the kitchen or dining room doing his schoolwork, but I didn't bother him too much about it. Jimmy was just an average student."[3]

His colleagues at Leschi remember Jimmy as shy but good-humoured, and easy-going with his friends. Terry Johnson was at Leschi and later went on with Jimmy to Garfield High and the Boy Scouts. Johnson spoke to author Mary Willix for her book Voices From Home. "Few people really knew [Jimmy]," Johnson told Willix. "He had a great sense of humour, was very sensitive, and very, very smart and streetwise. But he did not have a good early background in relating to people."[4]

Like many small children, Jimmy was drawn to art as a primary medium for expression. He also showed a marked propensity for imaginative writing. He said much later: "At school I used to write poetry a lot. Then I was really happy… . My poems were mostly about flowers and nature and people wearing robes … and then I used to paint a picture of, say, a really pretty mountain, then write about four lines of poetry about it."[5] He told another 1960s interviewer: "I've always loved painting. In fact it was my first love when I was a child. It was only when I got older that I took up music."[6]

His close interest in art during elementary (primary) school years suggests that his imagination was awakened early, and he turned to the nearest available medium: the school's art

Jimmy Hendrix at age three, Seattle, January 1946.

supplies. In this he was not unusual. Much more unusual was that he sustained this childhood fascination with his internal imaginative world into adulthood.

Jimmy's interest in art was no flash in the pan. All his close school friends remember him drawing regularly, and his family still has a large collection of early sketches. He took art at his last school, Garfield High, and also did more freely interpretative drawings and illustrations at home. His school friend Pernell Alexander, whom he met in 1952, told Mary Willix: "I lived with my grandmother across the street from the school. … She always encouraged us. She used to keep Jimmy Hendrix's drawings and Jimmy Williams's little stories. Jimmy Hendrix loved football, and he would draw football pictures."[7]

A gift from Hendrix's grandmother also provided a strong link with his adult life. "When I was small," Hendrix said later, "my grandmother, she's Cherokee, gave me a little Mexican jacket with tassels. It was real good and I wore it to school every day, in spite of what people might have thought. Just because I liked it. I used to spend vacations on her reservation in Vancouver, and kids at school would laugh when I wore shawls and poncho things she made."[8]

Hendrix claimed a fascination with music from an early age, saying once that the first instrument he liked was the harp. "I'd be about four, I suppose. Next it was violins. I always dug string instruments and pianos."[9] Like many young children he probably became fascinated simply with the sounds that instruments made. But at the time music was only part of a larger batch of interests, all of which he followed with enthusiasm.

He loved animals and had a passion for adventure and science fiction yarns – in books, on the radio, in films. Jimmy's dad enjoyed reading "those Amazing Stories-type comics with the rocket ships and people zapping each other with ray guns".[10] His son read them after him, but was especially taken with Batman and Superman comics. He followed Prince Valiant's adventures in his dad's newspaper and tried not to miss Flash Gordon at the Florence or Capitol theatres. On the radio it was more traditional fare: The Shadow, Dick Tracy and Gunsmoke. He would carry many of these early enthusiasms with him into adult life where they would reappear in his music, often in a light-hearted way.

According to Al Hendrix, Jimmy attended the Church of God Christ for a while, and at some stage he found an interest in church music – he sang briefly in a church group – and this too stayed with him into later life. (Al could not, however, recall his son singing there. "I don't know how Jimmy did in music at school, either," he wrote later, "but I know he didn't have a voice. He probably couldn't sing the scales."[11])

Freddie Mae Gautier was a daughter in the family who had looked after Jimmy for a while when he was a small baby. She recalled to Mary Willix later conversations with him about religion and the larger questions in life, as well as religious music. "I remember when Jimmy was little, he would sit by himself like he was meditating," Gautier said. "He talked about spirituals and the gospels – the depth of them – and the singing, and how much it meant. Sometimes he'd just sneak into churches. He said, 'I just go in and sit and listen to the choir and get an inspiration, and then I go on.'"[12]

As he reached early adolescence Jimmy became attracted more seriously to the music he heard around him in Seattle. During 1953 and '54 the family was a little more stable financially, with Al in regular employment and the three of them settled in a two-bedroom house on 26th Avenue. Nobody in the family owned an instrument, but Al did have a few singles – mostly blues and big-band jazz – that became familiar through repeated plays. Jimmy's friend from elementary (primary) school, Jimmy Williams, remembers that Hendrix "liked the old ballads, he liked blues and jazz; he liked ol' Muddy Waters, Louisiana-style music. He was really into that. I think mainly because Al, his father, had records that Jimmy probably heard a lot in those days. … Jimmy and I basically liked the same kinds of ballads. I mean, we're talking about the middle 1950s, right? Singers who were big in those days were people like Dean Martin, Perry Como, Nat King Cole, Sammy Davis Jr, and Frank Sinatra, of course."[13] These sessions with his friend helped Jimmy develop the habit of close listening. This is a timeless trend: children who may have had only a casual interest in music suddenly become obsessed with it as adolescence dawns and hormones kick in.

There were no instruments in the house worth playing, although Jimmy fooled around for a while on an old ukulele that Al fished out of the loft. His father also claimed in his later book to have made Jimmy a primitive guitar-like instrument at one point. Like most boys, Jimmy spent much of his spare time away from the family home, running with friends and exploring the neighbourhood's potential. Life was still harsh. Al was out working or relaxing with his friends a lot, and with little or no money to spare, Jimmy found that hanging out was often more interesting and less stressful than mooching indoors. As well as spending time with his school friends or at their houses, he would still occasionally go to stay with relatives to relieve the pressures on his father.

It was during one of these breaks, according to Al, that Hendrix discovered the music that would trigger his own enduring musical passion. Jimmy spent some time with Al's brother Frank and his wife Pearl and son Bobby in 1957, when he was 14 years old – a common age for boys to develop a taste for music. "They had a record player," said Al, "and Bobby remembers that that's when Jimmy became really interested in music."[14] His particular enthusiasms at the time were Elvis Presley ('Hound Dog' had been released in autumn 1956) and Little Richard.

When Elvis came to Seattle for a concert in September 1957, Al allowed Jimmy to attend. Jimmy drew a picture of Elvis in action, dated November 3rd: it shows Elvis strumming an acoustic guitar, with a plethora of his biggest hits named in the space around him. The early Elvis single sides include 'Hound Dog', 'Love Me Tender', 'Playing For Keeps', 'Don't Be Cruel', 'Too Much', 'Blue Suede Shoes', 'I Want You, I Need You, I Love You' and 'My

"I used to spend vacations on my Cherokee grandmother's reservation in Vancouver, and kids at school would laugh when I wore shawls and poncho things she made."

Jimi Hendrix

Baby Left Me'. Other songs written into the drawing by Jimmy include Little Richard's 'Rip It Up' and Gene Vincent's 'Be-Bop-A-Lula'.

Radio was another important source of the fresh sounds sweeping America at the time. According to author Mary Willix, Hendrix and his friends listened to a lot of rhythm and blues (R&B) on the radio. "The Seattle giant of R&B was Bob Summerrise, a popular disc jockey, who ran a record store called Summerrise Of Seattle that specialised in R&B. When Hendrix was in high school, Summerrise broadcast a rhythm and blues program from 9:00 to 12:00 every night on KQDE."[15]

Stimulated by the music he heard around him, Jimmy took the next logical step: he wanted to reproduce such sounds himself. Like many boys before and after, he began by fantasising. His father told the story many times of how he came back to their temporary lodgings at a boarding house on 29th Avenue to find Jimmy sitting on the bed strumming away at their domestic broom. Al recounted the tale in his book. "I'd told him to sweep up the room. When I came back he'd cleaned up, but at the foot of the bed was a little pile of broken straws. … Jimmy said, 'Oh, I did clean, and then I was sitting there making believe the broom was a guitar.'"[16] Jimmy's adolescent fantasising about his place in music must have been strong, perhaps at first even stronger than his desire to make music, for he was content to imagine himself as a player without ever producing a sound. However, he had an inner drive – and one that would soon manifest itself on real instruments.

Hendrix claimed later, in a 1967 interview, that his first experiences playing music were not with the guitar at all. "As a very young boy," he said, "I started my musical career playing drums and bass around Seattle, but when I was 15 I decided that the guitar was the instrument for me. I taught myself to play."[17] A couple of years later he said that after being attracted to violins and pianos for a while he "started digging guitars – it was the instrument that always seemed to be around. Everybody's house you went into seemed to have a guitar lying about. I was about 14 or 16 when I started playing guitar".[18]

There are no stories of a 15-year-old Jimmy playing drums or bass professionally around Seattle, but Charles Woodbury, pianist and vocalist with The Rocking Kings, a Seattle group in which Jimmy played, remembers him turning up at his first practice with the group and playing

"One day Jimmy said a neighbour wanted to sell him his guitar for $5, and he'd like to get it. And that was the first guitar he ever had."

Al Hendrix, Jimi's father

"When I was 15 I decided that the guitar was the instrument for me. I taught myself to play."

Jimi Hendrix

a bass guitar borrowed from a cousin. However, Woodbury remembers equally well that Jimmy was completely taken up by his passion for the guitar.

Hendrix was a musical adept who would quickly master the basics of any instrument and make a presentable sound on it. It is possible that he played different instruments borrowed from his Seattle school friends who were putting together amateur groups but always returned to the guitar because he identified most passionately with that instrument. His recollection of playing instruments lying around in other people's houses was confirmed by Pernell Alexander during an interview with Mary Willix. "The first guitar we played belonged to a guy named Robert McLamore – they call him Snake. His mother was a preacher. He was a hell of a dresser and a dancer. He had a guitar that he didn't play, so we practiced on it."[19]

Hendrix very quickly developed practical routes to playing the guitar. According to Al, he and Jimmy occasionally hung out with their landlady's adult son James who would play acoustic guitar on the back porch, accompanying himself as he sang old blues numbers. "One day," Al said, "Jimmy said to me, 'James wants to sell his guitar to me for $5, and I'd like to get it.'" Al said he gave his son the money. "And that was the first guitar he ever had."[20] Other versions of this story – including those told by Jimmy himself – mention that the landlady's son was a gambling crony of Al's. Hendrix said many years later: "I learned to play on a guitar that belonged to one of my father's friends who came to play cards. While the two men played, I would creep out onto the porch with the friend's guitar and see what I could get out of it. I didn't know that I would have to put the strings round the other way [because I was left-handed]. I can remember thinking to myself, 'There's something wrong here.'"[21]

Family friends have said that Al was pressured by other relatives before he would buy the guitar for his son. With the simplicity of a child's recollection, Hendrix said later: "One night, my dad's friend was stoned and he sold me the guitar for $5. I changed the strings around but it was way out of tune when I finished. ... After that I got tired of the guitar and put it aside. But when I heard Chuck Berry, it revived my interest. I learned all the chords I could."[22] Chuck Berry's songs formed the core repertoire for all the bands that Jimmy played with in Seattle, so the story has a ring of truth to it.

Young Jimmy – 15 years old by his own later reckoning – had his first acoustic guitar early in 1958, just months after the most traumatic incident of a troubled young life. In February 1958 his mother Lucille died, her body succumbing to the years of abuse she'd subjected it to. From all accounts Jimmy was deeply upset by this loss, though Lucille had been missing from his everyday life for some years. Even taciturn Al noticed his son's grief. "I told Jimmy about it. Oh, he felt sorrow over his mother's death, and he cried. I know her death affected him deeply, but I don't know what went on in his mind."[23] Neither husband nor son went to the funeral – Al from choice, Jimmy through practical circumstance. The boy had grown used to a pattern of loss and separation, but this was permanent. He was at a particularly vulnerable age emotionally and, with his father simply not equipped to assuage his son's grief, he had to fall back on his own resources.

From that point on Hendrix focused on learning the guitar. Gradually over the next three years he would translate all the sounds he'd heard in the air around him for the past decade into a competent guitar technique. But what were those sounds that swirled through post-war 1950s Seattle?

Jimmy with his father, Al Hendrix, snapped at home some time during the first few months of 1956.

music in the air

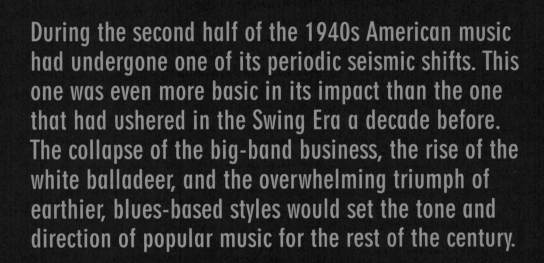

During the second half of the 1940s American music had undergone one of its periodic seismic shifts. This one was even more basic in its impact than the one that had ushered in the Swing Era a decade before. The collapse of the big-band business, the rise of the white balladeer, and the overwhelming triumph of earthier, blues-based styles would set the tone and direction of popular music for the rest of the century.

The arrival of Count Basie's band in New York and the release of their first commercial recordings in 1937 ushered in the simple, exciting Midwest riff style that had been gathering shape for nearly half a decade. Basie's band was seen then as a new extension of the Swing craze, but in retrospect what Basie and his band had developed was the first generation of a hybrid that eventually, via the likes of Fats Waller and Louis Jordan, would plug straight into post-war blues, R&B and rock'n'roll. Just a couple of years later the young pioneer electric guitarist Charlie Christian would emerge from similar roots, more or less fully grown musically.

While the Swing Era juggernaut was in place and proving immensely profitable worldwide, the musicians in the fledgling new groups played a secondary commercial and stylistic role. Late entries into the Swing Era like Glenn Miller, Harry James and Stan Kenton's bands notched up some of the most spectacular commercial successes of the period. The seeds of its dissolution were sewn when the United States entered World War II. The war didn't finish the Swing Era by itself – there are always a number of contributing factors to any great change in public taste and mood – but the war speeded up these changes.

As 1942 advanced, normal civilian existence became progressively more disrupted and the big-bands found it more difficult to sustain profitability. The costs involved in taking a 19-man big-band on the road full-time were substantial and continued to spiral as the war took hold. There was also a second set of major economic shockwaves. Military priority on all supplies of oil and petroleum made it extremely difficult to keep a band afloat with enough fuel to keep it on the one-nighter circuit. Shellac being a petroleum derivative, there was also a cut-back on its commercial use that limited the number of record releases. The only exception were the non-profit 'V-Discs' that were specifically recorded for the troops at the front.

Bands who lost income from live work were then hit in the summer of '42 by a Musicians' Union recording ban, perhaps the worst-timed event in the American union's history. For those artists and

T-Bone Walker (left), an early prototype for the electric guitarist as showman.

their sidemen signed to the largest record companies, Columbia and RCA Victor – in other words most of the biggest artists and bands – this ban lasted through to December 1944. Other companies, including Decca, had settled by the summer of 1943. A major source of income was taken away from sidemen and bandleaders. On top of this, there was a continual drain on personnel as musicians were drafted into the armed services. It was without doubt a harsh economic environment in which to sustain a living in the music business. Even radio, until then a big-band supporter, veered toward all-round entertainers and romantic balladeers such as Bing Crosby, Frank Sinatra, Doris Day and Perry Como.

Many bandleaders combined patriotism with economic good sense by enlisting their entire band in the service of the US military. Benny Goodman signed up in 1942. Glenn Miller ran his Army Air Force Band in the European theatre of war from 1942 until his death two years later, while Artie Shaw and his band had a torrid time of it in the Pacific war zone during the same period. Others toughed it out by diverse means: Duke Ellington subsidised his band through income from publishing royalties on his songs.

By 1945, star vocalists were undermining the popularity of the big-

Bandleader Lionel Hampton (centre), striking out a beat where jazz met showmanship.

Wynonie Harris, Willis Jackson, Al Sears and many others. The most important and influential of the converts was vibraphonist-drummer-bandleader Lionel Hampton, a Chicagoan who had come to international prominence as a member of Benny Goodman's Quartet.

During the late 1930s, Hampton had led groundbreaking recordings of all-star jump-style small groups that were full of a new drive and energy. In 1940 he formed a big-band that would change the course of popular music. From the start he decided to play music that expressed his personality – and he had definite ideas about what that music was and what that personality was. For one thing, he was in entire agreement with Goodman's old drummer, Gene Krupa, that showmanship was central to what you put over to the audience.

Hampton wanted a rock-solid rhythmic base. "I had Shadow Wilson on drums," Hampton wrote later in his autobiography. "I had trouble with Shadow from time to time. I liked my drummers to play backbeat, and that was not how Shadow wanted to play, and he didn't. I almost fired him, but the other guys liked him so much that I ended up keeping him on."[1] Hampton's insistence on a backbeat – that is, a heavy, regular accent on the second and fourth beat of each bar – would be central to the music he

bands they adorned. Originally hired to decorate the front of the stage and present some vocal relief for the crowd of dancers milling on front of the bandstand, they gradually metamorphosed into the main event. If any one vocalist encapsulated this change, it was Frank Sinatra. He emerged into international stardom while part of Tommy Dorsey's troupe of singers, just as Bing Crosby had emerged from Paul Whiteman's ranks a decade earlier. By the time he went solo in 1942, Sinatra's style of high romance and sentiment was sending whole audiences into the type of hysteria that comes along perhaps once in a decade – the next visitation would be Elvis in 1956, the one after that The Beatles in '64. Sinatra, with his own radio show and live appearances, soon personified the shift toward romance and reflection in wartime popular music, especially among white American audiences. There was also a handful of stars who would successfully bridge the gap between ballad and rhythm, often combining the best of both. Out of this middle ground emerged such major stars as Nat King Cole, Billy Eckstine and Dinah Washington.

Dance-oriented audiences were excited by new types of music. Jump-jazz was given clear popular shape by a string of hits from Louis Jordan and his pioneering shuffle-beat small-band sides for the US Decca label, including 'Caldonia ', 'Five Guys Named Moe', 'Saturday Night Fish Fry' and 'Let The Good Times Roll'. This new hybrid may have taken a fair chunk of the old Kansas City swing-shuffle-blues formula, but it added city humour and an edge that reflected the new energy and drive of 1940s urban youth culture.

As the decade went by, converts from previous eras took to this new musical strand alongside such new stars as Amos Milburn, Joe Lutcher,

fashioned in the crucial five years that followed. So would showmanship. "I'll take the credit for showmanship," he wrote, going on to detail some of the saxophonists who worked with him. "We had the crowds lined up to see us everywhere. ... I had Earl Bostic with me by that time, and Arnett Cobb. Arnett was a real showman. He and Johnny Griffin came up with a routine where they would throw their coats down when they really started into it. I encouraged this kind of showmanship. ... The audiences wanted good music, but they also wanted a show. I gave it to them."[2]

Hampton's cornerstone backbeat gave his band an incredible rhythmic drive – at times he would even use two drummers to generate lift-off. This helped shift the emphasis of R&B away from the shuffle of Louis Jordan and toward the rocking beat that would finally be called rock'n'roll. Hampton was well aware of the importance of what he was doing. "I tried a new direction in the middle 1940s," he said. "In January 1946 I recorded a rock'n'roll album for Decca called *Rock And Roll Rhythm*. But they never released it; they said it was too 'cacophonous'. I was ahead of my time on that. Rock'n'roll wouldn't be big for another ten years. In the 1940s it was still a black thing, which is why I was into it. Later on, Elvis Presley got all his stuff from Bo Diddley. I stayed in the black groove. You'd know my band was black just from listening to it. The crossover to the white audience hadn't happened yet. That came later."[3]

Of course, Hampton places himself centrally in this explosion of vitality and rhythmic excitement, and no doubt he was. But even he had to concede to Louis Jordan when it came to showmanship and hit-parade success. Arkansas-born Jordan came through Chick Webb's famous Savoy Ballroom big-band, playing third alto saxophone and doing an occasional singing routine. Frustrated at the lack of opportunities to shine, he went out on his

"During World War II many bandleaders combined patriotism with economic good sense and enlisted their entire band in the service of the US military."

own, forming his Tympany Five (never a five-piece, by the way) and getting a deal with the US Decca company in December 1938.

Jordan's recordings came out on Decca's Race Series, later retitled the Decca Sepia Series. After a slow start finding his distinctive style, Jordan began to have hits in 1941, starting with 'I'm Gonna Move To The Outskirts Of Town'. Three years later he was able to move to Decca's Pop Series label (selling for 75 cents instead of 35) and made a big-selling duet with Bing Crosby. Presaging post-1960s rock marketing, Jordan and his band evolved a technique for ensuring their records were hits. "I guess we were on top of the *Billboard* [charts] more than any other attraction over an eight-year period," recalled Jordan's manager Berle Adams. They all looked constantly for new material. "Much of it came from unknown writers. We favoured good lyrics, topical and meaningful, and we got them from both black and white writers. When we found something we liked, an arrangement would be made up and we'd play it on the one-nighters. The songs that the public asked for again and again were the songs we recorded. When we walked into a studio … we knew that the four songs would be hits – we had pre-tested the market. And everything we released was a smash because the public had already determined that they liked the song."[4]

Jordan remained a smash live and on record deep into the 1950s, becoming the single most dominant influence on the emerging R&B and rock'n'roll scene. His shadow hangs long over Bill Haley, for example, and not just in terms of the music. Haley first had the idea of mixing R&B and hillbilly styles when listening to Jordan's records in the late 1940s. Haley was a showman, as much in his antics on-stage as the way he dressed himself and his band. Jordan, who came to fame in the days of Cab Calloway and the zoot suit, was the most flamboyant showman of his day, even outshining Lionel Hampton's riotous stage act.

At the heart of Louis Jordan's style was the shuffle, a syncopated, railway train-like beat. As he explained to Leonard Feather, "We emphasised the beat mostly through a shuffle rhythm. The only thing that really changed was the intensity of the beat, particularly in the drums. Later they brought the bass up, and then the guitar."[5] Milt Gabler, the long-term label boss who produced most of Jordan's Decca successes, was also closely involved in launching Haley, and later readily admitted to deliberately modelling Haley's music on Jordan's. Much later, Gabler talked to writer Arnold Shaw about the rockabilly twist they'd given the Jordan-derived music. "All the tricks I used with Louis Jordan, I used with Bill Haley. The only difference between Haley and Louis Jordan was the way we did the rhythm. On Jordan we used a perfectly balanced rhythm section from the swing era – either they played shuffle or they played a good 52nd-Street [Swing] kind of beat. But on rock'n'roll, [Haley] had the heavy backbeat, which is what Lionel Hampton's band used to have, and I'd have to tone it down."[6] One of the prime streams for parentage of rock'n'roll could not be more plainly spelled out – especially when one remembers that Chuck Berry's favourite performers were Nat King Cole and Louis Jordan.

There was another direct offshoot from the hybrid that sprang up between Hampton and Jordan. This was the sudden emergence in the mid 1940s of small R&B groups led by honking, squealing, tenor saxophones. Spurred by the success of Illinois Jacquet and Arnett Cobb, at first with Hampton and later in front of their own small units, many saxophone players formed bands and began turning out simple but immensely frantic riff-based numbers. Often these were little more than crude showcases for three minutes of backbeat or shuffle mayhem from the horn of the sax player, who would usually overblow a single note or perform teeth-on-the-reed squealing.

During the late 1940s the genre's stars included Al Sears (late of Duke Ellington's band), Roy Milton, Joe Lutcher, Big Jay McNeely and, in 1949, Willis Jackson, whose work on 'Gator Tail', a single by Cootie Williams's band, gained him instant national recognition. These saxophonists would combine wild notes with outlandish live acts, often lying on the stage or in the aisle and honking, stripping off their sweat-drenched suits as they played on, and leading the audience in a conga line in and out of the venue. Chris Strachwitz, blues devotee and long-term Arhoolie record label owner, remembered now those saxmen "would jam a microphone into the horns and blow wild. I can see Big Jay McNeely playing on his knees, hear the bashing drums and three blasting tenors, and feel the floor bouncing up and down. He'd play 'Dirty Boogie' and the kids would be unzipping their flies".[7] It was all crude, wildly exciting, and a pure shot of adrenalin-fuelled entertainment. Its offshoots would reach all the way down to the R&B and soul routines of the late 1950s and early 1960s that the unknown Jimmy Hendrix would perfect before his rise to fame.

Underpinning all this new post-war musical activity was the blues. It had

The first rock'n'roller? Louis Jordan (playing saxophone, centre) on stage with his wild Tympany Six – a band that often included seven musicians.

Ike Turner, whose 'Rocket 88' single made with singer Jackie Brenston in 1951 is a contender for the first-ever rock'n'roll record.

been a presence in popular music since the runaway success of Mamie Smith's 'Crazy Blues' in 1920 and had been a talking-point internationally from the time of the Original Dixieland Jazz Band's sensational recording debut in 1917 and their subsequent post-World War I tours of Britain and Continental Europe. The searing intensity of the blues had been noted as early as 1919 by Swiss musicologist and conductor Ernest Ansermet when confronted with the wild blue phrases and smears of a teenage Sidney Bechet, playing in the James Europe Orchestra in France.

By the end of the 1920s, the decade of the so-called 'jazz age', with the entertainment world roughly divided into the 'sweet' and 'hot' styles, the blues had become an essential ingredient in 'hot' popular music – from the juke-joint boogies of the South, to the sophistication of the best jazz bands and orchestras, through to George Gershwin and his contemporaries. Looking back to those times, blues-cum-R&B artist Champion Jack Dupree delivered a lecture on his 1957 single, 'Old Time Rock & Roll', "Let's get wid' it. This here's what they call the rock'n'roll. We been doin' this since 1929. But the DJs and the teenagers just heard it. It just got new to them. I ain't gonna tell my age but I'll tell ya how long I been doin' it. Now I want all you folks to gather 'round this juke-box!..."[8]

So-called classic country blues first made it to records in the 1920s. It was paralleled during that decade by a variety of urban and semi-urban styles, in differing hybrid forms: the semi-jazz, semi-vaudeville of Ma Rainey and Bessie Smith, or even quasi-minstrel groups such as The Mississippi

Sheiks. Country blues itself – and many of its premier practitioners, looking for steadier incomes – had developed urban hybrids by the mid and late 1930s. Ex-country blues performers who had drifted into permanent residence in the large northern US cities evolved this style by incorporating instruments and ensemble routines which drew both from country blues and string-band practise and from contemporary jazz small-group styles. It became just as common in the 1930s for an urban blues pianist, for example, to have a kazoo or a mandolin in his front line as a trumpet or guitar.

With the emergence of the Midwestern style of blues-and-riff based jazz in the mid 1930s, for a time the worlds of jazz and urban blues drew closer together (often sharing the same instrumental line-ups and even the same musicians). But wholesale changes in the popular entertainment world and the bebop innovations of Charlie Parker, Thelonious Monk and Dizzy Gillespie would soon have them apart again, leaving jazz musicians to develop a new worldwide audience for their difficult and abstract new forms. Pre-war urban blues, meanwhile, gradually became absorbed into the fashion for R&B. Country blues had to find its own way and reinvent a new popular audience, in the tough urban styles of Chicago, Detroit and other big city centres of the late 1940s and '50s, typified by Muddy Waters, John Lee Hooker and Lightnin' Hopkins. These players would use the more traditional blues styles and forms as well as the electric-guitar innovations of T-Bone Walker to re-introduce raw blues to a younger urban audience largely unaware of the music's rural roots.

The invention of the electric guitar in the late 1930s had given guitarists the ability to sustain single notes and chords in a manner impossible on an acoustic guitar. It also allowed them to compete in volume with the loudest of instruments, from trumpet to drums. In jazz the applications were immense, from solo performers to small-group members and big-band rhythm-section sidemen. Eddie Durham, Al Casey, Les Paul and Charlie Christian all began to extract new and exciting sounds from the electric instrument, often liberally combined with blues phraseology. Durham is generally thought to be the first to have used the electric guitar professionally in jazz, as far back as 1935, but his approach remained that of an acoustic guitarist. Casey and Christian heard things differently.

Charlie Christian came out of Oklahoma City after pianist-composer Mary Lou Williams recommended him to John Hammond. "At the Ritz I met Charlie Christian," Hammond said later, "a tall young man, thin, dark, and wearing a purple shirt and bright yellow shoes. I listened to him and knew immediately. He was great. He was unique. To begin with, he phrased like a horn, which no other guitar did in those days … . He was endlessly inventive, although he needed equally big talents to stimulate him. As with every other great musician I have 'discovered', there was never a moment's doubt. I could hear the singularity of the sound. Always this quality seems so obvious. Lights flash. Rockets go off. Where is everybody? Why don't they hear it? This has always amazed me."[9] Maybe John Hammond and Chas Chandler were related?

Hammond inveigled the guitarist into Benny Goodman's small group in 1939 thanks to an unscheduled on-stage jam. Lionel Hampton, still with Goodman at the time, remembered meeting Christian that first night. "Hammond talked up Charlie to Benny, but Benny wasn't interested. So Hammond brought Charlie to Los Angeles himself. Charlie walked in, and he was a sight to see. He had on a ten-gallon hat, pointy-toed yellow shoes, green suit, a purple shirt, and a string bow tie. Benny took one look at him and left."[10] Christian's urgent musical creativity soon made Goodman change his mind. He fitted perfectly into what became the Goodman Sextet, staying with the group until his untimely death from tuberculosis in 1942. According to Hampton, "Benny never really approved of Charlie, and they never got along personally. But musically they inspired each other. … Charlie helped Benny make the transition from swing to bop."[11]

Christian's immeasurable contribution to the development of jazz is universally acknowledged, but his significance to the guitar is still little known in rock circles. His harmonic adventurousness and willingness to jam any time, any place, made him a major player in Harlem at the dawn of the 1940s when bebop was being formulated, but his tremendous rhythmic drive was straight out of the Midwest hybrid of blues, country and swing. He built his phraseology and melodic structures on the blues vocabulary of the time, extending it into new forms – just as Hendrix would in a later generation. Christian was a jazz player with an imagination that embraced a broad concept of sound and style reaching beyond his contemporaries. His musical language was adopted and adapted piecemeal by virtually every other new electric guitarist with a jazz, blues or R&B background in the following two decades.

The benefits of electricity were clear to blues players too, as T-Bone Walker soon demonstrated on stage and record. Blues guitarists were the first to realise that electric guitars didn't have to be electrified imitators of acoustic instruments, instead exploiting them sonically for their own unique qualities. T-Bone Walker was Dallas born and bred, but a habitué of Oklahoma City in the early 1930s and a friend of Charlie Christian. He made his first impact on the wider musical world as a singer with Les Hite's big-band in 1939. Already fascinated by the electric guitar's possibilities after hearing Les Paul's early efforts, Walker became ambitious with the instrument while on the road with Hite in 1940.

"Jump-jazz was given clear popular shape by a string of hits from Louis Jordan and his shuffle-beat band, including 'Let The Good Times Roll'."

According to band colleague Vida Lee, Walker "was backstage practicing and experimenting with the electric guitar. He had it in the dressing room, and it got so he could do just about what he liked with it. It was more exciting than when he played acoustic, and the sound was so new that people started talking."[12]

T-Bone's experience after launching his new guitar sound on-stage at the Little Harlem club in Los Angeles has close parallels to Jimmy Hendrix's early professional experiences. "Things were always jumping, and the chicks would be excited," said Phace Roberts of The Three Rockets dance act. "You'd see them crossing the floor, climbing the bandstand, and handing Bone money. When he went into the splits, they'd kneel beside him counting out their bills, putting them in his pockets or guitar! … People went wild. … Chicks would be lined up outside waiting for the Blues Balladeer. T-Bone pulled all the pretty girls. You could count on that, and it brought fellows into the club."[13] One of the first to spread the word about T-Bone Walker was well-connected jazz aficionado Marili Morden, and her reaction to first seeing his act was similar to that when Chas Chandler saw Hendrix 26 years later. "I hadn't expected to prefer the electric guitar to the acoustic, but the way T-Bone played it was fantastic," she said. "It was new to us all, and I was dumbfounded."[14]

Walker developed his own repertoire of guitar licks and used them extensively during a stint with Milt Larkin's band in 1942. "He played blues and other things," said Larkin. "We were playing swing, big-foot swing …. Any time there's a Texas band, blues and jazz fit together."[15] Morden remembered a similar mix in T-Bone's own band shortly after. "He'd get a blues guy on piano sometimes, but always jazzmen for the band."[16]

This mixture of blues and jazz, similar in intent but different in balance to that produced by Louis Jordan and Lionel Hampton, was crucial in determining the new blues and rhythm style that would flood the immediate post-war period. Recalling the impact of hearing Walker for the first time, B.B. King said: "When I first heard T-Bone's single-string solo on 'Stormy Monday', it drove me crazy. I could never believe a sound could be that pretty on an instrument. … T-Bone has a way of using ninth chords – nobody's done it ever yet. … I like his singing, too, but he always killed me with the guitar. Completely killed me."[17] Later, countless observers would say the same thing when they saw and heard Hendrix.

Most urban bluesmen of the immediate pre-war period had stuck to acoustic instruments and an earlier sound, and did not take advantage of the new electric instrument. Big Bill Broonzy, Joe Lee "Sonny Boy" Williamson, Tampa Red, Big Maceo, Blind Boy Fuller had all come to Chicago during the 1920s and '30s from various points south. They remained important artists in the '40s, and continued to mine the old blues seams, but those who were not dead by the end of the 1940s were either in obscurity or picking up on a new post-war demand for acoustic blues that raged through western Europe.

By 1950 the new blues and R&B forms were ruled by electric guitars, saxophones and drums as the piano's role waned. Among the later arrivals using these raw and exciting materials were the young Mississippian B.B. King, Lightnin' Hopkins from Houston, Texas, and Detroit's John Lee Hooker. In Chicago there was Muddy Waters – late of Clarksdale, Mississippi – at the beginning of his long local ascendancy. Robert Nighthawk (aka Robert Lee McCoy) from Arkansas was adopting the new sounds with enthusiasm, and

Rice Miller (the other Sonny Boy Williamson) was heating up cold days in hell with his harp-driven electric blues band.

Another denizen of Mississippi was Guitar Slim. Born plain Eddie Jones in Greenwood in 1926, Slim made little impact on music until he moved to New Orleans at the opening of the 1950s, making records for the Imperial and J-B labels before landing a deal in 1953 with Art Rupe's Specialty Records. Soon after this Slim hit with 'The Things I Used To Do', a million-seller at the time and a tune that became standard repertoire for all R&B groups of any persuasion for the next decade. Hendrix would record his own version in 1969 during a studio jam with Johnny Winter.

Guitar Slim's stage act was at least as wild as his slashing guitar playing. He used a specially-made 200-feet guitar lead (cord) that allowed him to wander into the audience to perform his outlandish stunts, borrowing from T-Bone Walker but embellishing his showmanship considerably. The young Hendrix certainly knew the music of Guitar Slim, as well as that of his acolyte Guitar Shorty. Playing in his first professional band in Nashville in 1962, Hendrix was already using his own 75-foot guitar lead to allow him to stroll out into the audience.

The most important figure of lasting influence during the transition from traditional blues to what would emerge as rock'n'roll was Mississippi-based Arthur 'Big Boy' Crudup. His role in shaping Elvis Presley's hybrid style is well documented – Elvis said throughout his career that he was in musical debt to Crudup – as are the shoddy deals that kept the older man from benefiting from his compositions and recordings. What is less well known today is the music itself.

Recording sporadically from 1941 onwards, Crudup combined unusually powerful imagery and expression in his lyrics with driving guitar playing – mostly electric from 1942 onwards – that presaged much of what was to follow. Crudup's career never really took off: he was an uncertain live performer and was unwilling to put up with the privations of early-1940s Chicago in order to advance himself. But he was influential among his peers, playing around Mississippi venues with Elmore James and Sonny Boy Williamson (Rice Miller), both of whom sought out Crudup after hearing his records, prior to their own moves to Chicago. Crudup also impressed many others who heard him on juke-boxes throughout the country: he sang on records with the intensity of the great 1920s Delta bluesmen, an intensity that would be echoed in years to come by Muddy Waters and B.B. King, among many others. Crudup's playing technique was that of an acoustic guitarist but his harsh, driving sound on electric guitar had a distinctly urban edginess, while his use of a drummer adept at jump-swing was greatly instructive to many aspiring bluesmen. This applied as much to young country-blues performers just beginning their peripatetic careers as it did to those already in the big northern cities.

Then there was Lightnin' Hopkins, from Texas, who had no interest in settling anywhere. Record producer Bob Shad remembered him in the 1940s as someone who would hop on buses, perform, and then walk around with a cup. "He had to be paid cash," Shad told Arnold Shaw for his great R&B study *Honkers And Shouters*. "Not only that, he had to be paid after each cut. He didn't want to know about doing a tune over. He didn't know the lyrics from one song to another, but made them up as he went along. A typical vagabond. Whatever hit his mind, he sang and recorded. ... Before he started

a new one, I'd pay him 100 dollars. He did another, I gave him another hundred. He refused to work any other way."[18] Blues enthusiast Chris Strachwitz preferred to remember the poetry in this way of life. "I took a trip to Houston in the summer of 1959 ... . I clearly recall that hot muggy summer day when I met Lightnin' in the afternoon in front of the house he was staying in and how he broke into verses addressed to us when Mack McCormick and I walked into the small beer joint where he was playing that night. He was singing a slow blues with a drummer behind him and as he saw us coming in the door Lightnin' sang "Woah, this man come all the way from California just to hear poor Lightnin' play" and from there this poetic genius told about the arthritis which was bothering him a good deal because it had been raining heavily that hot summer day. ... I had never encountered improvised poetry like this before, set to music about the things which were on the singer's mind – things which were no doubt on most of the customers' minds as well."[19]

Charlie Christian, the man who gave a new solo voice to the electric guitar.

Both have parallels with the later career of Hendrix. He would perceive himself as a rootless person, had little care for the business side of music, and was entirely concerned with living the life of a musician and entertainer – even if the terms of this entertainment had radically changed by the mid 1960s. Hendrix was also a musician who thrived on spontaneity and who was capable of incorporating any given event of the moment into his performing routine. He demonstrated this on hundreds of occasions while performing live, whether it was dedicating songs to people he picked out in crowds, changing the lyrics of songs to fit an occasion, or – in one very famous instance – abandoning a pre-arranged TV routine and playing a slashing instrumental tribute to Cream instead. Hendrix may not have copied Lightnin' Hopkins, but he came from the same American minstrel tradition, and was proud of the fact.

Big Joe Turner was another key figure in blending old forms of the blues with the newer sounds and rhythms of the 1940s and early '50s. A singing bartender in the wild days of 1930s Kansas City, Turner had been a national figure in the KC mould for over a decade, balancing his output between jump jazz, rollicking R&B, and boogie-woogie (he appeared as a duo with boogie pianist Pete Johnson for years). At the beginning of the 1950s he hit it big with a string of prototype rock'n'roll discs: 'Shake Rattle And Roll', 'Bump Miss Suzie' and 'Honey Hush'. These would be copied note-for-note at the marketing launch of rock'n'roll proper as young white musicians and singers hooked up to the infectious excitement that had already been at the heart of R&B for the best part of a decade.

The launch of rock'n'roll on an unsuspecting and predominantly white teenage audience in the mid 1950s takes us in another direction – and away from Hendrix's youthful everyday experience, because at the time, America was a largely socially segregated society, even though this was not officially acknowledged. The music and broadcasting industries of the time accurately reflected those social conditions.

When the young Jimmy Hendrix began listening to the vibrant new music going on around him, the record business was still largely divided along race lines, as was radio –no matter whether you were on the East Coast, West Coast, or anywhere in the middle. Bob Shad remembered: "At that time, if you brought a record by a black artist to a pop disc-jockey, you were dead. They would refuse to play [it]. I remember bringing up records, and I would refuse to tell them who it was. I would say, 'Just listen to the record.'"[20] Art Rupe, founder of Specialty Records, recalled a similar landscape. In 1944 he started his first label, Jukebox. "I called it Jukebox Records because the jukebox was the medium then for plugging records. If you got a record into the boxes, it was tantamount to getting it to the top stations today. The jukebox operator was also important because he bought in volume … a big op would have a thousand or twelve hundred locations. It was a sizeable sale if you made it." Rupe remembers the clear division between black and white at that time and later in Los Angeles. "Most of the stores that sold black records were little hole-in-the-wall places, owned by black proprietors. Since they couldn't get credit, they could buy only in limited quantity. The white distributors of the time didn't cater too much for them. I doubt that their salesmen even visited them."[21]

Rupe decided that what would sell in the black urban areas that he was investigating was the type of music that excited him. Both urban and country blues still had considerable markets in Los Angeles in the mid to late 1940s. "The urban music had horns and the country music was primarily percussion," said Rupe. "The urban was a little more organised and closer to the American popular Tin Pan Alley structure, except these were 12-bar versus eight-bar. The structures of urban and country music were the same, except – and I don't mean this disrespectfully – that one was very elementary and unpolished and the other was the same thing, but polished. The roots were there."[22]

The urgent, forceful sounds of black urban America continued to gather strength as the 1950s unfolded. One of the most potent shifts in style and fashion came with a gradual move in emphasis away from saxophone-and-piano-led bands, vocal or instrumental, to outfits led by guitar. This nationwide trend was already well established in Chicago blues, but as with so much else in this movement, the initial impetus had come from the Southern states.

Ike Turner was one of the first musicians to combine the Delta and Bayou rhythms and sounds with hard northern urgency. Turner was from Clarksdale, Mississippi, and followed in the footsteps of older men like Muddy Waters and Arthur Crudup. He had absorbed on-the-spot lessons from bluesmen such as Pinetop Perkins and Robert Nighthawk and by 1951 was making record dates in and around Memphis. One of these was 'Rocket 88', recorded in March that year at Sam Philips's studio in Memphis, and sold to Chess Records in Chicago. Released under the name of the singer on the date, Jackie Brenston, it was top of the American R&B chart by May. Turner was still just 20 years old.

He was soon picked up by Modern Records in Los Angeles, working as both recording musician and talent scout for the label for the rest of the decade. Along the way he made a string of prototype rock'n'roll records, following up on the success of 'Rocket 88' with its shuffle rhythm, raucous guitar riffs, blues vocal, and saxophone growls. Turner's familiarity with the music coming out of New Orleans and the surrounding regions suggests that the way 'Rocket 88' melded city and country rhythms had a black pedigree, not white. That city's unique ethnic and cultural history had long been recognised as a fundamental ingredient in the music created there. By the late 1940s the lilt and sway of New Orleans music that Jelly Roll Morton had referred to close on 50 years earlier as "the Spanish tinge" was taking a definitive new form, personified by Lloyd Price and Fats Domino.

Lewis Chudd, the (white) owner of Imperial Records based in Los Angeles, went to New Orleans in 1949 on a talent search. A friend in the music business took him to "Good Town, an unpaved, black section of New Orleans. We took a taxi. Because of the prejudice against white and black mixing, we lay on the floor until the cab dropped us at a club, a bar, or just a joint owned by an Italian named Duke Pania. I think it was called the Hideaway bar or Dewdrop Inn. There I heard a kid who worked Friday and Saturday nights for five dollars. Lloyd Price was on the same bill, and he was accompanied by the stout youngster we came to hear. I was offered Price, but I wanted the fat man who played the piano. He was so shy that he wouldn't come over to our table. … With [Dave] Bartholemew's and Pania's help, I finally got to talk with Fats Domino – that was his name – and signed him to a contract".[23]

Fats had his first (modest) hit, 'The Fat Man', the following year and remained a bankable recording artist well into the 1960s, crossing over to a substantial white teenage market by the second half of the 1950s. His companion that night, Lloyd Price, had his first major hit in 1952 with 'Lawdy Miss Clawdy' on Art Rupe's Specialty label. Rupe had been so impressed by Chudd's discovery that he made his own trip to New Orleans to see what he could find for his label. The trilogy of key New Orleans influences would be completed when Seattle's own Ray Charles, looking for a way to combine gospel and blues for his unique musical mix, travelled to New Orleans to record a bunch of songs in December 1953, discovering through the musicians he used exactly what he was looking for. It was the beginning of many crossovers in Charles's career, which would reach its peak in the early 1960s as he embraced so-called country & western and was discovered by a new and worldwide white audience.

While popular black music was undergoing a remarkable spurt of development and diversification in the 1950s, little or none of it was heard on

> ## "When I first heard T-Bone's single-string solo on 'Stormy Monday', it drove me crazy. I could never believe a sound could be that pretty on an instrument."
>
> B.B. King on T-Bone Walker

white radio. The mainstream of white popular music remained untouched by its vigour and energy. For middle-class white America it was the age of the novelty song and the cute singer. Stars of the 1940s like Dinah Shore, Doris Day and Frank Sinatra had continued to score into the 1950s, although Sinatra's career had taken a nosedive at the dawn of the decade that was only arrested when he moved to the Capitol label. He also re-launched himself as a serious actor as opposed to a romantic lead. Others regularly in the charts in the early 1950s included Johnnie Ray ('Ma Says Pa Says'), Mario Lanza ('Be My Love'), Al Martino ('Here In My Heart'), Kay Starr ('Comes A-Long A-Love'), Liza Rosa ('How Much Is That Doggie In The Window'), Eddie Calvert ('Oh Mein Papa'), Tony Bennett ('Stranger In Paradise'), Rosemary Clooney ('This Ole House'), and Frankie Laine with Paul Weston & His Orchestra and the Norman Luboff Choir ('Hey Joe!').

This type of music did not simply evaporate with the advent of rock'n'roll. The audience adjusted, shedding most of the teenagers and settling for people in their twenties and thirties who were already nostalgic for the sounds of their own early youth in the 1930s and 1940s. The arrival of white groups and singers playing black-inspired music did not knit the musical communities together. Few black performers had big successes in the mass record-buying market in the 1950s – with the notable exceptions of Chuck Berry, Ray Charles, Nat King Cole and, for a brief but glorious time, Bo Diddley and Little Richard. Ten years later, it would be the turn of Jimmy Hendrix from Seattle. Meanwhile, he had a lot of growing up to do.

strike up the band

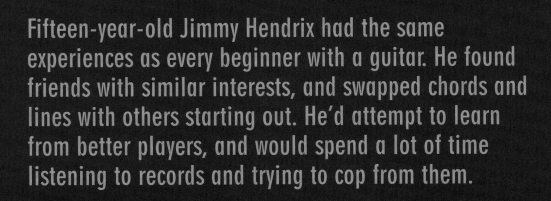

Fifteen-year-old Jimmy Hendrix had the same experiences as every beginner with a guitar. He found friends with similar interests, and swapped chords and lines with others starting out. He'd attempt to learn from better players, and would spend a lot of time listening to records and trying to cop from them.

Pernell Alexander, a school friend of Jimmy's at Meany Junior High School in Seattle, told author Mary Willix that he and Jimmy enjoyed playing Bill Doggett's 'Honky Tonk' and Richard Berry's 'Louie Louie'. "We both liked Chuck Berry, Eddie Cochran, The Everly Brothers, Mickey & Sylvia – 'Love Is Strange' – and Little Richard. … We listened to a lot of records. I had quite a collection."[1] (Alexander was one of many who spoke to Mary Willix for her prime source book on Hendrix's early years in Seattle, *Voices From Home*. Willix was a childhood friend of Hendrix. Motivated by their friendship and an urge to record his Seattle history, she interviewed childhood and adolescent friends, colleagues, acquaintances and family members for her unique work. The basis for any subsequent study of Hendrix's life and music, it is the source for many of the personal observations from Seattle in this book.)

Alexander's list of record titles, centred for the most part on 45rpm singles released in 1957, reveals Hendrix and his peers to have wide-ranging musical interests. Seattle was perceived by some in the outside world as provincial. Alexander himself, coming from Maryland and Baltimore, thought of Seattle as "a new experience – not only because of integration [at the high school], but the kids were naïve. It felt like some remote outback".[2] But the city's open outlook and a thriving local music network meant that these teenagers had a view of music that was anything but provincial. This would be reflected in the eventual emergence of a distinctive Northwest rock'n'roll style at the end of the 1950s.

Alexander started going down to Seattle's Jackson Street in 1958 when he was 15 years old. He and his friends would pick up any information they could from watching the acts there. "We didn't know about bass guitars back then," he recalled. "Jimmy and I would tune [the lowest string of] our guitars to low C for the bass part. I remember when we went to see [saxophonist] Big Jay McNeely … in 1957 or '58. He was one of my dad's favourites. That was the first time we'd seen a bass guitar; we were hooked."[3] Alexander's tastes ran to saxophone players and the gamut of music from rock'n'roll to jazz. Jimmy Hendrix, however, took a slightly different approach.

"Jimmy loved the blues," Alexander stressed, and said it was a neighbour, Mr Williams, who introduced Hendrix to playing the blues. "They used to sit out on Mr Williams's porch on 27th Avenue, and Jimmy would listen to him play the blues. I went over there with him a few times, but frankly I wasn't as interested in the blues as Jimmy was."[4] Jimmy's father confirmed his son's fondness for the

Jimmy Hendrix (second from left) with The Rocking Kings, Washington Hall, Seattle, February 1960.

blues. "Jimmy would put my 45s on that turntable and play along on his guitar," Al Hendrix recalled. "He'd try to copy what he heard, and he'd make up stuff too. He lived on the blues around the house. I had a lot of records by B.B. King and Louis Jordan and some of the down-home guys like Muddy Waters. I liked most of the guitar players and Chuck Berry. Jimmy was really excited by B.B. King and Chuck Berry. He was a fan of Albert King too. Jimmy also had some of his own 78s and 45s, but he never did ask me to buy him any records. He would buy his own."[5] Even at this stage, Jimmy was keeping his musical life separate from Al's. Chuck Berry's big hits were 'Sweet Little Sixteen' in February 1958 and 'Johnny B. Goode' three months later. 'Johnny B. Goode' was one of the earliest new releases that young Jimmy attempted to play along with on guitar. He would remember it in years to come.

"One of the songs we'd play back in those days was 'What'd I Say' by Ray Charles. That was a big one."

Jimmy Johnson, Jimi's schoolfriend

Through the blues, Jimmy would find his own voice as a musician. However, the wide musical taste that he and his friends enjoyed would also stay with him into his later years, and his personal synthesis of all these early enthusiasms was fundamental to what would make him a unique musician. In this he was not unlike a number of the musicians on the blues, R&B and fledgling rock'n'roll circuits in the 1950s. McHouston "Mickey" Baker was the Mickey of Mickey & Sylvia who recorded that January 1957 hit, 'Love Is Strange'. Not only had he contributed vibrant and authentic dirty blues guitar to a Champion Jack Dupree blues session for King Records in 1953, but throughout the 1950s and 1960s he was a featured soloist with Hal Singer, Esther Philips and Ruth Brown, and a top session man in New York City, appearing on records by Woody Herman, Jesse Stone, King Curtis and Ray Charles. He also played with jazz saxophonist Coleman Hawkins in Europe as a featured soloist in 1962.

Al Sears was a tenor saxophone player who went in the other direction: he hit the headlines with Duke Ellington in 1944, and moved later into R&B and rock. Sears had a genuine R&B hit single with Johnny Hodges' tune 'Castle Rock' in 1951. Soon after, he moved into management, promotion of R&B and rock'n'roll concerts, and publishing. Sears recorded scores of rock singles as a leader and as a featured tenor sax player with a host of frontline rock artists, including DJ Alan Freed's Orchestra.

Another Seattle friend who shared Jimmy's earliest enthusiasms in music and his first steps into public performance was Terry Johnson. The two had met in 1951. "He and Jimmy Williams and I were best friends for ten years," Johnson told Mary Willix. "We called ourselves The Three Musketeers. ... Our main bonding interest was music."[6] As with Pernell Alexander, Jimmy shared Johnson's enthusiasm for the latest hit singles. "We'd all go to my house after school and talk about the latest songs," said Johnson, "and what the words meant."[7]

Hendrix and Johnson were listening to and learning from musicians like James Brown, Fats Domino, Little Anthony, and Little Richard. "One of the songs we'd play back in those days was 'What'd I Say' by Ray Charles. That was a big one," said Johnson. "Ray Charles was one of our idols." Johnson remembers that they were very impressed by Little Richard's big hits, and liked The Chantels and The Shirelles. He also knew about Jimmy's passion for Elvis Presley's music, just as he saw his friend's deepening fascination with the great blues guitarists of the modern period.[8] The Ray Charles connection is worth looking at a little more closely, especially as Hendrix

later described him as "one of the all-time greats when you're talking of soul".[9] Charles recorded 'What'd I Say' in February 1959 and the 45rpm single entered the US charts that July, eventually becoming his first million-seller and certainly his biggest hit for the Atlantic label, for which he recorded all his classic R&B sides. The importance of church and gospel music in Charles's mature musical style is widely acknowledged, and 'What'd I Say' is one of the pieces most obviously from that tradition. The story of the record's evolution from live try-out to recorded hit was a kind of inverted version of the old Louis Jordan formula of road-testing potential new hit material before recording and issuing it.

Completely out of material after a long evening in Pennsylvania in late 1958, Charles just counted off a riff and told his band to follow him. "I said to the girls, 'Whatever I say, just repeat after me.' I started with that bass line," Charles recalled later, "the one you hear on the record, and we got to the part where the girls and me were going 'unnh' back and forth at each other, and it went on. To make a long story short, the people were dancing like hell off this thing. When the dance was over, a lot of them came up to me and asked, 'Where can I buy that record?' ... So the next night I thought, well, I'm going to try this thing again. So we kept trying it, going from town to town, and we got the same kind of reaction: people just went crazy. And they loved that little 'unnh, unnh', especially when the girls started doing it. The people would start to answer, too .... So it was a made-up song, made up on the spot – and you can tell if you listen, because the verses don't really have anything to do with each other."[10]

Charles's song is straight from the gospel's signifying tradition, although the lyrics and the musical context emphasise its rhythmic vitality and febrile sensuality. The song's overwhelming excitement generated by its call-and-response routine, along with the wonderful rolling bass line set up by Charles on his piano, made it a natural for teenagers everywhere – many of whom were entirely were ignorant of the routine's gospel origins. It was an object lesson for Jimmy Hendrix and his friends in Seattle in the creation of new musical hybrids that shimmered with vitality and the shock of the new. Not only did Hendrix hear Charles perform it on records, but he, Pernell Alexander and Anthony Atherton, a trio of thrilled if underage observers, sneaked into Seattle's Birdland venue to watch Charles's live act.

The third member of The Three Musketeers group, Jimmy Williams, remembered being involved in grade-school talent shows. "Terry [Johnson] and I were the only ones interested in performing. But Jimmy, I don't know. He never, never showed any interest in those kinds of things in those days. He would show up at the shows, the little festival shows, and he was very supportive when Terry and I were in a show."[11]

Johnson too has fond recollections of Hendrix's shy teenage personality, which may have been one of the reasons he would hang back at talent contests as a teenager. "As we grew older," Johnson told Willix, "I became more outgoing, and Jimmy Williams became more outgoing, but Jimmy Hendrix stayed kind of shy. I don't know if it was because of his home upbringing, or because of his social environment. Jimmy wouldn't open up to just anybody. I genuinely liked Jimmy. We clicked. We had the same sense of humour. We spent so much time together that I got to know him really well. There was so much to like about him. ... Jimmy was the type of guy who would never look you straight in the eye unless he knew you really, really well. He had a sense of insecurity that made it hard for people to get to know him. ... He had a great sense of humour, and was very sensitive and very, very smart and streetwise. But he did not have a good early background in relating to people."[12]

These reminiscences from genuinely close friends point to a part of Hendrix's character that is fundamental to understanding his entire career. Jimmy may in time have become the consummate showman – and for a time loved the effect that this had on worldwide audiences – but his concerns in life ultimately lay elsewhere. He was an intensely private man who knew the difference between real life and show business. For years, his closest relationship was with the guitar, although he was prepared to pawn any particular guitar for short-term money. What fed him was his inner vision of what he wanted to achieve in music, and when he came to understand this about himself it reinforced his natural sense of isolation, alongside a sense of purpose and ambition. Many years later, when asked by Dick Cavett whether he kept up with any of his old Army buddies, Hendrix made a point of saying that it was important to do so, but in such a way that when they met, it was as old friends, not rock star meets up with losers from the past. The ambition was personal, not social.

Jimmy Williams believed that Pernell Alexander encouraged Hendrix's earliest forays with the guitar. "[Hendrix] admired Pernell, and Pernell deserves credit for getting [him] started on the guitar. Pernell was quite a musician. We looked up to him. … If there was anything we needed to know, we'd ask Pernell."[13] Alexander himself credits another local youngster, Randy 'Butch' Snipes. "The kid was amazing," remembered Alexander. "He had great showmanship. He taught Jimmy the stunts. Butch was the first one here to play the guitar behind his back and with his teeth, and Jimmy learned those tricks from him. Butch taught us both a lot."[14]

Where Snipes learned about such things is open to conjecture, but the history of guitar showmanship stretched right back to T-Bone Walker and beyond. By the time Snipes was showing the teenage Jimmy Hendrix these tricks, they had been common stage parlance for black performers on the chitlin circuit for more than two decades. But Seattle was a hotbed of rock'n'roll and R&B enthusiasm. The city's own distinctive musical history had started a long, long time before the advent of Nirvana and the Seattle sound of the 1990s.

As in any musical or cultural history, the story of the Seattle music scene in the late 1950s has a small number of major streams of influence and development and many tributaries. One man who was central to the city's musical development in the 1950s, away from the already well established jazz and classical scenes, was keyboardist-bandleader Dave Lewis. Hendrix's colleague Luther Rabb recalls the impact of the Dave Lewis Combo on them all. "The musicians in the Dave Lewis Combo were our mentors. They were so advanced. I was studying music like crazy, and those guys were ahead of all of us….(they were) a model for genuineness and a calm, cool, relaxed attitude."[15]

Lewis, a well-schooled player from a family of musicians, touched every young aspiring Northwest musician in the late 1950s and early '60s. His outfit, The Dave Lewis Combo, was the most professional rock and rhythm group on the local scene, and led him to be described as the godfather of the Seattle sound. Lewis's band was the first in Seattle to play 'Louie Louie', Richard Berry's widely influential 1956 single. It was a basic component in the formation of the original Seattle sound, thanks primarily to the song's compellingly repetitive rhythm, and it was Lewis who first saw the simple tune's potential as a crowd-pleaser. "'Louie Louie' was so big here for so long," claimed Bob Hendrix, a cousin of Jimmy's, "that it was proposed as the official song for the state of Washington."[16]

Many local musicians point to what became known as the Seattle jungle beat as a defining characteristic of their city's music scene that kept it apart from any developments in California or New York during the late 1950s and early '60s. During that period, wrote Seattle historian Paul de Barros, "white kids in the Northwest seized upon black R&B with a manic, almost awkward ferociousness".[17]

Lacy Wilbon, who knew Hendrix when they were at Seattle's Garfield High School together, remembered Jimmy Pipkin as the first person in Seattle playing the 'jungle beat'. "[Pipkin] graduated from Garfield in '58 or '59. He had heard a rhythm in New Orleans that he liked," said Wilbon, "and he

reworked it, added nuances and perfected it."[18] This may be apocryphal, or just another step towards a definitive style. Seattle musician Barney Hilliard said that they would occasionally hear musicians who came through Seattle, but that prime influences came from records. "For example, we got 'Louie Louie' off the original record by Richard Berry."[19]

Lewis may have introduced the attractions of 'Louie Louie' to Seattle musicians, but the man who gave it a huge local impetus was white guitarist Rich Dangel. Dangel was born in Texas in the same year as Jimmy Hendrix, and his father was in the Marine Corps, so as the family moved around the country he would soak up the R&B he heard on US servicemens' juke-boxes. He was playing guitar before he hit his teenage years and by 1958, living with his family in Tacoma, Washington, had formed The Wailers, a high-school rock'n'roll band with enough fire and polish to land a US hit with 'Tall Cool One' in June 1959 – the first local Washington band to do so. They were followed in July 1960 by another Tacoma band strong on guitars, The Ventures, with 'Walk – Don't Run'.

Dangel's band made a recording of 'Louie Louie' in 1960 that was based on his rock'n'roll arrangement and featured a distinctive minor V chord and jungle rhythm – something that Hendrix picked up on and developed later. Dangel's guitar solo on the track was also widely imitated: The Wailers' recording of 'Louie Louie' was copied virtually note-for-note by The Kingsmen when they had their hit with the tune at the end of 1963 and into the first weeks of 1964. When Dangel moved from Tacoma to Seattle he left the band and began playing jazz with local guitarist Larry Coryell.

Both Dave Lewis and jungle-beat pioneers The Frantics made 45rpm singles and appeared on a television show aimed at teenagers, *Rock'n'Roll Party*, beamed out on Channel 13 to the Seattle area and devised by Seattle musician-turned-promoter Billy Tolles. Saxophonist Tolles and his friend Tommy Adams were originally jazz musicians, but were instrumental in

> # "The Dave Lewis Combo were our mentors. They were so advanced. I was studying music like crazy, and those guys were ahead of all of us."
>
> Luther Rabb, Jimi's childhood friend

bringing rock'n'roll to Seattle. They played Louis Jordan-type music in the early 1950s and then bar-walking rock'n'roll with their small group in clubs on Jackson Street. "I could just honk and walk through the joint, jump from tabletop to tabletop, honking my low B-flat," Tolles said later, "walk the bar, [go] outside and come back in the back door, all that kind of stuff. That really got us over. The white kids, they'd be in there clamouring for that."[20]

Musicians were taking the quasi-primitive drive of the so-called 'jungle beat' and edging it with the sophistication of other musical styles that they played alongside it on the stages of night-time Seattle. Dave Lewis himself was influenced by older jazz players, according to de Barros. "Lewis's tune 'J.A.J.', also covered by The Kingsmen, was a real musical oddity, a series of descending seventh chords followed by a 'circle of fifths' bridge. Lewis threw all manner of jazz riffs into his playing."[21] These influences gave Seattle's local rock variant a regional vitality that kept it closer to the music's roots than the watered-down pop music gradually dominating the charts as the first wave of rock'n'roll lost its intensity. The music may have stayed local for a few years, especially with Lewis based in Seattle all his life, but it would be exported in the next generation by players such as Hendrix and, shortly after,

Larry Coryell. Hendrix's early colleague Luther Rabb told author Mary Willix of the importance of the Seattle jungle beat and the vitality of the Seattle scene at that time. "We were isolated in Seattle," said Rabb in the 1990s, "so Jimmy had a whole different slant on music. We were doing things that were unique, ahead of their time. There was a lot of jazz, with a funky kind of rock thing with the guitar and bass. Seattle had the dual sax, and we used the jungle beat, which was 30 years ahead of its time. It was a syncopated rhythm [in 6/8], a cool thing because it could go with a lot of songs, and people could dance to it. Today people are calling it the New Jack Swing."[22]

Rabb felt that Seattle music directly influenced musicians in other places, but naturally he speaks as a local musician proud of his area's distinctive twist on a common stylistic stream. In a time when popular music had not quite become an exercise in global marketing, there were still regional shadings and identities to be found throughout the US, as well as in other countries. There is no reason to dispute that the geographically isolated Washington State music scene had its own identity. The extent of its influence on considerably later developments is, however, debatable. The influence

"We used to play stuff by people like The Coasters. You all had to do the same things before you could join a band – even the same steps."

Jimi Hendrix

tended to be felt through individual musicians rather than whole movements, at least until Nirvana's advent in the early 1990s. As Larry Coryell remarked to de Barros, "Seattle is not the real America. America starts on the other side of that mountain."[23]

The club that came to symbolise Seattle's musical life was Birdland. It was one of a kind in terms of Jackson Street's overall decline in the late 1950s. Pernell Alexander remembered: "Wilbur Morgan, the owner of the Birdland, lived one house over from my grandmother. He was more like a father to me than my own dad. In fact he was the most important figure in my life. He helped all of us with our music. The Birdland was very important to our music. The Black and Tan and the Four Ten were closed. They reopened in late '64. Jackson Street was where the gamblers and hustlers were. There wasn't anything happening music-wise on Jackson Street in those days."[24]

This was the local background as Hendrix began to grow as an aspiring guitarist. He was still at an early stage of mastering his chosen instrument, and like a sponge he soaked up every type of popular music that he could hear locally and on records. He was still a long way from innovation of any sort, as Paul de Barros noted later. "Hendrix had not developed even the germ of his distortion effects in Seattle. What Hendrix did derive from his local background was simple blues discipline and form, for which there were lots of able role models on Jackson Street .... It may also be that the easy interchange in Seattle between jazz, R&B, rock and blues – and the relaxed mixing of the races – had some subliminal influence on Hendrix's open-mindedness toward other experimental forms."[25]

During 1958 and '59, Hendrix continued to work out basic chord sequences and rehearse with his first bands. Luther Rabb remembered that Hendrix's idol was Duane Eddy. "Jimmy always carried his guitar around. He would show up at a party and just start playing." Rabb and Hendrix, who had known each other from childhood, regularly practised together. "Jimmy and I played songs that we learned by listening to the radio. We used to play in my

basement – until my mother told us to stop. We were so loud!"[26]

Hendrix and Terry Johnson were in a Junior High rock'n'roll band together, The Velvetones, and learned the words and music to the latest 45s. Hendrix would later recall those days in a number of interviews. "We used to play stuff by people like The Coasters," said Hendrix. "Anyway, you all had to do the same things before you could join a band – even had to do the same steps."[27] Schoolfriend and early bandmate Jimmy Williams confirms the thrust of this memory, if not the detail. "We played by ear, listening to 45s. And believe me, we wore out a lot of 45s on that old record player. First of all we had to figure out what key the song was in, then we'd let it play for a while, and then we'd take it off and start all over again. Jimmy would listen to the guitar part until he had it figured out and memorised. Then I'd play the piano part. We figured out C and D, and we got better and better."[28]

Robert Green, then a young pianist, was a founding member of The Velvetones, the Junior-High band that included guitarists Pernell Alexander and Jimmy Hendrix, Walter Jones on drums, Luther Rabb on tenor saxophone, and Anthony Atherton on alto. Both Green and Rabb had musical backgrounds in the church and roots in gospel music, just like Hendrix and many of his other friends. According to Green, the band started in 1958 with intensive rehearsing, then appeared at a high-school assembly, followed by their first paying gig at a women's-club event at the Polish Hall. "After that," Green recalled, "we got so many gigs we had to turn some down. Pernell's dad became our manager. We took part of the money we made to buy Jimmy an amp. He was always plugging in with Pernell." Green recalled the repertoire of the band. "Jimmy and Pernell were good. They had it down. They got a lot of their fingerwork by listening to Chuck Berry .... We did three or four Chuck Berry numbers – like 'Queenie'. We also played 'Lucille' by Little Richard and Fats Domino's 'Blueberry Hill'. We'd play blues for the grown-ups and whatever was jamming at that particular time for the youngsters. We played all the pop tunes."[29]

Exactly when The Velvetones bought Hendrix this amplifier is unclear, but it seems to have been some months after his debut with them. At first he wasn't even plugging in with Alexander. He started with The Velvetones in mid 1958, joining in on his acoustic guitar, with the inevitable result. "They drowned me out," Hendrix recalled later. "I didn't know why at first, but after about three months, I realised I'd have to get an electric guitar."[30] He probably realised a little more quickly than that.

Jimmy's fixation on the guitar showed no signs of going away – quite the opposite – and so during school summer holidays in 1958 his father finally gave in to his son's insistent requests for an electric guitar. "It was by chance," Lacy Wilbon said later, "that the day I went to Meyer's Music Store to buy a guitar, in August 1958, Jimmy was there buying a guitar."[31] Even then, ever-prudent Al Hendrix didn't exactly push the boat out. "I got him a Supro Ozark 1560S from Meyer's Store," said Al, adding rather unconvincingly: "I never did get him an amplifier, which I planned to, but that didn't make no difference."[32] (Jimmy later claimed he paid for the Supro by picking beans, often in tandem with Meany and Garfield school colleague Manual Stanton, but present opinion favours his father's version of events.)

By now Hendrix had the bug, wanting to do nothing more than play guitar every waking minute. His scholastic life, already faltering, began to wither as a result. He joined a second local band, The Rocking Teens, started by Webb Lofton, Walter Harris, Charles Woodbury and Lester Exkano. At first in that summer of 1958 Hendrix, still without his own amplifier, was as reluctant to join The Rocking Teens as were they to have him. "We were hesitant, because he didn't have an amp, but he always managed to find someone to plug in with," remembered Harris.[33] Just as in The Velvetones, Hendrix was sharing amps. Lofton, by then in the ninth grade, told Mary Willix that he and Harris "were the only ones in the group with any formal music training".[34] The

Rocking Teens played the same types of gigs as The Velvetones: Jimmy later claimed[35] that his first gig, a dance at Washington Guard National Armoury, was his first professional engagement. The other guitarist in the band was Junior Heath, while Robert Green occasionally subbed for Woodbury. At first Terry Johnson was, like Hendrix, a member of both The Rocking Teens and The Velvetones.

Everyone in both groups was aware that Jimmy and his family were poor. Heath recalled: "I never will forget one time we went by Jimmy's house, and for his dinner there was nothing there but a cinnamon roll on the table .... He and his dad lived in a sparsely furnished apartment. It had one bedroom and the other room was a living-room/dining-room/kitchen combination. ... By contrast to the rest of us, he was much poorer, and didn't have the support we had."[36] Walter Harris too was aware of the poverty Hendrix faced. "I felt sorry for him sometimes, like during the summer when he'd be working landscaping with his dad all day and [would] come to practice wearing the same clothes. But, as poor people, we were all in the same situation, trying to express our feelings through our music. It's just that Jimmy wasn't as fortunate in some ways as the rest of us."[37]

Hendrix was initially reserved on-stage, as he later admitted. "I knew about three songs and when [it was] time for us to play on stage, man, I was [shaking]. ... I couldn't get up in front."[38] It would be some time before he learned to lose his inhibitions and develop a stage act. Walter Harris corroborated this view. "Jimmy was a square, like most young kids. As time went on, Jimmy began to get into the group, and into the swing of things, and he started to clown, like the rest of us. One of Jimmy's idols was Chuck Berry, because of the way he performed and clowned with the guitar."[39]

Harris had met Hendrix in late 1955 when Jimmy was a seventh-grader at Meany Junior High. Harris learned music in church, had some musical training, but did not share Jimmy's taste for the blues when they first met. "At that time I felt only old people enjoyed the blues," said Harris. But Hendrix's passion slowly percolated through. "Blues wasn't my bag, but it grew on me as Jimmy played it. He was so expressive. It came naturally to him." The band was soon playing numbers by Albert King among the rock'n'roll of their normal stage routine. "We played a lot of Chuck Willis," said Harris, "The Midnighters, and Little Richard. ... At dances we played 'Rockin' Robin', 'Do You Want To Dance' and 'Yackety Yack', but not 'Charlie Brown' or 'Poison Ivy'."[40]

Appearing in two teenage Seattle bands simultaneously seems to have done little for Hendrix's confidence or sense of social ease, and he would rarely hang out after-hours. He said later: "You hear different bands playing around you and the guitar player seems like he's always much better than you are, you know? Then most people give up at this point because ... they get very discouraged, but it's best [to] just keep on. If you're very stubborn, you can, you know?"[41]

Jimmy's high school yearbook photograph, April 1958.

Webb Lofton of the Teens noticed that Jimmy was an "obedient kid. His dad had a good rein on him. If Al told Jimmy he had to be home at ten, he'd do it. Al always gave Jimmy a curfew, so we didn't participate in after-hours things. We played at adult dances ... but Al would meet him outside afterwards. Jimmy didn't drink and he didn't do drugs. If we got a bottle of wine, we had to twist his arm to get him to take a drink. One time we got some wine and Jimmy did not want to drink, but we insisted. He got drunk and threw his guitar down and said, 'I don't need you guys!'"[42] Jimmy's bad reaction to excessive alcohol – as opposed to other drugs – would often follow this pattern later in life. Lofton, along with pretty much everybody else who knew Jimmy at the time, recalled that he was bashful with girls and did not have a steady girlfriend until late in 1959, when he began to spend a lot of his free time with a Garfield High School girl, Betty Jean Morgan.

Both bands continued to play around the Seattle circuit, developing cohesion, a proper repertoire of tunes and something of a stage act. As young enthusiasts with little interest in any artificial divisions in music, they happily combined blues, rock'n'roll and R&B tunes in their sets. The Rocking Kings' occasional drummer Curtis Samuel recalled that Jimmy was crazy in equal measures about Duane Eddy's 'Ramrod' (from September 1958, Eddy's second smash hit after July's 'Rebel Rouser'), Chuck Berry's 'Johnny B. Goode', and 'Louie Louie', saying that Jimmy's face lit up in particular whenever they played the Eddy song. Jimmy's father Al remembered years later that one of his son's early conquests on the guitar was a 1950s TV theme, later a worldwide Eddy hit. "One of the first things that he learned how to play was the theme song from *Peter Gunn*, so even when he was just starting, he would make music out of the guitar."[43] The theme would stay with him, for close on ten years later he recorded a studio jam version of it with his last working group.

Bill Eisinger, another musician from Garfield High School, told Mary Willix about the variety of their early enthusiasms. "We started mixing rock'n'roll with R&B. We liked to play Earl King's 'Come On'. It was a kicking tune with a syncopated rhythm. Then there was Johnny Otis. Everybody knew 'Hand Jive' .... We liked the blues and R&B. Normally what we called the blues were slower tempo songs with a lot of guitar licks, like ones by Muddy Waters and B.B. King."[44] Johnny Otis had been a prime mover in West Coast R&B for well over a decade when, in 1958, billed as The Johnny Otis Show, he had a major R&B hit with 'Willie And The Hand Jive'. Recorded for the Capitol label in Los Angeles, it featured a five-piece brass section that The Rocking Kings could approximate with their two saxophones.

Walter Harris often saw how Hendrix would put his enthusiasm for everything he heard around him to good use. "He was living with Al in a little flophouse/hotel on East Terrace Street, between 12th and 14th. I saw he had a little radio. It turned out that Jimmy could play whatever was on the radio. Any number that came on the radio, he could play it. The same key. And he

practiced a lot, because that radio was all the company he had. He didn't have a TV."[45] Guitarist Lacy Wilbon, who never played in a group with Hendrix, remembered him as being "way ahead of the rest of us as far as dexterity goes, but he was weak on chords and theory. He wasn't proficient in chord-building. I suggested he get some books and teach himself. I said, 'If you do that, you'll be unstoppable.' He said, 'It would take too much time.' So I taught him six chords – and six inversions".[46] An inversion is a chord altered so that its notes are in a different relationship, useful for musical diversity and a more varied texture.

This exchange between the two youngsters was just like the conversations going on all over the world at the close of the 1950s as younger generations moved beyond adulation of their new rock'n'roll and R&B heroes and into emulation. Some kids naturally wanted to nail down basic music theory and elementary music-reading ability before they progressed to self expression. Others instinctively felt that such study would deflect them from a path that seems perfectly clear: a firm grasp of instrumental techniques, a good ear, and endless hours of practicing, using models readily available on records. For the vast majority of youngsters the second approach was faster, but it afforded them limited musical progress. They would eventually stagnate as they hit their heads on a self-imposed ceiling.

In rare instances, players thrive within their self-imposed limits and arrive at something unique and valuable. Hendrix was one of these. Others who come quickly to mind in this category are jazz trumpeter Chet Baker – who played entirely by ear – and early jazz cornetist Bix Beiderbecke. Bix

"He'd try to copy what he heard, and he'd make up stuff too. He lived on the blues around the house."

Al Hendrix, father of Jimi

was a poor reader but his amazing gift for melody and uncanny instinct for harmony allowed him to create beautiful, unique improvisations in the late 1920s. Paul McCartney could never surmount the tedium of learning to read music to the point of fluency, but his natural sense of musical structure and gift for melodic phrasing is unique. Like the young Hendrix, pianist Erroll Garner could instantly repeat anything he heard on the radio or records. Garner was also entirely self-taught and unable to read music, but successfully recorded with orchestras and vocalists during his long career – and even had a major hit with his composition 'Misty', a song Hendrix knew and played as a youngster.

In September 1959 Hendrix started at a new school, Garfield High. It was to be the last port of call in his formal education, and his attendance there would last just 14 months. In his years of fame, Hendrix would have little to say about these late schooldays. What he did say publicly was uncharacteristically bitter; he even claimed in a number of interviews that he left the school because of racial prejudice shown him by the staff after his romantic interest in a white girl student. This contrasts with much of what other pupils at the time remember. It also contrasts with an occasion when he gave a different twist to the story. Speculating in August 1970 about his rise to fame, he pondered: "I wonder what my old school mistress thinks about me? She looked pretty good, but got me excluded. In a lesson I spoke to a girl and the mistress got upset. 'What's wrong – are you jealous?' I asked. That was it."[47]

History teacher Ralph Hayes taught Jimmy at Garfield and was a neighbour of Jimmy's uncle, Frank Hendrix. Proud of Garfield's traditions of

openness and acceptance, Hayes felt sure that "Garfield was the most integrated school in the state of Washington…. Garfield students were unified, and the faculty worked together to help students."[48] Remembering Jimmy specifically, he recalled that the teenager was polite, well behaved, but very withdrawn. He showed little interest in history, although Hayes wondered whether that was because of his own teaching or because Jimmy simply wasn't interested in academic learning. Given Hendrix's mediocre scholastic record across most subjects, the latter is more likely to have been the case. Hayes, like all good teachers, took a personal interest in his students, and in this case it manifested itself with some unorthodox advice toward the end of Jimmy's stint at Garfield. "I remember saying to him, son, you really aren't interested in this class. Why don't you just leave this place called Garfield High School, get your guitar, and just make music? It's something that you thoroughly enjoy."[49]

A feature of Garfield's school life was the development of friendships across all social and racial lines. Jimmy was no exception. Steve Fletcher, who knew him through their mutually feeble attempts at the high-jump and maintained an easy friendship for the year Jimmy was there, felt that going to Garfield was the best experience he ever had. "The mix of wealth and poverty, the many ethnic backgrounds, the assemblies, the dances, the political environment … all of these things made the experience rich and rewarding. It was an opportunity to have friends from all categories …. Jimmy was someone who was unpretentious and accepting of all people, especially people who were different."[50]

Garfield student Dave Holden, who later became a an established musician, noticed a marked difference between race relations in Seattle and in the other parts of the US where he toured later. The difference would also affect Hendrix personally when he left Seattle. Holden said: "I totally missed out on [racial tensions in Seattle]. I heard about it, read about it, saw it on TV …. My first exposure to racism was on the [black-venue] chitlin circuit. I didn't go down there until '66. I certainly ran into the attitudes of the people that had been through that, other black people, 'cause they were real bitter. They had a lot of hostility. Not just toward whites, but toward blacks that burnt the black buildings up. I landed right in the middle of it and I didn't know which way to go. They were trying to figure out what kind of black person I was because I didn't have any feelings."[51]

Mike Tagawa, who is of Japanese extraction, also remembered Garfield as an oasis of cultural and racial integration, cultivated by a sense of unity that the school fostered among all its students. "We were different. Anybody who went to Garfield learned – way before it was popular, or way before it was mandated, or way before it was cool – as they say today – that diversity was really great. … Looking at the yearbooks I have from Garfield, I was amazed at the references there were to race – not in a negative sort of way, but in an innocent way – [that were] simply acknowledging that we were different from each other. … We were all different, and we could talk easily about it without being concerned about political correctness particularly."[52]

Tagawa had known Hendrix at an earlier school, Washington Junior High, and as a fellow member of a football team, the Fighting Irish. Hendrix was, by reputation, quite good at football, but not at other popular sports. "I remember distinctly that [Hendrix] was pretty terrible [at basketball]. I mean, he was really as bad as me at shooting hoops."[53] Tagawa also remembers Hendrix as an indifferent student, like himself, and someone immersed in music most of the time. "He wasn't a close personal friend outside of school, but we were friends at school. … Hendrix talked a lot about Webb Lofton, and the group called The Rocking Kings. I got the impression that Hendrix really liked Webb Lofton. … He'd tell me [that they] were a good group, and that he enjoyed himself. … Lofton's name stands out in my mind because he was one of the only – if not the only – person I heard Hendrix talk about in any extended way."[54] During Hendrix's first full year at Garfield, part of his life became simpler. "At some point The Velvetones broke up," recalled Robert Green. "I don't remember the timing exactly [but] it seems like The Velvetones and The Rocking Kings merged."[55] Soon after this, the new Rocking Kings acquired a manager, James Thomas. He was an older musician whom Jimmy and band members Walter Harris and Charles Woodbury had met when they heard Thomas and some of his band, James Thomas & The Tomcats, jamming in a nearby house.

Hendrix now focussed his ambitions on The Rocking Kings – no matter how many times he sat in with or did fill-in gigs for other Seattle bands. But the Kings made little money, most of it being swallowed by 'expenses'. Keyboardist Walter Harris thought they were pretty naïve at the time. "We were just young punks, but we were organised. We practiced together three times a week for at least four hours. Then we practiced by ourselves every day." Harris said they weren't interested in money, just playing, and a lot of adults pounced on that. "Our manager, James Thomas, would charge us transportation fees. We were probably only making five bucks for three hours, working at Birdland. … We probably would have played for nothing. On several occasions we probably came out with nothing. In the end we got ripped off. … But we didn't care back then. … If we had to do it again, we'd probably get ripped off again".[56]

"People have made Hendrix supernatural and superhuman. I remember him as just another guy, just like a lot of us at Garfield do."

Mike Tagawa, friend of Jimi's at Garfield High School

Al Hendrix remembered his son telling him about the arrangement the band had with James Thomas. "[Jimmy would] say, 'We're all gonna get paid $15 apiece,' but it was very seldom anything like that happened. The guys in the band would always end up with a zero, or maybe even owing James something. One time Jimmy left me a note saying that he and some of the group had gone to play in Vancouver. Walter Harris told me that the car broke down, and they ended up having to push it. After a whole lot of problems, Jimmy just said, 'Man, I'm so disgusted, I ain't gonna play with those guys no more.' But each time a chance to play came around, he just couldn't turn it down. He'd say, 'Well, maybe this time's gonna be better.'"[57]

Despite the rip-offs and shady deals, the Kings made good progress locally, becoming an increasingly efficient and popular combo that churned out sprightly covers of the hits of the day. They entered local competitions such as the ubiquitous Battle Of The Bands, performing creditably, and they played in a great variety of venues, mostly halls and social events. Eventually in 1960 they landed a Wednesday-evening residency at Birdland, a leading venue on Jackson Street.

Later on The Rocking Kings played a ballroom on the old Highway 99, half way between Tacoma and Seattle, called the Spanish Castle. It would be fondly if obliquely reflected in Hendrix's 1967 song 'Spanish Castle Magic'. The venue was worthy of his tribute. It was built in 1931 as a stucco imitation Spanish castle, battlements and all, and proved to be both a capacious and popular dancehall for the following 35 years. On most weekends the crowds filled the 2,000-capacity room. A dance-band-only policy was finally breached in late 1959 when Fridays became rock'n'roll dance nights, inaugurated by The Wailers under the auspices of local DJ Pat O'Day. The Spanish Castle quickly became a venue visited by rock'n'roll tours, the acts

passing through including Gene Vincent, Jerry Lee Lewis, Roy Orbison, Johnny Rivers and, later, Jan & Dean and Bobby Vee. Country artists like Ernest Tubb and Conway Twitty also headlined. Local bands appearing there in the early 1960s included The Casuals, The Checkers (with a young Larry Coryell on guitar), The Cut-Ups, and The Frantics. Along with Birdland, the Spanish Castle became a favourite haunt for Jimmy and he often tried to sit in with bands there – early signs of a habit that would stay with him for the rest of his short career.

Bandleader Dave Lewis remembered Jimmy Hendrix coming down to hear him at Birdland at the turn of the 1960s. "He'd always be there in the front, listening intently. Then he'd say, 'Dave! Hey, Dave, can I sit in?' So I'd say 'Sure.' But whenever he'd start playing something experimental, people would stop dancing. They didn't know what was going on. They weren't ready for what he was doing. They wanted to dance. So then I'd have to ask Jimmy to stop."[58]

Hendrix was beginning to think he might be able to make some sort of living out of playing music. Perhaps in pursuit of this, he and most of The Rocking Kings would work as James Thomas's backing band, The Tomcats, during the first half of 1961, for larger gigs such as outdoor events. The experience was making Hendrix increasingly confident of his showmanship as well as his musical accomplishments. Junior Heath recalled: "Jimmy was always a performer. He like[d] to play his guitar between his legs, and behind his back, and with his teeth."[59] Hendrix was maturing into a competent performer who had mastered the popular music of the day.

By this time, Hendrix had developed an ability to concentrate intensely for long stretches of time, practicing for hours on end and playing with anyone at the merest suggestion of a jam. In music, if not in school work, the hard work was paying off. Yet he was still prone to the usual vagaries of a band musician's life. During the spring of 1960 disaster struck when he lost his guitar, stolen one night from Birdland where The Rocking Kings were appearing regularly. He attempted to hide the fact from his father, who'd bought him the instrument, but Al quickly found out. In typical no-nonsense fashion, Al simply told his son he'd have to wait some time for the next guitar.

According to Al, Hendrix's uncle Frank and wife Mary saw to it that he quickly had a replacement. Jimmy and Junior Heath went and bought new electric guitars from Meyer's music store at the same time. Hendrix acquired this second electric guitar with a down-payment borrowed from outside the immediate family. Al Hendrix made him take the guitar back and return the down-payment. Furious and resentful that he'd been publicly humiliated, Al put his foot down. "I just felt that if I couldn't get a guitar for Jimmy, there wasn't going to be one," Al wrote later. "I don't remember how long it took me to get him another guitar – maybe [it was] a month or so."[60] The new electric guitar was a Danelectro 3012 model. Back in 1960, neither Heath nor Hendrix had the money for a guitar case, so they carried their guitars around on straps, often playing while walking or hanging around in the street.

As 1960 progressed, Hendrix was increasingly distracted at school and perpetually short of even the smallest sums of pocket money. Everyone who knew him in the late 1950s and early 1960s remembers he was always in need of money to take part in the simplest social occasions with his friends. Mike Tagawa: "One time he borrowed a quarter. You'd think, no big deal. But it actually created a little bit of distance between us because he never did pay it back. And then when we'd go down to the Burger King to eat hamburgers and french fries, he never had the quarter to pay me back. And it was like, man, aren't you going to pay me back the quarter? Well, I never said it like that, but it caused a little bit of discomfort. My family didn't have much money, and I don't think Hendrix's did either. I look back on it now and it's laughable."[61] Money was too tight to mention, something any teenager finds hard to bear. The aspiring teenage musician was becoming increasingly disillusioned with his circumstances. He was frustrated at the lack of forward movement for The Rocking Kings' career and their prospects of greater financial return. He was also getting into scrapes that would eventually bring him into close contact with Seattle's police. Things would soon come to a head. For most of 1960 Hendrix was a 17-year-old feeling his way through life like every other teenager. He occasionally hung out with kids looking for trouble. By this time his father had made it clear he little sympathy for his position. Years later Jimmy told Kathy Etchingham, "He didn't like the fact that I wanted to play guitar, always putting me down and telling me to get a job."[62] His father was fond of recalling the time in September 1960 when Jimmy and a friend broke into a store and stole some clothes. Al soon found out, making amends by insisting that he and Jimmy go to the store owner's house and do some work for him "as restitution".[63]

Tagawa felt people tend to forget that Jimmy was a young man like every other young man trying to make his way in life. "It's interesting to me that people have made Hendrix supernatural and superhuman. I remember him as just another guy, just like a lot of us [who were] at Garfield do. … It's hard for people that didn't see him as a student, doing student kinds of things, like carrying books – or not carrying your books a lot of times in Hendrix's case. Looking at him as somebody ordinary."[64]

Music and the absence of money were two key forces in young Jimmy's life. Whether they were the prime reasons that he left Garfield High School in October 1960 can never be confirmed, but there is little doubt they were major considerations. Tagawa saw Hendrix walking through Garfield's corridors shortly before he left, playing an imaginary guitar and with no school books in sight. "He gave me that nice, warm smile of his and said something like, 'I don't need my books. I've got my guitar.' I thought that was pretty cool, because I wasn't such a great student myself."[65]

Hendrix dropped out of Garfield and tried to make money by working for his dad. He quickly found his father a poor payer. Al claimed that Jimmy stuck with the work until the boy's induction into the Army in early summer 1961; others suggested that Jimmy came and went, using the work as a last resort where all else failed, or when he was particularly broke. In a 1967 interview, Hendrix claimed: "School wasn't for me. According to my father I had to go working. I had done that for a few weeks with my father. He had a not-so-good running contracting firm, and in me he saw a cheap labourer. I didn't see it that way. I had to carry cement and stones all day, and he pocketed the money."[66] Hendrix hinted that his father coerced him into leaving school – a common occurrence in poor families where schooling was seen as a luxury after a boy reached an employable age. Al was painfully aware of their poverty and no doubt expected his son to contribute financially as soon as possible. Hendrix, hardly the most dedicated of students and with interests outside the academic arena, gave in without too much persuasion.

This was a time of transitions as Hendrix began to glimpse the first contours of maturity through his adolescent existence. He'd moved forward personally in a number of ways. He'd met Betty Jean Morgan while they were both attending Garfield, and by summer 1960 they were going steady. She was one of the few Seattle people who would stay close to him for some time after he left the city in 1961. Her mother initially encouraged the relationship. "When my kids were growing up," Mrs Morgan told Mary Willix, "I opened my home to my kids' friends. I used to bake cookies and give them Kool Aid. Jimmy was one of my favourites of the kids who came over. He used to sit out on the porch and play his guitar. He was a typical teenager. He had a nice personality."[67]

Betty Jean Morgan herself said of Hendrix: "He was kind and very generous. We'd talk on the phone, and on the weekend he'd come up from 26th and Yesler to my house. I had a close-knit family, so we did things with my family."[68] Both Betty Jean and her mother confirmed that she and Jimmy were engaged, and that he continued to send letters to both of them well after he went way with the Army. "He bought her a nice ring," Betty's mother recalled. "When he went into the service he left his guitar with me. He used to write to me and keep in touch."[69] Betty still has the letters, along with photos he sent her during the first few months of his Army stint. They remain unpublished.

The 18-year-old Hendrix, seemingly poised on the edge of marriage yet with a hardly diminished drive to carve out a musical career for himself, decided in May 1961 that he would volunteer for the Army. Hendrix was apt to dismiss this later as something necessary to just get through. "I figured I'd have to go sooner or later," he said in 1969, "so I volunteered to get it over with so that I could get my music together later on. And when I joined I figured that I might as well go all the way, so I joined the Airborne. I hated the Army immediately."[70]

However there is good reason to believe that he joined the Army in response to two separate incidents late in the spring of 1961. He and some friends were detained for riding in stolen cars. With regard to the first offence, Al Hendrix was sure that only the driver of the car knew it was hot. No charges were pressed, but it seems that Hendrix was in custody at Rainier Vista 4-H Youth Center for a few days and was shaken up by the whole experience. Hendrix appeared in front of a magistrate after his second car-theft offence and, it seems, was given the option of a gaol sentence or induction into the Army.

His increasing disillusion with Seattle life does not seem in itself enough reason to want to join the Army. A little more credible is the notion that Hendrix knew he had to leave Seattle to further his career, but lacked the practical knowledge as well as the fortitude to simply take off. Probably the simplest explanation is the best: he and his father were following the magistrate's 'suggestions'. Al Hendrix later noted that his son, like many fellow blacks during the 1950s and 1960s when the US still had a vigorous National Service requirement, was classified 1A by the draft board, which meant that he could be called to serve at a moment's notice.[71]

> ## "When I joined the Army I figured that I might as well go all the way, so I joined the Airborne. I hated the Army immediately."
>
> Jimi Hendrix

While still at school Hendrix could have had the draft deferred, but now he was no longer a student he could be drafted at any time. The 1A status that Al remembered must have been something of a gaffe by the Draft Board, because Hendrix was chronically short-sighted (he had spectacles but rarely wore them – a contributory factor to his appallingly bad driving later in life). But this was hardly unusual when it came to drafting non-white US males. Hendrix joined up so quickly that, uncharacteristically, he missed a Tomcats gig where he was scheduled to play guitar, and the band had to find a replacement at short notice.

He and his father attempted to retain some control over his immediate future by deciding that it would be better to volunteer – an act which gave him the choice of service he was to enter. Al Hendrix recalled that his son started seeing a sergeant at the recruiting office, and that Jimmy decided he'd like to join the 101st Airborne Division, known as the Screaming Eagles. In mid May 1961 that is precisely what he did.[72]

the last train to clarksville

JUNE 1961 TO AUTUMN 1963

Private Jimmy Hendrix did not anticipate any immediate need for his guitar in the 101st Airborne: he left it in Seattle upon his induction into the US Army on May 31st 1961. He would soon realise that had been a mistake.

H endrix's first Army posting took him away from Seattle and the far Northwest for the first time since his early childhood. First he went to Ford Ord in California for basic training and to await his posting. Fort Ord was – and still is – the main Army Infantry Training Center in the US with a history that reaches back to the Mexican-US war of 1846. Even in Hendrix's time it was a gigantic base, covering over 28,000 acres, situated on the Monterey Bay Peninsula. It is bordered to the north by the city of Marina and to the south by Sand City. Monterey, Carmel, Pacific Grove and Salinas are just minutes away by car. (Other alumni of Fort Ord included actors – Clint Eastwood had been a swimming instructor there in the early 1950s – and musicians – Gary Lewis, of the Playboys, and Drake Levin, of Paul Revere & The Raiders. Even Bing Crosby's twin sons did their basic training there.)

All new recruits discover the shock of Army discipline and regulations, but it is likely that basic training was not as onerous for Hendrix as it would have been for many teenagers. He had received a strict upbringing from his father, doing the daily household chores that most teenage boys will spend their lives avoiding. Like other new recruits, Hendrix posed proudly for a photograph in full Army dress uniform.

During his first weeks he wrote to his father, making sure he hit all the right buttons, even enquiring how Al's gardening business was going. He then asked for small short-term loans until his Army pay caught up with his initial outgoings. His letters were full of comments about the new conditions that Army life imposed, including having to shave more regularly – clearly a source of pride as much as irritation for an 18-year-old.

During a short furlough at home at the end of the summer, he confided to his father that the Army "does teach you a few things, like self-reliance".[1] He paraded the new clean-cut image to his friends and hung out with Betty Jean. He made it back to Fort Ord from Seattle on September 11th, having left home about four days earlier, and on the 12th wrote a letter to his father that included a story about his trip back to camp. It is typical of Hendrix. "I just got back yesterday – here's what happened: when I got to San Francisco, I lost my bus ticket. I found out that I lost it just when I was standing in line – while I was searching and retracing my steps, the bus left – and the next one didn't leave until about two hours after my time to check in at the Company."[2]

He'd had to phone the base, report to the local MPs – and ended up arriving a day late. He finished

Hendrix was thrilled when he lined up for the Army flight that took him to his first parachute jump.

the letter by asking Al to "give everyone my love, including Betty, the sweet thing". But such instructions would soon cease. Perhaps alerted by gossip from other Seattle recruits at Fort Ord, Betty soon grew suspicious that he had "someone else down there – California girls are tuff, I know" and she would admonish Jimmy to "leave those 'sapphires' alone or you just better not come up here to see me".[3] Jimmy, deluged by a constant stream of letters from her, quoted this extract from one of them when writing to his father in early November, in an attempt to explain his increasing exasperation with her and to win Al's sympathy. The letter crossed in the post with one from Al bringing him news from home, and he diligently replied to that on November 2nd, making attentive comments about Al's domestic arrangements (including the arrival of a new TV). Jimmy tagged a request to the end of the letter asking Al not to pass on his comments on Betty to her. "She might get mad (smile)." He was already regretting his own outburst, but the break from Betty would not mend.

Such problems connected to his previous lifestyle were soon overtaken by events at the base. He spent another two relatively quiet months working as a clerk in the supply room at Fort Ord before being given a transfer to Fort Campbell, Kentucky, more than 2,000 miles away. Hendrix was soon readying himself for the journey to Fort Campbell, commenting to his father that he had to be there at 5:00pm on November 9th. For once, he made it. His bus left Ford Ord on the 4th and arrived in Kentucky four days later, where his training started immediately. Hendrix made his first dummy parachute jump on the 10th.

Fort Campbell was a very different camp to Fort Ord. It was smaller, with a distinct fighting and training tradition of its own. Named for the last Whig Governor of Tennessee it has a much shorter history than Fort Ord. It was constructed early in 1942 between Hopkinsville, Kentucky, and Clarksville, Tennessee, the location making for a much hotter and more humid climate than anything Hendrix had known before.

The 101st Airborne had been reactivated in September 1956 after disbandment at the end of World War II, and Fort Campbell became its first and only permanent base. Given Hendrix's ambitions, the posting was not arbitrary. In a letter home on November 13th, Hendrix wrote to his father: "Well, here I am, exactly where I wanted to go in the 101st Airborne. We jumped out of a 34-foot tower on the third day we were here. It was almost fun. We were the first nine out of about 150 in our group … it was a new experience. There's nothing but physical training and harassment here for two weeks, then when you go to jump school, that's when you get hell! Fussing and fighting everything you do. … That's how they separate the men from the boys. I pray that I will make it on the men's side."[4] The tone of the letter is calculated to appeal to his father's pride in his son's achievements. It also rather unsubtly suggests that Hendrix, who had ambitions for military achievement higher than his father's, was having to endure more than his dad ever faced. In fact, action was highly unlikely, given that the US was not then involved in any wars (although Vietnam would start up within a year of Hendrix's exit from the Army). But it points up that the 19-year-old Hendrix needed both to achieve and to be admired for his achievements.

Yet he was not simply aiming for glory. In a letter home written at Fort Ord just before his journey to Kentucky, he revealed a more equivocal set of aspirations. "I signed up for clerk, administration work, and stuff like that, because I really don't want to be in that infantry stuff, if I can help it – the AIRBORNE part of it is only the secondary pick. When I go to Fort Campbell, all I do is go to that jump school and if I graduate, all I will do is be sent or stationed there as a supply clerk or something – and then I just have to make that one jump a month for that extra $55 a month – and anyway, it would be a challenge … trying for something like AIRBORNE or Rangers – I'm leaving that Rangers mess alone (smile). Trying to make ABN is bad enough."[5] In an interview years later Hendrix confirmed this largely pragmatic viewpoint. Asked why he chose a parachute regiment, he replied: "You got more

money."[6] His willingness to use the system for his own ends was a variant on his behaviour back in Seattle, when he played with bands that allowed him to borrow their equipment, or hung out with people for the kick of it without completely committing himself to them and their collective cause.

Common to many teenagers, he had a similar utilitarian approach to his home and life there, while plotting how to achieve his aim of success in music. In the Army he had definite aims, but they were private aims and were quickly achieved through the routine the Army offered. Within a month of arriving at the camp he was making his first parachute jump. By the end of that month he was so practised that he was allowed to take photographs both on the plane and during the jump.

The initial thrill of parachuting had been enormous, but once he had acquired and mastered that skill – along with the concomitant fears – there was little else to look forward to. He later claimed to an interviewer that he quickly realised after joining up that the Army was the wrong place for him. Training to be a supply clerk was certainly not going to hold his attention for long. His letters up to March 1962 show him eager to give his father the impression that he was looking for advancement within the Army, including one dated January 17th in which Hendrix details his ambitions to reach Private First Class, which he expected to do by mid February. But he was well aware that a career of routine and boredom would stretch ahead of him should he elect to stay.

Meanwhile, he had to establish a private life – even in Fort Campbell, Kentucky. Within days of arriving, Hendrix was checking out the musical facilities and the unofficial side of music-making. "I had no musical training," he recalled later, "so I couldn't sign up as a musician. But I did play here and there."[7] He was soon sitting in with other musicians and borrowing guitars, often using equipment from the Army rehearsal rooms. As he became known around the camp he began to meet other people who had an interest in the styles of music he found most congenial, especially blues and R&B.

One of those he met in late 1961 while still borrowing guitars was bassist Billy Cox. "I was coming from a theatre and it was raining," Cox told a journalist many years later. "We all ran and wound up on the doorstep of Service Club No. 1, where you could rent instruments and go to little practice rooms. I heard this guy playing a guitar with a sound that I had never heard before. … I'd describe it as a mixture of John Lee Hooker and Beethoven. I went in and introduced myself, told him I played bass. I checked out a bass, started jamming, and that relationship lasted a long time."[8] The two of them hit it off both musically and personally. Cox recalled proposing that they get a group together to play gigs on the base. Charles Washington, a saxophonist and career soldier with the 101st Airborne (he later made it to the rank of Major), had a slightly different version of events. "I started a little group as a saxophone player. Two of the people I had work with me in that band turned out to be Jimmy Hendrix and Bill Cox."[9]

Perhaps there were two bands that quickly merged into one, or both bands had continually fluctuating personnel. Whatever its true origins, Hendrix, who until that point had been content to practice alone or at most jam with Army mates, was quick to join up. Soon afterwards he wrote to his dad asking him to send his guitar: now that he had the prospect of work with an Army band, he felt the need for his own instrument rather than relying on others. He'd also discovered that there were clubs and night-spots in nearby Clarksville where he could sit in with the bands and gain experience of the local scene. To do that on a regular basis he needed his own instrument, rather than calling favours from others or from the Army itself. This amateur freelancing would eventually lead to work in Clarksville for the band, but for the time being they appeared strictly within the camp, playing at Service Clubs No.1 and No.2 at Army-organised social occasions.

Hendrix and Cox clicked personally, but they also found a great deal in common musically – more in fact than most of Hendrix's earlier musical partners in Seattle. Cox said later that his record collection in the Army was strictly the blues. "Jimmy and I were not from the South, but our early influences were. We liked Jimmy Reed, and then we got more into a lot of B.B. and Albert King. … Albert King was a very, very powerful influence on him."[10] According to Cox, Hendrix's record collection then was quite small, but he would listen intensely to each of his discs. Hendrix said later that in the early phase of his career he was most influenced by musicians such as Muddy Waters, Elmore James, Eddie Cochran and B.B. King.[11] Of those, Cochran is the most surprising at first glance, but a young player still unsure of the way to his own musical goals may well have found value in Cochran's personal blend of driving rhythm guitar and adroit fills.

By the end of 1961 Hendrix was complaining of homesickness in his letters and working out ways to enliven his highly regulated existence. In the first month of 1962 he officially graduated as a parachutist and gained his Screaming Eagles Jumpwings badge. By January 17th at the latest the Army authorities had agreed that he could send for his guitar, for it is on that day that he wrote home asking his dad to send him his guitar. "I've been having dreams of coming home and seeing you and everybody – it seems kind of funny – I must *really* want to come home for a while – I can hardly wait until the beginning of March – that's when I hope to come home – I hope also that you send my guitar as soon as you can – I really need it now – it's still over at Betty's house – her mother and grandmother writes me all the time. They're real nice people."[12]

This may seem an odd place for him to have left the instrument, but Betty had after all been part of his daily life toward the end of his Seattle days. It was indicative of his quickly evaporating relationship with her that he didn't ask her directly to send his guitar, or even let her know that Al would be dropping by to pick it up. Hendrix had been so close to her that he'd proposed marriage prior to his move to Fort Campbell, though she had eventually turned him down because her mother insisted they were both too young.

By January 1962 at the latest, Hendrix was already looking around the towns nearest to the Army base, playing his guitar and meeting girls. Al remembered that on weekend leave "they'd go to town, he'd bring his guitar along and go to clubs and ask some of the guys if he could get in there and play with them".[13] Billy Cox remembered it as being a little more intensive than that. "We'd come into town every night; it's not like we had to wait for the weekends to come off post."[14] Eventually it became known to the gig bookers in Clarksville that there was a fair-to-middling band at the nearby base, so they came along to check them out. The name they used most frequently while in the Army was The King Kasuals. According to Billy Cox, the visit by the bookers led to offers of work for various low-paid Clarksville gigs.

The work brought its own set of problems, as saxophonist Charles Washington later remembered. "You know Jimmy was a left-hand guitar player. That being the case he would have to string his guitar backward with the strings upside down – the heavy strings on top, in reverse of what they normally should be. This was OK within itself, but [with] one exception: Jimmy somehow would always manage to pawn his guitar before a gig … and of course we'd have to go and re-pawn it, repossess it. Nothing else could be used! He had to have this specific guitar. And I think he played this particular angle against the band.

"It really appeared that Jimmy in many cases was never really with us," Washington continued. "He did a lot of concentrating on his music, and a lot of the small-talk that a typical group of guys would make, sometimes he would

not enter into. And of course we'd look over at him occasionally and there he is staring. And we wouldn't ask him for his thoughts per se, but this is what I would call being on cloud nine. You didn't get to know him that closely as far as the exact line of thinking."[15]

Corroboration of Hendrix's erratic attitude towards his guitar and his fellow musicians would come from Hendrix himself in a 1967 interview. He complained that he made no more money in the Army than he was making before he went. "So I had to sell my guitar – fortunately to a nice guy, who would lend it to me when I needed it."[16] Perhaps he was paying this 'friend' for the use of his old guitar when he needed it for gigs . Possibly he was borrowing it and claiming the money from the others on the pretext of having pawned it. When Hendrix was interviewed in later years about his Army experiences he invariably talked about his memories of parachuting and of the boredom of camp life – passing over the music he played there and the people he played with. Perhaps the band was simply a flag of convenience for a musician otherwise unoccupied.

"Well, here I am, exactly where I wanted to go in the 101st Airborne. We jumped out of a 34–foot tower on the third day we were here. It was almost fun."

Jimmy Hendrix, writing to his father

By spring 1962 he was making contacts outside the confines of the military. Although Clarksville was by far the closest town, the major musical centre of Nashville was only about 40 miles away. Singer-guitarist James Nixon was based in Nashville, at that time in King James & The Scepters, a band in which he was the only black musician. He was also later a founding member of the band NTS Ltd. "I met Jimmy Hendrix and Billy Cox at the same time in 1962," said Nixon. "I was doing shows at the Jumachi and the Top Six Club in Fort Campbell. They did shows there too – I used to sit in with them. They used to come to Nashville every weekend and sit in at the Del Morocco Club and places like that."[17] Nixon claims that Cox was at one point also the bassist with NTS Ltd, and considering the amount of doubling by many on the Nashville scene, this is entirely possible. During these forays off base, Hendrix and Cox met up with other musicians playing in the Clarksville-Nashville area, including Johnny Jones, bassist Charles Sherrell, guitarist Larry Lee, and singer Larry LaDon. Hendrix would play with all of these musicians at various times after he quit the 101st Airborne.

The group pressed on and began to play gigs at other military venues. Cox remembered that the reaction was limited. "We played at various service clubs but we got fired from the gigs 'cause we played real loud."[18] With the band working gigs both on and off the base, Hendrix started hanging out with girls from these newly discovered venues, distancing himself further from Betty and all his other Seattle contacts. The people he met from the Clarksville/Nashville area would be important allies in the difficult months after he terminated his Army stint.

In the spring of 1962 he served time with the Airborne in Hawaii, completing jumps there to develop his experience, but the thrill was not enough to distract him from the drudgery of routine Army existence. By March '62 he was writing to his father about the misery of Army training exercises in cold weather, and began to look for routes to an early discharge. In the end, he didn't have to connive his release. He simply had an accident during his 26th parachute jump, late in May. As he recalled some years later: "I got my ankle caught in the skyhook just as I was going to jump and I broke it. I told them I'd hurt my back too."[19] His leg in plaster and his acting on top form, Hendrix eventually convinced the Army medics that he would be of no further use to them. He earned the discharge.

"We liked Jimmy Reed, and then we got more into a lot of B.B. and Albert King. Albert King was a very, very powerful influence on him."

Billy Cox, on early Hendrix taste

The inconvenience of the broken ankle may have put an end to the Army regimen, but it didn't stop him from playing with The King Kasuals. A photograph of the group performing at Clarksville's Pink Poodle in June 1962, immediately prior to his discharge, shows his leg still in plaster as he sits on his modest amplifier. Hendrix is in dark suit and tie, playing the guitar, one foot on the floor, the other jokingly supported by a laughing lead vocalist so that the leg is stretched horizontally. Another band member is buttressing his back so that he doesn't fall backwards. Hendrix has a grin on his face as he mugs for the camera, firm in the knowledge that he was heading out of the Army and back into civilian life. "I was lucky to get out when I did," he recalled later. "Vietnam was just coming up."[20]

Hendrix's discharge from the 101st Airborne came on July 2nd 1962. He left the base with a small bag and his discharge pay in cash, but no guitar. His original idea had been to return to his father in Seattle, catch his breath and then plan his next move in the music business, possibly working with his Army buddy, Billy Cox. After all, Cox would be out of the military in a couple of months: maybe they could play the chitlin circuit together in different bands, or even form their own band. But he did none of these things, choosing instead just to kick around Clarksville and generally trying to sit in with some of the bands that he'd got to know through the work that he did there with The King Kasuals.

According to a later interview, his change of plan was down to financial embarrassment as much as anything else. "When I got out I didn't have anything to show for it at all," said Hendrix, "so I wasn't going to go back home."[21] He would tell another late-1960s interviewer a rather more complicated version of why he decided not to return to Seattle but rather to take his chances in the Clarksville-Nashville area. Glossing over a number of inconsistencies, he said: "There was this girl I was kind of hung up on. Then I thought I'd just look in at Clarksville which was near, stay there that night and go home next morning. That's what I did, looked in at Clarksville, which was near; stay there the night and home the next morning. I went in this jazz joint and had a drink, liked it, and stayed."[22]

Another latter-day interview brought a further expansion: "I would have left for Seattle but then there was this little girl, who kept me. And I stayed in Clarksville through the night, and had some wonderful times. I met a bunch of nice people who praised my singing – I gave drinks to them all. When I

woke up the next morning I had $13 left in my pocket. So I had to go back and borrow my guitar again, so that I could play my way to Seattle. But it was closer to go to Nashville. It [wasn't far] from Clarksville and Fort Campbell, where I'd started my way home. I stayed in Nashville: there were jobs for me there – lots of jobs!"[23]

The nightclub incident gave the 19-year-old the excuse not to go back home, and he certainly knew better than to phone his father for money. He later used almost identical words to explain his decision. "Nope. That was out. All I can do, I thought, is get a guitar and try to find work here. Nashville was only 20 miles away – you know, big music scene. There had to be something doing there."[24]

So there was young Jimmy Hendrix, stranded in Clarksville with a woman he was stuck on, planning to look for work 40 miles or so away in Nashville to try to kick-start his career. With no guitar. Hendrix would tell a number of variants on the story about regaining his old guitar, including one in which he crept back to Fort Campbell and stole it. None of them reflect well on him. But he talked most convincingly about selling it to an Army buddy and repeatedly borrowing it afterwards. In need of a guitar like never before, he "found the guy and told him I just had to borrow the guitar back".[25] There is no record of Hendrix returning it and eyewitnesses suggest that he used his old Danelectro guitar only as long as it took to get the money together for a better instrument.

Hendrix spent the next two months of 1962 in Clarksville with Joyce Lucas, the woman "who kept me", sitting in at professional engagements with some of the local musicians he'd met while in the Kasuals. Lucas was the first of a sequence of women who would play this role for Hendrix, prior to and during his years of fame, giving him not only basic needs like food, sex and a place to live, but also advice and encouragement at transitional points in his career. When Billy Cox emerged from the Army in September, he and Hendrix lodged together in a cheap Clarksville rental along with Lucas and some others, but regular work proved hard to find. Clarksville was a small town.

After an unproductive visit to nearby Indianapolis, Hendrix and Cox pulled together a new civilian edition of The King Kasuals in Clarksville, but the band wasn't up to much and got work only from the worst of the local agents. Hendrix later recalled the agency's name as W&W. "Man, they paid us so little that we decided that the two Ws stood for Wicked and Wrong."[26] Cox's recollections of the band's expertise make it clear that band and agency at that time were a reasonable match for one another. He maintains that the Kasuals were a covers band, keeping the customers happy with live versions of current and classic jukebox hits. "We were playing blues and R&B. ... Jimmy was too timid to sing and they laughed at me when I sang, so we had a singer named Harry Batchelor. We had two guitar players, bass, drums, and a saxophone. We were poor musicians then."[27]

Somehow, probably through word of mouth, these "poor musicians" got lucky. The Del Morocco (sometimes spelled Del-mor-roca) club on Nashville's Jefferson Street – just a block from where Hendrix and Cox ended up living – was looking for a new band. The Del Morocco was one of the better clubs on Jefferson Street, with a floor show and a stage large enough to accommodate a full size big-band replete with drum risers. Earl Gaines remembered it as one of the clubs on the first rung of the Nashville ladder, many of which stayed open 24 hours a day. "Everybody used to play those clubs," said Gaines, "Fats Domino, Little Richard, B.B. King – everybody."[28] The Del Morocco had a part-time band but wanted to upgrade to a full-time unit, and this suited The King Kasuals' needs. They were already known individually to the owners from the times they would sit in during their Army days. They auditioned and got the job.

Cox recalled the well-appointed club as not large, seating around 150.[29] The Kasuals often left their audiences bemused: Cox thinks it was because they were so loud – "at that time people didn't know whether to clap or walk out"[30] – but it was probably down to a combination of factors, including their relative lack of experience. They were hired primarily to provide backing music for shake dancers and as the support for bands coming through town, including those of Nappy Brown and Carla Thomas. On Sundays Ironing Board Sam, an early blues favourite of Hendrix's, played at the club, giving the young guitarist an opportunity to study his style.

Even within the limitations of this stereotyped club-band existence, Hendrix was constantly attempting to improve his music and the way he presented himself. He soaked up lessons from everyone he saw and heard. Like Guitar Slim and many other black musicians before him, he began to come off-stage and prowl around on the dancefloor while still playing. "I was the electronics man with the group," Cox said, "so I bought him a 75-foot cord at Radio Shack and put some quarter-inch plugs on the ends … so he could go off-stage into the audience. … He could even go out the front door and play on the sidewalk."[31]

The lack of audience response did nothing to dampen Hendrix's desire to play. Cox told stories of him walking the streets of Nashville with his guitar constantly in his hands, his face a mask of concentration as he ran through his licks. "I saw him put 25 years into the guitar in five years, because it was a constant, everyday occurrence with him."[32] Such obsessive behaviour is not unusual in an instrumentalist utterly determined to master his chosen horn, whether in classical, jazz or popular music. Many superior musicians get to that technical level by practicing eight hours a day for years on end, and Hendrix was putting in the musical miles to earn his virtuosity, like thousands of instrumentalists from before Vivaldi's time to the present day.

The band quickly moved into premises close to the Del Morocco. "A lot of mornings," Cox said, "we were right down here on Jefferson Street [in Nashville] – we lived over top of Joyce's House Of Glamour – [and] a lot of times I'd get him up mornings – we'd have to go for breakfast. I'd knock on his door – door'd be open – he's lying there in the same clothes he had on the night before, with his guitar lying on his stomach."[33] Jefferson Street was the main artery of the Nashville R&B music scene in 1962. The Joyce whom Cox mentions was very likely not only the manager of the House Of Glamor but also Joyce Lucas, the older woman with whom Hendrix had an affair that year and who appears in a relaxed picture with Hendrix taken in December 1962 at the Impressions Dance. Lucas may have been a regular companion, but she was not the only woman Hendrix was seeing in late autumn 1962 as he began to accustom himself to living in Nashville and took stock of his position in the world.

Later in his career, Hendrix had less benign memories of the stint at the Del Morocco. "We got in with a club owner, who seemed to like us a lot. He bought us some new gear. I had a Silvertone amp and the others got Fender Bandmasters. But this guy took our money and he was sort of holding us back."[34] He told another interviewer: "We used to have to sleep in a big housing estate they were building around there. No roofs, and sometimes they hadn't put floors in yet. That was wild."[35] Nobody seems to recall what happened to the accommodation at Joyce's House Of Glamor. Perhaps Jimmy and Joyce had gone their separate ways and the rooms had disappeared with her. Hendrix was already developing a mode of living remarked upon by many of his later companions. He kept different aspects of his life completely separate. Sometimes friends and associates were utterly unaware of one another's existence. Hendrix had checked out all the other musicians on Nashville's R&B scene, and he became part of a busy but small network of players. Even at this early stage of his career he was developing a reputation amongst his peers for the eccentricity he displayed in his manner of speaking and his dress sense.

In the early 1960s Nashville remained a provincial backwater to the larger US music industry, with the city only in the earliest stages of throwing off its long history of segregation. The white population largely preferred a very traditional type of country music, so the local industry focussed on satisfying that relatively affluent audience. Little of the music making from within that rigidly structured and conservative musical enclave had much resonance beyond a small radius of like-thinking southern American states. All this would change beyond recognition within a decade, but in 1962 that was still a long way off, and Nashville's local record industry had few heavyweight connections with New York and Los Angeles.

On the other side of the segregationist divide, however, there had been a vibrant R&B circuit since soon after the end of World War II. This scene, largely ignored by blues chroniclers until quite recently, was partly due to the hardiness of the chitlin-circuit joints and bars in the area, but its long-term popular strength was due mainly to the presence of Nashville's WLAC radio station. WLAC had been broadcasting the latest R&B releases since the late 1940s on a nightly show hosted by DJ Gene Nobles. His spot was sponsored by Randy Wood's Record Store, a retail and mail-order business based in nearby Gallatin. Wood's store offered a comprehensive service on what were then called 'race' records, as well as other more mainstream releases, including classical music.

"We played at various service clubs but we got fired from the gigs 'cause we played real loud."

Billy Cox, King Kasuals bassist

Radio reception could not be segregated and the response to Nobles' shows was large and sustained, especially from the young on both sides of the racial divide. These people wanted to buy the records they were hearing. "We proved that rhythm & blues could be commercial," WLAC DJ Hoss Allen told an interviewer. "We also initiated a new sound to white kids who probably never would have heard of it had it not been for the power of WLAC."[36] Within a short time the response from listeners allowed Woods to expand, eventually setting up Dot Records. His label prospered through the 1950s and had a string of hit cover versions, especially of white singers covering black rock acts. Pat Boone was Dot's biggest-selling singles artist during this time.

The reason for the nationwide response – accurately reflected by Wood's successful mail-order trade in the records played – was that WLAC had a very powerful transmitter (some 50,000 watts) with a phenomenal reach. It didn't need to be networked: people could pick it up from Montreal to El Paso to Jamaica. All the acts on the chitlin circuit across the US would tune in every night they were on the road driving from one gig to the next, checking out the latest releases. This gave Nashville a national importance in the development of new trends in black popular music that it would not otherwise have been able to sustain. It also gave local musicians employment opportunities and publicity outlets simply unavailable elsewhere. This helps to explain why Hendrix and Cox were trying to make a go of it in Nashville. But while the local live scene may have boasted clubs such as the New Era Dinner Club, Grady's Dinner Club, the Del Morocco and the Sugarhill Dinner Club, all on Jefferson Street, and the Stealaway nearby, it was certainly not well developed, with very little money filtering through to the musicians. Recording opportunities were limited to one-off deals with shoestring companies usually run from one room: none of the nationally-based companies had any interest in recording such acts.

Musicians working with the blues and its offshoots scuffled in a small number of clubs and bars. Hendrix had no good memories of them later, though he knew it was a proving ground. "In the bars I used to play in, we'd get up on the platform where the fan was, in one of them nice, hot, greasy, funky clubs … and you really had to play, 'cause those people were really hard to please. It was one of the hardest audiences in the South; they hear it all the time. Everybody knows how to play guitar. You walk down the street and people are sitting on their porch playing their guitar. That's where I learned to play, really; in Nashville."[37]

In the autumn of 1962 the band settled into their residency at the Del Morocco. Despite their versatility and enthusiasm, they were hardly setting audience attendance records, and Hendrix's attention soon began to wander as the notion of an endless engagement in a two-bit chitlin club didn't fit with his ambitions. In a bid to widen their appeal and provide the right mood music for dancers, Cox remembers that the band spread their stylistic net very wide indeed.

They incorporated the newly emergent Memphis soul style that had given The Mar-Keys a national No.3 hit in August 1961 with 'Last Night', an

"Jimmy was too timid to sing and they laughed at me when I sang, so we had a singer named Harry Batchelor."

Billy Cox, on King Kasual vocals

instrumental replete with blasting horns and a quasi-boogie riff combining elements of Bill Doggett's 1956 smash 'Honky Tonk', a song Hendrix knew well, with the theme from the TV series *Peter Gunn*. They regularly included songs to please an older clientele, such as 'Harlem Nocturne', a 1940s hit first recorded with a tenor saxophone lead, Erroll Garner's 1954 ballad 'Misty', and even repertoire from the better Broadway songwriters of the 1930s and '40s like George Gershwin, Vernon Duke, and Harold Arlen.

The residency slowly turned into a sort of informal prison sentence for a man with Hendrix's drive and ambition. One of the problems with long-term residencies is that, unless either the club or the band is already soaring, the sheer amount of time and effort taken up doing a gig seven nights a week means a band can die a very slow death. In a place like Nashville at this time, where live opportunities for black bands and musicians were limited, there were few escape routes. According to Hendrix, there were also complications related to the low-life that then passed for artist management and promoters in Nashville. "The promoters were the strangest and most crooked there," he said later. "They used to come right up on to this makeshift stage while we were in the middle of a number, slip our money into our pockets, and disappear. Then we'd find out afterwards that they'd only slipped us a couple of dollars instead of 10 or 15…. Nashville used to be a pretty funny scene,

with all those slick managers trying to sign up hillbilly singers who'd never been in a big town before."[38]

One kind of release for Hendrix was to sit in with other bands or jam after-hours with different musicians – easy enough to slip back into, given that he'd been keen on this sort of thing for a long time. Many musicians working the Nashville clubs in 1962/'63 remember Hendrix as something of a wild man when he sat in with their groups, trying ideas out, dressing unusually and generally trying to make an impression. Most remained at best bemused by his approach. With the indulgence of hindsight, Nashville vocalist Earl Gaines recalled Hendrix as "wild and loud. People didn't understand what was going on until the later years. He knew what he was doing. They liked the way he clowned, playing his guitar behind his head and all that. It was just so different, the way he played".[39]

Early on during his time in Nashville, Hendrix had made a valuable musical contact with guitarist Johnny Jones, then playing with The Imperial Seven (often simply called The Imperials), a band that had a residency at the New Era Dinner Club. Singer-guitarist Larry LaDon was also a member around this time (he claims to have later moved on to The King Kasuals). Jones was even then something of a veteran whose experience included early-1950s stints in Chicago playing with the likes of Junior Wells and Freddie King. He has often asserted that he functioned as something of a musical mentor for Hendrix during this period.

Another way to get noticed in 1962 was through that important Nashville radio station, WLAC. By 1956 its original R&B DJ, Gene Nobles, was on a sabbatical, his place taken by his understudy since 1949, Gallatin-born William "Hoss" Allen. Allen was on good terms with the show's sponsor, Randy Wood's shop in Gallatin – "The World's Largest Mail Order Phonograph Record Shop" – and was also friendly with a Nashville store, Ernie's Record Mart, that later began sponsorship of another R&B show on WLAC.

By 1962, Allen had many fans and an influential niche in the music business. Not only did he broadcast any new releases that came his way, but he also became a producer for many of the small labels recording local and not-so-local musicians. He ran sessions for the Athens, Hermitage, Excello, Old Town, and Brunswick labels, among others, and helped to get local musicians recorded on a regular basis – though few of these labels had wide enough distribution to cause a ripple on the national R&B charts. Allen was a very popular and well-respected personality in Nashville and the South until his death in 1997, and even managed to front a shortlived TV series, *The!!!Beat*, broadcast in Dallas, Texas, in 1966 which featured The King Kasuals as occasional support band. Despite subsequent stories, Hendrix did not appear; his place had already been taken in the band by Johnny Jones. Allen was also a manager, looking after the career of vocalist Earl Gaines among others during the mid 1960s.

That Allen was aware of such groups as The Imperial Seven and The King Kasuals is incontestable. He produced Johnny Jones's first two 45rpm singles between 1961 and 1963. The Imperial Seven cut 'Soft Shoe' / 'Midnight Tom' for Athens in 1962, while Johnny Jones & The Imperial Seven (with Billy Cox on bass) cut 'Really' Parts 1&2 for Hermitage in 1963. Allen not only reminisced about Jones and his men years later but employed them for various purposes during the 1960s, including a stint as backing band on that Dallas '66 TV show. By 1968, the two bands would merge personnel and record under the King Kasuals name. Allen was fond of telling anecdotes about his colourful career – often, according to friends, deliberately at his own expense. Allen recalled one session involving Cox and Hendrix that he says took place at King Records, from about one in the morning until late into

The King Kasuals, Hendrix's Army band, at the Jolly Rogers club in Nashville, spring 1962. The line-up varied; here are Jimmy Hendrix (left), Billy Cox (centre) and Leonard Moses.

the night. "It was Billy Cox's session," Allen remembered, "and he called me and said he had a guitar player he wanted me to hear. I told him I already had two guitar players, but bring him anyway."[40]

Allen gave the date as November 1962. Thinking Hendrix's contribution superfluous, he turned it off on the control board, with not a note recorded. This recollection is suspect, as it does not tally with recording practice at the time. The session has never surfaced on King or any King-related label, either commercially or on the collector's circuit, so everything about it remains a matter of conjecture.

King Records was controlled out of Cincinnati by Syd Nathan, enjoying great success with its Country & Western and R&B releases (the latter on Federal as well as King). James Brown, Hank Ballard & His Midnighters, Little Willie John and Freddie King made some of their greatest sides for Nathan as the 1950s gave way to the '60s. Nathan did most of his recording in his own excellent Cincinnati studio, not far from Nashville, and King had a distribution centre in Nashville.

That Allen's recollection is faulty is suggested by a simple fact: he took leave of absence from Nashville and WLAC between late 1960 and August 1963, during which time he was an on-the-road salesman for Chess Records of Chicago. Allen was not the most reliable witness when it came to dates and places, for he spent the 1960s living high and wild. Author Wes Smith says that Allen "was a wild man who drank until he couldn't stand, then sat down to have some more. His behaviour made for colourful, outrageous times at the

[radio] station, but eventually it caught up with him and nearly killed him." It is at least worth considering the idea that the session did not take place until Allen was back in town at the station in late 1963. He was undoubtedly making records for various labels at this time, and he may simply have had a faulty memory of the details of what he later specifically identified as "Billy [Cox's] session for King Records". Perhaps he embellished a story to poke gentle fun at himself for missing the world's greatest guitarist while he was living and working in Nashville. That idea is supported by Cox's later suggestion[41] that the A-side of a 45rpm single by Frank Howard & The Commanders, 'I'm So Glad / I'm Sorry For You' (cut for a production company based in Nashville and eventually released some time later on the New York-based Barry label) was composed by Billy Cox and features both Billy Cox and Jimmy Hendrix. Howard has recently confirmed the presence of Cox and Hendrix on the single.[42] This may not even be the session to which Allen is referring, but it at least substantiates Allen's claim that Cox was touting Hendrix around Nashville as a guitarist capable of making record dates. Whatever the truth of the matter, such openings at least gave Hendrix a taste of the next level in a musician's career : making music to be kept for posterity. But it would a while before he officially participated in a session that would see the light of day.

For the time being, however, there was only the faltering career of The King Kasuals to contemplate. The band's relative lack of popular success at the Del Morocco meant that they weren't making much money, and couldn't branch out to other venues. It seems that they stopped working together for a while so that individual members could try to find better work elsewhere.

Hendrix took this opportunity to take a break from Nashville. In December 1962 he traversed America, going back up to the Northwest corner and into Canada, where he stopped in Vancouver, living briefly there with his grandmother Nora. But even there the only work available was playing with obscure bands. It's hardly surprising that this visit failed to advance his career. He sat in regularly with a mixed-race band, Bobby Taylor & The Vancouvers, whose other claim to fame in retrospect was the presence on guitar of Tommy Chong, later to be half of the Cheech & Chong comedy duo that would later launch Blind Melon Chitlin on an unsuspecting world. The Vancouvers had a residency at a city venue, Dante's Inferno, co-owned by Chong and Taylor.

Guitar Shorty had also arrived in Vancouver during 1962, after the break-up in Los Angeles of Sam Cooke's band. Shorty had played in the late 1950s in Ray Charles's big band and more extensively with Guitar Slim, watching Slim every night for years and learning from his amazing stage act. Shorty recalled later: "Guitar Slim used to take his guitar at the end of the show, where he'd climb on the shoulders of his valet, who would walk out into the crowd while Slim was playing his guitar behind his head. ... When he got back to the bandstand, he [would] jump off his valet's shoulders and run back the same way he came." Shorty's wild stage act included an amazing somersault that he called a 'flip', performed while still playing. "One night I was feeling good and I said if he could do that, I could do the flips. My show is a take-off of Slim's: I just fortified it more."[43]

Shorty had cut a 45rpm single in 1957 for Cobra and three in 1959 for Pull in LA, but was not an established bandleader in 1962. He had a residency at The New Delhi in Vancouver. The chronology of Shorty's later recollections is questionable, but his claim that Hendrix used to accompany his step-sister Marsha to watch his act is credible. Less likely is his story that Hendrix used to go AWOL regularly from the Army to see him, as Hendrix had left the Army months before.

Young Jimmy must have been impressed by what he saw and heard of Shorty's act, but this was an isolated highspot in his generally low-key Northwestern winter of 1962/'63. Vancouver would be no more of a solution to his problems than Seattle had been. He made his way back down south in the early spring of 1963, working his passage with various bands, including dates in Biloxi, Mississippi and, in March, in Columbia, South Carolina. He arrived back in Nashville in early April and started up where he left off with Billy Cox. In the absence of anything else to do, they reconvened The King Kasuals at the Del Morocco.

During late spring 1963, Hendrix met local guitarist Larry Lee for the first time. "I was about the worst guitar player in Nashville," Lee later told Harry Shapiro, "and I was searching for somebody in my category, somebody to talk to." Lee caught The King Kasuals at the Del Morocco. "[Jimmy] was just doing nothing with that guitar, man. His guitar was an old Kay with strings about that high and I was sure that [he] was somebody in my calibre that I could talk to." A few nights later Lee went back to introduce himself to Hendrix. "He had another guitar, a new Epiphone, and I couldn't believe this

was the same cat that I'd seen. ... That's when I found out he really *could* play!"[44] Cox corroborated this change of instrument: he remembered going with Hendrix to a Clarksville music store some time in summer 1963 where Hendrix swapped his old Danelectro for this Epiphone Wilshire SB432 guitar.

Lee was acquainted with most of the musicians on the Nashville R&B scene, although he was not yet in a working band. He developed a friendship with Hendrix and accompanied him as he sat in with bands during 1963. He witnessed Hendrix jamming with Johnny Jones, then still playing in The Imperials and regarded locally as Nashville's top R&B guitarist. Doubtless Jones was the more accomplished and technically adroit player as he had been a professional for over a decade and could fit into any R&B and modern blues routine. Lee recalls that Jimmy was less predictable. "I was more impressed with Jimmy than Johnny. ... He had a sound that was more fluid than Johnny, he played more natural, he got more into it. ... He had a lot of nerve with his guitar."[45]

But Hendrix was still less than the complete guitarist he would soon become. In part this was because his ambitions were so much broader than those of any of his immediate peers, but also because he was young and still digesting his influences. At a 'cutting session' with Jones in Nashville's Club Baron one night, Hendrix demonstrated his inexperience in such situations by spending the night imitating B.B. King, coming off distinctly second-best in the process.

But it was his larger ambition that would keep him developing past the point at which others stopped. This itself would be the cause of some frustration during the next four years as his talents were either used for their own ends by a succession of leaders – well-known and obscure – or ignored by the music business in general. But as these agents, managers and record company big-wheels pointed out at the time, since when could a blues-based guitar player who didn't sing become a star? Especially one who was black.

There was no history in blues, R&B or rock'n'roll of guitarists being wildly successful purely because they were great guitarists. They had either to be able to sing or to have a gimmick. Even Duane Eddy had a gimmick, as well as the talents of people like producer Lee Hazlewood behind him. All R&B guitarists had similar gimmicks at this point, largely adopted from the flashy stage acts of R&B tenor sax players of the 1940s and '50s who would walk the bar during their solos and spin around on their back as they honked and tooted. But none of the R&B guitarists were celebrities outside a very small number of aficionados. By 1963 even Duane Eddy's career was on the wane. Hendrix would spend the rest of his early career in the United States trying to find a way to solve this problem.

Although The King Kasuals managed to find the occasional gig elsewhere, Hendrix would grab any opportunity to escape – specifically from the grind at the Del Morocco, and generally from Nashville's provincialism. Mostly he did this by asking for work from the touring acts that breezed into town looking for new musicians to fill vacancies in their backing bands. Billy Cox became used to his friend just taking off without a by-your-leave. "Jimmy hit the road six, seven times, and each time I'd [also] go and talk to the bandleader. ... So Jimmy'd go out and two months later he'd call me and say, 'Hey man, I'm stranded in St. Louis.' So I'd send him money and he'd come back."[46] Hendrix had similar memories. "I just travelled around. I played with different groups from Nashville to Los Angeles, Indianapolis and Florida."[47] He and Larry Lee began playing with another Nashville R&B group, Bob Fisher & The Barnevilles, repeating his Seattle habit of being in two bands at once. The Barnevilles at least managed an occasional support gig on a tour away from Nashville, thereby revealing ambitions that, however modest, outstripped those of The King Kasuals. Hendrix was losing patience with the lack

"I just travelled around. I played with different groups from Nashville to Los Angeles, Indianapolis and Florida."

Jimmy Hendrix

of ambition in the Kasuals. "I got tired of playing that because, you know, they didn't want to move anywhere. They just wanted to stay there."[48] By this time the Kasuals were inured to Hendrix taking off with each new offer to tour and had brought in part-time guitarists so they could continue to function without him. Johnny Jones, among others, doubled in both The Imperials and The King Kasuals around this time, and would eventually join the Kasuals permanently once Hendrix had quit Nashville for good.

One of Hendrix's attempted escapes occurred around the middle of 1963 when a tour headlined by Sam Cooke and Jackie Wilson and overseen by singer-promoter Gorgeous George Odell came through town. George was associated with the Supersonic Attraction agency based in Atlanta, Georgia, and was a well-known character on the Nashville R&B scene. A sometime boxer, he would perform way down on a tour's billing or work as a valet to the star acts, and was well known for his eccentric dress sense – he normally wore a blonde wig – and his ability to seek out musicians to fill any slots that opened up in backing bands and support acts as the shows passed through local towns. Cox recalled later that Hendrix "took off and wound up on the road with George. He got stranded in Atlanta, so he needed some money to get back. He came back, and we wound up playing again. He did that about five times".[49]

Cox may have dismissed this as just another false move by Hendrix, but it was an important stepping-stone for the guitarist. For a start, he got to witness first-hand two of the greatest black acts in showbusiness of the time, Sam Cooke and Jackie Wilson. Eyewitnesses recalled them on this tour as something awesome to behold. Cooke had recently returned from a European tour where he'd learned a thing or two about pleasing the crowd from his co-headliner, Little Richard. Cooke's manager, J.W. Alexander, remembered the

"Everybody knows how to play guitar in Nashville. You walk down the street and people are sitting on their porch playing their guitar."

Jimmy Hendrix

promoter asking if his artist would want to work with Wilson, given that last time the two had worked together Wilson had "kind of cut Sam up". Alexander said it would be OK. He later recalled: "Man, we cut Jackie up night after night! Before him, behind him, whatever. Jackie said, 'Man, you guys are killing me, what the fuck did you do?' But it was really because Sam had finally gotten into his gospel thing, you know? That fervent approach."[50] The lesson would certainly not have been lost on a performer as keenly observant as Hendrix.

Jimmy made a couple of tours under Gorgeous George's auspices in the spring and summer of 1963, initially contributing to George's own set in the Cooke/Wilson package tour but eventually playing in bands backing Solomon Burke, Jerry Butler and Slim Harpo, as well as Hank Ballard & The Midnighters. He even managed to sit in on an after-show jam session one night with Little Richard's superb backing band, The Upsetters. But it all came to an untimely end in Atlanta, and once again he needed help to limp home. Hendrix had few good recollections of these times when he looked back later. "I learned how not to get an R&B group together," he said. "The trouble

was, too many leaders didn't seem to want to pay anybody. Guys would get fired in the middle of the highway because they were talking too loud on the bus or the leader owed them too much money – something like that."[51]

With an irony typical of this part of his career, while Hendrix was still trying to find his way out of Nashville, The Imperials were involved in a live album cut in the city by one of the front-line female blues singers of the day, Etta James. Made for the Chess label, *Etta James Rocks The House* was recorded at the New Era in Nashville on September 27th and 28th 1963. Although the Ruppli Chess discography lists no personnel for the date, a recent CD reissue lists an out-of-town backing band for James. Vocalist Larry LaDon has claimed in interviews that The Imperials were on the date. Perhaps LaDon meant that the band was the warm-up act rather than James's backing band.

Wherever the truth lies, the album is an eloquent testimony to the incendiary atmosphere of the New Era in 1963. James is encouraged by a near-constant barrage of whistles, cheers and exhortations, her singing a step-by-step lesson in how to sing like Janis Joplin – some five years before Joplin's emergence. The album is sheer dynamite R&B from start to finish, proving that the Nashville R&B scene of the time was equal to anything going on elsewhere in the country. Nonetheless, it would be out-of-towner Hendrix who would eventually make the big breakthrough, while his old Nashville colleagues stuck to their familiar paths.

Hendrix and Lee spent most of November 1963 on the road once more as members of The Barnevilles. The band featured a trumpet and saxophone in the front line (leader and booker Bob Fisher, and Sam Higginbottom) and was hired as support for a tour by Curtis Mayfield & The Impressions. This was the first time Hendrix had worked on the same bill as an all-round musician of this calibre, and the exposure to Mayfield's charismatic professionalism had its impact. Considering that Hendrix freely admitted open admiration of Mayfield later in his career, and the evidence in his own songs of some close listening to Mayfield's output, he clearly listened closely during the course of that month.

But come the end of the Mayfield tour there were no follow-ups or offers of new work, so it was back to Nashville. In the meantime, President John F. Kennedy had been assassinated on Friday November 22nd, sending shockwaves through the nation and around the world. The main suspect, Lee Harvey Oswald, was murdered two days later. Kennedy's funeral on Monday 25th was broadcast live and took 93 percent of the US television audience. Just two days later, Jimmy Hendrix achieved his majority, quietly celebrating his 21st birthday with friends and colleagues in Nashville, thousands of miles from home and his family.

Just 21 years old and confronted in the most direct way by the ugly violence that was beginning to rip US society apart, Hendrix was now ready to abandon Nashville and the South for good at the earliest opportunity. That opportunity would not be long in presenting itself. As so often in his short career, it would not be exactly what he might have wanted, but it would have to do. He'd spent 15 months of his life nominally living in Nashville, although a good six months of that had been taken up by the road or Vancouver. He had no emotional attachment to the place.

Jimmy Hendrix was not the kind of person who meticulously planned his route to success. He was an opportunist who knew what he wanted and was unconcerned with the details of how to get it. He wasn't about to stop and ask questions of anyone who claimed they could help him reach the top. It was more important to believe that they could help him, rather than rip him off. Some things would never change.

highways to hell and back

Jimmy Hendrix was still living in the Nashville area as November gave way to December 1963, playing the Club Baron with The Barnevilles and looking for ways out. Then he received some encouragement from a visiting New York-based promoter who suggested he should try his luck in the Big Apple. Hendrix's guitarist friend Larry Lee remembers the man as someone who brought a show into Nashville from New York City. "He was a gay cat, you know? A sissy-acting cat," said Lee. "Anyway, this promoter told Jimmy he saw him play, and could get anything he wanted. If he would go back to New York, he could get Jimmy top money."[1]

I t was just the thing Hendrix had been looking for, and he quickly made plans to travel to New York City, however tenuous the connection. Clearly Larry Lee knew about the planned move, as did bassist Billy Cox, but few others noticed or cared. Lee said many years later that Hendrix seemed to be "in a kind of a rut, he wasn't going nowhere. He had big dreams, he always had big dreams. ... He always said he had some songs, but he never brought them up ... nobody would be paying attention. ... He did write me one letter from New York, he asked me to come up there, we were pretty good by the time he left, but I was in school, and my parents wanted me to finish school. He said New York is just a big country town and we can take this town, man. Jimmy had no responsibility, he was just footloose and fancy free. I knew it couldn't be that easy in New York".[2]

It wasn't. Hendrix arrived in New York City at a time when the entire US music scene was about to undergo wholesale upheavals. Basing himself in a cheap hotel, the Theresa on Seventh Avenue and 125th Street in Harlem, he was quickly disabused of the notion that the promoter had anything of substance to offer him, at least as far as work went. He had to make his own way, and with characteristic insouciance he decided against a humiliating retreat to Nashville. Of course, Hendrix would not have considered this an unfamiliar situation, considering his behaviour and lifestyle in the weeks after leaving the Army in 1962.

Hendrix (far right) plays a date in 1964 during his first stint as guitarist with The Isley Brothers.

New York City in early 1964 was not the most congenial of places for a young black R&B guitarist looking to further his career. There was an unofficial but universally acknowledged divide between work opportunities in different parts of the city, especially on Manhattan island. Uptown, the Harlem venues concentrated on a steady diet of soul and R&B, with a spattering of earthy jazz rooms as well. The plusher clubs and hotel lounges offered a more effete jazz, along with showbiz stars and downright cocktail music offered to a predominantly white clientele in midtown, while downtown continued its traditional mix of jazz clubs and a newly thriving folk scene in Greenwich Village.

"Greenwich Village was like Mardi Gras every weekend. During the summer, it was like that every day and night."

Richie Havens, folk musician

Folk had been a major part of the musical life of Greenwich Village since the 1930s and its popularity had been reinvigorated in the 1950s through the community-based politics of protest songs spearheaded by performers like Pete and Peggy Seeger. The folkies congregated in the coffee-houses and small cafés of the area, mostly scattered along Bleeker and McDougal streets. The folk factions were politically radical, but their music was often deeply conservative. Some of these Village venues intermittently presented black acoustic folk and blues artists, both old and new, from Lightnin' Hopkins to Len Chandler.

Richie Havens was one of the black performers who made the Village his operational base in the early 1960s. He was a refugee from Brooklyn, beguiled by the creative ferment he found downtown. "There were hundreds of painters, writers, poets, singers, comedians and songwriters developing ideas and perfecting their work," Havens wrote later in his autobiography. "There were all-day conversations about new books and experimental plays and there were all-night conversations about what was happening in our lives. …There was so much talent and energy in the Village of the early 1960s that we instinctively knew that big changes in our American culture were brewing all around us."[3]

Few of the Bleeker/McDougal clubs and coffee-houses paid more than a pittance: some simply left the performers to pass around the hat. Between 1960 and '63 popular venues included The Commons, The Third Street, The Cock'n'Bull (later to become The Bitter End), Café Raffio, The Gaslight Café, The Village Gate and The Village Vanguard (both mixing folk with jazz, comedy and other genres), One Washington Place (which decades earlier had been Café Society Downtown) and Page Three.

There was also the Café Wha?. Bob Dylan's chronicler Robert Shelton noted that "for a time, the hottest scene was in a basement *boîte* called the Café Wha?".[4] This opinion was confirmed by Havens. "The Wha? was no minor-league deal. Not many clubs in New York were doing as much business as the Wha? or were as skilful at milking dollars from their customers. The crowds began pouring in during the afternoon and continued to grow past midnight. There were so many tourists on the streets you couldn't walk in the opposite direction on the sidewalk…. The Village was like Mardi Gras every weekend. During the summer, it was like that every day and night."[5] These crowds watched the folk revolution grow and change on an almost daily basis during the first years of the 1960s. Shelton wrote that Wha? manager Manny Roth would regularly offer jobs to young musicians who simply drifted into the place, citing as an example the night in early 1961 when Dylan took his harmonica on-stage to accompany the gifted white blues songwriter and

singer Fred Neil.[6] Another young troubadour would take useful advantage of Roth's venturesome nature five years later.

By the fall of 1962 the younger generation of folk performers had established their own pecking order. Joan Baez and Bob Dylan had their status confirmed by recording contracts and headlining dates at the newly popular folk festivals, while Peter Paul & Mary had become early figureheads in the protest movement. This in turn had created a new clientele in the Village clubs, bars and coffee houses. There were newly politicised students from nearby New York University alongside cultural tourists, especially at weekends. The effect of all this on the Village was keenly felt at the Café Wha? where musician Victor 'Superman' Brady and his steel-drum band had for some time been headlining a bill featuring comedians, singers, solo performers and others. "He had a good thing going," wrote Havens, "but in a year or so, Brady was going to be blown out of the water by Bob Dylan, Joan Baez, Odetta, Peter Paul & Mary – a huge tidal wave of traditional and contemporary folksingers and songwriters."[7]

Peter Paul & Mary confirmed the power of this new movement internationally during 1963 when their version of Bob Dylan's 'Blowin' In The Wind' topped charts in many countries, reaching number two in the US that August. In May – while Jimmy Hendrix was trying to latch on to any chitlin circuit tour that would have him – Bob Dylan had walked out of Ed Sullivan's TV show just prior to broadcast in protest that CBS Television would not allow him to sing his 'Talking John Birch Society Paranoid Blues'. Dylan got national headlines as a result, and the politics of his protest were well aired.

During that summer of '63 America had been shocked by the murder in Mississippi of Medgar Evers, leader of the National Association for the Advancement of Colored People, provoking a sombre and self-questioning mood close to that found in Peter Paul & Mary's 45rpm single. In September, Trini Lopez scored a worldwide smash with his reworking of Peter Paul & Mary's hit of the previous summer, 'If I Had a Hammer'. Lopez's version reached number three in America and sustained the theme of social commentary. The assassination of John F. Kennedy that November brought the keening intensity of Peter Paul & Mary's performance back to public consciousness and the record became closely associated with the aftershocks of the president's death. During that month the trio had no fewer than three albums in the *Billboard* charts, and thanks to their popularity the author of their latest single, Bob Dylan, quickly became known beyond the confines of the folk scene, starting the process by which he would become a pivotal figure in rock music. The impact of 'Blowin' In The Wind' was universal. It made a direct hit on Sam Cooke – he wrote 'A Change Is Gonna Come' as a response to hearing Dylan's song. According to Cooke's manager J.W. Alexander: "Sam was taken aback by the message of the song. He said, 'Alex, I got to write something. Here's a white boy writing a song like this … .'"[8]

The timing of Hendrix's first spark of interest in Dylan is not known, but he certainly possessed a copy of *The Freewheelin' Bob Dylan* album, released in July 1963 and containing 'Blowin' In The Wind' as its first track. By the time *Highway 61 Revisited* came out in September 1965 Hendrix would habitually buy Dylan albums during their first week of release, regardless of how broke he was at the time. 'Blowin' In The Wind' was a single that crystallised the new mood of a nation willing to look at itself and consider its place in the world in a fresh light, and would prove to be as valuable a blueprint for Jimmy Hendrix's own creative development as it was for countless others.

While there have always been black artists operating in folk, most of the new young 'message musicians' of the early 1960s were white. Young whites for the most part showed little interest at the time in the contemporary urban blues coming out of Chicago, Detroit and other cities. Instead, these enthusiasts preferred the 'classic' forms of the music as played by veterans of the 1920s such as Robert Johnson, Mississippi John Hurt, Son House, Bukka White, Skip James and Tampa Red – all of whom were 'rediscovered' now by eager young researchers. Blues stars of the 1940s such as Lightnin' Hopkins and John Lee Hooker also enjoyed new attention, often in the guise of a different type of folk act; even Chicago's Muddy Waters made an LP for Chess around this time called *Muddy Waters – Folk Singer* in an effort to reach the new audience, which was normally not slow to show its disdain for contemporary blues artists. These new fans were victims of the time-honoured delusion that artists of the day weren't 'authentic' or 'pure' because their styles and influences weren't rooted in the music of 20 or more years ago. Contemporary musicians, as always, were fashioning their own new hybrids, and for the purists these were by definition culturally unacceptable. Somehow they were forgetting that the older styles they loved so much had been hybrids in their own time as well. For such reasons the electric blues that had become such a fixture in Chicago remained almost exclusively enjoyed by black audiences, just like its close relation R&B.

On the jazz scene the divide between uptown and midtown/downtown was dictated by the differing tastes of the clientele. English writer Francis Newton noticed this at the dawn of the 1960s. "Uptown there is the jazz of Harlem (the one that does not even get advertised in *The New Yorker*)," he wrote. "This is the sort of noise you hear coming out of the dark belly of The L Bar on Broadway and 148th, the visceral sound of Marlow Morris's organ playing, rather like crystallised glue, at The Top Club on West 145th. ... It is not very ambitious music, but by god the place jumps and the clients at the bar laugh and stomp their feet as men ought to do when they are enjoying themselves. Those who listen to this music are not 'fans'; they are just people who like to have some entertainment while they drink. Those who play it are craftsmen and showmen, who accept the facts of life in the jungle with disconcerting calm." [9]

In midtown and the Village, jazz musicians played other styles for a different clientele, and the far-reaching effects of the bossa nova invasion of 1962/63 were still being felt. There was also the continuing demand for Latin music of both Cuban and Puerto Rican inspiration alongside a thriving Latin dance scene in a variety of clubs and venues. At the close of 1963, clubs featuring jazz in New York City included Basin Street East, Birdland, The Five Spot, The Half Note, The Village Gate, and The Village Vanguard. Artists appearing as Hendrix arrived in the city at the end of 1963 included Ben Webster & Ruth Brown at Birdland, Thelonious Monk at The Five Spot, Charlie Byrd, Flip Wilson and Roland Kirk at The Village Gate, and Bill Evans at The Village Vanguard. By the middle of January 1964 Lambert-Hendricks-Bavan were headlining at The Village Gate. Up in Harlem there was the New York City version of the soul/organ jazz and chitlin circuit, at venues like The Apollo, Count Basie's, Minton's, and Small's Paradise, as well as numerous small clubs, bars, halls and lesser dives that featured talent of every description, from the stars of The Apollo to unknown locals plying their trade in virtual anonymity.

The 21-year-old Jimmy Hendrix initially stayed in Harlem for the same reasons as most other aspiring black musicians arriving in New York: Harlem had relatively cheap accommodation, it was the centre of the black music and entertainment business on the East Coast, and it was where everyone made their professional and social connections. Like most outsiders, Hendrix's first weeks in New York were anything but auspicious, and he even found it hard to persuade anyone to let him sit in at gigs. But in the first months of 1964 his luck would turn.

While Hendrix was reluctantly embracing penury in Harlem, the rest of the country was overtaken by a new musical fad that would prove more than just the latest dance craze. On February 7th 1964 The Beatles arrived in New York City to a welcome that took everybody by surprise – including their US record company Capitol. Two nights later they made their first appearance on Ed Sullivan's television show. Remarkably, 70 million people watched, about 60 percent of the country's entire viewing public. Many New York radio stations incessantly played Beatles music and pre-recorded interviews. The group was impossible to miss, even if you wanted to. Hendrix with his sensitive musical antennae would have noticed that The Beatles achieved their initial impact in the United States playing music patently inspired by acts that he'd been rubbing shoulders with and listening to for some time – and that most (but by no means all) of those acts were black.

The Beatles were important for Hendrix not so much for this initial impact on the music scene but because they focused white middle-class America's attention on R&B and its offshoots, a musical genre that until then had been completely off-limits to them since Little Richard had found God. It took a group of talented interlopers to show America its own riches, because they could be accepted in a way that no homegrown artists could be, with all their social, racial and economic baggage.

The so-called working-class lads from Liverpool were seen by Americans as exotic and fascinating, just in the way that American acts, black, white or in between, had been for decades in Britain. Meanwhile in this same month Bob Dylan, adding fuel to the fire, released his new album *The Times They Are A-Changin'*, once again laying down a challenge to his peers and society in general. That autumn, Peter Paul & Mary would transform the LP's title song into a worldwide anthem for a new generation.

The Beatles brought about a seismic change in US pop music. The pop-music year of 1964 had started with Bobby Vinton, The Murmaids and Bobby Rydell at the top of the charts (although the previous month had seen The Kingsmen's version of 'Louie Louie' and Rufus Thomas's 'Walkin' The Dog' making the Top 10, so it wasn't all bad news). From February to June The Beatles monopolised the number one spot in America – and often number two at the same time – with the sole interruption of Louis Armstrong's 'Hello Dolly'. Hendrix was on a unique and lonely drive towards creating his own personal hybrid of the different musics he'd grown up with and loved. In this, he found the examples laid down by The Beatles and Dylan to be nothing short of revelatory. He saw that it was indeed possible to break through to the larger public by using the music he loved in an entirely fresh way. The only trouble in his case was ... how?

"Those who play the music are craftsmen and showmen, who accept the facts of life in the jungle with disconcerting calm."

Francis Newton, writer, on jazz in uptown Harlem

New York City's tried and tested route for new black acts seeking fame was the Amateur Night at Harlem's Apollo. Held every Wednesday, it had been the stepping stone for many top artists since the early 1930s. Performers from every genre and generation had first tasted success there, including Ella Fitzgerald, Pearl Bailey, Sarah Vaughan, Ruth Brown, Clyde McPhatter, James Brown, Joe Tex, Gladys Knight, King Curtis, Ronnie Bennett of The Ronettes, and Inez & Charlie Foxx. Bobby Schiffman, son of the Apollo's co-owner Frank Schiffman, explained in a later interview how Amateur Night worked. "There was always a three or four-month waiting list to get on the

America's 'chitlin circuit' was a self-contained network of small venues right across the country for black entrepreneurs, performers and audiences. Pictured are Ethel's, Michigan (left) and Club Ebony, Mississippi.

show. Every Monday evening prospective amateurs would come in and register. When their turn came up, we'd send them a postcard and tell them: next week, be at the Apollo at seven o'clock. We would put them on in an order, and we always had six or seven left over that we would ask to come back the following week. You had to do that because you were on live radio and you couldn't take a chance on running out of amateurs."[10] Hendrix claimed in various interviews that he entered and won first prize of $25, and there is at least one witness to corroborate this. If he did, then his Amateur Night appearance must have been in March or April 1964 at the earliest, bearing in mind the lengthy process of registering and the chronology of his initial stay in New York. If that is the case, he did his turn in between tour dates with The Isley Brothers, whom he'd joined no later than March 1964, and quite possibly earlier. Whenever it was, the experience led nowhere. No one from the industry was there talent-spotting or checking the radio broadcast, or if they were, they certainly didn't spot him.

Meanwhile at the other end of Central Park, the hottest ticket in living memory was for The Beatles' first New York appearance, at the hallowed Carnegie Hall venue. Hendrix remained lodged at the Theresa hotel, working to get a break with one of the house bands in the bars and clubs he frequented. That winter, Harlem hadn't showed him its friendliest face, but this would soon change. In the entertainment industry, talent alone is never enough. Everyone needs luck, contacts and timing. His timing hadn't been much good since the previous December, but now it was about to turn. In February 1964 he was sitting in at the Palm Café, waiting as usual to be asked to leave or turn his guitar down, when he was noticed by guitarist Tony Rice, a musician in The Isley Brothers' circle. A meeting quickly led to Hendrix getting a job in their backing band. The Isleys were a hard-working group. They'd originally formed to sing gospel in the mid 1950s, but had moved from hometown Cincinnati to New York City in 1957. They first came to national attention two years later through their RCA 45rpm single 'Shout' which, though not a hit, was a widely influential record (for example, Australian rock'n'roll star Johnny O'Keefe had a major hit in his home country with a cover version in 1960). The Isleys followed it with their first US top 20 single, 'Twist And Shout', in June 1962. The Beatles would cover that one.

The Isleys' method was quite simple. They achieved all their early hits – and misses – by carefully emulating a particular style or performer of the time, and they brought a remarkable enthusiasm and chutzpah to live performances. Some of the models they'd already used by 1964 included Ray Charles, James Brown and Sam Cooke. Their January 1964 version of 'That Lady', released as 'Who's That Lady', along with 'My Little Girl' on the flip side, were closely modelled on Sam Cooke's singing style. The Isleys were not unusual in this blatant copying: many black chart acts of the day were content to imitate current fashions in order to penetrate the charts and become

consistent high earners. Only artists such as Brown, Charles, Cooke, Little Richard, Chuck Berry, Fats Domino, Bo Diddley and Curtis Mayfield had successfully combined a distinct musical personality with mass popularity.

The Isley Brothers were based in New Jersey but regularly did long tours that zigzagged the country. In mid winter 1964 they came back to town from their latest jaunt in need of a guitarist, a common experience for touring bands. Years later, Ernie Isley remembered that his brother Kelly asked around New York City for recommendations as to who might replace the guitarist who'd left. Kelly was told of a candidate who was better than the guy who played with Sam Cooke. "'What's his name?' 'Jimmy Hendrix'." Ernie recalled the conversation when Kelly went to see Jimmy at his hotel. "'Oh, glad to meet you, sure I've heard of The Isley Brothers. I love all your stuff.' Kelly says, 'I hear you play guitar.' 'Yeah.' 'Would you like to play with the Isley Brothers?' 'Sure!' 'Play something for me.' 'Uh, I don't have a guitar.' 'What do you mean? Where is it?' 'In a pawnshop.' So Kelly takes him to the pawnshop and they get the guitar out of hock: it's got no strings on it. OK, Kelly buys him some strings. Jimmy puts the strings on, tunes the guitar … 'OK, I'm in tune now.' 'Play something for me.' *Yayahh, didibadooo, whadabadooo, didooweee*. Jimmy Hendrix joined The Isley Brothers' band."[11] For once, the combination of Hendrix's natural talent and his insatiable curiosity and enthusiasm for other people's music had paid off. He already knew all the Isley Brothers singles and could quickly pick up the rest of their on-stage repertoire, even though he wasn't a New York insider. He was also lucky in the leaders who had chosen him for their band.

Although The Beatles were to change such perceptions for good, in 1964 most acts such as the Isleys still used back-up musicians in much the same way as big-name bandleaders had done during the swing era and the post-war R&B craze. The only faces in a band that mattered to the public were those up front, and that usually meant the singer(s) or other soloists. There had been chart success for doo-wop groups and mavericks like The Coasters, but there was little public identification with the individuals within these groups. When it came to the star-plus-backing-band package that Hendrix had just joined, a backing musician was just that. One guitarist was more or less interchangeable with any other guitarist, as long as a certain level of competence and discipline was obtained. The musicians themselves also saw things this way: there was constant movement between bands as they stayed on the lookout for better pay, a residency in a particular town, or a higher place in the pecking order on-stage. This to-ing and fro-ing would often occur during tours as well as at their beginning and end.

The Isleys were unusual in their attitude to their employees. Solid musicians themselves, they appreciated good musicianship in others rather than looking only for willing foot-soldiers to grind out so-so versions of the hit tunes while they grabbed the attention out front. The Isleys also encouraged

Like many black working musicians of the day, Jimmy Hendrix played out on the chitlin circuit during 1964 and '65 with a variety of acts. Pictured above is a typical chitlin venue, RJ's Place in Mississipi.

their band members to perform with enthusiasm and to exploit whatever stage gimmicks and tricks they'd picked up. For Hendrix, this was a positive development in many directions at once. Within days of Jimmy joining up, the band was back out on the road. He was about to find out the real personal and professional demands made of a touring pro. Ironically, his touring days with the top acts on the circuit would eventually coincide with the final development of his ambitions as a musician. He would soon reach the point where he wanted to run his own show and play his own style of music. But he had no resources, no contacts and no prospects of reaching that goal. Out on the chitlin circuit with a number of acts during 1964 and into '65, his

frustrations would mount as, week in and week out, he paid his dues and awaited his deliverance.

America's entertainment industry remained unofficially but effectively divided along racial lines until the long-overdue integration came during the 1960s. In the 1920s and early '30s this had led to the formation of an organised circuit covering the Eastern seaboard, the Midwest and the South, set up by black venue owners and promoters and known as the Theater Owners Booking Association (TOBA). The TOBA quickly became dubbed 'Tough On Black Asses' by the musicians and performers who played the circuit, thanks to the often less than satisfactory pay and conditions. That

Two more chitlin-circuit venues, similar to the kind of place where Hendrix found himself playing in the mid 1960s: The Busy Bee, Mississippi (left) and The Bright Lite, Arkansas.

circuit was in decline by the early 1930s due to the economic downturn and a shift in taste away from vaudeville entertainment packages, and it had collapsed by the advent of World War II. It was slowly replaced by a piecemeal collection of venues run and promoted by black managers and agents responding to the immediate needs of black communities across the United States. During the 1930s events at these venues – often the front room of a house or apartment – were called 'house rent parties'. Theatre director Brian Davis has said that this so-called 'chitlin circuit' was a network of houses, apartments, barns and old shacks.

"'I hear you play guitar.' 'Yeah.' 'Would you like to play with The Isley Brothers?' 'Sure!' 'Play something for me.' 'Uh, I don't have a guitar.' 'Where is it?' 'In a pawnshop.'"

Ernie Isley, of The Isley Brothers, reporting a conversation between his brother Kelly and Hendrix

"Musicians, singers, dancers and comedians would perform in these places during the Depression era," Davis remembered, "to raise money for suffering black families. The host would fix a big pot of chitlins to feed the entertainers and guests."[12] The 'chitlin' name became attached to a string of music and entertainment venues because chitlins (deep-fried pig intestines) and various other types of 'soul food' were sold at these places, particularly when a star attraction came through town. Journalist Phil Tajitsu Nash suggested[13] that Quincy Jones coined the term chitlin circuit "in referring to the life of an Afro-American on the road in the 1940s and 1950s", and historian Irwin Richman referred[14] to the 'borscht belt' when describing the analogous Jewish experience of musicians around the same time that "relied on its travellers to co-operate and care for each other".

The chitlin venues were close to the bottom of the entertainment tree. Although touring black musicians and bands were subject to habitual segregation for accommodation, service in restaurants and use of other public amenities, they would regularly play to white as well as black audiences, and were often handled by white agents and managers. In small towns the more established bands would perform at the biggest venues too, like the local theatre, while the chitlin musicians would play a juke joint, honky tonk or bar, in addition to larger places in the bigger towns. Organisation and logistics on the circuit were informal; the musicians simply wanted to earn a living.

There were chitlin circuit venues up and down the Eastern seaboard, across the North, and through the Rust Belt as far west as Chicago and beyond, down through Kansas City and Alabama to the Gulf, New Orleans and the Texas cities. There was also a substantial chitlin audience on the West Coast, especially in Los Angeles but also in San Francisco, Oakland and further north. Musician Leon Bibb knew the local chitlin joints during his youth in Cleveland, Ohio. "The chitlin circuit was the entertainment roots of black entertainers from the 1920s until the 1960s. Many inner-city clubs hosted black entertainment during that time. Cedar Avenue in Cleveland pulsed. ... It was the circuit where hip swingers swung."[15] Seattle musician Dave Holden recalled: "We went on the chitlin circuit with James Brown and Jackie Wilson. They called it the chitlin circuit. That was the Apollo Theater all the way down to Florida and all the cities down to Houston and Dallas."[16]

If there was a large enough black community to economically sustain an entertainment spot that provided live music, then that venue would sooner or later become part of the chitlin circuit. The artists would serve up music in the smaller places that was tailored to the clientele and was notably raunchier

and more wild-eyed than that heard in more well-heeled settings, allowing (or prodding) them to provide an exciting show. Blues singer Zora Young recalled the scene in Chicago. "The chitlin circuit was a black audience," she said. "Black audiences are verbal. They're hollering 'get on down' or something like that."[17] To some extent the musicians played music that varied according to region, depending on the taste of the locals, and it was often defined by different economic strata. During the late 1950s and early '60s a saxophone-and-organ trio might be the mainstay in a venue in Harlem, New Jersey, Pittsburgh, Chicago or Detroit, but it would be less welcome in some of the juke joints in Missouri or Tennessee where the taste was more for guitar-based vocal music with a strong dance beat. In Chicago, the blues circuit on the South and West Sides tended to be different from the chitlin clubs, which mainly offered a broader mix of music, and often hired comedians to entertain the audience between the music.

The larger venues in the cities were in an altogether different tier of the business, and only the top acts could fill them. The Apollo in Harlem, for example, was from the start owned by two whites, Leo Brecher and Frank Schiffman, both immigrants from Europe. Brecher was noted in the 1920s as "not only the landlord for the Cotton Club [a non-chitlin venue], but ... the landlord for all the show-business the coloured talent had up here in New York City. There was no competition."[18] Nevertheless, the groups headlining at the Apollo would play the smaller venues when they were out of town and mostly used the same agents for both types of venue. The determining factor was more likely to be the tier at which a performing act was operating. James Brown may have been king of the Apollo for many years, but he also toured constantly, playing the smaller places throughout the South and in Los Angeles during this whole period. The safest definition of a chitlin venue would include places such as the Apollo in Harlem, the Fox in Detroit and the Regal in Chicago, as well as the vast number of smaller clubs like The Rooster Tail and Mr Kelly's in Detroit, the venues on North Broad Street in Pittsburgh, and somewhere as far north as The Hi Way Inn in Roosevelt, New York, which featured acts such as Albert King, Sam & Dave and James Brown during the 1960s.

The chitlin circuit had largely expired by the early 1970s, ironically due to the success of the civil rights movement in breaking down the more blatantly segregated structures in US society. As rock and its attendant musical styles became more openly linked together in the public's mind and the performers more able to cross over and sell to every section of American society, mainstream booking agents began to pick up promotion contracts for black artists and institute booking policies that were not based on racial discrimination. Black artists were then able to play in bigger and better-paying venues and to enjoy healthier bank balances. The smaller venues on the old chitlin circuit simply could not compete economically, so the more successful black artists began to appear in larger venues in those areas, drawing away a significant proportion of the chitlin clientele. As a direct result of this change, the individual members of the informal chitlin circuit began to drop out and the communities that formerly supported them drifted into new ways of spending their leisure time. Of course it is a gross simplification to say that the chitlin circuit died at that point. Even today there are places scattered through the US that would answer to the description of a typical chitlin joint. But the economic and social pressures that forged the informal and intensely pragmatic networks that sustained the circuit as a separate and self-contained channel for black entrepreneurs, artists and audiences for nearly 40 years have receded.

According to Ernie Isley, Jimmy Hendrix came to live with the Isley family for a time early in 1964, soon after he joined their backing band. Ernie remembered later: "He had no place to stay, so he stayed at my mother's house. They asked him if he wanted a new guitar, what kind. ... So they got him one, and he said, 'Wow! I've got a new [guitar] and I'm playing with The Isley Brothers: this is everything.'"[19] From the beginning it seems that the Isleys were aware that their new guitarist was more than just another time-server in the backing band. He was not only a good technician but a flamboyant stage presence, and they could use this to their advantage. Part of the stage routine for most touring bands in those years was to start the show with a few warm-up numbers by the backing band alone. Hendrix, with his developing ability and showmanship, became a natural to feature in these preludes before the Brothers hit the stage. "When I was with The Isley Brothers," a rather jaundiced Hendrix told an interviewer years later, "they used to make me do my thing then, 'cause it used to make them more bucks or something – I don't know. I used to like to do it then, but most groups I was with, they didn't let me do my own thing, like feedback in 'Midnight Hour' or somethin' like that."[20]

Feedback or no feedback, Hendrix spent the best part of 1964 touring and recording with The Isley Brothers, regularly returning to New York City as each tour ended. Whatever irritations he expressed later, back then he was grateful for the exposure and the opportunity to cut other more established musicians – a novel experience for him. Ernie Isley recalled that there was an organ player, Gene Friday, in the band at the time who was also a good dancer. "So he'd be moving and stepping while he was playing. And it seemed like Jimmy, from the time he joined the band, was competing with that guy, cutting him, really pouring on the flash to put him down. See, when Jimi was playing all the time it was like he was in training, like an athlete, like Muhammad Ali. … He was enough of a musician and a technician so that he could always make his instrument do something that somebody else thought they could play but couldn't make theirs do – and do it spontaneously. Of course … the audience didn't see him practicing all day, and to them it just looked like it came out of nowhere."[21]

The Isleys quickly hardened up the new band on the road and took them into the studio for a session to cut their next single, for which Hendrix was certainly on board, thus making his first documented recording session. In January the group had come to the end of their contract with United Artists, a company for which they'd not been able to deliver any hits, and had decided to establish their own label. 'Testify Parts 1 & 2' was recorded some time prior to March 1964 (when distributor Atlantic took delivery of the tape master) and became the Isleys' first release on their own T-Neck label, a company whose early masters were soon after bought by its distributor, Atlantic. They reworked their old routines, informed by the R&B and soul techniques of records by contemporaries such as Curtis Mayfield and James Brown. The Isleys had already made 45rpm singles in two parts, like the fast and furious 'Shout' from 1959 which owed much to the call-and-response gospel routines that Ray Charles had incorporated into R&B.

The Isleys had concluded their work for United Artists back in January with an instrumental line-up of Al Lucas on bass, Bobby Gregg on drums and Gene Friday on organ. Now for 'Testify' they added a five-piece horn section, and on the resulting record the horns' full-bore blasts constantly punctuate the frenetic vocal expostulations and frantically driving rhythm. But this indifferently recorded single is something of a mess, with the Isleys so concerned to fit in their high-octane banter and all the impersonations of their subjects that it sounds more like an overheard conversation at a noisy party than a single. There is more than one guitarist present, and received wisdom points to Hendrix as the one who feeds in the occasional Buddy Guy-type licks between the patter. It seems a reasonable assumption.

The single's over-busy freneticism is its own worst enemy, making even Hendrix's simple riff patterns sound like an over-egging of the mixture. In that respect Part 1 is worse than Part 2, which at least finds the vocalists slightly less manic than before, though often out of tune, and the horn section a little less insistent with their interjections. Hendrix takes a four-bar solo break that

confirms his Buddy Guy leanings while also touching on Ike Turner-like techniques. But the most remarkable characteristics of this early effort are his instantly identifiable sense of time (or note placement) and his use of distortion and sustain. This last technique hints at an extension of the advances made by earlier players. There is also a driving single-note line taken from Earl King's 'Come On (Part 1)' – a tune that Hendrix had already played many times – that presages his own recording of the tune four years later. Perhaps the hysteria of the band's performance reflects their desperate search for a hit formula after years in the chart wilderness. If so, hysteria was not enough to score a hit. The single would make little impression on the charts that summer. 'Testify' and the September 1964 session that produced 'The Last Girl' / 'Looking For A Love' were later reissued on the Isleys' 1971 LP *In The Beginning*. 'Testify' was heavily remixed, recessing the band's contribution and boosting Hendrix's rhythm part. Perhaps the Isleys themselves realised that the original arrangement hadn't worked, or perhaps they were trying to cash in on Hendrix's posthumous fame. Some have claimed that Hendrix appeared on the final Isley Brothers session for United Artists, held on January 14th 1964, when 'Who's That Lady' received its first recording. Aural and chronological evidence suggests otherwise.

True to his Seattle habits, Hendrix wasn't working only with the Isleys. After a typical mix-up that left him stranded in Seattle in April 1964 he had to borrow money to return to New York alone and try to connect up again with the troupe. Once back he moved into a down-at-heel apartment on 81st Street, apparently in the same block as singer George Clemons and singer-guitarist Curtis Knight. All three were seeking studio work to make some extra money. According to Clemons, singer Don Covay used to visit clubs looking for suitable musicians for upcoming record dates, and Hendrix and Clemons were two of the players he pulled into a session. Knight missed out, although his brief time in the spotlight with Hendrix would come the following year.

According to writer Steven Roby,[22] Covay cut a number of songs during late spring 1964. These culminated in a US Top 40 hit, 'Mercy Mercy', originally appearing on the small Rosemart label, distributed by Atlantic, but purchased by Atlantic soon after when they signed Covay to an exclusive contract. Covay cut the single on May 18th. There have been a number of differing reports about the circumstances of the recording. In one later interview Covay said that he went straight into the studio the day after a riotous reception for the song at a live date, presumably without time to pick up new players,[23] making the single "in one or two takes."[24] At different times Covay has given varying accounts, sometimes placing Hendrix at the session,[25] and on others not even mentioning Hendrix as among the players present from his Goodtimers backing band of the previous night.[26] It should be noted that writer Peter Guralnik has described Covay as "a dreamy man who is capable of spinning the most elaborate fantasies around the most mundane events".[27] Whoever the guitarist is on the record, he certainly enjoys a prominent role – and perhaps this does suggest a regular band-member performing a well-learned routine rather than a last-minute substitution. Roby also records that Hendrix is on four other tracks from Covay's album *Mercy Mercy* and two from a separate session, unissued until a 1977 LP *Funky Yo-Yo*. The sessions for Covay's album were held in New York City from October 1st to 5th 1964, with the tracks linked to Hendrix recorded on the last two days. Hendrix was on tour with the Isleys from late September onwards – he posted a letter to his father from Columbus, Ohio, on September 28th – and left the band in Nashville in October. He is not listed in Atlantic files as being present at the October sessions.

'Mercy Mercy' itself is not much more than a competent stab at a Stax-like soul revue number, but the combination of Covay's impassioned vocals (imitated closely the following year by Mick Jagger when The Rolling Stones covered the song) and some fleet chordal work from the guitarist makes it a memorable recording. The guitar player uses rhythmic patterns that are tasteful modifications of the motifs favoured by Curtis Mayfield and Jimmy Johnson – and there have been suggestions that it is Johnson himself on the record. (Hendrix would recycle Mayfield-like and Johnson-like rhythms in new forms some years later on his own tunes such as 'Remember' from *Are*

You Experienced and 'Little Wing' from *Axis: Bold As Love*.) The guitarist on 'Mercy Mercy' has an assured technique, especially in the way he seems able to create unlimited time and space in which to shape his phrases and articulate the chords he is arpeggiating in a variety of rhythmic patterns.

If this really is Hendrix playing on 'Mercy Mercy', then it substantiates the notion of him as a professional R&B and soul stylist with his own identifiable sense of cadence and instrumental colour as early as mid 1964. Hendrix certainly had a predilection for the song: he would play it on gigs and in jams over the following two years, and even used it on occasion during early Experience dates.

Any studio activity with Covay did not prevent Jimmy from rejoining The Isley Brothers on his return to New York City: he stayed with them for around eight months during 1964. Despite his off-hand references to them during his years of fame, this first regular gig with a nationally recognised act was undoubtedly important to him at the time. The band travelled the length and breadth of the country, from Seattle to Florida, giving Hendrix a proper introduction to the routines and disciplines of road life. The brothers were able to observe their guitarist closely during this time. Ernie Isley has often mentioned since that Hendrix had obsessive practice routines and was clearly dedicated to his instrument. "He played all the time, all the time. It wasn't like a thing you were listening to, though; it was just a simple observation – like the sun is shining. Jimmy's playing the guitar. He would practice phrases over and over again, turn them inside out, break them in half, break them in quarters, play them slow, play them fast. It was just like a reflex. So when it came time to play, it was virtually automatic. Playing the guitar all day was just about all he did all day. He didn't talk too much – the instrument was the talker. Marvin'd say, 'How are you doing?' *Bading dada doo*, on the guitar. 'Is it cold outside?' *Wheeow*, on the guitar. This thing had its own conversation."[28]

The letters that Hendrix wrote home to his father at this time suggest a hopefulness and enthusiasm that his later comments about poor conditions and enforced regulations gloss over. A postcard from Columbus, Ohio, postmarked September 28th 1964 reads: "Well here I am again traveling to different places. I'm on a tour which lasts about 35 days. We're about half way through it now. We've been to all the cities in the Midwest, east and south. I'll write soon. Jimmy."[29] Just prior to this tour, The Isley Brothers had been on a long bill at New York's Paramount Theater with the latest beat sensation from England, The Animals. They made sure that their guitarist was given full licence to strut his crowd-pleasing stuff. On a package of that size it is doubtful that members of either band got past backstage nods, but Kelly Isley later recalled the Englishmen watching Hendrix in amazement from the wings, though the impression he made was obviously shortlived. No one from The Animals, including bassist Chas Chandler, recalled the event when they hooked up more meaningfully with Hendrix two years later, or in any later interview.

Just five days prior to the Paramount concert the Isleys had returned to a New York studio and cut a new single, 'The Last Girl' / 'Looking For A Love'. The A-side marks a radical stylistic departure from the previous single, suggesting that the band had reflected on the chart failure of that effort. For 'The Last Girl' the Brothers are accompanied by a studio orchestra, including harp and heavenly-choir backing singers. The ballad combines the compositional artfulness of the Brill Building with the orchestration skills of Burt Bacharach (indeed Dionne Warwick is one of the backing singers here), complete with unison strings-and-piano lines. It's a fine romantic single, but it has no guitar revelations. The guitar parts are so closely intertwined with the rest of the arrangement, with parallel guitar-and-flute and guitar-and-vibes lines at various points, as well as other counterpoint rhythmic figures, that the guitarist has no opportunity to display any individuality. The relatively complex arrangement must have been scored. (Imagine a Burt Bacharach session with everyone playing by ear. Exactly. It wouldn't have happened.) Given that Hendrix did not read music, there must be some doubt about whether he participated on this side. The flip, 'Looking For A Love', also boasts an orchestra and girl singers, but contained in a slow triple metre.

The song's style and construction is more typical of the 1964 Isleys, being something of a cross between a Sam Cooke soul ballad and Ketty Lester's 'Love Letters'. There are two guitar parts audible on this tune, one contributing a near-constant double-time skip beat, the other interjecting with biting, bluesy single lines in occasional obbligato, plus a few 'Walk On By'-like rhythmic punctuations.

Either two guitarists were present or a single player was overdubbed. Considering the normal studio techniques of the day, as well as the size of the ensemble and the costs involved, it seems more likely that we're hearing two guitarists. The rhythmic guitar part sounds scored, especially at the song's beginning; the other part could easily be played by someone relying on his ear, so it may well be Hendrix. The single was released on Atlantic both in the US and the UK, but never rose above cult status.

In late autumn 1964, guitarist Les Paul heard Hendrix playing with the Isley troupe at a nightclub in New Jersey called the Lodi. Paul, renowned for his early pioneering work with electric guitars and sound recording, was travelling with his son one afternoon to New York City on business and heard the band by chance. He later remembered being really impressed by what he heard. "Yes indeed, that dude was really working his guitar over. He was bending strings, playing funky as hell. I'd never seen anyone so radical."[30] Paul said he completed his business and dropped by the club on the way back, but by then the band had finished and Hendrix was gone. The band now on-stage featured guitarist Roy Buchanan, already well known to Paul. Buchanan recalled: "Les was just looking for some black guy who played left-handed guitar and did a lot of crazy stuff on-stage."[31]

In early October Hendrix wrote again to his father, this time from Cincinnati, Ohio, having accompanied the Isleys through the Florida/Texas leg of their current tour. He ended the letter by noting his address – now in Atlanta, Georgia.[32] However temporarily, Atlanta rather than New York City had become his home base. Some time between mid October and late November 1964, Jimmy and The Isley Brothers parted company. He later claimed that he'd become so disenchanted with the continual grind of the road and performing a set routine every night that he'd jumped ship, and it seems that he spent most of the remaining weeks of 1964 in and around Atlanta. Given his eternal restlessness, this desire for a change is quite plausible. However, the need to earn and eat soon drove him to re-establish contact with Gorgeous George Odell, the man who had managed to find work for Hendrix when he'd been trying to break out of the Nashville R&B scene. Odell obliged once more and landed Hendrix a series of low-profile jobs with tours working the South at the time. By the end of the year, Hendrix was operating mostly in and around Atlanta, which is where he met up with Little Richard's entourage.

On December 11th Sam Cooke was shot dead while staying in a Los Angeles motel. The sense of shock within the black music community was vast, for Cooke was not merely a singer but an artist interested in every aspect of the entertainment business. He was a partner in his own record company, he enjoyed producing records for other acts and he understood the financial side of music. Cooke had succeeded in Las Vegas and was about to take a step into the movies at the time of his murder. He was a symbol of what a black man who combined talent with sharpness could achieve in early-1960s America. Writer Peter Guralnik pinpointed Cooke's achievement. "As urbane as Duke Ellington in the world of jazz, and no less dignified, he was revered not just for his music but for his success, a notion that took a while to penetrate my preconceived ideas about racial solidarity and the purity of art. Sam Cooke was looking for white acceptance, because he was looking for wider sales and a broader market."[33] The motivation may not have been identical, but Hendrix was to capture exactly that market three years later. Some 200,000 fans came to view Cooke's body in its coffin and at the funeral there were heartfelt contributions from Lou Rawls, Bobby Bland and Ray Charles among others. Hendrix, aware of Cooke's contribution to contemporary musical developments and his importance as a role model, would have felt the impact of this senseless loss.

Cooke's death and funeral occurred when Hendrix was also soaking up the new sounds coming from the other side of the Atlantic. By his own later admission to band-member Rod Argent he greatly admired 'She's Not There', the first big hit by The Zombies: it reached the US Top 10 in the week of Cooke's murder. The Rolling Stones too were enjoying their highest chart entry so far, with 'Time Is On My Side'. The new energy in popular music was diversifying from that initial single stream of The Beatles as the US embraced the first so-called British invasion.

As 1964 gave way to 1965, Hendrix took the next big step in his career. He had somehow managed to hook up with Little Richard – the man who had shown Sam Cooke the way to express himself on-stage with true freedom. There are as many stories about how Hendrix joining Richard as there are witnesses to the event, most of them smacking of hindsight and attempts to readjust history to suit the teller. However, Richard himself has consistently claimed that Hendrix joined up with him in Atlanta. One way or another, Hendrix was on tour with Little Richard's backing band, The Upsetters, before Christmas had faded too far from memory. Within a year of leaving Nashville for New York City as a complete unknown, Hendrix had already toured extensively with one first-rate black act, The Isley Brothers, and had now joined the backing band of one of the greatest black performers of his generation. He was being fast-tracked through one side at least of America's still segregated music industry.

In a letter to his father postmarked January 25th 1965, Hendrix sent what is today the only known contemporaneous record of his joining Richard. "I received your letter while I was in Atlanta," he writes. "I'm playing with Little Richard now. We're going towards the West Coast. We're in Louisiana now, but my address will be in Los Angeles when I write again."[34] On the way to Los Angeles the troupe played in Houston, where Little Richard introduced him to guitarist Albert Collins. Hendrix asked to sit in with Collins at Club 500. "Ooh man, he was powerful then; he could play some blues," Collins recalled later.[35] A Dallas TV station, Channel 5, used Richard's Upsetters in February to provide support for Buddy & Stacy's cover version of Junior Walker's 'Shotgun' on the channel's *Night Train* show, which had been taped while the band was in Nashville and then broadcast out of Dallas. This was Hendrix's first appearance on television, and a surviving tape shows him already with the self-confidence to perform some sleight-of-hand tricks with his guitar, enough to steal some of the limelight from the singers up front.[36]

In mid February the Little Richard entourage arrived in Los Angeles from where Jimmy wrote again to his father, telling him he could write to his son at the Wilcox Hotel in Hollywood, care of 'Maurice James', the name he had adopted for professional use. At this time Hendrix began hanging out with singer Rosa Lee Brooks, who claimed to have met him one evening in the hotel's California Club room. Brooks was about to record a single for the tiny Revis label, and says she recruited Jimmy, quickly ensconced as her beau, to play guitar on both tunes recorded: the A-side 'My Diary' and the flip, 'Utee'. 'My Diary' has a disputed authorship but the weight of evidence supports the claims of singer Arthur Lee. Brooks said she used Lee as a backing vocalist on the session; Lee's own recollection suggested a deeper involvement in the recording's planning and execution. Lee even claimed later that it was Billy Revis, owner of the record label and the single's producer, who hired Hendrix for the date. Nobody can remember where Revis heard Hendrix, although one explanation could be that Revis simply turned up to see Little Richard and noticed Hendrix in the backing band.

Arthur Lee later claimed, "I wanted this 'Curtis Mayfield feeling' for the recording, 'like he does in 'People Get Ready,' that certain guitar feel. And this guy tells me there's a cat in town who could play that trip."[37] Lee and Hendrix hit it off immediately and remained on friendly terms, with Hendrix

becoming an enthusiastic supporter of Lee's cult band Love in later years. 'My Diary' finds Hendrix using a similar approach to that heard on the Don Covay single of the previous year, while 'Utee' is much more driving, capitalising on the dynamism he'd learned from playing live rhythm guitar behind two first-rate acts. The single went nowhere and became one of the rarest collectables in the Hendrix discography until a recent appearance of the two tracks on CD.

Meanwhile, Hendrix was busy holding down the job with Little Richard. Still based in Los Angeles and playing a number of dates around the city, he absorbed as much as he could as he watched his new leader wowing an audience, carefully adding this to what he had learned from The Isley Brothers about professionalism. Roger McGuinn, already a member of The Byrds in that early spring of 1965, remembers the group playing Ciro's club in Los Angeles as a local support for the Little Richard revue. "I saw Hendrix there playing as lead back-up guitarist," McGuinn recalls. "We were the support – it was early days for us then, we were unknowns, and he was an unknown. I noted him as a flamboyant guitar player in a conservative setting. He was obviously a good musician and a great band player, at that time in an Ike Turner style, touches of Motown, to suit the band he was in."[38] Richard himself was proud of the band he had then, telling biographer Charles White: "I put $16,000 into my new act which was very, very glamorous and elaborate. I was the star and singer of my own troupe of 17 musicians, singers, dancers and comedians. The Little Richard Show."[39] Most of the income was derived from advances for Richard's new recording contract with the Vee Jay label. That spring Bob Dylan, one of the major inspirations for The Byrds' coming musical innovations, had released his new LP, *Bringing It All Back Home*, a major step for him and in effect the birth of folk-rock. Dylan's updated sound made him an artist that the entire rock world could learn from. Hendrix would be no exception.

Dylan's latest milestone was one of the more important indications that Little Richard, only recently back in the world of secular rock'n'roll, was struggling to re-impose himself on what he found to be a very different music scene. His last US Top 40 hit, 'Ooh! My Soul', had been in 1958, following a run of greats like 'Tutti Frutti' (1955), 'Long Tall Sally' (1956), 'Lucille' and 'Keep A Knockin'' (1957), and 'Good Golly Miss Molly' (1958). Between 1958

"The chitlin circuit was the entertainment roots of black entertainers from the 1920s until the 1960s."

Leon Bibb, musician

and 1964 he had made no new rock records, concentrating entirely on gospel recordings. But from 1962 he had begun regularly touring Europe, including Britain (sharing the bill with the early Beatles on a few occasions), and had noticed the sudden surge of interest in older rock'n'roll styles. He began dipping his toes in the rock pool again.

By May 1964, Richard was ready for a worldwide resumption of his rock'n'roll career. He recorded 'Bama Lama Bama Loo', a spirited re-working of the main elements of 'Tutti Frutti'. Released in June on his old label, Art Rupe's Specialty, it made the Top 20 in Britain, catching the new waves of enthusiasm for R&B and rock that were washing through that country, but only crawled to number 98 in America before vanishing from sight. Anticipating success for the new single, he had put together a band in the summer and gone back on tour in the US for the first time since the late 1950s. "When 'Bama Lama' flopped, it was devastating to me," he admitted some years later. "It was like to've killed me. So I just got me a band together and went on the road. I went all over the country touring, one-night stands. I played in some dumps. I played in some snake holes, some rat holes, and some pig pens. Oh my god! The Domino Lounge, in Atlanta, Georgia; Soul City, in Dallas, Texas; I went everywhere."[40] It was in Atlanta that Jimmy Hendrix had been swept up by the revitalised Little Richard's troupe.

A deal in summer 1964 with Chicago-based Vee Jay had led Richard to make his first secular LP since 1959. Called *Little Richard Is Back*, it even started with a short declamatory monologue from Richard that announced his return after recent success in Britain and other points in Europe, tacked on to a new version of 'Whole Lotta Shakin'' (the first single taken from the album). This and other new singles, such as his rip-snorting October 1964 version of the oldie 'Blueberry Hill', received good radio airplay but sold poorly on both sides of the Atlantic. A second LP, cut in Los Angeles in December, met with similarly indifferent sales. The new tracks showed that Richard was aware of the emerging beat scene and its special emphasis on the role of the rhythm guitar, rather than the driving horn sections that Richard had favoured in the late 1950s. His model could well have been Ike Turner's recent records.

But this change of emphasis proved to be musically and commercially uneasy for Richard. The original Specialty recordings of 'Whole Lotta Shakin'', 'Lawdy Miss Clawdy', 'Tutti Frutti' and 'Long Tall Sally' had a brutally direct production with as much gain, or presence, as possible – and, in the case of Richard's voice, used distortion as a recording technique. This made both voice and band leap out of the speakers at the listener. Just as

Little Richard, and just regular rock. And he used to make his guitar sound like singing. That was really his approach."[42] This last point is acute, showing the perception of a discerning bandleader and talent-spotter. This is precisely what Hendrix would try to do during his brief career: to approximate the human voice in the intimacy and poetic power of his expression. That Richard heard this in a rhythm guitarist who was on the road with him for just six months says much for both bandleader and band-member.

Richard was like most consistently successful leaders: he ran a very tight ship and would not stand for infractions of discipline either on the road or on-stage. For Hendrix this must have been something of a contrast after the relative tolerance he'd enjoyed from The Isley Brothers, despite his later complaints to interviewers that he was fined by them for not appearing in an immaculate uniform on the bandstand. For one thing, Richard was not in favour of his band-members indulging in after-show jamming while on tour. He regarded it as a point of principle that the musicians were being paid by him to play on the tour, and they should look after themselves away from the show so that they were always ready to put in their best for their employer. This would rankle with many musicians, but especially Hendrix, who was always up for a jam no matter where he was or what time it was. The other area of potential conflict was upstaging the star. Like many other charismatic bandleaders, from Cab Calloway in the 1930s onwards, Richard most definitely didn't appreciate anyone in his band trying this on. He was the star, the people paid to see him, and his musicians were there to support him. If they wanted to be stars in their own right, then they should go and form their own bands.

There is conflicting evidence about whether Hendrix seriously tried out his routine of stage tricks while with Little Richard. Other troupe members remember that he would rarely turn it on during his pre-fame days, and then only when the mood was upon him. Richard's road manager, Hosea Wilson, said: "Jimmy was a real strong rhythm-guitar player. He was a hell of a

"When I was with The Isley Brothers they used to make me do my thing then, 'cause it used to make them more bucks or something."

Jimi Hendrix

importantly, Richard's Upsetters delivered a sensational beat on these older records, using either the old two-beat R&B feel or the even emphasis of boogie-woogie that Richard himself drove from the keyboard on songs like 'Lucille' and 'Long Tall Sally'. This suited Richard's vocal style, which had been built on the same rhythmic understanding.

The new recordings had a much more four-square beat, often with a drag-snare shuffle from the drummer in keeping with mid-1960s soul and British-beat trends. 'The Girl Can't Help It' exemplifies these features. Due to the drummer's use of fashionable common-time beat patterns in preference to the old 1950s cut-time beat, Richard's vocals have to be dragged out over a painfully slow tempo in order to make sense of the metre. The horns labour similarly, and the material simply can't cope with the treatment. When the band tries to duplicate the original rhythm, as on 'Rip It Up', the mediocre production and poor instrumental mixes undermine the energy in the performance. Nonetheless, these records were enough at the time to give Richard improved visibility and to remind listeners – old and new alike – that he was indeed back on the scene.

Richard appreciated the fact that he had a very talented new boy on guitar, saying later: "He wasn't playing my kind of music, though. He was playing like B.B. King, blues. He started rocking, though, and he was a good guy. ... He was never a precision guitarist. ... I regarded him as being innovative, creative, and something of a stylist."[41] Richard expanded on this to another interviewer. "He was outrageous in his playin' – you got to remember that at this time he didn't play the kind of music he played when he got famous. He was playin' blues – B.B. King type blues – he was playin'

talent. ... The thing is that when Jimmy was with the band he wasn't on the hard stuff. He wasn't flamboyant or anything then. He was all quiet – to himself. Most guitar players are introverted. Jimmy was like that. Richard brought Hendrix out."[43]

During the few seconds that he is visible on the Dallas TV broadcast with Richard in February 1965, Hendrix encourages the view that he was willing to advertise his presence. Richard himself was more equivocal when recalling his guitarist, revealing his overriding concerns as a star and bandleader. "I probably wouldn't have hired him if I'd knew that he was doin' all of that. I found that out on the stage one night, when I thought the people were screamin' over me and they were screamin' for Jimmy! I found that out the hard way! I loved him but I didn't want nobody to take my show!"[44] Exactly how much freedom Richard allowed this particular sideman on-stage is not made explicit, but the leash was a short one. One thing that Hendrix took with him when he left – and Richard has commented about this on many occasions since – was the singer's penchant for clothes and attempts to redefine the notion of standing out from the crowd. The louder the better was not just a maxim that applied to amplifiers.

Hendrix recorded with Richard while the band were in Los Angeles in February-March 1965 – the only time during his brief stay with the great rock'n'roller that they saw the inside of a studio together. The session was for a new single to be released by the black-owned Chicago label Vee Jay, 'I Don't Know What You've Got But It's Got Me', Parts 1 & 2. Other pieces apparently recorded at the same sessions include 'Dancin' All Over The World', 'You Better Stop' and 'Every Time I Think About You'. None of those three appeared on Vee Jay at the time – possibly because they are not very good. 'Dancin'' is a dispirited medium-tempo rocker with a desperate-sounding Richard trying to tie a litany of names from his early hits into dance steps fashionable in 1965, but the band is stodgy and the song threadbare. The tiny amount of audible guitar backing is suitably nondescript. The other two achieve little more.

The title chosen for release on Vee Jay, 'I Don't Know What You've Got But It's Got Me', is a slow ballad couched in the contemporary style of Sam Cooke or Otis Redding – no great surprise considering it was written by Don Covay, a man with a proven ability to keep abreast of musical development. (Covay is apparently also present on organ, though no one has yet worked out why he might have been in Los Angeles at this time.) The brass filigrees in the background are classic Stax licks, expertly played, while the simple arpeggio style of the guitar accompaniment is beautifully articulated by Hendrix in the manner of his models, Curtis Mayfield and Jimmy Johnson. Another notable feature of his playing is that he is completely at ease supplying obbligato fills between Richard's phrases. This is where his blues background pays off, for he never gets in Richard's way, completing graceful little fills that make their own point while amplifying the singer's, just like any top-rank blues guitarist. B.B. King indeed.

This single release went the way of all the other Little Richard material on Vee Jay, making a reasonable showing on the R&B charts (number 12 in November) but failing to make any impression on the pop chart. It proved to be the singer's last release on the label. Soon after, Richard began making sessions for the Los Angeles-based Modern label. By that time his guitarist would be gone.

Hendrix went back out on the road with Richard, who needed to pull in some money to cover the lack of income from his records, and they played a variety of venues, initially heading north to play in San Francisco and even reaching Seattle. Hendrix later claimed to have met Chas Chandler in Seattle on this tour, when Chandler, bass player with The Animals at the time, came to meet up with his friends in The Hollies who were sharing the bill with Richard. Hendrix apparently told Keith Altham that he and Chandler, embarrassed by Richard's behaviour at the hotel in which they were staying, went up on the roof and shared a joint. But The Animals' itinerary in spring 1965 would have made such a meeting close to impossible: Richard's subsequent short season in mid April at New York's Paramount Theater is a much more likely occasion: The Animals were in New York between April 13th and 15th taping a *Hullabaloo* appearance and for a few days afterwards, when Little Richard was on the Paramount bill with The Hollies.

After Seattle the Richard tour headed east, playing clubs in Atlanta and St Louis and passing through Nashville. Billy Cox, Hendrix's bass-playing friend in Nashville, claimed later that Richard and Hendrix dropped by his house and tried to enlist him as the band's bassist. Cox said he declined the offer, as he had done two years before when Hendrix had been clutching at every touring opportunity. Richard and band finally arrived in New York City in early April. Hendrix roomed back at the cheap and cheerless Theresa hotel where he'd stayed briefly early in 1964.

Richard's band based itself on the East Coast for the next three months. From April 17th to the 19th they were part of a package at New York's Paramount Theater that included The Hollies, Sandie Shaw, and King Curtis & The Kingpins. Curtis's bass player of the time, Chuck Rainey, noticed Hendrix during this engagement. Considering that Hendrix worked later for Curtis, it's likely the sharp-eyed and business-like saxophonist noticed him too, although this was by no means the only time Hendrix worked in a band

opposite Curtis's outfit. "I remember constantly going to my bass and trying to play lines the way I had just heard Hendrix play them," said Rainey later. "His lines were played with a lot of character – he didn't play them straightahead and simple."[45]

During May 1965, while still based in New York, Richard's revue played gigs on the college circuit in Schenectady and Syracuse, New York, and in June they worked a season at the Apollo. By this time Hendrix's days with the band were virtually over. He had few good things to say about them later, although he did suggest that he and Richard remained "friends". He told *Melody Maker* in 1968: "Bad pay, lousy living and getting burned – that was those days. With Little Richard, he was the guy out front and that was it. The King of Rock and Rhythm – that was him. And he said that he was the only one allowed to be pretty. ... That was when I got a fancy shirt because I was dragged at wearing his uniform. 'Take off those shirts,' he told me and another guy."[46]

Hendrix had become bitterly disillusioned with the pay and conditions that he and the other band members were forced to accept, no matter how glamorous the on-stage image may have been. He would write to his father in July: "He didn't pay us for five and a half weeks, and you can't live on promises when you're on the road, so I had to cut that mess loose."[47] It is quite likely that he did not disguise his disaffection with the set-up. He was just 22 years old and hardly the type to retain a discreet veneer of respectful deference to the leader and manager, let alone willingly submit himself to the petty disciplines that help such touring outfits to function. This would have alarmed and infuriated the management team, for friction within a working band always hampers its smooth running.

With the band in New York, this must have seemed to Richard the ideal time to look for a replacement, for the city always had a pool of willing and competent musicians seeking steady work. Richard's brother and road

> # "He started rocking, and he was a good guy. He was never a precision guitarist. I regarded him as innovative, creative, and something of a stylist."
>
> Little Richard, on his new guitarist, Jimmy Hendrix

manager, Robert Penniman, was delegated to do the deed. "I fired Hendrix, who was using the name Maurice James all the time I knew him," said Penniman. "He was a damn good guitar player, but the guy was never on time. He was always late for the bus and flirting with the girls and stuff like that. It came to a head in New York, where we had been playing the Apollo and Hendrix missed the bus for Washington, DC. ... So when Hendrix called us in Washington, DC, I gave him the word that his services were no longer required. We had some words. I explained why we were doing this. I was running the road for Richard and we didn't accept that kind of bullshit."[48]

Jimmy Hendrix had managed to last just six months with Little Richard, less time than he had spent with The Isley Brothers the year before. He was once again back in New York City, he had no money, and he still had an itch for personal success that he couldn't yet scratch. He faced the first weeks of summer 1965 with no particular place to go, but with two big advantages over the last time he'd been unemployed there, 18 months or so earlier. He had professional contacts he could follow up on and he had a new girlfriend, Fay Pridgeon. She would lend moral support and introduce him to her own circle of friends and acquaintances.

do the new york scuffle

By the middle of 1965 Jimmy Hendrix was becoming increasingly disillusioned with the music business after his experiences with Little Richard and his failure to carve out a career of his own. Once again he was scuffling around Harlem looking for work, but with little more success than the year before. During this summer in the doldrums he hooked up with a new girlfriend, Faye Pridgeon. (It has long been assumed that Hendrix first met her in early 1964, but summer 1965 more closely fits the few known facts.)

Pridgeon's memories of Jimmy's humiliations and battles against uncaring nobodies and hard-nosed club managers more accurately reflect the situation he was in at that time rather than in 1964, when he was in New York only briefly before going back out on the road more or less full-time for about 18 months. Their affair was to last, on and off, until Hendrix departed for London in September 1966.

The two met one evening at the Palm Café, a musician's hangout just a few doors down from the Apollo Theater. Little Richard's troupe, complete with Hendrix, had played the Apollo that June, and the Palm was a natural watering-hole for the musicians. Hendrix and Pridgeon took an instant liking to one another. She recalled later: "Those little stories and things he used to tell me, I started going for them, y'know? Really digging them, and liking him more than I was liking the fact that he was the cutie-pie with the guitar, y'know, the 'in' thing at the time – they were just getting to be the thing like with the processes fallin' in your face when you're playin' - he wasn't the average process wearer."[1] A 'process' was a hairstyle where the hair was straightened and styled using a chemical preparation. Hendrix, like Little Richard, had a 'process'.

Pridgeon was young, ebullient and attractive, and not the first woman to be first a lover, then a provider for Hendrix. The two spent an afternoon at her mother's, talking and listening to her blues records, then went to her temporary room at the Hotel Seifer. From the beginning, their relationship was strongly sexual, "hard and steamy like his music," she said. "There were times when he almost busted me in two the way he did a guitar on stage".[2] In the casual way he made most of his big decisions, Hendrix moved in to share the hotel room the next day. "He just moved in with me,"

Jimmy Hendrix (left), back-up musician with The Isley Brothers, plays a solo feature at an appearance in New Haven, Connecticut, in 1965.

commented Pridgeon. "It wasn't hard because he was carrying all his possessions in his guitar case."[3]

Like others before, she soon discovered that her new lover was as wedded to his guitar as to her or anything else. "Jimmy loved fooling about with his guitar as to her or anything else. "Jimmy loved fooling about with his guitar in bed, and he always slept with it," she said. "I used to think of my competition not as a woman, but as a guitar. Many times he fell back asleep with it on his chest."[4] At this point Hendrix relied almost totally on Pridgeon and her circle of friends and family for material support, and would twist her mother's arm for food. In his last months with Little Richard the band had received little or no wages. This dependency hardly endeared him to her relations and they soon decided he was using her, but she followed her own inclinations and ignored their advice to dump him. She was already used to the musicians' scene – she'd previously been a girlfriend of Sam Cooke – and she shared Jimmy's irregular lifestyle, sleeping late, eating irregularly, checking out scenes, looking for work.

The two of them had little or no money and moved around a lot. Pridgeon remembered how bleak it all was. "We used to go to Palm's … and places like Small's, The Spotlite, places around 125th Street in the Harlem scene, y'know? He told them he wanted to sit in, right. And these old fuddy-duddy rough-dried ain't-never-beens … they ain't gonna give him a break, so they just act like they don't even know he's there. So he'd sit there with this kinda look on his face for a few minutes, y'know? And I'd say, 'Don't say nothin' to these cats 'cause it's obvious they don't want you to play.' Finally they would let him come in and play, and then they'd get up and really just mess up so bad behind him it was incredible. He'd be lookin' all disgusted on the stage and he'd keep lookin' back at them; then the other guys'd come up and tell him he'd gotta turn it down and take him through all kinds of changes."[5]

June 1965 was not only the month that Hendrix was fired from Little Richard's band, but also saw the debut of two 45rpm singles that would be important to Hendrix. First was Wilson Pickett's 'In The Midnight Hour', a song that Hendrix would perform many times on-stage during the next 18 months. He would not be alone – just about every cover band of wannabes in the world would play that perfect dance number for the rest of the 1960s. The other single was Bob Dylan's 'Like A Rolling Stone', one that would haunt Hendrix for years and influence him deeply when he began composing his own tunes and writing his own lyrics. The month of June, like the one before it, was largely empty of work and barren of promise, though Hendrix spent the time fruitfully by plotting just how he could escape the chitlin treadmill. He became increasingly convinced that the only hope he had of making it big in the business was to go his own way and forget about being someone else's backing musician. Hendrix didn't mind trying to be a city-based freelancer, making some dough to get by while working on other things, but a career as a member of someone else's road band? That was a mug's game. He had the scars to prove it. So he began making contacts with other musicians and looking for a record deal that would lead to him cutting his own sounds. But life continued to be hard. Since he'd met Pridgeon, the two of them had moved around Manhattan, from one flea-flop to another, trying to stay ahead of the rent collectors. "We'd get our door closed to the hotel," said Pridgeon. "We'd get thrown out – we'd pawn the guitar – we'd come back – we'd borrow a guitar from some people – we'd play – we'd eat good … it was just that, y'know: on and off all the time."[6] By mid summer they were living in the same hotel as twins Arthur and Albert Allen, old friends of Pridgeon whom Jimmy eventually got to know. Later the Allens turned professional and would record with Hendrix as The Ghetto Fighters, and in the 1970s changed their names to Aleem, launching a second successful career.

During July 1965 Hendrix continued the pattern of the previous two months, hoping to do more jobbing work whenever it came along. Sure enough, at long last something did. But it was hardly an advance on his previous existence, as it came from a familiar quarter: The Isley Brothers again needed a guitarist. Still in a career downturn that would last for a good while yet, they continued to work hard for a turnaround and regularly put out new singles. Since Hendrix's departure the Isleys had revamped their band and updated their image. The lurex and satin of last year's uniforms had been replaced by white mohair suits, white shirts and thin black ties. Hendrix would repeatedly refer to this uniform in later interviews as one that he particularly resented wearing, but it was in fact quite tasteful as far as band uniforms of the day went. It was his attitude that had changed, and he no longer had the heart for such things.

The Isleys were preparing to record their next single for Atlantic and were once more in need of a guitarist for the road band: they had a great deal of work lined up for the summer around New York and New Jersey and wanted someone they could trust to deliver the goods. Jimmy was asked to cover both jobs. Still broke, he agreed. The gigs alternated between extended engagements and one-nighters, including the He-Jazz Grotto Hall in New Haven, Connecticut in July, featuring Jimmy out front in a brief solo spot, and the Essex County Country Club in West Orange, New Jersey, just across the river from New York City, in August. One of the long-term gigs was in New Jersey at Wildwood, a seaside resort that city dwellers of middling to low incomes from neighbouring states had turned into one of the most popular local vacation destinations. Wildwood boasted funfairs, hotels, entertainment centres and other forms of pleasurable activities, and during the summer holiday months usually had five or six different groups resident at the night spots in and around the town. During the summer of 1965 The Isley Brothers spent a month or so there with Hendrix in the band. Being about an hour's drive from New York City, the resort posed no great travel problems for any of the individual group members who might have occasional business in town during the day.

Hendrix didn't spurn the opportunity. He offered himself to some of New York City's independent record companies, probably as a way to find studio work or to make a proper record deal, or both. Pridgeon remembered this spurt of activity vividly. "He would sign a contract with anybody who came along and they had a dollar … and a pencil. He'd sign with them. Which got him into a lot of trouble later … with the companies and stuff."[7] But short-term dividends came quickly. On July 27th he signed a two-year deal (with options) with Sue Records and its affiliated management company, Copa. Sue was a label with a small but impressive roster of R&B and chitlin-circuit artists and a steady run of hit singles in the early 1960s, including 'I've Got A Woman (Part 1)' by Jimmy McGriff, which reached number 20 on the *Billboard* chart in October 1962. It was one of the few labels at the time owned and run by blacks. Owner Juggy Murray signed Hendrix, but nothing ever seems to have been recorded as a result. As Murray noted, "Reading a contract meant nothin' to Jimmy. He just came in and signed it and I didn't hear from him for months."[8]

Exactly what went wrong is unclear, for Hendrix claimed later that he actively worked on presenting material to Murray. Hendrix referred to it in a 1968 legal deposition. (The deposition was made in a New York City solicitors' office and was part of the American legal process where attorneys examine leading witnesses before a trial. Hendrix and Yameta Co Ltd were suing Capitol Records, PPX, Ed Chalpin and Curtis Knight in an attempt to have the PPX-controlled recordings featuring Hendrix withdrawn from sale. The existence of the deposition was brought to light recently by Joel J. Brattin.) Hendrix alleged: "I tried to write my songs so I could present them to [Murray], y'know, sing them to him." He also said he delivered to Murray "a demo. It's like you make a little rough thing, and I did". Murray apparently offered him time in a studio to record the songs properly but Hendrix demurred. Hendrix's reasoning, as given in the deposition, is bizarre. "I figured that since he was supposed to be my manager, and he was going to book a studio, he might be in the studio listening to me. And that makes me … you know, I just can't get it to go like that. So I said, 'No. As soon as I get my songs together I'll let you know.'"[9] Hendrix mentioned in the deposition that he made little effort to keep in contact with Murray, although he left the occasional message with the label owner's secretary. Soon after this Sue Records hit choppy financial waters, and not too long after was sold off to pay Murray's debts. The contract was never acted upon.

Hendrix's initial experiences with record producers and companies contrast markedly with those of Bob Dylan three years earlier. Dylan had been rebuffed by the folk music labels such as Vanguard and Elektra as too eccentric, too impure for them, but he'd been noticed by John Hammond, who twisted the arm of corporate giant Columbia to let him make Dylan's first two LPs. Dylan delivered on the deal, did the LPs, then got himself a good, tough manager in Albert Grossman. He had a clear idea of what he wanted and where he was going and quickly moved to protect his interests, especially the creative areas such as songwriting and production. Hendrix, by contrast, had little or no interest in the business end of things, presuming in all innocence that these would look after themselves. This non-method would result in him appearing on a haphazard string of mediocre recordings as a session man for a number of producers and musicians. Worse than that, some of the commitments he so casually made at this time were to cause him considerable anguish in his years of fame, and would indeed remain unresolved at the time of his death.

It is clear that at this point Hendrix either did not or could

Hendrix poses with Curtis Knight (centre) and fellow members of The Squires in a New York photo studio, late 1965.

not differentiate between a record producer and a record-company owner. It was a crucial difference. A producer then largely made records to sell on or lease to third parties for specific exploitation with no regard for the artists involved, most of whom were little more than hired hands. A label owner had (theoretically) at least a passing interest in building a long-term career for the artist in the hope that both parties would benefit from proper career development. Up to his departure for London in September 1966, Hendrix would mostly encounter producers during his hunt for a record deal to further his interests, and would fail to exploit his contacts with record-company men, of whom Murray was just one.

Hendrix wrote a revealing letter to his father on August 8th. It was a Sunday, so he presumably felt less pressure to be out on the networking circuit. He told his dad once more that he was out of work, but he also gave an unusually long and detailed account of his strategy – if that is not too strong a word for it – and it marks a turning point of sorts. "I still have my guitar and amp and as long as I have that, no fool can keep me from living," he wrote. "There's a few record companies I visited that I'll probably record for. I think I'll start working towards that line, because actually when you're playing behind other people, you're still not making a big name for yourself. But I went on the road with other people to get exposure to the public and see how business is taken care of. And mainly just to see what's what, and after I put a record out, there'll be a few people who knew me already and who can help with the sale of the record. Nowadays people don't want you to sing good. They want you to sing sloppy and have a good beat to your songs. That's what angle I'm going to shoot for. That's where the money is. So just in case about three or four months from now you might hear a record by me which sounds terrible; don't feel ashamed, just wait until the money rolls in because every day people are singing worse and worse on purpose and the public buys more

and more records. I just want to let you know that I'm still here, trying to make it. Although I don't eat every day, everything's going all right for me. It could be worse than this, but I'm going to keep hustling and scuffling until I get things to happening, like they're supposed to for me."[10]

The letter suggests that, in search of a breakthrough, Hendrix was putting in a lot of time and effort that never bore fruit and which today go largely undocumented. Given Pridgeon's assertion that his guitar was continually in and out of the pawnbrokers during this period, then he may have been economical with the truth in claiming to have both guitar and amp (and this may have been in reply to a pointed question in his father's previous letter). Al Hendrix did not like his son's singing voice and Jimmy goes to great lengths in the letter to disarm his father's inevitable reaction to hearing him sing on a record. The universal panacea – loads of money – will be the salve for his father's injured artistic sensibilities. The whole tone of the letter suggests something that had already been achieved, and Hendrix is clearly referring to Dylan's model when he writes of singing "sloppy" but having a "good beat". He claims to have visited "a few record companies" by the time of writing this letter in early August, and while this was probably an exaggeration, the Sue deal had been signed by then, so his optimism about making a record is at least in part justified. Writing less than two weeks after doing the deal, Hendrix could have reasonably assumed he was on the verge of a breakthrough. But nothing happened.

In the meantime, the Isleys recorded the 45rpm single 'Move Over & Let Me Dance' / 'Have You Ever Been Disappointed' on Thursday August 5th 1965. The personnel included a horn section: not a road-hardened unit, but chosen from top New York session musicians of the day, including trombonist Quentin Jackson, saxophonist Haywood Henry, and trumpeter Jimmy Nottingham who had played for jazz leaders such as Duke Ellington, Charles Mingus, Count Basie, and even Jelly Roll Morton. The lack of rehearsal time shows in some wobbly top-part trumpet playing. Even more apparent is the lack of a decent tune as the Brothers return to the overheated atmosphere of 1964's 'Testify'.

'Move Over' is a mid-tempo strut reminiscent of the Martha & The Vandellas hit 'Dancing In The Street', which had charted the previous September, although the brass patterns come from innumerable Stax routines. Compared to the balanced arrangements to be found on the United Artists sides the Isleys made before 1964 and the superb if formulaic clarity of the ensemble writing on most of their Motown singles immediately afterwards, the Isleys here sound shambolic, suggesting a dire need for an imaginative and disciplined musical director. Hendrix, one of three guitarists on this date, has little to do apart from play a riff in thirds (which he'd later re-use in more than one of his R&B-based songs, such as 'Wait Until Tomorrow'). The flip side, 'Have You Ever Been Disappointed?', is a ballad in the Curtis Mayfield/Sam

Cooke mould, sung with feeling and generally much more convincing in structure and in general arrangement. The band, used sparingly, plays with more discipline than on 'Move Over' and the song itself has a good deal more substance in its melodic line and harmonic sequence. Again Hendrix has little to do, supplying a simple arpeggio figure to add romance to the atmosphere. (As with the two Isley sessions from 1964, these tracks were subsequently released on a T-Neck LP, *In The Beginning*, in 1971, where they were subjected to drastic remixes and editing. 'Move Over & Let Me Dance' even sprouted a 'part 2' which is simply the same take minus big-band and vocal tracks and with Hendrix's guitar accompaniment mixed up front.)

Photographs taken at the session indicate a convivial atmosphere, even if Hendrix found himself returning to the type of employment he evidently wanted to put in the past. By contrast, the following week Dylan's

"Nowadays people don't want you to sing good. They want you to sing sloppy and have a good beat to your songs. That's what angle I'm going to shoot for. That's where the money is."

Jimi Hendrix, letter to his father

revolutionary new album, *Highway 61 Revisited*, was released. Hendrix bought it immediately, provoking a row with Pridgeon. As she related in *A Film About Jimi Hendrix*: "I said, 'You better tell me what you spent our last five dollars on, y'know. He wouldn't tell me nothin', he just kept flashing the thing. Then he finally took it out of the bag and he still wouldn't let me read it. But he took it out of the bag and was reading me some of the things it said off it up in the air like this. … I didn't recognise anything he said anyway so I went off and pretended I didn't give a shit. I went up to the bedroom or something and he finally came in and told me it was Bob Dylan, and I said 'Bob who?' 'Bob Dylan! – you never heard of Bob Dylan?' I said I never heard of Dylan, y'know? I said, 'What's with this weird cat…' 'cause … Bob Dylan was really a genius in his own right but I just couldn't get ready for it and I figured Jimmy was so heavy into what I was into, he would never like anything like that, y'know? But he just loved it to death. I wanted to get up and go to the bathroom; he would grab me by my arms and [tell me I was] gonna miss this part, y'know, listen – y'know, OK – I couldn't miss it: you could hear it on 42nd Street most probably. We almost got put out of the building behind Bob Dylan."[11] Hendrix later complained that being in the Isleys again drove him crazy with boredom, but he may well have been grateful at the time for the opportunity to escape a deteriorating relationship in New York City. The altercation regarding Bob Dylan and a letter written to Pridgeon on September 1st give strong hints that their friendship was under severe strain, and Hendrix seems to have decided to make a change. Their relationship moved into a different phase, with Hendrix often away on short tours and even taking up with other girlfriends. It was a pattern that would apply until he left for England in September 1966.

Hendrix found his second stay with The Isley Brothers personally memorable for a number of reasons, not least when he played opposite both Booker T & The MGs and the King Curtis band at different venues between July and October 1965. In both instances he met up with guitarists for whom he had only the greatest admiration: Steve Cropper and Cornell Dupree. He met Dupree during the summer-holiday season of engagements in Wildwood,

New Jersey, which the Isleys shared with King Curtis & The Kingpins. Curtis's group spent the last two weeks of August on tour in the US as a support act for The Beatles, and welcomed the New Jersey dates as an opportunity to relax in one location for an extended period. Dupree explained later that there were a number of acts at different clubs in Wildwood at the time, including Curtis, the Isleys and Fats Domino. "[Jimmy] and I stayed in the same hotel for about a month, and during that time we got acquainted."[12] Hendrix and Dupree did some quiet jamming in their hotel rooms during the day when there were no rehearsals, but would also play around on the nearby basketball court. "He wasn't much good [at basketball]," Dupree commented wryly, "but neither was I."[13] Dupree had an extended first-hand opportunity to examine Hendrix's guitar techniques, his favourite players and ideas. "He was influenced by some of the people who influenced me – for instance, Albert King. He loved those old Muddy Waters and Lightnin' Hopkins-type things: he was really into that. So we'd play a lot of blues, and he loved it. He was home-made, self-taught, like myself."[14]

Dupree was an acute enough observer to notice that Hendrix, though influenced by many different players, had his own musical signature by then. He was impressed that Hendrix's personal conception was so developed, even within the R&B framework. "[It was] more greased, I mean funky," Dupree recalled. "I mean, he could do some Albert King, but in a different definition. His clarity in his playing and what he was saying – it was there. I can't explain it. We'd just make parts up off the top of our heads, 1-2-3-go – he'd play what he played, and I'd play what I played, and somehow it happened."[15] Dupree's description of how the two gelled together is very close to the relationship Billy Cox and Hendrix shared during 1969 and '70 when they would create intricate riff and rhythm patterns together in hotel rooms and recording studios. Dupree, a superb and fluent player who would have blended perfectly with Jimmy's rhythmic style, was not the only one to note the Isley guitarist's expertise. For the second time in a year King Curtis himself had come across the band with Hendrix on-board, and when he came to re-assess his own musical direction at the end of the year and decided to expand the role of the guitar in his band, he would call upon Hendrix to supply the added punch.

Curtis and his band's supporting role for The Beatles' 1965 US tour was an apt prelude for what amounted to a second British invasion. This time the new intruders brought a more raw-edged and iconoclastic sound and approach to music-making, accompanied by fast-changing and irreverent attitudes to the American establishment who watched their sons and daughters embrace these English bands. In time, Hendrix would assume a pre-eminent position as the old assumptions about culture and society were overturned. For the moment, he could only watch from the sidelines and assimilate whatever came his way. As Billy Cox has repeatedly pointed out, Hendrix "was a sponge. You listen to his music and you hear country & western. You hear Curtis Mayfield and you hear B.B. King, and you hear Albert and Freddie King. You hear Chet Atkins. You hear a collage of guitar players. T-Bone Walker was one of his influences. Along with 150 others!"[16]

Hendrix confirmed his diverse interests in 1970 when interviewed by John Burks for *Rolling Stone*, telling him that he was a fan of the old Western Swing group Bob Wills & The Texas Playboys and that he used to watch the traditional country TV show, the *Grand Ole Opry*, in his Nashville days.[17] Someone else who witnessed at first-hand Hendrix's voracious thirst for new sounds of every description was singer/guitarist Curtis Knight. During 1965/66 Knight watched as Hendrix purchased many singles and albums on impulse. "He bought all the popular records from people like the Stones, The Animals, some Beatles records, 'cause he had a wide variety of taste. Also he had all the black blues records, like Robert Johnson, and all those guys. So he was always someone who spent a lot of money in a record store, always. I mean, almost every penny he got, he didn't spend it on a guitar, or an amplifier, he spent it on records."[18] The money was not wasted.

The Beatles had such an impact on America in 1964 that the white middle-class kids who bought the records, the ones who listened to the radio and sustained the pop-music industry, were happy to embrace subsequent new arrivals from Britain. This inevitably led to hits for any number of chancers and popular entertainers willing to adopt 'beat music' mannerisms and attitudes. There were such fleetingly famous acts as Gerry & The Pacemakers, The Dave Clark Five, Wayne Fontana & The Mindbenders, Billy J Kramer & The Dakotas, Brian Poole & The Tremelos, as well as more consistently successful acts who sounded as if they came from the easy-listening end of the musical spectrum, such as Petula Clark, Manfred Mann and Herman's Hermits. But the open arms of the new American fans also meant that groups at the vanguard of change were just as eagerly adopted. The Animals had been one of the first – so soon after The Beatles that they were considered part of the first post-Beatles wave – along with The Rolling Stones, The Kinks and The Moody Blues, among others. By the summer and autumn of 1965 an entirely new pack of bands and solo singers were knocking on the door of the US charts, playing urgent and muscular reworkings of tunes and routines with direct roots from the music that Hendrix loved as he'd grown up: modern, urban, black US blues and R&B.

By this time the Brits were applying such a personal slant to this musical alchemy that their music soon took on its own distinctive profile. The British were redefining primitivism. They had the sophistication of connoisseurs as they selected which music to perform from the black R&B repertoire, but then applied a consciously caveman approach to its execution, especially in the rhythm section. Such wild enthusiasm for relatively primitive sounds was unknown in the US at the time. Bands like Them, The Yardbirds and a newly inventive Rolling Stones were at the forefront of this redefinition of R&B hipness, with the Stones now writing their own material and in June 1965 delivering their first US number one, '(I Can't Get No) Satisfaction'. Parallel to this was the emergence of a distinct American reaction to the reinvigoration of popular music, typified in mid 1965 by The Byrds. Their brilliantly produced cover versions of Dylan songs and other folk-based material such as 'Turn! Turn! Turn!' directly influenced thousands of other bands worldwide – including, ironically, The Beatles themselves, the band who had inspired the formation of The Byrds to begin with.

All of this would have been fascinating to Jimmy Hendrix in New York City that summer, but perhaps most enticing of all was The Yardbirds. Since their first hit, 'For Your Love' in June '65, and the subsequent departure of Eric Clapton for the purer blues of John Mayall's band, The Yardbirds had been contemplating a US tour. They had released a second single that August, 'Heart Full Of Soul' (also a US Top Ten entry), at the same time that Hendrix was sweating away in his mohair suit with the Isleys. The Yardbirds specialised in a frenetic version of beat music that was given the name 'rave-up'. Few of their US hits were out-and-out raves – most of those were tucked away on their LPs – and their latter releases turned toward more pop-like formulas, but Hendrix was certainly aware of their capabilities. They arrived in the US in September '65 with Jeff Beck amply filling the lead-guitar position left vacant by Clapton. Beck was to prove the only guitarist as obsessed with sheer sound as Hendrix, both live and in the studio, and this was evident from his earliest forays with the band.

On 'I'm A Man' (November 1965) and especially 'Shapes Of Things' (April 1966) Beck demonstrated his tremendous imagination, hauling the guitar out of the old rock'n'roll patterns and into a new kind of popular music. George Harrison may have been the first to display a fascination with feedback on a hit single ('I Feel Fine', December 1964) but Beck was to systematically explore its uses on record in his own idiosyncratic way a year before Hendrix got the chance to display his own prowess. Jimmy must have been both heartened and frustrated when he heard Beck on Yardbirds records and realised he was not alone in his quest. Guitarist Mike Bloomfield, who

first met Hendrix in the summer of 1966, was aware of the direct connection between Hendrix's own use of feedback and the input of The Yardbirds. "There was no great electric guitarist in rock'n'roll that Jimmy didn't know of," said Bloomfield. "He knew every hot guitarist on record. … [Jimmy] had been fooling with feedback, but when he heard The Yardbirds, he realised its huge potential. Hendrix would add vibrato so that it sounded just like a human voice. [He] said that he went to England to wipe them out, and he did."[19]

The other 'rave-up' band, Van Morrison's Them, made a much deeper cultural impact than simply troubling the charts for a few weeks in the UK with their cover of Big Joe Williams's 'Baby Please Don't Go'. It was backed by an original, 'Gloria', a hit in Britain in January 1965 but not in the States. Within a few months 'Gloria' became one of the most imitated garage-band songs of the era, alongside 'Louie Louie' and 'You Really Got Me'. Hendrix himself would knock out a version in a studio jam within three years. Them followed that 45rpm single with 'Here Comes The Night', a major summer success on both sides of the Atlantic, and had an American Top 40 hit in December, the frantic 'Mystic Eyes'. They broke up soon afterwards.

The Isleys' crowded itinerary took them deep into the autumn of 1965, sharing dates along the way with a variety of bands. There was a gig opposite Booker T & The MGs at DePauw University in Greencastle, Indianapolis, on October 9th.[20] Eyewitness Rod Kersey noticed that the bands were stationed at opposite ends of the school gymnasium, making for smoother transitions and more or less unbroken dancing opportunities. The date also afforded Hendrix the opportunity to check out Steve Cropper's guitar technique while the MGs were playing. "Hendrix studied his every move on guitar," Kersey remembered. "He seemed to be making Cropper kind of nervous."[21] This suggests that Hendrix and Cropper were not personally acquainted at this time, contradicting the oft-told story that Cropper and Hendrix jammed in the Stax studios in Nashville for hours one autumn day in 1964 during a session that has never been issued and perhaps was not even taped. If this meeting of guitar greats did take place, then autumn 1965 now seems a more likely time.

During this period Hendrix once more came across a musician and hustler trying to make ends meet in New York City, albeit with more material success than Jimmy. While Hendrix had been out on the road, Kansas-born Curtis Knight had stayed in New York City trying to hit the big time, working odd jobs, and even hustling at the ping-pong table, according to one interview,[22] striving to keep his head above water. A man full of energy and personal drive, Knight sang in various groups and played occasional rhythm guitar, but his real gifts were for organisation and talent-spotting. By the time he again bumped into Hendrix he was running his own group, The Squires. Keyboardist Nate Edmonds's wife Sharon Soul recalled: "Curtis was a musician but more business minded. He formed the group and paid the guys a salary by the week. Curtis would generally set up the gigs and handle money collection – and then pay the guys on payday."[23]

Knight had been releasing 45rpm singles since the summer of 1961 but by summer 1965 was no closer to his first hit. Like most musicians, Knight had no particular personal vision, only a driving need to perform and to make a living through music. In mid 1965 he made a new deal, probably a one-off, with RSVP Records and its owner Jerry Simon, to cut the single 'Ain't Gonna Be No Next Time' / 'More Love', which became RSVP 1111. Hendrix was not involved, but they would soon work together. Soon after recording the RSVP single, Knight was introduced to producer Ed Chalpin, who ran the PPX production company and made his living turning out cover versions of other artists' hits. Knight knew very well about covers: he was playing them nightly in the clubs and bars around Harlem. Chalpin had the cover-version business down to a fine art, using a large pool of musicians to record quick-fire covers, or close copies, of new hits in order to make a few dollars on the back of the original. "That's the business Ed Chalpin was in," Knight said later. "He would get on a plane and come to Europe, and he would have the record out in Europe before the [American hit record got there]. That was legal. I mean, he didn't steal the record … he gave credit to whoever wrote the song, and he talked to the publishing company. He was a millionaire when I met him. …

He said, 'Well, say, who can you sing like? … Can you write?' I say, 'Yeah, I can write songs.'"[24] More important to Chalpin at this stage was that Knight had a ready-made outlet on RSVP for any new product in which he was involved. That autumn, Chalpin signed Knight to an exclusive management agreement. Not long after, Knight introduced Chalpin to this guitarist he knew, called Jimmy Hendrix.

Before his death in 1999, Knight told the story of this encounter with Hendrix a number of times, each with different details, but his memory was consistent on some matters. He said that Hendrix at the time was living with Faye Pridgeon in a rundown hotel, the America, just off Times Square on 47th Street – a seedy area in 1965 and one that still hasn't exactly been gentrified today. "He was down on his luck," according to Knight. "He had no money and he was about to get kicked out of his hotel." Hendrix later offered his own rather different recollection of their meeting. "I was standing in the lobby, and a girl came up and said, 'This is Curtis Knight.' And then I got his name mixed up with another person and I thought it might have been him. So I went up and started a conversation with him."[25] Hendrix asked Knight up to his hotel room, where Knight met Pridgeon. Hendrix, claimed Knight, talked openly about his lack of acceptance uptown in Harlem, his disaffection with the chitlin circuit, and his ambition to make it on his own. "I'm only explaining this," Knight said later, "just to give you an idea of what kind of frustration Jimmy was going through at that time. Not only was there not much money, there wasn't even a lot of prestige. The black artists were not playing in the football stadiums and in the big halls like some stars do today. … Everything was very narrow, so Jimmy was in the situation where he was completely smothered and was getting more and more frustrated. So when he got to New York, he had reached the end of his rope. … He pawned his guitar [probably the Fender Jazzmaster he'd played with the Isleys] and there he was sittin' in this hotel, broke and hungry."[26]

Knight also recalled events similar to some witnessed by Pridgeon when Hendrix attempted to sit-in with bands uptown. "Jimmy even had problems with black musicians in America," said Knight. "There was a place called Small's Paradise where people like King Curtis and all the top musicians would go, and Jimmy would go up there sometimes to jam, but they wouldn't even let him play, because he was so good he'd make them all look stupid."[27] Knight was impressed by Hendrix's obvious talent. Like others before him, Knight loaned Hendrix a guitar – an old Danelectro – and invited him to work in his group, Curtis Knight & The Squires, which he was in the process of re-organising.

Knight may well have exaggerated Hendrix's poverty in his re-telling of the story. After all, Hendrix had been working regularly with The Isley Brothers for much of the summer and autumn and was still playing gigs with them in October. Nonetheless, most people who knew him at this time remember that he was perpetually broke and usually hungry as well. He never had a fetish about money, seeing it purely as a means to various ends, and he may well have frittered away most of his earnings from the Isleys in his usual style, eventually pawning his guitar in order to keep eating. Knight and Hendrix may both have had a faulty recollection of their meeting. Hendrix claimed later to have gone into the studio the following day, October 6th 1965, to cut a single with Knight under Ed Chalpin's supervision. This suggests that Hendrix and Knight had some prior knowledge of one another's abilities and styles. The ad hoc nature of this studio session, three days before an Isley Brothers gig in Indianapolis, indicates a quick, low-rent production made for a specific purpose – another cover in the grand tradition – and one with a quick release planned to achieve the greatest number of sales on the back of the original.

This time, the song being covered was Bob Dylan's 'Like A Rolling Stone', the first single that Columbia took from Dylan's latest album *Highway 61 Revisited*, the LP that had meant so much to Hendrix on its release a few weeks earlier. The version that Knight and Hendrix recorded for Chalpin was given the title 'How Would You Feel'. Knight, evidently the tune's writer according to the single's label, apparently supplied only the new lyrics. Hendrix claimed Knight "sang the lyrics to me, you know, and gave me a

rough idea how the lyrics went, the melody went".[28] Hendrix then worked out the chords to the melody: not that difficult when it was a close copy of a Dylan song that he already knew and loved.

If one ignores Knight's vocals on the track and concentrates instead on the instrumental accompaniment, a very neatly-played cover version of the Dylan song becomes apparent, even down to the country-type guitar picking in imitation of Mike Bloomfield's work on the original. The only difference is the quality of the recording – Columbia managed a better overall sound for Dylan, naturally – and the entirely different lyrics. They constitute a clumsy and self-pitying attempt to paint a picture of the struggling artist ignored and vilified by society and asking for a break. Hardly what Dylan was on about. There is a clear difference in recorded sound between what the musicians are playing and what Knight is singing, and it may well be that the group originally attempted a version of Dylan's song, lyrics and all, only to abandon it when the vocals were tried and the gulf between original and copy was duly noted. Hendrix claimed that "the first session we did was one that I played all the instruments except the drums",[29] making it less likely that Knight was singing 'live' with the musicians and giving him the freedom to change his mind on his approach from one vocal take to the next.

The flip side, 'Welcome Home', is a straight lift from Curtis Mayfield's 'Can I Get a Witness' (which had been given new currency at the time in a cover by The Rolling Stones) combined with 'Don't Bring Me Down', a minor hit in the US for The Pretty Things the previous November. Again, Knight's vocal is mediocre, but at least on this side the recorded ambience of his singing matches that of the backing group. Hendrix plays a good solo that shows him already a master of driving R&B breaks in the manner of Buddy Guy. The 'How Would You Feel' / 'Welcome Home' single, which had to wait until March 1966 for release, would make no sales impact at all.

The session points up Hendrix's all-enveloping enthusiasm for Dylan, the pre-eminent singer-songwriter of the moment, and may even explain why he agreed to do the session in the first place. George Clemons, who often hung out with Hendrix around New York in 1965 and '66, was with him one evening in Harlem when the guitarist went into a club and put 'Blowing In The Wind' on the record deck. Clemons later told the story to Hendrix's friend Paul Caruso. "All these guys said, 'Get out and take your hillbilly music with you!' There was almost a fight. His girlfriend at that time, Faye Pridgeon, said that this hostility of the Harlemites caused him to sort of flee to the Village."[30]

Pleased with the session, Chalpin was quick to recognise the versatile talent this new guitarist had brought to it. He encouraged Hendrix to come back with other ideas, which he did a few days later. As Hendrix recalled it, "One time I was doing a demo. I wrote a song one night; and the next morning, you know, I wanted to record it; I wanted to make a demo of it."[31] Hendrix's attitude here isn't exactly consistent with his professed objections to recording demos for Juggy Murray with Murray present. Anyway, according to Hendrix, once the demo session was over Chalpin took him to his office and asked if he was signed to anyone. Jimmy came to believe that the simple document he signed with Chalpin's PPX company on October 15th did not conflict with his Sue Records deal, but merely allowed him to be paid for his PPX work. He admitted, though, that he never read it – for Hendrix never read any contracts.

The surviving one-page document confirms that Hendrix was living at the time at the Hotel America on 47th Street. It is not a standard form but a freshly typed page on PPX headed paper, identifying PPX as "Master Producers and Agents", with their logo adding: "Serving the record industry throughout the world." Across the bottom of the page is another PPX slogan, rendered in quotes: "Representing the largest and most diversified available library of Music Masters in the world." The terms of the contract include a clause that "Jimmy Hendrix will produce and play and/or sing exclusively for PPX Enterprises Inc, for three (3) years from above date [October 15th 1965]." He will also "make available his services at the request of PPX with a minimum of ten (10) days notice to produce no more than four (4) titles per session, a minimum of three (3) session[s] per year." For this Hendrix was to receive "one (1) per cent of retail selling price of all records sold for his production efforts, minimum scale for arrangements he produces." Perhaps most important of all in terms of PPX's intentions regarding masters that Hendrix produced for them was a phrase contained in the final clause: "PPX shall have exclusive rights to assign for all masters produced in conjunction with Jimmy Hendrix."

This is not a record deal like the one Hendrix had signed with Sue Records in July. It is a production contract with a company that produced master recordings for the primary purpose of assigning them, leasing them, or otherwise commercially exploiting them through third-party record labels. This sort of arrangement was not unusual at the time. Hendrix's deal gave PPX complete control over the form that any of his recordings would take (and continue to take), and Hendrix none at all. The contract is perfectly consistent with Knight's description of Ed Chalpin as someone quick to make low-rent cover versions of current hits, or low-cost masters in the fashion or style of a contemporarily popular act. Chalpin had spotted in Knight someone with the ability and desire to work that way, and it is clear that Chalpin thought that in Jimmy Hendrix he'd found another musician willing to operate under the same conditions. Nothing that Chalpin has done since October 1965 with the masters he owns is inconsistent with that perception. That it is an utterly bankrupt one from an aesthetic point of view probably could not interest him less.

The recordings featuring Hendrix and now under the control of Chalpin have been relentlessly subjected to re-editing, re-fashioning, re-constituting and doctoring under a constant programme of issuing and reissuing that started with Chalpin's licensing of PPX-owned Hendrix material to Decca Records UK and Capitol Records US in 1967. It continues virtually unabated to the present day. The Hendrix archive industry has been kept busy for decades trying to account for and log every release, known and unknown, discovered and undiscovered, of each basic studio performance. This activity, however meretricious, will no doubt continue. The only sessions that can be said to have 'original' versions that in any way comply with what the artists as well as the producer had in mind are the two RSVP singles released prior to Hendrix's ascent to fame: 'How Would You Feel' / 'Welcome Home' and 'Hornet's Nest' / 'Knock Yourself Out'.

Everything else was released later with the intention of selling records to fans of Jimi Hendrix. In the interests of clarity and sanity, only the most salient musical features in any selected performance will be dealt with here, even if this means silently conflating two, three or any number of multiple mixes, edits and re-edits of a basic performance to achieve this overview.

With Hendrix out of town with the Isleys and Chalpin busy with other projects, the PPX connection, like the Sue deal, remained dormant for a considerable time. It wasn't until late 1965 that Chalpin found Hendrix in town when he needed a guitarist for a session that, in itself, was hardly something that was going to move Hendrix's career forward. It was for a Jayne Mansfield novelty single, 'Suey', with Chalpin producing (and co-writing the B-side). Needless to say, Hendrix had little more than a functionary's role. After that, Chalpin would not use Hendrix on any other session independent of his work with Curtis Knight's band, The Squires. Knight talked later of his band as if it were something special on the New York City music scene of the day. But the aural evidence of the studio singles and on-location tapes made late in 1965 suggests that it was simply a competent covers band aimed largely at dancers in the clubs and bars of the city, with Knight's name used as a flag of convenience in recognition of his role as the outfit's principal organiser. That he apparently asked Hendrix in "as a co-feature artist, not as someone to be kicked in the background"[32] may have held some appeal to the hard-up guitarist, but this must be set against the fact that, even at this stage, Hendrix was ahead of most of the rest of the band in experience and

competence, let alone inspiration or musical thinking. Knight's apparent offer has never been confirmed by anyone else in the band at the time. Hendrix was quick to point out in 1968 that his fellow band-members were "very, very good, capable musicians". But he did not include Knight in that assessment, saying pointedly "as far as I know he's a singer".[33]

Hendrix didn't limit himself to Knight's band, taking better-paid work around New York City and environs whenever it came up. Given this and the ad hoc nature of the band's line-up, it is debatable just how much work Hendrix managed with Knight's band (which also gigged under the name of The Lovelights[34]) at least during late 1965, usually assumed to be the period when Hendrix worked most intensively with them. Knight hustled a fair amount of routine dance-gig work in and around New York City at clubs like Ondine's on 59th Street and, in 1966, The Purple Onion in Greenwich Village, as well as The Cheetah, which was close to Times Square. But Knight like most bandleaders in his position used a pool of players and a number of different group names to fulfil the bookings, and few of the musicians were ever-present. During October, for example, Hendrix was finishing his commitment to The Isley Brothers, and for a fair slice of November he was out on the road with Joey Dee & The Starlighters. A letter home to Al Hendrix in the last week of November 1965 informed him his son was "in Boston, Mass. We'll be here for ten days. We're actually playing in Revere. ... I'm playing up here with Joey Dee & The Starlighters."[35] The Starlighters had been long-term fixtures at one of the more popular New York nightspots, The Peppermint Lounge (hence the group's December 1961 hit 'The Peppermint Twist', a

"He would sign a contract with anybody who came along and they had a dollar and a pencil. He'd sign with them. Which got him into a lot of trouble later."

Faye Pridgeon, girlfriend

record with strong R&B overtones, especially in its second 'Part'). On this occasion they were taking a short tour and needed additional musicians to help out. As a result, Hendrix wasn't back on the New York City scene until late in the first week in December. That left him with little available time to play clubs with Curtis Knight's band before the end of 1965.

Knight's working group most often included drummer Marion Booker, bassist Napoleon Anderson, and Hendrix on guitar. Other musicians such as keyboardist Nate Edmonds and saxophonist Lonnie Youngblood would sometimes be called in specifically for a Curtis Knight & The Squires date or engagement, as well as when different combinations of the same musicians were needed for routine session work. Youngblood had known Knight in New York prior to a stint in the Army and met up with him on returning to the City after his discharge in 1965. Youngblood has even claimed in a number of interviews to have taken the band over from Knight and worked it under his own name. Given that they were all musical mercenaries, this is entirely possible if Youngblood had work on offer. His saxophone style, closely modelled on that of King Curtis, would have given the band a sufficiently fresh identity to work a separate gig circuit under another name – mainly in Harlem, according to Youngblood.

Nate Edmonds's wife Sharon Soul remembered a particular work pattern. "The Squires were a 'house band' type of group [at clubs] where they had to work four nights a week. Jimmy and Nate didn't star there or anything, they just played music that people that were into R&B music were into. Any recordings that they did may have been an attempt to make it, but the group was formed to earn money consistently as a house band. House bands provided a steady income for musicians while they worked on projects like recording."[36]

In this intensely pragmatic atmosphere, The Squires made a number of demo recordings. Hendrix recalled during a pre-trial deposition made in 1968 that he played on a little over half a dozen sessions with the band during 1965. Some were on-location live sessions recorded on a portable tape machine, and some sound as if they were made in a club but were probably demos made in a professional studio with crowd sounds added later for effect. Other selections seem possibly to be a combination of the two, with vocals and spoken comments added over material recorded live. Edmonds's wife Sharon Soul knew the reasons for this. "They ... could be used to shop to nightclubs for future gigs. ... If they audition the tape for a nightclub and it appears that they knew how to work the audience, then they had a better chance of getting the job. ... Most of the jobs that a musician got on Broadway were from word-of-mouth among musicians, but there were agencies such as Ka-Cole Enterprises that would book gigs for musicians and bands. Ka-Cole also had a photographer who would give the artists a professional picture to use."[37] The Squires had just such a picture produced.

Curtis Knight recalled later that they would use Chalpin's studio for such semi-formal work between booked sessions for Chalpin projects, though he preferred to dress it up in more dignified language. "With my manager Ed Chalpin owning the studio, Jimmy and I were able, whenever we felt like it, to go in that studio, that 10-track studio – which ... at that time was incredible – and create what I think is amazing music for that time. ... I did all the songs together with him, and Jimmy played most of the instruments. He played the bass. He didn't play the drums very often, but he played most of the instruments."[38] The absence of any surviving studio logbook makes it impossible to verify these claims, although in the case of the 'Like A Rolling Stone' soundalike single Hendrix himself later admitted to playing everything but the drums.

The tracks recorded in this fashion as demos for gigs must be regarded quite separately from those laid down during formal PPX production sessions for the purpose of licensing to third parties for commercial release as singles. 'U.F.O.', for example, is a voice-guitar duet on a tune with a simple structure and chord pattern. The recording quality is equivalent to a demo version and the song is unfinished. If it is indeed Hendrix playing guitar on this tune – and the playing is so unadorned that it really matters very little who it is – he could have played this simple run-through in a hotel room on to portable equipment, such is the sound quality. Knight has not even finished the lyrics to the verses, and when he forgets to come in with the hookline at one point the guitarist has to quickly cover for him by reverting to the verse pattern. So mediocre is 'U.F.O.' that RSVP's Jerry Simon's decision to sit on the master before re-selling to Chalpin and Knight in 1967 is entirely understandable. (The *earlyhendrix* website has noted a full-band studio version of 'U.F.O.' that first surfaced in 1997. Given its late arrival on the scene and the wonders of modern technology, determining the provenance of the accompanying instruments could provide a worthwhile area of study.) Other tracks fare better, although the informality is clearly evident in the relaxed, unpolished playing and singing, and the stilted nature of added spoken intros, comedy routines and other ad-libs.

There had been many precedents for this type of 'simulated live' recording in rock'n'roll, stretching back to the 1950s and including Chubby Checker's more recent 'twist' hit singles. By 1965 the idea was commonplace. Under normal circumstances such workaday recordings would never be heard again outside the artist's living room. With Hendrix involved, a large number of these demos would later surface in the guise of official Curtis Knight & The Squires releases, often with Hendrix's name writ large on the packaging. Among other things, such recordings show that saxophonist Lonnie Youngblood was a working member of the band. Later, he had a specific view on just what the Squires, and Curtis Knight in particular, had to offer back then. He remembered that, upon being asked to join the band, he said he'd

come along to a gig and check them out. "And I went, and that's where Jimmy Hendrix was, playing with this band. ... Curtis [Knight] was the bandleader, but he couldn't really ... he wasn't a very good musician at the time. He was more or less a hindrance to the band. ... That band had problems – and you know how bands have problems."[39] Youngblood's rather brutal assessment fits well with the pragmatic way in which Knight organised his band and their employment in New York City at the time.

Youngblood came late to the band, arriving probably at the beginning of 1966, just after the second series of studio appearances that Hendrix made with Knight under the auspices of Ed Chalpin and PPX. Although devoid of audience noise or spoken introductions, the three tracks recorded then are not dissimilar in sound quality to the demos that the band were making around the same time in the hope of attracting more live work. The three tracks were not issued as singles and were only released years later, after Hendrix had made his big breakthrough, suggesting that the third-party record company to whom they were initially offered (presumably RSVP) turned them down. 'Simon Says', 'You Don't Want Me' and 'Don't Accuse Me' do little justice to the band and are generally inferior to the 1966 sides made with RSVP's own producer, Jerry Simon. Their feeble quality may have contributed to RSVP's decision that they would themselves produce the next session with the band.

'Simon Says' sounds like an outtake from the October '65 session and is one of the worst of all the Curtis Knight recordings from 1965 and '66. 'You Don't Want Me' and 'Don't Accuse Me' are mediocre soul tunes that rely heavily on other contemporary models for their overall sound and construction, tarted up with some superficial arrangement features to give them a touch of British-Invasion hipness. The major gesture in this direction is a fuzz-effect guitar that plays simple lines to back the singer and lock in with the conventional R&B rhythm guitar, which is played very professionally by Hendrix. The identity of the rather heavy-handed fuzz guitarist has not been conclusively established, though many observers – including Knight – have suggested that Hendrix overdubbed it at the original session. 'You Don't Want Me' exists in two mixes, one burdened by Curtis Knight's uninspired vocals, the other with Knight's vocal removed. 'Simon Says' is a musical version of the old party game that could possibly have been an enjoyable novelty number had Knight not been such an inept party host. Considering that he is imitating Joe Tex's emotive spoken style, he might have tried a less laboured performance somewhat closer to his model.

The Squires continued to play the club circuit up to the end of 1965 – apparently appearing at George's Club 20 in Hackensack, New Jersey, on December 26th, although that date has recently been questioned[40] – while the individual members continued to pick up freelance work wherever they could. The repertoire consisted mostly of cover versions of current hits, pointing to the band's workaday function as a music machine for dancers. Recent and still-popular hits they churned out included 'Day Tripper' by The Beatles (US number one in December 1965), Otis Redding's 'Mr Pitiful' (number 41 in January 1965), 'Walking The Dog' by Rufus Thomas (number ten, November 1963), Joe Tex's 'Hold What You've Got' (number five, January 1965), 'Hang On Sloopy' by The McCoys (number one, September 1965 – Hendrix was a fan of guitarist Rick Derringer), 'I Can't Help Myself' by The Four Tops (number one, May 1965), Marvin Gaye's 'I'll Be Doggone' (number eight, April 1965) and 'Ain't That Peculiar' (number eight, October 1965), 'Woolly Bully' by Sam The Sham & The Pharoahs (number two, May 1965), James Brown's 'I Got You (I Feel Good)' (number three, October 1965), and '(I Can't Get No) Satisfaction' by The Rolling Stones (US number one, June 1965). A supplement to this varied but predictable dancefloor diet was a sprinkling of blues and R&B numbers. Hendrix plays with such verve on the surviving tapes that it seems safe to assume that he brought this repertoire to the band. He plays on (and occasionally supplies lead vocals to) tunes such as Memphis Slim's 'Every Day I Have The Blues', Howling Wolf's 'Killing Floor', and B.B. King's '(I've Got A) Sweet Little Angel' and 'I'm A Man' (the latter undoubtedly known to Hendrix in the versions by both Bo Diddley and Muddy Waters; Muddy called his 'Mannish Boy'). Listening to this collection of performances as a whole, as well as others from the same period claimed to

Hendrix (far left) around February 1966 with Curtis Knight & The Squires, a band with a fluctuating line-up and a clear role as a dance-music machine in the clubs of New York City.

be 'live', confirms Youngblood's musical evaluation of Curtis Knight as the group's weakest link.

The Squires' rhythm section is largely unidentified for the live tracks but probably includes various combinations of bassist Napoleon ('Hank') Anderson and drummer Marion Booker.[41] They are disciplined, clearly skilled in supplying dynamics as they interpret a tune, and responsive to what the frontline is doing. It's easy to imagine these musicians providing professional backing tracks to any number of recording sessions for a wide variety of artists and styles. But while the group generates a locked-in groove for tunes like 'Shotgun' and 'Mr Pitiful', they really explode when backing Hendrix's guitar-playing on the blues-based material. On a blues ballad such as B.B. King's 'Sweet Little Angel', Hendrix, heedless of Knight's sub-par vocals, brings off an inspired reinvention of King's own guitar style and technique. This performance alone is enough to put him in the front rank of blues guitarists of the day. The band also recorded the R&B song 'Money', first a hit in the US in 1960 for Barrett Strong but most notably covered by The Beatles (1963) and The Kingsmen (who had a number-four US hit with it in January 1965). On one take, Hendrix plays a burning solo that exhibits the rhythmic freedom and the ability to shape his phrasing in unpredictable and thrilling ways that would have such a devastating effect in England some nine months or so later.

Delivering both the lead guitar and vocals, Hendrix gives a frenetic work-out on Memphis Slim's 'Every Day I Have The Blues' (variously titled 'California Night' and 'Nobody Loves Me' on the PPX releases). It's a

staggering display of blues guitar playing that is worthy of mention in the same breath as his later efforts with the Experience and some of his all-star jams. Hendrix may still be unselfconscious about using a tone like Buddy Guy's and some of Guy's short, repeated phraseology in his solos and accompaniment, but his ability to spin out long and consistently surprising lines across the standard blues changes is already full grown. His attack – the actual sound of his guitar – is as ferocious as that found on, say, the late-1966 'Red House' recordings he would make in London. There are also moments when Hendrix uses string-bending, sudden pauses and other devices in a way that simply transcends any previous models, and breaks new ground. The same can be said of his early versions here of 'Driving South' and 'Killing Floor'. Hendrix would often record 'Driving South' live for the BBC with the Experience, in performances today regarded as some of his greatest blues outings, and he would play Howling Wolf's 'Killing Floor' at Monterey in 1967, as well as at selected concerts right through to his last tour in 1970. Regardless of what came later, the intensity of some of what he plays here with The Squires raises the hairs on the back of one's neck, generating that overwhelming level of excitement that would soon be his worldwide trademark. The arrangement here of Jimmy Reed's 'You Got Me Running' closely parallels that of 'Red House', down to the parallel-harmony bass part and the loping rhythmic feel.

These recordings, whether truly recorded live or made in a demo studio and played around with later, are conclusive proof that Hendrix had long moved on from an amateur or immature musical attitude and instrumental technique. He plays on the same level instrumentally as he would do soon after when running his own bands. Only the musical setting would change and the equipment – especially the amplifiers – would be upgraded. Hendrix would also gradually work out a way of singing that compensated for the limitations of his voice. Here his vocals are perfunctory, and he pushes too hard, for example, on 'Every Day', although his stab at 'Killing Floor' is characteristic, full of personality and largely comfortable.

What is frustrating about this whole group of recordings as one listens to them now is the absence of documentation. It is clear that they were not all made at the same time, and some could have been taped months apart. The presence and absence of Lonnie Youngblood's saxophone and occasional vocals alone suggest that different dates are involved. But until a definitive chronology can be established, Hendrix's development as an artist and musician can only be estimated rather than delineated in any conclusive way. The only assumption that is perhaps safe to make about all this material is that it was put down on tape earlier rather than later in The Squires' short existence, for as the band began to unravel and Hendrix lost faith in Knight's ability to partner him in his bid for success, the urge to preserve their efforts in the hope of advancement would have gradually evaporated.

RSVP label owner/producer Jerry Simon signed the individual members of The Squires (minus Curtis Knight, who is not mentioned) to a deal as late as June 10th 1966, some three months after the March 15th release of the Curtis Knight single featuring Hendrix's backing, 'How Would You Feel'. This single had been cleared for release by a one-off February contract with Knight and PPX. Five more selections were recorded before the end of that month, by which time Hendrix had stopped working with them. No further RSVP singles were released from this stockpile of material. In fact, only two singles were released from all the recordings made by the groups run by Curtis Knight while Hendrix was playing in the band. An anomaly typical of the period meant that the original 1967 British release of 'How Would You Feel' carried 'Don't Accuse Me' as its B-side, making it the third of the Ed Chalpin-produced tunes to be officially released, although by that time Hendrix was already famous in Britain.

That Hendrix was only ever partially committed to Knight's working band can be gauged by the fact that he felt able to work with King Curtis in early January 1966 prior to joining the saxophonist's band full-time. Hendrix would

"Hendrix had been fooling with feedback, but when he heard The Yardbirds, he realised its huge potential."

Mike Bloomfield, guitarist

have realised that joining Curtis's All Stars presented a number of advantages. First, he would be playing with a group of session musicians for whom he had very high regard. Second, the band would be based in and around New York City, working much of the time in the studio on Curtis's numerous projects as producer and performer, and as with The Isley Brothers the previous summer and autumn this meant Hendrix could avoid the back-breaking and demoralising tours he'd come to dread while on the chitlin circuit. Third, he would be earning some regular money again instead of starving on freelance oddments. Finally, Hendrix might have some more time to himself to plan his future. Curtis Knight's house-band worked what most jobbing groups of the day would have recognised as normal hours: at least four

sets of approximately 45 minutes each, with a 15-minute break in each hour. The first set would start between 9.30 and 10.00pm, which usually meant playing through until around 2.00am. By contrast, King Curtis, as a headline act, would be playing shorter sets than this and relying on support acts to fill in the extra time.

King Curtis's guitarist Cornell Dupree remembered how the bandleader, ever an astute reader of musical fashion and public taste, was well aware that it was time to update his sound. Dupree recalled: "At the time Curtis was trying to change the band, expand it, stay current you might say, and rather than [add] piano he chose to go with two guitarists."[42] King Curtis was already aware of Hendrix on the New York scene, through his own experience and Dupree's recommendation. At first, in December 1965, Curtis employed Jimmy Spruill as his second guitarist, but during January Spruill was unable to fulfil his commitments, allowing Hendrix to deputise. Sometime in the new year Curtis became tired of waiting for Spruill and instead asked Hendrix to change to full-time membership. The guitarist joined the All Stars at Small's Paradise up in Harlem. It was one of Curtis's favourite venues, though Hendrix's memories of the place were not so sweet, having so often been barred from sitting-in there. Bassist Chuck Rainey remembered a bonus from the new guitarist. "For the six months that Jimmy was in the group I gained an added feeling, which I label response."[43]

Hendrix probably should have been feeling more sanguine about his prospects given this heightened level of activity in New York City. Not so, judging by the postcard he sent to father Al on January 13th 1966. Perhaps it was those dank and dreary mid-winter hotel rooms. "Dear Dad, Well … I'm just dropping in a few words to let you know everything's so-so here in this big raggedy City of New York – everything's happening bad here – I hope everyone at home is alright – tell them I said hello – I'll write you a letter real soon."[44] Just why Hendrix was apparently so low at this point is not immediately clear. He should have been better off materially with the All Stars, but money evidently remained tight. Curtis Knight recalled that Hendrix was not really writing songs during this period, preferring to concentrate on his guitar playing, so he wasn't going through the frustrations of writing material and having it ignored. And while he was bound to stick by the collective musical discipline of the All Stars, when he had the opportunity to play a night with The Squires or with Youngblood he was able to play and sing centre-stage from time to time.

There was another area that still tyrannised Hendrix – that of stage apparel. Every black group he played with, from King Curtis to Curtis Knight, insisted on band uniforms. Hendrix could not escape a convention that had become anathema to him, especially when he looked to the freedoms in choice of clothing enjoyed by many of the young white performers whose music he enjoyed. Dylan not only wore whatever he felt like (as did his backing bands), he set trends in fashion. The new British bands brought innovations in stage dress and on-stage individualism to the US, but these completely bypassed the soul and R&B scene. There was more informality on Chicago's South Side. This must have grated on Hendrix, a man perpetually conscious of image, especially his clothes. He wanted to explore the new individualism not only of the second British invasion but also of Greenwich Village, an area of New York City in the forefront of such issues. "Jimmy was image conscious," remembered Curtis Knight. "That was the product."[45]

During January, Hendrix made his recording debut with King Curtis, contributing guitar parts to a 45rpm single 'Help Me (Get The Feeling) Parts 1 and 2' produced by Curtis, with vocals by Ray Sharpe, and released soon afterwards on Atco. Sharpe and Curtis were operating in the same way as Chalpin and Knight. "I was dealing with a friend of mine … King Curtis, from Fort Worth, Texas," Sharpe remembered many years later. "I went up [to New York City] and we sat around for about a month or so. He had some ideas on some stuff he heard me play, and we had a 'think fountain' going with King Curtis and Cornell Dupree about producing some stuff, and that was for him.

He had a contract with Atlantic, but my contract was with him, as my producer. I was considered an artist of his rather than of Atlantic. I had two sides released; there was much more in the can."[46] The 'think fountain' must have been short of water for 'Help Me', which merely rips off the chord changes from Them's 'Gloria' and the horn riffs from Herbie Hancock's 'Watermelon Man' while Sharpe delivers a sub-James Brown monologue, even recycling some of Van Morrison's lyric ideas. 'Help Me' is spread over both sides of the 45rpm disc and there is a short guitar solo, wholly within the Stax idiom, at the turnover point. The single disappeared without trace.

Curtis used Sharpe as a vocalist for another session in April that year but nothing was released from it at the time. A fire at Atlantic's warehouse in the early 1970s destroyed the masters, along with many other valuable Atlantic archives, so taped documentation of Hendrix's time with Curtis is sparse. (Curtis was hardly one to waste a good track; understandable, when he owned the master. 'Help Me', shorn of Sharpe's vocals, was later used as a basic track for Aretha Franklin to record 'Save Me', a song that appeared on her *I Never Loved A Man (The Way I Love You)* album from 1967. He also re-used the rhythm track, with minor alterations, for a later single of his own, 'Instant Groove', backed by 'Sweet Inspiration', a track from an unrelated session. It doesn't stop there: singer Owen Gray cut another version of 'Help Me', again using the original Curtis backing track.[47])

February 1966 found Hendrix on tour with King Curtis & The All Stars on the West Coast and in the Midwest. During Hendrix's absence, Curtis Knight signed a new deal with Jerry Simon's RSVP Records, authorising the release of a new Knight single. On March 15th the label released 'How Would You Feel' / 'Welcome Home', which had been recorded (with Hendrix present) the previous October. Not surprisingly given that it was an imitation of a hit from the previous summer, the record flopped. It's not known what Knight made of Jerry Simon's decision to release as a second single two instrumental tracks rather than anything featuring Knight's vocals – but what is clear from the single's label is that Hendrix co-authored both songs, 'Hornet's Nest' and 'Knock Yourself Out'. It is unlikely that Knight is present on these tracks.

Details about exactly when this new session took place have only recently become clearer. Hendrix himself thought it had been in June 1966. Given that the entire group signed a deal with RSVP that month and that Hendrix signed publishing contracts for a number of songs on June 21st, there is at least circumstantial evidence to back up this idea. 'Hornet's Nest' and 'Knock Yourself Out' don't appear on the contract list, but two otherwise unknown titles do – 'Station Break' and 'Flying On Instruments' – along with 'No Such Animal', another confirmed Hendrix composition not released until 1971.[48] It is likely that the titles were simply changed later on. Producer Simon took a co-writing credit on both RSVP tracks: this widespread practice in the recording industry dated back to its infancy in the 1920s, and Hendrix would have known about it long before this session. It meant that Simon could claim 50 percent of the songwriting royalty as well as his producer's fee and was in effect a form of bonus payment – one that many producers, managers and others in positions of power took advantage of in those days.

'Hornet's Nest' is a rudimentary riff-based song that uses minor blues changes borrowing heavily from the 'Green Onions' pattern. It starts at a medium tempo and speeds up quite markedly during its two-minute duration. Probably the song was composed in the studio and named for its swirling Hammond-organ treble figure played by Squires keyboard man Nate Edmonds at the start and conclusion. Hendrix and Edmonds both solo in spirited fashion, Jimmy frequently resorting to his fuzz-box for extra excitement, and the single makes for a good slice of action that would have come across well on a jukebox. The flip side, 'Knock Yourself Out', is another blues with an R&B riff pattern played in unison by the bass and guitar. The pattern had been heard in various incarnations a few times before and would be countless times afterwards, perhaps most notably though not identically on Cream's 'Strange Brew'. (The same basic pattern and rhythm is duplicated on a Curtis Knight track, a reworking of his 1963 single 'Gotta Have A New Dress', where Knight steps up for a mediocre vocal.) Again, the guitarist and

organ player are the major soloists, and both show they have ideas to spare in the short spaces allotted. The drummer is also allowed a four-bar break, elsewhere showing himself to be a fine, crisp performer.

One notable quality of both sides of the single is the smooth way in which the musicians interlock. These men knew each others' styles and were sufficiently attuned that they could complement one another with ease. 'Knock Yourself Out' works like a great advertisement for a first-rate instrumental group looking for a break, and perhaps that was its intended purpose. Hendrix later suggested that this and some other tracks were made in RSVP's studio. "There was one time, I think – they had a studio downstairs in the same building which was represented by RSVP … I think we recorded a song down there called 'Knock Yourself Out', and I think we recorded one called 'Hornet's Nest'."[49] The single was released later in 1966 but did nothing.

A track probably recorded during this same period, judging by the studio sound, composing credits and instrumentation – it lacks only a fuzz-box guitar overdub from Hendrix – was to lay unreleased until 1971. It appeared then as a single on the Audio Fidelity label in the US and on RCA in Britain, credited solely to "Jimi Hendrix" with no mention on the label of Curtis Knight, The Squires, Jerry Simon, or PPX. Like 'Hornet's Nest' and 'Knock Yourself Out', 'No Such Animal' is an instrumental, but runs over five minutes in length and was divided on its initial release across two sides of the 45rpm singles. Just why it appeared in this fashion and so relatively late, and why it has rarely cropped up on later compilations of Hendrix/Knight material, remains something of a mystery. Hendrix may inadvertently have shed some light on the matter during his 1968 pre-trial deposition when he said that on one occasion in this period "everybody was in the studio on my own money, like, to make a demo".[50] 'No Such Animal' awaits its CD debut at the time of writing, eluding collation onto the six volumes of the *Complete PPX Studio Recordings* released during the late 1990s and collected into a set in 2000. It was also left off the Jungle Records compilation CD *Knock Yourself Out* of the so-called 1965 studio dates. All this makes it doubtful that the track is in fact owned or controlled by Ed Chalpin, as everything to which he has legal access has been issued and reissued in many different versions and mixes in the intervening 30 years or so. It is also doubtful that it was sold on separately by RSVP's Jerry Simon at some unspecified date after Hendrix's rise to fame, as Simon seems to have sold his entire Hendrix holding to Chalpin in 1967. Of course, he may have sold it prior to that date, but Hendrix was unknown in the US at that time and would not have been an attractive commercial commodity, so there would have been little point in such a move.

Regardless of its undistinguished fate, 'No Such Animal' is one of the more focused and attractive of Hendrix's early studio outings. It also has a claim to be Hendrix's first recorded composition – he is the only credited writer on the 45rpm single label, Jerry Simon's name being absent this time – though it was quite possibly pulled together by the current members of The Squires during various jams, with none of their names making it onto the 1971 release. There is very little structure to the 'tune', which turns out to be a few short riff figures against a blues structure at mid tempo. However, after a near boogaloo drum-beat intro, Hendrix enters with a riff pattern very close to that of his later 'Ezy Rider'. His loose, flowing rhythmic style locks with the forceful drummer's beat before taking off on a solo where he uses the type of scratchy Fender sound he preferred early on for his blues performances (though he was yet to get his amplifier up to the volume levels that would give him the sustain he achieved in studios towards the end of 1966). Some of his playing on the second half of the piece, after organist Nate Edmonds's neat and professional solo, is loose and not rhythmically precise. It suggests that this may well have been a number The Squires used for jamming, and that it was recorded in the studio to use up time still available at the end of a session. It couldn't possibly have been recorded as a potential single release: five minutes of instrumental jamming stood no chance of making it in the charts in 1966. This track and the other two instrumentals from the same source show that, without Curtis Knight around, the band was efficient, spirited and wholly undeserving of the contempt usually directed at them for the sub-standard fare that Knight's participation usually guaranteed. The stockpile of unreleased material from these 1965-66 PPX/RSVP productions would only be revealed after Ed Chalpin bought up the masters in 1967 and began using them as fillers for the Knight/Hendrix albums he compiled and licensed to other labels. Of this material, the most interesting is '(I'm A) Fool For You Baby', a relaxed medium-tempo effort with a boogaloo backbeat on which Hendrix, given a very free accompanying role to one of Knight's more melodic vocals, spends the entire cut imitating a trombone with the help of his fuzz-box. Who else was trying that in pop music in 1966? No one on the East Coast, although Frank Zappa and Captain Beefheart were by then tilting at the established rock windmills over in Los Angeles. The only other parallels for such eclectic combinations were in the try-anything atmosphere of Greenwich Village. There, politically-driven bands with anarchic tendencies were becoming increasingly strident. In fact, Hendrix once mentioned in a later interview that he got his first sustain devices – two handmade fuzz-boxes – from Ken Weaver, an electronics fan and a member of The Fugs, a band nurtured in the agitprop atmosphere of the anti-Vietnam groups living on the Lower East Side and in the Village.

The Fugs played mostly in the Village, too. They became influential broadcasters of politically left-leaning musical and theatrical statements and were vigorous anti-Vietnam agitators. The band made two important and highly influential albums in 1965 and in '66, both released on ESP-Disk. This revolutionary New York record label had also been the first to recognise the importance of the second generation of avant-garde jazz musicians such as Albert Ayler, Pharoah Sanders, The New York Art Quartet and Sun Ra. The Fugs' debut LP, released in 1965 and simply titled *The Fugs' First Album*, showcased the group's performance poetry and folk roots. Neither of the key members – Ed Sanders and Tuli Kupferberg – were musicians at this point. The second, logically called *The Fugs' Second Album*, took the group away from the sleazy shock-verse of the first date, cemented their anti-war and anti-establishment stance while carefully keeping the language coarse and offensive to good taste, and grafted on some surprisingly effective electric rock accompaniment, including novel sounds like fuzz-guitar and fuzz-bass, soon to be exploited by thousands of other bands. Hendrix briefly signalled his awareness of the band's music in a 1970 Rolling Stone interview. Indeed, with The Fugs' near-constant presence at Village theatres and clubs in 1965 and '66 they would have been almost impossible to miss.

Hendrix viewed all this activity and agitation as a clear sign that important changes were taking place right through New York City amounting to more than mere shifts of fashion, but so far there was nothing in it that he could use to further his own ambitions. He continued to work with King Curtis, playing music for the people along the same old lines, keeping his band uniform respectable enough to wear, and making sure he did the right steps on stage. When time permitted he also played with saxophonist Lonnie Youngblood and with The Squires. Youngblood often moved in different music-business circles to Curtis Knight and had some independent recording projects on which he wanted to use Hendrix.

The fog of doubt and misleading information that infects the proper documenting of the PPX and RSVP sessions also obscures the circumstances of the series of recording sessions instigated by Lonnie Youngblood during 1966. So many dates have been suggested for them, from 1963 to 1966, that it comes as no surprise that at the time of writing their latest reissue, done apparently with Youngblood's full co-operation, has CD liner notes and personnel lists full of old and new inaccuracies and misinformation. (Anyone who wants to catch up on the latest research on these sessions should turn to the *earlyhendrix* website or *Jimpress* and *UniVibes* magazines. New information is being eked out all the time.) Youngblood offered Hendrix the same deal as he'd got with Knight and Chalpin, making backing tracks for a range of small-time vocalists, although there is a lone instrumental, 'Under The Table', thrown in for good measure. But it was paid work, and would help keep him going as well as providing studio experience. As with Curtis Knight's recordings, this seems to have been a series of sessions spread out over a period, and not a single intensive burst of recordings over a couple of days. Different singers provided the vocals. However, as opposed to the fate

of the PPX/RSVP material, most of the original versions of these songs were released on singles before Hendrix made it big: the fact that most of them did not trouble the charts made it a simple matter to meddle with the mixes on any number of concocted issues after Hendrix had become a star. But at least the singles still exist as evidence of the original intentions. There was plenty of scope for second thoughts and remixes of the original production efforts.

The original artists involved included vocalists Jimmy Norman's 'That Little Old Groovemaker' / 'You're Only Hurting Yourself' (Samar 112) and Billy Lamont's 'Sweet Thang' / 'Please Don't Leave' (20th Century Fox 45-6707), and duo The Icemen with '(My Girl) She's a Fox' / '(I Wonder) What It Takes' (Samar 111). None of these artists are unknowns in soul circles. Some tracks carry arrangements that include a substantial Stax-type brass section, often remixed close to inaudibility on later releases. In addition to these, Lonnie Youngblood's own singles as leader and featuring Hendrix were 'Go Go Shoes' / 'Go Go Place' (Fairmount F-1002) and 'Soul Food (That's What I Like)' / 'Goodbye Bessie Mae (Fairmount F-1022). Some of these singles were not put out until after Hendrix became famous, so from their very first release there is again the possibility that mixes were manipulated to emphasise the guitarist's involvement. (Niko Bauer of the *earlyhendrix* website has detailed some of the transformations that use, for example, basic tracks with 'new' and different combinations of lead instruments in place of vocals, or outtakes and alternative mixes. As well as identifying a number of later 'fakes', he has also noted that 'Please Don't Leave' does not involve Hendrix.[51])

Youngblood has given many different explanations over the years for the proliferation of this material in so many guises, but the root of it lies in the speculative nature of the sessions. As Youngblood once said, "[They were] my sessions, so I was paying [Hendrix], and it was my stuff. ... But, see, everybody was having sessions. As a matter of fact, we were all session musicians. So it wasn't like recording with a band. Even while I was recording for myself, I was recording solos for other people."[52] Youngblood consistently claimed that he set up a deal himself with the Fairmount label, a subsidiary of Cameo-Parkway, the Philadelphia label that had been the home for Chubby Checker's records. They had also released one of Carl Holmes & His Commanders' post-Atlantic singles. It is not widely known that Youngblood claims to have given Fairmount merely a distribution deal, leaving ownership of the masters with him. Considering the cost of compiling such a body of recordings at a professional New York studio, it seems unlikely that the saxophonist would have been able to finance the project entirely himself – after all, he'd only been out of the Army less than a year. This is probably where producer Johnny Brantley became involved. According to Youngblood, the sessions took place "on an 8-track [recorder] at Abtone Studio. It was on Broadway, between 55th and 56th [Streets] on the second floor".[53]

Once the recordings were complete, Youngblood had a bunch of tracks but an outlet only for his own sides. Fairmount did not release anything by the other artists. Brantley, a man Youngblood later blamed for cynically exploiting these recordings, "had a lot of access to a lot of different companies," said Youngblood. "Like if you cut something and wanted to get in the door somewhere, maybe Johnny could take it in for you". [54] More recently, Youngblood claimed quite bluntly that "we ran out of money and [Hendrix] changed his way of thinking. His concept was changing in the middle of what we were about. ... [Then] the tapes were stolen out of New York's Abtone Studio and sold to companies that have since earned millions of dollars".[55] The first part of Youngblood's claim fits with the rest of Hendrix's life at the time, but the story of the stolen tapes unravels on closer inspection. For a start, none of the singles that were released from these dates featuring other artists such as The Icemen, Billy Lamont or Jimmy Norman sold in sufficient quantity to trouble the R&B charts, and they have never been reissued in their original state.

Some of the performances have been edited and remixed with the vocals removed, making Hendrix's guitar more prominent and with additional saxophone lines by Youngblood laid over a more subdued background. These altered tracks appeared after Hendrix became famous. Credits on the original singles claim them to have been "produced by Johnny Brantley", or "produced by Johnny Brantley for Vidalia Productions". Clearly Brantley was by then involved at ground level. Youngblood must also have been party to at least some of the alterations and overdubbings that appeared on vinyl LPs after 1971, since he is playing new parts on them. The saxophonist was certainly the straw boss on the original sessions, for he is co-composer on a number of titles and is credited on the singles as arranger or co-arranger, along with keyboard-player Richard Tee, another busy New York session player of the day. Perhaps Youngblood is confusing these second thoughts on the tracks with the plethora of 'fake' Youngblood-Hendrix tracks that appeared on LPs in the early 1970s and which may have had their origins in unfinished Youngblood studio work that did not involve Hendrix.

The Youngblood material is a mixture of R&B and routine mid-1960s soul, performed professionally and middlingly well recorded, but certainly no big-budget operation. Youngblood has a good tone on his tenor saxophone and handles his King Curtis licks with confidence, while his singing, although rough and limited, is at least colourful. Youngblood's Fairmount single 'Go Go Shoes' / 'Go Go Place' is as good an example as any of the soul-style tracks. Hendrix opens proceedings with an unaccompanied quaver (eighth-note) pattern of see-sawing phrases in thirds, characteristic of his mature style. After that, he supplies a driving rhythm part, bedded down neatly with the bass and drums, while Youngblood shouts his vocals James Brown-style, then moves onto his sax for a professional King Curtis imitation. On the second cut, which is a continuation of the A-side, Youngblood refers specifically to James Brown's 'Papa's Got A Brand New Bag', a US Top Ten hit in August 1965, thus making it impossible that this track was recorded any earlier. He also refers to the latest New York dance craze, the boogaloo, which had become increasingly popular in the summer of 1965, especially with soul and funk audiences. Its rhythm was used for mid-1965 hits such as 'In The Midnight Hour', but it wasn't until early 1966 that it became one of those independently famous dance crazes – like the twist or the watusi before – that could sell a record simply by using its name within a song. Youngblood would not be using such a name unless it was a popular cliché, so this pushes the likely date of these recordings into the first half of 1966.

A similar musical approach is taken on the basic tracks that provided 'Sweet Thang' for Billy Lamont's 20th Century Fox single and three takes of 'Wipe The Sweat' for Lonnie Youngblood, all three of which first appeared on the 1971 *Two Experiences Together* LP. The James Brown-style rhythmic strut and the horn section's licks support a Lamont vocal that emulates the preaching passion of Brown without matching his charisma. All three takes of 'Wipe The Sweat' give Hendrix's guitar part an uneasily prominent place in the mix, with the second including new vocal monologues from both Youngblood and a rather over-excited Hendrix, who refers at one point to being "down here with Lucy Mae: we're doin' the 'scratch my back'", a reference to yet another 1960s dance fad. Once again the rhythm section is very impressive, especially the so-far unidentified drummer.

On the R&B numbers among the Youngblood recordings, Hendrix and Youngblood are relaxed and stylish. 'Under The Table (Take 2)', for example, is a walking blues kicked off by biting Buddy Guy-style guitar breaks from Hendrix punctuated by blasts from the brass section. The guitar has plenty of attack, the saxophone solo is sophisticated and assured, and the rhythm section is particularly tight and aggressive. The ballad 'She's A Fox' was claimed by Youngblood in 2003 as his own composition, but on its initial 45rpm 1966 Shamar release with The Icemen on joint vocals it was credited to the Poindexter brothers, a songwriting team. It is the most impressive product of all the Youngblood recording sessions, although it contains no Hendrix solo. A superior composition in the Curtis Mayfield tradition, it boasts a simple but effective arrangement, the most prominent feature of which is Hendrix's beautiful chordal accompaniment. It also helps that The Icemen are two competent and pleasant vocalists who

have a chemistry of their own. Hendrix gives us an unnervingly accurate presentiment of the devices and ideas he would employ when recording under his own name. In fact, his opening phrases bear an uncanny resemblance to his graceful and tender guitar backing to 'Have You Ever Been (To Electric Ladyland)', recorded 18 months or so later.

There is an odd rider to all this. Youngblood has repeatedly said over the decades that when he met Hendrix in New York in 1969 they not only jammed together at Small's Paradise (the photo of them playing together there on the 1971 LP *Two Experiences Together* bears out this assertion) but that they "hung around for three days at the Record Plant. … We cut enough material for three albums".[56] The latest incarnation of the Youngblood tracks at the time of writing is the *Two Great Experiences – Expanded Edition* CD on Empire Masterwerks, and it includes a previously unissued eight-minute slow blues jam erroneously claimed by the CD's liner notes to have come from the same "1965 sessions". On the CD it is given the title 'Mother Mother' but it was originally called 'Georgia Blue'. In it, Youngblood repeatedly sings a line about the fact that he was "born in Georgia 27 years ago". Youngblood was born in August 1941, making him 27 when he and Hendrix met up again in 1969. The track is unfinished, with a long section starting at 6:00 where Hendrix comps for a missing solo that has either been mixed out or was never added. Hendrix's style, plus his use of sustain and texture, is consistent with what he was doing in 1969, not 1966. Perhaps there is a grain of truth in what Youngblood asserted, after all. Considering what Hendrix would do for Curtis Knight in 1967, the possibility cannot be ruled out.

Hendrix made no mention of Youngblood's 1966 recording dates in subsequent interviews. He'd needed the money, he enjoyed the company, he did the gig, he moved on. As Youngblood commented, presumably not aware of the full truth of his own words: "Jimmy … he was a vagabond, man. He was one of the greatest guys I ever had the pleasure of working with. … Me and my wife … bought him a Fender amp. He wouldn't buy an amp – he didn't give a damn! If you wanted to play with him, you had to buy him an amp! He was that good. Jimmy was a light traveller."[57] Cornell Dupree remembers Hendrix using an enviable Fender Twin amp while he was with King Curtis, so this suggests that Jimmy was working with both sax players simultaneously (and that most of Youngblood's studio and live work with Hendrix was done in spring 1966, after Hendrix joined up with Curtis). Randy California, a member of Hendrix's group at the Café Wha? in the summer of 1966,

"Almost every penny he got, he didn't spend it on a guitar, or an amplifier, he spent it on records."

Curtis Knight, on the Hendrix budget

remembers Jimmy swapping to a Twin during their tenure at the club, though he didn't know where it had come from. Hendrix may have felt that appropriating an amp from Youngblood was a suitable 'payment' for the Abtone sessions, considering that he received $25 per session, according to the saxophonist. At least this time Jimmy had avoided signing a new contract with anyone. The amp-buying routine was hardly the first time Hendrix had allowed someone to procure equipment for him, and it would certainly help when it came to starting up his own band in the immediate future; either that, or it would make a handy item to pawn.

The parallel between Youngblood's description of Hendrix as a 'vagabond' and Bob Shad's identical description of Lightnin' Hopkins in chapter three is hardly accidental. Both men were feckless in their disregard for the conventional modes of conduct and were ruthless in serving their muse, ready to exploit anyone offering something of use. They both knew what they were worth. Youngblood was undoubtedly accurate in his assessment of Hendrix's expertise by this time. Guitarist Mike Bloomfield, who saw Hendrix play that August at the Café Wha?, remembers him even then being "by far the greatest expert I've ever heard at playing rhythm & blues, the style of playing developed by Bobby Womack, Curtis Mayfield, Eric Gale and others. I got the feeling that there was no guitaring of any kind that he hadn't heard or studied, including steel guitar, Hawaiian and Dobro".[58]

Part of Hendrix's evolving identity was linked to an active curiosity about drugs. Like most musicians who spent years on the road, he was no stranger to the substances commonly used to help musicians perform with enough energy or sleep when they had a chance. But there was a new wave of drugs hitting New York in 1966, including LSD. Hendrix had been discovering a new recreational use for drugs that year, such as the time he'd smoked weed with Chas Chandler of The Animals the previous summer. Both Knight and Youngblood have claimed in interviews that Hendrix was taking LSD in New York in the summer of 1966. This seems highly unlikely, for any number of practical reasons, and Hendrix is commonly assumed to have taken his first tab of LSD later, in London. But there were other drugs commonly and cheaply available that he and his circle were using, including marijuana. Knight knew that Hendrix and drugs made natural partners. "Obviously Jimmy was no stranger to drugs. I mean, he wanted to experiment and be part of a lot of things. … I'll tell you this, Jimmy had so much respect for me, he never took any drugs in front of me, never, because he knew I … used no drugs, nothing."[59] Youngblood also had a memory of Hendrix dabbling with new types of drugs that spring and summer. He thought it had something to do with the people Jimmy was meeting down in Greenwich Village. "He came to me one night," Youngblood recalled, "and said, 'Man, I tried something, you gotta try it man, because it is so great.' And I told him, I said: 'You know I could never do that because I'm scared to death of anything that might make me hallucinate.' I always wanted to be in control. He said it wasn't like that, but I never would try that. … I believe that when he did that, it helped to take his music to where he wanted to take it, [to] open up his mind."[60]

It's an interesting juxtaposition. Youngblood doesn't identify the drug used: it could have been anything. Youngblood is the straight operator who wants to retain control of his environment and get on with his business and his music, and so he tells the wayward, vagabond genius that he could never get involved – but then postulates that drugs may have helped Hendrix develop the music he later created. It apparently never occurred to Youngblood that Hendrix had an infinitely richer musical imagination to start with, and was desperately trying to find a platform on which to express it. There is absolutely no doubt that Hendrix often played when under the influence of a whole range of drugs and alcohol, at this time and afterwards. But there is no indication that as a result he played better or got better ideas. Paul Caruso, Hendrix's friend from those Greenwich Village days, thought drugs did not help. "[Being involved in drugs] caused so much confusion in his responses to reality. It may have fuelled his imagination to some extent, but Jimmy didn't need drugs to be imaginative. He used to just naturally shuttle back and forth between reality and what was almost schizophrenia. But I would prefer to call it an artistic, mystical, poetic and dreamlike sort of state, since he always retained a strong sense of self."[61]

Charlie Parker, an incontestably great musician and a big user (and victim) of drugs and alcohol, concluded that "any musician who says he is playing better either on tea, the needle, or when he is juiced, is a plain, straight liar. When I get too much to drink, I can't even finger well, let alone play decent ideas. And, in the days when I was on the stuff, I may have thought I was playing better, but listening to some of the records now, I know I wasn't".[62] While it's routinely accepted that it's possible for an artist to apply hallucinogenic-induced experiences to later creative projects, there is no objective evidence to support the idea that playing while tripping can produce superior music. Throughout history, the greatest artists in any field have always been voracious for experiences of all types, yet the process by which they translate those experiences into memorable works of art is one that

stands outside exterior stimulants and remains enigmatic, even to those blessed with extreme gifts. Again, Charlie Parker was aware of the process. He said, "Music is your own experience, your thoughts, your wisdom. If you don't live it, it won't come out of your horn."[63] He left the onlookers to make the other connections for themselves. Many people wake up highly elated after dreaming about writing wonderful symphonies. Very few ever actually write them.

Meanwhile Hendrix plodded on in New York, honouring commitments in which he had progressively less belief as the days went by. Still being part of the King Curtis All Stars, during May 1966 Hendrix played in the backing band for an Atlantic Records Showcase held at a hotel in New York City. Among the acts the All Stars supported that day were Wilson Pickett and Percy Sledge, so at least Jimmy got to play 'Midnight Hour', with or without feedback, for its originator. All Stars guitarist Cornell Dupree observed Hendrix during this period. He knew him as someone who kept to his own circles socially when not fulfilling a gig or rehearsal with Curtis. He also remembered that on occasion Hendrix could turn on the exhibitionist side of his playing, as he'd done with Little Richard and The Isley Brothers. But time was running out for Hendrix in Curtis's band. While he was more than capable of holding down the musical side of his brief in the group, his attempts to undercut Curtis's immutable dress codes and disciplinary rules only upset the leader. By the second week of May, Curtis had replaced Hendrix in the All Stars. The guitarist was back full-time to freelance scuffling. A week later, he was playing once more with The Squires. It must have seemed to him then that he would never make any lasting gains on this particular treadmill.

Hendrix played with Curtis Knight's band as Knight prepared his latest effort to advance his own career. New York musicians had been aware that a new nightclub was about to debut in late April 1966, using the premises of the defunct Palm Gardens venue on Broadway at 53rd Street. The large venue was refitted and renamed The Cheetah by two French entrepreneurs. True to its name, it was themed throughout with Cheetah-pattern décor, carrying the faux-primitive theme through to its wood fittings. In an odd conjunction, the new club was to premiere just two weeks after the opening night of Andy Warhol's arty and decidedly offbeat Plastic Exploding Inevitable at the Open Stage, in Greenwich Village's St Marks Place. An ad in New York's *Village Voice* newspaper proclaimed The Cheetah's opening night, Thursday 28th April, with three bands: Monti Rock 111, The Chambers Brothers, and Jon & Roy & Company. Richie Havens wrote in his autobiography that he played during the first two weeks at the Cheetah. "It was, in fact, the largest discotheque in New York with live music," wrote Havens. "At the time I had several friends that I jammed with, playing completely different music than I was performing in the Village clubs – and we managed to get a two-week gig there to open the club."[64]

Knight was determined to work the new club. He would recall: "The Cheetah was the first club to have top black *and* white bands regularly – to get in there you had to audition. Being thorough, Jimmy and I decided that since the décor was cheetah, we would go down to the garment district and buy some material that looked like cheetah. So we had some outfits made up of white bellbottoms and cheetah shirts."[65] Whether Hendrix did in fact show enthusiasm for designing and acquiring these new uniforms is debatable, given his long aversion to such things, but there is no doubt that Knight saw the project through. They got the gig and they wore the uniforms: there are pictures of Hendrix, Knight and The Squires playing at the Cheetah in their cheetah-design outfits. One of them shows Hendrix playing the guitar with his teeth and Curtis Knight looking on, a big smile on his face. Hendrix is still playing the Fender Duo-Sonic guitar that Knight had loaned him the previous autumn. Some things never seemed to change.

Curtis Knight's name (minus The Squires) appeared in the Cheetah's ads in the *Village Voice* for the first time on May 12th 1966, playing opposite The Denims. They managed two weeks there. In a place as big as the Cheetah (the bar alone was 100 feet long) there were two stages, each with a band so that the music and dancing was in effect non-stop. This was not a new idea – the vast Savoy Ballroom, "the home of happy feet", had been doing it back in the 1930s – but it was unusual enough to catch the dance crowd's initial enthusiasm in a town with a long history of top-flight dance establishments and a thirst for the latest generation of dance clubs – quickly becoming known as discothéques.

But in a world dominated by quick changes of fashion, and with a bill that hardly took the breath away, the Cheetah fast ran into problems attracting enough punters to establish an atmosphere. Out of curiosity, Havens went down the week after he finished his opening stint and found it more or less empty. "There was a band playing. Not bad, I thought – when suddenly I noticed that the guitar-playing was unusual, and that wasn't all. The guitar player had the instrument upside down and somehow was clipping the strings with his teeth, or his tongue. I couldn't believe my eyes or ears. Was he really playing the thing with his teeth? I found myself crossing the empty dancefloor that could easily have held 2,500 dancing people. ... A few tunes later and I knew that this was not a circus act, this was quite simply the greatest guitar player I had ever seen."[66] It may well have been, but with so many good acts competing for attention that spring and summer, it was not enough to draw the dance crowds while Curtis Knight remained the band's frontman. Apart from the huge music festivals that were running in New York all through that summer, just one week before Curtis Knight's group had started its two-week residency at the Cheetah, the Café Au Go Go had launched its Blues Bag event on Sundays, featuring Chuck Berry, Muddy Waters, John Lee Hooker, Judy Roderick, Bo Diddley, Jesse Colin Young and others.

As The Squires limped un-noticed into May at the Cheetah, Hendrix finally began to gather around him the things he would need to break out of his artistic chrysalis and reveal himself to the wider world. That spring he had met Carol Shiroky at a mutual friend's house. Hendrix had been in and out of a string of affairs and was no longer living full-time with Faye Pridgeon; Shiroky was the first

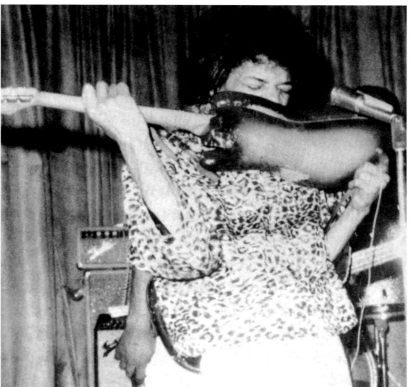

At the Cheetah club in New York City with Curtis Knight, May 1966, complete with suitable outfit.

white girl with whom he became seriously involved. At first she'd found him a turn-off, but she would drop in occasionally at the Cheetah as she was friendly with Curtis Knight. One evening Hendrix came over to her table and went through a gentle seduction routine that Shiroky found irresistible. "He said, 'I know you're gonna laugh.' I said, 'I promise I won't laugh.' He said, 'Well, I wanna kiss you on your knee.' So of course I laughed – I mean how many people tell you they want to kiss you on your knee? And he said, 'Well, you see, I told you you were gonna laugh.' That was it. Three days later we moved in together and it was like an instant fire kind of thing."[67]

The affair was shortlived but came at a crucial time for Hendrix, because Shiroky quickly did two things for him. She claims to have bought him his first white Fender Stratocaster and she boosted his confidence sufficiently for him to leave Curtis Knight's group. In later years Curtis would never suggest tensions between himself and Hendrix; others remembered differently. George Clemons has suggested that at the time Knight was not as indulgent of Hendrix's on-stage antics as he made himself appear in hindsight. Hendrix would have found any criticism dispiriting, expecting his obvious talent to

lend him more latitude with such a musical lightweight. But bands are rarely democracies. Shiroky had similar memories of Hendrix's discontent. As she recalled, "Jimmy was having a lot of trouble with Curtis and he was unhappy, having had fights with him, not being paid, or getting paid a pittance, you know. ... I said, 'Why are you with Curtis, you don't need him, he needs you.' And he said, 'Because it's his guitar.' Two days later I bought him a white Fender Stratocaster, that's what he wanted, that was the love of his life ... . Then he left Curtis, and Curtis never forgave me."[68]

There may have been more complex reasons for Knight's anger. She and Hendrix acquired the white Fender Stratocaster at Manny's musical instruments store on 48th Street a couple of days later, as guitarist Jeff Baxter, who worked at Manny's at the time, remembered later. "I made a guitar trade with Hendrix," said Baxter. "I traded him a white Stratocaster for a Duo-Sonic."[69] That Fender Duo-Sonic was probably Knight's. It's likely he never did get his guitar back after Hendrix left The Squires on May 20th 1966, midway through an engagement. If so, Knight had a legitimate reason for being more than a little annoyed with Hendrix.

Hendrix got out of town with another group trying to recreate better times, Carl Holmes & His Commanders. He made it as far as Gettysburg, Pennsylvania, with the Commanders before accompanying them back into the Cheetah club. Ironically Holmes's group followed Curtis Knight in there, but only completed a single week before heading back out on the road. Hendrix had been through this a hundred times before and knew it led nowhere: he quit Holmes and at last determined to put his own group together. With his guitar in part courtesy of Knight and the Fender amplifier donated by Youngblood, at least the guitarist was now properly equipped to go out on his own.

By early summer 1966 Jimmy Hendrix was finally ready to show his true musical colours and demonstrate through his music the sum total of his reflections on life. In the past month or so a number of friends and fellow musicians had offered support for such an idea, including Richie Havens. "I told him he should not be the backup in any group," Havens wrote later. "He was good enough to be out front with his own group. ... I told him to get down to the Village. That's where he could find many young musicians looking to play."[70] Havens was not telling Hendrix anything he didn't already know, but his advice and subsequent help spurred the hesitant guitarist forward. Years later, Hendrix enthused over Greenwich Village to an interviewer: "Nice there, man. The people were more friendly there than in Harlem. Harlem is cold."[71]

Havens claims to have introduced Hendrix to Manny Roth, the owner of the Café Wha?, before Hendrix had even pulled his first group together. Hendrix was on the verge of forming his first 'power' trio, unaware that in London three other musicians were thinking along similar lines. His first group would last a matter of weeks and be forgotten in as many months, whereas Cream would help rewrite rock history during the next two years. But Hendrix's first trio would take him a step further towards fame, which was now only months away.

the birth of jimi hendrix

JUNE TO OCTOBER 1966

During early 1966 Jimmy Hendrix had been living in hotel rooms close to New York's downtown districts and Greenwich Village. He was looking for a more congenial climate than Harlem had been providing for him. "I couldn't stand it there," he said later, "because they talk about you worse than any place else."[1]

Hendrix's friend and neighbour Arthur Allen recalled of the guitarist: "He was very self-conscious about … the things that he wore 'cause he was kind of different, … especially in comparison to a lot of the brothers uptown at that time. So he was very sensitive to the places he'd like to be, and he found that the people would tolerate him a little more [in Greenwich Village]."[2]

Another friend who met him at this pivotal time was Paul Caruso. He said later: "When we first met and started hanging out together in the Village, [Hendrix] was often sort of oddly dressed in calypso shirts and ratty bell-bottom jeans. … He had a 'marcel' ['process' hairstyle] like Little Richard, as well as Little Richard's thick moustache. Yes, the good Reverend Penniman taught him a lot about how to be free and wild onstage. … [Hendrix] was pathologically shy. He would stare at the ground and almost shuffle his feet when he met someone, but he had the courage to break through all that."[3]

While the guitarist's social life continued the drift downtown, he felt that his New York professional career would make no progress while he slaved away at the pit-face, playing support roles for bands at uptown and midtown venues. Most of these clubs offered different types of entertainment from that which interested Hendrix. The midtown places usually provided first-rate dance-based bands playing precise covers of chart hits and other popular material for their patrons. Uptown, where R&B, soul and funk predominated, a finer balance was struck between music for dancing in larger venues and music for relaxing over a drink in a tiny club or bar. Hendrix was professionally equipped to play these venues, and certainly continued to do so in order to earn whatever pittance he could manage. But by summer '66 he had slipped into a very different way of thinking about music and performance. This guaranteed that his on-stage persona no longer sat comfortably with the demands of the mid-town club clientele.

Each new musical genre generally goes through the same pattern of inception and development. It starts as a new folk-based hybrid (using 'folk' in its broadest sense) created and shaped unselfconsciously as a means of entertainment. After a period, the new genre will have been around long enough to grow a sense of its own history and identity, allowing its practitioners to reflect on its intrinsic nature and their role in its development. At some point, a generation emerges who regard themselves quite consciously as 'artists', serving their own muse first rather than the public's short-term

Chas Chandler (second from right) playing bass with The Animals, shortly before he left in 1966 and became Jimi Hendrix's first manager.

needs. This does not mean that the music they make is by definition any better or worse than the music that this genre and its previous generations have already provided. Nor does it mean that all practitioners suddenly become self-conscious in their craft, proclaiming it 'art'. A great diversity of intentions and conceptualisations remain – indeed they have to if a musical genre is to stay vital.

In the years following the advent of The Beatles, rock and its concurrent popular genres – derived loosely from blues and other musical streams – became conscious of itself, its style and its origins. This had something to do with the presence of a second generation of performers playing music in the style of previous innovators. The Beatles, The Animals, The Rolling Stones and their peers emulated their own role models such as Little Richard, Chuck Berry, Bo Diddley, Elvis Presley, Jimmy Reed, Gene Vincent, Ray Charles, Buddy Holly and many others.

There was also a geographical factor: this second generation was largely nurtured in a country far removed from the source. They saw the music their models played as automatically elevated above the commonplace, making it the iconic expression of their own search for identity. This shift in perception began to percolate back into the US and the way musicians there thought about rock and pop, although the process was slower and more fragmented – partly for social and demographic reasons, and partly due to cultural perceptions.

By 1965 a number of US pop musicians were increasingly prepared to regard what they were doing as important in its own right and were primarily creating music to please themselves more than their audiences. Bob Dylan, Phil Spector and Brian Wilson are obvious examples. In 1966 the floodgates opened. The Beatles stopped touring and went public with their desire to concentrate on self-expression and inner explorations. Within weeks it became fashionable for every pop musician to do the same – whatever the level of musical expertise or talent. For black musicians working the popular genres, this turn towards conscious self-expression was still some years away, although ironically avant-garde jazz players in New York City were radically reasserting the role of improvising musician as artistic icon, something begun in the 1940s by Charlie Parker, Thelonious Monk and their circle. Yet in soul and R&B such notions were not taken seriously, even when they were broached at all, and pragmatism prevailed.

Hendrix may not have been the first black musician to aspire to the elevated musical status that white rock musicians and their attendant media were claiming, but he was by far the most important and innovative of that first wave. His indifference towards the mechanics of building a career in the music business – in direct contrast to, say, Bob Dylan or even Phil Spector – meant that his artistic ambitions had so far been frustrated, and he would eventually succeed through sheer musical determination and stubbornness. In the summer of 1966 his timing finally locked into place. Later he would be quoted regularly in interviews as saying that he had felt that 1966 *had* to be his lucky year, but that is of no significance. Hunches remain hunches, even when proved right. Hendrix finally made the right moves at the right time.

In early June 1966 he went down to the Café Wha?, going as directed by Richie Havens on an evening early in the week when things would not be too busy or crowded. He introduced himself to the owner, Manny Roth, as the guitarist Havens had told Roth to look out for. Hendrix, calling himself Jimmy James at the time, had arrived with his new guitar but without any backing musicians: he was intent on keeping this new initiative separate from any other current affiliation. Roth suggested that when the house band took a break he get up on-stage and play solo. Hendrix did just that, starting a slow blues suited to solo performance.

The house bassist, Tommy 'Regi' Butler, came back from his break and, interested in what he heard, joined the guitarist on the platform. According to Butler's wife, "At the end of the song Jimmy turned to Regi and said, 'Hey man, can you play this?' and proceeded to let loose with one of his infamous riffs."[4] They played, she claims, for around an hour. She doesn't mention a drummer, but it seems that the house drummer also came into the jam, for he also joined up to create Hendrix's first trio, a group that later became the house band at the Wha? and also started touting for work in other venues in New York City.

Hendrix thus arrived at the personnel for his first band as a leader through happenstance and instinct rather than design. Jimmy played guitar and delivered the vocals, Butler played bass and Danny Casey drums. Hendrix chose the name Jimmy James & The Blue Flames while they worked at the Wha?, but they often used different names – including The Rainflowers – for other venues so that Roth wouldn't be easily alerted to them working outside their residency. Jimmy and the Flames debuted at the Wha? probably in the second week of June 1966. The previous week had seen Joni Mitchell make her US debut at the same club.

The Café Wha? had dropped in status from its early 1960s peak as the most fashionable Village hangout for those interested in folk and the attendant post-beat scene, but it was still a popular destination for people from the suburbs and further afield who came to the area at night and on weekends looking for something a little exotic. Being squarely among all the Village nightspots, it was also a regular on the tour of the Village habitually undertaken by visiting UK pop acts. But it was still trading largely on its past reputation. The club's small-ads in local papers rarely if ever named the current attraction, relying instead on its credentials as a left-of-centre cellar featuring performers of a different stripe. Hendrix certainly fitted that description. He was earning peanuts, had no name to make him an attraction, and had to start by working as the leader of a house-band rather than as a featured artist at different venues in the way that Richie Havens, a man with a track record in the Village, was able to do. Hendrix soon discovered that he was on another treadmill of sorts, and that he would again have to manoeuvre some kind of escape.

One route was to find work for the group away from the two nights a week at the Wha?. Butler remembered organising one gig for the band at Connie's Ballroom in Harlem, an upstairs club where they managed one set of their music before the owner, flanked by his bouncer, asked that they play dance music – like every other band that played there. After getting the inevitable reply that the band didn't know any, the owner told them, "You all just pack this noise on up, and take it back downtown."[5] That was the end of Hendrix's involvement with professional music-making in Harlem until after his ascent to stardom.

His last lingering connection with Harlem was Faye Pridgeon, with whom he maintained a close if occasional relationship until he left for London later in the year. She remembers her Harlem friends talking about Jimmy moving downtown. "I'd been on the scene a couple of times," she commented to an interviewer, "and people … were sayin' … Hendrix is playin' at the so-and-so in the Village, and they said, 'Oh yeah that's nice, yeah, shine on,' just shining it like it ain't no big thing. But they had no idea … it was just a matter of time, y'know, all he had to do was get out of fucking Harlem and all those places and go somewhere with somebody with some bread and had eyes for talent."[6] Pridgeon would look critically at his involvement with white girls down in the Village during that summer, but mainly kept away from downtown, coming there only when Hendrix asked her. As always, he was careful to separate out an increasingly complex personal life.

Meanwhile Jimmy's ideas about his own band were beginning to develop. He made friends with a variety of young men around the Village and midtown, often for arbitrary reasons. Writer and blues harmonica player Paul Caruso came into that category. "When I first saw Jimmy," said Caruso, "he came right up to me and said that I looked like Bob Dylan with my freaked-out hair. What he didn't know was that I considered Bob Dylan to be the greatest writer in the world at the time. Dylan was a fountain of brilliant images. Jimmy and I would carry on about him."[7] In fact, Hendrix and Butler met up with Dylan in those first few weeks of gigging at the Wha?. Hanging out at another Village venue, The Kettle Of Fish, they bumped into the man who had released *Blonde On Blonde* the previous month. Hendrix referred to it in a later interview[8] as a very stoned evening, and said that all he and Dylan managed to do was giggle uncontrollably. Another great encounter.

Hendrix found another like mind, this time hanging out at Manny's instrument store. Randy Wolfe was 15, newly arrived with his family from California, and a devotee of Delta blues. Wolfe had gone to the store to buy a guitar. "There was this tall, thin, black guy standing there playing a new guitar – I think it was a [Fender] Telecaster. I asked him if I could borrow it, and I started playing. While he was listening to me he got really excited about what I was doing. So he told me his name was Jimmy James, and invited me down to the club that night, the Café Wha?, to play with him. [He told me it] was his first gig not playing behind somebody else."[9]

Wolfe went down to the club that evening. Ignoring the fact that he was underage, Hendrix taught him a clutch of songs backstage before the next set began – including 'Like A Rolling Stone', 'Wild Thing' and 'Shotgun' – and they went out to play. Jimmy also made time soon after to teach him 'Hey Joe', a song Wolfe had not come across before. The 15-year-old stuck strictly to a support role, often using slide effects and gradually building confidence to work twin lead passages with Hendrix. The teenager blended well with him and was ushered in as a fourth member of the group. Regi Butler was often absent now; while sometimes Jeff Baxter from Manny's would sub for him, but Randy Palmer was now the regular bassist. Hendrix renamed the group's new second guitarist Wolfe as Randy California to differentiate him from Palmer, a Texan, whom he dubbed Randy Texas. California retained his new name when he returned to San Francisco with his stepfather Ed Cassidy to start the band Spirit, and would use the name professionally until his death in 1997. Drummer Danny Casey didn't need or seek a name change.

As The Blue Flames expanded into a quartet, Hendrix was working much longer stints at the Wha?. Shortly before the band was augmented, they were playing four nights a week, though California thought they might have got up to "about five or six sets a night … six nights a week".[10] He remembered his time with Jimmy James & The Blue Flames as "tough: the band made about $60 a night, and Jimmy split it equally four ways. I think he had to borrow guitars to play on for the first couple of weeks, which was hard on him because he had to re-string them".[11] In these early weeks, Jimmy's white Strat was stolen from the stage and he was once again reduced to borrowing an instrument.

Playing with names and swapping them around was something Hendrix had been doing for some time now (Maurice James had long ago become Jimmy James). But he was about to make a further and more significant change. As the band line-up began to settle down to a consistent quartet of members, he made a decision about his own working name, changing the spelling of Jimmy to Jimi.[12] This was not a marketing decision brought about by record company or management pressure: it happened before anyone had ever heard of Hendrix as a solo act.

All his life, Hendrix liked toying with words and using unusual spellings. His adoption of 'Jimi' may have been influenced by the fashion for re-spelling given names among some blacks in the US at the time. For example, a look down the list of musicians on *The Heliocentric Worlds of Sun Ra Volume 1* album released in late 1965 on ESP-Disk, the label that released the Fugs records Hendrix knew and enjoyed, finds percussionist Jimmy Johnson re-spelling his given name as Jimhmi. Contemporary American poets were toying with changes of spelling. Dylan played with such devices, and Hendrix could have been moved to experiment himself through that connection. The new spelling of his given name would stick because he would be world-famous before he got the opportunity to play around with it again. Of course, such a relatively subtle change often failed to register with the managers of the clubs in which he was playing, and they consistently advertised the band on their billboards as Jimmy James & The Blue Flames.

California recalled some intriguing snippets of the repertoire the Blue Flames played.[13] Hendrix's love of Dylan's music and his demonstrated familiarity with 'Like A Rolling Stone' from the previous autumn made that song an obvious choice. 'Shotgun' was kept on from his R&B days, while 'Wild Thing' was a brand new arrival. It had been a hit for The Troggs as recently as May that year in the UK, reaching the US Top Ten in the first week of July. Hendrix's girlfriend Carol Shiroky recalled that he learned it direct from the radio in their hotel room during the last two weeks of June, shortly before the couple split up. It's a very simple song with a limited chord progression, so it was quickly pressed into service with The Blue Flames. California remembers Hendrix teaching him the tune just before his first gig with the band – so despite California's recollection that Hendrix had only just started at the club when he joined, he probably came on board two or three weeks into Hendrix's debut season at the Café Wha?, when The Troggs' record had received radio airplay and entered the charts.

"Hendrix was pathologically shy. He would stare at the ground and almost shuffle his feet when he met someone, but he had the courage to break through all that."

Paul Caruso, friend

'Hey Joe' was another song in the Blues Flames' repertoire. Various people have recalled Hendrix hearing Tim Rose's version of 'Hey Joe' while in Greenwich Village, and this may have been his first contact with the song. But Curtis Knight is adamant that Hendrix knew another version first. "'Hey Joe' was originally recorded by a … group called The Leaves," said Knight. "I was with Jimmy when he bought the record, at a record store in New York. He always had some idea of what he wanted to do with that record. … We never played it … but this is how it happened, this is where it started."[14] Clearly Hendrix was struck by the song; he immediately began playing 'Hey Joe' with his own group in New York and retained it in his repertoire on moving to England.

Hendrix continued to indulge his career-long love of jamming while playing at the Wha? and hanging out in the Village , studying other groups' routines at different clubs. Musician Bob Kulick, a member of The Random Band then playing Village clubs, often saw Hendrix about. "He was constantly at one club or another, either hanging out or picking up girls. Jimi was a consummate musician who would jam with anybody any time. When he watched bands, he would even take notes. He'd pick up stuff from everybody – no matter how bad they were. … There wasn't anybody around who could play like him. No one could even figure out what he was doing. He played tons of blues, but his signature song was 'Hey Joe'. He also did a primitive version of 'Third Stone From The Sun'. I asked him who his biggest influence was, and he told me Curtis Mayfield."[15] Kulick observed that Hendrix already had a louche lifestyle and often relied on girlfriends to pay for him when earnings at the club were thin. "He was doing fine playing all the … places, and he always had plenty of women taking care of him. When Hendrix wasn't hanging out with bands, the girls were all over him. I think between what he made playing, which wasn't a lot, plus what his girlfriends gave him, he did all right."[16] A new twist on that lifestyle was about to arrive.

On Thursday June 23rd 1966 The Rolling Stones and their entourage arrived in New York to prepare for the band's fifth US tour. They were by this time a highly successful and affluent band with a flamboyant American manager and a burgeoning social status on both sides of the Atlantic, and had a retinue of friends, girlfriends and others travelling with them. Keith Richards had brought along his girlfriend, fashion model Linda Keith. The following evening, the 24th, with the Stones performing in Boston, Linda Keith joined up with two New York friends and went out on the town, dropping in at The Cheetah towards the end of the evening. (Keith's recollection of this evening's events is consistent with parallel facts and chronologies; Curtis Knight had a quite different recollection which is not.) As usual, the club was running its two-band routine to keep the dancers happy. Keith's later recollection was that she wasn't sure why she and her friends went to the Cheetah that night, but along they went. "It was a place we didn't normally go to. … It was [an] enormous place, like a ballroom. Very few people were there, and a regular sort of band [was] playing – not very well in fact. I didn't take any interest in the band at all. And then suddenly I saw the guitar player … and from that moment I just became completely involved."[17] The guitar player was, of course, Hendrix. He still wasn't working a full week's stint at the Wha?, and so to make a little more money was probably picking up work wherever he could and with whoever would hire him.

Keith asked a friend in the music business to get Hendrix over to their table. "He was very naïve. He was very shy and nervous and he didn't look at you when he spoke to you,"[18] she recalled. He had plenty of charm and quickly made an impression on Keith. Swept off her feet by this quiet but charismatic man, she invited him back to the hotel suite she was staying in courtesy of her boyfriend. "He came back to the apartment and [we] played a lot of Dylan, who Jimmy idolised – he thought Dylan was the greatest."[19]

The two struck up an instant rapport and Hendrix became more or less a constant presence. Keith was splitting her time between her friends' Manhattan apartment and her hotel room during the week when the Stones were out of town playing in neighbouring states. "[Hendrix] would stay at the 'Red House' [apartment block], as we called it, for days on end. I would play loads of music, trying to motivate him, something he desperately needed. It seemed silly, me, a middle-class white girl, playing him the blues."[20] She has claimed that their relationship was not a romance – she was Keith Richards's girlfriend, trying to help out someone who she believed in but who seemed to have little belief in himself. She told one interviewer: "He was completely lacking in confidence and terribly indecisive. … He was confused about his

would only refer to her as 'Auntie Faye', not in a deceitful way, but nonetheless I was never quite sure if she was his aunt or his girlfriend. … As it was, his life in Harlem was strictly off-limits to me."[22]

It was obvious to the more perceptive of his friends who saw them together that Hendrix and Keith had a special chemistry. Paul Caruso remembers that Hendrix "felt very strongly about Linda Keith. I spent time with [Jimi] and Linda when they were together in New York, before [he] went to England, and I saw a very pure, very strong – you know when you're around two people whether they're deeply in love or not."[23] This closeness would not last long, but proved pivotal for the direction the rest of his life would take. It also proved fatal to his affair with Carol Shiroky. She was well aware that he was not the most faithful lover in New York, but found his absorption in Keith too much to bear. Like his previous girlfriends, Shiroky was conscious of Hendrix's ability to compartmentalise his private life and carry on with what amounted to a series of parallel existences in different parts of town. But his relationship with Linda Keith was of a different order. Soon after Hendrix played 'Wild Thing' to her on her birthday, 26th June,[24] their relationship cooled to the point where they were just good friends. What she had to offer him was no longer what he needed most.

When The Rolling Stones arrived back in New York City to play at Forest Hills on Saturday July 2nd, Linda Keith persuaded them to come on from the concert to see The Blue Flames at the Café Wha?. Bill Wyman wrote later in his autobiography that he at least was impressed with what he saw that night, but the Stones were back on tour within two days and were not scheduled to come back to New York as a group during that trip. They were not in a position to help Hendrix.

That same weekend, another group of players saw Hendrix perform, and although they too were not placed to help him, the memory stayed with one guitarist in particular. In fact the experience was burned into his memory. The Butterfield Blues Band had spent the spring and early summer on the West Coast and then worked their way east across the country. Now they were booked for a week at New York's Café Au Go Go, playing their first three nights (July 1st-3rd) opposite The Blues Project. Al Kooper was playing keyboards with The Blues Project, and later remembered the Butterfield band vividly. "There was an intense rivalry between the Butterfield Blues Band and The Blues Project. … We played the Café Au Go Go [with them] on a double bill over a weekend for three nights, and it was the only time we ever did that. It was very tense. But it was remarkable in that if they played a bad set, we'd play a bad set, and if they killed, we killed. It was very evenly balanced."[25]

During this time, Butterfield guitarist Mike Bloomfield was tipped off about a wild guitarist playing in the nearby Cafe Wha?. He wandered over to escape the tense atmosphere at the Au Go Go by checking out the band: instead, he got the shock of his life. Hendrix was prepared. As well as knowing him from records, he may well have seen Bloomfield in New York City the previous year, as Butterfield's band had held down a short residency at the Café Au Go Go during July 1965. Bloomfield recalled, "I was performing with Paul Butterfield and I was the hot shot guitarist on the block – I thought I was *it*. I'd never heard of Hendrix. … I went right across the street and saw him. Hendrix knew who I was, and that day, in front of my eyes, he burned me to death. I didn't even get my guitar out. H-bombs were going off, guided missiles were flying – I can't tell you the sounds he was getting out of his instrument. He was getting every sound I was ever to hear him get, right there in that room with a Stratocaster, a [Fender] Twin [amplifier], a Maestro fuzz[box], and that was all – he was doing it mainly through extreme volume. How he did this, I wish I understood. … I didn't even want to pick up a guitar for the next year."[26]

It had turned out to be a pretty tough three days in New York for Bloomfield, yet he had sufficient presence of mind to contemplate what he was witnessing and penetrate to the core of what made Hendrix unique. "That

"I asked Hendrix who his biggest influence was, and he told me Curtis Mayfield."

Bob Kulick, Greenwich Village musician

ethnic identity and there was a great conflict between his musical roots and desire to play the blues and then wanting to be this sort of middle-class pop star."[21] Linda Keith loved the blues – not surprising, considering her involvement with Keith Richards, a musician who has had a deep respect for the blues throughout his long career – and she attempted to steer Hendrix in this direction. But he would not be pushed when it came to music. He took his own course.

Whatever differences of opinion the two of them had about music, Keith understood the extent of Hendrix's talent. On a more personal level, she also showed a subtle understanding of his complex and elusive inner character, being perhaps the first person since his childhood to do so. "He seemed petrified to make an honest commitment to anyone," she said later. "He would be in Manhattan with me and then uptown with Faye Pridgeon. At first, Jimmy day, Hendrix was laying things on me that were more sounds than licks," said Bloomfield. "But I found, after hearing him two or three more times, that he was into pure melodic playing and lyricism as much as he was into sounds. In fact he had melded them into a perfect blend."[27] Nobody has explained Hendrix's genius more concisely or pithily – and Bloomfield seems to have been the first musician to witness Hendrix using extreme volume, distortion and feedback in a controlled and intentional way. The timing of Bloomfield's observation fits in with Hendrix's own statements that he first learned to control and use feedback during his stint in the Village in summer 1966.

Hendrix formed a band to play at the Cafe Wha? club in New York City's Greenwich Village in summer 1966.

removed from what Hendrix was attempting that the rejection seems entirely consistent with his approach to hit-making.

Keith's second industry contact, Seymour Stein, just months into setting up Sire Records, was a more complicated case. Keith has always maintained that he showed no interest in Hendrix and that was the end of the matter. Stein, talking later to author Sean Egan, had a different story to tell. He saw Hendrix twice at the Café Au Go Go, and both nights ended with Hendrix and Keith rowing over the damage Hendrix was inflicting on the guitar she'd borrowed for him from Keith Richards. "I thought he was an amazing guitar player," said

The tours by bands such as the Stones, The Animals and Herman's Hermits, as well as the Au Go Go's Blues Bag series of gigs, were by no means the only big music events in New York City that summer. US beer producer Rheingold sponsored a summer festival at the skating rink in Central Park. Running from July 1st to September 5th, there were concerts every Monday, Wednesday, Friday and Saturday evening, plus a Sunday matinee. There was a mouth-watering array of talent on display across a broad range of styles, from Duke Ellington to Nina Simone, Muddy Waters to Otis Redding, King Curtis to Miriam Makeba, plus Mongo Santamaria, Bill Evans, Jackie Wilson, Thelonious Monk and others fitting somewhere in between. It seems likely that Hendrix would have seen some of this summer festival: it wasn't far to go, and the entrance fee for an entire concert was just $1.00. The following summer he would be one of the festival's headline attractions.

Back in the Village things were unravelling. The entourage accompanying the Stones tour dispersed out of New York during July and went their separate ways, with Linda Keith planning to head for London and resume her modelling career. But she was determined to do something about Jimi James before she left. She replaced the stolen Stratocaster by lending Jimi one belonging to Keith Richards from their shared hotel room. She was instrumental in organising a showcase for The Blue Flames at a slightly more salubrious club than the Wha?, which she felt was not an ideal setting for the band.

The showcase occurred early in the third week of July 1966, after the Blues Project had finished their month-long stint at the club on Sunday 10th. Keith attempted to use what record-business contacts she had in New York to Hendrix's benefit, but she met with indifference. The obvious first choice was Andrew Loog Oldham, who obliged her by dropping in at the Cafe Au Go Go, but quickly turned her down, to Keith's bemusement.

She recalled later: "I told this record producer [Oldham] that there was this fantastic guitar player ... playing in the Village and would he come down and listen to him because he was really going to like this. He was a very materialistic man [and] he came down – he thought I was mad. He did not see what I was talking about. When he saw Jimi he thought, 'This is nothing.'"[28] Oldham later explained his reaction, saying that he recognised Hendrix's talent without it moving him: he felt he could do nothing for him. "I didn't fall in love with him and that's what it takes for me to work with people. ... My day job was The Rolling Stones. In terms of making somebody a star, I couldn't have done that because of my agenda with The Rolling Stones."[29] He was also aware of an undercurrent between Keith and Hendrix that he didn't feel was either resolved or altogether constructive. He wasn't even sure that she was offering Hendrix to him. Judging by the music Oldham's own Immediate label released during the next few years, his taste was so far

Stein. "I really liked what I saw and heard. I think she's forgetting that I saw him under the worst possible conditions. I've fucked up over the years, but this wasn't one of [those] occasions."[30] Stein gracefully retreated. Deflated but undeterred, Keith kept at her self-appointed task. The Blue Flames went back to their house-band spot at the Café Wha? while she cast around for new openings, increasingly unsure as to how she might manufacture them.

Usually, in fact, timing is all. That summer, Keith's perseverance paid off and Hendrix got lucky. The Animals had arrived in the United States on June 27th for their final pre-disbandment tour, staying briefly in New York before moving on to Hawaii and the West Coast to begin the tour proper. They were out in tandem with Herman's Hermits, a group then at the peak of their popularity on both sides of the Atlantic.

After spending all of July on the road through the West, Midwest and South, the tour came into New York via Chicago and Baltimore. Herman's Hermits spent three nights separately in a short season at a club in Atlantic City, New Jersey, leaving The Animals to deviate briefly from the package scheme. Monday August 1st was a day off for the group, their first since the beginning of July in Los Angeles, but the following night, August 2nd, saw them flying to play a single appearance in West Hyannis, Massachusetts. The gig was poorly reviewed by the local press, but the band didn't hang around to read the reports, flying back to New York City the same night. Upon their arrival, the group's bassist, Chas Chandler, decided to go out to some clubs while he had the chance. He and some of the others ended up outside Ondine's in midtown. Just as they were about to enter, they bumped into a party including Linda Keith. Here was an opening for her. She decided to buttonhole Chandler about Hendrix.

"I didn't know [Chandler]," she said later, "but I knew [he] was one of The Animals." What she also didn't know was that Chandler was already planning his post-Animals future and was thinking of going into management. Musically astute and with a good deal of plain common sense, Chandler was keeping his eyes open on his last Animals tour for potential acts to manage. Keith had struck blind but lucky. Chandler was sufficiently interested in what Keith had to say to agree a rendezvous at the Café Wha? the following afternoon, even though The Animals had an important gig that same evening in Central Park at the Rheingold Festival. "I think [Jimi] was getting quite desperate to record or at least make another step," Keith recalled, "and so Chas came down to see him and was, like ... it was instantaneous; there was no question in his mind."[31]

Chandler's own recollections of what he saw on the afternoon of August 3rd were just as positive. "I went there with her the next day to a little club called the Café Wha? in Greenwich Village, which was a little coffee house really with musicians playing downstairs." Chandler may not have been overly impressed with the venue, nor was he awestruck by the raggedy band onstage, but the guitarist whom Linda Keith had been talking about was something else again. "I thought immediately he was the best guitarist I'd ever seen," said Chandler. "He was playing with a little pick-up band. … The first song Jimi played onstage that afternoon was 'Hey Joe'. He had it all. You just sat there and thought to yourself, 'This is ridiculous – why hasn't anybody signed this guy up?'"[32] Shades of John Hammond and Charlie Christian. Unfortunately for Chandler and Hendrix, more than "anybody" already had "signed this guy up", even if they had done nothing of note with the artist they'd signed. But that trauma was still in the future.

Straight after that first set, Chandler introduced himself to Hendrix and called him to a table where they could talk. He said he was at the beginning of a tour – in fact he was more than half way through it – and would be unable to act immediately, but he was seriously interested in managing Hendrix. Chandler had already decided that Hendrix should divorce himself as quickly as possible from the rest of the group, whom he regarded as a poor lot. His plan was that, once his Animals tour was over, he would take Hendrix back to London, where he had many contacts and potential sources of finance. There he would look for deals and set him up in a band.

For Hendrix this must have been a pleasant surprise. No one from the music business had said such things to him since the sweet-talking no-show manager in Nashville who had convinced him his future was in New York but delivered nothing. Like most Americans, Hendrix had not been out of his native country (except for vacations in Vancouver, just over the border) and had little idea what England was like. He just knew the music. He was understandably reluctant to throw in his lot with a hard-talking man from Newcastle in the north-east of England whose 'Geordie' accent you could cut with a knife and who was only in town for a day. He must have wondered how Chandler could follow through on such ideas.

Chandler, excited about his discovery but mindful of his current commitments, promised Hendrix that he would catch up with him again in New York at the end of the tour and make arrangements for them to travel together to London. How much Hendrix believed this promise and committed himself to leaving New York can be gauged from the fact that he did absolutely nothing to prepare himself for such an eventuality. Considering Linda Keith's passionate belief in Hendrix's talent and her desire to see him succeed, she must also at first have thought little of Chandler's initial meeting with Hendrix, for she too failed to set in motion any basic tasks such as acquiring Hendrix a passport.

On the face of it, they were right. Chandler was in Fort Wayne, Indiana, on the evening of August 4th as The Animals resumed their US tour with Herman's Hermits. Hendrix remained fixed in the Café Wha? during that hot August 1966 with no clear idea of how he would make his way out. Jimi James continued with The Blue Flames, but there was no prospect of advancement through the Wha?, and money remained very tight indeed. He watched while bands with record deals and good rhythm sections such as the Butterfield Blues Band and Jesse Colin Young's Youngbloods gigged at more prestigious Village venues like the Café Au Go Go and the Gaslight; for one memorable week Muddy Waters played opposite The Youngbloods in mid August. But he heard no more from Chandler, and no other prospects presented themselves.

The Beatles came to Shea Stadium in the City during their last US tour, on August 23rd, supported by The Ronettes among others, while Jimi James played to 60 or so people in the Wha?. To make some extra money, he returned to one-nighters with other groups, probably including those of Curtis Knight and Lonnie Youngblood, though his heart was no longer in it. He continued to compose new tunes so that The Blue Flames were not just a covers band. People around him at this time remember Hendrix playing embryonic versions (or at least portions) of 'Third Stone From The Sun', 'The Wind Cries Mary' and 'Remember' in addition to 'Red House' and 'Hey Joe', although The Blue Flames didn't actually perform them all. Linda Keith said that when *Are You Experienced* was first released none of the tracks were a complete surprise to her, because most featured riffs, patterns and ideas she'd first heard in Greenwich Village that summer.

But Jimi's circumstances were about to change. In the first week of September bluesman John Hammond Jr came in from a long solo world tour around Europe, the Near and Far East and Japan to play the Gaslight Club in a repeat booking from his season there the previous autumn. The week was successful and towards the end of his run, as he remembered, "One night between shows – it was a warm evening out – I went upstairs, and my friend who was working at the Playhouse Theater on McDougal Street right next to the Café Wha? came over and said, 'John, there's this band playing downstairs that you've got to hear. This guy is doing songs off your old album and he sounds better than you.' So I thought I'd check this out." Hammond discovered that Hendrix was playing tunes from Hammond's 1965 LP *So Many Roads*, "playing the guitar parts better than Robbie Robertson had".[33] At the end of the set Hendrix, who had recognised Hammond in the small audience and quite likely chosen his set's repertoire to reflect his guest's presence, came over and introduced himself as Jimi James.

Hammond was the blues-playing son of the famous Columbia Records A&R man John Hammond. He'd built a reputation as a fiery, knowledgeable and authentic player of traditional blues styles, in much the same way as his counterparts in Britain, Alexis Korner and John Mayall. On his album *So Many Roads* Hammond had explored music not just of the bluesmen of the 1920s and '30s, but also more recent repertoire from Muddy Waters and Howlin' Wolf. Hammond said later that he felt this may have been the first exposure Hendrix had to this material. "I had all those Muddy Waters and Howlin' Wolf tunes on [the album], and he had gotten them from my record – at least, this is what he told me … and he went from there. I'm sure as he got more and more well known, I became less important to his reality, and he had to say, 'Oh, I got this from Muddy Waters and Howlin' Wolf,' which I can understand. But Robbie Robertson's guitar playing on that album is what really inspired him."[34] Hammond's recollections were not entirely impartial: Hendrix certainly knew Muddy Waters from the original, as he proved six months later when talking to Val Wilmer. "I liked Muddy when he had only two guitars, harmonica and bass drum. Things like 'Rollin' And Tumblin'' were what I liked, that real primitive sound."[35] Hendrix's listening habits were far broader than Hammond could possibly have known.

Hammond was a natural act for the Gaslight club, still largely a preserve of acoustic folk and blues traditions. Hendrix's electric guitar would not have been a welcome addition. Nonetheless Hammond, impressed with the man as well as his playing, wanted to join up with him in some way. "He knew who he was, but he was kind of quiet," said Hammond. "He was an intelligent guy, and he had the kind of sophistication of somebody who'd been around but wasn't stuck in something. He knew what he liked and he knew that he was going to make it – I mean, he knew it, I knew it, anyone around him knew it. The intensity and the fact that he was so intent, his demeanour – he was not a young kid who didn't know anything, he had been around, and he came from a scene that was very sophisticated."[36] That same night, when both men had finished work, Hammond suggested that they pool their talents. Hammond's idea was for the two of them to co-lead Hendrix's existing band, using a new name. Hammond, who had built up excellent contacts in the Village for some years, would rustle up some work. Hendrix immediately agreed: there was nothing about the deal where he could come out behind.

Hammond moved on to a short season at one of the nearby clubs and began networking furiously. He concentrated on the Café Au Go Go because, as he said, it was "the rock'n'roll place at the time".[37] According to Hammond, his band with Hendrix was booked to open about a week later, so they fitted in a few quick rehearsals – even though they didn't need much, with the repertoire mostly blues material they already knew. Hammond was "just playing the harmonica and singing because [I knew that Hendrix and California] were heavyweight electric guitar players".[38] He was particularly impressed by Randy California's slide technique.

The band, dubbed by Hammond as The Screaming Night Hawks, opened at the Go Go around September 13th, playing opposite blues singer Ellen McIlwaine, a mainstay in the Village over the past year. Hammond remembered it as an unqualified success. "We just rocked the house out for about two weeks. All these bands came to see us. ... There was a lot of jamming done."[39] McIlwaine has a different recollection. "That lasted for about six days. We'd hang around and make friends backstage and [Hendrix] said, 'Can I come and play on your sets?' and I said sure. When he was with a band, he was a real cut-up kind of guy, and when he played with me he just sat on a barstool and played very tastefully. He was a nice guy."[40]

Hammond also remembered Chas Chandler arriving at the club to prepare Jimi for his removal to London. To Hammond it seemed just happenstance; for Chandler it was the result of four days spent in a constant search for the elusive Hendrix. Chandler's band had played an extension to the initial Herman's Hermits US tour, completing a further month of extra work on their own. They came back into New York City on September 6th after finishing in the same Atlantic City club where Herman's Hermits had completed their US jaunt a month before. Chandler was at last free to start his new career on the business side of rock, and knew that the best way to kick-start it would be to find that Greenwich Village guitarist he'd last seen in early August at the Café Wha?.

Chandler – and Animals manager Mike Jeffery, according to Hendrix's later recollection[41] – met up with Hendrix at the Café Au Go Go and immediately began serious discussions with him about relocating to London. Hendrix remained interested but unconvinced, playing for time and looking for advice from his friends. After all, to him it seemed that he did now have some alternatives, even if they were the usual long shots. Ellen McIlwaine had promised to speak to her manager about him, and did so during those six days at the Au Go Go. "[My manager] wanted me to put a group together", she recounted. "I called him – and I can remember making the call from the club on the pay phone – and I said, 'Guess what? You won't believe it, there's this great guy and you've got to come down and hear him!' And the manager said, 'No, I know who that is. You don't want him in your group. He's black.' And I said, 'Actually, I don't want you as my manager,' and he said, 'Oh, you have an attitude!' And I thought *I* have an attitude? Puh-leese! ... It shows you where people's heads were at. Even in New York. It was still 1966. Even in the Village. It was still weird."[42]

Considering that Hendrix was now co-leading his group with John Hammond Jr, it's not surprising that Hammond's father had come down one evening to check them out. Hammond Sr was steeped in blues tradition and had been responsible for Bessie Smith's last recording session as well as a host of other important blues records during the intervening decades. His taste was perhaps for more traditional blues, but he had a keen ear – after all, not only had he signed Bob Dylan to Columbia, but also, in March that year, George Benson. Hammond had also been the first to record Aretha Franklin a couple of years earlier.

Hendrix arranged for Faye Pridgeon to make one of her very rare excursions down to the Village, with Linda Keith apparently now long gone from the scene, and they met up with John Hammond Jr plus Hammond Sr and his wife. "We were in this little bar in the Village," Pridgeon recalled. "Jimi was so nervous. ... He wanted me to meet John Hammond Sr because he thought they were wild about him. That really impressed him."[43] It is not known why nothing further came of the meeting. Perhaps by then Hendrix was so caught up in Chas Chandler's preparations for his departure to London that there was no time to follow up. But it's also possible that Hendrix, though immensely flattered by Hammond's attentions, was realistic enough about his own desires and attitudes to know that Hammond Sr did not share his musical vision. Hammond and his son, like Linda Keith before them, appreciated Hendrix as a blues artist and would have wanted to pursue that for his career, especially with the current American fashion for blues bands such as the Butterfield group and The Blues Project, both of which had enjoyed commercial success in the past 12 months with their uncompromising modern

electric blues. But Hendrix already knew he wanted more than that. He was looking for an all-inclusive musical language. Chas Chandler's encouragement and advice suggested that he could encompass those ambitions. The future, it seemed, was with Chandler.

"The band made about $60 a night, and Jimmy split it equally four ways. I think he had to borrow guitars to play on for the first couple of weeks."

Randy California, The Blue Flames

According to Hendrix, Chandler had already involved Animals manager Mike Jeffery to back up his words to Hendrix. Hendrix claimed later that it was Jeffery who negotiated his leaving the States and removal to England, saying that Chandler and Jeffery "would spend money on me, the promotion plus the expenses, plus equipment. And I had a salary a week. It was like hotel bills were paid, clothes, you know. And this indicates to me that, you know, I had a very good thing, a good chance. And it gave me belief in them".[44] Received opinion has it that Chandler didn't introduce Jeffery into the picture until after their arrival in London. Kathy Etchingham, Hendrix's first English girlfriend, recalled in her autobiography, for example, that she and Hendrix were introduced to Jeffery in London. However, what Hendrix claimed points to an earlier involvement by Jeffery, even if they had never personally met in New York.

Hendrix met with Chandler's music publisher (Schroeder) and his lawyer (Leon Dicker) in New York, and they in turn introduced him to the roomful of mirrors called Yameta. This was a company that had been set up in Bermuda to handle The Animals' profits and avoid British tax laws. In time it would become Hendrix's own Bermuda triangle, but for now no one, not even Chandler, was aware of that. Instead, they had to attend to more basic matters.

Obtaining a passport was made complicated because Hendrix hadn't known that he'd been registered at birth by his mother as Johnny Allen Hendrix, leading the initial search for a birth certificate to come up with nothing. This quick resolution of a potentially tricky bureaucratic process gives an even stronger hint of an early involvement from Jeffery. His skill at resolving all manner of such diplomatic and procedural matters is well documented. The misapprehension corrected, a birth certificate was conjured on September 19th, which in turn led to a passport, and by the third week in September Hendrix and Chandler were able to start planning exactly what they would do in London.

Chandler, who could still not believe that such a great talent could come unencumbered, badgered Hendrix to let him know about any deal signed in the past that needed unravelling. Hendrix recalled a few, including the contract with Sue Records that had never been acted upon. Chandler and Jeffery began buying them out with money taken as an advance against probable future earnings. But one slipped through the net: the production deal with Ed Chalpin's PPX. Hendrix probably regarded it as insignificant and thought the tangible musical product risible. Just one single, 'How Would You Feel', had been released under the PPX deal by the time Hendrix left New York. There was further work as a session player on a Jayne Mansfield single that was never released in the US and failed on its release in the UK in 1967. He probably had no real understanding of the nature of the contract he'd signed, and even less inclination to understand it. In fact, it would turn out to be a major thorn in his side during his few years of success.

By this time Chandler and Hendrix had spent many hours talking about what they would do once in London. Chandler was insistent, overriding Hendrix's objections, that they begin with a clean slate, hiring the best British musicians rather than taking members of the Blue Flames. In this, Chandler was probably being as much pragmatic as musically astute, for he knew that it would be a big enough problem getting Hendrix a work permit in Britain, let alone a complete band of unknowns. Hendrix was clearly reluctant to agree to this. He made offers to virtually the whole band prior to his departure. Guitarist California had no desire to leave his stepfather, Ed Cassidy, and indeed they soon relocated to San Francisco to start up their new band together, Spirit. Hendrix also asked bassist Butler, just three or four days before leaving, but Butler too turned him down.

Butler felt he had a secure gig at the Wha? and didn't want to chuck it in for a vague promise of fame in unknown London. Like Billy Cox and the rest of The King Kasuals three years earlier, he chose to stick around the place he knew. Only Hendrix, with a burning ambition and no emotional centre to his life, was prepared as usual to gamble so recklessly. Soon afterwards he revealed his own rather different perspective. "I said I might as well go because nothing much was happening," he told Val Wilmer. "I only hope that the guys I left behind are doing all right. The way I left was kinda wrong – they all thought they were going, but this way it was easier for me to go alone. I kinda feel rotten about leaving just like that because we weren't living too much, you dig?"[45]

Chandler wanted Hendrix to reassume his real surname, and was relaxed about Jimi retaining the unusual spelling of his given name. He felt the name Jimi Hendrix should be the focal point of the new band. Like just about every event in this early period, the credit for inventing the new band's name is now disputed. Drummer Mitch Mitchell wrote in his autobiography that 'The Jimi Hendrix Experience' was dreamed up by Chandler in the Gotham Hotel in New York just after he met Hendrix.[46] Hendrix in his 1968 pre-trial deposition[47] said that Mike Jeffery, Animals manager and Chandler's partner, came up with the name.

On the evening of September 23rd 1966 Hendrix and Chandler departed New York City's Kennedy airport on a Pan Am flight, accompanied by Animals roadie Terry McVay. They flew into the night with no real idea of what the next day would bring. They should have known it wouldn't be that easy.

Arriving at London's Heathrow airport the following morning at 9.00am, they made it to the passport desk but no further. Her Majesty's Customs remained unconvinced that this louche looking black American had anything beneficial to offer Britain, especially as he had no work permit, no accompanying papers, and only Chas Chandler's word that he wouldn't be a burden on the United Kingdom's welfare state. McVay claims that he carried Hendrix's white Fender Stratocaster through Customs to avoid it being impounded (the guitar was in Jimi's possession courtesy of a still unsuspecting Keith Richards). After close to an hour of frustrating dialogue with a suspicious group of Customs officers, Chandler finally managed to convince them that no, Hendrix had not come to play music in England and therefore deprive a musical British citizen of an opportunity for gainful employment. He was in fact the composer of a number of tunes and was coming to England to collect royalties due to him.

Considering the legendary toughness of a suspicious Customs official, Chandler must have had something tangible to back up his story. The only claim Hendrix had to publishing royalties in late 1966 would have stemmed from the 'Hornet's Nest' / 'Knock Yourself Out' RSVP single released earlier that year as by Curtis Knight & The Squires. Both A and B-side were co-written by Hendrix and RSVP owner/producer Jerry Simon. This opens up its own hornet's nest. In June 1966, Simon had signed The Squires to the RSVP label, having already released the PPX-produced 'How Does It Feel' under Curtis Knight's name. Hendrix must have mentioned this contract to his new management team, given Chandler's customs story and Jeffery's subsequent approach to Simon to buy the RSVP masters. Just how Simon could sign Hendrix to an exclusive deal when he was already a PPX artist remains

unexplained. It is intriguing to note that when Jeffery eventually declined to buy the RSVP masters in 1967, PPX's Ed Chalpin stepped in and bought them up instead.

Once free of Heathrow, Chandler and Hendrix drove into London, on the way visiting keyboardist and bandleader Zoot Money in his Fulham house and finally booking into the Hyde Park Towers Hotel in Inverness Terrace, Bayswater, across the road from Kensington Gardens. That night Chandler took Hendrix to a favourite haunt, The Scotch Club Of St James, tucked in Mason's Yard just north of Pall Mall. It was "a split-level disco that had replaced [another club, the] Ad-Lib as the top spot, and came across with a touch more chic than the Cromwellian, which was number two".[48] Chandler intended to start networking immediately and get Hendrix noticed. He got noticed.

Although Hendrix was on a seven-day visa with no permission to work in Britain, he gave an impromptu seated solo performance at the Scotch that impressed the rock elite in attendance that night – including Zoot Money, George Fame and The Who's Keith Moon – before Chandler, nervous about the visa restrictions, dragged him off the small stage. Hendrix also got noticed on a more personal level. On this, his first night in London, he met Kathy Etchingham at the club and eventually spent the night with her. Etchingham had not been in London long herself but was already becoming involved in the fast-moving social scene of the city's rock world. She knew immediately that Hendrix was to be taken seriously on every level. Like Linda Keith, she quickly grasped how he had been affected by his childhood and how this had shaped the adult now before her. "It was evident," she wrote later in her autobiography, "that he, like me, had never had a normal, cosy family life as a child and had been left feeling insecure and vulnerable. ... He opened the door for me to become myself. ... The paradox was that he was probably the most insecure person I had ever met. But together we made an anchor for each other even though we were both independent, scared of commitment and really too young to understand any of it."[49] They were to be lovers for the following two years.

This unlikely sequence of events led directly to Hendrix losing the guitar he'd brought with him from New York. Linda Keith, piqued that he had rejected her so soon after his arrival, claimed it back. He'd been in this new city for just one day and already he was scuffling for a guitar.

He and Etchingham moved into Hyde Park Towers. Neither of them had much money and scraped by from day to day. For Hendrix, it was like a repeat of his existence in New York City, but at least his new mentor Chas Chandler was working hard to get his career off the ground. For a man who had never once been delivered what was promised by manager or agent, this was a novel experience.

Growing accustomed to London nightspots, Hendrix spent more time over the next three days at The Scotch Of St James and the Birdland club (in a basement in Jermyn Street, quite close to The Scotch), sitting in with bands known to Chandler. It gave Hendrix continued exposure and made a convert of Animals lead singer Eric Burdon. During the daytime, Hendrix and Chandler split their time between playing *Risk* and plotting the best way of pulling a band together around him.

Hendrix had already attracted the interest of music businessmen Kit Lambert and Chris Stamp, managers of The Who, who were thinking of setting up their own record label. They saw Hendrix sitting in with a group, probably The VIPs. According to Chandler it was at the Scotch on September 27th, but it might have been at a different club on a date in October if Chris Stamp's memory is better. Lambert and Stamp were sufficiently impressed – and astute – to offer a contract to the guitarist the same night, and Chandler recalled the deal being done in principle on the spot. "Kit [Lambert] practically knocked tables over to get across to talk to me," said Chandler, "and said, 'I've got to sign that guy.' We sat that night and made out a deal. And he agreed to pay £1,000 in advance for The Jimi Hendrix Experience. That was sort of worked out on a beer mat."[50]

Chandler's colourful story isn't borne out by the sequence of events. Lambert knew Hendrix "was after a deal with Decca [Records] and wasn't interested in a new record company that didn't even exist".[51] For that reason alone Chandler could not have done an instant deal at the Scotch in late September prior to the Experience was even formed. It would be a month before Lambert and Stamp could persuade him that they and their new independent label could give him the promotion and chart success that he felt he would be more likely to get with an established major British record company. Eventually, the Jimi Hendrix Experience would need a deal with Track, simply to get the money to record the B-side of 'Hey Joe', which was taped on 23rd October.

In the meantime Hendrix and Chandler had to put a band together. At that point neither man knew precisely what he was after, but Chandler was keen to provide Hendrix with a backing band that would showcase his talents, much in the way that American soul and R&B bands were built around a frontman. In the event, something quite different emerged.

On Thursday September 29th, five days after arriving in England, Hendrix attended auditions for The New Animals at the Birdland club in central London as an observer. He took a liking to one of the applicants for the group, 21-year-old guitarist Noel Redding from Folkestone, Kent. Redding wasn't so sure about him. "I was hanging around hoping," Redding recalled later, "when Chas Chandler – bassist with the chart-topping Animals, TV star and all-round god – came over and asked if he'd heard me before. I reminded him of the night at John Bentley's club on Baker Street when Eric [Burdon] had sung with us. Chas asked if I could play bass and sit in with this other guy, gesturing to a bloke who was pacing uneasily in a distant corner. He was dressed in a horrible tan raincoat and grotty black winkle-picker boots and zips! Awful! In London in those days, we all wore [theatrical shoemakers] Annello & David's Cuban/Spanish short boots and

"I thought immediately he was the best guitarist I'd ever seen."

Chas Chandler, future manager

squared toes."[52] Nevertheless, Redding said he'd have a go. He was introduced to a pleasant-mannered Hendrix as well as drummer Aynsley Dunbar and keyboardist Mike O'Neill, who was sitting at a Vox Continental electric organ. The music the quartet made was desultory in the extreme. "Jimi mumbled the chords of a song called 'Hey Joe' and we ran through it two or three times," wrote Redding, "before briefly trying a couple of sequences in the same vein as ['Mercy Mercy']. Jimi was amazed I remembered the chords so easily. But what's a blues progression when you've been in Germany learning new songs between sets? No one sang. It didn't seem much of an audition."[53]

Hendrix explained later to many interviewers that what he really liked was Redding's hairstyle, which was a little like Bob Dylan's. Hendrix's references to hairstyles and fashions were not as whimsical as they seemed – he and Chandler had arranged for their respective girlfriends to attend the auditions to check out each musician's fashion status. All approved of Redding. So Hendrix asked Redding to have a chat. They quickly established that they had mutual enthusiasms in music – Booker T & The MGs, Sam Cooke and so on – and that they could get on tolerably well together. Hendrix asked him to return the next day, as did Chandler. By the following day Redding had been told by Chandler's partner Mike Jeffery that he was the bassist in The Jimi Hendrix Experience – a band with no drummer, a question mark over the inclusion of a piano player, and with no gigs lined up. Nevertheless, Redding was thrilled. He began planning to move to London.

Redding's impressions of these very early days show that there was genuine uncertainty as to what kind of group would best suit Hendrix's musical needs, and that there were problems with availability among top-flight London musicians. After all, Hendrix was an unknown. There was no work lined up and no repertoire to speak of, let alone a singer to deliver it. Chandler and Hendrix were uncertain enough about the participation of in-demand drummer Aynsley Dunbar to canvass actively for a back-up early the following week.

Mike Jeffery's role in Redding's hiring confirms his early involvement . Jeffery had managed The Animals for the best part of the previous four years, during which time Chandler had experienced success, even if he'd seen little money as a result. But that was such a common story in rock'n'roll in the 1960s that it was more or less considered normal by young musicians in the business. As Noel Redding succinctly put it, "Bands get headlines about million-dollar advances but few can touch the cash. Some managers and producers have access to ways of preventing anyone from knowing where it is and who can spend it. High taxes and large lump sums breed these piranha companies which feed off innocents who think being a musician has to do solely with playing music. In reality, it's a business, and a pretty sharp one at that."[54]

Jeffery had been involved in The Jimi Hendrix Experience at the earliest possible opportunity by Chandler because he knew his manager had the contacts and business channels necessary to prepare the legal and business ground for a successful attempt at creating a new star. Chandler had enough experience to know his own strengths and weaknesses and was aware that he needed financial help. Jeffery was an obvious choice. He was a tough-minded man from Chandler's hometown who had flair and imagination as well as a degree of charm and attractive mystery.

Redding said later, "Jeffery as an agent/manager was brilliant, but his 'sheer confusion is best' policy haunted us. A real charming wheeler-dealer, he rarely let his left hand even know he had a right hand."[55] Kevin Ayers, singer and guitarist with Soft Machine, an act signed to Jeffery around this time, was also a songwriter signed to Jeffery's publishing company. His recalled Jeffery and Chandler more bluntly. "We never got the royalties for our first record, and that sold a lot of copies. Chas Chandler died just as we were getting a case together. ... I didn't like either of them after a while, Chas Chandler or Mike Jeffery. I mean Chandler was quite charming in a way but he was a villain. So was Jeffery. No other word to describe them."[56]

On the first day of October Hendrix made a move that was to have a long-term impact on his career in Britain. As usual with him, it came about through a somewhat casual combination of luck and timing. Even before coming to London, Hendrix had made Chandler aware that he admired guitarist Eric Clapton on Yardbirds and John Mayall recordings. Chandler assured Hendrix that he could effect an introduction. On the evening of Friday September 30th he did just that.

At the Cromwellian club in South Kensington, central London, Chandler ran into Clapton and lost no time in telling him about this amazing American guitarist he'd just brought to London. In the time that Chandler had been away on tour with The Animals, Clapton had joined up with Jack Bruce and Ginger Baker to form Cream. His new band had made its debut in late July 1966 in Manchester and its first major impact at the Sixth National Jazz & Blues Festival, at the Royal Windsor Racecourse on July 31st. Since then Cream had played London clubs and the occasional out-of-town gig, busily expanding their live repertoire and recording their first single, 'Wrapping Paper' / 'Cat's Squirrel', for the Reaction label.

Cream had been the talk of the Jazz & Blues Festival, London's rock journalists wrote ecstatically about the group, and they were packing out the small clubs, breaking the house record at London's influential Marquee club in mid August. Despite all that, for most people they remained an unknown quantity with much expected of them. They were not instant superstars and would have to work hard to establish themselves. Clapton was interviewed by *Record Mirror* for the paper's August 13th issue and was asked to summarise the current British scene. "Who do I rate as guitarists? Jeff Beck and John Mayall's new guy [Peter Green]. He's good. He's got out of all this muck. He's going in the right direction. … If I was sure that everything George Harrison played was his own ideas, I'd say he was good, but I've got this feeling it's Paul McCartney telling him what to do. There are only about four groups in the country who are developing their own directions – The Beatles, The Kinks, The Small Faces and The Who, I suppose. … I'm tired of being called a specialist musician. People thought Cream was going to be a blues band, but it's not. It's a pop group, really. We were a bit ragged at Windsor. It'll take about two months before we're OK. We've got about four good numbers and a few standards."[57]

Clapton, with a healthy respect for Chandler and a guitarist's curiosity in other guitarists, showed interest in the new American. "He said I had to bring [Hendrix] down to the Regent Polytechnic," Chandler recalled, "because Cream were playing there the next night."[58] He agreed to do so. According to Jack Bruce, Hendrix, primed and ready for a jam, approached him late the following afternoon in a pub close to the Poly and introduced himself. Bruce was at that point moderately well known in Britain and virtually unknown in the US, so it seems likely that Chandler and Hendrix had come across him in the pub and that Chandler, pointing him out, suggested Hendrix approach the Cream bassist.

Hendrix asked Bruce if he could sit in with his band that evening. Bruce agreed, warning that "you'll have to ask the other guys" first.[59] Having already got Clapton's OK the night before, the two plotters decided against approaching Cream's drummer, Ginger Baker, prior to the gig. This was

"He was very, very flash."

Eric Clapton

something of a tactical mistake because Baker, at that time a man with a short temper and not averse to showing it, had been the guiding force behind Cream's gestation. He assumed seniority and felt he should decide such things as whether or not someone was allowed to jam with the band. Having been a jazzer on the London scene, he was loathe to allow any such thing: people had to earn a jazz musician's respect, and few managed it. Confronted with an unknown guitarist mounting the stage to play with his group, Baker objected strongly, taking a dim view of Hendrix's showmanship and dismissing him as a clown. He made his negative feelings towards Hendrix known for a good time afterwards. In June the following year he was asked by *Record Mirror*'s Norman Joplin to compare Clapton and Hendrix. His reply was brief and to the point. "I don't just think Eric's better than Jimi – I think he's in a different class altogether. Jimi is first of all a showman [rather] than a musician. But Eric is a musician first."[60]

Clapton remembered Hendrix appearing in the dressing room prior to start of the gig. "He was very, very flash," Clapton observed. "He stood there in front of the mirror combing his hair. He asked if he could play a couple of numbers. I said, 'Of course,' but I had a funny feeling about him."[61] Clapton's instinct was right, because Hendrix, normally the most co-operative and considerate of players in jams, went for the jugular from the moment he mounted the stage midway through Cream's set. He counted off Howlin' Wolf's 'Killing Floor', a frantic blues into which he could pour all his blues technique and outlandish showbiz antics. This was the Hendrix determined to waste the opposition, just as he'd wiped Mike Bloomfield's musical ego into oblivion the previous July in Greenwich Village.

Like Bloomfield, Clapton would remember the experience distinctly decades later. "He played just about every style you could think of, and not in a flashy way. I mean he did a few of his tricks like playing with his teeth and behind his back, but it wasn't in an upstaging sense at all. And that was it. … He walked off and my life was never the same again, really."[62] From that time on Clapton made a point of seeing Hendrix whenever he could.

Hendrix had astounded an unsuspecting Poly audience, none of whom knew who this unannounced black guitarist was, but the only immediate benefit to him was that the best British musicians were suddenly aware of a new presence in their midst and began talking to each other about him. The talking would become louder in the following weeks, finally reaching the music press and translating into print, but for the week ahead Hendrix was back to the business of trying to form a band. A further unplanned but significant benefit was his exposure to Cream's trio format. After he'd played, Hendrix became convinced that this was the set-up he should be aiming for. He would form a trio, not a quartet or a larger group. It would be another week before he could communicate that desire to his management.

With the drummer's stool still vacant, Chandler cast around for more names. The day after Hendrix had jammed with Cream, British keyboardist and singer Georgie Fame played the last date with his own Blue Flames, a group he'd been running for more than two years. The next day – a Monday – the entire band was told by Fame's management that they were being fired. Their 20-year-old drummer, John 'Mitch' Mitchell, was confronted with the all-too-common experience for jobbing musicians of suddenly dropping from a wage of £120 per week to nothing. Mitchell went home to his parents' house in Ealing, west London, wondering what to do next. His career in music had not been a particularly long one, but as an erstwhile child actor he'd been performing for most of his life.

During his stint with the Blue Flames, Mitchell had discovered the best of contemporary jazz drumming – Elvin Jones, Max Roach, Roy Haynes and others – and yearned to play in situations that would allow him that type of expressive space, but he was not part of the British jazz scene. John Hiseman, then of the Graham Bond Organisation and later drummer with his own band, Colosseum, recalls: "[Mitchell] wasn't known as a jazz drummer and didn't play on the jazz circuit in London. I've never met anybody who ever played with him on the jazz circuit. So, liking that type of drumming is one thing, but whether he'd ever done it up to then I doubt."[63]

On Tuesday October 4th 1966 Chandler contacted Mitchell through a mutual friend, asking him to attend an audition with his new signing the following day. Mitchell was unaware that the band held its first rehearsal on the Wednesday at a music publisher's premises in Denmark Street on the edge of Soho, central London, with Aynsley Dunbar occupying the drum stool for at least part of the session. Noel Redding remembers that he and Hendrix had been jamming over those two days, often without a drummer, getting to know each other's style. Redding, a guitarist who had been asked to move to bass, was coming to terms with his new role and the technique required to hold down the job. With Dunbar's involvement increasingly doubtful, the group needed to clarify who would be the drummer in the new group.

Mitchell recalled later that his audition was every bit as strange as Redding's the previous week. Mitchell had done some phoning around to see what the feeling was about Hendrix. "It turned out they'd auditioned every bloody drummer in England, near enough, including a lot of people I knew. … I hadn't heard a word about this guy and he'd been in the country a couple of weeks up to that point. He'd played with Cream and Zoot Money and people that I knew and it really fazed me. The drummers they'd auditioned, who were mates of mine, hadn't mentioned anything to me."[64]

At the rehearsal room Mitchell met Hendrix and Redding. Hendrix was still wearing the Burberry raincoat that had so underwhelmed Redding the week before, but Mitchell was impressed by his gentle, generally polite manner. The first number they ran through was 'Mercy Mercy', and the group played on through acres of R&B material that they all knew. Mitchell was struck by the guitarist's complete mastery of every style he played. "I really like Curtis Mayfield & The Impressions and I was astounded that he knew that style really, really fluently. He wasn't that flash a guitarist on that occasion, it was more just going over rhythmic structures."[65]

Later the same day, according to Mitchell, Chandler phoned and offered him the job, saying that the group had a short tour in France supporting French singer Johnny Hallyday the following week. They would pay him £20 a week; would he be able to make it? It was not immediately appealing to Mitchell but the group seemed to have some promise, and with not much else to do apart from one-off freelance gigs, he accepted.

Chandler said in many later interviews that when he and Hendrix tried to decide between Mitch Mitchell and Aynsley Dunbar they eventually flipped a coin, which fell for the former. This colourful account was backed up by Hendrix's new English girlfriend Kathy Etchingham in her autobiography,[66] but it doesn't entirely square with the run of events. Dunbar had been around since before Redding had showed up for the September 28th audition, but a week later Chandler approached Mitchell about auditioning: what's more, Mitchell had got the job. There may have been a fashion issue here. Dunbar was also at that time still a member of John Mayall's Bluesbreakers and a thorough professional. To him it may have been a case of helping out until Chandler had sorted out a band for his new signing. After all, for Dunbar it would have meant leaving an established and in-demand group for the uncertainty of an untried and unknown American, as well as working for a manager with no experience and a band with no work and no record deal. If there was a flip of a coin, it may have been to decide between going with Mitchell or making an effort to prise Dunbar away from Mayall's Bluesbreakers.

Rehearsals began the following day. In a last attempt by Hendrix to resurrect the quartet line-up he'd found so comfortable in Greenwich Village just a month ago, Procol Harum bassist Dave Knights was brought along for a try-out, with Redding reverting to guitar. But things had moved on and he no longer wanted to be locked into that structure: the trio format was agreed for The Jimi Hendrix Experience.

Both Mitchell and Redding remember these first rehearsals as desultory. Redding recalled that Jimi would communicate a new idea by telling them the basic chord structure and tempo, leaving him and Mitchell to find their own parts within that framework. By this method, a song and arrangement would emerge. "Luckily," said Redding, "our concepts meshed."[67] Mitchell was now free to indulge his penchant for jazz musicians such as Elvin Jones and Max Roach, and he relished the freedom that this new attitude to music-making gave him – an attitude almost unknown in rock at that time. "The second or third time we played, things started to stretch out considerably," Mitchell wrote later. "That's when I started to feel it was a real chance, having come from such a structured unit as The Blue Flames. ... To have that much freedom was like being released from prison, and to have another musician prepared to give you that freedom was a most fortunate thing."[68] Hendrix must have been feeling pretty much the same way.

There has been much general discussion – from the time the group was formed to the present day – about the suitability of The Experience as a vehicle for Hendrix and whether the two musicians he chose were worthy of him. Such discussions ignore the situation in which Hendrix found himself at the time – he was a brilliant but unknown and untried black American with no clear musical format in mind – and denigrates the roles that Mitchell and Redding played in helping Hendrix realise his musical ambitions.

Both Mitchell and Redding were imaginative and responsive musicians prepared to go wherever Hendrix went musically and give him not merely sympathetic support but inspired responses. Importantly, they had the technique to go there with him and keep pushing. From the off, the trio was a better proposition than anybody had the right to expect, Chandler and Jeffery included – even if Mitchell's cocky character occasionally caused the sparks to fly, especially with Chandler.

Mitchell was aware that he rubbed people up the wrong way, but wasn't concerned. "Mitch was completely different to Noel," Kathy Etchingham wrote in her autobiography. "He had developed a stagey sort of [posh] accent which at the time we all assumed as genuine, none of us having had any first-hand experience of the upper classes. ... Jimi would become infuriated with Mitch's patronising attitude, which led to him sometimes not even turning up for rehearsals. At one stage there was talk of sacking him ... but it was

decided to give him another chance and somehow they just kept going."[69]

Proof that they all knew how well the trio blended came in the form of a management contract they signed on October 11th with Mike Jeffery and Chas Chandler, agreeing to work as The Jimi Hendrix Experience. The same day, publishing deals for all three were also signed. There were now only two outstanding matters to settle before they began gigging. What were they going to play? And who was going to sing?

The group had been selecting rock, blues, soul and R&B standards for their set and had also by this time worked out 'Hey Joe' in the slow treatment that Hendrix and Chandler admired so much from the Tim Rose single they'd both heard earlier that year. Mitchell had vociferously objected to them playing 'In The Midnight Hour', having his first row with Hendrix when the guitarist wanted to include it in their regular sets. "Being a cocky little bastard at the time, [I] said, 'Oh fuck! Not this *again*. I've just come from doing "Midnight Hour" for two years. We've got a new band, can't we do better than this? Please?'"[70]

It wasn't quite so easy to decide who was going to sing. Hendrix evaded the issue, so Redding and Mitchell each had a try-out, but neither felt up to the job. Chandler argued that Hendrix was the focal point of the band and the reason it existed at all, so there was never a question that a singer would be pulled in from outside. Hendrix simply had to sing. Redding remembered that, at first, Hendrix "would crank his guitar up really loud to cover his singing, but gradually he gained confidence and found the right balance between voice and guitar. He was very pleased and relieved he could do it, and so were we".[71]

"'Kit Lambert practically knocked tables over to get across to talk to me and said, 'I've got to sign that guy.'"

Chas Chandler, with Jimi in London

Singer, songs and – eventually – amplification were sorted out to everyone's satisfaction. A set of small Burns amplifiers that Chandler obtained were rejected out of hand and eventually Marshall was agreed upon as the brand of choice. Singer-songwriter Kevin Ayers witnessed Hendrix testing some Marshall equipment around this time. "I was in The Animals' office one day on Shaftesbury Avenue in central London and we went out into one of those big guitar shops – Shaftesbury Avenue was full of guitar shops in those days.

"Jimi was going to buy some amps, or they were going to buy some amps for him, to get him on the road," Ayers continued. "He went into this well-established guitar shop and asked them to put up these Marshall stacks. So the guy got a 100-watt stack and one speaker out, and Jimi said no. So he kept building this thing up – he had something like four or five speakers and two amps linked.

"Then Jimi started playing and all these other guys – the assistants in the shop and everybody else – just sort of went, 'What's that!' It was an incredible noise but it was incredibly dextrous guitar playing: skilful and exciting, really exciting. And I asked, 'Can he sing, can he sing as well?' and I think Chas Chandler said, 'Oh, he sings like a dream.'"[72] Whatever Hendrix thought of his own voice, Chandler never seemed to have any doubts.

The group flew out to France before even venturing a live performance in front of an audience in Britain. The debut of The Jimi Hendrix Experience would take place in France as support band for French star Johnny Hallyday. Mike Jeffery had arranged the permits and visas in lightning time. It would be a memorable few days.

live in paris
and london

Of all the places to make a debut, The Novelty Theatre-Cinema in Évreux would not have been on the list of many would-be rock stars. Évreux was a decidedly provincial if pretty French town, two-thirds of the way between Paris and Rouen, and it was here that The Jimi Hendrix Experience met up with the Johnny Hallyday tour on October 13th 1966. Hallyday was a huge and enduring star in France, guaranteed to pull the crowds wherever he appeared there. His support acts were usually intended to keep him as of-the-moment as possible.

H allyday had seen Hendrix in London, jamming with Brian Auger's Trinity. According to Auger's guitarist Vic Briggs this was at the Scotch Of St James club, while Hendrix's girlfriend Kathy Etchingham recalled sitting next to Hallyday watching Jimi at Le Kilt Club, a venue in Baker Street run by the same management as the Scotch. Hallyday knew Hendrix would add to the spectacle of his shows, which otherwise included Long Chris, and The Blackbirds.

Mitchell had mixed feelings about the short French tour. "You'd do these grubby little cinemas, right out in the sticks, much worse than the cinema tours you did in England, real flea-pits. [Hallyday] was treated like royalty, however – given the keys to the city, and all that. We also got treated very well."[1] The Experience closed the first half of the show. They had fifteen minutes to play their cover versions: 'Land of A Thousand Dances', 'Midnight Hour' (both originally by Wilson Pickett), 'Mercy Mercy', and 'Hey Joe'. Hendrix had left America to get away from this type of repertoire, so it was ironic that on his first tour with his new band his set was made up entirely of soul covers. He had little choice: according to Mitchell, the group only had about half a dozen songs rehearsed and ready at that point. There had been no time and little inclination to look into more wide-ranging, let alone original, repertoire.

The French must have thought they were seeing a new Anglo-American soul act, minus the horn section and dancing-girl singers. A music critic for a local paper seemed to think so. "Johnny

Bag O'Nails reception, London, November 25th 1966, in front of Paul McCartney, Eric Clapton and others.

Hallyday's latest discovery … was a singer and guitar player with bushy hair, a bad mixture of James Brown and Chuck Berry, who pulled a wry face on-stage for a quarter of an hour and sometimes played the guitar with his teeth."[2] At least Hendrix got noticed, although the critic thought he was describing The Blackbirds. Yet these few column inches of print were more than he'd ever received in the US. The audience reaction was equally unnerving at first. Experience drummer Mitch Mitchell, who had played on TV in France before, had some idea of what to expect, but for the debut of a new band it took some courage. For a start, he recalled later, French audiences don't applaud. "You'd finish a number and … silence. You'd think, 'Christ, what's this?' On the first few gigs they really didn't know how to take us and didn't really want to see us. But … we'd have been told pretty damn quickly if they really had hated us."[3]

The following night's concert was at the Cinema Rio in Nancy, a town in eastern France about a half-hour's drive from Strasbourg and the German border. Experience bassist Noel Redding claimed that this was the night he introduced the rest of the band and manager Chas Chandler to some new varieties of 'uppers' to help them through the night. No one remembers much about the gig so they must have worked. Mitchell recalled sharing some marijuana with the French musicians in Johnny Hallyday's horn section, which broke the ice and got the band accepted as part of the musical fraternity of the tour. Next they played Villerupt, a small town in north-eastern France on the border with Luxembourg, not far from Longwy. Passing on unnoticed but with three 15-minute spots behind them, they spent Monday October 17th hanging around at the Olympia in Paris, waiting for their soundcheck and rehearsal slot. The next day saw the final appearance of the tour. This time, the Experience played just three tunes in their 15 minutes: 'Killing Floor', 'Hey Joe' and 'Wild Thing'.

The Olympia concert was taped for broadcast by French radio – as was just about everything of any moment played at the Paris venue from the 1940s onwards – and copies have been in circulation among collectors for some years. Two tracks, 'Killing Floor' and 'Hey Joe', were given their commercial debut on the four-CD boxed set *The Jimi Hendrix Experience*, released in 2000. In his between-songs patter a nervous but happy Hendrix shows his appreciation to a relaxed, responsive crowd. The music they play sounds rushed and still in the process of being formed between the three musicians,

but it carries a characteristic edge that would distinguish the Experience as a unit for the next three years. The outstanding French photographer Jean-Pierre Leloir was present that night, taking the first known shots of the Experience in action. Leloir's pictures reveal Hendrix still with his Little Richard-like 'process' hairstyle, wearing a silk shirt and patterned trousers that would not have seemed out of place in a US soul band of the period. The tour proved a positive episode for the band, confirming that they worked well together and could instinctively hit a pleasing musical balance. Hendrix, ever the student of fame, studied Hallyday's stage act closely, picking up further valuable hints about how to make personal contact with an audience and take them along with him.

Back in London the following day, the band prepared for their first recording session, booked at the studios of De Lane Lea Music in London's Kingsway, a major north-south traffic thoroughfare that separates Covent Garden from Lincoln's Inn Fields. Chandler and Jeffery had decided on a strategy of piecemeal recordings until they'd nailed down a record contract and been paid advances. This meant that Chandler and his partner Mike Jeffrey enjoyed the advantage of owning the masters because they paid for them, although they still had to find the cash. The up-front outlay further encouraged Chandler's already finely-honed approach to recording: get in, lay it down, and get out again. After all, 'House Of The Rising Sun' had taken The Animals just 20 minutes to record, and it'd sold a million. Of course, The Animals had been a working band for a considerable time prior to that record, while the Experience had been a working band for just one week, but the general principle was hard to fault.

Chandler's natural flair for publicity was reinforced by the infinite pains he took to work out his tactics so they could achieve maximum exposure for whatever single came out. To his mind, if there was no unified image to present to the world then you were working at a disadvantage. It had worked for The Animals, The Beatles, The Rolling Stones and the rest, so it would work for the Experience. Following this logic, he tailored the three personalities to suit the stage act and the records he hoped they'd soon be making. Redding remembered, "[Chandler] spent hours grooming and creating 'HENDRIX, the PR man's dream'. We all had to refine our roles. Jimi would be macho man, Mitch the bouncy type, and I'd be the quiet one."[4] The scheme formalised one of the golden rules of running a successful pop group in any age: each member of a band, even on-stage, must have a clearly defined identity for the audience to consider. Thus millions of fans worldwide would prefer Paul to John, Brian to Mick, identify with Ringo because he was the ordinary bloke at the back, and so on. All this was new to Hendrix, who had never been more than a backing musician supporting the one and only star at the front of the stage. But he was lucky enough to have a shrewd amateur psychologist in Chandler who gave each musician an on-stage role that they could live with. Only with time and success would these roles become worn and contentious.

"Jimi would be macho man, Mitch the bouncy type, and I'd be the quiet one."

Noel Redding, on Chandler's role-casting

The first Experience recording session took place on October 23rd 1966, almost exactly a month after Hendrix had arrived in Britain. Just one tune was attempted: Tim Rose's slow version of 'Hey Joe' that both Chandler and Hendrix had admired that summer in New York City. The song itself, written by Billy Roberts, is in the key of E minor and uses about as basic a structure as it is possible to get. It has just one cycle of five chords – the most common chords in the repertoire of rock guitar, C, G, D, A, E – which repeat for the entire length of the performance. A simple but effective blues riff decorates the tonic chord and adds impetus after each cycle is completed. The only deviation comes with Hendrix's opening guitar runs and the two-bar unison chromatic runs by bass and guitar after the short, B.B. King-inflected guitar solo. Even though the song's basic building-blocks are simple, there are numerous modifications and inversions to keep things interesting. Hendrix changes the chord voicings on his guitar, for example, and there is a continual suggestion of the minor key from the parts that the three-voice female backing chorus are given to sing. In addition, Mitchell interprets his role quite freely, bringing fills and emphases in unexpected places.

But it is the vocal performance upon which the whole song hangs – perhaps surprisingly, given the difficulties in deciding who should take care of lead vocals for the new band. Hendrix brings to his telling of the story of Joe an infinite variety of vocal slurs, hesitations and speech-like moments. His relaxed delivery makes listeners feel as though they are overhearing a conversation in a bar somewhere in America. Hendrix acts the parts very convincingly, with an appropriate climax towards the end where Joe vows: "They ain't gonna hang me / They ain't gonna put a rope around me." For many fans who bought the single on its release, this statement of freedom defined Hendrix's initial and enduring appeal as the outsider who would win against the odds. Hendrix may not have been a confident singer or even one with much of a range, but he had the gift of intimacy with his audience such as few singers possess. In that, at least, he was Dylan's peer.

In his later autobiography Redding remembered this first recording session as a difficult one, with 'Hey Joe' needing many takes before the band could capture the mood they wanted. Mitchell recalled the job being done quickly. Although a few takes were taped, he thought it was the first that was eventually used: there simply wasn't the budget to spend on endless recording.[5] Chandler's recollection of this first session chimes with Mitchell's, though a reported altercation with Hendrix probably accounts for Redding's feeling that it had been tricky. The band was now equipped with Marshall amps and used them with a purpose: "He was getting uptight because he wanted to record it louder and louder," Chandler recalled. "We just couldn't get it onto the tape because it was too loud, and he threw a tantrum."[6] This was Hendrix's first recording session as a leader and he was largely ignorant of the way in which studios functioned, let alone their limitations. Hendrix considered the argument as a straightforward battle of egos between himself and his producer. In the event, producer Chandler won by offering Hendrix his passport and visa, freshly acquired that day. "I said, 'Well, fuck off then.'"[7] Chandler's bluff was not called.

Recording at De Lane Lea studio, London, 1966.

Hendrix laughed instead and went for a compromise. The backing track was quickly finished. At this time, Kathy Etchingham recalled, Hendrix was still willing to consider – or at least to seem to consider – other people's opinions, especially his manager's. "He allowed Chas to believe he was going along with his ideas, but if there was one thing Jimi hated, it was being told what to do, whether it was by a manager, an audience or a girlfriend, and if he was forced into an option he tended to do the opposite. As he became more successful this character trait grew to be more of a problem."[8]

For the B-side of the planned single Hendrix suggested one of the covers they were currently playing, but Chandler quickly scotched that idea. Having

sunk his own money into the record, he was not going to hand over publishing royalties to a third party. He told Hendrix to come up with a song quickly. That same evening, October 24th, Jimi knocked out 'Stone Free', a paean to freedom and the gypsy life, but for the moment nothing was recorded. Chandler had hit a wall over the proposed deal with Decca, the record company that he and Hendrix favoured. Not for the first time, Decca didn't like what it saw (or heard) when it looked a gift horse in the mouth. "The A&R man who turned it down," Chandler remembered wryly, "told me 'I don't think he's got anything.'"[9] Without a deal and with no prospect of being picking up a major label, Hendrix and Chandler turned back to Kit Lambert and Chris Stamp. Lambert and Stamp had been managing The Who from the beginning of the band's success and were looking to broaden their business by starting an independent record label. Such operations had been common in the US for decades but had not been part of the UK rock and pop scene, which was largely dominated by the major companies such as Decca, Pye, the EMI group of labels (Columbia, Parlophone, and His Master's Voice were best known in pop circles), plus CBS and RCA, two giant US labels that had distribution in Britain. There was also the Philips/Polydor/Deutsche Grammophon group, but this had only been a presence on the pop scene for a couple of years and had some distance to make up with the other majors.

In the latter part of 1966 a few independents started up, including Stones manager Andrew Loog Oldham's Immediate and Chris Blackwell's Island labels. Stamp and Lambert followed, believing that their more imaginative and attuned approach to the new music being created in Britain could deliver major new stars and outstanding music. What they needed to do was to convince artists and managers that they were a good bet, as well as persuade one of the major companies to inject capital, assist with record-pressing and provide distribution. A big disadvantage for the duo was that, with little capital themselves, they could not afford lavish publicity campaigns or pay large advance sums to their signings. For this reason they had looked into the possibility of receiving funding from a major. After a hectic round of meetings and discussions they had a positive response from Polydor UK. The company's marketing director at the time was Alan Bates, a man still very active in the recording industry today and with a fine track record of his own over the years. He remembers Polydor eventually agreeing to finance the start-up of Track "to the tune of £250,000, as I recall: which was a considerable amount of money in those days".[10] Bates felt that Polydor, which until recently had been called Deutsche Grammophon in Britain and was something of a fledgling on the UK pop scene, "saw people such as Stamp and Lambert as a way of getting quickly involved in what was happening", especially at the cutting edge of pop, somewhere the two men knew well in late 1966.

With Decca out of the picture and little interest elsewhere, Chandler, Jeffery and Hendrix became convinced that they should go with Lambert and Stamp's Track Records, soon to be underpinned by the Polydor money. In the final days of October 1966 they signed a deal that gave Lambert and Stamp exclusive use in the UK of recordings produced by the Hendrix/Chandler team for Yameta Productions, the holding company to which the Experience were all signed. On Wednesday November 2nd, with the money from Track's advance now in the bank, the Experience went back into De Lane Lea studios and cut 'Stone Free' in one session to complete their first 45rpm single. With events overtaking them, Lambert and Stamp eventually arranged for Polydor to release the record on its own label while Track was properly formulated. Unsure initially about this idea, the larger company reluctantly agreed. The single was assigned a release date of Friday December 16th, giving Chandler, Stamp and Lambert just over a month to co-ordinate their publicity campaigns. They knew they had a killer single – but they also knew that plenty of killer singles failed every week in the music business due to inept campaigns, poor timing or sheer bad luck.

'Stone Free', a modified blues, was a rough composition that nevertheless captures a real sense of burgeoning excitement through its structure and the band's playing. The recorded performance has drama, good light and shade and a storytelling sensibility that leads the listener through the song stage by stage in a state of mounting excitement. The form is intro/verse/pre-chorus/chorus/interlude/verse/pre-chorus/chorus/guitar-solo/chorus/outro. The tune starts in the key of E minor, using one of Hendrix's favourite guitar chords, an augmented 9th, to add flavour to the mix, before modulating to D for the chorus. The beat is close to a boogaloo, but the group interprets it very freely, with Mitchell's cowbell rhythm stressing each beat, making it swagger, while his bass-drum pattern accentuates the blues-based riff variations of Hendrix and Redding. As with 'Hey Joe', Hendrix chooses an almost conversational delivery for the melody of 'Stone Free', toying with blues intervals in the way that John Lee Hooker would build a blues phrase rather than delivering any defined melodic pattern. This is also surprisingly close to the angle Otis Redding was using on his songs at the time – especially in the chorus, with its driving on-beat pulse, and the little whoops and hollers that were Otis's trademark and which keep the listener's heart beating fast.

Noel Redding's bass maintains a powerful rhythmic drive, especially in the chorus where he uses a double-stop ostinato, and Mitchell constantly underlines Hendrix's vocals and guitar parts in dramatic fashion. Even after just a month playing together, this band is uncannily able to anticipate and support each other's musical moves. Considering their well-documented reluctance to rehearse much more than the absolute minimum, this was more than simple coincidence or luck. It demonstrates a meeting and sharing of talents on a par with the dynamic telepathy of Cream, who were releasing their first singles at this time.

'Stone Free' ends with a nicely unanticipated shift to an F5 chord and a fade that sounds like the Lone Ranger riding into the distance. It's a rough and ready recording, evident for example on the introduction to Hendrix's guitar solo where there is a pause at the end of the chorus and a sustained chord: as it hangs in the air, its tone changes as Hendrix switches on his fuzz-box. Then he swoops in with his slashing solo using that same tone. Six months later, such bare threads would never have been left showing on a Hendrix record. The solo itself, across a bass riff in A, is exciting but not particularly distinguished by Hendrix's standards. It is as if he's determined to impress by flash and sound rather than ideas, playing patterns that are frantic but hardly ingenious. Only the razor-sharp tone and the use of sustain arrests the listener and demands attention. In total, 'Stone Free' is a successful B-side by a group finding its feet very quickly indeed. It quickly became a counterculture anthem, with its lyrics praising the footloose and fancy-free life. That this was not mere posturing from Hendrix, as he stressed in a number of interviews. He told Val Wilmer: "I stay one or two months in a place and then I must have a change. ... I couldn't even think of a place where I'd like to live for the rest of my life. I just get so restless, man – I might leave right away even if I don't have any money."[11]

Mitch Mitchell, Jimi Hendrix, Noel Redding; London 1966.

It's worth stressing today just how original and fresh this music sounded in late 1966. Hendrix himself was unique in his instrumental and vocal delivery, but as a band the Experience were doing things that no other group could get close to, including Cream. The audaciousness of Mitchell's fills and changes of rhythmic emphases had no precedent, even in his own playing with previous groups. Hendrix had never played with a drummer like Mitchell, who fused the alert responses and musical dialogues of a jazz drummer with the heavy stressing of the snare beat that was at the core of every competent rock drummer's repertoire. With such dynamism at the core of the band's playing, Redding – who has often been derided in hindsight – provided an essential anchor, but he did not follow the conventional values of rock bassists who usually provided a strong emphasis of the beat through simple patterns in the instrument's bottom register. Redding preferred to alternate between such simple patterns, often played in the mid-register, and a bassline that functioned as more of a harmonic guideline than a simple bottom-end riff, in the manner of a rhythm guitarist or jazz bassist. If Mitchell was Hendrix's Elvin Jones, then Redding was his Jimmy Garrison. As for what Hendrix himself was doing on 'Stone Free', Jeff Beck said many years later: "It's got bits of Buddy Guy; it sounds like Les Paul in places. Jimi does every trick in the book and nails it all together so tight that you can't even see the joints."[12] Presumably when Beck referred to Les Paul he meant the unexpected sweetness of Hendrix's guitar playing behind the "got to, got to, got to ..." vocal refrain, rather than the jagged solo.

After the group completed 'Stone Free' they played three days at a venue in Munich – their first appearance in Germany – to a generally enthusiastic welcome. Arriving back in London in the middle of November, Hendrix continued to work on new original material as the publicity machine gathered pace. Much effort went into mounting a promotional appearance at the Bag O'Nails, a club in Kingly Street in London's Soho, just east of Regent Street and a stone's throw from the fashion centre of Carnaby Street. By this time the Experience had recruited Gerry Stickells, a drinking-mate of Noel Redding's, as road manager and general factotum for the band. It was a wise move: Stickells proved to be one of the most loyal and resourceful of all the people employed in a support role for the guitarist.

In late November they recorded 'Love Or Confusion', a piece with a perfect balance between almost unbearable build-ups of tension and constant dynamic devices to provide temporary relief. It is also the first of Hendrix's compositions where he constructs a complete accompaniment from multiple overdubs instead of relying on sheer sonic power and cutting-edge sound to bring to life a riff or a section of a song. There is a constant dialogue between all the guitar parts, the bass patterns and the drums, all of it intimately connected to the direction in which Hendrix takes his vocal line. The listener is continually swapping attention from one part to another as the piece tells its story through statement and sympathetic interjection. Given the turbulent subject-matter of the lyrics, this is an entirely apt musical translation.

The guitar solo on 'Love Or Confusion' shows a different side of Hendrix's artistry compared to that on his first two studio efforts. Recorded a couple of weeks before Cream's 'I Feel Free' was issued, it shows Hendrix pursuing a melodic direction with the aid of fuzz-box sustain not far removed from the type of playing Clapton would reveal on that new single. Both men take advantage of 'raga-rock', introduced at the end of 1965 by George Harrison's sitar work on 'Norwegian Wood' and a current rage in 1966 (even The Rolling Stones had endorsed the style with 'Paint It Black' in May). The inevitable transfer of the sitar's snaky melodicism to the electric guitar had come with George Harrison's playing on The Beatles' *Revolver*. That album, released in

August, contained not only the sitar-laden 'Love You To' but also the more closely relevant and very beautiful sitar-influenced guitar playing of 'I'm Only Sleeping', backwards tapes and all. This was a tune Hendrix would only just have picked up on: he could not have heard it in the US because it was left off the Capitol America edition of *Revolver*, the last Beatles album to be doctored in this way by EMI's US arm.

Hendrix and Clapton reveal their different improvisational methods as they absorb this new influence. For his 'I Feel Free' solo Clapton concentrates on crafting a number of restatements of his original melodic phrase during the opening bars, most of them rhythmically conservative and symmetrical in shape, then finishes up with a sweeping blues-based line that is much longer than anything so far in the solo, resolving the listener's expectations in what is a very 'up' song with ecstatic lyrics. From the start of his solo on 'Love Or Confusion', Hendrix is much more rhythmically adventurous than Clapton, bringing triplets, grace notes and trills into a long opening melodic line that envelops more than half the solo's length before pausing. It is an audacious thing to do, but Hendrix plays with assurance and all his customary fire. The solo ends with a slight cooling of the emotional tension, in line with the more turbulent and questioning nature of the song. Often overlooked in favour of the more spectacular triumphs included on Hendrix's first album, 'Love Or Confusion' is a little masterpiece.

The following day The Jimi Hendrix Experience played at their reception at the Bag O'Nails, where the combined efforts of Chandler and his helpers ensured an enviably large turnout, including key members of British rock's meritocracy – Paul McCartney, Mick Jagger, Jeff Beck, Pete Townshend, Brian Jones, Eric Clapton, Jimmy Page, and John Lennon. Kevin Ayers, who was in attendance, remembers an air of stunned disbelief: "All the stars were there and I heard serious comments, you know: 'shit', 'Jesus', 'damn' and other words worse than that!"[13] Yet people were prepared to acknowledge overwhelming talent when it was thrust down their throats in this fashion. As Jagger said much later, they all felt that they'd discovered Hendrix and wanted to bring this fabulous musician to the attention of the world. "He came

out of nowhere and we just adopted him 'cause he was great," said Jagger. "He was ours, y'know?"[14] Such opinions helped immeasurably in the short term to get the group's name out into the world as the stars began telling the British music media that Hendrix was something special who was about to happen in a big way. That couldn't come soon enough for the band; money remained tight and work was scarce. Mitchell resorted to doing jobs on the side to keep money coming in, occasionally to the detriment of band rehearsals. This infuriated both Chandler and Hendrix to the point where they actually considered throwing him out.

During this limbo period Hendrix relied financially on Chandler, and Chandler in turn was feeling the squeeze. As Kathy Etchingham explained, "Chas … didn't have the money to launch an act quickly. Pop groups did not make huge sums at the time unless they wrote their own material, and The Animals had run into considerable financial problems. Even in those pre-video days it was expensive to launch a new act. You needed to be able to hire studios and backing musicians and you needed to pay the act enough to live on while you waited for the deals to come and the money to roll in. Even our modest daily expenses were becoming more than Chas could afford."[15] All those involved needed the band to get out and start working in order to pull in some cash.

Hendrix had never been interviewed during his early US career, and the Bag O'Nails launch provided him with his first, published in *Record Mirror*. The music paper's piece, headed "Mr Phenomenon!", came out on December 10th, just one week before the release of 'Hey Joe'. "Now hear this," exclaimed Peter Jones, "and kindly hear it good! Are you one of those fans who think there's nothing much happening on the pop scene? … Then we want to bring your attention to a new artist, a new star-in-the-making, who we predict is going to whirl round the business like a tornado. Name: Jimi Hendrix. Occupation: guitarist-singer-composer-showman-dervish-original. His group, just three-strong: The Jimi Hendrix Experience. [*Mersey Beat* newspaper founder] Bill Harry and I dropped in at the Bag O'Nails in Kingly Street to hear the trio working out for the benefit of Press and Bookers. An

The Jimi Hendrix Experience at BBC Lime Grove studio (Area C), London, December 29th 1966, performing their first single, 'Hey Joe', for the TV chart show *Top Of The Pops*.

astounded Harry muttered, 'Is that full, big, blasting, swinging sound really being created by only three people?' It was, with the aid of a mountain of equipment."[16]

Jones went on to quote from his interview with Hendrix and Chandler. Jimi stressed the potential of his group. "We don't want to be classed in any category," he said. "If it must have a tag, I'd like it to be called 'Free Feeling'.

"A singer and guitar player with bushy hair, a bad mixture of James Brown and Chuck Berry, who pulled a wry face on-stage for a quarter of an hour and sometimes played the guitar with his teeth."

Jimi Hendrix Experience, first review

It's a mixture of rock, freak-out, blues and rave music."[17] Chandler had some worthwhile points of his own to make, in his typically blunt way. "We brought him over, auditioned to find the right musicians to follow his style, and gave the three of them a chance to find their feet on the Continent. ... You just can't get bored with him. It's the first time I've seen such a brilliant musician who can put on such a brilliant visual performance. He has this unique stage appeal. ... We want to stick with just the two musicians working with him. Noel and Mitch follow his every mood – if we got even one more it would spoil the understanding. Make it slower."[18] November 1966 closed with Hendrix celebrating his 24th birthday on Sunday 27th.

In those comments to *Record Mirror*, Chandler was addressing one of Kit Lambert's few initial concerns when he'd first seen Hendrix – that he was simply too good ever to make it big, and that his music would remain overly complex for the majority of fans to grasp quickly. Chandler was convinced that this would be no problem because Hendrix, in addition to his musical brilliance, wanted to communicate to every audience and had the kind of charisma possessed only by an élite few. It seemed that the writers attending the press launch agreed. Tony Hall, in his column for *Record Mirror* in that same issue, had an equally positive opinion. "Remember the name Jimi Hendrix. ... I saw him at the Scotch Of St James one night recently. A most striking visual performer. And a helluva blues player and singer. He even plays guitar with his lips or elbow. But I thought he'd be difficult to record. So Chas took him in the studio. The result is quite the funkiest rhythm feel I've ever heard in this country. Very Atlantic-ish. It was so exciting to hear how Hendrix had inspired the musicians with him. Especially Georgie Fame's drummer. Terrific."[19]

December was spent in and around London. Hendrix and Etchingham moved from the Carlton Towers hotel on Bayswater Road to Ringo Starr's flat at 34 Montagu Square in Marylebone, just north of Marble Arch, sharing it with Chandler and his girlfriend. The move brought them closer to London's West End and imposed upon them a faint semblance of domestic living. The Experience picked up a spattering of gigs around the capital, from The Ricky Tick in west London's Hounslow to The Upper Cut in Forest Gate, part of the East End. They even ventured as far as Southampton, on the coast some 80 miles to the south-west of London. But the highlights of the month came on Tuesday December 13th, with their first appearance on television, on ITV's

pop chart show *Ready Steady Go!*, and some further studio recordings the same evening, followed three days later by the release of the first single, 'Hey Joe' / 'Stone Free'. The early TV outing came through Lambert and Stamp at Track Records. They had excellent connections with the television chart shows and used them to good effect as soon as the deal for 'Hey Joe' was done. This was no altruistic gesture: they were trying to show Polydor Records not only that they could pick talent but that they had the industry clout to justify the financial backing Polydor were committing to. 'Hey Joe', labelled "a Yameta production", came out on the Polydor label as an interim arrangement – Track Records was simply not far enough advanced to be the label that released this first Jimi Hendrix Experience effort.

Hendrix would have enjoyed the irony of appearing on the same TV show as The Troggs, whose 'Wild Thing' had been one of the summer's biggest surprise hits. It was a song Hendrix would make an integral part of his live act. Other artists appearing on *RSG!* that night included The Merseybeats and The Escorts, BritBeat bands with home hits that never translated fully to overseas markets. Also present was a young Marc Bolan, debuting on the show with his third single, 'Hippy Gumbo'. As he told PR man and journalist Keith Altham in 1970, "It was Jimi's first appearance too. I took one look at what he was doing and it affected me so badly I went into a rapid decline."[20] Bolan revived his spirits by joining John's Children and writing 'Desdemona' for them, a record banned by the BBC for the line "Lift up your skirts and fly". Some things never change.

After taping the TV-show spot, the Experience went into CBS studios in Bond Street, central London to record 'Foxy Lady', 'Red House' and an early version of 'Third Stone From The Sun'. These three pieces suggest something of a change in recording strategy. 'Foxy Lady' and 'Red House' could easily be reckoned as A and B sides respectively of a potential second single, but the ambitious 'Third Stone From The Sun' could only have been considered as an album track. The very opening of 'Foxy Lady' – used eventually to kick off the original UK release of the *Are You Experienced* LP – demonstrates Hendrix's new obsession with sound and his absolute control of his instrument. It is like a statement of artistic intent for his entire career. Tapping the neck and fingering the strings onto the fretboard to generate feedback from his amp, precisely judged to give out the upper harmonics of the song's opening chord, he gives a mesmerising demonstration of his complete mastery of the guitar's electric sound production.

Many people, from Linda Keith onwards, have commented on the large size of Hendrix's hands and the facility they gave him, but later David Lee Roth's bassist Billy Sheehan put it into a technical perspective. "I think it was the strength of Jimi's hands that made him so great. It allowed him full control of the guitar, to derive his sounds right from the wood and steel. Ironically, for such an electric player, Jimi never seemed to rely on amplification tricks. The real magic was in his fingers that took command of his hands, the pick and strings, the amp and speaker."[21] Mike Bloomfield expanded on this. "What really did it to him was early Muddy Waters and John Lee Hooker records – that early electric music where the guitar was hugely amplified, and boosted by the studio to give it the effect of more presence than it actually had. He knew that stuff backwards."[22] Bloomfield also specified Hendrix's precise control of every physical aspect of his guitar. "I have never heard a sound on a Hendrix record that I have not seen him create in front of my eyes. ... Somehow, by tapping the back of his guitar neck – which he constantly did – and by using the [vibrato] bar, Jimi could control feedback. You would hear a rumbling start – he knew which note would feed back and what harmonic he was shooting for, and then he controlled it. ... He was listening for such things and I believe he heard them on the English records, especially by The Yardbirds and Jeff Beck. He was very modest. He never said he took it further than the Yardbirds."[23]

Perhaps not, but Hendrix certainly used volume and feedback for a very individual purpose. On 'Foxy Lady', once into the tune proper, he uses an overdriven amplifier to give an extreme cutting edge to his sound in addition to a fuzz-box tone and string manipulation. Those chords howl out the simple, slinky message of the lyrics. Matched precisely by drums and bass, with Mitchell providing expert drum fills at crucial moments, Hendrix creates such a thrilling soundscape that it really doesn't matter who he is addressing in his singing: the intention is perfectly clear from the instruments alone. The tune's construction is extremely simple, based on chord progressions used many times before and after in rock and blues. But as Mahogany Rush guitarist Frank Marino explained later, that simplicity provided the perfect platform for Hendrix to unveil his musical alchemy. "You can see how really simple the stuff is. It's rhythm and blues, raw and with fuzz-tones and stuff. ... From a guitar player's point of view, it's easy enough to play those kind of chops [or techniques]. The thing about Hendrix was the uniqueness of the chops: they're not technically hard to do, it's just that nobody thinks of doing them that way. If a guitar player analysed his lines, he'd see that Hendrix plays each one just a little bit differently from the norm. He doesn't do the habitual licks, or if he does he changes a note here and there."[24]

In the guitar solo Hendrix recorded for 'Foxy Lady' – the fourth he'd put down on tape since arriving in England – he combines aspects of the first three ('Hey Joe', 'Stone Free' and 'Love Or Confusion'). He casts the whole solo in the blues vernacular, using bent notes and glisses, or slides, between notes primarily within blues or pentatonic scales. To that he adds the new melodicism he had been hearing on recent British rock records, a style that helped to give him a complete and mature approach to improvising. Moving between middle and high registers, and using extreme sustain to give his melodic construction an unlimited flowing lyricism, he brings the same ecstatic emotion to his bluesy playing that B.B. King could achieve at his best. But

First British TV, performing 'Hey Joe' on the ITV show *Ready Steady Go!*, December 13th 1966.

Hendrix does it in a different, non-traditional context and uses such rhythmic daring in his asymmetry of phrase as to take the listener's breath away. This is not entertainment: it is pure burning desire filtered through a musical instrument. Was there a model for 'Foxy Lady'? Not exactly, but Hendrix possibly drew a lesson from 'Wild Thing', a tune primordial in its simplicity and focused on its straightforward declamatory vocal. The record had excited him for the past six months.

Models abound for the other song released from that session – the slow blues, 'Red House' – because it is one of the most traditional in sound and form of all his official recordings. But again, Hendrix takes a traditional form and injects so much of his own vision as to make it an intensely personal – and highly contemporary – creation. Hendrix's raw and simple approach to 'Red House', just adding a few production mannerisms, set it aside from much of what was being recorded by his blues contemporaries in Chicago and elsewhere by 1966. The shape of contemporary blues was personified as much by The Butterfield Blues Band and the various Kings or the Buddy Guy recordings of the day as by the generation that Hendrix had listened to so intensely. 'Red House' is the blues as Muddy Waters, Lightnin' Hopkins and their peers would have played it in the late 1940s and early '50s – raw, simple and sparse, with a nice turn of irony in the lyric. But Hendrix adds a remarkably sophisticated blues conception in his guitar accompaniment and solo, along with the high-octane sounds always associated with him.

One of the principal devices that Hendrix took over from his models was the close approximation of the human voice in his playing. In this December 'Red House' solo he offers a literal version of the old phrase "screamin' and hollerin' the blues", scooping and bending his phrases to maximum expressive effect. There is also a wonderful mixing of repetition with variation, simplicity with extreme sophistication, both in what he chooses to play and how he chooses to connect it all together. It is as if some supreme conversationalist picked you specially as the listener for his story. 'Red House' is another little masterpiece, its roots and subject matter seeming to stretch back to summer 1966 and Hendrix's time with Linda Keith in Manhattan. It provided a template for all the slow blues he would play for the rest of his career. Hendrix would record a studio remake of 'Red House' the following March, a version of which would be the first released in the US, but this December 1966 effort is by common consent the definitive studio rendition.

Redding recalled that as the release date for 'Hey Joe' approached there were constant post-gig discussions with Chandler during the first half of December, picking over the performances and working on the finer points of presentation.[25] Impromptu gestures from a particular evening were built into a progressively more formidable stage act. The Experience were now working as recording partners with Lambert and Stamp, the team that had The Who under management contract, and so members of both bands met casually on a number of occasions and the different managers could plan ways of intensifying each group's dynamic act without diluting individuality. Hendrix probably picked up ideas about stage drama and the wilful destruction of equipment to create a new type of spectacle as he watched The Who and talked to their managers during the course of this month: The Who and The Move had both been smashing things on-stage for some time now. Certainly Hendrix's stage act was becoming wilder rather than calming down. This fitted with the character that each member of the Experience was supposed to be projecting and which PR man Keith Altham was now busily selling to the media upon instruction from Hendrix's management. Besides, it was fun at first, as Pete Townshend suggested at the time in an interview about The Who's smash-'em-up act. "We've got to the stage when we end the night by destroying everything – which is expensive. I think in pop, though, it's good because it has a big impact and, personally, we find it a great laugh."[26]

With the release of 'Hey Joe' and its attendant hype, Hendrix became the subject of a series of interviews. Some show him moving on from what that single represented, even before it had become a hit. He was eager to progress to his own material and assert his own musical character, even while one typical reviewer was rating his first single as "the most genuinely soulful record ever made in Britain. Jimi has really inspired the other two musicians. Dig the way the bass comes through. The best record Polydor has issued. A must".[27] With the help of the *Ready Steady Go!* spot and a further appearance on *Top Of The Pops* on December 29th, 'Hey Joe' entered the charts, peaking at number six as the year came to a close. The Jimi Hendrix Experience finished 1966 with a gig in Folkestone, Kent – Noel Redding's home town – and the band stayed at Redding's mother's house to bring in the new year. By then, Hendrix had already written what would become his second single. It was called 'Purple Haze'.

get experienced

Four days into the new year of 1967, the Experience appeared at the Bromel Club venue in a hotel in Bromley, a south-eastern suburb of London. Hendrix was interviewed there by Richard Green for Record Mirror and his piece appeared in the January 14th edition. Green reported Hendrix's uncharacteristically patronising ideas about how little the British knew about the blues. "My main thing is the blues," Jimi said, "but people like Elmore James and a few others the people here wouldn't know."

Hendrix lost no time in distancing himself from the current single, 'Hey Joe', claiming: "That record isn't us. The next one's gonna be different. We're working on an LP which will mainly be our stuff."[1] Chandler must have loved him for that one, with the single then high in the charts. However, Hendrix was in the midst of a writing spree, converting new ideas into songs at a prodigious rate now that the coming album offered a guaranteed outlet. Some of these ideas may well have had roots in lyrics and other writings he'd started in New York the previous year, while some of the musical devices he used as building bricks for the tunes could have been based on riffs and chord sequences from back in Greenwich Village that summer. But until now there had been no motivation to bother completing anything, so he had achieved little of worth. And he knew that.

Now it was very different: he had a keen audience for anything he presented on stage or in the studio. In Noel Redding, Mitch Mitchell and Chas Chandler he had people willing to work hard to bring the songs to their best possible conclusion. Mitchell felt that some earlier ideas were being re-crafted and developed for the new band. "I think he brought over a scrapbook with ideas and some of those got translated into proper songs, or at least sketches for songs that we worked out in the studio."[2] This last point is important in grasping the full extent of the metamorphosis from Jimmy Hendrix in the Village to Jimi Hendrix in London. He was now working with musicians who – for whatever reason, including sheer laziness, according to Redding – resented rehearsing and tried to get things out of the way as quickly as possible.

What made the Experience different from Hendrix's New York colleagues, indeed lazy bands the world over, was that they took his sketches and ideas and, with Hendrix guiding them, turned them into

The Jimi Hendrix Experience (left), on-stage at the Marquee club in central London, March 2nd 1967, filming for German TV.

manifestos for musical change. Looking at the constituents of the band, it is truly remarkable that it fast became so good and so creative. It must have surprised Hendrix as much as it did Chandler and British music fans. After all, the hiring process and the rehearsals had been haphazard, the musicians that Hendrix ended up with hardly coming from illustrious headlining careers in the industry.

"Hey Joe' isn't us. The next one's gonna be different. We're working on an LP which will mainly be our stuff."

Jimi Hendrix

Yet somehow Hendrix had chosen two musicians who had imaginations of their own and who could respond to him in ways that were not stereotyped. They brought a collective sense of creativity to music that would have been beyond 99 percent of rock or R&B or soul players on either side of the Atlantic at that time. In the process they helped to redefine the roles of guitar, bass and drums in rock as much as the individual members of Cream were doing at the same time. Their more perceptive peers in Britain recognised this. Pete Townshend said that January: "There are two groups at the moment which I like very much – the Cream and The Jimi Hendrix Experience. In a way they're a bit alike in that they both have fantastic guitarists and drummers. They're also alike in that they both have tremendous records out at the moment, and they are both laying down some great stuff – what more can anyone want?"[3]

These qualities came across particularly well in the studio, as shown on the next single, 'Purple Haze', begun on January 11th, the same day that Hendrix signed with Kit Lambert and Chris Stamp's new label, Track Records. The song's subject matter was extrapolated from the science fiction stories that Hendrix and Chandler both enthused over: there is a picture of Hendrix in his London flat at this time reading a paperback of Penguin science fiction. The first draft of lyrics for the new piece, starting: "Purple haze – Jesus saves…", were long and discursive and thus far too extended for the three-minute singles of early 1967, but with Chandler's help and advice Hendrix pared them down to manageable dimensions. While in consequence they may have lost many levels of meaning from the original script, they were now simple, focused and striking. They also allowed the music to tell the larger story. Poised effectively between the twin intoxicants of drugs and desire, they could be interpreted to the listener's taste, but there was no mistaking the basic message of supercharged delight. The recording was characteristically quick. "Hendrix came in and kind of hummed us the riff and showed Noel the chords and the changes," Mitchell remembered. "I listened to it and we went, 'OK, let's do it.' We got it on the third take as I recall."[4]

As with his other early songs, Hendrix went to some trouble to come up with an arresting introduction. This time he started the song with two bars of a repeated tritone interval on bass and guitar (E and A-sharp) that gives an urgent, menacing sound from the outset. This interval had long been associated in western music with illegal and nefarious pursuits and feelings, and was reputedly banned from use in religious music during the Renaissance and for some time afterwards. In the early Baroque period in western music 'the devil's interval', as it became known, was exploited for its notoriety by composers and virtuosi, shocking and thrilling audiences with its

daring usage. In the early 20th century it underwent a complete transformation in importance as a building-block for composition as Arnold Schoenberg developed his 12-tone theories. He made the tritone interval of fundamental importance to his music because it lay exactly in the middle of the 12 tones between octaves. Hendrix knew nothing of this history, but was keenly aware of the emotional effect the interval conveyed, as were many others of his generation. In 1965, teenage drummer Tony Williams had recorded 'From Before' on his album *Spring* with a first section that consists entirely of two saxophonists, Wayne Shorter and Sam Rivers, repeatedly playing the tritone interval in octaves.

With 'Purple Haze', after the startling two-bar tritone intro, the bass maintains a pedal E while Hendrix plays a simple but hypnotically tuneful guitar riff which is perhaps even more famous than his vocal line. Again the song is simplicity itself, consisting of just three chords in the verse, with a bassline hovering around G and E that repeats constantly under the blues-drenched vocal line, which is not so much sung as hoarsely shouted. The intensity is terrific, the churning drums further whipping up the emotions through a series of rolls and fills that punctuate the riffs and vocals.

The guitar solo arrives as something of a release rather than a further racking up of the atmosphere. Hendrix uses an Octavia effect on his guitar: this adds an identical line to what is being played, only an octave above. (The Selmer Varitone pickup and amplifier had been marketed the year before for brass players, adding a sub-octave below the line being played.) The Octavia effect brings a brilliance to Hendrix's spiralling melodies as he gives the impression that the guitar notes are flying off into the ether. This is perfectly in character with the song's lyrics, of course.

'Purple Haze' had a powerful impact on many guitarists at the time, as John Scofield explained in a recent interview. "When I first started to play guitar – this was before Hendrix – there was a chord known as the 'Hold It' chord, an E sharp 9. It was based on a … Bill Doggett song from the 1950s. You can hear [that chord] on 'Purple Haze'. So the 'Hold It' chord became the Jimi Hendrix chord … . Now, that's a big influence right there."[5] The Doggett song was a 1958 hit single and the title track of Doggett's major LP release for that year. There is a further link between the two in the shape of Henry Mancini's brooding theme tune for the late-1950s TV show *Peter Gunn*. Duane Eddy and Lee Hazlewood fashioned it into a downright menacing rock anthem and made it a hit. An early Hendrix favourite, it uses the devil's interval in the verse. The melody, raspingly delivered by Jim Horn's sax, has a bridge section that Hendrix seems to have used as a starting-point for his famous 'Purple Haze' guitar riff.

"We still had nights when the audience hated us and every note we played."

Noel Redding

The Experience recorded the B-side of 'Purple Haze' on the same day. '51st Anniversary' was a curious song set up as a monologue from the singer to an un-named 17-year-old girl. The singer attempts to persuade the girl that it's too early for them to get married and settle down and he cites a number reasons. Given a medium tempo and a simple chord sequence, always resolving to the tonic B major, the piece features two main sections and a brief connecting passage (bridge), carrying the only vocal line that comes close to a hook: "I'm gonna change your mind." Hendrix concentrates on the verbal message of the song, leaving no time for even the briefest of solos. This decision is sound, for the tune retains a close unity as it sticks to the narrative. The lack of variety is a plus, not a defect.

He prevents the listener's attention wandering by deploying a number of embellishments such as substitute riffs and other variations, sometimes played in unison between bass and guitar and sometimes using the two instruments separately. Mitchell's drums are intelligently varied from verse to verse, with his elaborations on the "So you … want to be married" bridge adding much to the urgent atmosphere. As with so many early Hendrix recordings, there is an unexpected twist at the end where the band shifts to G. Over a repeated guitar figure, Hendrix terminates the talking and, after inhaling a large quantity of unidentified smoke, asks to be allowed to "get back in my … groove". The track fades appropriately. On its release as The Jimi Hendrix Experience's second single in March, 'Purple Haze' was recognised instantly as the wildest and most frenetic 45rpm disc made to date, eclipsing even The Who's 'My Generation' and 'Substitute', 'Mystic Eyes' by Them or 'Happenings Ten Years' Time Ago' by The Yardbirds.

The same session that provided the basic track for 'Purple Haze' was also responsible for backing tracks for 'Third Stone From The Sun' and Hendrix's first

Mitch Mitchell, Jimi Hendrix, Noel Redding in Hamburg, Germany, March 1967.

worried either of us much; I guess we had both listened to enough of them throughout our childhoods not to take them too seriously. We could be shouting and screaming one moment and forgetting about the whole thing the next. … Both of us operated on very short fuses and neither of us was ever willing to climb down so we could only end them by one or other of us storming off – usually me." On January 9th they rowed about Etchingham's cooking – a frequent source of friction at the time. After dispatching a few plates in his direction, she stormed out. "He followed, trying to persuade me to come back, but I refused to listen. I found a taxi and jumped in, and without letting Jimi hear told the driver to take me to Angie and Eric [Burdon]'s place in Jermyn Street. When I returned the next day, having cooled down, I asked him what he had done while I was away. 'I wrote a song,' he said and handed me a piece of paper with 'The Wind Cries Mary' written on it. Mary is my middle name, and the one he would use when he wanted to annoy me. … It was about the row we had just had, but I didn't feel the least bit appeased."[6]

Although there have been assertions from Carol Shiroky[7] that 'Mary' was composed the previous summer, Hendrix had simply made rough sketches of ideas back then. His songwriting methods rarely shifted much during his short career: he would sketch an idea on his own and then work hard on it in the studio with his group of the day to bring it to completion. There may have been a germ of an idea for this particular song prior to that row with Etchingham, but there is no reason to doubt that the argument was the direct catalyst that led to his taking up the fragments and constructing a complete piece from them.

recorded ballad, the wistful 'The Wind Cries Mary', eventually to appear as the band's third single. 'Mary' showed another new side of Hendrix's creativity, but one that in retrospect is consistent with his love of Dylan and acoustic blues. Once more it shows his concern for presentation and arrangement, for the song is ushered in with a series of softly flighted chords that settle the reflective mood even before the start of the Curtis Mayfield-type chord progression that underpins the vocals.

Again Hendrix opts for a conversational approach to his vocals on 'The Wind Cries Mary', using Dylan's dramatic inflections as a way of punctuating and underlining the image-laden lyrics. The melody for the verse is simplicity itself, with intervals of seconds and thirds represented in various combinations at its core. Starting from the sixth and fifth notes in the scale – notes traditionally associated with lightness, aspiration and concord – his vocal moves into the lower intervals of the scale, looking for the 'blue note' pitch in between the well-tempered notes of the conventional scale and stressing the song's emotional ambiguity. Hendrix sings with a previously unsuspected sensitivity, allowing the proper weight in his voice to emerge and communicating with disarming honesty. There are no histrionics, bearing out Hendrix's repeatedly stated contention that he was in the business of communicating his deepest feelings and thoughts rather than merely adopting convenient poses.

The restrained guitar solo is built around fingering positions on the fretboard that allow Hendrix to play with different chord extensions. The solo has some of the world-weariness that would later be found in Otis Redding's 'Dock Of The Bay'. The story behind the writing of 'Mary' bears out this similarity, as his girlfriend Kathy Etchingham recalled: "Having rows never

Mitchell recalled the rushed recording of 'Mary' at the end of the 'Purple Haze' session. "We did a demo version at De Lane Lea studio on a Friday night and it was ragged, to put it mildly. We went off for the weekend, did some gigs, went back the following Tuesday and got it right, but the initial feeling wasn't there. So the original was released, warts and all."[8] Chandler too remembered a rapid recording. "There was 20 minutes left in the studio. And Jimi had written 'The Wind Cries Mary' the night before at home. Mitch and Noel had never heard the song [before, and] it was recorded, including overdubs, in the 20 minutes. And that was all part of the session for 'Purple Haze'. We had the third single right there and then."[9] Chandler may have been exaggerating to claim that the song was completed, overdubs and all, in 20 minutes, but there is no doubt that it was finished in short order, with little or no attempt to correct defects. These are easy to spot, from ragged entrances to wavering beats. But, as Mitchell claimed, the song is alive with feeling, transcending any such weaknesses with ease.

The looseness of this first try at 'The Wind Cries Mary' might be explained in part by the successful recording that same day of the backing track for one of the band's wildest and most imaginative of pieces, the predominantly instrumental 'Third Stone From The Sun' (to which various overdubs would be added in April). On first listen it seems a rather formless jam across a minimal bass riff, pulled together by one of Hendrix's most insinuating guitar melodies. Listened to closely it reveals a more cohesive form than one might expect – possibly due to the presence of Chandler, who wasn't prepared to stand around while the group experimented with a few notions and then edit it all together later.

'Third Stone From The Sun' is a structured group performance with a definite beginning and end. It is divided into two basic sections, both having further subdivisions. The first section (up to about 2:30) is almost wholly pre-set, with little improvising. It alternates between guitar chord work and melodies – picked in a quasi-sitar fashion, amid sympathetic open strings and set against a jazz-derived drum rhythm – and a more formal melodic statement against a relatively conventional 4/4 rock beat. There is also one brief four-bar burst of blues-drenched guitar improvisation immediately before the ghostly "kinky machine" voiceover. Amongst all this, Hendrix and Redding imaginatively swap between variant bass and guitar riffs. The structure contains effective contrasts, such as when the mixolydian-mode melody is played over a jazz beat, followed by a Wes Montgomery-type jazz guitar melody – right down to the trademark Montgomery octave picking – over a typical 1967 rock beat. But what is so satisfying is that at no point does the band sound merely like a group of musicians imitating other styles. They have their own musical identity.

This is underlined emphatically in the second section of the piece, from about 2:30, where Redding holds down a simple three-note riff while Hendrix and Mitchell play musical catch-me-if-you-can. Mitchell here provides pure contemporary jazz drumming in an emotionally heightened environment, allowing him the sort of explosiveness normally reserved for a handful of jazz drummers – most of them leaders of their own groups such as Art Blakey, Max Roach and Elvin Jones, who by then had left John Coltrane's band and in early 1967 was running his own power trio, albeit an acoustic one.

At times the excitement overwhelms Redding and Mitchell and the beat wavers, making it a likely candidate for Mitchell's comment years later that "there are several sessions that make me cringe, but you learn by experience".[10] That this doesn't really affect the track's success has a lot to do with the approach that Hendrix takes, for this is not an orthodox guitar solo. It is more akin to a soundscape forged from his control of amplified feedback and the way he manipulates the Stratocaster's physical characteristics, including its switches and vibrato arm. As such, the solo is largely independent of the metre offered by Redding and Mitchell, instead using the forward momentum of the bass and drums, over which he drapes his constant rumbles, interjections and shrieks. The short monologue he delivers half way through this improvised section is part Vincent Price, part prankster Hendrix, portraying a visitor from another world who – strangely enough, for such a cosmic presence – wishes us never to hear surf music again. An alternative mix of this section included in the 2000 four-CD box set *The Jimi Hendrix Experience* gives us this monologue stripped of its unearthly effects and allows us to hear Hendrix cracking up afterwards, adding amid general studio laughter: "Sounds like a lie to me!"

'Third Stone From The Sun' is brought to its end by a repeat of the sweeping Wes Montgomery-style melody followed by what was possibly the Experience's version of Armageddon. Tumultuous drum explosions lead to the most frenzied series of shrieks and whoops from Hendrix's guitar of the whole six-minutes-plus performance. A gentle fade on what sounds like a spectral freight train wheeling into the distance concludes the adventure. This recording would spawn a thousand freak-out imitations around the world, but few of those imitators would realise that, equal to inspiration, such essays in sound need a structure if they're not to become prolix and dull.

The Experience's early live performances may not have enjoyed the unqualified success of the studio sessions. Mitchell, who knew the British club circuit well from his days with Georgie Fame, felt that when the band were away from the in-crowd of the inner London clubs they struggled a little to win over their audiences. One early gig was in Hounslow, west London, at the Ricky Tick, part of a chain of nightclubs using the same name and run by a friend of Chandler's. "As I recall," Mitchell wrote later, "the audience didn't exactly know what to make of us. Most of our early gigs were like that. We were playing to audiences largely composed of mohair-suited mods and sort of proto-skins in boots and braces. They really didn't know how to take us – Jimi especially – at all."[11] This was partly a problem of fashion and partly of presentation. From the earliest appearances, Hendrix and his cohorts wanted to dress in entirely different ways to the latest London trends. This meant they were not easily pigeonholed, but it also meant that they didn't have a natural, ready-made audience. They had to forge their own and wait for people to catch up with what they were wearing.

> ## "Hendrix came in and kind of hummed us the riff and showed Noel the chords and the changes. I listened to it and we went, 'OK, let's do it.' We got it on the third take as I recall."
>
> Mitch Mitchell, on 'Purple Haze'

A number of difficulties with live presentation took some time to be resolved. The first concerned amplification. The group had switched to Marshall amps and tried to upgrade their volume and power, slowly learning to find a workable balance. At the time, drums were rarely miked at all – so far there had been little need for it. Foldback or monitoring for on-stage communication was similarly unknown. PA systems were rarely adequate to the task of pulling the vocals above the level of the guitar and bass amps, while live mixing desks were still a thing of the future. With the band still discovering its internal balance and developing its musical dialogue, there were often sonic inadequacies and unsatisfactory compromises. Kathy Etchingham remembered occasions when Hendrix, annoyed at Mitchell's overplaying, would hit a cymbal with the end of his guitar in order to rein back the drummer. Mitchell was aware of his tendency to overplay, but felt that it was important to play rather than pull back, in order to work out an approach that properly suited the music. "I always felt completely at home with Jimi, right from the beginning, and him with me, right through to the end," said Mitchell. "I always knew where he was leading me and he was always prepared to be led by you. He was never frightened about going off in unknown directions, unlike a lot of otherwise very good players."[12]

Drummer and bandleader Jon Hiseman, who heard and saw the Jimi Hendrix Experience during this early stage, feels that the band had major problems playing live. "I had joined Graham Bond in 1966," says Hiseman, "and in early 1967 we must have done a show with the Experience. It really came across to me like a steam train how inadequate the bass player and drummer were for what Jimi was trying to do. Not technically, but power-wise. It was so weak. First of all you have to remember that the amps in those days were woefully inadequate. I mean, I played to 4,000 people at the Bath festival with un-miked drums. So, Jimi had these Marshall cabinets and of course he was coming across like hellfire, whereas the semi-acoustic drums and the bass – which I never liked – sounded so weak to me."[13]

This is a different picture of the early Experience compared to the usual assumption of a triumphant progress towards superstardom. Clearly, The Jimi Hendrix Experience was not the only group having such problems with their live sound, given the unsophisticated nature of their amplification and the way they rode it to its limits every night. Although the Experience was possibly the loudest band of the day, many bands suffered from exactly the same limitations. Redding noted a disastrous gig at the start of February in South Shields, north-east England. Hendrix's new amp blew up as they were tuning, so he took Redding's, who in turn borrowed a tiny amp that buzzed and objected as the set started. Roadie Gerry Stickells improvised by swapping the bass into the PA amp, and put the vocals through the small amp. "Of course," said Redding, "from then on we couldn't hear a word, except in the breaks where we were singing and not playing, [and] even then we just heard a tiny whisper."[14] Mitchell too was painfully aware of the enormous handicaps the band had on their early live dates. "I could barely hear anything at all, you really had to rely on watching people's hands move and hope you were playing in the same time: very difficult. You couldn't hear any vocals and half the time neither could the audience."[15]

Jon Hiseman is aware of an irony here. As many drummers were forced to play louder on stage, they would habitually play that way in the studio, too, and sound the worse for it. "But the sound of the drums on the Hendrix

records is fantastic," Hiseman feels, "because Mitchell played so quietly compared to some others. There must have been a corollary between the two. So, live he always seemed very weak sonically – which is not necessarily a problem: Charlie Watts is a very weak drummer. Today you can mike the drummer, you can sample the drums, you can trigger samples off the drums, and the drummer sounds like the side of a house. But on those Experience records Mitch sounds fantastic."

Hiseman feels that in those early days the drums put the other instruments in context, especially if the rest of the band was playing loosely. "If somebody's playing very fragmentarily, they have to be steady," he says. "If they're playing steady, you can be fragmentary. The trick to Cream was that Jack and Eric would go out and out and out, and actually you had Baby Dodds on the drums, who just didn't shift. And that was the key to their success." Dodds was the first great jazz drummer and played with Jelly Roll Morton and Louis Armstrong, making some of the greatest jazz records of all time with these two men in Chicago in the 1920s while deploying his characteristic metronomic beat and rhythmic verve. "After the Hendrix Experience was all over," Hiseman continues, "I heard Mitch live with Jack Bruce and I think he played the best drum concert I've ever heard. His playing was just fantastic, with something untouchable about his drum

Backstage at Brian Epstein's Saville Theatre, central London, January 29th 1967, with The Who. Hendrix is holding Pete Townshend's Rickenbacker 12-string guitar.

control. But the times I heard him with Jimi I thought Jimi needed a much more powerful rhythm machine in front of him to actually go where he wanted to go. He needed the power and simplicity of Ginger Baker."[16]

The other constituent of the Experience's on-stage sound was Redding and his bass amp. One of the big problems with on-stage amplification – and this remains true today, especially in small venues – is that the bass can easily get lost in the maelstrom, even for the player himself. Unless the speakers are at ear level and the tone is firm, the bassist's own sound can go straight under him and get lost out in the crowd. He turns up to compensate and engulfs the rest of the group. The result is an impaired sound. In 1966 and '67, before the advent of smaller amplifiers and speakers combined with proper foldback systems and someone out front balancing the levels, the whole live sound and the way it held together (or not) was more or less left to chance and instinct, especially as most venues had appalling acoustics. Within this context, Hiseman feels that Redding had many problems to deal with. "It was too diffused a sound. There was no meat on it. You couldn't hear the beat. Every time I saw them you couldn't hear the bass because the sound was too diffuse. It needed an anchor. Billy Cox, the bassist with Hendrix towards the end, could be that anchor because he had the sound at the bottom the group needed."[17] One advantage Cox would have over Redding was that by 1970 Hendrix had long abandoned the idea of tours consisting of tiny clubs with seemingly non-existent acoustics.

Redding himself was aware that the group suffered from inconsistent sound and were not always a success everywhere they played. At the Bag O'Nails reception, Redding noted that "for only three people, the sheer volume was breathtaking. Some of the audience fled. Part of the problem was gear. Our future set-up hadn't been invented yet".[18] At the Ram Jam club in Brixton, "we totally freaked the regulars [at this] all-reggae, black, smoker's pub – who had no idea what to make of us".[19] On other occasions it was worse. "We still had nights when the audience hated us and every note we played,"[20] Redding wrote in his autobiography. Things remained hit-and-miss until they quit the club circuit later in 1967.

There are very few recordings of the group playing live at this very early stage of their career, so the evidence is not plentiful, but what does exist suggests that most of the routines were kept brief and simple. Mitchell was a very busy drummer still learning exactly when to provide extra drum fills and embellishments, and exactly what shape they should take, but his energy level alone made sure that the music surrounding Hendrix's guitar and vocals was effervescent. A performance of 'Foxy Lady' recorded in late March 1967 at the BBC for radio broadcast finds Mitchell filling every small crevice and gap in the song, with cymbals splashing and fills around the kit at each cadence, not only punctuating Hendrix's guitar work but cranking up the intensity to a point of near frenzy.

It is certainly over the top, and few other drummers in rock could even have conceived of playing what he does, let alone executing it, but it is certainly a valid way to support Hendrix.

Within the past half-decade a revolution had occurred in jazz drumming, led by Elvin Jones in his work with John Coltrane, where he made the drummer an equal partner with the frontline soloist, developing a vital and wildly exciting dialogue along the way. This had been quite shocking for the jazz community of the day, many of whom felt that Jones was over-playing non-stop, that he was too loud, and that he had no taste. Within a few years, however, his

style had influenced the entire contemporary jazz scene to the extent that most young drummers brought their instrument to the fore in their respective groups, making it part of the frontline. This in turn paved the way for the drumming that accompanied jazz-rock and, later, fusion.

A similar change was happening in rock through Mitchell's work with Hendrix and Baker's work with Cream – and in Robert Wyatt's work with the lesser-known Soft Machine, still to make their first single (in fact Chas Chandler would produce it) but a big hit on the underground scene. For two or three years some explosive drummers had been filling in the gaps between vocal lines and interjecting among the guitar riffs, with Keith Moon in The Who and Viv Prince in The Pretty Things the most obvious examples. But what Mitchell, Baker and Wyatt were doing came from a different tradition. As with any revolution, some nights it worked better than others. The Experience's BBC recording of 'Stone Free' from February 13th is a good example of what Mitchell must have sounded like then on-stage with Hendrix. During the guitar solo, which is in 4/4 like the rest of the tune, Mitchell breaks up the rhythm into units of at most two bars at a time, introducing cadences and breaks through elaborate snare and small-tom patterns that virtually no other drummer of the time would have devised. It makes this section of the song highly charged and exciting, but at the same time delivers a choppy background for Hendrix's solo – and Hendrix's undistinguished playing here may be the result of his inability to develop longer melodic ideas over the constant rhythmic shifts.

As with most revolutions, some people wanted to know about it; others didn't. BBC radio declined to get behind the 'Hey Joe' single, but the new so-called 'pirate' radio stations were quick to spot the single's appeal and, along with Radio Luxembourg which was beamed into the UK at night, were undoubtedly instrumental in its strong showing in the charts as the new year got underway. Strangely, Chandler was unable to get Hendrix's band into the 'underground' London clubs where the more experimental groups were flexing their muscles, possibly because he lacked personal connections in that world, or thought it unimportant given the quick build-up after 'Hey Joe'. Mitchell remembered this period as somewhat perplexing. "The thing with the UFO and Middle Earth type of underground clubs was that, for whatever reason, they didn't want to know us at that time … . Looking back we might have had more in common with that audience, but maybe Chas thought they were marginal. … In the long term it was probably a smart move."[21]

Other smart moves at this time included the continuing development of Chandler's publicity strategy and the refinement of the band's image, off-stage and on. To this effect, Hendrix was allowed free reign when it came to his unique clothes sense, the other two band members following in his wake. The constant efforts to promote Hendrix as the wild man of rock met with considerable success (one oft-used epithet was 'the black Elvis', a line that perhaps showed the relative age of the copy editors rather than the accuracy of the slogan). On-stage, Hendrix was certainly smashing up equipment and indulging in noise for noise's sake, at least for a time. As so many rock outfits have discovered before and since, very little publicity early in a career in any shape or form can be construed as bad publicity. It was only later that Hendrix chafed under a public image so ill-fitting of his private persona.

In February Chandler made a tentative switch to Olympic studio in Barnes, a London suburb about five miles west of the centre, bordered by a large loop of the

Hendrix in discussion with his manager, Chas Chandler, during a soundcheck, London, March 1967.

river Thames at the north, east and west and the Upper Richmond Road to the south. Although the band would bounce between De Lane Lea and Olympic until April 1967, it would prove a good move for the immediate as well as the long-time future. Olympic was still a 4-track studio, but it offered superior sound reproduction to De Lane Lea, thanks in part to the equipment and in part to the engineers who worked there. It is no accident that in May Olympic became one of the very few studios where The Beatles would record outside Abbey Road. The Rolling Stones and Eric Burdon were also enthusiastic about Olympic's results: Burdon had re-launched The Animals as Eric Burdon & The New Animals and was preparing material for a new album to be released later in 1967, *Winds Of Change*. Produced by Tom Wilson, it was recorded at Olympic by engineers Ami Hadani and Ed Kramer, with remixes by Gary Kellgren and Ed Kramer. Kellgren and Kramer would both work at Olympic with Hendrix who, along with Chandler, came to value their fine ears and imaginative approach.

The first job undertaken at Olympic was to complete the work on 'Purple Haze' – mostly vocal and guitar overdubs – before turning to new material. As with so much to do with Hendrix's career, this move of studio and the new relationships are considered in retrospect as the stuff of legend, especially as Kramer has been intimately involved in the posthumous preparation and release of Hendrix material up to the present day. But at the time the changes seemed almost mundane. Kathy Etchingham was concerned to give her perception of the working relationships in her autobiography. "It irritated me in later years," she wrote in 1998, "when I heard that people like Eddie Kramer – the recording engineer at Olympic studios – had been credited with 'creating' Jimi's sound. I had always thought that Roger [Mayer] and Jimi had invented it … . Unlike Eddie Kramer, Roger was a close and personal friend. He used to go down to the Speakeasy and other watering holes with Jimi, discussing all the possibilities of electronic sounds."[22] Mayer supports this perception of the Olympic sessions, saying recently: "Eddie Kramer was the engineer on the sessions. He wasn't a personal friend of anyone. He never hung out socially with Jimi. He never went back to the flat, he never went down to the clubs. When it came to mixing the records, most of the ideas came from Jimi and Chas."[23]

The first song started at Olympic was 'Fire', which would quickly become a staple of the Experience's stage sets. Its fast pace, simple construction and cheekily suggestive lyrics lent themselves well to the excitement of live performances. This combination of sly, almost humorous suggestion and a driving beat is one of the band's early innovations often overlooked. Because Hendrix did not have a powerful singing voice, he was obliged to find other ways of communicating his personality. On earlier recordings he had used a largely conversational approach that made listeners feel he was talking to them; on 'Fire' he is still addressing a second person with a conversational tone, but the speed of the music and the dynamism of the performance demand a deftly gliding, swooping vocal. Everything is delivered with a knowing smile, including his quip, "Move over Rover, and let Jimi take over," just prior to the short guitar break. When 'Fire' was released later on *Are You Experienced*, many read this as Hendrix staking his claim to be the new rock messiah. It's quite probable this was among the levels of meaning suggested in the phrase, but it's also simply a high-spirited joke. Chandler was always at pains to stress in interviews after Hendrix's death that his main memories of the man were of fun, laughter and playfulness. We forget this side of Hendrix at our peril.

The arrangement of 'Fire' relies greatly on the drummer supplying much of the musical interest. The riffs devised for guitar and bass leave great gaping holes where the drums simply have to do something exciting, otherwise the performance would wither and die. Mitchell is up to the task, using contrast, cross-rhythms and a series of patterns to reflect the pell-mell feel of the piece

without simply steamrollering through on an unvarying backbeat or on one simple repeated two-bar pattern – as most rock drummers of the day would have done. This means that the passages where the trio settles into a storming, constant rhythm together are even more of an adrenalin rush, while leaving enough juicy gaps into which Hendrix can drop his vocal phrases.

'Fire' was guitarist John Scofield's first experience of Hendrix's music, and he found it irresistible. "I heard this on the radio and was instantly knocked out. It was coming out of a little transistor radio but it completely blew me away, so I went out and bought *Are You Experienced* the next day. I wasn't a jazz guy yet; I was into Clapton and Jeff Beck. But Hendrix seemed to be on another level. I'd never heard anything that strong and I was just fascinated by it – the guitar playing and the beat and the whole thing. It seemed to me to be an extension of soul music and psychedelia combined with great blues guitar playing that related to B.B. and Albert King."[24]

Just prior to this recording session, Jimi's first major interview with *Melody Maker* appeared in the January 28th issue, in one of the paper's regular features, 'Pop Think In', where a series of specific topics elicited responses from different stars each week. The subjects for Jimi included Freak Out, Teeth, Mexico, The Monkees (prophetically, as it turned out), In-Clubs, Jazz, Bob Dylan, and Vietnam. Hendrix's humour shines through. For example, toying with the idea of Freak Out, he suggested: "I think for a new freak out people should get really high and dig a Mrs Mills single on 33rpm. Then they can talk about that for two weeks until they're bored."

"Jimi was never frightened about going off in unknown directions, unlike a lot of otherwise very good players."

Mitch Mitchell

On The Monkees, he cut to the chase. "Oh God, I hate them! Dishwater. I really hate somebody like that to make it so big." He felt differently when talking about Bob Dylan and Cream. On Dylan: "Oh yeah! I think he's too much. Really out of sight. … Dylan's got a lot of feel. … I have one or two Dylan singles that were withdrawn from the shops just a few days after release. They're too much." On Cream: "That's the first group I saw and sat in with when I got to London. No, wait a minute: I played with them about a week after I got here. I think the one I like best is Eric Clapton. I don't know too much about the other guys … but I have a feeling that we're on a different scene than the Cream – in sound as a whole. I think Eric and I possibly think along the same lines but it's hard to get it across to [others]." He had some interesting opinions on jazz. "I like to listen to it. But to play it – I don't think that way. I like Roland Kirk – he's the only cat I dig in jazz. … I don't happen to know much about jazz. I know that most of those cats are playing nothing but blues, though – I know that much!"

Considering he'd only been in England for six months, his understanding of the British pop scene was unusually comprehensive and thoughtful. "I think if it weren't for Spencer Davis, the scene would really drop down. … You see, The Beatles, man, they were where it was all at. When they dropped out altogether, things changed because they were the group that really kept the scene going. They were holding it up. … The only ones holding it up at the moment, coming through in any way, are the solid performers like Tom Jones, Dusty [Springfield], Spencer Davis and all that. The Troggs and that scene just aren't solid … a group like them will never really get any respect. The Who – they're solid – but I'd have to listen to more of your singles to go any further than that."[25] This early fondness for Spencer Davis suggests he may already have warmed to the talents of the group's vocalist and keyboardist Steve Winwood, then just 18 years old and thinking about striking out on his own. But Hendrix's intelligent comments on the pop scene contrasted glaringly with his attitude to Vietnam, where he simply parroted US government thinking prevalent since the early 1950s about China, communism and the Domino Theory.

One of the more significant things to emerge from this and interviews with *Disc*, *NME* and other UK music magazines at the time was the clear indication that the British scene was rapidly polarising between what musicians like Hendrix regarded as 'serious' music and the chart fluff that was represented for him by bands like The Monkees. While such divisions have always existed in popular

Mitchell, Hendrix and Redding moving through some psychedelic changes with drums, guitar and bass.

a fond private tribute – almost a wave goodbye – to that style. The performance is very much in character. Even Mitchell keeps to simple, strutting soul patterns while Hendrix has fun with the vocal line and makes his guitar mimic the kinds of horn lines routinely played by Stax brass sections.

More evidence of the quick spread of Hendrix's fame came with the front cover of *Record Mirror*'s February 11th issue, entirely taken up by a kaleidoscopic head-and-shoulders shot of the guitarist – although there was nothing inside to justify such a prominent display. Readers had to wait two weeks for that, when an interview appeared under the heading "Jimi Doesn't Think He's A Big Name Yet". The feature concentrated on what

music, the separation of musical aspirations had not been so stark until 1966 and '67. Even The Beatles, who were deadly serious about the standards of their music, did not decisively cross the border between music primarily for entertainment and music primarily for self-expression until they quit touring in 1966. The very first tune they completed after the end of their touring days was 'Strawberry Fields Forever', in November 1966, one of their most complex achievements and a clear break with the past. They had thrown down their gauntlet for all to see. The most prominent of the many reasons for this turnaround was Bob Dylan's rising importance in rock and pop circles. Hendrix, as a Dylan advocate and devotee, was one of the first to audaciously press home this distinction between art and craft. Hendrix simply did not record anything that he didn't feel strongly about. He was desperately keen to communicate with his audience and to be successful, but his starting point was self-expression, not entertainment. He felt that success ought to be a natural consequence of self-expression. As he later told Val Wilmer, "When it comes to writing songs, I have to wait 'til they come to me, even if I've got a record date minutes away. I couldn't keep going just for money. I can't feel pop – I couldn't call myself that."[26]

Whatever the method used, success was now arriving in a hurry, evident from the reception Hendrix received when the group played the Saville Theatre in London's Shaftesbury Avenue in late January 1967. Supporting The Who that night and plagued by PA problems, they still had the crowd on their side according to *Melody Maker* reviewer Chris Welch: "The crowd were so keyed up they laughed sympathetically while Jimi searched for a mike that worked." Spurred to rise to the occasion, The Who "played their best for months". Welch also noted that "the smoke bombs and amplifier smashing [were gone]. In their place were good singing and playing".[27] The Who closed the evening with a complete rendition of 'A Quick One While He's Away'. The world was expanding rapidly for both groups, and there would soon be another opportunity for them to go head-to-head in a competition for the crowd's favour. Eric Clapton later recalled this Saville concert as the one that inspired Jack Bruce to come up with the famous riff to 'Sunshine Of Your Love' in response to what he heard from Hendrix's band, although Bruce himself has disputed this version of events.

Hendrix's next snapshot view on the world was recorded at Olympic studio on February 8th. Of all the material he released from his first year in England, 'Remember' was closest to the R&B and soul music he'd played until recently in the US. The structure, accompaniment and vocal line are all similar to those found on many of Otis Redding's recent Stax hits. The song can be seen either as a throwback to a time when the band were short of material and casting around for tunes with which to fill the first album, or as

Hendrix had been up to in the recording studio. In it he fretted a little about what his new fans would make of the as-yet unreleased 'Purple Haze', wondering "how people are going to take the next [single], because it's so different from 'Hey Joe'. I think everyone will think we've used different instruments on it, but it's still two guitars and drums – at one point the guitar sounds like a flute. I recorded it exactly as we do it on-stage. Everything we do on record we can do exactly on stage. ... Our third record will be even more different".

The lottery of predicting which records would be hits was revealed when Hendrix let slip that they'd planned to release a different second single. "They'd picked ['Love Or Confusion'] to be our next single, but I had this thing on my mind about walking on the sea. Then I wrote 'Purple Haze'." This may well have been true, considering that 'Love Or Confusion' had been completed in December, prior to the release of 'Hey Joe', leaving a choice of B-sides between 'Red House', 'Can You See Me' and 'Foxy Lady'. 'Love Or Confusion' would have made a strong follow-up to 'Hey Joe' had 'Purple Haze' not come along.

Hendrix was also uncertain about the choice of tracks for the first album when the interview took place. He said the LP "will be different and all the songs will be mine except for 'Like A Rolling Stone' and maybe a Muddy Waters number". Presumably he meant 'Catfish Blues' or a variant, but neither song appeared on the finished record, probably because Hendrix was in full compositional flood. "Up to now," he told *Record Mirror*, "I've written about 100 songs, but most of them are in those New York hotels I got thrown out of. When I go back I'm going to collect them from those hotel rooms where I missed the rent." Now new ideas were constantly coming out of his head, and the urgency to go back to old ideas was fast receding. "I can't write no happy songs," he continued, saying that 'Foxy Lady', at that time still unreleased, was "about the only happy song I've written. [I] don't feel very happy when I start writing. ... I'm writing a number 'I Don't Live Today', it's really weird, man. I hope we can get it ready for the LP".[28]

At the Montagu Square flat Hendrix talked to Kevin Swift about related issues for a piece in the British musicians' monthly magazine *Beat Instrumental*. Why didn't [Jimi] complete the obvious image by engaging two blues-soaked men as drummer and bassist, Swift asked about the Experience. Hendrix had an entirely logical reply. "If I'd had two bluesmen with me we would have gone straight into one bag, the blues. That's not for me. This way we can do anything and develop our own music. We might do our own arrangement of a Howlin' Wolf number followed straight away by 'Wild Thing', or a Bobby Dylan number. We'll do things our own way and make our own sound."[29] This refutes the idea put around later that Hendrix had

"I don't happen to know much about jazz. I know that most of those cats are playing nothing but blues, though — I know that much."

Jimi Hendrix

Redding and Mitchell thrust upon him by management, or that at this stage of his career he really didn't care who he played with, as long as he was allowed to record and reach out to a wide audience. Although he rarely talked about it, Hendrix had weighed up the potential compatibility of his drummer and bassist and decided that they were the people he personally wanted to work with. That he was no bad judge of such things is demonstrated plentifully on the records the group made, both in the wide stylistic territory they covered together and the consistently high quality they achieved.

On February 20th, after these interviews had appeared, the band went back to De Lane Lea studio to record 'I Don't Live Today' between club dates, TV appearances and interviews. It would be one of the stand-out tracks on the first album, bringing side one of the original vinyl LP to a close. Today, when CDs can easily contain in one unbroken programme the entire contents of what were often double vinyl albums, the importance of such demarcations is usually lost or forgotten. But 'I Don't Live Today' was a climactic piece with which to conclude the first part of the adventure and was clearly positioned on the LP with that in mind.

Considering the amazing musical imagination displayed and the disciplined organisation of the constituent parts on 'I Don't Live Today', it's fascinating to reflect that a few miles away at EMI's St John's Wood studios in Abbey Road The Beatles were deep into their recording sessions for *Sgt Pepper's Lonely Hearts Club Band*. In that same week in February they were working on 'A Day In The Life', wrestling in particular with the problem of how to end it. Chandler and Hendrix clearly thought equally hard about how to end 'I Don't Live Today', as early takes recorded before Hendrix's vocals were added make plain. These recordings, still available only on bootlegs, are some of the most exciting and revelatory Hendrix tapes to have come to light since his death. They are too important to languish on bootlegs, and it must be hoped that one day the Hendrix Estate will release them officially.

'I Don't Live Today' is based around a descending six-note riff that enters after a two-bar drum-only intro and an extra two bars of misleadingly bright chord work from Hendrix. The blues-drenched riff sounds like Ike Turner twisted

Close to his audience: Hendrix exploits a long lead at the Star Club in Hamburg, Germany, March 1967.

through some illegal substances and cranked up a further few notches. It follows the simple chord progression and underpins the vocal line, which itself is short and simple but considerably more developed melodically than any Hendrix had undertaken in the past six months of recording – as well as being a variant of the opening riff. As Hendrix had told *Record Mirror*, the melodic shape and the lyrical content of the song are depressing. It is one of Hendrix's bleakest statements, equal to Lennon's 'Yer Blues' or one of Dylan's more apocalyptic downers from his 1965/66 output. Hendrix claimed many times later – including repeated on-stage announcements during his regular concert tours – that it was about the plight of native American Indians, perhaps underlined by the ironic drum pattern on those opening bars that follows the Hollywood idea of American Indian music. Nearer the time of its first release, Hendrix would be a little more revealing about how the song evolved. "The beginning came to me, you know … and then the music just made me feel like these words. The words and music, they go like that."[30] Hendrix was aiming the song at a specific subject, but its application is universal: the 'I' in 'I Don't Live Today' could be him, you or me – or anyone who has ever suffered utter desolation, then or now.

Yet, finally, the track is not depressing. It is fierce, it has real rage in its heart, but it has a sense of dignity and poise – perhaps grace is the best word for it – that is rare in rock music, a form more familiar with hyperbole than balance. This is most clearly spelt out in the solo section, which for its entire length sustains a heartbreakingly elegiac lyricism. As with all master improvisers working within set lengths and specific structures, Hendrix is remarkably economical with his material here, teasing at a number of short rhythmic phrases, inverting and varying them, embellishing and reducing their shapes. This gives the solo great continuity as well as the balance that comes naturally from working with a restricted group of motifs. Additionally, Hendrix invests his playing with intense emotion, not only through his guitar technique but through the sound he has chosen, thickened with the Octavia and probably altered by the recording board's tone controls for a weirdly appropriate 'manual' wah-wah effect.

After another coruscating chorus the tune comes to a halt, around 2:15 on the released version. The studio outtakes reveal that the song originally stopped here, presumably because no one had thought of an appropriate ending. A subsequent take added the free-for-all double-tempo section at the end, underpinned by the opening riff and given over to unprecedentedly wild guitar soundscapes. The version that appeared on the original UK vinyl release of *Are You Experienced* added some control – and irony – by fading the free-for-all in and out at whim and allowing Hendrix to make some spoken observations and laconic comments. This released version also shortened the section considerably; the outtakes reveal that as originally played in the studio it was at least as long again as the entire song up to the 'halt'. It would be by far the most avant-garde, tortured and frenzied music on the whole album, including the as-yet unfinished 'Third Stone From The Sun'. It becomes a wall of sound, a constant wail of pain and anguish punctuated by tumultuous drumming from Mitchell. It was unparalleled in pop music up to that time, the only music to come anywhere close being by The Beatles and, oddly, also destined to remain unreleased in its original form for decades, until their *Anthology 2* in 1996. The weird closing section to 'Strawberry Fields Forever', as first recorded, is like a long trip into a nightmare from which you simply can't escape.

Hendrix's wild, unvarnished ending for 'I Don't Live Today' did have some precedents in New York avant-garde jazz, which was led by Sun Ra, Albert Ayler, and John Coltrane with his final great group. Perhaps Hendrix and his management had no interest in being associated with such figures, preferring to travel a little closer to pop music's progressive mainstream by making the final changes to the track with those fadings and spoken interlude. But the musical parallels are unmistakable. Like members of The Beatles, Hendrix was aware of Coltrane's music, and knew of the *Ascension* album. Mitchell recalled that Hendrix turned him on to many blues player he didn't know, and that in turn he played Hendrix records by Roland Kirk, Miles Davis, and Coltrane. Hendrix's wildness sounds nothing like Coltrane's, but the approach to sound and emotion is similar. It is idle speculation, but if this unvarnished version of 'I Don't Live Today' had been released back in 1967, Hendrix's affinities with the most avant of the musical avant-garde would have been writ large. Whatever musicians like Jeff Beck, Frank Zappa and Captain Beefheart were doing in response to the new soundscapes opening up in pop music, Hendrix was creating his own sonic booms.

"I'm writing a number, 'I Don't Live Today', it's really weird, man. I hope we can get it ready for the LP."

Jimi Hendrix

A different angle on Hendrix's jazz affiliations can be heard on his other classic recording of February 1967, 'Manic Depression'. This fast tune in 3/4 time has breathtaking playing from each member of the trio and shows just how free-ranging Hendrix's imagination could be. For a start, the idea of playing in triple metre even today remains rare enough in popular music to immediately raise eyebrows. At that time it was a marked novelty, although the members of Soft Machine had been doing such things in the relative obscurity of Canterbury for some years. The Moody Blues had managed a hit in 3/4 with 'Go Now' in 1964 and The Beatles had mastered the metre in 1965 for 'Norwegian Wood'. Yet, apart from Soft Machine, with their prototype jazz-rock, such time signatures were usually only attempted for gentle waltz-type ballads, where the listener would probably be largely unaware of the metre.

With Hendrix the metre is thrown in the listener's face from the first frenetic bar. This could have posed an insurmountable problem for the tune if he'd had the standard rock rhythm section of the day: one has only to listen to Eric Burdon & The New Animals' tribute to Hendrix, 'Yes I Am Experienced', recorded shortly after this, to hear the pitfalls. The Burdon band, though excellent rock musicians, had no idea what to do with a fast beat in triple metre: the drummer repeats a couple of wooden patterns for the whole track while the rest of the group tries to hold the beat together and not get lost. Compare this to what the Experience achieve. The beat comes alive from the start as Hendrix and Redding combine to play supple riffs amid Mitchell's spectacular and beautifully varied drum part. Here the jazz

influences are out in the open, especially with Mitchell whose patterns are largely based on those of Elvin Jones but honed to perfection for the rock context that the song creates. Ex-Animals organist Alan Price certainly noticed it, commenting to *Melody Maker* about the drummer's playing with Hendrix: "It has been great to see Mitch Mitchell come out of Georgie [Fame]'s band and be let loose. It's rather like a civil servant becoming a demolition worker."[31]

As with so many of the tunes that would be released on *Are You Experienced*, 'Manic Depression' has a clear, simple and very effective arrangement, focussing on the voice during the verses but presenting entrances and exits for each part of the song that give the listener a clear guide to what is happening and where it is about to go. The opening false start remains effective after thousands of listens because it is so dramatically played and relates directly to the riff that ties the whole song together, allowing the listener to anticipate with relish what is to come. Each subsequent guitar riff and melody is memorable, including the long, singing, upward-climbing line that introduces the devastating guitar solo.

This is one of Hendrix's most resourceful solos on record. Its apparently random wildness masks tremendous rhythmic sophistication in its conception and realisation. One of the marks of a master improviser is the amount of rhythmic variety they manage to inject into even the shortest solo while retaining overall coherence. Hendrix's solo on 'Manic Depression' gives the impression of complete rhythmic freedom, as if he could pluck any phrase from his head and instantly execute it with verve and perfection. The bar lines dissolve as he unwinds fantastic long phrases and slashing melodies beyond anything played in rock prior to this session. At the solo's climax, after a scrambling repeated triplet figure from a single fingering position on the fretboard – often used by guitarists to generate the illusion of speed – Hendrix plays a series of jagged single notes on and around off-beats, in a pattern that – apart from being impossible to notate on paper – describes extreme manic tension, climaxed by a ripping, screaming high note from whence he winds the brief solo downwards. As with so much of his playing on *Are You Experienced*, he is breaking new ground as he is recording. Even at the solo's conclusion, the change from the earlier savagery to a keening, singing melody (with a voiceover urging "cry on, guitar") is closely judged, not only bringing a balance and emotional resolution to the solo, but linking back with a variation to its opening bars as well as to the concluding instrumental tag of the song.

The stark lyrics are among Hendrix's most direct expressions of a basic human dilemma. For the most part, *Are You Experienced* would contain lyrics about everyday subjects, unpretentious and not especially deep, but there are exceptions where he reaches a more profound level. This song is one. Its subject matter remains unusual for rock: even more unusually it is happily free of self-indulgence in its direct statement of Hendrix's angst. He was learning quickly from his models, especially Dylan.

In the February 25th issue of *Melody Maker* Paul McCartney reviewed the latest crop of singles, The Jimi Hendrix Experience's 'Purple Haze' among them, even though it would not be released until the following month: presumably McCartney, a fan, wanted to plug it for Hendrix. "So, Jimi freaks out and sounds all the better for it," said McCartney. "It's breaking out all over the place, you know. I thought it would be one of those things that people might keep down but it's breaking through all over. You can't stop it. Hooray! … This is yet another incredible record from the great Twinkle Teeth Hendrix!"[32] The whole feature reads as if it was dictated over the phone, but the Beatle's desire to help Hendrix's career is unmistakable.

The Experience started March with a further session at De Lane Lea studio where they attempted to put down an acceptable version of 'Like A Rolling Stone'. This was followed by a week in France and Belgium

Hendrix shares a pew backstage with some unlikely fellow travellers on his first UK package tour, March 31st to April 30th 1967: Cat Stevens (with gun); Gary Leeds (Walker Brothers), Engelbert Humperdinck.

supporting the release of 'Hey Joe' there with gigs, TV appearances and interviews. Later there was a quick visit to Amsterdam. That same month Stevie Winwood left The Spencer Davis Group and began considering his future, laying the foundations for what would become Traffic, one of Hendrix's favourite bands. Meanwhile the Experience's live set was filling up with more and more of the originals that Hendrix was completing for the first album. As Mitchell noted, the album "became the basis of the live act for some time to come. There were a few we didn't do live, such as 'Remember' and 'May This Be Love', because in all honesty they were album fillers".[33] This implies that it was a strategic rather than strictly aesthetic decision to leave the Dylan and Muddy Waters covers off the album. There are indications that the decision had been reached before the band even recorded 'Like A Rolling Stone', as *Melody Maker* dated March 4th carried a short news piece about *Are You Experienced* stating that "all the tracks have been written by Jimi".[34] Both Hendrix and his management wanted to send out a single message uncomplicated by cover versions of other people's songs.

Toward the end of March, Mitchell had his hair permed in a frizz to blend in with the other two. More importantly, 'Purple Haze' was released as the follow-up single to 'Hey Joe'. *Record Mirror* was in two minds about the new track. Peter Jones wrote: "Not, to me, as consistently communicative as 'Hey Joe', but it is rather a stronger showcase for the wild-haired talent."[35] In a bid to boost the chart potential for 'Purple Haze' the Experience appeared on the BBC's chart-based show *Top Of The Pops* on March 27th with a marginally slower, more overtly sexy version of the single that added little to the studio interpretation and was without the Octavia effect on the guitar solo. More substantial progress was made the same day with a scorching 'Killing Floor' recorded for BBC radio and broadcast on *Saturday Club* on April Fool's Day. It was an outstanding version, not only for the bite in Hendrix's guitar playing but also for the power and precision of Mitchell and Redding in support. Its pace, ease and punch, as well as Hendrix's notably more accomplished, less strained vocals, compare favourably with the live version that they would play at Monterey four months later.

Perhaps in an effort to keep 'Purple Haze' as the focus of the public's

attention for a little longer, Chandler along with his partner Mike Jeffery and Lambert & Stamp of Track Records decided to delay the release of the *Are You Experienced* album. The reason Chandler gave to the press was transparently specious. "Due to a fault," he said, "we have decided to re-record all but six of the LP tracks. But Jimi has also written about 15 more numbers since we started work on the LP so we're going to record all those as well. I'm afraid it's starting from scratch all over again – and will mean that the release of the album is going to be delayed for over one month."[36] Needless to say, nothing apart from 'Red House' was ever re-made, and eventually the original December 1966 version of 'Red House' was used on the album.

In mid March, Hendrix and Kathy Etchingham along with Chandler and his wife-to-be Lotta moved out of Ringo Starr's flat on Montagu Square in Marylebone and into a flat in a mid-century purpose-built block just south-west of Montagu Square at 43 Upper Berkeley Street. It was so close, Etchingham remembered, that they were able to move in by simply walking around the corner with their scanty possessions.

That same month the band started to notice screaming teenage girls at their gigs, mobbing their performances and clawing at the musicians afterwards. This coincided with their ascent to the package-tour level of fame thanks to the success of their first single. Until then they'd been a band desperate for a break as they put together a solid-as-a-rock live act; now they were beginning to metamorphose into a successful band trying to live up to their own image.

That image would become ever more heightened and was thrown into sharp relief during April when The Jimi Hendrix Experience set out on its first and last package tour of the UK. They would be the lowliest support for The Walker Brothers, who were on their final UK tour before disbanding, but it was an important opportunity for the Experience to get their groundbreaking stage act across to new audiences. Perhaps it was simply the best chance on offer at the time. Lining up alongside The Walker Brothers and the Experience were Cat Stevens, still in his 'I Love My Dog' and 'Matthew & Son' period rather than his *Tea For The Tillerman* second coming. There was also a group called The Californians, plus the man with the biggest selling

British record of 1967, Engelbert Humperdinck, whose 'Release Me' had spent 56 weeks in the charts. The Experience's set included 'Can You See Me', 'Foxy Lady', 'Fire' and 'Purple Haze': the contrast between Hendrix and his fellow professionals could not have been much greater. Mitchell remembered that "it was definitely not our kind of audience – but, then, what audience did we have at the time?"[37] Redding recalled in his autobiography that it was a fractious tour but that it marked the point at which things began to consolidate for the band and Hendrix's publicity began to sink in with a public who read more widely than *Record Mirror* and *Melody Maker*. A surge of national press interest came primarily from the infamous occasion when Hendrix first set light to a guitar. On the opening night of the tour, at north London's Finsbury Park Astoria (later to become The Rainbow), journalist and PR man Keith Altham suggested tongue-in-cheek that Jimi might use lighter fluid to set fire to his guitar on-stage and that this might make an impact. It certainly did.

The continuity of the package show was chaotic – hardly surprising considering the personalities involved. As Hendrix said to Altham at the time, "This is a silly little tour. I go on and tear up the stage so that the audience are jumping up and down and then on comes Engelfluff and stops the show dead with 'The Last Waltz', and damn me if Scott Walker follows that by being even more miserable."[38] To Chris Welch, interviewing him for *Melody Maker*, Hendrix admitted: "The bosses of the tour are giving us hell. The organisers don't give us a chance to tune up before we go on-stage. They say we are obscene and vulgar, but we play our act as we've always played it. ... We refuse to change our act, and the result is my amplifier sometimes gets cut off at the funniest times. I wonder why? ... Just before I go on I turn round and find a guitar string is broken, or I find my guitar is all out of tune. ... But they are not getting rid of us unless we are officially thrown off the tour."[39] It's easy to forget that all rock stars, however precipitous their rise to fame, must retain the will for battle to complete their climb to the top. At this point, Hendrix was still near the bottom of the pile, even though his popularity was building quickly. He and the rest of the band had to endure all the sly and dirty professional tricks that have always been played on support bands. They also had to suffer the egos of the other stars. Mitchell remembered, for example, that Cat Stevens refused to travel on the bus with them for a while, before relenting, much to the Experience's disappointment.[40] Hendrix's resentment – and his mental toughness – showed through in that interview with Welch.

The Experience somehow made it through to the end of the tour on April 30th, despite the occasional escape from over-zealous fans off-stage or frosty relations with fellow stars. In the meantime, during time off, they finished *Are You Experienced* by recording the title track and 'May This Be Love', also taping a B-side, 'Highway Chile', to couple with 'The Wind Cries Mary'. Like 'Stone Free', 'Highway Chile' quickly became a favourite of Hendrix fans, partly due to its 'let's get lost' lyrical content – though in fact the subject matter is straight from traditional blues – but also because of its unselfconscious raunch.

Starting with a declamatory guitar line, Hendrix launches immediately into a verse telling the highway chile's story – left home when he was 17, and so on. The way he disarmingly relates the narrative brings to mind his recent comments to Chris Welch about singing. "I just wish I could sing really nice," he said, "but I know I can't sing. I just feel the words out."[41] He feels them convincingly on 'Highway Chile'. He also solos convincingly over an entire verse, starting with a bold flourish that he repeats with small variations in shape until he suddenly throws in a rhythmic variation that catches one out the first time. It's an asymmetric line, ending on a weak beat and then launching off again towards the final improvised bars where the even emphases of the rhythm return the listener to rock convention. For Hendrix it was a casually produced solo, but one full of interest. By the final chorus, as the band head for the chorus repeats and the standard fade, they have speeded up noticeably – something they rarely did in the studio, even in the early days, and something Hendrix as producer would never have allowed later in his career.

'May This Be Love', the ballad that originally kicked off the second side of the original UK vinyl release of *Are You Experienced*, is often overlooked among Hendrix's quite frequent wanderings into tender love-songs. The reasons are simple but not entirely obvious. This is a melodic, romantic composition that borders on the sentimental, especially in the lyrics which are hardly Jimi's most inspired or subtle, notwithstanding the image of the waterfall. But the song's arrangement tends to accentuate the unusual and at times bizarre ideas that Hendrix and Chandler devised to enliven the tune.

The opening glissando down the fretboard, helped along by the vibrato arm, may suggest a waterfall in motion but is about as romantic as melting ice-cream. The opening verse introduces the pretty melody, held well by Hendrix's partially double-tracked voice, but at the end of each phrase there is a pause while Hendrix drops in some more water effects. Clever, for sure, but they break the song's spell. Also at fault is the mix, which recesses the vocals too far, over-promoting the rather threatening drum patterns and generally overplaying the sound effects. Only during the beautiful guitar statement of the melody does the song flow properly, as its true beauty is revealed through Hendrix's gentle guitar caresses: this instrumental ideal is something to which his vocals can only aspire. The cushioned ending is well executed, as Hendrix softly picks out a perfect major cadence while Mitchell makes his cymbals gently simmer – a portent of more elaborately shimmering endings to come.

The last new tune recorded for the LP was also one of its most original. 'Are You Experienced?' is played almost entirely against a drone A chord (though it sounds like A-flat because this was the first recording on which Hendrix tuned his guitar lower than standard pitch, here down by a semitone or half-step). The use of the drone once again invites a comparison, at least superficially, with Indian classical music, while the drums sustain a military snare pattern against a piano chord.

'Are You Experienced?' has a strange air of unreality for many reasons, not least the liberal use of backwards-recorded guitars and other instruments, including drums. But the entire sound of the track is deeply affected by an absence that, to put it crudely, you only notice when you notice it. There is no bass playing on the track. This creates a gap between the very congested mid-range occupied by the guitar and the steady boom of the bass drum. Perhaps Hendrix wanted the song to be more like a disembodied marching band coming out of the mist and retreating back at the end. Perhaps he was aiming for the rather ethereal feeling that the finished track possesses, rather than the warmth that a bass holding down the pedal tones would have supplied. Perhaps the absence of a bass in Indian music had an influence. Perhaps Noel had gone for a pint. But there is no bass guitar. Instead, there are myriad guitar effects that visualise the double and triple meanings of the quasi-visionary (and quite likely drug-induced) lyrics. Hendrix is taking on the role of knowing guide for the listener, introducing us all to the extravaganza, just as The Beatles were doing on *Sgt. Pepper*. But this guide is wayward, a beguiling spirit rather than a theatrical barker.

And then there is the backwards guitar solo. Using 1967 technology, the most obvious way to produce a backwards-sounding solo would be for the backing tape to be played in reverse while Hendrix familiarised himself with the new geography of the piece. He would then have to rehearse and try a few phrases, bearing in mind the way the 'shape' of the notes change when reversed. The guitarist would then record a part against the backwards-running tape – which afterwards would, of course, be played in the standard direction. The new guitar part just added would now sound 'backwards' against the regular track.

However, for reasons that remain unexplained, that is not what happened on this track. On 'Are You Experienced?' the entire piece of tape with the guitar solo runs backwards: Hendrix has not only imagined a guitar solo that runs counter to the prevailing rhythm, but imagined his phrases running backwards as he plays with Mitchell in normal studio conditions. The crude studio fades in and out either side of the solo barely conceal a track that is running backwards in its entirety: Mitchell's cymbals and every other sound is rushing backwards, along with the guitar solo. Then there is a muddled transition, and suddenly everything is running normally again. Regardless of

During his first UK package tour in April 1967 Hendrix still seemed to enjoy acting the showman in front of the Experience. Later he came to resent the crowd's expectation that he would go through the hoops.

the primitive studio conditions under which he was operating, this solo is one of the most brilliant and arresting creations of Hendrix's entire career.

There is no doubt that the solo on 'Are You Experienced' was conceived from the outset to be heard backwards. This can be easily substantiated. Anyone who has a vinyl copy of the album and a regular turntable and is prepared to manually wind the album backwards with the stylus in the right grooves (or has some nifty digital gear) can verify this, for they will hear the solo as originally played – 'forwards' – in the studio. Heard like this, it seems to be a series of set-piece ideas with no particular continuity, often stopping abruptly, and with obvious attempts to bend and slur notes for maximum effect. Heard the other way around, as on the finished recording, it has a distinct flow and extraordinary logic.

There are some astounding phrases and ideas, certainly pre-conceived by Hendrix, that remain unprecedented. The physical properties of a stringed instrument dictate that, for the most part, any sliding or bending of notes will normally raise pitch. For it to be the other way around, a player has to articulate the note (or the sequence being played) so that it starts at a fingering position where it is already 'altered' – and somehow not only get it in tune but also make the transition between altered and normally executed notes sound natural. Considering the technical challenge involved, guitarists mostly opt to start an altered note from a standard fretted position and bend it upwards in pitch from there. In this way, whole phrases of 'bent' notes can be articulated.

At a number of points in this solo, Hendrix includes outrageously bent notes which, listened to as originally executed forwards, sound somewhat staged, especially in the way he clips both the beginning and the end of the note. But he knows how this will make the notes 'form' when heard the other way around. Listened to backwards, as released on the album, they're

breathtakingly effective, coming out of the speakers as pure white-hot howls of angst from his soul: psychedelicised hellhounds on his trail. As well as all this, the whole shape of the solo is masterful, rising from small, whispering phrases through to an agonised climax of distorted melodic shapes, and back down again to mesmerically tumbling small phrases. Again, the conception is simple but the manner of execution, and the detail therein, makes this a highlight in Hendrix's recorded legacy.

The sessions at Olympic studio on April 3rd and 4th completed the recording work for *Are You Experienced*, including songs rejected and not reworked for any subsequent release during Hendrix's lifetime. Pieces taped between November 1966 and April 1967 but left unissued either on *Are You Experienced* or as singles include 'Here He Comes' [aka 'Lover Man'], 'First Look Around The Corner', 'Midnight Lightning', 'Gypsy Blood', 'Like A Rolling Stone', 'La Poupee Qui Fait Non', 'Teddy Bears Live Forever', '# 3', 'Go My Own Way', and 'Hound Dog'. (There was also a session to remake 'Red House' on March 29th that provided a version for the song's initial American release on the US issue of the *Smash Hits* LP the following year. 'Red House', as well as 'Can You See Me' and 'Remember', were not included on the original US release of the *Are You Experienced* vinyl LP; in their place were the A-sides of the first three UK singles, 'Hey Joe', 'Purple Haze' and 'The Wind Cries Mary'.)

The team made final mixes of the *Are You Experienced* album at Olympic and finalised the song sequence on April 9th and 10th, with the 10th also taken up by press and radio interviews for Hendrix. The Walker Brothers tour ate up most of the rest of April, finishing on the last day of the month at a cinema in Tooting, south London. During May, Hendrix would reach a new stage of his rapid ascent to international acclaim, obviating the need for any more package tours – at least in Britain.

from marylebone to monterey

MAY TO SEPTEMBER 1967

Freed from the petty constraints of the Walker Brothers tour and waiting for Are You Experienced to hit the shops, Hendrix and his management team were buoyed by the release on Reprise of their first US single, 'Hey Joe', on May 1st 1967. As was the custom of the time, the American company couldn't resist interfering with the British release, putting '51st Anniversary' on the flip side instead of 'Stone Free'.

W ith no live shows from the band or a major marketing campaign, it failed to chart. Four days later, on May 5th, Track Records released the next British single, 'The Wind Cries Mary' / 'Highway Chile', following the strategy of pushing a new single out as soon as the previous one began to falter. 'Purple Haze' had peaked at number three in late March and had also scored heavily right across Europe. The Experience was one of the hottest bands that side of the Atlantic.

As the Experience went back into Olympic studio in early May to continue recording new material, their management were already set on making a dent on the American market. Managers Chas Chandler and Mike Jeffery based their ideas on the spectacular success British acts had enjoyed in Europe and America between 1964 and early 1967, but no one was prepared for the sudden changes in lifestyle and habits of consumption (music as well as drugs) and the way these would fragment the pop music scene in the next six months.

In later years, Chandler put considerable distance between himself and the long and short-term career strategies that his partner Mike Jeffery devised for Hendrix. But there seems little doubt that both men initially shared the view that the way to break the Experience in the US was to get them onto a package tour where they would work relentlessly, just as The Animals and so many other British Invasion bands had done to achieve success, adding in some TV and radio appearances along the way in time-honoured showbiz fashion. This, they figured, was the key to the States. Two events – one good, one disastrous – would disrupt such plans, but the result would be a breakthrough in America much faster than anyone could have predicted.

Like any other region in a big country, the West Coast of America had always sustained its own identifiable strains of popular music, reflecting the different attitudes and lifestyles of the coastal states such as California, Oregon and Washington. California had a larger national and international reputation because of its pre-eminence in the entertainment business. The state was wealthy and had

Meeting the neighbours in Montagu Square (left), Marylebone, central London. Hendrix had a flat in the Square at the time.

a relatively large local population that normally supported a variety of musical efforts. By the mid 1960s West Coast pop was dominated by Los Angeles and came mostly from two streams: the surf-music-inspired reinvention of early 1960s New York big-production ditties, popularised by Brian Wilson and The Beach Boys, Jan & Dean and others; and the rougher R&B-influenced music played and enjoyed by the black community. The streams were largely divorced from developments in the Midwest, Chicago and the East Coast, especially New York City which was still recovering from successive British 'invasions' and was re-configuring its teen-pop fodder into acts like The Shangri-Las and The Ronettes. Of the cities in California, Los Angeles had usually taken the lead in post-war musical entertainment and innovation. The city's own popular music reflected the tastes and mix of its population. The Byrds were harbingers of change as they joined together many different styles and ideas: they had studied the way Bob Dylan had married rock and folk, grafting some of the serious intention of folk onto pop music and making their own conclusions.

Given the immodest ambitions of the bigger rock stars, it was only a matter of time before singles ceased to be regarded as the 'little symphonies' of the Phil Spector era and LPs became the only format that could encompass

"Like most acid-heads Jimi had visions and he wanted to create music to express what he saw. He would try to explain this to people but it didn't make sense because it was not linked to reality in any way."

Kathy Etchingham, girlfriend

rock's new ambitions. A significant part of the audience who had tuned in to The Beatles and turned on to the so-called permissiveness of the era were excited and intrigued by these developments, eventually becoming able to sustain their interest beyond a single three-minute tune.

During 1966, developments that had been brewing in the north of California, mostly around San Francisco, began to bear fruit in remarkable ways as the search for a distinctive and purposeful new approach to pop music took hold. Local and transplanted acts began identifying themselves with what was fast being described as a counterculture, based in the Haight-Ashbury district of the city. A number of venues in inner San Francisco at this time, particularly Bill Graham's Fillmore, actively promoted young and daring bands that shared the values of the new audience.

This counterculture was not so radically different to the Beat movement based in San Francisco throughout the 1950s, which had been closely involved with sexual and social freedom, eastern religions and philosophies, experiments in artistic pursuits, and the politics of protest and drug-taking. There was a strong streak of hedonism in the new movement of the 1960s, and it attracted people looking for good times as well as supplying a new cause to rally around – America's involvement in the Vietnam war. Until now the criticism of US foreign policy had been the preserve of the usual left-wing media and intellectuals: the War had been largely ignored before the massive escalation of US involvement during President Johnson's first elected term of office following his landslide victory of late 1964. Now, with the draft threatening the nation's youth, the disaffection was spreading to college campuses across the States and would soon become not only a powerful political force at home and abroad but also an extension of the fashion

industry as various symbols and icons were adopted as part of the counterculture.

Early in 1967 a group of people in California decided to take a leaf from the jazz world and stage a festival that would showcase this new talent alongside more established names. They knew that a number of singular talents had come to early maturity but until now had been largely ignored by the US media and music business. Bill Graham and other promoters were successfully staging concerts and package events featuring artists such as The Doors, Jefferson Airplane, Quicksilver Messenger Service, Big Brother, Buffalo Springfield, Mother Earth, and The Grateful Dead, as well as more established performers such as The Byrds and The Mamas & The Papas. It was felt that a collective statement of intent would help the new movement to come together.

There had been a jazz festival at Monterey since 1958, run by Jimmy Lyons, a man well known in jazz circles. Monterey is a coastal Californian town about 75 miles south of San Francisco. In January 1967 a young rock impresario by the name of Alan Pariser had the notion that the coming summer would be the right time to stage a major rock festival at Monterey, and he began to set the wheels in motion. Of the many people involved, Derek Taylor, an ex-publicist for The Beatles who had moved to Los Angeles, was given the task of finding some fresh new British talent to debut at the three-day Monterey Pop Festival. Using his Beatle contacts, Taylor talked to Paul McCartney to see if he would consider a role on the Festival's board of governors and represent the British contingent. McCartney agreed. Taking a break from the almost-finished *Sgt Pepper* sessions at Abbey Road, McCartney spent ten days on the West Coast in mid April 1967, making suggestions for the best examples of cutting-edge British rock. A huge fan of Hendrix even at this early stage, he insisted that the Festival would be incomplete without him. He also supported an appearance by The Who, a band that had enjoyed spectacular singles success in Britain and other parts of the world during 1965 and '66, but had yet to register significantly in the US. Incredible as it may now seem, anthems such as 'My Generation', 'Substitute', 'I Can't Explain', 'I'm A Boy', 'Pictures Of Lily', 'Anyway Anyhow Anywhere' and 'The Kids Are Alright' had all failed to puncture the US Top 40.

This endorsement of Hendrix by McCartney guaranteed an approach from the Festival committee. Chandler explained, "You've got to remember how huge The Beatles were in them days. They were a colossus. The Mamas & The Papas and John Phillips … asked [McCartney] to be part of it, [to] guarantee the Festival. Paul said, 'I'll join the board at Monterey if the Jimi Hendrix Experience are on the show.' Brian Jones was a good pal of Jimi's and mine, [he] used to be about the house at the time. It was Brian who answered the phone from California when it was John Phillips on the phone asking us to go to Monterey. Because Brian answered the phone we said, 'Yeah, Brian will do the announcing … ,' and Brian went out with us and announced Jimi on-stage."[1]

Meanwhile, the new single 'The Wind Cries Mary' was out in Europe and in need of support through live appearances. On May 7th the Experience appeared again at Brian Epstein's great central-London talent showcase, the Saville Theatre, topping the show and supported by Denny Laine, Garnet Mimms, and 123, an experimental Scottish troupe. David Bowie, a young man just starting out on his own road to rock salvation, was present at the Saville gig and wrote a letter to *Record Mirror* with his less than flattering impressions of Hendrix's appearance. Objecting to the highly favourable review given

An interview with the Danish press in Copenhagen, May 1967. Hendrix told one journalist that his debut album was "different to anything ever heard in the world before". He wasn't far wrong.

Hendrix by *Mirror* journalist Derek Boltwood the week before, Bowie claimed: "I was treated to a proverbial feat of journalistic insanity in last week's review of the Saville show. ... Like a can of knowledgeable Windowlene, he wiped off the cloud of mystery surrounding Jimi 'out of sight' Hendrix and 123. How, I ask myself, could the 123, with their chromiatic [chromatic], quarter-tone and chordal harmonies, hope to compare with the ethnic, emotion-filled E chord of Mr H? Why should they think that open harmony and subtle colouring could hold a light to the volcanic battery of one's senses and involved tongue-wiggling from the tentacle-headed flower show from Greenwich Village?"[2]

Looking back now, it is difficult to find any negative reviews or impressions of the Hendrix performance at the Saville Theatre. One wonders about the motivation behind Bowie's distaste, beyond the fact that he obviously enjoyed 123 and *Record Mirror* didn't. Perhaps it was a case of Bowie being caught off balance and out of step with the latest fashion to hit the pop world? His own records at this time are notably short on features such as overdriven amps, screaming guitars and blues-ridden melody lines. That would come later.

With their third successful single in a row, near-unanimous critical raves for *Are You Experienced* in Britain and Europe, and a lightning tour around specially chosen key cities in France, Germany and Scandinavia organised to promote all this activity, Hendrix's management could feel with justification that they had the group's European career under control. During this time Hendrix and the other band members were giving interviews almost daily, in Britain as well as across Europe. Some of them prove today to be goldmines of information; others are embarrassing period pieces. Kathy Etchingham noted: "As he got more into drugs, I would sit and listen to Jimi giving interviews, spouting the most ridiculous acid-inspired stuff which the journalists would soak up as if it were timeless wisdom. Like most acid-heads he had visions and he wanted to create music to express what he saw. He would try to explain this to people but it didn't make sense because it was not linked to reality in any way."[3]

The quandary over how to break Hendrix in the US had begun to ease: there was the invitation to Monterey and the leverage which this gave

Chandler and Jeffrey with Reprise, the American record company now committed to making Hendrix a star in the States. Management figured that the next most important step was to get Hendrix onto a package tour that would put him in front of audiences across the whole country. After all, no one had a clue if Monterey would have any impact. At this point it was simply a convenient lever. Jeffrey set to work plotting that next step.

But a much bigger problem was about to engulf them. Just ten days after the release of *Are You Experienced* in Britain, Ed Chalpin of PPX began to make his feelings known about Hendrix absconding to England and becoming a star – while Chalpin claimed to have him under exclusive contract. Chandler and Jeffrey thought that they had flushed out all the old contracts and claims from Hendrix's period as a nonentity in New York City and earlier. Now they were presented with their worst nightmare: a seemingly valid contract that might take their artist away after they'd spent close on a year's hard work (and a fair chunk of money) establishing him. All Hendrix could do was to smile lamely and tell them he hadn't thought it important enough to mention.

The results of this oversight would be a series of artistically questionable releases over the next few years issued under Hendrix's name, often in tandem with Curtis Knight. But the suits and counter-suits to resolve the dispute would not be finally resolved during Hendrix's lifetime. There is no doubt that Hendrix was as deeply embarrassed and angered by the subsequent issue of the Chalpin/PPX-owned material as anyone else in his circle. For someone of his exacting artistic standards the appearance of this material must indeed have been painful. Meanwhile, the band had to prepare for their first US trip while under this legal cloud, not knowing what effect it would have on their chances of cracking the American market.

Despite this, nothing could stem the flow of music coming from Hendrix, who was presently enjoying the musical benefits of a supercharged imagination. On May 4th, the day before 'The Wind Cries Mary' was released, the band went back into Olympic studio to cut basic tracks for tunes that would eventually be considered for the second album. On the following day another long session produced four more contenders. Exactly a week later, on May 12th, *Are You Experienced* was released. This new studio activity underlines what Chandler, Mitchell and Redding would all say later: none of their recording activity in the first couple of years was aimed at specific projects or concepts. They recorded all the time, whenever they got the chance, and only afterwards would they assess what they had and decide what to do with it. Most bands in the Experience's position in May 1967 would have taken a break while the first LP was released and their singles were still buoyant in the charts. But here they were, working on new material in an effort to strike while the iron was white hot. In two days the band recorded

"The Cream shouldn't worry because they are playing what they like."

Jimi Hendrix, on another great trio

basic tracks for no fewer than seven separate songs. Although only three of these would eventually appear on *Axis: Bold As Love*, the material that remained unused would probably have been released by most other bands of the era. One of these, 'Mr Bad Luck' (also known as 'Look Over Yonder'), was a medium-tempo blues in the modern Chicago tradition that quite likely dated from Hendrix's days in New York. This May session, his first shot at getting down a definitive version, saw a spirited run-through, but as with the earlier 'Here He Comes' (or 'Lover Man'), Hendrix would never sanction release of any of the various studio versions he made. This first attempt at 'Mr Bad Luck', released for the first time decades later, has a curiously Cream-like sound to it, with Mitchell playing a straight contemporary rock beat in his Keith Moon style, while Hendrix comes as close as he ever would to sounding like Eric Clapton in Bluesbreakers mode. Perhaps this explains why 'Mr Bad Luck' would not appear on *Axis: Bold As Love*. Hendrix – and Chandler, no doubt – wanted no such comparisons to be made, however competently the track was played.

Another song with a decidedly Cream-like atmosphere about it – but from a completely unexpected direction – was 'Takin' Care Of No Business', a slow knockabout oompah-like piece. Its English music-hall overtones would have fitted nicely alongside Cream's 'Wrapping Paper' or some of Ray Davies's efforts for his near-contemporary *Village Green Preservation Society* project. Lots of fun, but hardly a serious contender for the altogether more focused final mood of *Axis*. Other pieces left in various stages of incompletion and started on these two days include 'The Dragon From Carlisle' and 'Cat Talking To Me'.

The first of the three tracks that would make it to the next LP was 'She's So Fine', a Redding composition, the first from a group member other than Hendrix. Redding proves himself no great singer and the song itself is hardly a masterpiece, but it's played with great gusto by the whole band. Mitchell's drums are particularly splashy, in Keith Moon fashion, suiting well the post-mod style of the song. Hendrix plays with heightened enthusiasm in this different style, his rhythm guitar passages humming with energy but without the least glimmer of self-indulgence or scene-stealing. His short solo is tremendously exciting but very simple, a clever and successful imitation of the British power-rock guitar styles prevalent the previous year.

'EXP' is an indication of the high spirits in the Hendrix camp at this time. It begins as a spoof radio interview acted out by Hendrix and Mitchell

(who had been a child actor). It's as if the interviewer and interviewee – and the listener – had just drunk some coffee laced with acid. After a jokey namecheck for Hendrix's old Village friend, Paul Caruso, and references to the existence of UFOs – no doubt another result of Hendrix's passion for science fiction – Hendrix gives us his idea of what a spaceship would sound like should it come within earshot. Screaming guitars, sparks of feedback and other effects move between the two speakers (this is one of the first rock albums consciously mixed for stereo listening) and successfully create the illusion of a UFO floating in front of us: a ball of light and a cathedral of sound. 'EXP' would eventually be used as the kick-off track for *Axis*, and while the routine palls a little today, its good humour is at least entertaining and the guitar sound effects still arresting, standing as some of the wildest music Hendrix ever released.

The other *Axis* track more or less completed at these May 1967 sessions was 'If 6 Was 9'. The title and lyrics referred to the then-fashionable *I Ching*, the book used to interpret an ancient Chinese system of divination. Much has been made since by commentators about Hendrix's references in this song to life and death, but that is the danger of hindsight. When he wrote this song, Hendrix had no intention of dying for a very long time, and the references in the lyrics to death are part of the list of paradoxes and unlikely events he itemises. The song is a celebration of individual creative power. Hendrix is saying he doesn't care what else is going on out there – including whatever fashion the hippies decide to follow next – because he's going to stick to following his own muse.

The composition itself is one of Hendrix's most complex. It starts with a spare, dramatic riff, the vocal line matched by a rough-hewn guitar in octaves. The opening verse is a direct lift from the piece known variously as 'Experiencing The Blues' and 'Catfish Blues', Hendrix's own down-home take on Muddy Waters and John Lee Hooker and one that he had been playing regularly on-stage with the Experience for the past six or more months. Here he gives it an entirely different lyric and a fresh rhythmic emphasis. The stealthy, almost stalking rhythm, with Mitchell keeping the beat on hi-hat and snare and punctuating with spare bass-drum explosions, takes us through two

"One song is about the earth being invaded by space creatures, who find human beings so unsuitable for running the earth that they destroy all human life and let the chickens take over."

Jimi Hendrix, on his debut album

verses that establish the subject. After the build-up of tension in this manner, Hendrix releases it with what amounts almost to a sigh on the guitar – and the start of his spoken section: "White collared conservative…". It's a welcome release that leads into a lyrical guitar solo played over brightly resonant chords. At its end, we are back into that opening, stalking riff, now overlaid by a drum solo and interwoven with Hendrix's mumbled comments – including the famous line, "I'm the one that's gonna have to die when it's time for me to die." The tune then doubles back to the open-chord pattern of the guitar solo, Hendrix playing intensely lyrical guitar over an octave-pattern walking bass and jazz drumming.

In an inspired departure designed to lift this to its natural wild climax he overdubs descant recorder, an instrument known then to most schoolchildren but here played with complete abandon, sounding like nothing other than whirling dervishes or the speaking-in-tongues musical lightning of jazz saxophonists Albert Ayler or Pharoah Sanders. This final part of 'If 6 Was 9' is akin to an ecstatic musical celebration of his creative delivery.

Four days later the first studio sketches were made for the next single, 'The Burning Of The

Mitch Mitchell, ever the percussive match for Jimi's dexterity, playing in Copenhagen, May 1967.

City, and found themselves immediately plunged back into the small-time gigs that had typified their work pattern prior to the US trip. The Move would never make an impact in the States, and Pink Floyd's early incarnation left American audiences bewildered. Zoot Money and Geno Washington would remain British-based artists with no real effect on the US. The Spalding gig proved to be something of an endurance test for bands and audience alike because the Auction Hall was possessed of uniquely awful acoustics that did unforgivable things to every band's sound. Perhaps, in the spirit of a true Barbeque, it should have been staged in the open air. But then it might have rained. California this was not.

Midnight Lamp', alongside further work on 'If 6 Was 9'. In one sense, 'If 6 Was 9' encapsulates the end of Hendrix's first phase and 'Midnight Lamp' the start of his second. The first is bursting with energy and ideas as Hendrix is impatient to realise the visions inside him; the second is a doleful calculation of the costs of experience. Both are powerful statements, but Hendrix would rarely revisit the sheer wild abandon of 'If 6 Was 9'. Of all the groups working at the peak of their powers in rock at this time, only The Beatles stand comparison with this work-rate for high quality in such quantity.

There was a brief European tour – the Stockholm concert of May 25th provided footage eventually used as a bonus on the DVD release of the film-short *Experience* – and the band was ready to fly to America. The future of the Experience's music was already well in hand, months before the band's past recordings were laid before the public in the US with the release there of *Are You Experienced*.

On May 22nd Ed Chalpin filed his lawsuit against Yameta (the holding company to which the Experience were all signed) and Reprise (their US record company). The same day, a Swedish journal published an interview with Hendrix, done at the Karlstad concert on the 20th. Hendrix claimed that *Are You Experienced* would be "different to anything ever heard before in the world. One song is about the earth being invaded by space creatures, who find human beings so unsuitable for running the earth that these visitors destroy all human life and let the chickens take over instead."[4] Apart from having fun at the expense of his interviewer (and chickens) Hendrix was right: the lyrics of 'Third Stone From The Sun' were new territory for pop music. Science fiction was still something of a bastard child in the publishing world, just like rock in the musical world. By marrying the two in his lyrics Hendrix was making something new that would be picked up by many songwriters in the so-called psychedelic period during 1967 and '68. But *Are You Experienced* would have some heavyweight psychedelic competition to contend with just two weeks later, from pop music's heavyweight champions.

For now, there was an engagement to be fulfilled that represented something of a mini Monterey, at least considering the talent on display. In typical English style, Spalding, a small town in Lincolnshire, found its Tulip Bulb Auction Hall taken over for the day for an event bizarrely dubbed Barbeque '67. For the princely sum of £1.00 the happy music fans could avail themselves of the opportunity to see The Jimi Hendrix Experience along with Cream, Zoot Money & His Big Roll Band, The Move, Pink Floyd, and Geno Washington & The Ramjam Band. Of this line-up, only Hendrix's group would subsequently appear at Monterey. Cream had just arrived back in the country from their first American tour and the recording of *Disraeli Gears* in New York

On June 1st The Jimi Hendrix Experience went into rehearsal at London's Saville Theatre. That same day, The Beatles' *Sgt Pepper's Lonely Hearts Club Band* was released, their eighth album in four years and easily their most ambitious. On a technical level alone it inspired and challenged every other pop musician who wished to use the recording studio in new and musically satisfying ways. Most were not up to the task, able only to imitate the trappings and style of what The Beatles had achieved. The Rolling Stones had released the sub-par *Between The Buttons* in January and would follow with the desperately uneven and at times pretentious *Their Satanic Majesties Request* in December. Of The Beatles' traditional rivals only The Kinks, with *Something Else* in October 1967, produced something that was distinctive, lasting and different.

The Who, perhaps wisely, released no new album until *The Who Sell Out* in January 1968, an ambitious attempt to create an album that was a radio programme, a concept rarely attempted since and never bettered – partly because it was done with humour. Among the more recent arrivals, Donovan managed a worthy summer album with *Sunshine Superman*, Pink Floyd served notice with *The Piper At The Gates of Dawn*, an album drenched in the imagery The Beatles had been playing with on *Pepper*, and Cream came up with the important, influential and accomplished *Disraeli Gears* in the autumn. On the other side of the Atlantic, the older generation of bands was withering. Brian Wilson abandoned *Smile* when faced with early evidence of *Sgt Pepper*'s artistic advances, while the newer acts had polarised. There was the pop froth of The Monkees, blues-driven progressive bands like The Blues Project and Butterfield Blues Band, and psychedelic shockers such as The Doors, The Grateful Dead, Jefferson Airplane and Love, all of whom revelled in the wake of the creative freedoms opened up by the change in pop culture forced through by The Beatles. Hendrix, meanwhile, went his own way.

Jimi being Jimi, he had a copy of *Sgt Pepper* the day it came out and was busy learning the title track to play at his Saville concert three days later. The Experience were top of a bill on June 4th that also featured Procol Harum (about to hit it big with 'A Whiter Shade Of Pale'), The Chiffons, Denny Laine, and The Stormsville Shakers. Paul McCartney and George Harrison were in attendance and the concert became something of an unofficial celebration of *Sgt Pepper*'s release. Hendrix opened his set with a rousing rendition of the title song – a piece that on that night would only have been known to true believers. But the show didn't go exactly as planned. *Melody Maker* reported: "It should have been such an exciting event … but there was little magic about the Procol's set, while the Hendrix Experience teetered on the brink of disaster."[5] They suffered severely from "a series of long delays" when mikes and amps repeatedly broke down. One particularly long break was filled by an impromptu drum solo from Mitchell. The Experience's set was professionally recorded with the intention of extracting a live EP, but the uncertain performance that night and the speed of events overtaking the band that summer sank the idea.

All three members of the group were invited back to Beatle manager Brian Epstein's London home to join in the private celebration party after the concert. It proved to be a farewell show for the Experience, their final date prior to departure for America. That trip – on legitimate professional business – was timely in more than one sense, for Hendrix's UK work visa was not far short of expiry. The American visit would give management some breathing space to sort out a more permanent visa on his return. One of Hendrix's final PR tasks before leaving was to review new singles for *Melody Maker*, among them Cream's 'Strange Brew'. Hendrix was enthusiastic: "Ooh, that's nice. … It has a strange sort of West Coast and San Francisco sound. I like this record because I like the way he [Eric Clapton] plays anyway. … It sounds very nice to me, but I don't know about the little kiddies. The Cream shouldn't worry because they are playing what they like."[6] That theme was to echo increasingly through his own music as time progressed.

"Well, if this is the best they can do, we can't wait to play."

Mitch Mitchell, on seeing the competition at Monterey

The Jimi Hendrix Experience left London's Heathrow airport on Tuesday June 13th, flying first-class to New York's JFK airport, accompanied by Chandler, Brian Jones and journalist Keith Altham. Mike Jeffery had gone on ahead to deal with publishing and copyright matters, tying them all to the Bermuda-based Yameta company that swallowed so much of the Experience income (as Redding and Mitchell would later find to their regret).

After a hunt for a good hotel and a freshening-up, Hendrix typically headed for his favourite record stores and bought a stack of the latest US releases. Later he went back to his Greenwich Village haunts, dropping in on Richie Havens at the Café Au Go Go and catching The Doors at The Scene club. Redding and Mitchell, new to The Big Apple, spent the evening on board a luxury yacht moored in the harbour, just as The Rolling Stones had done almost a year earlier. No one apart from Hendrix would have known about or noticed the irony.

The following day the troupe flew out to San Francisco and on the 16th arrived at Monterey airport. That day the Pop Festival started, with Simon & Garfunkel, Eric Burdon & The Animals, and Lou Rawls headlining a long and diverse bill. An atmosphere developed of willing co-operation and open drug-taking of the chemical and organic kind, along with a conscious effort to evoke the era of flower-power as 100,000 orchids were flown in to the site for distribution among festival-goers.

The presence of The Beatles was hard to escape, from badges claiming "A splendid time is guaranteed for all" to the group's contributions to the festival's lavish official programme booklet. John Phillips made the opening speech, nominating three themes: music, love and flowers. It was a Festival of birth and rebirth for many artists. On this first day Eric Burdon shed his old Animals image and staked a formidable claim at the forefront of the psychedelic generation, playing much of the material from his as-yet-unreleased *Winds Of Change* album, including 'Warm San Francisco Nights'.

The second day – the first that Hendrix and his group attended – was split into afternoon and evening sessions, with virtually the entire San Francisco freak contingent represented that afternoon, from Big Brother and Quicksilver Messenger Service to Country Joe & The Fish and Steve Miller. Mixed in were the finest new-blues players, from Al Kooper to Canned Heat, with Buddy Miles's Electric Flag thrown in for good luck. The evening's

highlights included Paul Butterfield, Jefferson Airplane, Booker T & The MGs, Moby Grape, and Otis Redding, as well as The Byrds who dedicated their rather rushed version of 'Hey Joe' to "a number of performers … Love, The Leaves … and a cat who's gonna perform here, Jimi Hendrix".

Mitchell took the opportunity to study some of the American acts he'd heard only on records, including Otis Redding, Booker T, The Byrds, and Jefferson Airplane. "We were aware of the West Coast movement," he recalled later, "but hadn't paid much attention to it until then. Some of them turned out to be very good, but we still thought, 'Well, if this is the best they can do … [we] can't wait to play.'"[7] Roger McGuinn of The Byrds remembered Hendrix hanging out at Monterey that day, and watched the Experience the following evening. Bassist Harvey Brooks noticed Hendrix, Brian Jones and Mike Bloomfield backstage together. "We were just sitting in this room, and everybody was tripping on a little acid and talking about how groovy everything was," said Brooks. "That was the whole thing: how groovy everything was. … I had known Jimi from New York, so it was like this big get-together. You looked around and you saw people smiling and having a nice time … and then someone stole my bass from the stage. It was a Fender Jazz Bass. That brought me back to reality." [8]

The entire afternoon of Sunday 18th was given over to master Indian sitar player Ravi Shankar. Hendrix is reported to have been in attendance alongside Mike Bloomfield; he apparently "nodded appreciatively" while "Bloomfield sat rapt on the side of the stage".[9] The complex, uncompromising music that Shankar played in a series of ragas must have made a considerable impression on a musician of Hendrix's sensitivity, underlining the basic notion that music could be a three-hour raga as much as a three-minute pop tune. Shankar received a lengthy ovation at the conclusion of his set. The evening's programme was long and varied. The Blues Project, now in its last throes of activity, kicked off the proceedings, followed by a second Monterey set from Big Brother & The Holding Company, substituting for a last-minute cancellation by Dionne Warwick (and with their first set not filmed, Big Brother were determined now to be preserved for posterity). Then came Buffalo Springfield, already missing Neil Young. The major action was packed into the end of the evening with the last four acts, in order of appearance: The Who, The Grateful Dead, The Jimi Hendrix Experience, and The Mamas & The Papas. Considering that Hendrix's group was unknown in the US, this billing reflected considerable faith in Paul McCartney's judgement.

Hendrix and The Who had already appeared on a bill together and, well aware of their respective acts, were determined to up-stage one another – not only because this was their introduction to America (though The Who had appeared fleetingly in the spring) but also through sheer professional pride. There are as many stories about the backstage trading that resulted in The Who going on before Hendrix as there were people present, but it probably amounted to nothing more than the usual stand-offs and amateur dramatics when up-and-coming bands are looking for any kind of advantage in hitting big with a crowd. Nobody in either band was stupid enough to take it personally. If anyone lost out, it was the group who became the meat in the running-order sandwich, The Grateful Dead. They came on after The Who's wildly successful smokebomb-and-mayhem set-closer that had finally won over a crowd who earlier had been disinclined to take them to their hearts. After all, this was by far the meanest, toughest music they'd been subjected to in three long, drug-filled days. The Who had been introduced by Eric Burdon as a group that "had been passed by slightly in America but they won't after this. … This is a group who will destroy you in more ways than one". How right he was. The Grateful Dead, not at their best, tried hard to recreate the hypnotising musical mantras that had made them San Francisco's favourite live act. Despite the crowd willing them on and an unscheduled walk-on announcement from The Monkees' Peter Tork during the set, the Dead failed to achieve lift-off.

Then it was the turn of the Jimi Hendrix Experience. After a fey but affectionate introduction from a blissed-out Brian Jones, the Experience took the blitzkrieg approach, kicking off with a 'Killing Floor' fuelled by adrenalin, nerves, acid and various untold extras. It was the musical equivalent of a fast ride in an E-type Jag. Hendrix was dressed in clothes as exotic as any on display elsewhere during those three days, though he still had his Little Richard moustache. He was not only something utterly new musically, but an entirely original vision of what a black American entertainer should and could look like. The crowd were used to the smart suits of Motown and Stax acts, just as Otis Redding had worn the previous day; now they were forced to suspend judgement on every level and accept what they saw and heard as an unprecedented event. Hendrix with his consummate stage craft, charisma and musical ability had them completely won over long before the end of his set.

The aural record reveals a distinctly patchy performance. Tuning problems abound. 'Foxy Lady' is taken much too fast, losing a lot of its raunch in the process, and 'Rock Me Baby' is uncomfortably fast, though very disciplined and containing a fiery Hendrix solo. For the full impact of the Experience that evening one must view the film shot by D.A. Pennebaker and released as *Monterey Pop*. On a confident and controlled run-through of 'Hey Joe' the band gets the tempo just right, transforming it from the rather strident up-tempo rant delivered by The Byrds two days earlier into a classic piece of pop storytelling.

All through the songs, and between numbers, Hendrix constantly makes contact with the audience in a relaxed and intimate way, disposing of the conventional "thank you, you're a great audience" routines and instead involving them in his own feelings about being at Monterey, about coming through New York on the way, about having been to England, about having to tune up. His success in building this relationship is clear from the good-humoured response throughout. They applaud generously as he introduces Redding and Mitchell while conceding that "nobody's gonna know us, OK". The crowd wants this to work, even before the famous lighter-fluid ending. Unusually for a Hendrix gig, and despite out-of-tune guitars for virtually every number, it's mostly the slower songs that work best: 'Like A Rolling Stone' takes on a completely different character to that created on the original studio recording by Dylan, and 'The Wind Cries Mary' develops a genuinely haunting quality through Hendrix's delivery of the melancholy lyrics and the band's relaxed handling of the dynamics.

Hendrix announces that they have just two numbers left, and the band tears into 'Purple Haze', a little fast but not unsettlingly so. Hendrix concentrates on his stage impact and in his solo sticks quite closely to the studio version before taking an extra chorus to whip things up. The tune is full of power, the band is bursting with visual excitement, the crowd is completely with him. Only Hendrix and his management know what's coming next. He switches to an audibly inferior Stratocaster while Redding runs through the riff to 'Steppin' Out', a Clapton performance that Hendrix would have known. Was this a wind-up or an in-joke?

After a long preamble praising his audience, Hendrix announces his last number, saying: "There's nothing more I can do – look at these beautiful people out there." He then begins the feedback sequence that introduces 'Wild Thing'. The performance is certainly full of raw excitement and swaggering sexuality, but its musical worth is nowhere near the rest of the set: it's the spectacle that matters, and the spectacle of the burning guitar, famous as it is, still has the power to stun when viewed through Pennebaker's lens, close to 40 years on. With that in mind, it is important to remember that for those watching on the night and for the performers themselves this was an unknown band making its bid for fame. The bid succeeded with that audience that night, giving Hendrix a gilt-edged introduction to the American music industry. There were influential people watching from the wings – Bill Graham went straight backstage and arranged for The Experience to play The Fillmore. But it was only in retrospect that it became something momentous. Everybody knew that Hendrix was special that night and that they'd witnessed the beginning of something, but there was a considerable debate about exactly what was special. Nobody knew if he'd even have a single hit, let alone a sustained US career.

Jann Wenner, still a few months away from founding *Rolling Stone* magazine, filed a report on the Festival for *Melody Maker* in England, headlined on the *MM*'s front page. Wenner wrote: "Jimi Hendrix made a memorable return to America. Although he handled his guitar with rhythmic agility and minor drama, he is not the great artist we were told. His real art is in his presence." Wenner's preferences were made clear in the very next paragraph. "The San Francisco groups were distinguished by their artistic maturity, a thoroughly professional approach, mostly original material, and musical quality. They stand out for their sheer sound in a musical, rather than an existantial [existential] way."[10]

In contrast, Barry Hansen was well aware of Hendrix's expertise as he wrote a report for US jazz magazine *Down Beat*. "This was the American debut of his English group and quite possibly the major event of the festival. Hendrix's roots are deep in blues and soul; yet he has learned the best licks and tricks from the white blues and psychedelic guitarists: Bloomfield, Clapton, and all the rest – an unprecedented and very likely unbeatable combination. His tone and phrasing on the guitar, which he plays left-handed, are amazing. ... The audience, taken a bit aback at first, cheered more loudly with each number. ... The climax came with a lightly regarded rock tune of a year ago, 'Wild Thing'. This had the audience screaming at every line before Hendrix even started his coup de grace ... [and] if The Who had not done some of this before, there might well have been a riot."[11]

Hendrix didn't close the evening; that was left to festival headliners The Mamas & The Papas who received a rapturous welcome from the crowd that had so recently been steamrollered by The Who and Jimi Hendrix. A perfect chill-out for a great night's entertainment was capped by Scott McKenzie's guest vocal on the John Phillips-penned hit '(If You're Going To) San Francisco'. To put this event into perspective, the entire Monterey Pop Festival and its aftermath

Park Experience: wallowing in the virtually unanimous UK raves for the *Are You Experienced* LP.

would be overshadowed a week later by an unprecedented media and music event, the first ever simultaneous worldwide live broadcast involving television companies across every continent. The programme, *Our World*, had invited just one pop group to contribute, and they were The Beatles. Performing in front of an invited studio audience in London, among whom were a fair sprinkling of pop stars, the world's favourite group premiered a song that would be their next smash hit single, 'All You Need Is Love'. Their audience was estimated at 400 million. On release, the single went to number one in countries worldwide

Capitalising on the Experience's Monterey debut and the word-of-mouth approval that followed, 'Purple Haze' was released in the US the following day, Monday 19th, with 'The Wind Cries Mary' as the American flip side. The Experience were rush-booked into Bill Graham's Fillmore venue in San Francisco for a five-day season starting the day after that, June 20th, supporting Jefferson Airplane, a band hot from Monterey and with 'Somebody To Love' at number five in the national charts that week. But the Experience cleaned up, to Chandler's delight. "Jefferson Airplane were top of the bill,

Phoning from New York, he caught Chandler and the group just as they arrived back in their San Francisco hotel after deposing Jefferson Airplane from the Fillmore bill. "He phoned … to tell us he'd pulled off this fantastic thing," Chas recalled, "[that he'd] got them on the Monkees tour. Jimi and I just sat there stunned."[15] As far as the band's musical credibility was concerned, this was suicidal. In terms of audience and style, it was a mismatch. But there was a certain twisted logic, and we know now that Jeffery was not the prime mover, only the opportunist who enthusiastically exploited the idea. Chandler may also have been more aware of it in advance than he later cared to admit. After all, members of The Monkees had been present all through the Monterey Festival and certainly saw Hendrix do his stuff. Not only that, but Monkees drummer Mickey Dolenz had known about Hendrix a year prior to Monterey. He later told an interviewer, "I first saw him in New York at a club called the Café Au Go Go. He was playing with John Hammond as Hammond's guitar player. I was just invited down by somebody, and they said, 'Let's go see John Hammond, there's this guitar player who plays with his teeth.' And sure enough, there he was. I said, 'That's fantastic,' and didn't

Jimi at the Monterey Pop Festival in California, June 18th 1967. He introduced the band to the American audience by saying: "Nobody's gonna know us, OK?" Maybe so, but not for long.

Jimi Hendrix Experience was second, and Big Brother & The Holding Company were the opening act. We'd done two nights there and Jefferson Airplane cried off 'cause Jimi just crucified them, murdered them. And they pulled out of the last show, and we got back to the hotel after the second show, after being told we'd be topping the bill on the last night – and we were really ecstatic, it'd been a fantastic night."[12]

Mitchell's memory was considerably less triumphant. "The original Fillmore bill was Gabor Szabo, us and the Airplane, but it was strange: poor old Gracie Slick, her voice went haywire after the first gig, just couldn't make it after that. I think that's why Big Brother with Janis [Joplin] ended up playing with us. Janis was just great."[13] Hendrix's group had triumphed at the American headquarters of the counterculture almost two months to the day before Cream would arrive there to make it their West Coast home-from-home – even though Cream had already been to the US and had made their second album there. It was quite a coup, and a great portent for the immediate future. Surely more live triumphs beckoned for the Experience?

Well, almost. As Mitchell later commented, "Breaking it in one place – at Monterey – didn't cover the whole of America, as we were later to find out."[14] Yet enthusiasm for The Jimi Hendrix Experience was coming from the most unlikely quarters, and Mike Jeffery was the man to take advantage of it.

think too much more about it until a few months later when I was at the Monterey Pop Festival, and suddenly they say here's The Jimi Hendrix Experience, and out they came, and I said, 'There's that guy who plays with his teeth!'"[16]

Mike Nesmith, the most musically gifted of the quartet, had learned about Hendrix in London some months earlier from no less a source than John Lennon. "I was having dinner in London with John Lennon, Eric Clapton and a group of people," Nesmith said later. "In the middle of dinner John produced this portable tape recorder and requested that the restaurant turn down the piped-in music, and then proceeded to play 'Hey Joe' on his recorder, saying, 'You guys gotta check this out.' … Everyone was reverential. Hendrix had taken off on his own and done it in such an artistic and creative way. Like everybody said, 'Gee, if we could really play music like that, we would!'"[17] It seems that Hendrix was yanked onto the Monkees tour because three Monkees wanted to be taken seriously as musicians and make a mark in the rapidly evolving pop and rock scene. Dolenz, Nesmith and Tork, fresh from the embarrassment of not playing on their first hit single, felt that an association with Hendrix would help reposition their reputation and perhaps give them the credibility they craved. Even if Hendrix was dragged kicking and screaming to the deal, his bill-topping partners walked into it with eyes wide open, encouraging their management to set it up. But their reasoning proved hopelessly naïve.

The gap between what by now was termed 'bubblegum' and the emerging 'underground' music had widened into a chasm by mid 1967. These two strains of popular music served utterly separate audiences. Chandler and the band members looked at the chasm from the other side and were horrified both at the damage that could be done to their own credibility and the certain suicide a support spot on such a tour offered. After all, everyone in the business knew that on such a bill you were on a hiding to nothing – as any of the support bands for The Beatles' various tours could have told Mike Jeffery. But the contract was signed and had to be honoured. After unsuccessfully trying to record a basic track at Houston Studios in Los Angeles for 'The Stars That Play With Laughing Sam's Dice', which would eventually become the B-side of the next single, and playing a night at the Whisky A Go Go in the city supporting Sam & Dave, the band flew over to New York for rest and recreation prior to the Monkees tour.

New York City in early July 1967 was still a long way from the forefront of pop fashion, as Hendrix had ironically noted to the audience at Monterey. Nothing much had moved on from the previous year as far as Hendrix was concerned. "It's ridiculous [to have] people standing laughing at us at New York airport when they're dressed in ill-fitting Bermuda shorts," he told *Melody Maker*'s Michael Wale. "If they knew how stupid they look they wouldn't stare at us so much."[18] The group played two successful gigs at the very fashionable Scene club in New York, where they performed alongside Tiny Tim among others. Jeffery had managed to get Hendrix added to the Rheingold Festival at the eleventh hour as support for The Young Rascals, appearing in Central Park on July 5th. His successful performance was photographed for posterity by freelancer Linda Eastman, later to become Linda McCartney. Dates like this, plus the Monkees tour support, were helping to finance the US trip, for although their expenses for the trip to and from Monterey had been met by the festival committee's fund, no performance fee was paid to any artist apart from Ravi Shankar. The Experience needed income to help mount a sustained attack on the American market, and such appearances would help.

In the short time between the Rheingold gig and the beginning of the Monkees tour, the band began serious work on the next single, 'The Burning Of The Midnight Lamp', in New York City's Mayfair studio, a small facility up a few floors in a building close to Times Square. Hendrix had written much of the intensely personal lyrics on the coast-to-coast plane journey. In between sessions, Hendrix and Redding checked out Frank Zappa at Greenwich Village's Garrick Theatre, while Mitchell went to see Miles Davis and Dizzy Gillespie elsewhere in the Village. Hendrix immediately became fixated on Zappa's use of a wah-wah pedal for his guitar and used one that same evening for overdubs on the new single.

The Monkees tour started in Jacksonville, Florida, on Saturday July 8th. It was bankrolled by Screen Gems who in a year had made The Monkees into a massive phenomenon for teens and pre-teens, so the touring party enjoyed lavish facilities. Relations were friendly between the two groups. Mitchell remembered, "They were a nice bunch of chaps, even though we thought they couldn't play. We shared the private plane and all that, but god, did their audience hate us. Eight-year-old kids with their mums and dads: no wonder they hated us."[19] The Monkees themselves were genuinely embarrassed at what they'd inflicted on Hendrix and his group. Peter Tork, later a friend and regular companion of Hendrix on the occasions when their professional lives coincided, recalled: "Poor Jimi, they booed him off the stage. The Monkees were designed to bring rock to the next level below where it was standing. So you had kids who were 16, 17 and 18 years old who liked rock: The Monkees were designed to bring 14 and 15 year olds into the fold and not scare the living daylights out of mama."[20]

There are conflicting stories about how and why the Experience came off the Monkees tour so quickly (they lasted just six venues, finishing on July 16th on the last of four nights at Forest Hills Tennis Stadium in New York) but their employment was terminated through mutual consent. Redding said, "The tour manager nagged Jimi to tone down the act. Jimi acquiesced at the Forest Hills gig by turning off completely. Usually intolerant of his on-stage moodies, this time I agreed with his tactic. We were told to get off the tour, or else … or else what? Get thrown off the tour? Second prize was being asked to stay on. … Getting thrown off the Monkees tour was as good as not being invited to the White House as far as credibility went."[21] Chandler and Jeffrey, hardly shrinking violets when it came to exploiting notoriety, concocted a story – with the consent of promoter Dick Clark and the Monkees management – that right-wing pressure group The Daughters Of The American Revolution had objected to the Experience's act. The Daughters at that stage didn't even know of the Experience's existence, though doubtless they would have objected given the opportunity. The exit was designed so that no one came out feeling overly abused. Hendrix let off steam the following day in an interview with Britain's *New Musical Express*. "We got screams and good reactions, and some kids even rushed the stage. But we were not getting any billing, all the posters on the show just screamed out MONKEES. … We decided it was just the wrong audience. I think they're replacing me with Mickey Mouse."[22]

The group now had time to kill after dropping out of the tour early, and while waiting for replacement gigs to be arranged they took to New York City for entertainment. Mitchell later told *Record Mirror* that he and Redding had visa problems. "We were restricted to H2 visas and that meant we had to get permission for every job. I was offered a couple of recording sessions in Hollywood but had to turn them down. Also, we couldn't go to radio and TV studios for interviews or we'd be in trouble with the unions."[23] Hendrix was an American and a union member, so he didn't have these problems. Instead he had old friends to revisit and debts to pay. A few days' work had been organised for the band at the Café Au Go Go, a year almost to the day after he'd debuted his first group there in the unsuccessful showcase arranged by Linda Keith. John Hammond remembered: "I saw him in New York when he

"Hendrix's roots are deep in blues and soul; yet he has learned the best licks and tricks from the white-blues and psychedelic guitarists."

Down Beat reviews Monterey

had just blown out [the Monkees] tour, and he was totally depressed by it. He came into the Gaslight and jammed with me there. I had a little band there at the time, and we talked about old times."[24]

In the days prior to this social call, the Experience had gone back into Mayfair studio to finish off the next single, 'The Burning Of The Midnight Lamp' backed with 'The Stars That Play With Laughing Sam's Dice'. 'Midnight Lamp' had been under construction for some time and had already been the subject of a number of re-thinks. At these sessions they finally decided on the overdubs and additional instruments needed, Hendrix completing the A-side by adding what amounted to a harpsichord obbligato. The resulting single, released a month later, was something of a strange choice considering the alternatives already committed to tape or the other possible singles languishing on *Are You Experienced*, but it had a deeply-felt if somewhat obscure lyric with a strong sense of place and circumstance, plus an intricate accompaniment. Unfortunately, much of the detail was lost in the sub-standard recording process. Mayfair studio was not exactly state of the art, although the group did use Gary Kellgren on the session, an engineer who would work extensively with Hendrix at New York City's Record Plant studio in the near future. Replying to a reader's letter in *Melody Maker*, Hendrix detailed the equipment on 'Midnight Lamp': "We used a … Fender [Dual] Showman amplifier with two 15-inch speakers and I used a … wah-wah pedal with my guitar. We also had straight rhythm guitar, harpsichord, and a Mellotron to produce the girl's voice. The secret was manipulation of the wah-wah pedal and the tremolo bar on the guitar. No other electronic equipment was employed."[25]

'Lamp' begins oddly for a single, trailing a long and rhythmically repetitive phrase that sounds as if it is an excerpt from a chaconne by Pachelbel or Purcell rather than a pop riff. It is repeated in its entirety before the full group joins in, with Hendrix adding his vocal line. He sings across a chord sequence that is straightforward but again unusual for pop singles in its movement, providing the vocal line with some ungainly changes to negotiate

"There's nothing more I can do — look at these beautiful people out there."

Jimi Hendrix, announcing his last song at Monterey

but adding to the general sense of frustration and despair suggested by the lyrics. The atmosphere is summed up by the haltingly delivered aside from Hendrix after the guitar solo: "Loneliness is such a drag."

Musically, the song has always been noted for the first recorded use by Hendrix of a wah-wah pedal. He uses it as part of the instrumental accompaniment in a way that suggests a subsidiary conversation. At times it is distracting, but the new toy comes into its own during the solo. Here, all the yearning and passion that rumbles around the rest of the performance comes pouring out, wrapped in this tumbling, plaintive, ever-changing framework of distorted wah-wah sound. The solo is full of blues phrases and intervals, as well as abrupt changes of pitch, but Hendrix uses these devices in a fresh way in what is essentially not a blues context. The contrast is satisfying.

The B-side, 'The Stars That Play With Laughing Sam's Dice', was titled purely to give everybody a chuckle at the initials: STP with LSD. (STP is, like LSD, a hallucinogenic drug, also known as angel dust.) Nobody in the band took the song very seriously. Mitchell said "it was just a filler, done in one take with the background vocals done by people in the studio. … There is really nothing to be read into the song. Just a quickly written B-side, so needless to say it was never done on stage."[26] It would be fair to describe the sound of the original 45rpm single release of 'STPWLSD' as muddy, as if it had been mixed in a hurry. For a track with so much going on there could have been a more concerted effort at separation, but perhaps it wasn't a priority. The song was at least thought about long enough to receive an arrangement, for it starts with a nicely worked triplet riff shared between guitar and bass before the short verse has Hendrix expounding some nonsense about the stars and the zodiac simply to justify the title.

Still, the band plays with great zest before bringing this section of the song to an end some 40 seconds into the track. Then a wah-wah phrase introduces a strolling blues tempo, Hendrix calls everybody to order, the party begins and, over a three-chord jam background, he takes one of his most outrageously brilliant blues solos ever committed to tape. That he saw it primarily as an accompaniment to the party being held in the foreground shows just how confident he was of his own powers – and the direction of his

career at this time. Virtually every other guitarist in 1967 would have killed to have been able to play such innovative, incendiary blues guitar, and some of the phrases that emerge above the general hubbub still raise the hairs on the back of one's neck. Praise is also due to some outstanding bass and drum work from Redding and Mitchell in this section.

On the single's release, this B-side became something of a hipster's code for super-cool: few people investigated far enough at the time to discover – and then relish – this remarkable guitar solo, let alone Hendrix's laconic hitchhiker's guide to the zodiac … "Don't open that door!". 'Laughing Sam's Dice' was first gathered onto LP on *Smash Hits* in 1968 and has since had two posthumous remixed releases. It appeared on the generally ignored *Loose Ends* compilation of 1973, with the guitar track mixed much higher and the whole piece bathed in echo. Much later, in 1998, it appeared on the CD *South Saturn Delta*, again with the guitar mixed high but (thankfully) less added echo. Oddly enough (or perhaps not, given Hendrix's original design) the solo still sounds most exciting in the single's mix, slightly buried and poking out from time to time in outrageous musical fistfuls.

The 'Midnight Lamp' / 'Laughing Sam' single did nothing on release in the US, though it managed to (just) breach the Top 20 in Britain, getting to number 18 in early September 1967. All that work for so little return. Redding later noted wryly, "It was a sign of the times that it took 42 hours to record 'Burning Of The Midnight Lamp' while 'The Wind Cries Mary' had taken six minutes."[27] In one final anomaly connected with this most singular single, 'Lamp' was left out of the reckoning for the next LP, *Axis*, but was added to *Electric Ladyland*, an album otherwise made up entirely of pieces recorded after the *Axis* sessions. Track Records released 'Lamp' twice on a single in Britain, the second time (in 1969) substituting 'Fire' (mis-titled 'Let Me Light Your Fire') from *Are You Experienced* as the A-side and making 'Lamp' the B.

All three Experience members, still in New York after the Monkees tour, continued to lap up what the city had on offer. Mitchell went and saw jazz drummer Elvin Jones in a miserable little club where "nobody showed any interest at all. They've got the best in America, but they don't show any enthusiasm for their artists. … He came over [to my table] and said, 'English pop group, huh?' But when he saw we were genuine he came over and kissed me. I think we were the first people to take any interest in months".[28] Over the next few days Hendrix hung out in Greenwich Village and checked out old friends, catching up with the past year's worth of New York life and repositioning himself in the eyes of his American peers. During this short break, John Coltrane's death on July 17th reverberated through New York's music community. The funeral took place in Manhattan four days later; there were thousands of mourners, and performances by the Ornette Coleman and Albert Ayler groups. Hendrix must have been aware of the shock of Coltrane's death at just 40 years old, although his reaction is unrecorded.

That evening the Experience played two shows at the Café Au Go Go. During down-time Hendrix continued to visit old friends and colleagues, but amid this satisfying round of old haunts he was to commit an act of gross stupidity. Of his own volition, in late July Hendrix went into a recording studio with Ed Chalpin and Curtis Knight. Chalpin, owner of the PPX record company, was suing Hendrix, his current managers and his US record label over his claim on Hendrix through a contract signed in 1966. Considering Hendrix's position at the time, it seems incredible that he could be so feckless about his career. But he was. With all the subsequent statements and counter-statements made by interested parties (including Hendrix) it is impossible to establish a credible motivation for him, but a close listen to the music that resulted, in conjunction with those memories, at least puts us on the road to a possible conclusion. As with so many pivotal events in his short life, a plethora of dates and even locations have been suggested for the reunion of

Jimi Hendrix (right) awaits his turn to go on at the Monterey Pop Festival, California, June 1967.

Hendrix and his old New York colleague Curtis Knight, usually between July 17th and 25th. There were two separate sessions that resulted in less than an hour's worth of taped material as originally performed.

Hendrix plays a Hagstrom eight-string bass for the duration of one of the sessions (generally regarded to have been the first, possibly on July 25th, though no one knows for sure or is prepared to prove it by releasing the session log). From this, six separate pieces of music were released. Hendrix ambles his way through the second session, on a heavily wah-wah'd guitar for most tracks, although there are occasional precise rhythm-guitar additions to the tunes that are not simply recorded jams and which could conceivably be from him. Just five numbers emerged from the playing committed to tape on the second day. On both days there is a mix of structured songs and directionless, aimless (and pointless) jams. The jams consist simply of friends and colleagues messing around and were never intended (by Hendrix at least) to be heard by the public. The structured songs sound like demos that Knight had worked on previously, and it is entirely possible that Hendrix agreed to add some touches to them as a favour to a friend. Supporting this idea is a surviving studio dialogue taped during the second session where Hendrix attempts to extract a promise from Ed Chalpin, who is listening in the control room, that Chalpin would not use Hendrix's name on any release. Chalpin recorded the lot, as he was legally entitled to do, and has used the tapes as the basis for his seemingly endless edits and re-edits of the material ever since, providing the world with successive floods of re-assembled Hendrix-related bits and pieces.

There are six tracks from what is presumed to be the first session, the one with Hendrix on eight-string bass: 'Get That Feeling', 'Future Trip', 'No Business', 'Odd Ball', 'Flashing', 'Day Tripper'. Of these, only Lennon & McCartney's 'Day Tripper' and 'No Business', a very simple soul-style ballad, could be described as songs or pieces with any more than an incidental structure. The others are all jams, with no fewer than four ('Get That Feeling', 'Future Trip', 'Odd Ball' and 'Flashing') in the same key and sharing the same rhythm as the 'Day Tripper' recording. They seem to be either remixes and/or edits of the basic track, or edits and fade-ins of jams that came out of work done on 'Day Tripper'. On 'Get That Feeling' Knight begins the track still singing "Got a good reason…", an obvious left-over from work on 'Day Tripper'. The two guitarists have the same tone and attack used on the 'Day Tripper' master. Hendrix's work on eight-string bass – an unusual instrument with four paired strings designed to give a rich, strong sound – is disciplined and tight throughout, playing simple patterns and very supportive of the group effort. He is the perfect celebrity guest.

The Knight version of 'Day Tripper' is an attempt to deliver the song back to the soul roots of Lennon and McCartney's composition. Drummer and bassist are up to the task, but neither guitarist has any idea about how to augment the rhythm and build a treatment or arrangement. The track is also hampered by Knight's sub-par vocals: unfortunately for him (and us), the man was simply without talent or charm as a singer, however hard he tried. The same can be said of 'No Business', the other 'song' made that day and a Knight original. It is closely modelled on Otis Redding-style power-soul ballads, and Hendrix obliges with a perfect imitation of a Stax bass line. But whatever charm this simple, plaintive ballad might have had in the hands of a superior performer like Redding is entirely dissipated by Knight's witless vocals. This is sub-garage rock made worse by Knight's less than subtle imitation of Hendrix's singing style. Knight also mentions Hendrix's name in the lyrics, though this is quite probably a later vocal overdub: it's hard to believe that Hendrix, who wanted to be an anonymous sideman, would have been happy for Knight to identify him in this way.

On what may be the second studio date with Knight a similar pattern emerges, only now Hendrix is on guitar and messing with his wah-wah. It was still a new toy for him, and one that so far he'd only used on the 'Midnight Lamp' session, so he may have seen this as a relaxed way of exploring the gadget's tricks and listening to the results while at the same time helping Knight out. Two instrumental titles, 'Hush Now' and 'Love Love', share the same key (concert C) and sound like different portions of one loose jam, the former pretty much sticking to the opening sequence of chord changes as well as the overall form of the first part of Hendrix's own composition 'Somewhere' (as that tune is represented on posthumous Hendrix releases).

Once again only two structured tunes are played at this session. 'Gloomy Monday' starts as a driving rocker – Hendrix's pulsing rhythm guitar is unmistakable on this track. There is a short section of the song (six bars, repeated just once) in a slower waltz metre that also, bizarrely, seems to feature a sitar (or an instrument imitating one), perhaps in some weird deference to the Beatles of *Rubber Soul* from some two years earlier. Knight's

Peter Tork of The Monkees with Hendrix on their US tour, July 1967.

pedestrian vocal is double-tracked in an effort to give it some power and presence. The recording quality on this track is quite different to anything else made for PPX that summer, and Hendrix uses no wah-wah, suggesting that the backing track (and probably the song) was old – perhaps dating back to the previous year – and that Knight asked Hendrix to help finish it. Some of the devices used in the song suggest models from 1965. Hendrix once again does a sterling job as sideman, playing unselfishly and with plenty of drive, lifting the performance several notches as a consequence. But the song is essentially banal ("I can't wait for the weekend" sung in schoolboy manner, for example) and could never have reached any level of real musical satisfaction.

Two other pieces, 'Happy Birthday" and 'Love Love', derive from the same basic track. There is only the most elementary structure: merely a riff, down one simple tone (whole-step) for four bars, loosely-played wah-wah guitar and Knight's vocals around a couple of well-known blues intervals. Once again Knight is feeling sorry for himself. The two tracks sound like different portions of the same jam, with Knight supplying identical vocal lines but different lyrics. Of all the miserable Knight vocals on the PPX material between 1965 and '67, this is perhaps the least inept, although that hardly makes it pleasurable. We have no proof this is the vocal that Knight recorded on the day Hendrix was present in the studio – he may well have tried for a better subsequent performance. The reason for this element of doubt is a song called 'Ballad Of Jimi'. The performance has been released with two completely different sets of lyrics, both sung by Knight.[29] The first, on Capitol's *Get That Feeling* LP of December 1967, has mundane rags-to-riches lyrics. On its second release, after Hendrix's death, Hendrix had suddenly become the subject of a Knight lament describing him as his 'best friend'. Hendrix had a lot of self-declared 'best friends', and few of them did him much good, alive or dead.

On August 9th the Experience left New York City for a short series of cross-country gigs, at first in Washington DC, thence to Michigan, and finally Los Angeles, where they played the Hollywood Bowl on August 18th as support to The Mamas & The Papas, and at Santa Barbara the following evening, with Moby Grape and Tim Buckley among others. Within two days the band flew back to London, bringing their first American adventure to a close. Redding said later, "Jimi lost a lot of drive once we broke in the States. He seemed content enough to have conquered the place where he had struggled so hard."[30] He felt that some of the heart went out of the band as the pressures of overnight celebrity in America took their toll. "We had conquered America, but at high cost," wrote Redding. "We had our act worked out, but we were doing it night after night and [were] unsure about where it was getting us."[31] Of course, Redding's view here was given in retrospect. The high energy of the shows the Experience played at this time speaks of hope rather than deflation.

Back in Britain the workload hardly dropped, with the band as hot as they had ever been. *Melody Maker* in its August 12th issue anticipated their return to the UK with a news item announcing that the "Jimi Hendrix Experience appear at London's Saville Theatre on August 27th after their return from their extended tour of America. The Crazy World of Arthur Brown and Tomorrow are also on the bill". Alongside this item was a picture of Steve Winwood's newly-formed Traffic, gathered around a studio microphone to record 'Hole In My Shoe'. "It's due for release," the PR item continues, "on August 25th and features a vocal from guitarist Dave Mason. A Mellotron is used in the backing, and the track includes a recitation by a six-year-old girl in a

Soundcheck with white Strat, preparing for a concert at the Hollywood Bowl, California, August 18th 1967.

'dream sequence'." One of the best bands to emerge from flower-power and the acid-tripping mentality of 1967, Traffic would have a strong impact on Hendrix: he would see them at the Saville a month later. But the biggest shock for British rock that month was the death of Beatles manager Brian Epstein, whose body was found in his London flat on the day of Hendrix's Saville concert. The Experience's second show at the Epstein-run theatre that night was abandoned as a mark of respect. The Beatles, away in Wales meeting the Maharishi, hastily re-convened in London. Meanwhile, a letter from Jimmy Page was published in *Melody Maker*'s September 9th issue while he was still on tour in the States with his band The Yardbirds. The paper turned the letter

September – after a delay of some months – of the *Are You Experienced* album, replete with its different cover design and altered track listing.

The band devoted the first half of September 1967 to a full-scale tour of Germany and Scandinavia, arriving back in London on the 13th. Good-quality radio and TV recordings from this tour reveal them with a renewed appetite for live work and overwhelmingly positive responses from the audiences. In Stockholm for a live radio-studio concert on September 5th, the Experience opened with a wild stab at 'Sgt Pepper's Lonely Heart's Club Band' and played an exciting but ragged 'I Don't Live Today', specifically "dedicated to the American Indian". They debuted 'Midnight Lamp', with Hendrix using his wah-wah pedal to great effect, but the song's introspective atmosphere was not conducive to live performance and they only played it live a few more times. The set was wrapped up with a spectacularly wild 'Purple Haze'. In the same town two days later Hendrix met up with two Swedish musicians, Bo Hansson and Janne Karlsson, at a jam in Stockholm's Club Filips. Out of this session came the instrumental 'Tax Free', a study in time changes and chord movement that Hendrix would enjoy playing live with his group and recording in a fine studio version the following year.

The second half of September turned into a hectic round of publicity and interviews. Hendrix was voted Top World Musician by *Melody Maker* and received his award in person from Jimmy Saville on the 16th. Later that month, the *Guitar In* at London's Royal Festival Hall on the 25th boasted one of the most eccentric line-ups ever to include the Experience. The concert was staged in aid of International Liberal Year and was attended by the leader of the British Liberal Party, Jeremy Thorpe. On the bill were flamenco guitarist Paco Peña, British folkster Bert Jansch, and guitar duo Tim Walker & Sebastian Jorgenson, all of who played acoustic sets prior to the interval. The second half of the concert was

"They were a nice bunch of chaps, even though we thought they couldn't play."

Mitch Mitchell, on The Monkees

into a feature, detailing the band's close brushes with the violent side of American life. Quoting examples of race riots, beatings, bomb scares and lootings in cities across the US, Page pointed up the paradoxical nature of American society at the time. "At Griffith Park, just outside Los Angeles, we attended a huge Love-In," he wrote. "There were loads of people with flowers in their hair so we were expecting a peaceful time. But it didn't stay that way for long. A riot broke out – we never discovered the cause – and many innocent bystanders were hurt."[32] The acid-laced summer of love was feeling the first cold winds of autumn.

Reviews of Hendrix's fifth British single, 'The Burning Of The Midnight Lamp', were mixed but mostly sympathetic upon its August debut. *Record Mirror*'s Norman Joplin commented that "despite all the gimmickry, an atmosphere of haunting lonely despair seeps through. I think this is Jimi's best record yet but not as commercial as his earlier hits".[33] A low-key reaction in the US was offset to some extent by the release there on the first day of

given over to the Experience.

Seasoned music-industry man Barry McCann was present and remembers that many in the sell-out crowd had come solely to see Hendrix. The Experience, alerted to the excellent acoustics in the hall during rehearsals, had stripped their gear down to basics, with just one amp-and-speaker stack for each instrument and the usual two PA columns. Nonetheless they certainly made a change from the acoustic recitalists. "The most striking thing," recalls McCann, "was the contrast between the two halves. We all filed out for the interval after this pleasant but low-key acoustic music, but then the most thrilling thing was coming back in, knowing what was about to happen, looking at those huge amp stacks on-stage and listening to the hum they were giving off. The anticipation was just incredible."[34] Sometimes you can just see the future. A few days after this, Hendrix and the Experience began once again to map out their own future in the studio, with Chandler at the helm, as work on their second LP, *Axis: Bold As Love*, began in earnest.

turning on
the axis

On October 1st 1967, a day after the launch of BBC Radio-1, the Experience went back into Olympic studios in west London to resume work on what was to become their second LP, Axis: Bold As Love. The album would receive overdubs and be given its final mixes by the end of the month. First up was the track that would take the penultimate slot on side two of the original vinyl release, 'Little Miss Lover'.

L ittle Miss Lover' is a lusting-song that reflects the almost endless sex available to the band during the recent US tour. It boasts one of the defining rhythm-patterns of the era, played during the intro and verse by the drums in unison with bass and guitar to a skipping 4/4 beat. Emphases fall across off and on-beats in a way that was completely novel for rock at the time, especially in the way it stresses the bass-drum pattern. At other points the rhythm falls into a more conventional strut, including the short but effective guitar solo. Hendrix's solo comes across like a high-spirited whoop and develops into nothing less than a seduction in sound, intensified by heavy use of the Octavia and accompanied by his cheeky spoken asides. One of Hendrix's most inventive interludes, it is full of constantly surprising twists to the phrases he develops, almost as if he is conversing with himself. Such wonderful intimacy and freshness would become progressively rarer in Hendrix's work as he sought bigger and bolder statements to top his previous achievements. For now he could still think small – and be incredibly creative as he did so. The song is wrapped up quickly after the solo: a short recap of the first line of the verse leads to a vamp across the verse patterns where Hendrix plays delightfully inventive, darting lines in obbligato to the vocal exhortations that carry the tune to its closing fade. His mastery of the guitar is evident as he effortlessly toys with small phrases in this final section of the song, inventing slight variations and paraphrases that keep the listener fully engaged.

Two other songs were successfully attempted during that session, 'You Got Me Floatin'' and 'One Rainy Wish'. 'You Got Me Floatin'' has a series of R&B-inspired riffs underpinning the otherwise unremarkable but quite charming melody and lyrics. The hazy, will-o-the-wisp opening grabs attention before the entry of a scorching guitar-and-drums riff. It is another driving rock tune, with heavy snare-drum emphasis on each beat in the bar during the opening before Mitchell brings in a snaking Latin beat in the verses of the type closely associated with Mongo Santamaria. The arrangement of the tune is not simple, and a sense of enormous drama and variety is encouraged throughout the piece: it's a short composition, lasting less than three minutes, with a basic harmonic framework and form, but it's

Members of the Hendrix Experience, The Move, Pink Floyd, The Nice, Amen Corner, The Outer Limits, and Eire Apparent on a late-1967 tour.

packed with incident and variation. Although the lyrics contain a simple "I dig you" message, the elation transports the lyrics to higher levels of feeling. The song's ending is properly thought out, a shift to A providing an appropriate lift as if to suggest the whole group is floating with the sweet delirium of desire while they fade into the distance.

'One Rainy Wish' is a 3/4 ballad that has been unfairly neglected in favour of 'Little Wing' from the second album, perhaps because 'One Rainy Wish' was rarely played live. But it is one of Hendrix's most winning creations, from the shimmering suspended entry at the beginning to the carefree shift into a freely jazzy triple time at the end as Hendrix plays C and C-sharp-minor chords behind his spoken narration of the dream that inspired the song's lyrics. The melody itself is one of Hendrix's most beautiful, stated first in the most loving, caressing way by his guitar in the tempo-less, suspended opening against ringing guitar chords, almost like waterfall notes from a shower of clear rain. Across a pedal tone sustained by a bubbling bass note and cymbal shimmers, Hendrix picks out the melody on two separate guitar tracks, one in mid-range and in a sequence of fourths, the other an octave higher (its Octavia effect doubling it further), almost in the manner of a round answering its delineation. Then the vocal enters the piece, on a medium waltz tempo and decorated with beautiful guitar arabesques throughout the verse, before a pause and a swoop into the chorus – which hits common time and turns the song bluesy for a moment.

At the conclusion of the chorus there is a gem of a throwaway Octavia-effect guitar solo, the line it pursues close to bird-call in its freedom and ebullience. At its close, the solo gracefully links up with the underlying guitar and bass riff that signifies a return to the verse. The concluding part of the song, back to 3/4 again, picks up the birdsong motif as guitar sounds and melodic phrases float and dart around the partly-sung, partly-spoken narrative. The song dissolves in a repeated spiralling guitar phrase that has the dream evaporating in front of us. One of the longer pieces on *Axis* at 3:40, it is also one of its happiest creations.

Billy Idol's guitarist Steve Stevens was impressed by Hendrix's gift for brief but entirely apposite guitar statements during 1967. "There was a lot of excessiveness in Hendrix's playing that I don't like at all, like the way he'd play solos that would go on and on," Stevens said. "But the Experience wasn't like that. They did those three-and-a-half minute songs, really tight. That was one of the best aspects of Hendrix, the way he knew how to incorporate his style of guitar playing into the songs he was doing."[1] Jazz guitarist Mike Stern saw something else in 'One Rainy Wish', specifically its personification of Hendrix's gift for lyricism. "It has that same singing quality that I dig in Jim Hall's playing or in Wes Montgomery's playing, but the thing about Hendrix was that he had that sound: he would articulate that lyrical feeling with a fatter sound on his Strat than you would get with a regular hollow-bodied guitar. Jimi was definitely a legato player, and whether he intended it or not, he started a movement among guitar players with his long, sustaining, legato lines. He sounded more like a horn player than anyone before him, and he influenced everybody that followed him."[2]

The following day, October 2nd, the band took on 'Bold As Love' which became the title track for the new album. This is possibly the most ambitious piece on *Axis*, the extravagant metaphors of the lyrics suggesting a growing confidence in Hendrix's handling of words – there is even a sly reference to Donovan's hit 'Mellow Yellow' at one point. But the piece tends to founder on its own ambition. His desire to make a big statement puts undue emphasis on the song's structure, and the moments of true inspiration are too few to carry

listeners along. Its lack of real cohesion conjures images of the group and Chandler discussing how to arrange the bits and pieces and saying: "Well, if we put this ending here, that'll be a good send-off." Such transparency suggests that a structure has failed to engage the listener's attention at the deeper levels.

The piece starts dramatically as Hendrix goes through a series of colour definitions and reaches a logical climax with the first chorus, singing: "They're all bold as love: just ask the Axis." But then he has no idea where to go and so the whole exercise is repeated, simply with different words; that this works is mostly due to Hendrix's disarming singing. After this we get the guitar statement of the second theme. It's not one of Hendrix's most inspired melodies, sounding a touch grandiloquent though beautifully articulated. Next comes the highlight: a simple and heartfelt melodic solo punctuated at

"When came the final freak-out on 'Wild Thing' James went spare, knocked over amplifiers, flung down his guitar, and wrestled with his bass player."

Melody Maker, on an October 1967 show

its close by drum and bass. The song comes to a logical end. Only it doesn't. With 'Bold as Love' intended as the final track, something more show-stopping was required. After scratching of heads, the team came up with a solution, of sorts. At 2:47 there is an edit point and a drum intro to a further minute and a half of music: mostly this is a rehash of themes stated earlier in the tune at a slightly brighter tempo and with tape-phasing thrown in to provide a heady effect. All this fades into the distance like a Busby Berkeley vision, over-ripe, faintly ridiculous and straining too hard to make its point. Perhaps this was the consequence of having to deal with the aftermath of *Sgt Pepper* in London in the latter half of 1967.

Six months earlier the Experience would perhaps have whipped up a free-for-all finale like that on 'I Don't Live Today', but that was no longer appropriate. Hendrix had since moved away from such tactics, at least in the recording studio: the most radical music to end up on *Axis* would be contained in 'If 6 Was 9' and 'EXP', two tracks recorded back in May. Hendrix was now attempting to establish different channels of self-expression. Indeed, while there is a great diversity of style, tone and mood on *Axis*, the dominant impression is of beautiful sound quality and effortless control. It is a wonderfully crafted album, fulfilling the public pledges Hendrix made after the first album that he would smooth out the production wrinkles and make the next LP as perfect as he knew how. That polish, added to the less adventurous nature of most of the material, makes it his most cohesive and unified album, as well as his happiest, but it also makes it his most conservative. Hendrix's sense of discretion on *Axis* was sensed by Taj Mahal's guitarist Jesse Ed Davis, who saw Hendrix live and listened intently to his records. "It wasn't until *Axis: Bold As Love* that I thought Jimi hit his full stride in the studio," said Davis. "He made use of every trick in the book, but with such subtlety and finesse. Tape-delayed echo, phasing effects whooshing from left to right with the use of pan-pots, some of the wildest equalisation I've ever heard – all combined to make a very well-produced recording of excellent music. His main trick seemed to be to make use of every effect, but with extreme moderation."[3]

The following day's activities included a BBC Radio-1 session, broadcast in part on the *Top Gear* programme a week later. Mixing new and old, the band

Live at the Saville Theatre (left) in central London, October 1967 took the opportunity to try out the newly-recorded 'Little Miss Lover', played very close to the studio version but with a guitar solo that harked back to the rip-'em-up style of Hendrix's live work and the early singles. A version of 'The Burning Of The Midnight Lamp' goes off the rails in the intro to the second verse where Hendrix fails to articulate the guitar pattern correctly, improvising his way out of trouble but losing Redding in the process. They more or less stumble into Hendrix's vocal. The song's arrangement is awkwardly exposed by this sparse treatment, the guitar-bass verse intros dragging somewhat, but Hendrix's vocal is committed and his guitar playing incisive as he uses his wah-wah with great taste and imagination. On 'Catfish Blues' Hendrix does a respectful imitation of the kind of "well well" and "oh well" asides that Muddy Waters and John Lee Hooker used for precisely this type of haunted, slow blues – it's a Waters song, after all (although some have since catalogued a myriad of blues influences on Jimi's 'Catfish Blues', no doubt well-meaning but ultimately meretricious). The solo here is pure Hendrix and typically intense, pointing to the volcanic blues performances to come in 1968, especially on 'Voodoo Chile' where the blues melody and overall feel would be very close to this. Mitchell even takes a solo that presages some of the rolls and patterns he uses on 'Chile', making a reasonable blueprint for what was to come. Regardless of its context, this is a fine blues performance in its own right.

No such claims could be made for the next recording laid down that Tuesday at the BBC, where the trio has fun with 'Hound Dog', complete with imitation scratchings, mewings and barks (pekinese rather than hound, at a guess).

'Driving South' is a different matter for Hendrix, as always. On the two takes made that day he paces the song beautifully, starting with a delicate theme statement before cutting in the fuzz and sustain like a buzz-saw and scorching the earth with his second theme of descending thirds. The broadcast version runs for nearly five minutes with plenty of heat and wonderful continuity. Hendrix never lets up for a second, breezing through the pre-arranged key change and drum break before diving back in to bring things to a peak as the vehicle goes as far south as it can on this journey. Nonetheless, he plays little that he has not committed to tape elsewhere, suggesting that this is a

Recording at the Playhouse Theatre in London for BBC radio's *Top Gear* show, October 6th 1967.

showpiece performance rather than an exploration for him. The other surviving take sounds like a warm-up only, replete with missed cues and sloppy execution.

An informal jam also recorded that Tuesday with Stevie Wonder, present at the BBC to record his own latest hits, has seen official release after years of circulation only on bootlegs. Wonder is on drums for the predictably titled 'Jammin'', a medium-tempo instrumental based on a simple bass riff. The musicians take a minute or so to get off the ground before a short but blistering blues solo from Hendrix where he looks forward in style and timbre to what he would do in the studio for 'Voodoo Child (Slight Return)' a year later. After that, it drifts to an inconsequential close. 'I Was Made to Love Her' again has Wonder on drums, and gives the impression that the musicians

enjoyed themselves, though there is little of value apart from novelty for the uncommitted listener. Redding was unhappy about the tape's eventual release. "Some enterprising person suggested an 'informal jam' between Jimi and myself, with Stevie on drums," he wrote in his autobiography. "Of course they forgot to turn the tape machines off. This jam was aired a couple of times and then bootlegged. I feel a jam is an impromptu musical creation and is therefore co-written, but when the songs were registered after Jimi's death, my part in them – surprise surprise – wasn't."[4]

Management had been busy putting the finishing touches to the Experience's first headlining tour of the UK, with support acts including The Move, Pink Floyd, The Nice, and Eire Apparent. There would be a lightning visit to France and the band would fit in further one-offs, including a return to the Saville Theatre, their first appearance there since the night of Brian Epstein's death. One of the two shows there ended with Hendrix rolling around the stage in a mock wrestling match with a reluctant Redding. As *Melody Maker* noted, "Our Jimi, feeling somewhat piquey, ... decided to conclude his musical performance by grappling with bass player Noel Redding, dragging him to the floor and assailing him bodily. Presumably all good clean fun, and in the interests of psychedelic experience, [but] one still had the feeling that Jimi meant it – or at least half of it. The Experience had been playing exceptionally well. ... When came the final freak-out on 'Wild Thing' James went spare, knocked over amplifiers, flung down his guitar, and assaulted the said bass player. Apart from these asides, Jimi played fantastic guitar with every trick imaginable."[5]

The following three October days were spent in and around Paris on a variety of promotional exercises, including appearances on TV shows and the shooting of a video to accompany 'The Burning Of The Midnight Lamp' and 'The Wind Cries Mary'. The most enjoyable aspect of the short trip was a show at the Olympia, almost exactly a year after their first Paris appearance on the Johnny Hallyday package. Hendrix acknowledged this from the stage and also gave the French audience credit for their early acceptance of the Experience. "Let's say we're having a little first-anniversary thing today," he tells the crowd. "I'd like to say thank you very much for last year, for letting us play here – instead of booing us off the stage, y'know, you gave us a chance, so thank you very much." The commercially issued performances from this concert reveal the band as relaxed and happy. 'The Wind Cries Mary' has ineffable calm and a vocal performance that is full of feeling. Hendrix prefaces 'Catfish Blues' with a cheerful series of exhortations. "Have you heard of Mississippi?" Yes!! reply the crowd. "Have you heard of Muddy Waters?" Yes!! again. "How about John Lee Hooker?" Yes!! for a third time. "So we'd like to do this little blues, mix it in with our own kind of way, we'd like to do it our own way – the Experience way, y'know?" Yeah!!!

As with 'If 6 Was 9', 'Catfish Blues' would eventually supply elements of another of Hendrix's best-known originals, this time 'Voodoo Child (Slight Return)', which would be recorded the following August, sharing the same melody line. There was a similar aspiration in the lyrics, too, a mojo-like

Studies in concentration: Jimi on-stage at Sussex University in Brighton, southern England, November 11th 1967, just before the start of the band's UK package tour with The Move, Pink Floyd and four other bands.

power that in 'Catfish' is explicitly a sexual hold over women, in 'Voodoo Child' a more general sense of omnipotent ease. An unaccompanied wah-wah coda for 'Catfish Blues' brings howls and cheers of delight from the Paris crowd heralding many similar on-stage blues codas to come. A further performance, the set-ending 'Wild Thing', filmed and later added to the DVD release of the TV film-short *Experience*, confirms the impression given by the audio recording that both band and crowd were in very high spirits, delighting in the heady derangement that by then was a staple of the Experience set.

Back in London by the evening of October 12th, the band went straight into more interviews, some TV and radio recordings, and a spattering of live gigs in the build-up to the November UK tour with The Move. The concerts had been front-page news in *Melody Maker* back in September, the paper noting: "The Move will be making their first ever British concert tour in the first two weeks of November. Last year the Rank Organisation banned The Move from playing in their theatres because of the group's loud and explosive, TV-smashing act. The Move will co-headline with The Jimi Hendrix Experience."[6] Good to see that it wasn't only Jimi's cigarette lighter fluid that was getting into trouble at the time.

Before the tour, though, there was an album to finish at Olympic. Mitchell remembered this as a good time for the band. "I felt happy to be in a studio, particularly Olympic. Working on *Axis* was the first time that it

became apparent that Jimi was pretty good working behind the [mixing] board, as well as playing, and had some positive ideas of how he wanted things recorded. It could have been the start of any potential conflict between him and Chas in the studio. Chas was fair, though, and realised that Hendrix knew what he was doing and that there were engineers, like Eddie Kramer, ... who could really improve things."[7] One recording that no one yet had the opportunity to improve upon was the first pass at Hendrix's ballad 'Angel'. Unaccountably mis-identified by the Hendrix Estate as 'Little Wing' upon its first official release in 1997, this August 15th session has just a single Hendrix guitar track accompanied by Mitchell's drums, with no vocal overdubs. This was a common method of recording for the Experience, according to Mitchell: other instruments would be added where and when they were needed. Hendrix's guidelines, expressed through his rhythm-guitar part, were usually comprehensive. Guitarist Mike Bloomfield admired this aspect of Hendrix's artistry. "Jimi's musical approach, as he explained it to me, was to lay out the entire song and decide how it should be – horns, strings, the way it should wind up," Bloomfield told *Guitar Player* in 1975. "Then he would flesh the pattern out by playing it with chords and syncopation. He was extremely interested in form – in a few seconds of playing, he'd let you know about the entire structure. That's why he liked playing rhythm guitar so much – the rhythm guitar could lay out the structure for the entire song."[8]

This is precisely what happens with this unfinished trial-run of 'Angel'. It is mapped out like a highway, so clear are the signs pointing the way in which Hendrix wanted to develop it. The song has carefully controlled dynamics, with steadily built crescendos and equally adept decrescendos placed in the verses and choruses. As he plays 'Angel' in this way it seems almost to be caught in structure and style between the approaches of the first two albums. He uses instrumental methods like those found on, for example, 'May This Be Love', and even includes the climbing guitar-and-bass riff from the end of 'Hey Joe' in order to drive things along. But Hendrix also touches at the textural clarity and R&B guitar feel that he often favoured during the making of *Axis*. Perhaps it was this equivocation over the exact nature of the tune that led Hendrix to postpone its completion and, eventually, to leave it off *Axis* altogether.

Two days later there was another session for the BBC, this time for broadcast on Alexis Korner's *Rhythm And Blues* show on the corporation's World Service network. A couple of cover versions – Dylan's 'Can You Please Crawl Out Of Your Window' and Willie Dixon's 'Hoochie Coochie Man' – were tossed off in fine style, with Hendrix's R&B guitar style very evident in his accompaniment to the Dylan piece. The Dixon song featured Korner himself adding some authentic wobbly slide guitar and Hendrix using his fuzz box, now sounding just a little dated in late 1967 but bringing a suitably savage edge to his white-hot solo. The informality of this session is evident with the inclusion of short solos from both Redding and Mitchell before the collective blues playing at the song's close. More convincing is 'Driving South', here in its longest outing for the BBC at 5:31. The guitarist eases himself into the performance quite playfully before switching on the fuzz box and going for broke. For the first half of the solo Hendrix sticks closely to more or less conventional modern blues guitar phrasing, just as the top British guitarists were playing at the time. But after a pause and a whole-tone shift upwards he turns on his wah-wah, leaving it half-open to give a series of cutting overtones to his sound as well as a more vocal quality. Longer and more characteristic phrases follow as he juxtaposes blues lines with chunks of sound, chords and vibrato-arm effects, pushing the envelope for this song as far as he ever would. A jagged pause gives Mitchell a drum break and the track is quickly faded. Incomplete it may be, but this is still a stirring blues journey taken at considerable speed.

That Hendrix's fertile mind was working in other directions at this time is indicated by more recordings made at Olympic just after this. Committed

said later: "He had the tendency to play with his fingers very flat [on the guitar's fingerboard], and he had a very long thumb, so he could come over the top of the neck to play bass notes. That left his fingers in a likely position to do all his chordal-type stuff. Playing with his fingers flat also got him that

"We'd like to do this little blues, mix it in with our own kind of way – the Experience way."

Jimi Hendrix, announcing 'Catfish Blues'

double-stringed effect every time, like in 'Castles Made Of Sand' or 'Little Wing'. That's an R&B thing."[9] Hendrix's "chordal-type stuff" was among the most refreshing aspects of his playing, especially on 'Little Wing'. He uses his unorthodox fretboard technique and finger positions to play double and triple-string pickings of extraordinary beauty and delicacy, unlike any other rock player of the day (and very few in soul and R&B). It is a technique that has now fallen into disuse in rock. 'Little Wing' is a simple act of worship for an unnamed woman. The lyrics read like something from the Pre-Raphaelite school of poetry, their decorum and striking images shot through with light and remaining in the mind long after the short track has concluded. There is an introduction, two verses and a singing, richly melodic guitar solo over open guitar chords that shimmer above the drums and bass. This is a magic carpet of sound upon which the melody can fly away, once again showing how Hendrix could conjure such a strongly visual realisation of his words, especially in the ballads.

'Wait Until Tomorrow' is a medium-tempo ballad of immense charm, not least in the way Hendrix chooses to sing as if he were addressing his hesitant lover, fretting as he goes through each situation. Again he displays his verbal gift for painting vivid pictures with a modicum of lines. It is a ballad in the traditional sense, telling a story to its listeners. The 'flat fingering' style again allows Hendrix to create a beautiful R&B-type chordal figure for an opening theme, accompanied only by bass punctuations. This leads into the verse proper with the complete trio as Hendrix pictures himself "standing here, freezing, inside your golden garden". He could have suffered such a fate in a Seattle winter as easily as in London, especially with a girl named Dolly-Mae – though by 1967 he'd outgrown overprotective fathers. His delightful rhythm-guitar patterns are kept up for the entire length of this short song (almost exactly 3:00) and solos are eschewed. But this is such a busy and varied track, with so much from every instrument embedded in the arrangement, that the listener only realises this later, with no accompanying sense of loss.

'Ain't No Telling' is the *Axis* equivalent of the first album's 'Remember', Hendrix's more or less straightforward 'filler' song that sat half

"Chas was happy for layers of overdubs to be put on a track, but he tried to draw the line over simply doing more and more takes of the same thing."

Mitch Mitchell, on studio strain

to tape in the space of five days were 'Little Wing', 'Wait Until Tomorrow', 'Ain't No Telling', 'Spanish Castle Magic', 'Up From The Skies' and 'Castles Made Of Sand'. 'Little Wing' was a tune conceived during the heady days spent at Monterey that summer and infused with the festival's sense of hope and anticipation. The track has been a favourite of fans and fellow musicians alike since its appearance and continues to fascinate. Guitarist Frank Marino

way between contemporary British rock and R&B. 'Ain't No Telling' encapsulates the frustrations of being on tour and wishing you were back home. The simple form – two verses, bridge, verse, outro – is fleshed out with a scintillating though spare arrangement, this time at a relatively fast clip, with the guitar overdubs functioning more as an echoing Greek Chorus on the action than a separate, independent line. This is especially evident during the instrumental passages, where Hendrix provides contrast rather than a set-piece solo. 'Ain't No Telling' really is very concise – just 1:46 – and would serve to pace the first side of the album rather than shine as a highlight, sitting in the running between 'Wait Until Tomorrow' and 'Little Wing' to bring a nicely-judged change of pace and to keep things moving. Chandler must have been pleased.

'Spanish Castle Magic' is an affectionate portrait of a venue Hendrix frequented back in his Seattle days, its lyrics suggesting he had learned a thing or two about lyrical whimsy from John Lennon's 'Lucy In The Sky With Diamonds'. The accompaniment is hard-edged and suggestive of a rock'n'roll palace rather than a psychedelic bolt-hole but remains steadfastly optimistic and playful, like the words it supports. The strutting riffs and clanging chords, augmented by an acoustic piano, keep a fine balance between pomp and urgency, and the uncluttered arrangement based on staccato patterns and silence under the vocal verse is a master-stroke of pacing and dramatic effect. There is a powerful and eloquent guitar solo that sticks mostly to distorted variations of blues phrases, but it breaks no new ground for Hendrix. The song's power and memorably simple riffs made it a natural for live trio performance and an instant hit with audiences, and it became it a staple of Hendrix's live set for the rest of his career.

On October 29th, the last day of new recording for *Axis*, the group put down two satisfyingly diverse tunes. 'Up From The Skies', which became the first track on *Axis* after the introductory 'EXP', must have been something of a homecoming for drummer Mitchell with its slinky jazz-blues in the manner of Mose Allison, Grant Green, Jimmy Smith/Kenny Burrell and England's Georgie Fame. Hendrix later acknowledged in interviews that it was Mitchell who brought the jazz feel to this number. However, only Hendrix could take this rootsy genre and make it the perfect vehicle for the coolest of cool science-fiction stories. Hendrix has since been accused of lifting the initial melody of the verse of 'Up From The Skies' from guitarist Grant Green's 'The Selma March', recorded in May 1965 and released on Green's album *His Majesty King Funk* (which, incidentally, featured on organ Larry Young, later a jamming partner for Hendrix). There is no mistaking the similarity between Hendrix's verse melody and one of the themes of Green's song, but it is such a common gospel-blues phrase – hardly unique to Green in jazz-funk circles – that it could be regarded as part of the collective heritage of musicians working in this genre and its derivatives. In any case, Green and his colleagues state their theme and then clear the decks for eight minutes of improvisation. Hendrix carefully constructs a wise and amusing critique of the follies of the world. The whole band manage the shift to lightly greased jazz-funk with ease, making for a delightfully laidback jazz-blues as the lazy flicks of the guitar are echoed in the vocals and the drummer's brushes. No other rock group in the world at the time could have laid down a track like this and made it sound so

Versatility: soundcheck at the Albert Hall, London, November 14th 1967.

utterly in character. Add to that the ineffable ease and good humour of Hendrix's vocals and the result is a uniquely memorable offering. The relaxed poise of 'Up From The Skies' would have been inconceivable on *Are You Experienced*. Maybe, as Jimi suggests, it's just a change of climate.

The last new song recorded at Olympic during these October sessions was 'Castles Made Of Sand', another minor miracle. Its deft changes of pace and texture, its shifting moods and ironies are all perfectly handled by players and arrangement alike. Stevie Ray Vaughan said later that the track exemplified some of his favourite things about Hendrix. "He always had the ability to get every kind of tone that he could ever want on his guitar," Vaughan enthused. "My favourite is what I call the 'King' tone, something that I've heard out of Albert King, B.B. and Freddy. That's where I first heard it, but Hendrix took it further. It's a breathy tone, it sounds more like bells but it's not harmonics. It's just a way of playing with the skin of your fingers and part of your fingernail, and part of your pick sometimes. It's not a harmonic and it's not a false note, it's just a very pure tone. And he'd get it, like in the beginning of 'Castles Made Of Sand'. *That's* the tone."[10] Hendrix's playing at the beginning of 'Castles' is a reminder that his music was essentially simple, and that what made it so special was the way in which he applied this simplicity. The opening guitar-chord pattern is played with a single fretting shape across the fretboard which is then simply moved up and down to the correct positions. Easy as pie – but it's the conception that takes the breath away. The imagination one needs to frame such a simple idea so brilliantly has been beyond all but a handful of musicians in any generation.

The lyrics of 'Castles' caused some offence on the song's initial release, with Hendrix accused of cruelty in his final verse where he describes the suicidal depression of a young girl "crippled for life / And she couldn't speak a sound." But that is to misread the lyric's intent and to miss the simple paradox in the situations that each verse depicts. Hendrix is describing reversals of fortune, with the first two verses about the fragile nature of hope and expectation. The third and final verse reverses the negative, giving the girl hope unawares. After all, having been dismissed as dumb for life at the outset of that verse, she speaks through sheer exaltation: "Look, a golden-winged ship is passing my way!" At that point in the song the music pauses while Hendrix concludes his monologue and his guitar picks up its accompaniment in the style that so captivated Stevie Ray Vaughan. Then the guitar takes off into the skies, chasing that golden-winged ship to the horizon. Here was a perfectly realised vignette, painted in bright musical pastels that would summarise the overall mood of the album.

Axis: Bold As Love was a record completed at a point of equipoise. The musicians felt confident and at ease with themselves and each other; the record company had faith in whatever the band might do; their producer made a valuable input that was taken seriously; and the recording studio they used gave the music a rich fullness and a new transparency. This was perhaps the peak of Hendrix and Chandler's relationship in the studio, albeit one that would not last much longer. Mitchell later remembered a good balance at this time, though not without the occasional flare-up. "Where tempers did start to get a little frayed was over re-takes," he wrote. "Chas was quite happy for layers of overdubs and effects to be put on a track, but he tried to draw the line over simply doing more and more takes of the same thing. ... Chas did his best to put up with us, which can't have been easy. I think he and Jimi were still sharing a flat together and consequently living in each other's pockets. I think that's going to put a strain on any relationship."[11] This is a debate as old as the availability of magnetic tape in recording studios. One school of thought is that perfection is attainable and should be achieved, whatever the cost (and costs). The other view is that any freshness will very soon fade after a number of takes, and that if someone has a basic competence to play what is required then more often than not

In the studio, late 1967: Hendrix and Redding adjust headphones (above); Jimi goes for a take (opposite).

their first or second efforts are usually going to be the ones with the extra 'spirit'. The debate continues.

Hendrix's tendency to go for seemingly endless re-takes – something that came to a peak during the making of *Electric Ladyland* in 1968 – irritated both Chandler and Redding. Redding was not given to studio experimentation and would take off to the nearest pub if Hendrix showed signs of getting stuck on a particular item. Chandler simply thought differently to the increasingly meticulous Hendrix. Kathy Etchingham felt that Hendrix, once he was famous, listened to Chandler more and for longer periods of time than anyone

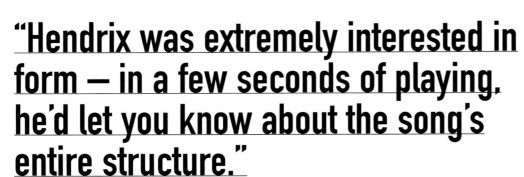

"Hendrix was extremely interested in form – in a few seconds of playing, he'd let you know about the song's entire structure."

Mike Bloomfield

else close to him, not least because Chandler had shown complete faith in him from day one. "It was demonstrations of support and friendship like that which made Jimi willing to take more interference in his work from Chas than from anyone else," Etchingham said. "He knew that Chas truly had his best interests at heart. Their relationship lasted longer than any other Jimi had with a male friend."[12]

October 1967 ended with the final mixing sessions for the new album. According to Chandler this followed a scare when Hendrix had contrived to

leave the finished master tapes to Side One in the back of a taxi the night before the cutting session that would make them ready for vinyl pressing. Other people around at the time felt that Hendrix, unhappy with the short time devoted to mixing the master tapes, had deliberately lost them in the hope that he'd buy more time for a better mix. In fact he achieved the opposite, for the side had to be remixed in one fraught and continuous session. This resulted in some songs being mixed in less than optimum conditions – 'If 6 Was 9' was especially poorly served, being the last cut on the side and done as the clock ticked down. But as November began the album was finally out of the group's hands.

November would be a month of rest, live concerts in the UK and abroad, and the Experience's second UK tour of the year – this time as headliners. The usual round of interviews would deliver good publicity for the album when it appeared. Hendrix told Nick Jones in an interview published in *Melody Maker* in early December that *Axis* had been produced with special consideration for the potential offered by stereo sound, then a new experience for many record buyers. "I hope everybody can dig it in stereo because that's what it's all about," said Hendrix. "We've tried to get most of the freaky tracks right into another dimension so you get that sky effect coming down out of the heavens, you know?"[13]

The opening week of that month was something of a rarity: Hendrix and the group had some time away from each other and from professional activities. Hendrix split his time between Kathy at their flat, on one hand, and playing music, jamming with whoever was around, on the other. One very unusual musician he jammed with one evening that week was American multi-instrumentalist Roland Kirk, then appearing for two weeks at Ronnie Scott's jazz club in Soho, central London. Kirk was not only prodigiously gifted but a charismatic performer able to excite just about any audience. He was a consummate instrumentalist, responsible for as many innovations on flute, saxophone and his other instruments as Hendrix was on the amplified guitar. Often, Kirk would play three instruments at once. He was a natural for Hendrix to jam with, being conscious of the history and legacy of music and a passionate devotee of the blues – a recent record he'd made live in Copenhagen had featured Sonny Boy Williamson guesting on harmonica.

Hendrix knew Kirk's music from records Mitchell had played him. Kirk had been in the country for a couple of weeks during an extensive European tour, appearing as well on one half of a Jazz Expo 67 bill in London, supporting the all-conquering Charles Lloyd Quartet with pianist Keith Jarrett and drummer Jack DeJohnette. Kirk had cut a singular figure at that gig, appearing on-stage "erotically encased in a sort of black PVC boiler suit – a space outfit for blowing space music" according to Val Wilmer in *Down Beat*.[14] Jimi sat in with Kirk at Ronnie's, the two musicians meeting on the common ground of blues changes. Contrary to some

claims, no tape has ever surfaced of this jam, but both men enjoyed the music they made, and from that time spoke only well of one another. Hendrix told one interviewer: "[The jam] was, y'know, what can I say? Because, y'know, I really got off. I was so scared; I mean, he gets all these sounds and so forth … but we got along great, I thought. He told me I should have turned up [my volume] or something."[15] Kirk later opined, "They put Jimi Hendrix in a bag. They called him a pop artist. But Hendrix was a stone blues player."[16]

A quick promotional dash to Holland for the Experience led to a TV-show recording where they played 'Foxy Lady', 'Purple Haze' and 'Catfish Blues'. The band was in fine fettle for the first two songs; they hadn't played this repertoire intensively in the past few weeks and there is an edge of excitement here common to so much of their live work in 1967, even though they suffer from considerable tuning problems during 'Purple Haze'. 'Foxy Lady' is at the correct slowly-swaggering tempo and forms an all-out attack on the audience's sensibilities, with Hendrix's guitar tone awesomely blistering. 'Catfish Blues' is the standout performance, with Mitchell especially exciting and adventurous as he tries out bass-drum fills and patterns that would be a feature of the studio jam titled 'Voodoo Chile' the following year. He also gets off a convincing solo. Hendrix sticks to guitar basics but is incandescent and incredibly funky. His wah-wah work after the drum solo is impressively vocalised and amazingly relaxed, and much of his phrasing also anticipates 'Voodoo Chile'. The band then launch into a mid-tempo rave-up that points to the extended jams of later Experience tours. At over eight minutes, this 'Catfish Blues' is one of the longest Experience live cuts in existence from 1967 and something of a milestone.

Hendrix was back in England by the next day, readying the band for the UK tour starting on November 14th, but he found time to start another demo of 'Angel' – now titled 'Sweet Angel' – using just a drum machine and playing all other accompanying instruments himself. The song's conception is complete in this version and would change little in structure or treatment, although Hendrix's lightness of touch and spirit, such a feature of this period, would be lost in later versions. Hendrix himself would revisit this version at Olympic in late December, but it would remain incomplete.

The poster for the UK tour gave The Jimi Hendrix Experience and The Move joint headline billing, with Pink Floyd and Amen Corner second, and The Nice, The Outer Limits and Eire Apparent bringing up the rear. The opening night was at London's cavernous Royal Albert Hall, and many music journalists made the trip. *Melody Maker*'s Chris Welch was not entirely impressed by the package, commenting that it "thundered off on its trip of Britain with a deafening start … . The Floyd gave one of their colourful and deafening displays of musical pyrotechnics, and indeed all the groups were painfully loud, with the agony increased by the horror of the Albert's acoustics. The Eire Apparent practically damaged my hearing system for life; The Nice, my favourite group, blew their cool. … Jimi was great, and

Mitch Mitchell at his kit in the recording studio, towards the end of 1967.

deserved the ovation, but really Mitch and Noel shouldn't make announcements. Sorry, lads, but Jimi sounds better with the chat."[17]

The problems highlighted by Welch suggested fierce competition between the bands. Pink Floyd had threatened to pull out of the tour when they learned that their lightshow would have to be sacrificed in order to fit more people at the rear of the Albert Hall's stage. There was also a change occurring in the climate of British rock. Bands no longer considered themselves as an extension of vaudeville, all in the same boat together, but would jealously protect what they saw as their own personal performing environments. Mitchell was convinced that the tour simply didn't gel. "In a way the tour was more absurd than the previous one," he wrote later, "because none of the bands on this one were package-tour material. … Syd Barrett, who was still with Pink Floyd, didn't talk to anyone during that time. In fact, David Gilmour, who was ultimately Syd's 'replacement', joined the tour half way through."[18] A backstage photograph of the entire cast of performers from this tour – it opens this chapter – has most of the musicians trying to out-cool one another in sour looks. There are just three smiling faces, one of which is Mitch Mitchell's. At least they managed to mark Hendrix's 25th birthday, on November 27th in Belfast, where he was presented with a cake backstage. The tour was a major popular success, confirming The Jimi Hendrix Experience as A-list pop stars and winding up with a rip-roaring night in Glasgow on December 5th. Publicity generated from the tour would last right through the Christmas period and into the new year as the interviews granted by group members filtered out into the media and recordings made for TV and radio were broadcast. The end-of-year British music papers traditionally ran readers' polls, and they reflected the Experience's huge impact in the past 12 months – even if some results were slightly eccentric. *Record Mirror*'s poll had Hendrix as third best guitarist, behind Hank Marvin and Jeff Beck, and the Experience as fourth best group, behind The Shadows, Booker T & The MGs, and Herb Alpert's Tijuana Brass.

By now Hendrix had already attracted the interest of a number of film and TV-programme makers and his management had agreed to the production of a film for television that came to be titled *Experience*. The half-hour programme was narrated by Alexis Korner and included footage shot mostly at a show in Blackpool. A sequence filmed in photographer Bruce Fleming's studio in Great Newport Street, central London, in mid-December has Hendrix playing an acoustic 12-string guitar for the first recorded version of the blues 'Hear My Train A'Comin'', one that he would play many times in the years to come. This acoustic version is 100 percent country blues, reflecting a knowledge of Leadbelly, Robert Johnson and Skip James, as well as more contemporary acoustic players. Hendrix sings with great feeling, however artificial the circumstances of the session may have been.

Although the pace slackened in December after the tour was finished and *Axis* was released, the Experience appeared at a major end-of-year show,

OCTOBER TO DECEMBER 1967

playing two performances on the same day at London's Olympia exhibition arena. The line-up listed on the poster for *Christmas On Earth Continued* reads like a cast of thousands. In addition to the Experience, The Move and Pink Floyd, veterans of that recent UK tour, there were Eric Burdon & The Animals, The Who, The Graham Bond Organisation, Soft Machine and sundry other entertainers. The Experience headed the bill and were filmed, both front and backstage, for the *Experience* programme; the footage would be used, without the original sound, as a background for the narrator or other music.

Showing no let-up in their creativity, the group had gone back into Olympic studio for the two days before the *Christmas On Earth* concert to record a basic track for a new Hendrix song, 'Crosstown Traffic'. This would be a key title on the follow-up album, *Electric Ladyland*, and the second single released from it (in spring 1969). The Experience also started work on two Noel Redding tunes, 'Dream' and 'Dance'. Neither was completed, now or later, and no vocals were ever added. Hendrix would recycle the opening riff and other sections of 'Dance' in his 1969 tune 'Ezy Rider', virtually the entire bridge section of the latter song coming from this tune. Redding's name would be absent from the credits on the first release of 'Ezy Rider', after Hendrix's death. 'Crosstown Traffic' enjoyed a happier fate. As one of Hendrix's most radio-friendly songs, it has been closely associated with him ever since its release. In more recent years it was even licensed by the Hendrix Estate for use in a TV commercial. It is just possible that Hendrix would have found this decision puzzling.

Given a dazzling, multi-layered production that heightens the effect of the arrangement, the song enjoys production values that approach those of The Beatles. Another of Hendrix's songs to address a second-person presence – like 'Foxy Lady', 'Wait Until Tomorrow', 'Up From The Skies' and many others – its lyric finds Hendrix at his most wry and acerbic. Dave Mason, a founder member with Steve Winwood of Traffic, gives a strength and presence to the backing vocals that is unusual for a Hendrix recording. It makes possible some pleasing touches such as the vocal-and-guitar riffs that introduce each verse, as well as the counter-melody "crosstown traffic…" lines in the chorus, echoing the techniques used in Traffic's own recordings. The song is short – under 2:30 – but is busy and engaging, disguising the essential simplicity of its form.

The end of the year was a time of quiet triumph for Hendrix. He was the largest figure on the cover of *Melody Maker*'s Xmas Bumper Issue that summarised all the year's major pop events. Featured inside in an interview with B.P. Fallon, he offered opinions on the groups of the day and expressed a preference for The Nice of all the bands on the recently concluded UK tour. The records he'd enjoyed most that year were varied: singles by The Small Faces, Pink Floyd, Marmalade and Cream received strong endorsements. American acts he approved of included Albert Collins and a girl group called Ace Of Cups. One topic of great interest – and something he mentioned in other interviews published around this time – was his desire to take time out to learn more about the fundamentals of music. He told Fallon, "I'd like to take a six-month break and go to a school of music. I'm tired of trying to write stuff and finding I can't. I want to write mythology stories set to music, based on a planetary thing and my imagination in general. It wouldn't be similar to classical music but I'd use strings and harps, with extreme and opposite musical textures … . I'd play with Mitch and Noel and hire other cats to supplement us."[19]

This sounds suspiciously like one of Jimi's stoned raves that Kathy Etchingham had noticed him visiting upon the occasional unsuspecting music journalist. If so, he certainly said it on more than one occasion. Assuming he was sincere, the comment was a strong indication that Hendrix at this early stage of his fame was finding his own limitations frustrating. He needed to know more to progress. He was aware of other people out there who were better equipped theoretically and technically to express themselves more fully in music. He felt that he owed it to his music to improve this area of his life. But nothing was to come of it.

In adolescence he had been unable to summon the patience to learn such things and the same would apply this time. Life was moving too quickly now for him to cry a halt, however temporary, and the incentives were overpowering to simply carry on as he was. Besides, there were other distractions – such as appearing as Father Christmas on the front of *Record Mirror*'s issue dated December 23rd. Much more fun. Five days later at Olympic studio he made more progress on his November demo of 'Angel', though it is still titled 'Sweet Angel'. The mood of the song is much more upbeat than the remakes he would record in 1970 – but a step away from the robust treatment he had given the song back in October. Hendrix uses alternative readings of the lyrics that suggest a pleasant confusion over the origins of the angel in question. Perhaps the silver wings belonged to an aeroplane as much as anything extra-human, and the sweet succour on offer was more earthly, delightful not just to the senses but to the soul as well.

With Chandler away from London for the festive season, Hendrix enjoyed a quiet Christmas in the Marylebone flat alone with Kathy Etchingham. For

"They put Jimi Hendrix in a bag. They called him a pop artist. But Hendrix was a stone blues player."

Roland Kirk, jazz individualist

new year's eve they attended a party at the hip Speakeasy club in central London. Trombonist and musicologist Chris Barber was present that night, having come on from his own gig at Birdland, near the Scotch of St James. He remembers the jam that ensued between various celebrating musicians. "The Speakeasy had a band every night," he says, "with a junior bar and a restaurant, which was very good. Upstairs there was a room where you could have a session if you wanted to. We did. Zoot Money, Georgie Fame, Speedy Acquaye, Jimi and I played. No one knew what to play, so we finally decided to have a go at 'Auld Lang Syne', appropriately enough. We quickly realised as we ran through it that it was the same changes as 'Trouble In Mind' – and the whole number lasted for something like an hour."

This unlikely combination does make sense, given that all participants were firmly committed to the blues, including Barber, a lifelong evangelist for the music. But the evening (or early morning) was not yet over. "There were two black American guys sitting down watching," Barber recalls. "They were songwriters, and had managed some hits. One of them asked if he could come up and sing, so we did a blues and he sang with us. It was Isaac Hayes and his brother. Apparently he hadn't sung much in public before that. This went on for an hour or something like that, then it wound down, like all jam sessions do, petered out, and we all went home."[20]

Chris Barber remembers the jam as a relaxed and open meeting of musical minds, a typical product of the late 1960s – as was Hendrix. "He was an exceptionally good blues player who found a way of projecting himself that got to people," says Barber. "He was someone I'd go a very long way to listen to. It was a lot to do with the generation, and the time. I knew all three of the guys in the band in those days. Mitch was trying to turn it into a Buddy Rich band; Noel was out of his head most of the time – he wanted it to be a pop band, I think, and didn't seem to be particularly interested in music one way or the other. Jimi was very interested in music, and so was Mitch. They wanted to get on and make music all the time."[21] The following year would provide plenty of opportunities for them to do just that.

the road to electric ladyland

The first major business in the new year of 1968 was a two-week Experience tour of Scandinavia. After flying out on January 3rd to Gothenburg the group gave some interviews, allowing familiar themes to crop up. Hendrix confessed to one newspaper, "I think I would like to run away from it all for half a year and just study music. I'm tired of trying to write music only to find out that I can't. People think that I'm a sulky guy. That's because I think about music all the time. If I suddenly get very quiet and serious, then it's because I've just got an idea for a song."[1]

Promotional duties completed, the group went out to a local club. By this time Hendrix's consumption of drugs had escalated to the point where he needed to be on something virtually all the time. Redding's recollection of Hendrix's evolving drug usage during and after *Axis* suggests someone with no knowledge of his own limits and little interest in trying to establish them. "Jimi seemed to have higher tolerances than me. We always took the purest we could find. ... Know your source was the rule. If I took two tabs, Jimi took four. We got crazy on pills and got thrown out of hotels. ... It was about this time I was offered a snort of coke which turned out to be heroin. I knew it wasn't for me and never knowingly touched it again. ... People who like the same highs hang out together. Musicians who liked heroin formed little groups together, but I never could relate to having a basin in the middle of the studio for spewing up. That distanced me from Jimi, who was always longing for an escape, even for a few hours of 'the next best thing to being dead'."[2]

Heroin was becoming relatively popular on the British rock scene in 1967 after devastating the international jazz community for over 20 years and being something of a chic drug among intellectuals and drop-outs in New York for most of the 1960s. By the time it had taken its course through British pop life at the beginning of the next decade, a number of A-list rock heavyweights would experience its strangulating grip, including John Lennon, whose 'Cold Turkey' is about him beating his addiction. By all accounts Hendrix never injected – like many people he had a fear of needles – but other methods were available, and it was around this time that he added heroin to his list of recreational drugs. With

Jimi and Stratocaster in action sequence at the Fillmore West, San Francisco, February 1st 1968: hitting the high notes (left); taking advantage of that close-at-hand vibrato arm (right).

a tight control on supply of illegal drugs in Denmark then, there was little point in even looking for such things. The only widely available alternative was booze. Redding and Mitchell were quite at home with this substitute, but as most of his colleagues and friends over the years observed, Hendrix and alcohol did not make for a successful mix.

Back at the Gothenburg hotel in the early hours, a drunken Hendrix was about to inflict some serious damage on his hotel room and on his personal reputation. According to Redding – the only vocal eyewitness to the events rather than their aftermath – the entourage had returned from the club "rotten drunk". He said: "Jimi'd been hanging out with this gay Swedish journalist. Perhaps he was putting ideas in Jimi's head, but Jimi suggested we should have a foursome. The Swede was really pushing it, and the vibes got stronger and stranger. Jimi made an advance to me – I passed on it. The tension built up until Jimi started dashing about, smashing everything in his room. It was terrifying to see." [3]

After a period of confusion and destruction and several attempts by people in Hendrix's troupe to calm the guitarist, the police were called and Hendrix was taken off to the local lock-up. Through a combination of Chandler's Swedish contacts and professional charm, Hendrix was allowed out to fulfil his concert engagements. But at the end of the short tour, on January 9th, Hendrix and Chandler had to return to Gothenburg to answer further questions relating to the event. In all, he was detained a further eight

days before being found guilty in Gothenburg Municipal Court of causing damage to a hotel room. He was heavily fined. Only then, on January 17th, was he allowed to leave the country. This was the first public sign that all was not well with Hendrix and that the pressure of events over the past 18 months was getting to him in new and worrying ways. He had been moody or visibly pissed off before, as had everyone else in the group, but he'd never completely lost control. It seemed out of character. He was known to be a quiet, relaxed man in company, always ready to party but – unlike many other rock stars – not obsessed with making the biggest noise in a group of people or insisting on making others accept domineering, boorish behaviour.

Typically, Mitchell looked positively on the enforced time-off. "In some ways," he wrote later, "it was the best thing that could have happened. Not for Jimi, really, but we'd been working solidly without a break for over a year and were totally knackered."[4]

Redding's account of the "foursome" incident posed difficult personal questions, but these seem to have been allowed to drop by all concerned. Hendrix would probably have been attractive to some gays: his dress sense alone would have appealed, let alone his general demeanour. Kathy Etchingham remembers that "quite a few people thought he was gay because of his appearance (although 'gayness' was an unheard-of concept in all but the most sophisticated corners of the country), and the words 'pansy' and 'queer' could be heard here and there. Jimi probably didn't know what they meant, and if he did he certainly wasn't offended, being more confident of his sexuality than any man I had ever met".[5]

Musically, the Scandinavian tour was uneven. For the first two nights Hendrix was supported by a couple of local groups, The Baby Grandmothers and The Mecki Mark Men (the latter soon recorded two Hendrix-influenced albums for the US Limelight label, one of which found its way into Hendrix's own record collection in London). Remarkably, the Experience gave good value that first evening in Gothenburg; they played two long sets and, according to all reports, were on especially good form. The following day, in Sandviken, their set lasted just 35 minutes, with Hendrix claiming a sore throat. That he was worried about the effect his hotel rage would have on Scandinavian fans was shown in an interview he gave the following day in Copenhagen to Claes Hanning of *Expressen*. "Usually I can drink a lot of booze," he told Hanning. "Someone must have put some kind of tablet in my glass. ... I really hope the Swedish audience overlook this."[6]

Later in the interview, Hendrix confirmed that he was still aspiring to new musical pastures. "After Stockholm, I'll take it easy for a while, as I need to calm down. Since my breakthrough, everything has gone so fast that I've never had a chance to relax. I want peace and quiet to maybe write the pop musical I have in mind. The business needs something fresh: the audience is tired of seeing bands just standing on a stage." [7] He expanded on this idea when talking to Carsten Grolin for *Ekstra Bladet*. "I have also thought about changing our stage act completely. In the future, I'll present a stage play with colours, which is going to play one part, [and] dancers and other groups, who are going to play different parts, either with or without instruments. I'd like to have Procol Harum with me. They appear like a troupe of Shakespearean actors when they get on stage."[8]

The vision was becoming complicated and unwieldy, which probably accounts for its eventual removal from Hendrix's plans. But his expressed interest in such ideas not only underscores his musical ambitions but confirms that he was, as ever, acutely aware of all that was new in contemporary music. Many of the newest rock albums had unified concepts at their heart, from the embryo of The Who's *A Quick One* through *Sgt. Pepper* and The Moody Blues' singles and albums, to The Pretty Things' *S.F. Sorrow*. These would feed into works like the second side of The Small Faces' *Ogden's Nut Gone Flake* and eventually the brilliant *Who Sell Out* and its follow-up, *Tommy*. Hendrix was keen to compete, even if at this point he seemed not to want to try it on an album, but rather on stage.

He told Lars Bengtsson, "There isn't a single theme to [*Axis*]. I don't think so. I don't know ... 'let your body drift', maybe. We don't plan an LP with a theme – the songs are made without any connection." He was aware that he wanted more consistent quality from himself. *Axis: Bold As Love* had begun to reveal the obsessive perfectionist in Hendrix, but the things he

Hendrix at the Fillmore West: urging feedback from his guitar becomes a two-handed job.

worried about in interviews were different to those that would cause such rancour within the band when they came to record during 1968.

He told Bengtsson, "It's easy for me to write songs today, in contrast to the beginning when I was afraid that the things I wrote were not what I really felt, or that they said what I felt but were in danger of being censored. But even now I wish from time to time that I could correct a verse in a song when I hear it on record and know it's not what I feel. Or if I suddenly discover ... that some people have misunderstood the words."[9]

Hendrix hints here that his early songwriting in London was, in part at least, specifically aimed at pleasing his management and record company – one recalls the drastically edited lyrics to 'Purple Haze' as well as the hurriedly written 'Stone Free' and 'Highway Chile' – and that somehow his lyrics had failed to get his points across. There is also the question of verbal and syntactical sloppiness, something of which Redding was aware during the *Axis* sessions but was unable to persuade Hendrix to correct. Hendrix was certainly guilty of errors that are relatively simple to rectify, like the changing tenses throughout 'Long Hot Summer Night', or the way he leaves conflicting singular and plural endings on phrases, as in "Castles made of sand / Melts into the sea" and other similar losses of grammatical continuity. It is hard to believe that Hendrix would not have wanted to improve such things when his attention was drawn to them on his records, especially given his intense admiration for Dylan, who used endless verbal shortcuts and was brilliant at exploiting the vernacular of the day, but whose use of conflicting syntax or tense was never unintentional and always had an alternative point. What remains so unusual about Hendrix – and so touching – is that he was prepared to admit such failings publicly.

Meanwhile there was a tour to finish, jams to be jammed, and court appearances to be made. Two shows a day in Copenhagen and Stockholm rounded out the tour. A version of 'Catfish Blues' from the first show in Copenhagen on January 7th (issued on the 1995 UniVibes CD *Jimi In Denmark*) suffers from poor recording balance and a distant vocal, and while it offers savage blues guitar playing and a cohesive band effort, it follows the established format for the tune, offering no great surprises. The following night's shows were also excellent and represented something of an effort to act on the eternal dilemma of the performing pop star: pleasing the audience, but without relying exclusively on old numbers that the artists are tiring of playing. For both January 8th concerts the band played the opening three selections of *Axis: Bold As Love* intact, including Mitchell's spoof radio-interview spot and Hendrix's reaction. The experiment was not repeated.

Hendrix, with time to reflect during the week of relative quiet as he waited for the court case, talked in one interview about the music that currently most impressed him. "If I should mention someone who inspired me it would be people like Bob Dylan, Muddy Waters, Elmore James. I like free-form beat like the Swedes Hansson & Karlsson."

This was keyboardist Bo Hansson and drummer Rune Carlsson. "They are truly fantastic. We – Noel, Mitch and me – played for five hours with them in Sweden. I also like the new album from Traffic. I think that the future is rock and blues – modern rock and blues."[10] If that was to be the future, then it was certainly convenient for Jimi.

"I want peace and quiet to maybe write the pop musical I have in mind. The audience is tired of seeing bands just standing on a stage."

Jimi Hendrix

Back in London on January 17th, Hendrix and his group prepared for an upcoming American tour for which they were due to leave on the 30th. They also resumed recording at Olympic Studios. Hendrix had begun to welcome musical and non-musical visitors to studio sessions the previous autumn, often to the disquiet of other group members and Chas Chandler. This new series of sessions involved Traffic's Dave Mason again, with Brian Jones of the Stones also contributing, although most of his efforts were either quietly dropped at a later stage or left out of the mix when it came to finalising tracks. Six pieces were committed to tape between January 21st and 28th, two of which were later incorporated into *Electric Ladyland*. One would also become his best-selling 45rpm single; most of the others were either released soon after his death or many years later on CD compilations.

Just two selections are still only to be heard on bootlegs: a jam that has been titled 'Have You Ever Been To Electric Ladyland (Electric Ladyland Blues)', although it bears no relation to the ballad with the similar name, and 'Little One (Mushy Name)', of which there are two versions. Neither consists of music that Hendrix would have wanted the rest of the world to hear on an official release. He made no subsequent attempt to shape and complete these try-outs for possible release, giving a clear impression that they were experiments, meant as guides to how a new piece could be developed. However, 'Little One (Mushy Name)' is fascinating in that it includes the first recorded appearance of the main melody, chord progression and basic structure for 'Cherokee Mist', an instrumental tune that Hendrix attempted to record definitively on a number of occasions but which he never completed. This first version features driving drums from Mitchell, a sympathetic sitar background from Jones and a close co-ordination between bass and rhythm guitar that provides great forward momentum. There's also a hint of the 'Mist' melody at the outset of the so-called 'Electric Ladyland Blues' jam, confirming that the 'Cherokee Mist' theme was much on his mind that day.

On the first night of these new Olympic sessions Hendrix attempted his own arrangement of Dylan's 'All Along The Watchtower', one of the tracks on Dylan's new *John Wesley Harding* album, released in the US that same month: Hendrix had got hold of an import copy on his return from Sweden. Kathy Etchingham remembers his excitement. "We played it over again and again," she said. "Jimi particularly loved a track which went 'I dreamed I saw Saint Augustine, alive as you or I' but felt that it was too personal to Dylan for anyone else to be able to cover it. Then he thought he would do 'All Along The Watchtower' but he was terrified that

Dylan would laugh at him and the critics lay into him." She told him to stop worrying and just do it. According to Etchingham, Hendrix "would often book studios himself when he was in London and we would go down with any bunch of musicians he could raise. I used to roll joints and lie down on the long padded bench seat behind the console and fall asleep, we were there so long. They would jam together for as long as they could manage".[11]

On that night, January 21st 1968, Hendrix rounded up a posse of musicians including Mitchell, Dave Mason and Brian Jones. Etchingham said that Jones brought along a giant sitar,[12] but the finished mix of 'Watchtower' betrays no hint of that instrument. However, the two jams of January 28th that ended the week's recording certainly feature Jones on sitar, probably with Dave Mason on bass. Jones may well have used the sitar on 'Watchtower' only for it to be left out of the mix, though he initially tried a piano accompaniment for that song. The entire evening was devoted to getting down an acceptable backing track and then adding overdubs. In the next few evenings various jams were taped, and these have since appeared on bootlegs. One night's recordings – with Dave Mason and an unidentified drummer whose style is certainly not that of Mitchell's – consisted of jams on blues changes and drones, or snatches of themes that Hendrix was dallying with at the time. One of these undistinguished blues has elements of the title track to *Electric Ladyland* within its sprawling mass, while another piece, 'South Saturn Delta', has a promising structure of riffs, breaks and themes, but the form is clunky, with no real musical development to take it to a meaningful resolution. However, the attempt impressed Hendrix sufficiently for him to take the master to New York later that spring and arrange for a horn section to be overdubbed. Nonetheless, the track was never issued during his lifetime. It certainly didn't reach the smoothly executed standard that Hendrix demanded at the time and the problems of its form were never resolved. It remains an interesting but failed experiment.

Another instrumental was much more successfully attempted that week, on the 26th: 'Tax Free', a composition by Swedish duo Bo Hansson and Rune Karlsson that Hendrix had picked up during his recent Scandinavian trip. It was recorded by the Experience as a trio, and their fine co-ordination attests to the group's continued compatibility. It may have been left off *Electric Ladyland* due to Hendrix's tendency to race in one of the rhythm guitar tracks, and there are also small link sections that sound as if they need further guitar support, indicating that the track may was left unfinished. The construction of 'Tax Free' – with its different sections, the break-and-pauses formula of the main theme, and its strutting, jazzy, rhythmic feel – suggests that Hendrix's own 'South Saturn Delta' may have been his own attempt to compose something similar. Both typify his determination to grow as a musician. 'Tax Free' is certainly a more sophisticated construction than the

"I think that the future is rock and blues – modern rock and blues."

Jimi Hendrix

Hendrix piece, its varied pace and metres fascinating players and listeners alike. There are only a couple of brief improvisations: the first comes over a jazzy 3/4 beat; the other is more of an improvised accompaniment part towards the end. But the piece is so cleverly structured, and so imaginatively arranged by Hendrix, that this does not become apparent the first few times one hears it.

'Tax Free' is something of an object lesson in how Hendrix began to evolve his arranging technique. He uses different guitar tracks, each with a distinctive role and timbre, to play the part of different voices, much as the arrangers of swing-era big-bands did, where each instrumental section – trumpets, saxes, trombones – would play melodies, chords and counter-melodies in response to one another. The piece's three basic sections break down further into sub-sections, and its success rests in part in the subtlety with which Hendrix orders and links them. His wonderful arranger's ear continually juggles the way in which the main themes of each section are heard, keeping the experience fresh for the listener.

Also on January 26th, 'All Along The Watchtower' was given a preliminary 'final' mix by Hendrix and Chandler. This mix would be taken to New York and work done there to complete the master that was released as a 45rpm single and on *Electric Ladyland*. But Hendrix's overall conception for his version of the Dylan song was complete and in place by the end of that night's work. It's instructive to compare Dylan's original with Hendrix's cover. Dylan, on acoustic guitar, uses a simple but haunting descending minor-chord progression as a prop for his story, delivered by a masterful vocal. The bass and drums supply the drive, the drummer stressing every beat with a snare stroke. The only punctuations are Dylan's traditional harmonica breaks. He's taking an almost troubadour-like approach, distinct from the more striking instrumental colours of his productions of the previous two years. After he has told his story there is a concluding burst of harmonica, then the band simply stops. One's imagination is left reverberating with the images released by Dylan's verbal conjuring. This original version of the song lasts 2:28; Hendrix's lasts 4:01. Hendrix has no extra verse of lyrics; there are no repetitions. What makes it so much longer?

Hendrix's version takes a musicianly approach, logically enough. Adopting the same equal-beat snare pattern for the drums, he constructs an introduction and wrests from Dylan's bursts of harmonica a beautifully melancholic, swooping guitar line that is independent from the vocal but as memorable as any other element of the piece. In doing this, Hendrix sets a precedent in rock – in some ways rather unfortunate – for such introductory melodic ploys. Luckily for Dylan, his guitar playing is wholly sympathetic to the mystery and drama that are the song's core strengths, perhaps more to do with musical traditions associated with Dylan's heritage than Hendrix's.

His major guitar overdub, full of shifts of 'voice' and musical vernacular, runs a close commentary on the words, as well as adding the introduction and the solo. He continually draws on elements of hillbilly music and western swing. Although Hendrix certainly listened to and admired some of his great contemporaries in country guitar-playing, such as Clarence White (in his pre-Byrds career as well as with The Byrds), he also heard and absorbed the often heavily blues and jazz-inflected slide-guitar playing found on pre and post-war hillbilly and western swing records. This type of hard-driving and frequently beguiling vocal music with improvised guitar (and violin) accompaniment thrived on the West Coast in the 1940s and early 1950s, where Hendrix would have heard it on the radio. No less an R&B stronghold as the Modern label released many such hillbilly sides in that period.

Throughout the song, Hendrix substitutes his sensitive guitar work for the cadential harmonica passages Dylan had supplied between verses, but he also incorporates the swooping melody shapes of western swing guitarists. Hendrix's solo is a soundscape that paints as accurate a picture of looking out into "the cold distance" as Dylan's lyrics. The break he plays between verses one and two is almost pure western swing in its long, elegiac, singing phrases,

echoing the keening of the lyric. The second break, four times the length of the first, incorporates Hendrix's major soloing on the track. It begins with some purely traditional slide-blues phrasing before changing tone and moving into a ghostly country-and-hillbilly sequence, suggesting perhaps another presence in a conversing group. Then Hendrix once again abruptly swaps styles – almost as if a third voice has entered this conversation – with a wah-wah passage that is more bluesy and colloquial in nature, convivial and eager to catch up with the others. After a concluding vocal verse the performance fades with a trademark Hendrix touch: a high guitar note, howling out into that cold landscape. This type of sustain was what Hendrix searched for and indeed found in various musical contexts throughout his career – and in this instance it shows again a direct knowledge of violin playing in western swing and hillbilly music (Dylan's harmonica on the original is not itself ignorant of such roots). Hendrix's high note on the fade is accompanied by the acoustic guitar that has underpinned the entire piece, as if the gypsy-style messenger has delivered his narrative and is now moving on to his next audience. This is a masterful combination of elements, painting as complete a picture of the scene evoked by Dylan's imagination as Hendrix could encompass. It is so seamless a construction of so many seemingly disparate parts as to be one of his most dazzling – and most popular – single creations.

'Have You Ever Been (To Electric Ladyland)', another key element of the next album, was given a decisive start during that week of studio work at Olympic in west London. This compelling ballad is often overlooked, coming straight out of the howling chaos of the album's opener, '…And The Gods

"He thought he would do 'All Along The Watchtower' but he was terrified that Dylan would laugh at him and the critics lay into him."

Kathy Etchingham, girlfriend

Made Love', and then merging into the start of 'Crosstown Traffic'. However, it is one of Hendrix's most artfully constructed ballads, full of unorthodox but pleasing chord movement, often on unexpected beats. It is blessed with a vocal melody that elegantly descends from the tonic in a manner not unlike the memorably warm and soulful ballads of Smokey Robinson and Curtis Mayfield – influences also prevalent in Hendrix's supporting vocals. Yet the context is different, providing a kind of added value. For a start, the common-time (4/4) metre is disguised in the first verse by the drums, often through triplets and unusual off-beat emphases. Mitchell's imaginative fills and cymbal splashes, greatly aided by electronic alteration of the cymbal and drum sounds, seem to cut across his constant 4/4 snare beat, enhancing the slow, dream-like quality of the piece, almost as if it simultaneously exists on two rhythmic levels between which listeners can slide as they choose.

The recording of this piece completed the band's work at Olympic for what would become *Electric Ladyland*. While Redding remembered this as a time when the band-members were unhappy with one another as tempers frayed and Hendrix drew away from Chas Chandler, the months of December and January had nonetheless been enormously productive. Just three months after the finalisation of *Axis: Bold As Love*, they had produced complete or near-complete versions of 'Crosstown Traffic', 'All Along The Watchtower', 'Have You Ever Been (To Electric Ladyland)', 'Dream', 'Dance', and 'Tax Free', and were working on other new pieces. On the eve of the Experience's departure for an extended US tour – plus two shows first at the Paris Olympia

– they had what Chandler at least regarded as half of the next album. But Hendrix had other ideas.

The Paris Olympia shows were booked as a warm-up; the Experience's regular US support, Soft Machine, were not present, their slot taken by Eric Burdon & The Animals. The Olympia had been the venue for the band's first ever gig and usually elicited a relaxed and free-flowing performance from the band. The January 29th event was no exception. Released later in the boxed set *Stages*, the music shows Hendrix and his cohorts bursting with vitality and enjoying a warm relationship with the responsive crowd. Perhaps in recognition of the French propensity for the blues, Hendrix leans heavily in that direction, kicking off with an almost frenzied 'Killing Floor' and directly following with a spare, intense 'Catfish Blues' where Mitchell's drum solo receives continuous cheers from the typically ebullient Parisian crowd. A wonderfully slow, knowing 'Foxy Lady', marred only by some approximate singing, shows just how heady this band could be when it clicked, a point underlined by two more blues in succession, 'Red House' and 'Driving South'. This 'Red House' performance is something of a neglected classic, with Hendrix employing a slashing tone reminiscent of his early guitar heroes Albert and Freddy King. He plays with astonishingly fluid phrases and a gift for paraphrase at a level shared only by the greatest instrumentalists, from Louis Armstrong to Miles Davis and onwards. Here Hendrix displays that skill by using his own recorded solo from the *Are You Experienced* 'Red House' as a basis for further variations, inventing new and fitting shapes for familiar phrases. His own satisfaction is reflected by the freedom he brings to 'Driving South' immediately after this, followed in turn by the perfect calm of a haunting 'Wind Cries Mary'. Even Hendrix's tuning problems hardly detract from the overall mood.

Another notable achievement at the Olympia on the 29th was 'Little Wing', positioned immediately before the usual mayhem of the set-closer, 'Purple Haze'. A year before the beautiful live version recorded at London's Albert Hall, the band already have a proper ending worked out for 'Little Wing' to get around the problem of the album's studio fade – a half-step down, followed by a touch of low feedback and a decisive tonic chord – but it is still being finessed, and is a long way short of the grace and elegance that they would exhibit in London. Still, with a wildly positive crowd – Parisians were getting ready for a very hot summer indeed, and one that President De Gaulle would not appreciate – and a triumphant conclusion to this unusual set, things were looking very good. It was a highly satisfactory way of gearing up the band for a long and important US tour, which had taken Mike Jeffery's office a long time to plan. It would last to early April 1968, when Mitchell and Redding returned to London for a break while Hendrix stayed on in New York City. Hendrix would not return to London until May 27th, after extensive studio work at the Record Plant in New York and a brief Italian concert tour. The US tour would break the band conclusively across that country, in the process putting intolerable strains on everyone involved. Hendrix in particular would emerge a changed man, with different professional and personal objectives. It was not the typical US package tour that every British band (except The Beatles) had been a part of since 1964. This was a Hendrix headlining tour, run by his own management and overseen by his own people. They chose support groups with the sole purpose of putting on a show that climaxed naturally with the Experience, who naturally sent everyone home happy. No one was going to overshadow the main act, even though the support bands were first rate.

On this tour, the main support group was an English band admired by Hendrix and under contract to the Jeffery-Chandler team. The Soft Machine were a good match for the Experience in that they offered a near-whimsical mix of contemporary jazz and rock while retaining the occasional snatch of song form. The members of Soft Machine – keyboardist Mike Ratledge,

drummer Robert Wyatt and guitarist Kevin Ayers – had been a fixture of the underground scene for some years, a major attraction in Canterbury since the mid 1960s before arriving in London and appearing at clubs like UFO – the same venues that the Experience couldn't get into a year earlier. "I was with the same management," recalls Ayers. "I was signed to Mike Jeffery as a songwriter before Soft Machine. He was a weird guy, Jeffery."[13] The Soft Machine quickly became aware of Hendrix's impact on the British music scene. They were also aware of the time being spent on the Experience by the Jeffery-Chandler management. Ayers says the band worried that their managers were going all out for Hendrix, and as a result might not continue their interest in Soft Machine. But they did. "Hendrix said it's fine with me, or something like that," says Ayers. "He liked us, because we were weird. Weird and very white. We weren't like a rock'n'roll band and absolutely no threat of any kind. Not that he'd worry about that. And we were cheap."[14]

Soft Machine didn't make a great start on the tour, booted off the bill at San Francisco's Fillmore Auditorium after Robert Wyatt argued with the venue's owner, Bill Graham. But the Hendrix Experience fulfilled all expectations, playing a set that stuck to the formula of the previous summer. The next day, February 5th, the Experience were in Arizona, supported by

"Hendrix was an amazingly ostentatious, outgoing and energetic showman and at the same time he had this very moody, sensitive and often perceptive side."

Kevin Ayers, Soft Machine guitarist on tour with the Experience

Soft Machine. The pattern for the tour was set, normally a gig a day followed by high-energy partying and substance abuse, then the following day some bleary-eyed interviews with local or national media. Much of the questioning from US journalists aimed to catch up with events that had been covered a number of times already in Britain. Hendrix, Mitchell and Redding mostly gave patient and intelligent answers to their inquisitors, especially when the journalist showed an above average grasp of the subject. More than once Hendrix eluded attempts to label him, from suggestions that he was only interested in the blues to the charge that he was going to abandon rock for avant-garde jazz. He quietly insisted that he would continue to draw inspiration from every suitable source and play his own ideas.

The pace of the tour was unrelenting, but that didn't deter the touring party from indulging in everything offered to them and more besides. Kevin Ayers remembers it as "two months non-stop – a real bash. We did top to bottom, coast to coast. I don't think there was a main city we didn't play. Punishing itinerary? Not at that age. You can do anything when you're 20. I remember the poor roadies used to have to set off after having broken down the gear at about three in the morning and then be there for the next gig, having driven for 600 miles or something, tanked up with speed or whatever. They needed *something*".[15] The roadies weren't the only ones who were tanked up. As the tour settled down, Ayers remembers a day-to-day pattern emerging. "Our drummer, Robert Wyatt, became very friendly with Mitch Mitchell. And with Noel Redding, for that matter. I became friendly with Jimi

Hendrix himself. We used to go out to nightclubs together. I think that must have been something to do with me being basically a lyric writer in those days, and he liked that. He was struggling to write words and express all these things he felt and all the new experiences. Also, I was a pretty blonde white boy. I think he went both ways, actually. Any way possible, in fact, not just

"The 1968 American tour was the one that did us in. We stopped making music and started doing time."

Noel Redding

both! Yeah – we used to knock around together. Not on a regular basis: it was far too punishing for me. I couldn't cope with the intake or the hours that they did, every night and every day. Because of his aura, his ability and his stature, he was sort of led. He was a leader, but he was led quite easily by other people of similar stature. He was led by fast talkers and people with nice pockets, and packets of nice things in their pockets."[16]

Redding remembered an unfolding nightmare on the tour, waking stoned after little sleep and starting the cycle again. They were offered drugs everywhere, he said. Commerce, marketing and more sinister forces were taking over the supply lines for drugs. "Even acid was succumbing to commercial pressures which drove out fellow freaks and opened things up to dealers with an eye on the methedrine content," lamented Redding. "With pure acid you could eat and sleep to rest the body if not the brain. Not any more. And we mixed chemicals so badly, too. Mostly from necessity. Just how do you get down after the show so you can sleep?" Sex was liberally available too, though again things were going wrong. "Before, the girls had been companionable people who liked hanging out with us, but gradually they became women whose presence was strictly sexual, and we too became less men than famous fucks, another notch in the knickers."[17] Mitchell seems to have faced the same problems but was more sanguine about the solution. He enjoyed watching Soft Machine's warm-up set, and considered them a hard act to follow. He was grateful to drummer Robert Wyatt, who turned him on to jazz pianist Cecil Taylor.[18] But he remembers partying most nights away, and trying to get by on an hour's sleep per night before having to clear out and catch the plane to the next location.

The repertoire on the tour varied from night to night, with Hendrix occasionally interweaving 'Spanish Castle Magic' from *Axis: Bold As Love* into the set in an effort to move his crowd on from last year's hits. This was a considerable problem for the band: during the spring and summer of 1968, many in the US were still just discovering *Are You Experienced* for the first time; it stayed in the Top 100 for close on a year following its release the previous summer. Understandably, Hendrix's stage announcements were becoming somewhat standardised. During the introduction for 'I Don't Live Today', for example, he would always describe it as dedicated in some way to the contemporary plight of the native Indians of America – something he hadn't seen as mandatory when playing the song in Europe. From time to time tunes such as 'Tax Free' and 'Catfish Blues', recorded in the studio but never commercially released during Hendrix's lifetime, were worked into the set for occasional relief. Hendrix also ensured

representation for Dylan on this tour by regularly playing 'Can You Please Crawl Out Your Window', a song the Experience had recorded live for the BBC the previous year.

By February 12th the tour had reached Seattle, where Hendrix was met from the plane by his family. A number of eyewitnesses have spoken of the ambivalence with which Hendrix greeted this return to his home city. He was undoubtedly pleased to see his family again, especially as his father Al had remarried, giving Jimi a new bunch of relations. But he gave a subdued performance with the Experience that evening, aware of his family's presence. And an appearance the next day to address the morning assembly at his old school, Garfield High, was more or less bungled. He managed to answer two questions from the school populace after being introduced by the principal, and then left the assembly. Hendrix found this attempt to reconcile his past failings with his present eminence too unsettling: underneath the flashy exterior there evidently remained a sensitive and very private man.

Difficulties balancing public and private lives were occurring regularly on this tour. Kevin Ayers is convinced that Hendrix's continual struggle to sustain his public image was at the root of the unsettled, unhappy nature of the trio during the US visit. Probably at the time they all thought of it as a passing phase brought on by such sudden fame. Unfortunately, it lasted longer than any of them could have imagined. Ayers recalls, "Sometimes I visited Jimi in the morning in his room, when we were in the same hotel, and what struck me was that when he woke up he seemed to be very vulnerable and very shy, and then would construct this character called Jimi Hendrix by a gradual application and intake of various substances. And girls and things around and stuff. One time when I went there he was besieged by guitar manufacturers. They would try to get him to endorse stuff by playing it, so they'd leave him these guitars which he'd promptly give away to his groupies. And you could see this almost inarticulate kind of very shy behaviour, touching his mouth and looking down and looking away. I was struck by the difference between the guy who got up on stage at night from the guy who woke up. It seemed a huge difference, and it was like he was building this new person, filling this thing he'd developed. Everyone has that to a certain degree, especially in the performing arts where you're not the same person on stage as you are when you're at home with your family or friends, but I was quite shocked by the extremity of the change and what it took to get there.

"I think he was struggling very much because he was taking so many mind-expanding experiences," Ayers continues, "drugs as well as the other thing of playing in front of so many people and being adored, of having this

"Hendrix was just a nice guy who wanted to play the guitar in small clubs."

Jon Hiseman, drummer

incredible response and trying to live up to that. Needing to express his private feelings about the cosmos and man's position to his fellow man – that sort of thing. I think he was very concerned about it, and in his private moments he was a deep thinker. But then he was an odd sort of combination. He was an amazingly ostentatious, outgoing and energetic showman and at the same time he had this very moody, sensitive and often perceptive side."[19] Hendrix was touring this huge and varied country at a time of upheaval. On

Performing to the crowd's expectations during a two-shows-a-night three-night season at the large Winterland venue in San Francisco. These photographs were taken on the last night of the run, February 4th 1968.

the most superficial level, there was a fashion revolution taking place. Everyone on the tour noticed how it was this year rather than 1967 that marked the full spread of hippie and flower-power dress, as well as changes to codes of conduct and language, right across the States. More fundamentally, post-war culture was being remodelled in a way that would lead to a schism within the society, and one that would not heal for a generation. There were places on the tour where no more than lip-service was being paid to the so-called new freedoms. But the idea that to be hip you just needed some beads, incense sticks and trendy reading material in your tie-dye bag seemed to be gathering strength, even in some redneck areas.

In Texas, Mitchell recalled, the easygoing casually-clothed personal security guard assigned to them for four days turned out to be a prominent member of the state police force. In other cities there were less happy scenes: fights, thefts, awkward Union officials, constant problems with amplification and equipment, and the ever-present demands of local and national media. All of this told the individual members of the Experience that they'd made it very big indeed, but the overall effect was coruscating. They also had little guidance or protection from their management team, who did not see it as their role to accompany the musicians through each phase of the tour. That was left to the roadies. In some ways the road crew suffered more physical hardship than the musicians, driving to every concert and working flat out to

set up and then break down the gear before moving on to the next venue. Such routines would later become smoothly-oiled and reliable. In 1968 it was still a new and far from perfect industry and the equipment constantly caused problems. There was little time to check and make sure all was well with Jimi, Noel and Mitch, who were flying from gig to gig. Meanwhile Chas Chandler was getting anxious about pushing ahead with the next LP, adding to their sense of daily pressure.

Redding felt that this tour signalled the end of the group's original attitude toward what they were doing. "The 1968 American tour was the one that did us in," he wrote later. "We stopped making music and started doing time."[20] Kevin Ayers witnessed this at close quarters, and while he remembers how thrilling it was to watch the Hendrix Experience from the wings, he says: "Hendrix got very, very bored and even angry and upset with having to do stuff that the management told him to do. Like he didn't want to keep biting his guitar, he didn't want to keep humping amplifiers. He said he just wished they'd leave him alone to get on with things. But he was made to. … If you don't hump your amplifiers we don't pay you – stuff like that."[21]

The bootlegs that have surfaced from this spring and summer US tour in 1968 confirm the band's professionalism and intensity, but reveal them only occasionally deviating from what was too quickly becoming a formula. This was the first time it had become a major problem for Hendrix, but it was to get a lot worse, especially after the hit singles dried up and he relied on album sales to spread his musical message. In time it would mean that his fans were not clamouring for new hits, just the old ones. Hendrix was by no means alone in having to deal with this phenomenon, but he felt it acutely, being determined to play at his best at all times, and through the medium of personal inspiration rather than mundane professionalism. This dilemma between creativity and repetition damaged many musicians of the era. Jon Hiseman, then drummer and leader of British jazz-rock band Colosseum, saw it in action. "There's an old type of entertainer," he recalls, "who I've met doing the more commercial circuit, before I turned professional, and they hold the audience in a kind of contempt. They're punters; you're suckering them. You have an act; you develop this act; you know it works. It's very simple.

"But then a breed of new guys came along who had been inspired by music they'd heard which had somehow reached them and pulled their insides out. And they wanted their own concerts to be the same, every night, when they made it in the industry. You assume that when you reach that point, that's what it will be like. That the good times, the creativity, will be unlimited. Then you're suddenly faced with the business of going out on-stage every night and trying to re-create those good times that you had when you were first starting out and able to come up with fresh ideas all the time. You're now on a big stage, wanting to be appreciated and wanting to replicate earlier successes. People back in the 1960s had a real problem with what they called 'being creative'. In the end, what they'd thought was a creative act simply became a show. It actually comes across professionally as a creative act, which is what they couldn't accept. A lot of the painful problems that I saw at close hand were to do with that, and the managements all thought that you could work the creative process. But the artist always felt that he was in the moment of creation, and of course as he found out what worked he narrowed his range dramatically, so he ended up presenting an act. You create a persona and people come expecting to see that persona. So if you're being creative for nine months but you're actually going to go on for four or five years like this, all the creation stops after nine months and you go around reliving what you created. They found that psychologically this was a serious problem for instrumentalists. It's not a problem with singers – but for instrumentalists it becomes a serious problem."

For Hiseman it led ultimately to the break-up of his band, Colosseum, because they felt they'd done everything they could and it was possible for them to move on to other things. For Hendrix and the Experience, it was nowhere near as simple. "Those guys were much more successful than we were," says Hiseman. "They had become icons for taste, clothing and posture, and attitude to the establishment. But at the same time they got seriously caught in their own trap. They were expected to be like that on and off the stage. The Beatles created a persona: I don't know how much it was down to them, but it was important to what they were. Hendrix probably did the same thing. And, of course, he was just a nice guy who wanted to play the guitar in small clubs."[22]

For most of the tour, Hendrix's way of dealing with this type of pressure – apart from drugs and casual sex – was to jam after-hours as much as possible. Nearly everyone who became at all close to him, either professionally or personally, was struck by just how much importance Hendrix attached to sitting in with groups or convening an informal jam – anywhere, at any time. A number of recordings of these jams would surface in later years, taken from tapes made sometimes by nightclub owners, sometimes by members of the audience, and occasionally by Hendrix himself. He had a tape recorder that he took along to as many places as possible so that he could record for personal reference any new idea he came across or any jam he got into. Guitarist Rick Derringer of The McCoys (Derringer would later play with Johnny and then Edgar Winter) remembered one such jam. "He used to come down to The Scene in New York a lot when [The McCoys] were playing at night. After the set was over he would come up and jam and try out riffs for new songs. I came pretty much from a country music background and Jimi played a lot of country kind of guitar riffs. I respected his country influences."[23]

Some of the tapes that Hendrix made were stolen from him while he was still alive, others were stolen from his apartment after his death. Hendrix was never the most organised and careful person, with a clear disregard for a great many of his possessions, always believing that if one went, another would come along. But some things were irreplaceable, and the thefts he knew about hurt him deeply. A jam at The Scene, taped by Hendrix himself, apparently on March 13th, was later stolen and has been made available many, many times. It features him with various members of The McCoys, and unfortunately includes a couple of numbers where a very drunken Jim Morrison of The Doors insists on burbling a combination of lyrics and obscenities over the jamming musicians. As a private tape in a musician's own collection it would have had its point, but as a commercially available record of an informal night's worth of music-making it has serious aesthetic problems. Hendrix would doubtless have been appalled by the tape's release and subsequent exploitation.

As his life began to centre increasingly on recording, Hendrix turned to jamming as a means of working in the studio as well. This in turn placed an increasing strain on his professional and personal relationship with Chandler, who believed that studios were not palaces designed for self-indulgence. Both Chandler and Redding became sick of the hangers-on in America whom Hendrix, for one reason or another, could not or would not shake off. Hendrix was quickly identified as an easy touch, never happy to say no until pushed too far, at which point he could become quite ugly or brutal in his responses. But for the most part he suffered alone. "I'm sure he had a lot of fun," says Kevin Ayers, "but he also had a lot of bad times with hangers-on and groupies who would rip him off terribly – I mean, sadly. They'd just walk away with his whole wardrobe. He was very conscious of his clothes, he loved his fancy clothes. They'd walk away with them, and his money, and his guitars. It must have been really heartbreaking for him."[24]

Redding and Chandler continually told Hendrix about the disruption that was being caused and the money that was being wasted, but as he withdrew in order to protect himself, he paid less and less heed. At this point he was not even attempting to look for help from the few people who actually cared and who could have guided him through the worst of it. Relationships within the band stagnated or deteriorated. There was intense business and legal pressure building up from a number of sources, and no one had any idea how to deal with it. They were musicians, and like most group-members of the day they only wanted to think about music and having fun. As Redding commented later, "Not having an ounce of business know-how between us, we relied on our feelings to make all our decisions. We knew this was no way to do business, but we didn't know what else to do."[25]

Private recordings from this spring tour – at Clark University in Worcester, Massachusetts, on March 15th and the Capitol Theatre in Ottawa, Canada, four days later – have in recent years been made available to collectors by the Hendrix Estate on their Dagger label. The tapes reveal a fiery band willing to give a good account of themselves, but there is only occasional evidence to suggest that their performance had evolved much further from the set they'd delivered at Monterey the previous summer. Both sets include 'Wild Thing' and 'Foxy Lady' and Ottawa has an almost ten-minute 'Red House' where a clearly inspired Hendrix delivers superb undiluted blues guitar. The tune was a relatively new arrival in the Experience's live set, no doubt added to give the band a chance to stretch out, relax, and abandon the showmanship for a few minutes. It receives respectful applause at its conclusion. 'Fire' was played at both gigs. The Ottawa version, taken very fast, features a scalding guitar solo that is phenomenally well articulated considering its velocity, and consequently very exciting. The Clark University version, by contrast, is just a little overcooked, its tempo frantic, the short ending-solo used as a showpiece for some on-stage antics. This contrast between band-pleasers and crowd-pleasers is consistent with the growing tension between musical progress and entertainment. Hendrix also includes 'Tax Free' and 'Spanish Castle Magic' in the Ottawa concert. Neither piece would have been well known by the audience at that point: one had not been released at all; the other had only been available for a month or so on the new LP. This live take of 'Tax Free' is an uneasy combination, the band sticking to the musical script while trying to inject crowd-pleasing elements of excitement and slick phrasing that don't necessarily mesh with the tune being played.

While in Ottawa, Hendrix came across Joni Mitchell, playing opposite him at the Capitol Theatre. They had not crossed paths professionally since they both started out in Greenwich Village in June 1966: Mitchell with husband Chuck at the Gaslight; Hendrix with the first edition of The Blue Flames at the Café Wha?. By now Hendrix was intent on documenting what he discovered in the musical world around him, and he decided to add a recording of Mitchell to his own private tape collection. He did it in an open and honourable way, asking Mitchell's permission. "He introduced himself very shyly and said, 'Would you mind if I tape your show?'," Mitchell recalled many years later. "I said, 'Not at all.'"[26] It is probably no coincidence that it was during this US tour that Hendrix kept a reasonably regular diary, for the only time in his professional career. Like the narrator in 'Up From The Skies', he wanted to hear and see everything – but more than that, he wanted to document it for his own reference and use. This voraciousness had always been a part of the development of his unique style and approach, and he was intent on developing its practical uses by all possible means. Taping other musicians was one such method. Hendrix's diary entry covering his meeting with Mitchell reveals his excitement at discovering her music and his pride at being resourceful enough to have his tape recorder at the ready. He wrote: "Talked with Joni Mitchell on the phone. I think I'll record her tonight with my excellent tape recorder (knock on wood). Went down to the club to see Joni, fantastic girl with heaven words. We all got to party."[27] Hendrix, Mitchell and drummer Mitch Mitchell spent the rest of the night back at their shared hotel talking about music and playing together, much against the hotel management's wishes and in the face of their objections. It is revealing that Hendrix was drawn to Joni Mitchell's ability with song lyrics, an area in which he felt there was constant room for improvement in his own writing.

In the same week as these North American concerts, in Britain Hendrix appeared as an interview subject in the March 16th issue of *Melody Maker*. He told Frank Simpson that the tour was "completely successful" and Simpson was informed by the band's management that the tour had been a total sell-out. Despite this upbeat message, Hendrix also took the opportunity to moan about his "mechanical life" and the treadmill of endless concerts with no breaks in between. Simpson concluded: "Jimi still reacts to music. [Drummer and bandleader] Buddy Miles dropped in to see him. ... Both Buddy and Jimi want to get out and jam in a club for the evening. The first thing Jimi did, arriving in New York and finding that Eric Clapton was there, was arrange to jam with him. 'You can do this in New York,' he explains."[28]

Just a couple of days prior to this, while still in New York, Hendrix had made it into the studio for a session with Mitchell, Redding and some American friends, including Paul Caruso and Stephen Stills. Early work-outs on '1983' and 'Little Miss Strange' were recorded but left undeveloped; later versions would take their place. Two new tunes were attempted; neither made the cut for *Electric Ladyland*, and one of them was left a long way short of complete. The new songs were the autobiographical 'My Friend' and 'Somewhere', and they show a very strong concern for striking images in their lyrics. 'My Friend' is an easy-tempo'd, convivial but subtly-constructed blues number in the vein of Bob Dylan's stream-of-consciousness songs of the mid 1960s. Hendrix, slightly more world-weary, tells his story over a backing from old Village Vanguard colleague Caruso on harmonica and Stills on piano. He devotes one whole tape track at the introduction and fade-out to ambient sounds designed to conjure a local bar on a friendly night. The elaborate language is at times a little too self-consciously literary ("A stagecoach full of feathers and footprints / Pulls up at my soapbox door"), as if a recent swig of Dylan had not quite been fully digested. But other more tellingly personal

lines ("Haven't I seen you somewhere in hell / Or was it just an accident?") bring to the song the emotional intensity normally associated with Hendrix. The earthiness of the backing and the confidential way he sings, accompanied by sympathetic blues licks from his guitar or Caruso's harp, make this a convincing picture of celebrity loneliness.

'Somewhere' is equally downcast, dealing with a desolation that seems to have been Hendrix's frequent companion from this time onward. The song is patently unfinished: the guitar and bass are often not in sync with each other or with the later drum overdub from Mitch Mitchell; the edited fade provided by Alan Douglas as an ending for the song's appearance on *Crash Landing* in 1975 shows that Hendrix never figured out how to close the piece. The words to 'Somewhere' are bleak, initially indicating collective despair that suggests compassion for the deeply troubled state of American society in 1968, at home and overseas in war. A later verse personalises the misery: "As far as I know / They may even try to wrap me in cellophane and sell me." Of course, "they" did worse. This follows a guitar break that is competent but sounds like a filler, keeping the place warm for a later version that never came. The bass playing is officially unidentified, but sounds very much in the style of

"Hendrix introduced himself very shyly and said, 'Would you mind if I tape your show?'"

Joni Mitchell

Hendrix himself, simultaneously busy and melodic. Although Hendrix abandoned work on this piece, he clearly valued the lyrics, recycling them in part 18 months or so later for 'Earth Blues'. This being a less-than-Experience session, it's doubtful that Chandler was present. Considering that Chandler had been trying to arrange sessions for the band but Hendrix had not been co-operating, this studio foray would not have helped clear the air between the two as the tour dragged on and tempers frayed.

On April 4th an event of the first magnitude put all such concerns and frustrations into proportion. Martin Luther King was assassinated in Memphis. The Experience tour was in Virginia that day. They witnessed a split in American society as some people laughed, cheered and toasted the assassin, while others walked around in shock. The following day the entourage flew to Newark, New Jersey, to prepare for a major concert in Symphony Hall. Newark was an area with a large black population and there had been some violent confrontations between ethnic minorities and state and government authorities. In 1968 the violence in the US that The Yardbirds had noticed while on tour the year before became overt, centring on two great political questions of the time, both of which had become explosive issues. There was the peaceful protest and advance of civil rights advocated by Martin Luther King. King was assassinated in a pointless bid by racists to hold back an unstoppable process. There was also the heat and fury of a Presidential nomination race with, at its heart, the problem of America's involvement in Vietnam. The President incumbent, Lyndon Johnson, would eventually withdraw, while Vice President Hubert Humphrey's candidacy would be fatally undermined as he failed to distance himself from Johnson's pro-war stance. Senator Robert Kennedy, fiercely critical of the government, would himself be assassinated in early June.

Hendrix's own stance on these issues had shifted considerably since his rise to fame. No longer in favour of the Vietnam war, and forced by events to confront the race issue, as usual he chose his own highly individual path. By all accounts Hendrix was not political, but he was certainly aware of the crosscurrents affecting society and had his own opinions, often expressed through sardonic humour and carefully phrased wit. But the concert at Newark on the day King died was hardly an occasion for levity. Redding felt it was "when the whole black thing hit Jimi right in the face. He couldn't turn away. Jimi was never heavy about being black. He was into being Jimi – human being, pop superstar. ... In my experience, Jimi had blackness thrust upon him in certain respects. ... He was disillusioned enough to be cynical and he was no more keen on letting black people use him than he was willing to be exploited by white people".[29] That night in Newark, Hendrix made his own statement about how he perceived the world. Mark Boyle, who provided the light show for the tour, remembered later the extreme tension and grief that confronted the group that night. "The streets of Newark were silent and deserted when we arrived," said Boyle, "except that there seemed to be an enormous black man on each corner, as though he was a sentry or policing the block or something. There was an immense crowd at the auditorium. ... Mitch and Noel were already on stage and they were playing very quietly, and Jimi came on and went to the microphone and muttered, 'This is for a friend of mine.' He then began an improvisation that had a beauty that was simply appalling ... and within a very short time the whole audience was in tears, and the stage hands came in from the back of the stage, what they call the redneck stage hands, and they were standing there: white people, old men, with tears running down their faces, at the back of the stage, as this incredible music was played."[30]

There was just one more date, in White Plains, New Jersey, before the band were due to take a break. The next gig was on April 19th, in Tory, New York, on the night of Martin Luther King's funeral. The rest of April was given over to jamming, partying and recording. Jazz guitarist Larry Coryell recalled many evenings jamming with Hendrix, especially at The Scene club in New York City. "I once got to play with his rhythm section, Mitch Mitchell and Noel Redding. That was incredible, because they could really swing."[31] Soft Machine's drummer Robert Wyatt witnessed such a jam. "Larry Coryell, a wonderful guitarist, came in and started unpacking his guitar," Wyatt recalled later. "He was going to take on Hendrix. ... Coryell was one of the first people in jazz, in Chico Hamilton's group, to use rock guitar technique. Coryell thought well, if I can do what they do, I can do it much better than them. A lot of jazz guitarists thought that about Hendrix, and I have to say: you're all wrong! Anyway, Coryell got up, fingers flying trying to duet with Hendrix. Hendrix was just sort of looking and playing and doing his lines. Poor Larry Coryell, the more he was busting his fingers, up and down the guitar, feeding back ... it just sounded silly and incoherent. Hendrix was playing strong, graceful lines. And everything Hendrix played sounded more weird, more modern, actually more jazzy, and more coherent, where Larry Coryell just sounded panicky. It was quite embarrassing. It was really funny to see that technique is not actually about how fast you can play, it's about what authority you have over what you're doing."[32] Coryell must have been doubly mortified at this, being both a friend and an ex-Seattle boy like Hendrix.

Mitchell and Redding went back to London for ten days while Hendrix worked alone on song ideas. Versions of these songs, taped by Hendrix himself in his hotel room, include 'Long Hot Summer Night', '1983', 'Voodoo Child' and 'Gypsy Eyes'; others sketched at the time, such as 'Cherokee Mist', 'Angel' (again) and 'Getting My Heart Back Together', would not appear on any album sanctioned by Hendrix during his lifetime, though he did attempt studio recordings of all three.

Mitchell was interviewed by Melody Maker's Chris Welch and was typically forthright in his views about the American tour. "Let's be honest. It's not a question of neglecting our fans at home. We don't want to stay away, but we've all got to earn some money. And America is the country that can afford to pay more. Once we've got more bread we will be able to spend more time

on recording, writing, rehearsing and preparing a new stage act. When Jimi comes back, we're going to lock ourselves away for a month. We're very tired. We have played 47 cities in nine weeks." Mitchell seems also to have been bitten by the self-improvement bug that had prompted Hendrix to consider writing a "pop musical" earlier in the year, for he told Welch: "I'm going back to study at the end of the year. I'm going for a five-week drum course at Juilliard School in New York with Grady Tate and Elvin Jones."[33] As with Hendrix, the dream was not realised.

Hendrix kept up his jamming in New York City in early April, including a mammoth blues blow-out at The Generation Club, the venue he and Mike Jeffery were later to buy and transform into Electric Lady studio. He made his own recording of the night's proceedings on his portable tape machine, including two jams in which he did not participate. After this he joined guitarist B.B. King and keyboardist Al Kooper on-stage, along with vocalist and blues-harpist Paul Butterfield and three of Butterfield's band: guitarists Elvin Bishop and Buzzy Feiten, and drummer Phil Wilson. Kooper had been a friend of Hendrix's since his Village days. Three separate blues jams from that evening have become available on bootleg releases, mostly in cut-up form and lacking the continuity of the evening's actual events. As usual in such jams, Hendrix equally enjoyed playing a purely supportive, which is what he did in two of the three blues jams, allowing others to shine, as well as on 'It's My Own Fault'. One tune on which he did step forward and take a lead was an impassioned run-through with Kooper, Feiten and Wilson of Dylan's 'Like A Rolling Stone'. Hendrix knew of course that Kooper had been on the original Dylan studio recording of the song, so this slow, brooding performance, with Kooper's restrained organ giving it an atmosphere different from any other Hendrix rendition of the song, must have meant a great deal to him – as would the tape in his own private collection.

In an interview with Beat Instrumental around this time he referred to his passion for jamming and his rapidly evolving ideas of its place in his music. "I like this touring," said Hendrix, "but I don't like the touring. Know what I mean? ... But sometimes I get to meet other musicians and we kind of exchange notes. We worked a lot early on in the tour with the Electric Flag, who are real groovy over there on the West Coast. One guy, Buddy Miles, is someone I like talking music with. What you can do in America, specially in New York, is meet up with guys and just go out and jam somewheres. The club scene is so informal – you just go in, wait your turn, and get up there and

"The first thing Jimi did, arriving in New York and finding that Eric Clapton was there, was arrange to jam with him."

Melody Maker, on a favourite Hendrix pastime

blow."[34] There is an irony in Hendrix's remarks, because almost all the stories of people sitting in and jamming with him in America, or of others allowing him to do the same with their bands, came after he achieved worldwide fame in 1967: in other words, when it was cool to be seen or heard jamming with him. When he'd come to London an unknown in '66, with Chandler's help he sat in with virtually every musician of consequence in the city, from Eric Clapton downwards. Before that, in New York City, he'd battled to get any form of recognition on the most basic musical levels, and spent most of his early musical maturity between 1964 and '66 being exploited, either by leaders of bands constantly out on the road, or by musicians a long way below his level of attainment and understanding. Hendrix may have taken his belated acceptance at face value in order to get on with what mattered to him most – jamming with musicians he admired – but it seemed that the

Time off from the long American tour that took up all of February and March 1968 and finished in early April. Roger Mayer (far left) was Hendrix's friend and sonic ideas-man who came along to lend a hand.

harshness of the old American dictum, "When you're hot, you're hot; when you're not, you're not," contained an uncomfortable element of truth.

By April 18th the band were again all in New York City and ready to record. This time it was at the Record Plant, a studio newly opened by a consortium headed by engineer Gary Kellgren, with whom the band had worked so amicably at New York's Mayfair studio the previous year. This first day of new recording was given over to 'Long Hot Summer Night', a composition that would first be heard as the B-side of the British release of 'All Along The Watchtower' before appearing on *Electric Ladyland*. It is one of Hendrix's most beguiling songs, thoroughly well crafted from start to finish, possessed of an unusual harmonic construction, and full of extra little touches that catch the ear and deepen its appeal.

The first evening of recording probably consisted of just Hendrix and Mitchell, who put down rhythm tracks, with keyboardist Kooper overdubbing some acoustic piano – Hendrix returned to 'Summer Night' many times for preliminary mixes, further recording and various adjustments, through to its conclusion in August. During an interview at this time he specifically drew the attention of *Beat Instrumental*'s readers to Mitchell's wider musical abilities. "The ideas come from all directions when we're doing an album or even a song. Mitch has this 'feel' for sounds, like knowing exactly what other instruments to use."[35] The panoply of sounds in 'Long Hot Summer Night' suggests that Mitchell's involvement was more than simply a drummer and that he helped Hendrix realise his ideas for the piece. But as with 'Burning Of The Midnight Lamp' the previous year, this was still a very personal song, its pain and loneliness only alleviated by some extravagant and occasionally humorous imagery in the lyrics.

From the opening guitar riff – a skewed blues passage as if Lightnin' Hopkins had been slipped an acid tab – there is a dizzying sense of a private world spiralling out of control, the song's chords and harmony undermining the macho strut of the soul-flavoured rhythm. The tune has two personalities vying for dominance, often reflected in the sinuous and constantly altering vocal melody: this friction between the two states of mind makes it endlessly fascinating. Hendrix allows optimism to triumph ultimately, but it sounds like a close-run thing, with his lover phoning in to say she's on her way back, that she's "been a fool" and is "tired of crying". One wonders whether this might be a transference of self to the other. Hendrix, after all, had been playing the field a long way from home for nearly half a year.

The dream-like quality of 'Long Hot Summer Night' is emphasised by Hendrix's various musical sleight-of-hands. These come at us like a series of shocks or tricks – similar to those we experience in our dreams, like falling down lift-shafts and other such terrors. There is a two-bar stop-time passage at the end of the first verse that has an overlapping out-of-tempo guitar lick sticking out like a loose thread, outrageously free, sliding right across the bar-line and, for an instant, reversing the beat. No matter how many times you listen to this piece, your inner sense of the beat is turned around in an exciting way, momentarily disorientating you as if you've been on a fairground ride for a couple of seconds. In the equivalent break at the end of the next verse, no such outrageous risks are taken, and this time the song's continuity remains intact.

Hendrix accentuates the sense of tumbling pell-mell through this song by using an arresting triplet pattern at each verse-end, similar to that George Harrison would favour later on Cream's 'Badge'. The vocal chorus echoes

Hendrix's "where can you be", increasing the sense of disconnected mirror-like unreality. This chorus makes several subtle but vital contributions to the tune – especially where single sustained notes pick out harmonies indicating the major/minor tonalities, shifting the song's mood from dark to light with just a single tone's difference. Hendrix's guitar solo continues this misterioso mood as the song is raised a tone, preparing for the happy ending that the narrator craves. It is a brilliantly thought out and arranged track, with another highlight the accompanying bass lines, played by Hendrix himself. They are often as arresting as anything else going on in the piece, combining great

"We're very tired. We have played 47 cities in nine weeks."

Mitch Mitchell

rhythmic invention with independently rewarding melodic patterns, in much the same way as Paul McCartney at his best could grab the attention in Beatles songs. It points up the difference between Hendrix and Redding, a more sparse player concerned with sticking to agreed riff patterns or plotting a logical harmonic path through a song. Certainly Mitchell appreciated the difference. "Jimi was a fine bass player," he wrote, "one of the very best, very Motown-style. He was a very busy bass player, which in retrospect was so good for me to have played behind as it stopped me overplaying, which I did do, particularly on several of the album tracks."[36]

The differences between Hendrix and Redding were also demonstrated in the following few days of recording as the group worked on Redding's 'Little Miss Strange', eventually to become the second of his songs to appear on an Experience album. It is immediately noticeable that the piece is imitative rather than original in conception, in clear contrast to Hendrix's songs. The instrumental introduction combines ideas from Traffic and Cream while the vocal verse and its accompaniment (fuzz guitar melodies with parallel harmonies) sound like a Cream song filtered through the vocal organisation of The Small Faces. The form is not particularly cohesive, leaving long gaps for Hendrix to enjoy himself by imitating several current guitar styles.

'Little Miss Strange' would be used to start side two of the original four-sided vinyl double-album, a bright and energetic introduction to the far heavier fare contained on that side – 'Long Hot Summer Night', 'Come On Part 1', 'Gypsy Eyes' and 'Burning Of The Midnight Lamp', a sequence that seems to chart the emotional peaks and troughs of Hendrix's often long-distance relationship with Kathy Etchingham in those touring months. That this may well be more than speculation is underlined by the explicit reference to Etchingham in the long soundscape that swallowed the vast majority of side three of the original vinyl issue, '1983, A Merman I Should Turn To Be'. Hendrix had written the first draft of the words some months before, prior to the US tour. Etchingham noted this later in her autobiography. "We were sitting on the bed together when he read me the lyrics ... 'So my love Katherina and me decide to take our last walk through the noise to the sea, not to die but to be reborn, away from lands so battered and torn, for ever...'. 'What do you think of that?' he asked when he'd finished. 'I'm not coming with you,' I told him, making him laugh. 'You can go to the bottom of the sea by yourself.'"[37] Etchingham felt the vision was a result of taking acid. "'1983' had this strange rushing, buzzing noise going through it, just the sort of sound you hear when you are tripping. He also talked a lot about 'the other side' and about death, which people later interpreted as being about suicide, but was really only about being in an altered state of mind."[38]

It is hardly a new idea to take altered-state visions and translate them into works of art, whether verbal, musical, pictorial or otherwise. It has been an active pursuit of creative people for millennia – and Hendrix was not the first gifted person to have trouble realising those visions. When he talked

about '1983' a few months later to Yardbirds guitarist Jim McCarty, he was very concerned about the mechanics of trying to make the music correspond exactly to his original ideas. McCarty complimented Hendrix on managing to evoke a feeling of the ocean in '1983'. "He told me that was how he approached a song, especially if it was a specific thing, like a house burning down or an ocean or waterfall. His whole thing was visual. He visualised: 'What do I have to do on the guitar to create a house burning down?' That's how he viewed the guitar, basically the same way as Picasso would view a canvas. He had the ability to pull it off because he was brilliant."[39] While it's impossible to know whether Hendrix felt that he had precisely translated his insights into an independent existence within this music, or whether he'd lost much of it on the way (as Coleridge claimed he had with *Kubla Khan*), the only worthwhile assessment to be made is one based on the work itself, not Hendrix's hopes for it.

'1983' was planned as an extended-form piece. A private demo tape made in his New York hotel room in spring 1968, with just a guitar and vocals running through the structure, lasts nearly eight minutes. The master studio recording is no mere 'let's see what happens' jam, but has a definite shape. First comes an intro on three chords – A, C and D (with Jimi as usual tuned down a half-step or semitone), and then the first verse ("Hooray I awake...") sung against chromatically descending harmony, from D down to Asus4). This intro and verse then repeat ("Oh say..."). Another repeat of the intro leads to a repeated bridge ("It's too bad..."). An out-of-tempo instrumental interlude, starting at 3:13, leads to a recap of the verse (with spoken words, "So my darling...") and then a guitar break over the intro chords. The piece moves at 4:15 to the sound-painting section, as the narrator musically evokes his descent into water and what he finds there, among sounds of dispersal and dissolution. For around a minute, Mitchell's drums supply the underpinning for drifting tides of little sounds, weird whistles and bells, many guitar-generated though heavily disguised and with wavering pitches, and all intended to approximate the ebbs and eddies of water currents. These are the rushing trip-like sounds referred to by Etchingham.

Around 5:48 a set metre emerges at medium tempo, entirely on cymbals, accompanied by a guitar melody. Played idyllically over an F-sharp drone, it is reminiscent of the Indian music that Hendrix had admired and used the previous year and is counterbalanced by exquisite backwards-guitar passages that carry the timbral qualities of Indian bowed instruments. Toward the end of this melodic section a flute enters (Chris Wood of Traffic) before the tranquillity is swept aside at 8:12 by hectic guitar and a fevered drum passage of considerable force and rhythmic complexity – with Mitchell demonstrating his grasp of the solo techniques of jazz drummer Elvin Jones. A slinky bass-drum rhythm emerges as if sauntering out of the water, firstly as a background for a brief bass solo, probably by Hendrix himself. Eventually at 11:24, after seven minutes of the instrumental diversion, the original intro/verse and tempo are reintroduced, but in a shortened form. This is resolved in a spectacular climax with multitracked guitar lines. Hendrix does not make the mistake of 'Bold As Love', this time allowing not only a more free-flowing climax but also a gradual relaxation as the musical storm subsides. It is as much a sound-painting as Debussy's Livre 1 Preludes No.10, *La cathèdrale engloutie*, with its spectacular imagery beneath the waves, except that this time the undersea vision is Hendrix's rather than Debussy's.

The finished piece is more the result of genuine inspiration than musical aspiration, and stands as a perfect realisation of one of Hendrix's most ambitious projects. The tag 'Moon Turn The Tides ...Gently Gently Away' originally concluded side three of the vinyl release, flowing uninterrupted from the ending of '1983'. It allows for a gradual subsidence of the vision conjured by the 13-and-a-half minutes of music in '1983' and a re-entry into the world, like the slow dissolving of a vision. On CD reissues this effect is hampered by the fact that the next track, the groove-hard rocker that opened side four of the double LP, 'Still Raining Still Dreaming', follows hard on its heels, shattering that temporary suspension of 'normal' time. In the days of vinyl, listeners could leave the stylus to go round and round on the centre groove as they took their own time to find solid earth once more.

As with so much else on *Electric Ladyland* – and the other two Experience albums – there has been nothing else in rock like the music of '1983'/'Moon Turn The Tides', although plenty of individuals and groups have attempted to take elements of its construction and plot a different direction. It could be argued, for example, that this 1968 epic was the starting point for what became New Age music in the following decades. That is not to lay the blame for New Age excesses, pretension, faux-naiveté and pomposity at Hendrix's door. No one who influences others can be blamed for the followers' failings. It is just that Hendrix made it OK to look beyond the existing boundaries of what people were supposed to do within rock and pop. The year before, he'd done it at times with sheer noise and a reinvention of what the amplified guitar could do. This year he was looking in other directions.

'1983' was absolutely not just a stoned rave (there were plenty of those to follow, most of abysmal musical quality): rather, it is a careful construct designed to deliver a vision. No matter how many drugs he was ingesting at the time and how many hangers-on were disrupting recording efforts, Hendrix stuck to his pre-arranged scheme for this work, building, embellishing and enriching it in overdubbing sessions before the final mix in June. It was a high-water mark of Hendrix's musical explorations. In his short life he never again completed such a long and relatively complex musical construction, although he would play very long solos within simple ballad structures, and play extremely extended jams. He would also continue to push the boundaries of sheer sound manipulation and innovation.

Chas Chandler – still officially the producer for now – must have been wondering what was going on. Here was a piece lasting 13 minutes and more that would swallow close to the entire side of a pop LP. Avant-garde jazz nutters did that sort of thing, not rock idols. To his credit, Chandler did not attempt to hinder these efforts. He always encouraged Hendrix's creativity. But the current working methods were wearing his patience thin, and it is clear that Hendrix meant this to happen. The guitarist wanted to work for himself with no restrictions, no interjections, and no one telling him to move on and stop wasting studio time. This would have been negotiable if Hendrix had been able to articulate what he was doing, but he wasn't. According to Redding, "He'd lose his train of thought, skip to something else, fail to convey what he was up to. ... I told him he was being silly to try to do so much at once – writer, producer, singer, guitarist, arranger – but he took no notice. Things had to be done Jimi's way or no way, and Jimi's way was getting more and more unproductive."[40]

As to the question of having so many people around him in the studio, mostly hangers-on, there was again perhaps an underlying notion, if not a method or an aim. Hendrix was building buffers between himself and the people from whom he wanted to wrest control. Having these hangers-on around helped Hendrix to distance himself from others. Apart from the simple desire to have good times, Hendrix was positioning himself for his own idea of his future. Being constitutionally incapable of confrontations, and certainly in awe of Chandler's temper and physical strength, he would never have directly confronted his nominal producer, but he did push him over the brink. Fellow guitarist Larry Coryell remembered that the star was having to perform something of a balancing act. "I watched [Hendrix] record the album *Electric Ladyland*; I went to a few of the sessions. I tell you, he was a hell of a man in the studio – and in spite of everything going on around him. I mean, he had to put up with groupies, all the kids from the Village, sitting around the studio. He had a Christ-like appeal; he was more than just a guitar player, he was a personality. He had the kind of charisma that I imagine Charlie Parker had. ... All of us were attracted to him like a magnet whenever he came to New York."[41] The strain between Hendrix and Chandler in the studio came to a head with the new song 'Gypsy Eyes' begun in April. On the face of it, there

was nothing particularly complex or demanding about the rhythm track to this tune, although there were adroitly placed breaks and novel rhythmic patterns played in tandem by guitar and drums. Redding, bored and frustrated like Chandler with the endless re-takes on other material, didn't attend the first day's work on the piece, but Hendrix and Mitchell still got through 41 takes without managing a performance good enough to call a master. Considering that the majority of pieces on *Are You Experienced* needed just one or two takes to complete a rhythm track, this was guaranteed to set Chandler's teeth on edge. After a blazing row that changed nothing – Hendrix and Mitchell resumed attempts to get a master take of 'Gypsy Eyes' the following day – Chandler decided he'd had enough and immediately began his withdrawal from active production on Hendrix sessions.

Years later, Chandler told Etchingham that it had become impossible for him to get Hendrix to do anything in American studios. According to Etchingham, Chandler said he would tell Hendrix to get into the studio to record, and Hendrix would just shrug and say, "Yeah, when I feel like it."[42] Etchingham recalled: "Sometimes he would disappear for days on end and then he would invite different people to be his manager or producer or take part on his albums, none of whom his actual management wanted. He would

"Things had to be done Jimi's way or no way, and Jimi's way was getting more and more unproductive."

Noel Redding

make glowing promises he couldn't keep, to anyone who happened to be around."[43] Chandler told Hendrix writer John McDermott: "I was sitting there listening to him play the same song over and over again, thinking to myself, 'What is going on?' Jimi had wanted this to be a double album, and I distinctly recall being glad that I had done so much at Olympic, because at this pace, the album would never be finished."[44]

Hendrix had told journalist Pete Goodman in mid April 1968: "I'm so tired I could drop, but I find the relaxation comes from thinking more about music. Nothin' else moves me. But sometimes I have this feeling I'm getting too mechanical. Each day on a tour like this kinda moves into the next. ... This I gotta avoid. But you can't help thinking back to a couple of years ago when I met up with Chas Chandler in the Village. The responsibilities are greater now. I guess I wouldn't have it any other way."[45] Possibly Hendrix had not yet realised how heavy a set of responsibilities he was fashioning for himself. Defining exactly what a record producer does is difficult, but the absence of a good one is noticeable on any recording session. Much later, Rat Scabies of The Damned caught it perfectly when talking of producer Nick Lowe: "His real art was knowing *that* was the take: the unquantifiable art of a producer, the taste of knowing what to go with."[46] Until now, during Hendrix's brief two years at the top, Chandler had been a more than adequate conjuror in the studio. Now he was excess to requirements.

Chandler stayed around long enough only to see through the last of the already-booked US gigs. Afterwards he soon headed back to London and began the complicated process of extracting himself from Hendrix's management and production team. This all took place during a period when there was considerable legal activity over the long-pending PPX lawsuit, which would finally be settled that summer. Chandler eventually sold his interests to Mike Jeffery, who thus became the major business presence in Hendrix's life. Hendrix may have thought that he'd got what he wanted, but in fact he didn't really know what he'd landed himself with. Once he knew, he would like it even less.

america calling

During the week where April ran into May 1968 the Experience worked intensively in the recording studio on sessions intended to bring the next album to completion. It didn't work out that way, partly because Hendrix would not allow any errors, poor recording mixes or other blemishes to be left on the tapes, but also because of his now chronic inability to determine when he had achieved the high quality he sought.

The first day of May found the band at the Record Plant studio in New York City working on another version of 'Tax Free', because the January session at Olympic in London had failed to satisfy Hendrix the perfectionist. Yet again 'Gypsy Eyes' was attempted and at last an acceptable rhythm track was completed, this time in a mere five takes. Perhaps Hendrix was surprised that he'd managed to get what he wanted so quickly, and so with time still available he and Mitch Mitchell put down the basic tracks to another song for *Electric Ladyland*, 'House Burning Down'. Both songs are testaments to Hendrix's rhythmic inventiveness. As ever, he uses simple basic elements but juxtaposes them with sophisticated arrangements and instrumental accompaniment. 'Gypsy Eyes' has a breezy tempo and starts with a cut-time beat where the first and third beats are stressed on the bass-drum and the second and fourth on the hi-hat. In the verses Hendrix cuts between a rock backbeat and cut-time, giving the song tremendous forward momentum and natural drama. He takes advantage of the initial bass-drum/hi-hat emphasis to play some delicious down-home blues riffs and slide guitar parts, also providing slide accompaniment to his vocal. 'House Burning Down' has a modified tango beat at its base, though Hendrix and Mitchell put it through a series of developments and variations as they make liberal use of one of their favourite devices, deploying sudden breaks and pauses that give the music its grammar and punctuation.

Hendrix had demo'd 'Gypsy Eyes' for himself back in the spring. At that point few of the distinguishing musical features of the finished song had been created, the lyrics were quite different, and the basic beat was closer to a John Lee Hooker boogie, even if the chord structure was more like standard rock. The 'Gypsy Eyes' nominally completed in May and given a first 'final' mix in mid June (and eventually to become available on the 2000 four-CD box *The Jimi Hendrix Experience*) has in place most of the structure, lyrics and melody of the song as released on *Electric Ladyland*, but the treatment is considerably different. Hendrix's vocal, although strengthened with artificial-double-tracking, is recessed and much more emphasis is given to parts of the guitar accompaniment that would be left out of the final album version. Much of this accompaniment darts in and around the vocal line, obstructing it and giving the sense of an overburdened tune. Some of Hendrix's lines – especially those used in the breaks – are unimaginative and not up to his normal standards of the time. He even uses guitar clichés that he would only have resorted to in the absence of anything else to play. The faded ending is different, too. The song feels uninspired, with no sense of mystery or excitement, and sounds curiously dated, possibly because it lacks the usual spark. It seems more like something from the previous year rather than the cutting-edge piece it would eventually become. No doubt Hendrix took away this initial mix and discovered where he had gone wrong, although he would not complete the track until August.

'House Burning Down' was more readily brought into shape, receiving a rough mix just three days after its initial appearance in the studio. However, Hendrix again did not complete the finishing touches and final mix until August. He sets a great deal of intensity into the playing and delivers some curiously whimsical lyrics that deal with knotty social and personal issues. The piece had not appeared on the early-spring demo tape, and it is possible that Hendrix wrote it in response to the assassination of Martin Luther King and the intense, varied reaction to that event among America's black population. He again deploys the imagery and surreal exaggeration he so enjoyed when following Dylan's lead, but the kernel of the message is spelt out unequivocally: "He shouts, 'We're tired and disgusted / So we paint red through the sky.' / I say, 'The truth is straight ahead / So don't burn yourself instead / Try to learn instead of burn / Hear what I say.'" This is the first direct social comment Hendrix makes in a song, in reaction to the most appalling violence and conflict in his homeland.

The tune starts with a wonderfully full-blown overture that places an echo-drenched guitar melody amid strumming guitars, like a character delivering a melody in a traditional Spanish folk setting. Appropriately enough after this, the song then segues into an old-fashioned 4/4 beat for the first chorus, followed by a fast tango for Hendrix's opening verse, though this never settles completely because the bassline consistently bursts the boundaries of the rhythm pattern with varying melodic lines, like a jocular commentator carrying on a conversation of asides with a bystander. The guitar-drum pattern continually evolves and shifts, bringing rich variation to the accompaniment. All this is on display to be taken in before one even starts to listen to the overdubbed guitars.

Hendrix's guitar commentaries on this track are remarkably inventive and intense. The opening statement in that overture has a bluesy guitar line, soaked in echo and with an immense sweep. Twin guitar parts commence in the first chorus, prior to the entry of the vocal, different in timbre and treatment but producing some elegantly lyrical intersections. Hendrix does not draw attention to them, instead building the impression of many different conversations taking place – just as in the lyrics. The brief solo between the chorus and the second verse is a vivid, searing depiction of the song's landscape. The closing section marks the return of the heavily echoed guitar, this time screaming over the flames of the insistent rhythm now pounding out an almost martial beat that was first heard in the opening chorus. Once again Hendrix uses extreme sustain to create scorching, lyrical lines as the rhythm shifts more than once beneath him. Then suddenly the backing instruments stop, and the guitar launches into a solo effort that completes Hendrix's depiction of the riot that he wants the friend with whom he converses in the lyrics to avoid – helicopters, sirens and other ambient noises included.

The following day, May 2nd, the band recorded some pieces that didn't make it to *Electric Ladyland* but instead were added to the stockpile of material that Hendrix could return to at a later date. The studio was filled with hangers-on as the Experience started a long, untitled jam that included at least three identifiable tunes, among them the instrumental 'South Saturn Delta' which had been given a run-through at Olympic. 'Three Little Bears' is also in there, a tongue-in-cheek nod to the habit of soul and R&B musicians to take commonplace or nursery-rhyme subjects known to all and dress them up in the latest musical fashion. (The year before had seen these ideas

crossing into the US rock Top 40 with 'Hey There Little Red Riding Hood' by Sam The Sham & The Pharoahs.) Hendrix's vocal on this jam is so desultory and foolish (as well as stoned) that he stops singing at one point to intone, "I don't feel like going through with this, this is really silly." One can only agree. Yet he clearly had ambitions of some sort for the song because at some point he bothered to overdub a second guitar part.

Another much more serious attempt at realising a new piece was made that day. Hendrix had for some months been toying with the idea of an instrumental that would paint a mournful picture of the legacy of the Cherokee nation but so far had not come up with a definitive form for the piece. The New York spring demos had included a raw and partial realisation that at least included the basic melody, echoing some of the Hollywood-style conceptions of native American Indian music that the Experience had featured in 'I Don't Live Today'. This first studio attempt at 'Cherokee Mist' has no bassline. Noel Redding had rowed with Hendrix after the conclusion of the jam, "letting him know what I thought of the scene he was building around himself. There were tons of people in the studio, you couldn't even move. It was a party, not a session. He just said, 'Relax, man….' I'd been relaxing for months, so I relaxed my way right out of the place, not really caring if I ever saw him again."[1] Redding would be back on board the next day. Meanwhile, 'Cherokee Mist' had become a seven-minute cry of pain and anger. Whatever the state of Hendrix's head that evening he spent considerable care and time to get this track right: there are at least three guitar tracks to be heard in addition to Mitchell's drums. Mitchell plays throughout with mallets, his snare loosened from the snare drum to give it a more 'ethnic' sound.

The track divides loosely into two sections. Over a 'Running Bear' drum pattern Hendrix plays a guitar melody that at first sounds so naïve as to be almost gauche, delivered with a tone that Hank Marvin would appreciate. But before the shock has worn off, he has let rip on an overdubbed track with a searing and insistent burst of guitar feedback, holding a sustained screech for minute after minute and adding extra distortion and weirdness from time to time with the vibrato arm. After almost four minutes of this mayhem the backing track abruptly stops, followed by the feedback, which for a few seconds actually sounds like someone crying. Hendrix then starts a second melodic pattern at a slower tempo, simpler and on a rising two-note pattern, as if a mourning parade has been set in motion. Mitchell's drums join in the slow march, building the tension for more than a minute. Hendrix then reintroduces the first melody, now revealed as a desolate lament played on what sounds like an electric sitar, or a guitar played in imitation of that sound. Once again piercing shrieks and screams are emitted by the guitar overdub, this time in short, teeth-rattling stabs. Mitchell breaks off, the melody ends and the performance dissolves into a fine mist of little sounds, picked out on a celeste.

Although 'Cherokee Mist' has been available on a variety of bootlegs for well over a decade, it has never been officially released in its complete and unedited form and few people other than Hendrix collectors have ever heard it. It is patently unfinished; an out-of-tune guitar line near the end would never have passed muster if Hendrix had been moved to return to the piece and prepare it for mixing, effects and completion. But it is a shattering performance, in a style that Hendrix did not otherwise attempt, and for those reasons should be made officially available – especially when one considers the sub-par jams, remixes and other ephemera that have appeared officially in the past 30 years and more. Presumably it is the deeply weird and unsettling nature of this undoubtedly uncommercial track that has kept it from the public ear. The Hendrix Estate should reconsider, because 'Cherokee Mist' is a tune Hendrix evidently wanted to complete to his satisfaction and release on one of his albums, and this is easily his most effective version, however incomplete it may be.

It is surprising in retrospect that so much was successfully recorded at the time. There were personal differences within the inner circle of the Hendrix Experience and his indulgent approach in the studio, often resulting in carnival-like scenes with hoards of hangers-on. The band's optimist, Mitch

Mitchell, was aware of the conflicts and frustrations around him as well as the absurd waste of money and resources, but felt that the experience was a good one. "The security at the Record Plant wasn't terribly good," he wrote later, "and Hendrix would turn up with endless streams of people, so to get any kind of work done was really difficult. Looking back it was amazing that [*Electric Ladyland*] was finished. In the end the bulk of it got done in about a month, although at the time it seemed to take forever. Not just the album tracks; there were loads of out-takes …"[2]

All through this period and well into the summer, prior to the band's return to Europe and London, Hendrix spent many nights and early mornings jamming with everyone who came through New York City. The jamming was especially intense at The Scene, a club whose relaxed atmosphere Hendrix particularly enjoyed. He became determined to replicate this jamming vibe on the new album. The approach had already produced results in Britain at Olympic studio earlier in the year with the sessions that had kick-started 'All Along The Watchtower' and he was anxious to try more elaborate combinations. Unfortunately, it became another area of conflict within the band, because Redding didn't enjoy having guest musicians either on-stage or in the studio. Redding's concept of recording was closer to Chandler's: have your ideas worked out within the group in advance, go in, get it done quickly while the spirit is there, then get out. This was more or less the opposite of what Hendrix – and, increasingly, Mitchell – was finding to be the most congenial way to work. Hendrix by this time saw the studio as his natural habitat, a place where he could control the creation of his music in a way that was impossible on-stage. It was only natural for him to ask other musicians along to play on his projects. As Mitchell wrote later, "It was one of the finest things in life – I mean, how lucky can you be – to work with all those people, in and out of the studio."[3]

After an extended break on May 2nd, the same day that 'Cherokee Mist' was recorded, Hendrix brought a collection of musicians back to the studio from The Scene to record a workout on 'Voodoo Chile', a down-home blues he'd been refining privately for some months. In addition to Hendrix and Mitchell there was bassist Jack Casady (Jefferson Airplane), keyboard player Steve Winwood (Traffic) and jazz guitarist Larry Coryell. Coryell was asked to sit in, but has said since that he declined Hendrix's offer and preferred to watch from the control booth, feeling that the music simply didn't need him. Engineer Eddie Kramer, brought over from Olympic in London to work at the Record Plant, was now concentrating on the new Hendrix project, so it fell to him to scramble together the equipment needed for the session to start.

'Voodoo Chile' is a slow blues in the electric country style of players like John Lee Hooker, Muddy Waters, Elmore James and Lightnin' Hopkins. The song takes the form of the 'Catfish Blues' that the Experience had been playing live for over a year, even down to Mitchell's drum solo around two thirds of the way through the performance, although the derivation is somewhat obscured by the addition of Winwood's organ and the different bass style that Casady brings to the group. (Instrumentally, the line-up for this session is the same as for Blind Faith, the so-called supergroup formed in 1969 when Cream and Traffic broke up, but the resultant music is a world apart. It was an open secret that Hendrix and Mitchell would have welcomed a closer and more regular musical liaison with Winwood.) Hendrix wanted to give 'Voodoo Chile' the easygoing atmosphere of an informal late-night jam at a club, so he and various colleagues later added an audience-ambience track. It certainly sustains the illusion of a live 'performance' and adds to the studio frisson, but appears mildly self-indulgent at the close when the inconsequential studio chatterings seem like they will never end. Hendrix's lyrics for the piece are taken from the blues tradition where male potency and sexual magic combine into an almost supernatural ability to effortlessly please any carnal partner. Hendrix gives them an individual twist with his references to "the outskirts of infinity" and "Jupiter's sulphur mines" – hardly standard blues phrases – but otherwise this is very traditional blues content. One has only to hear 'John The Conqueror' by Muddy Waters to understand the territory in which Hendrix is travelling. All this would be inconsequential if not for the alchemy that exists between the four musicians. Hendrix and

Winwood individually had the ability and musical presence to shape a performance by force of their personality and innate sense of form, and both move faultlessly together during the 14 minutes and more of 'Voodoo Chile', allowing the music to climax, unwind and then find a proper resolution in a further climax. There is so much incident, so much variety in what is played – especially as Winwood and Hendrix swap lead roles and use their own special instrumental attacks – that the pace never flags and the listener's attention never wavers. Winwood's opening phrase for his organ solo alone is one of the most arresting moments of the entire piece.

The other vital ingredient in this constant shaping and re-shaping of the performance is Mitchell. He is on inspired form, responding with alacrity to every phrase and musical lead. He stokes an enormous fire under the group through his constant rhythmic shifts, his abrupt percussive explosions, and his ability to revel in a deep blues groove when called to do so. Hendrix of course remains the focal point throughout 'Voodoo Chile', his voice oozing confidence and power while his guitar work runs a huge gamut of emotions as well as being innovative in redefining precisely what could be construed as modern blues guitar playing.

The older generation of electric blues guitarists – from Hubert Sumlin to Muddy Waters and B.B. King – never aspired to the kind of playing which Hendrix had now mastered. On slow blues numbers their guitar had always been at the service of the vocalist, dedicated to underlining the mood of the piece and providing screwed-down rhythm guitar to keep the excitement bubbling under. Younger blues guitarists like Lightnin' Slim, Buddy Guy, Elmore James and Freddy King were more extrovert in their playing and often used a tremendously exciting attack in their sound. But their phraseology was only a small step away from those older players, limited by the lack of sustain from their amplification and by their reliance on what for the most part were traditional electric blues licks. They would simply run these licks together to form a coherent and satisfying solo or accompaniment rather than attempt to forge new extensions to the blues-guitar language.

On the other side of the street were the young guitarists, black and white, who came to the blues through R&B. They were much more interested in what Hendrix was doing and where he was taking blues playing, but were also apt to take their lead from Eric Clapton's very personal but more conventional amalgamation of earlier approaches. Of these young guitarists, only Peter Green seemed to want to take the transforming power of extreme amplification and distortion deep into the blues. It would be another year before the release of Green's own groundbreaking contribution to the genre, Fleetwood Mac's 'Oh Well (Part 1)'.

'Voodoo Chile' was later transformed by what Hendrix and Kramer did to its sound. After selecting the best of the three takes, they added tape-delay effects to the guitar and deepened the drum sound to give an extra dimension and impact to the playing. Meanwhile, Hendrix's standout performance on this piece had an unexpected tag the following day. The Experience were back as a trio at the Record Plant, improvising for a film crew brought in by ABC television who were making a TV short about the band's runaway success in America. Rather than go over old ground, the trio worked up a medium-tempo blues with a distinctive, moaning guitar lick and two verses of lyrics that extended the themes Hendrix had been articulating the day before with Winwood and Casady. By take 20 the film crew had got what they wanted – and the band had produced what all three agreed was an acceptable master. The track was dubbed 'Voodoo Child (Slight Return)' as a nod towards the slow blues of the day before, and the piece was eventually used to conclude the *Electric Ladyland* album.

Once again Hendrix and Kramer used production techniques on the basic track to build up the sound of the group, especially the guitar, which often has delayed echo added to its arching melody lines and blues phrases to make them sound almost larger than life. There is no doubting the impact on the listener's imagination of these techniques, but what really takes the breath away on 'Slight Return' is the sheer power of Hendrix's sound. It is so raw, so exciting and so big that it seems to engulf the speakers, as if it were stepping into a new dimension of sound production. Only after a few times through such a spectacular exhibition of sound manipulation does one even bother to note that this is, in fact, a boogie-type riff blues with a simple three-chord bridge. And one is inclined to add "as if that matters", so completely does Hendrix's musical expression transcend matters of genre and form. In retrospect, though, it mattered a lot. 'Voodoo Child (Slight Return)' was the last studio creation Hendrix released in his lifetime that became popular in concert. Obviously pleased with its impromptu creation, Hendrix began using the song in Experience sets almost immediately and it quickly became a live favourite. It was the perfect way to climax a concert (as well as the album) without having to play 'Wild Thing' any more and trash a guitar in the process. 'Wild Thing' was never entirely abandoned by Hendrix, but immediately after the creation of 'Voodoo Child (Slight Return)', live appearances of the old Troggs song became progressively more sporadic, until by 1969 and '70 it would turn up on special occasions only as something of a golden oldie.

The new tune's success also dictated to some extent the direction in which Hendrix would channel his more extravagant guitar explorations in the next two years. In this way *Electric Ladyland* charts not only the extent of his musical advances and ventures, but their limits. Beyond this point, with the sole exception of the multitracked unaccompanied 'Star Spangled Banner' of March 1969, Hendrix would not try to cross new musical boundaries, instead consolidating and extending the musical territory he had already claimed for himself. This is not to suggest that everything from now on is inferior or less successful – this is demonstrably not the case – but that his aims became more modest. After all, Hendrix had a career to nurture and a public to satisfy. Placed in the same position by a different set of pressures, The Beatles were contemporaneously creating a fascinating patchwork of delectable musical miniatures for the double album eventually called *The Beatles* and released within a couple of months of *Electric Ladyland*. For the first time a Beatles album broke no new ground – with the exception of the musique concrète of 'Revolution 9' – but it stands today as one of their finest and most diverse collections of songs.

The rest of the Record Plant sessions up to May 17th were concerned with the overdubbing and mixing of already recorded tracks. In between, there were sporadic engagements to honour. Mike Jeffery had begun making arrangements for a series of live concert recordings of The Experience. He was conscious

Stratocasting at the Fillmore, May 1968.

of the pressures on the group and the increasingly strained relations between the individuals, and was aware that Chas Chandler was about to fly back to England and out of an active role with Hendrix. Just like Cream – who were recorded extensively in the spring of 1968 on what became their farewell tour of America – the Experience were perceived by their management and record company as near to the end of their collective existence. Both The Jimi Hendrix Experience and Cream were working in different New York studios making albums that their respective managements feared would be their last; making live recordings would guarantee further releases and income after any break-up. Chandler was disarmingly frank with Redding when he told the bassist that the group's management thought they were on the way out and that live recording served as an insurance policy for the future.[4] In Hendrix's case this was especially important because of the continuing legal wrangles with Ed Chalpin's PPX and the likelihood that some sort of financial settlement would be reached that required extra income.

One of the concerts due to be recorded was the Miami Pop event where the Experience were slated to headline over The Mothers Of Invention, Arthur Brown and Blue Cheer for two consecutive evenings on May 18th and 19th. The first concert was one of the Experience's best gigs that year, but the second – the one to be recorded – was cancelled because of a mini cyclone and torrential rain. Eddie Kramer had come along to oversee the recording but, unable to do anything, saw Hendrix calmly jotting down the lyrics to a new song as they all watched the rain, powerless to change the elements. A month later these lyrics would be used in a Record Plant jam with Buddy Miles and Mike Finnegan's group as the basis for 'Rainy Day Dream Away' and 'Still Raining Still Dreaming'.

In the meantime the group made their separate ways to Italy, picking up in the process a new roadie, Eric Barrett, through Redding's contacts. While the Experience played their three nights in Italy, Mike Jeffery finalised the lease purchase of a New York City nightclub, bought in his and Hendrix's joint names. Jeffery had run nightclubs in Spain and elsewhere and saw this as a new opportunity for commercial success, using Hendrix's name as the come-on. It would also provide Jeffery with a useful new base in America. Hendrix too had let it be known among his inner circle that he would prefer a permanent address in New York City, so to own a nightclub there with a small recording facility attached seemed to him a positive move. The club never happened, but the plan slowly evolved into the building of a state-of-the-art studio for Hendrix's own use and for hiring to outside artists and productions. Thus was the idea of the Electric Lady studio conceived, although it would be years before the project was completed.

After the Italian shows there were appearances on May 30th and 31st in Zurich as the Experience topped the bill at the *Monster Konzert* supported by a strong cast that included Traffic, The Small Faces, The Move, John Mayall's Bluesbreakers, Eric Burdon's New Animals, and Eire Apparent. Finally, on June 1st, the entire band returned to London, although they would be there for just one week. It was the first time Hendrix had been in London since January. During the weeks before his return, Kathy Etchingham had been looking for a new place to live; when a disgruntled Chandler had come back he'd told her to move all her and Hendrix's belongings out of the shared Upper Berkeley Street flat. The new flat she found comprised the top two floors of an 18th century Georgian terraced house, 23 Brook Street, Mayfair, between the T-junction with South Molton Street and the intersection with New Bond Street. High up in what would have been servants' or children's bedrooms 250 years earlier, Etchingham had found Hendrix an ideally located retreat, within easy walking distance from the London clubs and venues where he enjoyed hanging out. Etchingham lived at the Brook Street flat for the next year and it would be Hendrix's base during the infrequent occasions he was back in London before he and Etchingham broke up in spring 1969.

During his week in London, Hendrix barely discussed with Etchingham what had been going on during the lengthy American tour just concluded, avoiding especially the schism with Chandler, but he did talk about his dissatisfaction with matters in general. At this, Etchingham would write in her book, he was something of a past master. "As far as his career went he was always complaining about something. If it wasn't Chas and the management putting pressure on him to record things he didn't want to record, it was the

Larger than life: Jimi competes with his image on-stage at the Fillmore East, with Mitch Mitchell and Noel Redding, New York City, May 10th 1968.

fans asking to hear stuff he didn't want to play. His ideal situation would have been to be able to get up on-stage in front of huge crowds and just jam away like he used to in the clubs, among friends. The demands of having to do things he didn't want to do put enormous pressure on him."[5] In the months and years to come Hendrix would actively pursue this idea of running his live and studio career as a kind of lengthy public jam, before realising that it provided no lasting solution to his problems.

Hendrix spent just six days in London before flying back to New York City. On June 5th Senator Robert F. Kennedy, already declared the victor in the Democratic Presidential Nomination Primary in California, was assassinated while leaving a Los Angeles hotel. America was once again in shock at the violence that seemed to be guiding its future and crippling its government. A service was given in New York on the 8th at St Patrick's cathedral where Senator Edward Kennedy gave an oration, before his brother's body was taken to Washington for burial. That evening, Hendrix jammed with Buddy Miles's Electric Flag at the Fillmore East in a city still in shock. Two days later, on June 10th, Hendrix was convening another new session aimed at completing more material for the new album. This time he decided to take something of a trip to the past with the help of Buddy Miles and organist Mike Finnegan. Finnegan's group, completed by saxophonist Freddie Smith and percussionist Larry Faucette, had been introduced to Hendrix by legendary R&B producer Tom Wilson. Finnegan later explained to Hendrix chronicler John McDermott: "[Hendrix] joked, 'We're going to do a slow shuffle in D. You be Jimmy Smith and I'll be Kenny Burrell.'"[6]

This was a reference to some notable organ-trio records that jazz organist Jimmy Smith made for the Blue Note and Verve labels in the early and mid

1960s, often featuring the great jazz guitarist Kenny Burrell. Smith's albums also regularly featured guest saxophonists such as Stanley Turrentine and Lou Donaldson. Hendrix knew those records well: he even approximates some of Burrell's favourite fingering patterns in his opening flurries. While the style of organist Finnegan is not really that close to Smith's, and Miles's drumming bears no relation to the cool swing of Smith's regular trio-date drummers Donald Bailey and Grady Tate, the relaxed groove that the Miles/Finnegan group establishes has the same after-hours cool that permeated the great Smith recordings. Another quality that the Hendrix session shares with a typical Jimmy Smith workout is the sense of building excitement. Smith possessed a formidable keyboard technique and when he was in the mood he could blow up a storm, often experimenting with the electric sound of his instrument as he went along. The way Hendrix carefully builds the climaxes and deploys his relentless rhythmic playing has parallels in Smith's organ playing as well as Burrell's gritty blues soloing.

The group managed a number of complete jams on that day, but just one – the best, of course – made it to *Electric Ladyland*, although in an unusual form. At a later date, Hendrix decided to cut the jam called 'Rainy Day Dream Away', originally clocking in at 8:06, into two pieces. The first section, keeping that title, delivered a bright kick-off for side three of the vinyl original, ending in a fade that dissolved into the primeval beginnings of '1983'. The second section, beginning at the pause that signalled the first section's fade-out, was given the new title 'Still Raining Still Dreaming' and provided a declamatory start to the vinyl album's final side. Both sections worked beautifully in their edited forms. Indeed, if one takes the trouble to patch the two halves back together into the original complete performance, it is revealed as slightly repetitive and hardly as gripping or effective as the edits that Hendrix prepared and approved.

The rest of June's studio work was dedicated to mixing and overdubs on already recorded tracks. The exception was the creation of '...And The Gods Made Love', the sound-effects track that would preface the album. This 90-second soundscape is another piece of good-humoured Hendrix radicalism, evoking flying saucers and other extra-terrestrial existences without a guitar in sight. It was achieved by editing and manipulating taped sounds, mostly using as sources recordings of Mitchell's drums and cymbals and Hendrix's voice, and then running them at different speeds, looping and splicing the tapes into strange sequences and applying bizarre levels of echo, delays and reverberation. Here was a nicely confusing beginning to match that of *Axis*.

Just days before, Hendrix's management and record company had reached a settlement of sorts with PPX/Ed Chalpin, the complexities of which have been well documented elsewhere. The main musical consequence was that The Jimi Hendrix Experience and their management team were now obliged to supply Chalpin's company with a complete Experience album of new material that they could exploit commercially.[7] In time, this would lead to the only official non-Experience Hendrix LP released before his death. In a parallel and not entirely unrelated business development, financial connections were severed between Hendrix, Mike Jeffery and Yameta, the Bahamian offshore company that Jeffery had used for many years apparently as an agency and tax haven for his pop groups, including The Animals and the Experience. With Chandler's withdrawal, Jeffery decided it was time for some restructuring in order to develop a more direct business and managerial relationship with Hendrix himself and to leave Yameta dealing only with tax and banking matters.

July 1968 was designed by the Experience's management as a slow month to give the musicians some rest and private holiday time. *Melody Maker* carried the news that Hendrix would appear at the Woburn Music Festival on the 6th, but added that a projected September tour of Germany had been postponed due to "a massive offer to appear on further dates in September during his new American tour which starts in Dallas on July 31st".[8] The American dates were simply more lucrative. The Experience's performance at Woburn – alongside such acts as Tyrannosaurus Rex, Family, Geno Washington, Pentangle, Little Woman, and Dolly Collins – contained a more adventurous mixture than normal, including both 'Tax Free' and 'Red House' (and resting favourites like 'Foxy Lady', 'Hey Joe' and 'Purple Haze'). They finished with 'Voodoo Child (Slight Return)'. Although this concert was recorded, it has never been heard by the public.

Two days later Hendrix was interviewed for *Melody Maker*, this time with Alan Walsh asking the questions. Hendrix confirmed that the Woburn set "was really only a jam, we hadn't played for so long". At this point he was optimistic that the next LP – now described as a double album – and its first single would be finished within the next two weeks. Hendrix was asked why there had been such a delay between new albums – no one counted *Smash Hits*, released in the spring to fill the gap between *Axis* and the next album and containing no new material . He gave a revealing reply. "They felt we were in danger of becoming too pop-orientated," he said. "People were starting to take us for granted, abuse us. It was that what-cornflakes-for-breakfast scene. ... I was tired of the attitude of the fans that they've bought you a house and a car and now expect you to work the way they want you to for the rest of your life. But we couldn't just say, 'Screw them,' because they have their rights, too, so we decided the best way was to cool the recording scene until we were ready with something that we wanted everyone to hear."

Hendrix was clearly very proud of the forthcoming record. "All the tracks are very personal ... they're us. That's why we want to get them out as soon as possible, because this is how we are ... now! I want them to be heard before we change." He was aware of the fragility of the group's existence, evident when he talked about Cream's imminent break-up. He admitted he knew that one day the band would move on to separate things, and that it would be good for all of them. But "Mitch is becoming a little monster on the drums. He's involved in his Elvin Jones thing. He's the one I'd worry about losing. He's

becoming so heavy behind me that he frightens me!" That must have been comforting for Redding to read in his copy of *Melody Maker*. Hendrix was also drawn into talking about the fact that he was an American but had first tasted success away from America. Did he want to settle in the US? No, he replied, at this point in his life he wanted to stay free, with no roots. "The earth's my home; I've never had a house here. I don't want to put down roots in case I get restless and want to move on." As for politics, specifically American politics, "I just want to do what I'm doing without getting involved in racial or political matters. I know I'm lucky that I can do that ... lots of people can't."[9] A musician's first responsibility, as always, was to his music.

After a short holiday Hendrix flew back to New York City on July 24th and straight into further work on the album, spending the evening on a new rough mix of 'Gypsy Eyes'. By the 28th the Experience were reassembled in Los Angeles, this time to receive gold records for *Are You Experienced* as a prelude to the start of their second US tour of the year. The dates started the following evening in Baton Rouge, Louisiana. Soft Machine were once again the main support band and Eire Apparent, the Irish band under contract to Chandler and Jeffery, opened most of the shows. Chandler was present during much of the tour to solve on-the-ground problems, making sure everyone did what they should and that no one got hurt, though he was in the process of winding up his connection with the strategic side of management within the Hendrix organisation. The tour would last until mid September and had its accustomed share of weirdness. After a short rest there would be individual concerts through October and November to support the US release of *Electric Ladyland*, as well as further recording. By then, everyone involved would be in need of a major recuperative break.

With *Electric Ladyland* regarded as close to completion at this point – final mixes of the remaining tracks went on into late July – it seems remarkable that the tour was planned to start before all the loose ends had been tied up. Hendrix had mentioned to his *Melody Maker* interviewer that he expected there to be "17 pieces" on the new record. In fact there would be 16 – and this was the tally after the last track, 'Come On Part 1', was recorded at the end of August. Clearly there were some last-minute rearrangements, in part perhaps for purely pragmatic and mercenary reasons: some immediate income from touring was needed to help defray the substantial bill for the recording of the new album, as well as providing for the PPX settlement and the projected outgoings on the club/studio project.

The first three gigs on the US tour were in Louisiana, and featured only Soft Machine in support. This was an unusually slick piece of tour planning on management's part, who on previous tours were more likely to have had the group travelling 500 miles or so between shows. The repertoire marked a return to material from the first album and the first few concerts were somewhat shaky, with Hendrix apparently not well and unhappy during the gigs that followed in Texas. In Dallas he played half of Traffic's 'Mr Fantasy' before abruptly dropping the theme and playing 'Rock Me Baby' instead. After 'Foxy Lady' he turned 'I Don't Live Today' into an excuse for another dedication to "the American Indians". The following day, August 4th, the band was in Houston and the dedication had grown to a litany he would recite often enough during the following year or more: "This next song," he announced, "is dedicated to all the soldiers that are fighting in Detroit, and Seattle and Washington. Oh yeah, and the soldiers fighting in Vietnam too." He also slipped in a mention of the American Indians "and all minority groups" before starting the song for the Houston crowd.

A few days off in New York went some way to recharging the group's batteries and allowed them to be photographed in Central Park by Linda Eastman. Hendrix liked her shots sufficiently to request that one be used on the front cover of *Electric Ladyland* – a request later ignored by the US album designers. On August 11th in Davenport, Iowa, Hendrix and the Experience toyed with bringing 'Tax Free' back into the set, getting as far as announcing it but for some reason launching into 'Red House' instead. Most of the rest of the show consisted of standard Experience repertoire for the time. The band was playing to sell-out audiences everywhere but were beginning to appear as if they were going through the motions. Hendrix's on-stage announcements made it plain that he wanted to move the stage presentation and repertoire forward, but he had not yet found a way to do so that would satisfy the crowds and his management.

Redding gave up looking for a way out. "We were the travelling salesmen of music," he wrote later. "At times, simply bored brainless with The Experience Show, we could hardly imagine going on a minute longer. The management insisted that our growing (younger) audience only wanted to hear the same cranked-out hits. If we tried to change we got static. Somehow we did some very good shows, jamming our way through our standards. We'd lost that driving energy, though, and strangely, Jimi and I were both thinking ahead to softer, more melodic songs played on a variety of instruments."[10]

After attending a benefit at The Scene club for the beleaguered African region of Biafra, Hendrix made a trip to the Record Plant studio to attempt a first pass at 'Room Full Of Mirrors', a song with some of his most striking lyric imagery. On this date the words to the song had already been penned, but the music was obviously not settled, the form on this first run-through being entirely different to later versions. But Hendrix was not in good shape, either through over-indulgence in unnamed substances or sheer exhaustion, allied perhaps with a touch of despondency. Hendrix's old friend Paul Caruso was on hand to add his sensitive harmonica playing to the brew. Caruso recalled many years later that it was "not a good day for [Hendrix]. We had been working on 'Hear My Train A Comin'' and 'Roomful Of Mirrors' at that time. ... When it was just the two of us in a hotel room, the result was very simple

"There were tons of people in the studio, you couldn't even move. It was a party, not a session."

Noel Redding

and pure, like Lightnin' Hopkins's earlier work. We developed 'Room Full Of Mirrors' into a very introspective blues and went into the Record Plant to record it. There were ... three takes, each one getting a little better. But Jimi just completely lost it. He lost physical control of his instrument. For me it was a tragedy. We didn't have many opportunities to work together."[11]

The final version of 'Mirrors' from this session, lasting just 1:25 and palpably incomplete, was included on the 2000 four-CD box-set, *The Jimi Hendrix Experience*. It is moody, sensitive and intimate, hinting at similar sensibilities as the occasion when Hendrix had played 'Hear My Train A'Comin'' on an acoustic 12-string in London some nine months earlier. His voice is unsteady and he is under strain, and, in retrospect, the vulnerability this uncovers is touching, although it is doubtful that he would ever have wanted the tape made available for anyone else to hear.

The tour resumed a few days later in Maryland, moving on to Atlanta, Georgia, on the 17th, where the rationale for events became murkier. The bill in Atlanta featured support acts The Amboy Dukes and Vanilla Fudge. Although Hendrix was known to admire the Fudge's early singles, such as their 1967 hit arrangement of 'You Keep Me Hanging On', there was no other obvious reason as far as the Experience were concerned for the band to be added to the Atlanta line-up. Two weeks later, at the end of August, Vanilla Fudge were announced as permanent additions to the support acts for the tour. Not only that, but they were to get second billing. Kevin Ayers from Soft Machine recalls, "A lot of things happened on that tour that were very weird – we suddenly realised that Jeffery was in with some darker forces. Once when we were playing on the West Coast we were suddenly told that Vanilla Fudge were playing with us, between Soft Machine and Hendrix. ... There would often be groups that would come and play for a particular show. Jeffery

was being used, or using ... he was tough, he handled it OK. He made a great deal of money out of it all."[12]

Hendrix and his band made another dash back to New York City in a four-day gap near the end of the month, using it profitably to complete final mixes on all outstanding *Electric Ladyland* tracks. In addition, on August 27th they romped through 14 takes of Earl King's old hit 'Come On (Part 1)'. They also worked diligently on a Redding original, 'How Can I Live', that was never used on a Hendrix album but appeared later on the first LP by Fat Mattress, Redding's post-Hendrix band. 'Come On (Part 1)' was a fittingly up piece with which to finish work on the new album, for it distils everything Hendrix had learned from the R&B masters of the past as well as all the advances he had made himself to the genre. More simply, it is a thrillingly exciting performance, making the heart leap as the sheer power of Hendrix's sound and rhythmic thrust pours out of the speakers. Captured live-in-the-studio, the band is full of the instinctive cohesion and dynamism that had been among their most impressive traits back in 1966 and '67, here feeding off each other's excitement and ideas to produce a track definitive of the era in every respect.

Hendrix sings the pared-down lyrics with panache but the real fireworks come in his guitar playing. He fills the song completely with his ideas and sound. Each of his solo breaks, though completely couched in the harmonic and melodic language of the blues, is more daring and impossibly brilliant in conception than the last. His grasp of rhythmic fragmentation here equals that of his work on 'Manic Depression' back in 1967 and reminds the listener of Sonny Rollins's tongue-in-cheek dissection of metric time in the previous few years when the saxophonist was at his adventurous peak. Hendrix's precise control of time on this track allows his playing to become almost indistinguishable from speech, so natural and fluent are his lines, no matter how hard-pressed he is by the pulsing rhythm behind him. 'Come On' is an achievement of a rare order and one of the great recorded treasures that Hendrix left for us.

The following day the final masters of *Electric Ladyland* were prepared and sequenced, and soon after dispatched to the US record company, Warner Bros/Reprise, in preparation for a rush September release. To help things along, Hendrix sent in from "somewhere in America" his own handwritten credits, suggestions for the cover, and liner notes. All of his proposals for the inside of the gatefold album would be used, but the outside cover would be entirely different, to his great disappointment. But that was nothing to what Track Records would do in his name over in Britain.

As in Europe that summer, across America it was impossible not to feel the shock waves from momentous political events. On the day before Hendrix recorded 'Come On (Part 1)' the Democratic Convention had opened in Chicago to identify their nominee for President. In this most turbulent and troubled of years, the peace platform would be defeated and Vice President Humphrey nominated on August 28th – followed by the Chicago police force's brutal quelling of peace protests on that and the next day. This was on top of the chaos over in Paris that had filled most of May and nearly toppled President De Gaulle, as well as the assassinations of Martin Luther King and Robert Kennedy, and the Russian invasion of Czechoslovakia in mid August that had swept away recent moderate reforms.

Such political and social upheaval would have affected any creative artist not living as a hermit. To add still further to the mix, at the 1968 Olympic Games black American athletes had signalled their willingness to show solidarity with the emerging Black Panther Party by raising their arms Panther-style on the winners' podium. All the rooms were full of mirrors. Hendrix was living more or less permanently in America now, meeting people directly involved in these struggles and witnessing the upheaval at first hand. He could not remain detached, and this shift in his views would be increasingly reflected in the interviews he gave that autumn.

the sun ain't rising

At 4.30am on September 2nd 1968, with the finished masters for the new album delivered to Warner Bros and a lacklustre performance at the gig that evening behind him, Hendrix sat down in his Denver hotel room and wrote 'Letter To The Room Full Of Mirrors'. This was a free-flowing prose piece heavily indebted to Bob Dylan but with a significantly different sensibility at work. Hendrix's gentle sense of humour and fun could never remain dormant for long and his wordplay is more obvious than Dylan's, as is the imagery and simple warmth of his piece.

In a scurrying series of images and statements, the final flourish is the most memorable. Hendrix rebuffs the demands of his "old lady" that he should explain himself ("what's physical?!") with a typically oblique personal response: "and he stutters, smiles, and retaliates with ... well ... er ah ... what is music m'love (puff puff) And they probably found out that it was. by this time." The grammar and syntax throughout the piece are hardly free of errors, but the liveliness and character make up for that. Hendrix wrote on his notepaper that he finished work at 6.10am, although this included a separate letter to his record company detailing exactly how he wanted the new LP sleeve to look, giving the song listing and all the musical and production credits for the record. He puts "Directed and produced by Jimi Hendrix" in a prominent position, omitting to mention that Chas Chandler had a role in many of the sessions. The notes are in fact different in several respects compared to the way the LP sleevenotes ended up. Hendrix gives the title as *Electric Lady Land* and isn't sure if he should put 'Gypsy Eyes' before or after 'Come On (Part 1)'. (He got it wrong, putting 'Gypsy Eyes' first, with a note to the record company to check the order themselves.) This uncertainty may have arisen from the last-minute rearrangements of the song order made necessary by the late inclusion of 'Come On (Part 1)'.

Hendrix had told *Melody Maker* back in July that there would be 17 tracks on the new album; the record was released with 16. He said later in interviews after the album's release that there was a great deal more material he would have liked to have included, but that it would probably have required a

Hawaiian guitar: the Experience play a concert (left) at the Honolulu International Center, October 5th 1968.

four-LP set. This all suggests considerable soul-searching about the record's definitive form. Certainly there would have been enough material to comfortably fill a three-LP set, like George Harrison's *All Things Must Pass* of 1970, though even two-LP sets by rock artists were unusual enough in 1968 to give record companies the jitters. Missing from this album were 'Dance', 'Dream' and 'Tax Free', all three written by people other than Hendrix; tapes of these were transferred from Olympic to Record Plant in February in preparation for more studio work on them. Others that failed to make the album were 'Angel', 'My Friend', 'Somewhere', 'South Saturn Delta', 'Three Little Bears', 'Cherokee Mist' and a first version of 'Room Full Of Mirrors'. In addition a number of jams of varying quality and success remained unused, few of them ever achieving the dignity of a title. The songs alone accounted for around 40 minutes of extra material, comfortably enough for two sides of a third vinyl disc. Perhaps the prospect of the effort that would be needed to knock tracks like 'South Saturn Delta' and 'Three Little Bears' into shape – combined with the battle to convince his management and record company that it would be worth the wait – helped persuade Hendrix that he didn't need the hassle. Significantly, he relegated six out of eight of these pieces to the past, never returning to them again, with just 'Angel' and 'Cherokee Mist' receiving later studio treatments with a view to being included on the never-completed follow-up studio disc.

Electric Ladyland was released by Reprise on September 17th while the Experience were deep into their second US tour of 1968. They had already played most of the West Coast, including San Diego, Seattle, Vancouver, Spokane, Portland, Oakland, Sacramento and Los Angeles, where their return to the Hollywood Bowl was a major success that obliterated the poor showing of their previous visit – and even included a performance of 'Come On (Part 1)'. The strange aggregation of groups on that US tour managed to rub along together as best they could: even the band members of Vanilla Fudge seemed friendly at times. Soft Machine guitarist Kevin Ayers remembers his second tour with Hendrix as every bit as debauched as the first – only this time he'd opted out. "Second trip I went macrobiotic," says Ayers. "Brown rice and green tea and none of the other stuff at all. No drugs; no women, even. I was straight and they were stoned all the time. I didn't have any contact with any of them."[1] None of the musicians came away with very good memories of the concerts and few noticed even which city they were in, with little time to note their location on the way from airport to hotel to venue and out again.

base between tour dates until the end of October, when the band's focus once again shifted back east. The break allowed Hendrix to gather together a few new ideas for songs and to absorb what was going on around him in the US. A traumatic political year was climaxing in the tragi-farce of the build-up to the November Presidential election. In subsequent interviews Hendrix would allow himself decidedly more latitude to talk about issues outside of music.

"I still love America – quite naturally – but I can see why people put it down. It has so much good in it, you know, but it has so much evil, too."

Jimi Hendrix, on US politics '68-style

After a round-trip to Hawaii for a concert in Honolulu on October 5th the group returned to Los Angeles on the 8th and flew to San Francisco to open for Bill Graham at his Winterland venue in San Francisco. They played there for three nights, two shows per night, each one of which was professionally recorded by a team hired by Mike Jeffery, implementing the insurance policy of live recordings that Chandler had mentioned to Redding. The Experience listened to the resulting tapes on the 15th but decided against their use. They were shelved until the 1980s when a handful of tracks appeared on Alan Douglas's *Concerts* collation and, later, a single CD selection was officially released as *Live At Winterland*. This series of evenings in San Francisco is a prime candidate for the construction today of a complete boxed edition of every tune played, especially when one considers the all-inclusive retrospective documentation accorded to such music greats as Miles Davis and even Captain Beefheart. Under such conditions it would be possible to study the band functioning over a brief time span on relatively similar repertoire, but always taking slightly different approaches and hitting different moods.

It could be said that one 'Purple Haze' performance is going to be very similar to another, but there are always variations to enjoy, especially in Hendrix's more expansive repertoire such as 'Red House' (of which three versions were performed at Winterland that October). 'Are You Experienced' enjoyed a rare revival, being played twice, once with guest Virgil Gonsalves on flute in a performance lasting close on 16 minutes and once with the Experience, lasting a mere six-and-a-half minutes. The Experience-only cut appeared on *Concerts* (1982); the former is available on bootlegs, unedited and with Gonsalves audible. The luxury of two extended recordings from consecutive nights would offer much to the Hendrix devotee. As it is, the material that has been released allows for only a partial view of these concerts and with none of the continuity that tapes of full shows would provide. Nonetheless, highlights remain and some conclusions can be drawn. The versions of 'Red House' released – the October 10th version on the *Variations On A Theme: Red House* CD (Hal Leonard 1986) and the 11th outing on *Live At Winterland* – are expansive, powerful, deep blues experiences with Hendrix fully connected to his material. This is simply wonderful playing, by any standards. The Experience's tribute in San Francisco to Cream, 'Sunshine Of

"Music has to go places. We'll squeeze as much as we really feel out of a three-piece group, but things happen naturally."

Jimi Hendrix

All three Experience members made good use of a two-week break in late September, with Redding and Mitchell returning to London to catch up with friends, colleagues and family and Hendrix staying on in Los Angeles at a house he'd rented in the hills of Benedict Canyon. He would make this his

Your Love' (October 10th; *Live At Winterland*), sees the band using the instrumental as an excuse not only for a free-flowing jam but as a showcase for a real rarity: a Noel Redding fuzz-bass solo.

Other highlights from the Winterland tapes are a 'Killing Floor' (*Live At Winterland* CD) that features Jefferson Airplane's Jack Casady guesting on bass and a 'Little Wing' (*Concerts*) that for sensitivity and perfection of touch approaches the February 1969 Albert Hall version. There are also some fine versions of 'Like A Rolling Stone' (*Winterland+3*). 'Tax Free' (*Live At Winterland*) as ever inspires the whole group to flamboyant playing and sharp collective musical turns, and even 'Wild Thing' (same CD) is wheeled out for a spot of fun and feedback. Hendrix had started to play 'Star Spangled Banner' regularly on this tour, and it was performed in more than one set at Winterland. (Hendrix wasn't the first to use it – Duke Ellington had been playing it at large concerts since 1943.) On the tracks so far made available the band sounds absorbed and willing to excite. They are far from a spent force on the material where all three – and especially Hendrix – are fully engaged, such as the slow blues numbers. Mitchell in particular seems utterly inspired and at the top of his game, whether playing all-out or offering spare accompaniment and punctuation on the quieter pieces. On this evidence it's clear why Hendrix spoke openly to interviewers about his fear of losing Mitchell.

Redding in his autobiography was dismissive of the standard of the group's playing during the entire Winterland engagement. He pointed to irreconcilable personal differences to explain perfunctory playing from them all. One wonders if, even at this stage, Hendrix had privately taken the decision that Redding had to go and, in the way he behaved towards him, was letting the bassist know. Redding felt "we were past the point of being able to leave our problems off stage while we played … . I stood there fading in and out of a deep resentment. I was terminally bored with Jimi's style and his moodiness".[2] Mitchell, needless to say, had a more positive take on the shows, concentrating on the music rather than the personal frictions. "We always tried to do something special at the Winterland or Fillmore," he would write later. "On these gigs we probably jammed more and had lots of guests up like Jack Casady and Virgil Gonsalves and Herbie Rich, from Buddy Miles's band."[3]

During the Winterland season Hendrix was interviewed by phone for a number of publications. His discussion with *Circus* magazine showed he had given thought to the social and political turmoil in the US that year. Not only was he considering composing a song for the Black Panthers that "doesn't just pertain to race but to

symbolism … and to what's happening today" but he was already thinking of The Next Album as "a double set again" with "about 20 tracks on it". Questioned about possible links with the Panthers, he gently put some daylight between his own beliefs and theirs. "They come to the concerts and I sort of feel them there – it's not a physical thing but a mental ray, you know? It's a spiritual thing. But I don't care if people are white – let me tell you something. I don't care as long as people are doing their jobs. … I'm for the masses and the underdog, but not for just trying to get the underdog to do this or to do that, because I tried that before and I got screwed so badly millions of times."

Hendrix wondered where people's common had gone in America in 1968, and compared his experiences in the US with those in Europe. "I was digging America so much," he mused, "until I went over there and came back again … and saw why people put this country down. I still love America – quite naturally – but I can see why people put it down. It has so much good in it, you know, but it has so much evil, too, and that's because so much of it is based on money. That's really so sick. People here are losing their peace of mind. … In Europe, people have a little more contact with one another. There's a little more communication, and everything's not all freaked out. In just saying hello and goodbye, there's more warmth." He stressed that he lived "all over, though, so no place is really my home" and emphasised his frustrations with the narrow-minded 'blame culture' infesting America at the time. "The black person argues with the white person that he's been treated badly for the last 200 years. Well, he has – but now's the time to work it out, instead of talking about the past. We know the past is all screwed up, so instead of talking about it, let's get things together now. … There are some evil folks around, and they want you to be passive and weak and peaceful so that they can just overtake you like jelly on bread. You have to fight fire with fire. I mean, I'm getting myself personally together in the way of music and what I'm going to do."[4]

He made similarly optimistic noises about his own situation to an interviewer for *Guitar Player* magazine on October 10th. Talking about the way the Experience worked, he commented: "Most of our practice is thinking about it. They might hear the same tune I have, so they throw it around in their minds and picture the fingerboard. So then, when we to go to the studios and I give them a rough idea, maybe Mitch and I will lay a track down completely by ourselves and then add the rest. … I just keep music in my head. It doesn't even come out to the other guys until we go to the studio." He went on to reveal the breadth of his musical

Peace, love and a wah-wah pedal at the Civic Auditorium, Bakersfield, California, October 26th 1968.

thinking. "You can't get stuck upon guitars, you have to use a little bit of imagination and break away. There's millions of other kinds of instruments. There's horns, guitars, everything. ... Music has to go places. We'll squeeze as much as we really feel out of a three-piece group, but things happen naturally. We've got about four tracks that we haven't released yet. One has a very simple rhythm with a funky horn pattern in it [this has to be 'South Saturn Delta'] and a tiny bit of echo to make the horn sharper. ... But we haven't been able to get these things together because we've been on tour."[5]

Not surprisingly, Hendrix was back in the studio almost immediately after completing his commitments at Winterland. By October 18th he'd started a new round of recordings on fresh material. This time the studio was TTG in Hollywood, Los Angeles, which had been block-booked on Jimi's behalf by his management for two purposes: to oversee the completion of Eire Apparent's first album, and to begin work on the Experience's fourth. In the event, although most of the Eire Apparent album was laid down in readiness for its eventual completion in New York, nothing intended for the next Experience record was finished and, while there was much jamming and a few tunes were run through, no fourth album was underway by the end of the month.

The Eire Apparent LP, called *Sun Rise* and eventually released on Buddha Records in early 1969, remained something of an obscurity in the Hendrix canon until its reissue on CD in 1991. It was Hendrix's first production credit for a non-Experience album and, after initial hesitation, he enjoyed the experience immensely, getting on with the group members very well, making suggestions, and even adding some guitar overdubs of his own to help things along. Guitarist Mick Cox had been drafted into Eire Apparent to replace Henry McCullough, who had run into problems after a drug bust and had to leave the US in a hurry. Cox got on particularly well with Hendrix, who quickly took him under his wing and, among other things, sat down in the studio to sort out Cox's guitar. "He asked me if I minded if he messed with my guitar a little bit and try to get a sound," Cox told

Laying down a guitar part in the main room at TTG studio, California, October 1968.

Guitar World later. "I had just bought a Strat, and he sat down with it, fiddled around with it for an hour, worked for a bit on the action, raised the pickups, telling me exactly what he was doing as he was doing it. He had a very natural thing about how to get the very best out of any guitar, setting up the bridge – the kind of knowledge very few people had at that time. And of course, when he handed it back to me it sounded a thousand percent better than it did when I gave it to him. That was my introduction to him."[6]

Hendrix made significant contributions to *Sun Rise* both from behind and in front of the mixing desk – and this despite the fact that he had never worked at TTG before and got off to a difficult start with Jack Hunt, the staff engineer allocated by the studio to the Eire Apparent album. In a calculated snub, Hendrix, in Hunt's presence, asked Angel Balestier, another TTG engineer whom he'd never previously met, to engineer the coming Experience sessions. Hunt quit the project that day. Cox recalled Hendrix adding a beautiful backwards-guitar track to the composition that would open the

album, 'Yes I Need Someone'. "When we came in at 11 in the morning he'd been up all night doing Christ knows what, as much as he could get up his nose and down his throat. We played the tune through and he asked if we'd mind if he'd put something on it, and of course I said, 'No, go ahead.'" Hendrix added the backwards guitar track in one take, according to Cox. "There's this amazing guitar on it that just fitted perfectly. First take. On the whole album there's fills and things he did where he tried more or less to sound more like me and less like himself so people wouldn't say it was Hendrix playing all over our record. He tried to simulate my style and play just a little bit better to make me look good."[7] Eire Apparent's album is dogged by mediocre songs but the musicianship is good and the occasional flashes of Hendrix's guitar that peek out from the mix or help along a chord change make it an essential item for the dedicated Hendrix collector. It marked a promising debut for Hendrix as a producer and must have given him considerable confidence in his ability to bring out the best in the work of others.

Jams taped on October 16th and 17th with a variety of musicians, including Jack Bruce and Graham Bond, were apparently plagued by technical difficulties in the studio that rendered the music commercially unusable, although that hasn't stopped the bootleggers. There was also a jam with Stephen Stills, but the master tape has vanished and the music has yet to appear privately among Hendrix collectors. Paul Caruso has said that he was involved in a further October 1968 session at TTG but there is no official log of it. "We made another abortive attempt to record 'Roomful Of Mirrors'," Caruso remembered. "We were at TTG studios. Jack Casady was there on bass and there was an organist who I can't recall. The same thing happened [as last time], only this time, instead of Tuinal, a barbiturate, it was a nasty combination of STP and cocaine, an unfortunate set of circumstances which made him paranoid and caused a mood shift. He could no longer ... he just lost the music, and said, 'I can't get it together.' Jimi left the studio very upset."[8] Unfortunately for Caruso, who accompanied him, Hendrix apparently then took out his frustrations on his old friend, accusing him of stealing things from his house in Los Angeles and then punching him hard in the stomach. "He hit me. He knocked all the wind out of me. It took me a couple of minutes to get my breath back. It is upsetting for me even now to think about it. This really seemed like the end of our friendship. A few minutes later inside the [Whiskey A Go Go] he showed no sign that he had just flipped out. He just sat there smiling, surrounded by his women while I was furious."[9] After a confrontation at the club, Caruso left.

October 18th saw the release of 'All Along The Watchtower' as a single in the US, backed by 'Burning Of The Midnight Lamp'. The music Hendrix recorded that same day has fared a little better than that of the previous days, with the masters still in the possession of the Hendrix Estate. Two new structures were tried out by the Experience: 'Izabella' (a different song than the later Hendrix composition) and 'Messenger'. It would be inaccurate to call them finished songs as the recordings don't go any further than work-in-progress, even though both were given overdubs by Hendrix and Mitchell. Perhaps they were just trial runs to see what the tunes would need for completion. The Experience also indulged in plentiful jamming at TTG that October without any guests sitting in. This was probably done with the intention of developing new tunes as this was rapidly evolving as Hendrix's preferred way of generating fresh material, but none of the ideas from these sessions subsequently surfaced in other songs. Redding thought it was all down to the level of drug-taking. "Jimi was trying too hard to be experimental, but he was so out of it he changed his mind every other second, not even knowing when he had it right."[10]

made, it would be to 'The Stars That Play With Laughing Sam's Dice' with its party scenes and general madness. The piece was put together by Hendrix and Redding and starts with an ominous guitar riff that sounds as if it has been developed out of 'Foxy Lady'. There follows a bridge and chorus section with a number of breaks, variant riffs and chord sequences. There are no vocals, but the tune is played so tightly by the band that it is at least possible that no words were ever contemplated. After nearly three minutes of this trio work-out – with no guitar solo in sight, nor even an opening for one – the bass and guitar fall into a rising three-note figure while Mitchell does his Elvin Jones impression. Party noises are introduced, with laughter, yelling and

Hendrix at the controls for a playback session during an extended stay by the Experience at TTG's Sunset-Highland studio in Hollywood, California, October 1968.

The music played and recorded on October 21st included a series of jams that for the first time found Hendrix using the phrase 'electric church music' to describe what he was doing. In the room with him were organist Lee Michaels and drummer Buddy Miles in addition to the usual Experience line-up. Despite almost incessant tuning problems, the musicians were in good spirits and at one point Hendrix announced the personnel in the studio over his vocal microphone as if they were giving a concert. His announcement was later edited onto the version of 'Red House' recorded eight days later that was widely bootlegged before making its official appearance on the 1994 CD compilation *Blues*.

Another track routinely bootlegged from October 21st is 'Calling All Devil's Children'. This is one of the Experience's more off-the-wall outings and, while it is not top-flight Hendrix, the recording is of sufficient interest to have merited commercial release by now. No doubt its non-appearance stems from the subject, a simulated drug bust. If any fruitful comparison were to be

whooping. Hendrix says to someone, "Listen, the devil is gonna take over," among other snippets.

A photograph taken at the session has Hendrix standing on a high stool in front of a microphone as he conducts everyone through this and the following segments. After around five minutes the drums move into an all-out assault and the guitar and bass produce long drones. At the party, meanwhile, it sounds as if a drug bust is taking place (simulated, of course). At 6:00 or so every instrument ceases and a few hardy souls continue talking until they all make siren-like whoops and pretend to be busted again, just for fun. Then the track quickly fades. The recording represents Hendrix's anarchic side as well as his mischievous sense of humour. At that time he was rarely in full and sober control of his senses thanks to a high drug intake, so it is probably no accident that this is one of the more fully realised items from a generally unproductive and highly uneven couple of weeks in the studio. A great deal of effort was taken to make 'Calling All Devil's Children' work: the group completed no fewer than 27 takes of the musical section of the piece before they were satisfied with its performance and moved on to have fun with the party scenes and manic dialogues. Hendrix was putting his own twist on the absurdist routines he'd heard by The Goons, the radio-show madmen to whom Redding had introduced him. Other 1960s rock musicians who benefited from *Goon Show* writer Spike Milligan's crazy humour were The Bonzo Dog Band and The Beatles. Brian Jones would have told Hendrix about the Beatle piece 'You Know My Name (Look Up The Number)' as the Stone had played saxophone on it.

The following day the Experience were back to traditional pop methods, getting through 19 takes of 'Mr Bad Luck', an R&B-style song they had played sporadically since 1966 and had now retitled 'Look Over Yonder' with different lyrics. It is a slick, fast and power-packed performance by the trio, recalling what they had been capable of when Chas Chandler was still lurking in the control room. On top of a surging and precise rhythm track Hendrix deploys imaginative guitar overdubs, full of a wide variety of instrumental colour and fresh melodic invention. Backing vocals recall the falsetto harmonies of 'Crosstown Traffic' and *Axis* tracks from a year earlier, hinting at the song's early Experience vintage. One possible reason that this track was dropped from contention for subsequent albums is the rising bass and guitar riff used after the first two choruses and guitar solo, when a chordal shift and a halving of the tempo is introduced for a complete verse: the riff here eventually became the basis for the second half and all the guitar soloing of 'Stepping Stone', recorded the following year and briefly released as a single. 'Look Over Yonder' itself was used by Mike Jeffery to kick off the second side of the so-called soundtrack album to the film *Rainbow Bridge*, released a year after Hendrix's death. To round out the day's recording, Mitchell and Hendrix jammed with Carol Kaye, the great soul and Motown bassist. The results remain unreleased at the time of writing.

On Wednesday 23rd Hendrix divided his time in TTG studio between two sessions: one for more jamming with organist Lee Michaels and an unnamed harmonica player; the second for some attempts at two more fully structured pieces. The first, 'Peace In Mississippi', is perhaps the first recorded instance of Hendrix at work in a recording studio on a tune that is quite blatantly an imitation of himself, or at least an attempt to reproduce or reconstruct something that used to come spontaneously and successfully to him and the band. It consists of a blues-drenched and aggressive riff played at medium tempo and punctuated by angry-sounding chords and drum breaks. The guitar sound is laceratingly raw, just as Hendrix intended, the bass and drum parts

"Hendrix had a natural thing about how to get the best out of any guitar — the kind of knowledge very few people had at that time."

Mick Cox, Eire Apparent guitarist, on Jimi as guitar-tech

are very basic, and the melody — when it finally appears more than a minute into the piece — is another in his faux-American Indian series, touched also by blues intervals and string bending. In its original form this track lasted over seven minutes, during which Hendrix spends a great deal of time trying to reach the inspired heights, as well as the weight and depth of sound, of his solo work on 'Voodoo Child (Slight Return)'. But in this instance his playing is bereft of inspiration and he generates more noise and fury than any sense of excited purpose.

The thundering, thumping megalith of 'Peace In Mississippi' shows just how tiny a gap there was between the light-as-helium inspiration of his best work and the earthbound drudgery of so many of the heavy-metal acts who followed in his wake. Hendrix left the track incomplete, and it has had a wayward history since on official Hendrix releases. It was one of the tracks that suffered the Alan Douglas treatment on 1975's *Crash Landing* – the original bass and drum tracks were replaced and it was edited from 7:10 to 4:20 – and then subsequently appeared on Douglas's swansong for the Hendrix estate, *Voodoo Soup* (1995), this time with Mitchell and Redding restored and in a longer edit running to 5:24. So far, the current producers working under the direction of the Hendrix family have not elected to reissue it in any form and the complete version is only available on bootlegs.

Decidedly more successful is 'New Rising Sun'. For this ballad Hendrix used the same method of studio accretion as he had for predecessors such as 'Have You Ever Been (To Electric Ladyland)', 'One Rainy Wish' and '1983'. The tune arises from a static, guitar-generated mist of electric sound. Over the slow, pellucid and beautifully played chord sequence of his rhythm guitar track, Hendrix lays a series of exquisite accompanying guitar lines, more than one of which was recorded on a backwards-running track. After a complete harmonic sequence the cycle is started again, this time with a drum accompaniment subjected to the types of slowed-down effects he'd used on a number of earlier tracks, again including 'Have You Ever Been (To Electric Ladyland)'. Some deliciously melancholic and sweetly lyrical guitar playing emerges from the mix. (This describes 'New Rising Sun' as released on *Voodoo Soup* in 1995, running a little over three minutes; another version is in circulation that lasts for more than eight minutes.) Hendrix never revisited this recording, perhaps regarding it as too regressive as he moved on to other musical styles and ideas in 1969. But for the time being he may have seen it as part of a larger design for the as-yet unnamed follow-up Experience album to *Electric Ladyland*, because on the same day he recorded three more musical snippets, each titled 'Introduction' and dissimilar to one another in nature and instrumentation. None of them was subsequently used, but they do add up to four introductory pieces – potentially one for each side of a new double-vinyl-LP album.

"Jimi was trying too hard to be experimental, but he was so out of it he changed his mind every other second, not even knowing when he had it right."

Noel Redding

Like so much of the material not commercially issued in Hendrix's lifetime, 'New Rising Sun' has suffered a chequered history and serves as an illustrative example. In the years immediately following his death there were a number of separate investigations of the tape archive and some editing work was done. Engineer John Jansen took parts of three separate and unrelated Hendrix compositions and jams that he'd discovered and edited them down into a short ad hoc 'suite'. This was then set aside because it was thought that such editing and interference with Hendrix's original work was inappropriate. One of the sections in the 'suite' was 'New Rising Sun', which thus picked up a different title, 'M.L.K.', on the tape box in which it was stored – although by all accounts this was not a title ever contemplated by Hendrix. Jansen used around half of the original track as an appropriate way to finish up his compendium. The untitled 'suite' was found later, worked upon further (mostly by replacing rhythm tracks on the other sections), and issued by Alan Douglas on *Crash Landing* in 1975 under the title 'Captain Coconut'. Twenty years later, Douglas reconsidered this decision. Using the original TTG master, he remixed and issued 'New Rising' as the introductory track on *Voodoo Soup*, Douglas's stab at what Hendrix's studio album of 1970 might have been had he lived to complete it. The track also appears in the 1972 film *Rainbow Bridge* at a low level in the mix behind some voiced-over transcendental twaddle; the film then cross-edits on the soundtrack into the instrumental beginning of the July 1970 studio version of 'Hey Baby' that appeared on the *Rainbow Bridge* album. Mercifully the narration stops at this point as a hippie rides around a field on a horse.

A few more days of inconsequential recordings at TTG – mostly jams, but also a short session where Hendrix played bass on a Robert Wyatt tune, 'Slow Walking Talk' – led to another attempt at a useable studio version of 'Lover Man', by now a thoroughly grooved item in the stage show. Six takes were recorded, with takes three and four agreed as the best efforts, both sustaining the ferocity of the live Experience. Yet neither seem to have been considered later by Hendrix for release and he would attempt a number of subsequent studio versions in the next two years.

With the energy levels stoked up and a general feeling of bonhomie ruling in the studio that day, the group bombed through an impromptu version of the Them hit, 'Gloria'. It lasts nine minutes and is full of near-obscene storytelling from Hendrix. Instead of Van Morrison's original stentorian mid-song narration about Gloria coming to meet him "around midnight", walking to his door and so on, Hendrix substitutes scurrilous memories of Redding and Mitchell's early days on the road in Britain and the groupies they met. There is no doubt that the only reason this performance was taped was because Hendrix now insisted that every note played on every session was properly recorded. A take like this would never have been given a second thought for the next Experience album: it was much

too rough, too sprawling – and possibly libellous. Its first commercial release came as a bonus track on a vinyl single accompanying a mid-1980s greatest hits compilation. It adds nothing to the Hendrix legacy apart from demonstrating that he had a wicked sense of humour on occasion.

Something that certainly did add to the Hendrix legacy was a jam version of 'Red House' that concluded the day's activities. By then the group had been augmented by the arrival of organist Lee Michaels once more, along with well-known reedman Jim Horn on flute. A number of takes of 'Red House' were attempted: take six was later edited down into a complete performance, to which was added the Electric Church introduction of October 21st. The edit is quite brutal, ushering in a performance already underway. It was frequently bootlegged before eventually debuting officially on Alan Douglas's 1986 CD *Variations On A Theme: Red House*, a collection of seven different versions of 'Red House' intended for specialist study. Later, the same mix was issued on the 1994 *Blues* album. None of these issued versions include Jim Horn's flute playing, but Hendrix's guitar work is urgent enough for the listener not to regret the editorial interference. In fact, Hendrix's playing could almost be called belligerent in places, so slashing is his phrasing and so cutting is the edge to his tone, which is closer to Buddy Guy than usual at this time. There are moments here when he is pushing at the extremes of 12-bar blues expression, mimicking speech, screams, shouts and singing in his headlong determination to drive on the piece. In this he is well matched by Redding in particular, who has rarely played better on this number and helps motor the tune through to an explosive ending.

Although the performance continues on its highly charged way and reaches a satisfying climax, Hendrix suddenly decides to terminate the session brutally while the others seem happy to play on. He does this by playing a cadential blues run at full volume that compels the rest of the group to hurriedly curtail proceedings, toeing the line as the master loses patience with events. Some of Hendrix's guitar playing on this track is so wonderfully inventive within a traditional blues context that it's a natural impulse to laugh and smile in pleasure at what one is hearing. However, the track itself is not a happy one, and the sudden ending strongly suggests Hendrix's frustration, either with himself or with his peers. Michael Fairchild's notes for the official 1994 release of this 'Red House' quotes writer Sharon Lawrence, who claims she was present when the track was cut. "I dropped by TTG Studios to watch Jimi at work," said Lawrence. "He was dejected by what he heard, obviously annoyed with himself. He put on his jacket and prepared to leave. Abruptly, he took it off again and purposefully strode into the main recording room. He picked up his guitar and started..."[11] Hendrix himself discussed his preference for working ad hoc like this in an interview he gave soon afterwards to *Beat Instrumental*. "It's satisfying, working this way," said

Jimi's feedback-on-the-floor routine, here at Yale University in New Haven, November 17th 1968.

Hendrix. "I'd start with just a few notes scribbled on some paper and then we got to the studios and the melody is worked out and lots of guys all kick in little sounds of their own."[12] What Hendrix didn't seem able to grasp completely at the time was that only some musicians could respond to this method in an entirely sympathetic and creative way.

This great blues track was the last throw of the dice at TTG for the Experience. The remaining sessions there, to the end of October, were concerned only with further work by Hendrix on the Eire Apparent album. On November 1st the Experience were back out on the road to complete their touring for the year, which would last more or less without a break until December. Personally, Hendrix, Redding and Mitchell were by now running on empty and in need of a restorative break. Soft Machine guitarist Kevin Ayers had observed at close hand the toll that the Experience's lifestyle was taking on them. Ayers was aware that no one within their shared management team seemed to realise the damage that was being done, and few of them cared to change things. "They all seemed very happy to keep Jimi Hendrix very stoned with whatever type of drug he wanted," Ayers recalls today. "I later found out that basically they'd give him any money he wanted – go out and buy a new car or, y'know, this that and the other, and a big supply of drugs, so he was constantly stoned."[13]

This was a low point for Hendrix. He was contemplating breaking up the band, even though he had little clear idea of what he wanted to replace it with, but was under pressure from his management to keep things as they were. Interviews given in the first week of November made it clear that the group was about to go its separate ways, and the news was splashed over the music

"They all seemed very happy to keep Jimi Hendrix very stoned with whatever type of drug he wanted."

Kevin Ayers, Soft Machine guitarist, on tour with the Experience

press on both sides of the Atlantic. *Melody Maker*'s Laurie Henshaw quoted Hendrix as saying the band had come to its natural end. Hendrix described the split as a logical consequence of Redding and Mitchell's desire to try something different – in effect transferring his own wishes to them and spreading misleading stories if not downright lies. "Mitch and Noel want to get their own thing going," said Hendrix, "so very soon, probably in the new year, we'll be breaking up the group – apart from selected dates."[14] Pressure was being exerted by the media – in Britain in particular – because that same month Cream delivered their farewell performance in London and it must have seemed only logical that the other great guitar trio must be in trouble too. But the Experience held together. Just.

The month's touring took the band through Minneapolis, Cincinnati, New Haven, Rhode Island and a number of venues in Florida before finishing up with gigs in Detroit and Chicago. The Chicago date on December 1st was the last Experience gig of 1968. The Detroit performance nearly didn't happen at all, with a stressed and reluctant Hendrix deliberately missing the plane and urgently pressured into catching a later one to fulfil his commitment. The concert was taped, the result revealing the band playing the usual numbers, including 'Foxy Lady', 'Hey Joe' and 'Purple Haze'. While the Experience were raking in record box-office receipts, on-stage they seemed to be playing on autopilot.

In Britain *Electric Ladyland* had been released on October 25th, while the band were struggling through their TTG commitments, and had caused an immediate furore, exactly as the record company had intended. The cover was entirely different to the US edition and completely contrary to Hendrix's designs, showing 21 naked women in a photographic studio, some of them holding the artworks of previous British Hendrix LPs. Within weeks *Electric Ladyland* had gone to number six in the UK album charts; as usual, notoriety had translated into healthy sales. Track, Hendrix's record company in London, trumpeted the success of their publicity-mongering in a full-page ad taken in the music papers, headed "Revolutionising The Recording Industry" and reproducing Tony Palmer's pop column from *The Observer* newspaper of November 10th 1968 that proclaimed Track's position as industry leaders.

"Two years ago," wrote Palmer, "Hendrix was a down-and-out in Greenwich Village. The grandson of a Cherokee Indian from Seattle, Washington, he is the Black Elvis. His music is electric religion. ... On stage he looks like a bird of paradise, with his multicoloured clothes, his witchcraft charms dangling abundantly from his sweating neck and his hair standing up as if in fright of his face. His new LP has a cover photo of 21 nude women, snapped by photographer David Montgomery, who also photographs the Queen. ... With records like these, Track have cornered six percent of the British market at a gross of nearly half a million pounds a year. Arthur Brown's single, 'Fire', will shortly be a million seller and got to number two in the American charts – all of which is an amazing triumph for Chris Stamp and Kit Lambert, son of Constant and godson of Sir William Walton. Together they are revolutionising the recording industry by demonstrating that quality alone counts, which, with careful promotion and devoted musical production, can bring just rewards. ... Technically, they are already in the future. While everybody talks about making stereo singles, Track have actually done it. Jimi Hendrix's latest single ['All Along The Watchtower'], although the label doesn't mention it, is in stereo."[15]

Hendrix distanced himself from the album cover when questioned by the media. It was another blow, because he regarded *Ladyland* as his most complete – and completely personal – record to date. All this furore merely cheapened it and put a distance between object and creator. In an interview with *Beat Instrumental* published in December he registered bemusement at what had been done in the UK. "First, I'm happy with the content of the record," he said. "But it seems that folks in Britain are kicking against the cover ... and all I can say is that I had no idea that they had pictures of dozens of nude girls on it, 'cause [in the US] there's just a picture of me and the boys. ... Why I'm kind of proud of [*Electric Ladyland*] is that I really took the bulk of it through from beginning to end on my own, so I can't deny that it represents exactly what I was feeling at the time of production. Only a couple of tracks come from British sessions."[16]

As November wore on, the band had a planned TV appearance on *The Ed Sullivan Show* cancelled, but some good things emerged too, including Hendrix's second credit as an album producer. During the time he spent in New York between tour commitments Hendrix had produced *The Street Giveth & The Street Taketh Away* by Cat Mother & The All Night News Boys. On its release early in 1969 the album spawned a chart single and made it to number 55 in the *Billboard* album charts, further underlining Hendrix's good ear and taste as a producer.

Late in the month, on the 28th, the Experience appeared at Philharmonic Hall in New York City on a programme that included harpsichordist Fernando Valenti and The New York Brass Quintet. For Mitchell and Redding it was a memorable highlight, though for different reasons. Redding enjoyed the trappings of this different musical world as he compared it to the regularly sordid circumstances of rock venues. "The plush velvet comfort of the Philharmonic Hall was a dream come true," he wrote in his autobiography. "The red, deep-pile carpeted dressing rooms, with a grand piano as polished as our personal uniformed waiter, was built to accommodate an orchestra. Why was I in a rock band? The acoustics were impeccable. The subtlest nuance carried distortion-free to the furthest corners. We'd been bashing it out in fields and barn-like sports halls to miles of people who couldn't hear us well enough to bother listening."[17] Mitchell was similarly flattered, but had a different viewpoint. "We'd always wanted to play Carnegie Hall, but they wouldn't have us. In lieu of that we were offered the Philharmonic, which was great. Lovely hall, very prestigious, no rock band had ever played there. Only one problem, a member of the band had to play in a symphonic context. Jimi and Noel flatly refused, so I thought OK, what the hell, *I'll* do it. Would I mind having tea with Leonard Bernstein? Which I did; charming chap. He suggested that I might like to play with The New York Brass Ensemble. ... It was a great gig and the whole thing was filmed and I'd love to see it."[18] (The film was shot by Gold & Goldstein, whom Jeffery would also engage to shoot the February 1969 Albert Hall appearance; this explains why it is not available, because until relatively recently the film-makers were in almost constant litigation with various generations of Hendrix representatives since the original projects ground to a halt.)

What the members of the Experience were perhaps unaware of at that time was that Leonard Bernstein was one of the first of the prominent classically-trained musicians of the day to embrace pop culture. Bernstein had a long history of populism stretching back to his Broadway offerings of the 1940s, and now he was tiring of the internecine wars between rival avant-garde classical camps. He had recently proclaimed publicly that he derived more pleasure from and found more creativity in new pop musicians such as Bob Dylan and Simon & Garfunkel than in the latest works from contemporary classical avant-garde composers. He felt these composers had a stranglehold on compositional style in the US and mostly operated from within comfortable academic sinecures, thereby avoiding the thorny problem of making a living from their music. This was tantamount to a declaration of civil war in the classical community – and did not go unnoticed in New York by young composer renegades such as Philip Glass and Steve Reich. Their creative instincts would eventually bring them into touch with the more sophisticated end of rock and pop music during the next decade.

Meanwhile, the appearance of The Jimi Hendrix Experience at Philharmonic Hall was another shot across the bows of the avant-garde intellectual establishment. It was a fine feather in the cap for the band, followed as the year ended by many more, including the *Billboard* Group Of The Year award, and for Hendrix the *Rolling Stone* Performer Of The Year award. Yet all was far from well with Hendrix himself: in fact he was wilting under the pressures he now faced. On top of the normal business of touring, recording and making himself available to the media, he seemed incapable of controlling his love of constant good times and was allowing no time for his body and mind, let alone his feelings, to recover. He was also unable to shake off litigation. Ed Chalpin and PPX were bringing a new action, this time in Europe, against Track, Polydor and Jimi Hendrix after claiming a loophole in the US settlement that did not specify "for the world". Hendrix now found himself directly in the firing line, as Mike Jeffery had previously obtained his signature on a disclaimer that freed Jeffery of any liability in the matter. There had also been a few paternity suits from women claiming they carried Hendrix's baby or had already given birth. Hendrix had wanted none of this when he'd yearned to be a star: he'd been looking for recognition, craving a lifestyle of complete indulgence and limitless opportunities to create the music that he cared about so much. He was not equipped for or inclined towards dealing with such vexatious and demanding distractions.

To add to his isolation, precisely at the time he needed confidants to ease the pressure he felt, Hendrix was no longer close to the other two members of the band. There were precious few others he knew well enough to trust. Inevitably, he folded. "Jimi suffered badly from depressed panic attacks,"

Redding wrote later. "I believe he felt threatened and hounded. ... Whatever it was [that triggered it], he slashed his wrists. This was kept very quiet, but we all felt horrified."[19] Redding attempted to talk to him, explaining that he needed to talk things through to retrieve a sense of perspective. But Hendrix kept his own counsel.

The tour commitments ended and the two English members of the group flew back to London in early December for a holiday and to work on their own projects for a while. Mitchell arrived in time to become involved in the plans for The Rolling Stones' *Rock & Roll Circus*, an extravaganza originally planned as a BBC TV special but never broadcast at the time. Invited to be part of a supergroup for the evening alongside John Lennon, Eric Clapton and Keith Richards (on bass), Mitchell acquitted himself with élan on Lennon's 'Yer Blues' and the considerably less charming 'Whole Lotta Yoko'. This is the only known recording featuring Mitchell and Clapton in the same group. Clapton plays a scorching solo on 'Yer Blues' and Mitchell's dexterity makes a convincing case for him as one of rock's great catalysts of the time. He certainly stimulates Clapton musically in a decidedly different way to Ginger

"I took the bulk of it through from beginning to end on my own, so I can't deny that it represents exactly what I was feeling at the time of production."

Jimi Hendrix, on Electric Ladyland

Baker, following the guitarist's musical patterns hand-in-glove as he did with Hendrix. Mitchell's boss was not around to see this meeting of the rock aristocracy. Considering his Stones connections and his friendship with Brian Jones it is odd that Hendrix stayed in New York City throughout this period.

While in London, Redding gave an interview to Val Wilmer in which he was very diplomatic about the group, but the underlying tensions crept out all the same. "That's what I want to get into: just writing and playing. Jimi is interested in recording and Mitch – well, no one knows what Mitch is doing," Redding smiled. "I feel that if we stop playing concerts, what are we going to do? At least I'm attempting to do something. I had one song on the last LP and I'll have about four on the next one, so I feel like I'm working at something."[20] That Redding expected four songs on the next Experience album suggests that some sort of new accommodation had been struck between the band members at the end of the recent US tour.

Hendrix stayed on in New York City right through Christmas and into the new year. He kept a low profile and did not go out much, possibly recuperating from the incident when he slashed his wrists. A report in the music press in early January mentioned that he had fallen and torn his ligaments in New York, but this may have been about as truthful as the story concerning the 'outraged' Daughters Of The American Revolution. There had been disagreements within the Hendrix camp about the necessity of a European tour in early 1969, with some questioning whether it was worth the effort. After all, the real money was in the United States and that was where Hendrix now wanted to spend his time. Only Redding and Mitchell wanted to work in Europe. Hendrix's 'fall' in New York may also have been an attempt to dodge the European commitments. If so, it only delayed the inevitable. He flew out of New York on January 2nd 1969 to face a future every bit as uncertain as the one that had awaited him in September 1966. This time, however, everyone was watching.

playing with the
massed alberts

JANUARY TO MARCH 1969

Hendrix was met at London's Heathrow airport on January 2nd 1969 by his girlfriend Kathy Etchingham who took him back to their flat in Brook Street, Mayfair. "I had everything ready for Jimi's return to the country," Etchingham wrote later in her book Through Gypsy Eyes. "When the day came I hired a limo – a job I was getting practiced at – and headed down to Heathrow. Each time the routine was the same; Jimi would emerge from among the other passengers, guitar in one hand and travel bag in the other, his main luggage left for others to deal with."

"The car would be circling outside," Etchingham said, "waiting to sweep us up when we emerged from the airport into the daylight. Jimi was absolutely delighted with everything we had done [at the flat]. 'This is my first real home of my own,' he said, and I knew just how he felt."[1] What she may not have been aware of was just how much Hendrix needed somewhere more like a home than he'd had in America, and Hendrix himself may not have been fully aware of it until he got there. As it turned out, he had just a week in London before the European tour started. He spent it mostly at Brook Street, either relaxing or giving a stream of interviews. It was his first time in town for six months.

The Experience quickly accepted a couple of promotional opportunities, one of which was an appearance on BBC TV's *Happening For Lulu* show on Thursday 4th. Hendrix was in fine form personally for the appearance, talking to *Melody Maker*'s Chris Welch in the BBC canteen prior to the performance about his admiration for all three ex- members of Cream and Ginger Baker in particular.[2] With no new record to plug, the TV appearance was no more than a routine engagement designed to alert the public to the upcoming tour. It was planned as a three-song spot where the hostess would sing a duet with her guest to finish the show.

Although he said nothing about it, even to his fellow band members, Hendrix had other ideas, with only his pre-broadcast chat with Welch hinting at what he had in mind. Banking on the fact that the show was broadcast live – a relative rarity in television, even then – Hendrix played 'Voodoo Child

At the Royal Albert Hall (left) in central London, February 1969.

(Slight Return)' and then started 'Hey Joe'. Just a short way into the routine rendering he abruptly stopped and, eyes half-closed, declared dismissively: "We'd like to stop playing this rubbish and dedicate a song to the Cream regardless of what kind of group they may be in: we'd like to dedicate this song to Eric Clapton, Ginger Baker and Jack Bruce." He then dived immediately into 'Sunshine Of Your Love', a Cream hit the Experience had often played in an instrumental arrangement during their US tour. This surprise performance closed the show. The Experience managed to shock the studio bosses, thrill Hendrix's watching fans and make the headlines the next day as the papers decided that Lulu had been insulted. Lulu wasn't fooled by Hendrix's dedication to Cream, a band that had broken up with a final concert at London's Albert Hall on November 26th – he was determined not to do the show-closing duet – but she was not the type to take offence. In fact, straight after the show the band returned with her to the flat that she and Maurice Gibb shared and together watched a video of the proceedings.

Hendrix had talked a good deal to Chris Welch about the Experience and his plans, denying all rumours of a split-up that he'd helped initiate the previous November and asserting that the next studio album would be out in a couple of months. Welch explained that the title of this record, *First Wave Of The New Rising Sun*, "is a reference to Jimi's successful attempt to achieve composure and maintain the good nature necessary to retain his sanity. And this can be difficult when one is not white and crewcutted in America." He then quoted Hendrix: "A lot of people in America are looking for a leader in the music field. The Beatles can be a positive force and they could really get people together. They've got power because they are performing for the masses and they should use their power. I'm trying to use my power. I could buy myself a house in Beverly Hills and retire, but I just want to go on trying to communicate. The *First Wave Of The New Rising Sun* is my new life. Everybody has something to give of themselves and it's not just money."[3] Unfortunately Hendrix did not reveal any details of what this next album would consist of, although he did say he wanted it to be another double LP rather than the single his management were suggesting. The proposals for the record would change a number of times in the next few months before it was quietly dropped as a concept during early summer as his circumstances changed.

this Brook Street flat in the 1700s (in fact Handel leased No.25, next door, from 1723 until his death in 1759, and there is a blue plaque outside to commemorate the fact). A parallel that Short failed to draw was that both men had left their native lands to find fame as expatriates in London. But he did describe Hendrix in the flat in great detail. "The attic of the house, which has become Jimi's favourite room, contains an assortment of bric-a-brac and a bed with a Victorian shawl pinned to the ceiling as a canopy. At two in the afternoon, Hendrix is making the bed, neatly folding back the black sheets and straightening the colourful Persian bedspread. Then he grins and calls his girlfriend Kathy to open a bottle of wine. Kathy Etchingham is a 22-year-old redhead from the North who shares the flat. Jimi explains her presence: 'My girlfriend, my past girlfriend and probably my next girlfriend. My mother and my sister and all that bit. My Yoko Ono from Chester. We won't marry. Marriage isn't my scene; we just live together. Those bits of paper you call marriage certificates are only for people who feel insecure. ... One day I wanna become a parent,' Jimi announces. 'Now that is what the world is all about. Having kids. Like planting flowers.'"

This theme lingered in Hendrix's mind, inspiring him as he talked about his latest musical projects. He mentioned that his next album would aim to "simplify it all and bridge the gap between teenagers and parents". Just how he intended to do that he did not say, although he revealed that he was "moving away from what I've done so far". The conclusion of the interview was spent discussing the front cover to the British edition of *Electric Ladyland*, a copy of which Hendrix proceeded to bite in mock anger for the benefit of the *Mirror* photographer. Short ended his article by asserting that "Hendrix won't need a plaque for any of us to remember him by".[4] Ironically, in 1997 that is exactly what Kathy Etchingham and Pete Townshend unveiled on the front wall of 23 Brook Street, right next to Handel's plaque, as a TV film-crew shot a documentary to commemorate the occasion. The rooms that made up the flat are today under the aegis of the Handel House Trust, confirming just how far perceptions have shifted.

Hendrix seemed to recover a measure of personal equilibrium while living in Brook Street, although the stay was punctuated by a month-long European tour, more recording sessions and, in February, two major concerts at London's Albert Hall. The Albert Hall dates were announced in *Melody Maker*, which noted that "Hendrix is looking for support groups for the two shows planned and hopes to have Spike Milligan as compère. Among groups suggested so far are Eire Apparent and the new Dave Mason-Jim Capaldi group, Wooden Frog. ... It is hoped to record the Albert Hall concert and the group also plan to release a new studio album within the next two months, called *First Wave Of The New Rising Sun*".[5] The European tour this year took in Sweden (three concerts over two days), Denmark, Germany (ten concerts), Austria, and France (a single date in Strasbourg). It was extensively filmed by Steve Gold and Jerry Goldstein, the duo who had shot the New York Philharmonic engagement in November and who would go on to film at the

"We'd like to stop playing this rubbish and dedicate a song to the Cream regardless of what kind of group they may be in."

Jimi Hendrix, halting 'Hey Joe' on the Lulu TV show

Two days later, on January 6th, Hendrix gave an interview for *The Daily Mirror* newspaper in his Brook Street flat and the feature was published on the 11th, the same day the *Melody Maker* piece appeared. To the *Mirror* he made it clear that he wanted his relationship with Kathy Etchingham made public – a complete reversal of previous policy and something regarded in pop circles at the time generally as a bad career move, where even the hint of a 'steady' could wreck a pop idol's career. That was of course to seriously misjudge both him and his fans, who were most definitely not teenybopper girls. In any case, the women he attracted couldn't have cared less if he had a 'steady' or not.

The *Mirror* writer, Don Short, lost little time in pointing out both to his readers and Hendrix that the composer Georg Frederick Handel had lived at

Albert Hall in February. The shows in Sweden on January 8th and 9th and in Denmark on the 10th were later bootlegged, largely illustrating the lassitude now prevalent in the band's playing, although a radio interview in Denmark displayed good humour and camaraderie among the trio, undercutting some of the misery they remembered in retrospect.

More than anything the group probably needed a break professionally from one another in order to recharge their creative batteries and rediscover the chemistry that made them such a force two years earlier. It all had to do with perceptions. The three musicians saw themselves on a par with each other; both Noel Redding and Mitch Mitchell saw little reason for Hendrix to be singled out as the star: they had been through much together and somehow stuck it out. No one had any idea what they would do next outside of the

The Experience relaxing on a sofa somewhere in London as they ready themselves for assorted media duties around their appearances at the Albert Hall in February 1969.

Experience, although separately they all talked about it to the press. Redding planned to get his group Fat Mattress off the ground – they would become an occasional support band on the Experience's next US tour – and Mitchell wanted to play with some British musicians he admired. Hendrix intended to record and jam more.

Of the three, Hendrix was by a long way the most eager to express himself to interviewers and be understood by them, even when he affected a lack of interest. Redding often used such opportunities to be an Eeyore, answering an interviewer's questions simply by asking where all the beer had gone. Mitchell now tended to try to mystify and embarrass the journalist, showing little interest in talking about music and his views about it. Hendrix always tried. An interviewer in Denmark asked if he envisaged expanding the group. "New musicians? Roland Kirk, Lee Michaels; there would only be jams," Hendrix replied. "I don't want to play with anyone for a lengthy period of

time. We have jam sessions wherever we go. It's not to show we can play, it's for the communication between the musicians. It's just so nice to play with other people."[6]

Yet the rest of the world saw Hendrix as the star and the other two as the sidemen. Including the management. The situation was ripe for change but no one knew what to change to. So the tours and recording sessions continued and the quality drained away. In Copenhagen the critics were underwhelmed. "It was The Jimi Hendrix Experience's last big tour," wrote one reviewer. "Sure. The typical sounds were there. The vibrations and the sound painting. The guitar playing by itself and the erotic openness. Jimi stood there in the spotlight and played his songs and in some way it was tragic. Maybe he has reached a turning point in his career. A turning point when he wants some peace and quiet and the ability to develop his music and interests. Jimi has done a lot since his breakthrough. He has revolutionised pop and blues music and created a new sound dimension. He has explored all the possibilities of his instrument, worked with space and industrial sounds. Maybe he is unable to take it any further on that road. He seems to have found himself in a dead-end street. He stood in that street and tried to make himself heard in Copenhagen. … Between shows he threw himself on a sofa together with Noel, Mitch and a Danish blonde, the only alert one of the four."[7]

That same winter, in a studio just outside London and later in their own studio in Saville Row, another even more famous band was in the throes of breaking up. The Beatles had assembled to make a film and a new record intended to return them to their musical roots, a 'live' album recorded more or less the way they used to at the beginning of their career. Looking for inspiration, they turned to outside musicians and found keyboardist Billy Preston. The project quickly unravelled and became their musical low-point. Put on the shelf for a year, it then had its name changed from *Get Back* to *Let It Be* and was finally released. By then they'd made and issued another album, *Abbey Road*, as their true swansong, and had broken up. They had read the signs of their own decline and knew it was time for a new challenge. Rock was going through one of its periodic shifts and new artists and acts were emerging. Led Zeppelin would be voted top band of 1969 by British fans. Traffic broke up in January and Steve Winwood would join forces with Eric Clapton and Family's Rick Grech to form the shortlived Blind Faith.

In this atmosphere of uncertainty and change the Experience readied themselves for a new round of recording at Olympic and made preparations for the Albert Hall concerts, one of which was planned to deliver a new live album by the group. (The recording may have been earmarked as the settlement for Ed Chalpin/PPX after the relative failure of the Winterland recording project, which Hendrix had vetoed due to his frequent tuning problems.) The plan was also to film the Experience at the Albert Hall, for publicity use and possible worldwide cinema release – and, finally, as a sop to British fans who had not had the opportunity to see the band live since December 1967 (apart from a one-off gig at Woburn in July 1968).

While the Experience had been on tour in Europe, manager Mike Jeffery had requested a rough edit of the best of the Californian TTG sessions for them to mull over. It made for thin listening. There were 'Messenger', 'Mr Lost Soul', 'New Rising Sun', 'Peace In Mississippi', 'Izabella', 'Calling All Devil's Children' and no fewer than four separate jams, mostly with drummer Buddy Miles and keyboardist Lee Michaels. This was hardly an improvement on the

"I could buy myself a house in Beverly Hills and retire, but I just want to go on trying to communicate."

Jimi Hendrix

the Express. Hendrix had flown to New York City on January 30th for a short visit, primarily to see and make a decision about the proposed nightclub that he and Jeffery were toying with.

He also intended among other things to honour an agreement he'd made back in Los Angeles in October to produce the second album for The Buddy Miles Express, *Electric Church Music*, having already written the liner notes for the first, *Expressway To Your Skull*, an album made at Coast Recorders in LA while the Experience had been at TTG. Members of the Express recalled that Hendrix was around for just a few of the tracks, delegating the rest to Mercury staff producer Anne Tansey.[8] The tracks overseen by Hendrix were 'Miss Lady', '69 Freedom Special', 'Destructive Love' and 'My Chant'. Miles's band were well into drugs at this time. Guitarist Jim McCarty remembered, "We were all pretty crazy back then … let's say that The Buddy Miles Express was [makes an aeroplane sound]. … Virgil Gonsalves was a baritone player who used to play with Billie Holiday. That's where he got his smack problem from. In the Express you had a diversity of chemical stimuli that would defy belief. From one end of the stage to another, you could say that we covered it all. There wasn't much that was missing."[9] With all this extracurricular stimulant in the air – and in the musicians – it is perhaps understandable that Hendrix got only half the album produced but still fitted a large number of jams into the agenda.

On the evening of February 11th, after finishing production work on 'Destructive Love', Hendrix jammed with members of Miles's group in the studio. Perhaps inevitably the music that resulted was heavily blues-based. Although 'World Traveler' was instrumental and focused on guitar-organ dialogues, 'It's Too Bad', a variant of the brooding riffs and feel of 'Hear My Train A'Comin' / 'Voodoo Chile', contains a deeply-felt vocal from Hendrix who recounts a recent incident between himself and a sibling. The piece is closer to a jam than a structured blues: there is a double-time instrumental section after the vocals and, just as the selection is about to end, the organist starts up another bass pattern and the other two musicians pick up on it. This was not an attempt at a useable master but just a try-out of ideas in the guise of a studio jam among friends, following the path Hendrix had been taking for at least the previous six months. Hendrix indicated his approval of the

"We have jam sessions wherever we go. It's not to show we can play, it's for the communication between the musicians."

Jimi Hendrix

outtakes from *Electric Ladyland* and certainly nowhere near enough – either in quality or quantity – for the next studio album, no matter what Hendrix may have been telling the UK press. More recording was clearly a necessity. The sessions at Olympic combined attempts at new material for the forthcoming

direction of this particular session when he used the general feel and part of the lyrics during formal Experience sessions upon his return to London and Olympic studio just a few days later. Unfortunately the steady personal deterioration between Hendrix and Redding in particular made the four-day

LP with rehearsals for the Albert Hall gigs (two were planned, on February 18th and 24th) but they were desultory at best, with the group members having trouble even making it to the studio at the same time. In fact, Hendrix's first fruitful sessions that February were not with the Experience at all and not even in England, but with Buddy Miles and members of his band, booking completely unproductive. Nothing from these sessions was worked up later for release.

Hendrix and Mike Jeffery had shifted their stance on the nightclub idea in New York City, now favouring the development of a recording studio there. On February 14th, back in London, he tried out a solo demo of the blues 'Midnight Lightning' using lyrics that in part were taken from 'West Coast Seattle Boy', one of his old song ideas dating back to his Village days and written under the influence of Bob Dylan's stream-of-consciousness talking blues. Hendrix had tried somewhat unsuccessfully to describe it to Meatball Fulton in London in 1967. It was, he said, "a song about … 'I've did this' and 'I've did that, blah blah' but, y'know, its something like, y'know, but like one line, yeah, 'I get stoned and can't go home and they call long distance on the public saxophone' and all this man, y'know…".[10] He could certainly sing it better than he could talk it.

The following day at Olympic all the Experience members managed to be in the same place at the same time long enough to record a medium-tempo Hendrix song provisionally titled 'Shame Shame Shame' (no relation to the old R&B song by Jimmy Reed). In part it reprised the blues 'It's Too Bad' from his New York jams containing the desolate lyric detailing Hendrix's fractured relationship with his sibling Leon. Hendrix sings: "It's a shame shame shame shame shame / My brother can't be with me today / Well the last time that I seen him / He asked me for help / And I turned him cryin' away / He asked me for help and I turned him away." This performance has been bootlegged, although none of the versions released so far is complete, the longest running to just 1:52. It's a little faster than the New York jam version, and has a similar tempo and feel to the 'Room Full Of Mirrors' played at the Albert Hall a matter of days later. The piece is a drone blues in classic Hendrix style, using a minor variation on the 'Voodoo Child (Slight Return)' guitar riff, though muted and lonesome in this context and with a melody line close to that of the verse in 'Gypsy Eyes'. It's a low-key performance and quite touching, although this could hardly be classed as essential Hendrix. ('Shame Shame Shame' is part of a group of recordings known among Hendrix collectors as the Chandler Tapes. There are around 17 titles from 1966-1969, all recorded in England. During the last decade of his life Chandler apparently found them one day in a cupboard at home. At one time it seemed as if they would be officially issued but at the time of writing they are only available on bootlegs. In 1988 Chandler hired Noel Redding and Mitch Mitchell to add some new bass and drum tracks to unspecified titles among this material – most likely the February 1969 tunes – but nothing else is known about these recordings.)

The rehearsals at Olympic for the Albert Hall gigs reveal a band attempting to get back on an even keel and put themselves in a better mood – 'Spanish Castle Magic' and 'Hear My Train A'Comin'' from February 17th were subsequently released on the *Jimi Hendrix Experience* boxed set of 2000. The recordings add nothing of significance to the Hendrix legacy, apart from some fine turns of guitar phrase on 'Spanish Castle Magic'. They sound exactly what they were: rehearsals. The Olympic studio sessions came to an end on February 26th, two days after the second Albert Hall concert, and the material recorded that evening smacks of desperation. The Experience attempted 'Sunshine Of Your Love' in the absence of anything better to do, but the version they mustered is one of their most lacklustre. 'Gypsy Blood' (also known as 'Cryin' Blue Rain') is another slow blues in the vein of 'Hear My Train A'Comin'' or 'Voodoo Chile' but very subdued, almost as if Hendrix is playing to himself rather than Redding and Mitchell. 'Room Full Of Mirrors' follows the contours of the Albert Hall recording, although it is much shorter, settling at a comfortable mid-tempo and once more relying on the melodic twinning of vocal and guitar and some riffing rhythm-guitar patterns. Hendrix's vocal is relaxed, showing none of the strain exhibited on the later studio versions of this piece. But as with the other Olympic material from this February the tune

was unfinished, with no overdubs attempted. Redding noted later in his book that Mike Jeffery was expecting to be able to release a new Hendrix Experience LP called *First Wave Of The New Rising Sun* in April to coincide with the start of the next US tour. To Redding's mind there was, however, nothing new worth releasing.

But Hendrix may have had a different idea of what the new LP should be. He referred to it in a March 10th interview conducted at the Brook Street flat by Jane de Mendelssohn for *International Times*. "That's where I write some of my best songs, in bed, just laying there," said Hendrix. "I was laying there thinking of some when you came in. [It's] a really nice piece of music that I'm getting together for this late-summer LP that I'd like to do with this cat named Al Brown in America. It's called *The First Ray Of The New Rising Sun*, and it gives my own solution."[11] Brown was a friend of Hendrix's from New York, apparently a trained musician (and excellent cook), and Hendrix's comment may simply have been typical generosity to a friend.

New Rising Sun was one of three projects he regularly talked about at this time, the others being a second studio LP and a live album. Regrettably, nothing came of them. Perhaps the reasons lie not only in the dispirited atmosphere within the Experience but also in Hendrix's continuing drug intake. De Mendelssohn could recall seeing that day "the biggest collection of alcohol and drugs. I mean there were three different types of hash, grass, amyl nitrates, pills and lots of different kinds of bourbon and whisky. We just helped ourselves. He was constantly smoking joints and we were both drinking … . Then at one point he offered me some amyl nitrate and we both went out of our skulls."[12] Maybe the album projects went the same way. But there is a hint both in Hendrix's January interview with *Melody Maker* and the way he jammed with other musicians during the encores at the February 24th Albert Hall concert that there may have been a fundamental disagreement between Hendrix and those around him as to what form the studio album should now take. He had told *Melody Maker*: "Jamming is the thing now

"We've all been through the teenybopper group scene. But there will still be a need for good permanent groups."

Jimi Hendrix

because everybody wants to create some music. We've all been through the teenybopper group scene. But there will still be a need for good permanent groups."[13]

At least the Albert Hall concerts took place, although to this day there is serious debate among Hendrix devotees and the musicians who played as to whether the shows were good, bad or indifferent. The first, on February 18th, was presented by the Experience with no guests sitting in. They were supported by Soft Machine and Wooden Frog (the band Traffic's Dave Mason, Jim Capaldi and Chris Wood had formed after the departure of Steve Winwood). The preparations had been riddled with arguments between the company shooting the film, Gold & Goldstein, and Jeffery's appointed team. Hendrix was so alarmed that on the 17th – the day before the first show – he turned to Chas Chandler, by now severed from all business and management ties with the band, and asked Chandler to produce the shows.[14] Chandler came in and resolved the most vexing technical problems, thereby allowing calm to descend, but it was too late to ensure a smooth return to live performances in Britain for the band.

Both Redding and Mitchell later recalled a subdued performance that night. Mitchell claimed: "The first [of the two Albert Hall gigs] was appalling. One of those gigs where you wished you could go back the next night to make up for it, but you had to wait a week. I don't know what it was, it just didn't feel good."[15] The set-list was 'Tax Free', 'Fire', 'Get My Heart Back Together', 'Foxy Lady', 'Red House', 'Sunshine Of Your Love', 'Spanish Castle Magic', 'Star Spangled Banner' / 'Purple Haze' (the same sequence that Hendrix would expand and use to great effect at Woodstock some six months later) and an encore of 'Voodoo Child (Slight Return)'. Redding remembered Hendrix as "relaxed and happy"[16] and intent on trying a new stage routine where he would strike a series of poses rather than go through non-stop movements. As for the set they played, though, Redding regarded it as "listless – polished but lacklustre". Chandler was blunt, calling the show "among the worst I had ever seen Jimi play. And it wasn't his fault, it was Mitch's and Noel's. They were lifeless: Mitchell's timing seemed totally off, he was coming in late so often it seemed he was out of his brain, and Redding was trying to show how awkward he could be. ... Up until that point I had been one of the supporters of the group, because I thought that they made for a good unit. Now I felt it was time they got thrown out. If I had still been in charge, Mitch and Noel would have been sacked the next day."[17] But the crowd enjoyed it, no doubt happy simply to have the band back in London and playing live again.

Possibly as a reaction to what was perceived as a let-down, when the Experience returned to the Albert Hall for the second show on February 24th they were armed with a slightly different set of tunes and a few friends to help out. There was also an entirely different support line-up this time: Redding's group Fat Mattress, and Van Der Graaf Generator. The Experience's segment of the show –

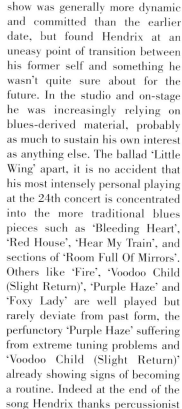

which, as planned, was recorded for a potential live album – started with 'Lover Man', a song that in the past had often been used to kick-start proceedings. Then Hendrix introduced 'Stone Free' as a "blast from the past", facetiously imitating a typical British DJ's hyped-up verbiage in what even then was a radio cliché. A week after the concert, Hendrix told *Record Mirror* interviewer Valerie Mabbs that he was seriously considering re-working 'Stone Free' as an extended single, playing a tape of the Albert Hall version to demonstrate his ideas. This 'Stone Free' was stretched to over ten minutes, allowing all three Experience members to solo. It also gave Hendrix the space to try an innovation he'd recently been working into some of his improvisations as he begins at one point to pick out related scales, something he had perhaps picked up from the countless jams of the past year and which he would certainly have heard used by musicians he admired such as Roland Kirk. From now on he appeared to enjoy introducing a couple of such scales into jams and solos to provide extra light and shade.

A sequence of gig-hardened material came next: 'Getting My Heart Back Together' followed by 'I Don't Live Today' and 'Red House'. After that long and involving blues, Hendrix ramped up the adrenalin once more with 'Foxy Lady' and 'Sunshine Of Your Love' and then took the pace back down again

The Experience live at the Falkoner Centret, Copenhagen, Denmark (left and above), January 10th 1969.

with the debut concert performance of 'Bleeding Heart', announced by Redding as "a slow blues in C sharp". This wonderfully paced and inventive blues led to 'Fire' and an exquisite 'Little Wing' before 'Voodoo Child (Slight Return)' began – all nine minutes of it. For this piece, designed by Hendrix as the show's closer, the first of the evening's guests, percussionist Rocky Dijon, was brought out. The audience reaction was overwhelming, keeping a visibly tired Hendrix on-stage. However, instead of calling a halt, he invited the audience to either stay and clap or leave. They stayed.

On the impromptu 'Room Full Of Mirrors', Chris Wood and Dave Mason joined in for some jamming. At last, the musicians left the stage. But still the long concert was not over, ending instead with two encores demanded by the crowd. Hendrix sent them home satisfied with 'Purple Haze' and a brutal demolition of 'Wild Thing' (later erroneously identified on the posthumous live album of the show as 'Smashing Of The Amps'). This second Albert Hall show was generally more dynamic and committed than the earlier date, but found Hendrix at an uneasy point of transition between his former self and something he wasn't quite sure about for the future. In the studio and on-stage he was increasingly relying on blues-derived material, probably as much to sustain his own interest as anything else. The ballad 'Little Wing' apart, it is no accident that his most intensely personal playing at the 24th concert is concentrated into the more traditional blues pieces such as 'Bleeding Heart', 'Red House', 'Hear My Train', and sections of 'Room Full Of Mirrors'. Others like 'Fire', 'Voodoo Child (Slight Return)', 'Purple Haze' and 'Foxy Lady' are well played but rarely deviate from past form, the perfunctory 'Purple Haze' suffering from extreme tuning problems and 'Voodoo Child (Slight Return)' already showing signs of becoming a routine. Indeed at the end of the song Hendrix thanks percussionist Dijon for contributing and then asks the audience if there is anyone who wants to play guitar "'cause I'm finished". He really does sound tired and ready to stop.

But the audience demanded their encores, and Hendrix has the nerve to try something new with 'Room Full Of Mirrors' as the first offering. Joined on-stage by Dave Mason and Chris Wood, the Experience give the audience nearly nine minutes of jamming. Wood's flute is flat and Mason's guitar solo is not one of his most memorable, but their playing allows Hendrix to move out of the spotlight for the first time that night. The result is some staggeringly inspired guitar work from him as he interweaves among what Mason and the others are doing. This interplay is what Hendrix absolutely loved, his snaking lines becoming overwhelmingly exciting and disarmingly subtle at the same time. At one point he takes over from a Mason solo with a simple circling phrase that he uses to turn the rhythm inside out and round and around, in the manner of a master improviser from India or a Charlie Parker, before resolving the tension once more with some powerful rhythm guitar.

Mitchell takes all this in his stride, never losing his place and stoking the rhythmic fires higher than before. Contrary to some reports of the concert at the time, on the evidence of the recordings Mitchell is in outstanding form all evening, providing terrific drive and huge levels of imagination and energy through his drumming.

The film that was shot on the 24th was part of a project for which Hendrix had been 'on call' for the previous couple of months. He had already been filmed extensively at the Brook Street flat and in other off-stage locations, which was something Kathy Etchingham remembered well. "[Steve Gold and Jerry Goldstein] also filmed two Albert Hall gigs which Jimi wasn't too happy about because it meant having the lights up in the auditorium, which he thought spoilt the atmosphere."[18] Photographer David Redfern was shooting on that night, remembered the light. "It was absolutely fantastic for taking photographs, because film was slow in those days. The lights from the film crew flooded the

Jimi displays good-humoured distaste for the British sleeve of his *Electric Ladyland* double LP – but he really didn't like it.

entire stage."[19] Great for filming, but a bad atmosphere for establishing intimacy with your audience, which was what worried Hendrix.

Some films involving Hendrix shot over the next year or so were poor efforts, often badly edited, sometimes empty of wit and ideas. Some have never been issued commercially, and the Gold & Goldstein film is one of them. Hendrix's management has often been roundly criticised for their part in these projects. However, film footage of virtually every other band operating around this time (The Beatles, as ever, proving the exception) is very scarce, in concert or otherwise. This makes Mike Jeffery's scheme seem remarkably far-sighted: he intended to shoot plenty of Hendrix footage and to

to understand his music. His strange business deals may even have resulted in some of this footage not being available over 30 years later. But the Hendrix audio-visual legacy is infinitely greater for his efforts. Only in the 1970s would others follow his lead and start to create films of headlining rock acts for commercial release.

Hendrix spent the rest of his stay in London prior to the next US tour relaxing at Brook Street, giving interviews or planning his future with a variety of business and legal associates. There was even a series of meetings with Chas Chandler and the rest of the band to consider Chandler taking over once more as manager, ousting Mike Jeffery.[20] This came to nothing as no one could settle upon a method of dislodging Jeffery. Back on more solid ground, Hendrix talked to interviewers about the current recording projects, and in conversation with *New Musical Express*'s John Grant said that what he now called *The Last Rays Of The Morning Sun* was not the only planned release.

"There's another album to come from the Experience – I'm dropping my name as a prefix, we are a three-piece group and not enough credit is given to it – titled *Little Band Of Gypsies*. It's a jam-type album."[21] This sounds like another attempt to profitably use all those hours of taped studio jams stacked in studios on both sides of the Atlantic. The notion vanished almost as quickly as it appeared. Hendrix worked hard at composing new songs in the flat, taking advantage of the relative calm enforced by Etchingham. The situation on the top two floors of the building was ideal for insulating them from unwanted visitors. "There wasn't even a doorbell at street level," Etchingham wrote later, "so no one could drop in on us without prior arrangement. I knew how fragile our tranquillity was; that if ten people came and knocked on the door Jimi would let them all in, regardless of whether they were friends or just passing weirdos. I used to make a point of keeping the downstairs door closed when he was playing music or had his earphones on, ensuring that unwanted visitors couldn't get to us. … Since we had no neighbours, Jimi was able to set up his amplifiers and play to his heart's content."[22] This comparative calm didn't last. Before long he'd given out their address and phone number to all and sundry and a steady stream of people were

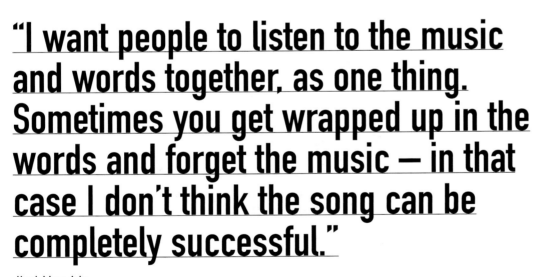

"I want people to listen to the music and words together, as one thing. Sometimes you get wrapped up in the words and forget the music — in that case I don't think the song can be completely successful."

Jimi Hendrix

use it to create a proxy world tour that would visit places the Experience could never get to. Hendrix himself certainly approved. In the light of his early death, the decision seems an especially valuable one today. If we only had to rely on the usual media outlets for Hendrix footage there would be just a handful of television appearances from Europe and America, his sets at Monterey and Woodstock, and perhaps one or two other festival appearances – and that would pretty much be that. Jeffery may have been a crook and one who robbed Hendrix blind, and he may not have understood or even wanted

coming through the flat: some were genuine friends; many others were out for whatever they could get.

Hendrix talked to *Melody Maker*'s Bob Dawbarn about live music and the future in a two-part interview published in late February and early March. He had a remarkably relaxed attitude towards live performance. "I always enjoy playing, whether it's before ten people or 10,000," said Hendrix. "And I don't care if they boo, as long as it isn't out of key. I don't try to move an audience – it's up to them what they get from the music. If they have paid to see us then we are going to do our thing. If we add a bit of the trampoline side of entertainment then that is a fringe benefit, but we are there to play music. If we stand up there all night and play our best and they don't dig it, then they just don't dig us and that's all there is to it."

He now had significantly different aims for his latest songs compared to a year or so before. "I've not written too many heavy things recently. Most of what I have done will come out on the next LP in the late summer. I don't try to make a thing about my songs when I put them on a record. I try to make them honest and there doesn't seem too much point in talking about them. … I don't mean my lyrics to be clever. What I want is for people to listen to the music and words together, as one thing. Sometimes you get wrapped up in the

At home with girlfriend Kathy Etchingham at their flat in Brook Street, Mayfair, central London, for a *Daily Mirror* interview, January 1969.

words and forget the music – in that case I don't think the song can be completely successful."[23]

A man as committed to jamming as Hendrix found plenty of opportunities to jam while in London. During February and early March his partners included Billy Preston, who had concluded his recording stint with The Beatles on February 22nd; Hendrix found him playing at a favourite jam-station, the Speakeasy. There were also sessions with Dave Mason, Jim Capaldi, The Gods, and Roland Kirk, who once again was playing a week at Ronnie Scott's. Hendrix was one of a number of guests entertained by Kirk at the jazz club in the first week of March. Critic Brian Priestley caught Kirk's act that week and noted: "He is a very 'traditional' jazzman … , shown not

only by his organic use of showmanship but also by his inherent feeling for contrast and his readiness to accept all kinds of sounds into his frameworks." Apart from the term 'jazzman'– Hendrix was never a jazz musician – it would be hard to find a more apt description of Hendrix's own working methods at this time. Priestley continued, "Kirk made himself many new friends during this latest trip to England by jamming (on separate occasions) with Jimi Hendrix, Eric Clapton and Stevie Wonder."[24] Kirk had also recently jammed successfully on-stage in Boston with Frank Zappa & The Mothers Of Invention. Kirk's bassist Vernon Martin later recalled the Hendrix jam that week as "an onslaught … a very high gospel of mixing elements of rhythm and country/blues guitar with tremendous energy".[25]

When Hendrix got involved in such jams, there seemed a complete justification of his insistence that jamming was the future for the music he wanted to play. Byrds man Roger McGuinn confirms that by this time he was widely respected by musicians from many genres. McGuinn remembers Hendrix and bluegrass guitar genius Clarence White as a mutual admiration society. "Clarence was doing in country rock what Jimi was doing in blues," McGuinn recalls. "They both took it to a new extreme. Clarence's playing was brilliantly executed and freshly imagined: Jimi was fascinated by it." McGuinn also remembers a particular jam in New York. "Jimi, Eric Clapton and myself had been hanging out at a club, and we all wanted to play. The three of us went back to a loft and jammed until morning. It was acoustic guitars only, and it was the blues. No one else was there – just the three of us. It was an astounding experience; no one talked much, we just played, and it was very, very cool – egos were checked at the door, and it was just pure music all the way. No need for anything else, or any other instrument."[26]

With such encounters occurring regularly in his musical life, it is understandable that Hendrix was losing patience with the stereotyped sets of tunes he had to deliver to the people who came to see the Experience wanting to hear the hits. Perhaps if he changed his playing situation, he reasoned, those expectations would also change. Similarly, if he delivered a new album that stood quite apart from the first three, then surely his fans would come to expect diversity from him rather than what he saw as the narrow – and now dated – stylistic range from which he had to choose at every gig. After all, the majority of his stage repertoire still came from the first album. The problem was how to sustain his inspiration sufficiently to complete a project to his exacting musical standards at a time when his attention was divided and his precise direction uncertain.

Returning to New York on March 13th to prepare for the new tour, Hendrix first plunged into a new round of recording. It was divided into three main strands: completing his production duties for Buddy Miles; attempting once more to record new material, both alone and with the Experience; and fitting in as many recorded jams as possible in the time available. With the other members of the Experience still back in London, Hendrix first of all used the Buddy Miles band as a convenient means to get into the groove, recording a jam with them on March 15th as well as an early version of 'Message To Love' that trod a fine line between a jam and some sort of preordained structure. The next undertaking, three days later at the Record Plant, consisted of a solo session and another run-through of ideas using elements of the Buddy Miles band.

The solo session gave birth to Hendrix's extraordinary multitracked version of 'The Star Spangled Banner', a piece remarkable enough purely from the terms of its conception. Although the Experience had been playing snatches of the piece on-stage in recent months, this studio version fleshes out the stentorian melody, in the process becoming vast in its scope. There are no new studio tricks: all the techniques applied here to his guitar had been used on tunes dating back to *Electric Ladyland* the previous summer at the very least, with the exception perhaps of recording a guitar track at half-speed and then running it at normal speed to raise the pitch by an octave. It was a brilliantly simple way of stretching the remit of the guitar to produce a fully orchestral range of colour. Hendrix also brings his wry sense of humour to the piece. As the thunderous old melody is brought to its natural concerted conclusion, Hendrix begins to introduce all manner of guitar commentary and ironies. He imitates the sounds that were dominating American minds just weeks after Richard M Nixon had become the latest President, at whose inauguration ceremony 'The Star Spangled Banner' was played jubilantly and fed over the airwaves into virtually every American home. Hendrix interjected sounds of war, protest and division, howls of pain, the screams of bombs and ricocheting of bullets – the dreadful turmoil of a bitterly divided nation. All this would become much more explicit in his later and more famous live versions of the tune, but the seeds were all clearly sewn at that Record Plant session.

'Bleeding Heart' was another tune in transition at the time and Hendrix gave the blues piece a workout this evening, using the same arrangement played at the Albert Hall just three weeks ago but at almost medium tempo rather than the ultra-slow treatment Hendrix had favoured before. The next stage of the song's evolution would involve another hike in tempo and a more sophisticated casting of the song's blues form to take it away from this traditional approach and further towards a blues lament.

A new ballad – unfinished at this point but sufficiently developed to be sketched in the studio – was tried on the same date, March 18th. Called '(Hey) Gypsy Boy' it contained the first draft of the words later used for 'Hey Baby (New Rising Sun)'. The band played it very slowly and with no introduction – they didn't reach a conclusion, either, in any of the eight attempted takes. Hendrix plays a very simple melodic guitar solo, clearly as a guide for the bass and drums. Of all his recent material it was one of the most thought-through pieces, though it patently needed much more organisation before it could be called finished. Based loosely on the verse chord-changes of his beloved 'All Along The Watchtower', it is a song in need of contrast – something the next version he

attempted would provide. A composite version of this ballad combining basic tracks from this session and one from ten months later was eventually released with additional overdubs from session musicians on the *Midnight Lightning* LP produced by Alan Douglas in 1975. That version exposes its weakness as a performance, mostly due to chronic tuning problems and an unclear form that requires a fade-out, along with various edits and melodic figures recycled to decorate the bare bones of what Hendrix had left unfinished. Perhaps '(Hey) Gypsy Boy' should never have been released in anything but its original work-in-progress state. This 'unimproved' version is only available on bootlegs at the time of writing.

The next day Kathy Etchingham flew into New York to meet up with Hendrix, reversing her policy of never following him to the US. It would precipitate their break-up and propel Hendrix into a new phase of both his career and his private life, and one that he would fail to survive. Etchingham had vivid memories of finding herself alone at Hendrix's hotel suite. "I was just dozing off when Jimi arrived back, trailing an enormous entourage like the colourful leader of some circus freak show. From that moment on there never seemed to be less than 20 people hanging out around us. If we stayed in the room, they stayed with us; if we went out to eat, they all came too – at Jimi's expense. They were the loudest, nastiest bunch I had ever come across. Many of the women were obviously whores and the men all appeared to be pimps and drug dealers, with their cool shades and their little spoons handing around their necks like badges of office. I was startled by how relaxed Jimi seemed among them all, a king presiding over a court of fools. If I tried asking him to send them all away, he would become defensive. 'These people are my friends,' he would say. It was clear they disliked me, Jimi's 'tight-assed white English bitch', just as vehemently as I disliked them." Within a few days Etchingham had moved on to lodge in another hotel with friends, only to find that they too were caught up in the spiral of drug dependency. This fast-living New York set that now included her boyfriend seemed no longer able to enjoy themselves without maintaining their expensive highs. "Their whole lives revolved around where the next lot of stuff was coming from. I wanted to get

"They were the loudest, nastiest bunch I had ever come across."

Kathy Etchingham, girlfriend, on Jimi's latest crowd of hangers-on

out and party, but they couldn't go anywhere until they'd got their stash. They spent days waiting for unreliable flakes and criminals to turn up."[27]

Hendrix's personal and professional life were headed for change, and there would be hard times ahead. Unwilling or unable to directly confront his problems, he prepared for the upcoming tour by taking every opportunity to dive into the Record Plant. On March 25th he enjoyed another jam with members of The Buddy Miles Express, including guitarist Jim McCarty and bassist Roland Robinson. One of the jams from that night was released in

Live at the Albert Hall in London (above, and opposite page) with the film-maker's lights up full as Hendrix and the Experience blast out into the hall's notoriously cavernous acoustics.

heavily edited form by Alan Douglas and given the title 'Jimi/Jimmy Jam'. Nothing of any great musical consequence occurs during the 17 minutes or so that has been released on bootlegs, apart from the first appearance of the theme later titled 'Villanova Junction', though this was edited out of the greatly shortened commercial release. McCarty remembered the evening well when talking to Mark Renusch. "It was one of those nights where Jimi had been jamming at a number of clubs. We ended up at Ungano's and after it closed we went down to the Record Plant. It was four or five in the morning and we were just playing. It wasn't a question of Jimi saying, 'OK, we're going to try this.' It was just people playing."[28] Most observers place this as the night of a jam including Hendrix and guitarist John McLaughlin, but McCarty, who has very clear memories of the 'Jimi/Jimmy' jam and of who was present, remembers little about the circumstances of the McLaughlin session at which he was also present, which suggests that it was a different occasion.

This workout set the pattern for the jams that would take place at the Record Plant for the rest of that spring at the same time as the Experience's attempts to work up new material of sufficient quality for *The First Wave Of The New Rising Sun* proved as fruitless as those of February and the previous October. By the final days of March, Hendrix was already talking publicly about completely different recording projects, showing just how volatile his plans had become. He told a Los Angeles radio show: "We have to go to New York to record on [April] 1st and 7th to get our new LP and single together. Yeah, 'Freedom' and 'Both Ways'. The LP will probably be called *Freedom* or *Band Of Gypsys* and the single's 'Freedom'."[29] This was probably just the first thing that came into his head. He wouldn't write 'Freedom' for another nine months and there is no known song titled 'Both Ways'. Only *Band Of Gypsys* had previously been aired as a possible idea for a recording project.

Once they completed the latest US tour at the end of June, the original Experience would be history and all current recording projects abandoned. Hendrix meanwhile took advice from his old idol: he would not look back. Instead, he became fixed on embracing change as he attempted to grab a future for himself – however obscure that future might seem.

jam today, no experience needed

APRIL TO JUNE 1969

As March turned to April 1969, Hendrix upped his activity in the studio. Yet another jam came about in typically spontaneous fashion, this one featuring bassist Dave Holland and guitarist John McLaughlin. Both musicians had been recording with Miles Davis in late February, although McLaughlin was currently the guitarist in drummer Tony Williams's trio, Lifetime.

L ike Hendrix, Mitch Mitchell was always up for a jam, especially when it involved sitting in with some of the people he admired in the jazz world. "We'd go down to The Scene and I would play with Larry Coryell, Jimi would play with Larry Coryell, Charles Lloyd," Mitchell said later. "I got Tony Williams in … [and it] was interesting for me to hear another drummer working with the man. It was the one chance I got to hear the band. Plus through that I got to do some sessions with Miles Davis, like an incestuous circle, but surely that's what music should be about."[1] Mitchell was directly responsible for McLaughlin jamming with Hendrix. McLaughlin had come to New York on the invitation of Tony Williams to set up a jazz-rock band with the drummer alongside organist Larry Young. A day after arriving, McLaughlin accompanied Williams when he visited Miles Davis. Davis was in the middle of a drastic change in his approach to making music, deeply influenced by what Hendrix had been doing on the guitar. He asked McLaughlin to come down to Columbia studios the following day for a session. On February 20th McLaughlin showed up and, under Davis's tutelage, recorded the beautiful melody to Joe Zawinul's 'In A Silent Way'. The following day he started rehearsals with Williams to get their band, Lifetime, underway. Within a month Lifetime was playing clubs around New York and nearby cities, turning up the volume to rock levels and sending a series of shockwaves through the New York jazz scene. Up to that point most jazz musicians in the city had fought shy of amplification.

"I was playing at the Village Vanguard with Tony Williams and Larry Young," McLaughlin recalled, "and Mitch Mitchell came down to see us. I knew Mitch from the Georgie Fame days back in England."[2] Mitchell enthused about what Lifetime were doing – according to McLaughlin he "was really nutty about Lifetime. He came over and said, 'You better come down to the Record Plant because we're recording tonight: just come on down.' When I got there, Mitch wasn't actually there at all. There was a guy named Buddy Miles playing drums. I didn't know Buddy at the time: I just saw this guy who was playing some boogaloo. So I played, then Jimi came and joined in. Dave Holland was there, and we played all night. … I was using a flat-top Gibson [acoustic guitar] with a pickup on it. We worked some chords out, but nothing complicated. We were just jamming".[3] A recent interview with bassist

Drummer Buddy Miles (left) was one of Hendrix's regular jamming partners during 1969.

Dave Holland suggests that McLaughlin's memory may not be comprehensive about this studio jam. Holland said: "I knew [Hendrix] very slightly. ... The opportunity I had to play with him was a call I got one afternoon to come down to his studio and just have a jam session with John McLaughlin and Buddy Miles. It was very loose and a lot of fun, and that was the extent of it. It's

"Hendrix had this really long cord [lead] and would walk up to cats and give them a little riff to play and then he'd walk up to someone else and give them a little riff to play."

Dave Holland, bassist, on jam-session technique

interesting, though – he had this really long cord [lead] and he would walk up to cats and give them a little riff to play and then he'd walk up to someone else and give them a little riff to play – and that's exactly what Miles did, that same kind of intuitive orchestration."[4]

When in the early 1970s McLaughlin finally heard the tapes of what was played that night he vetoed their release. He has explained his decision many times since. "What I heard is not up to it. It was four o'clock in the morning and everybody was a bit tired. But it was fun,"[5] he told Bill Milkowski in 1985. More recently he described using his amplified acoustic instrument alongside Hendrix's amplified solidbody guitar as an "absolutely no-go situation; as soon as I turned the volume up, my guitar was just freaking out; the drums, the bass, everything was so loud, and I regret that I didn't get a chance to play with him after I got into my own particular electric sound".[6]

His judgement is backed by Alan Douglas, who later in 1969 signed McLaughlin to his record label, Douglas Records. Douglas knew both guitarists well. "Nothing really heavy came out of that jam," said Douglas. "There were some spots where they got off but they were just kind of feeling themselves out. It wasn't serious. Jimi was jamming all the time, and John was just another good musician who came in. But if they had developed a rapport and spent time together they could have done incredible things together."[7] McLaughlin has consistently withheld the jam from general release. Back in 1975 he said, "There's been a lot of bad stuff around [Hendrix's] name, not the least of it being people who have been releasing his music. You see, he wouldn't like it without his having quality control."[8] For that reason McLaughlin has stuck to his decision, and the bootlegs that have appeared (usually under the name *Hell's Session*) indicate that his principled stand is the right one. Hendrix himself would never have wanted this music made commercially available.

Meanwhile, Hendrix continued to record new tunes he hoped might reach the standard he required for commercial release. On April 1st the Experience started the first of four straight nights of recording at Olmstead studio in New York City. They attempted a series of takes of 'Bleeding Heart', all at medium tempo rather than the slow blues treatment of the tune they'd played at the Albert Hall, but the results were poor. Even though the studio had been changed, the party atmosphere and lack of cohesion between Experience members all too readily derailed proceedings. One instrumental was completed to a reasonable standard. 'Midnight' is a medium-tempo tune built mainly around the augmented 9th chord that Hendrix used so liberally in his tunes (most notably in 'Foxy Lady'). In fact, this is the 'Foxy Lady' strut,

only slightly altered and put through a modulation sequence. After running through this cycle once Hendrix begins his solo, playing hell-for-leather as the opening three chords repeat twice. Then the Experience go to a bridge of commonplace chord changes, playing at a stalking tempo. After this they return to the opening sequence, running through it three more times. Over all this Hendrix plays some heated, swashbuckling guitar, reaching a considerable climax in the final verse before allowing the track to fade out. It is one of the more impressive of Hendrix's later studio outings with the Experience. Edited down from a longer take it is simple in the way of most of his best work, but imbued with sufficient bite, swagger and grandeur to achieve lift-off. It also benefits from a superb recording, with Noel Redding's bass never sounding better. That it covered old, well-trodden Experience ground rather than indicating a new route for the band was perhaps only of concern to Hendrix at that point. 'Midnight' was shelved until 1973, when it appeared on the posthumous compilation *War Heroes*.

The following six nights were spent in fruitless attempts to record presentable versions of 'Hear My Train A'Comin'', 'Midnight Lightning', 'Trashman', 'Earth Blues' (at that point known as 'Lullaby For The Summer') and 'Ships Passing In The Night'. A whole sequence of jams loosely based on 'Peace In Mississippi' was recorded but to no great effect. Virtually none of this material has ever been officially issued apart from a heavily edited 'Trashman' on *Crash Landing* in 1975 and a painfully out of tune 'Hear My Train A'Comin'' unfortunately released on *Midnight Lightning* in the same year. The instrumental 'Trashman' is based on a single chord but otherwise has a first section identical to 'Midnight'. It then moves into a second section with a simple but effective rising melody, harmonised in major thirds by a second guitar part. But it is musical gruel compared to what Hendrix had been achieving regularly in the studio in 1968. It even pales beside 'Midnight' recorded a couple of days earlier.

During the time the group was involved in these unproductive sessions the sixth Experience single on Track, 'Crosstown Traffic' / 'Gypsy Eyes', was released in the UK. Hendrix was irritated: not only did he feel that *Electric Ladyland* should not have its eyes picked out in this way, but the A-side was now over 15 months old and no longer represented what he was doing musically. Yet what he was doing musically now was hardly translating into releasable singles, let alone albums. The record company was simply trying to plug a gap in their release schedule that for the moment was somewhat inconvenient but not yet alarming. It would be, in time.

The Experience moved back to the Record Plant on April 7th, but with no evident improvement. The only near-complete master from this and the next two nights was a disciplined but spiritless new version of 'Stone Free'. This was Hendrix's shot at the extended single he'd mentioned a month earlier in London. Appropriately enough, it would see the light of day in highly reassembled form on the controversial *Crash Landing* album of 1975 (and later the *Jimi Hendrix Experience* box-set). Still the band ploughed on, occasionally augmented by other musicians. They reached a preliminary mix of 'Stone Free' by the 14th and had another stab at 'Ships Passing In The Night', a slow blues with no clearly defined shape. On one occasion this piece included an unidentified trumpeter playing through a Harmon mute. Later, his careful noodlings would be mistaken for the work of Miles Davis, but this proved to be wishful thinking: pictures taken at the session reveal a trumpeter bearing as little physical resemblance to Davis as does his playing. Many people dream of discovering tapes of a jam between Davis and Hendrix, but there never was one. Frankly, if this session was it, those people would have been mortified by its poor quality and lack of all energy or ideas.

Neither Mitchell nor Redding recall this period in their respective memoirs, probably because so little of any worth was recorded, but it was a crucial time in the band's history. The wheels were coming off and Hendrix was looking for escape routes. He gradually brought in other players he could rely on as he continually shifted personnel through his long sequence of jams. In this way his old friend Billy Cox, for example, was introduced into some Record Plant sessions, the first one with the bassist falling on April 21st when a spirited but necessarily loose version of 'Roomful Of Mirrors' was jammed upon with a drummer who had a technique equal to that of Mitchell but in style was closer to Tony Williams. Amid the general party atmosphere and lack of focus, such moves were either ignored or not seen for what they were – certainly not by Redding, at least, who was participating in his last Experience sessions and, while he did not know it, was soon to play his last gig with the band. On April 17th Hendrix tried once more to record 'Midnight Lightning'. Paul Caruso was in the studio that night, as was Hendrix's New York girlfriend, Devon Wilson, who contributed the occasional back-up vocal. The rough jam that was given this name has stayed in the can ever since for good reason.

By this time, Devon Wilson had established herself as a major player in the travelling circus that had so dismayed Kathy Etchingham on her arrival in New York in March. Wilson was aggressive, intelligent, sexy, dominant and ruthless. She had come up through the West Coast school of hard knocks and now had reached a position of note thanks to her sharp mind and street savvy. What is more, she was unhesitatingly ready to use her access to drugs, sex and famous people for her own ends. Wilson had first been introduced to Hendrix back in the summer of 1967. Gradually they grew closer as the guitarist spent increasing amounts of time in New York City: she impressed and attracted Hendrix with her sexual voraciousness, sheer sass and the attention she lavished upon him. She was a young woman of great ambition but – like Hendrix – had little control over her own personal needs, from hard drugs to emotional requirements. Wilson indulged the aspects of Hendrix's lifestyle that were leading him to a creative impasse. Although she was dead

"Maybe I'll never get to take that break; all I know is that I'm thinking about it most of the time now, and that doesn't help create the right mood."

Jimi Hendrix

Hendrix tried out two new songs on April 24th, in between jams. One of these, 'Crash Landing', contained lyrics with direct references to her. Their uncommon power came from the simplicity and emotional honesty of the stark images that derived directly from the hard-hitting tradition of the blues. Later, a portion would be inserted into the bridge of 'Freedom': "You don't love me girl / You just want me / So let's make it baby so I can leave / You don't need me / You just want to bleed me / So take out your dagger and cut me free / Cut me free / You don't love me girl / You're just trying to suffocate me / So hand me your blankets and take your dirty sheets …" and so on.

The original recordings of 'Crash Landing' feature a line-up of guitar, organ, bass and drums. Producer Alan Douglas replaced much of this instrumentation and added a female chorus when he re-edited and assembled the version that became the title track for the 1975 Crash Landing LP. He also winged in a guitar solo from another take because the original take he used as a basis for his edit was without one. "I want to tell you something that we did on Crash Landing," Douglas told this author in 1992. "You are probably the first one I've ever told, just so that everybody will understand. That record has been out there for a long time, and we flew that solo in from another take. If I was in the studio with Jimi and we listened to the two takes of 'Crash Landing' which I had to deal with, and we decided that the rhythm track was better on this one and the solo was better on that one, we would have done the same thing. It's normal recording procedure, you know? It wasn't easy to do, it was difficult to do. I'm making it sound like it was a matter of splicing in something. It wasn't. We had to fly a solo from another take, and the tempos were just different enough to make it difficult. But I had a great engineer and the right people around me."[9]

The first two posthumous albums produced by Alan Douglas were Crash Landing (released September 1975) and Midnight Lightning (December 1975). Douglas had studio musicians overdub fresh parts on top of the original rhythm sections and also added rhythm guitar and occasional

"We had to fly a solo from another take, and the tempos were just different enough to make it difficult."

Alan Douglas, producer, reassembling Hendrix recordings

set against what she saw as exploitation by his uptight and very English management, she unwittingly saw to it that he was never sufficiently alert to take proper control of his life and to cut through all the music-business crap that surrounded him. Perhaps in some strange way he wanted it like that. He would hear what he wanted to hear: that none of it was his fault, and that he would be all right if it wasn't for The Man. Perhaps this was so. But however weak a character Hendrix may have been and however uninterested in the detail of business, he grew to realise that this was no solution. He would eventually have to fight his own battles if he wanted to win and preserve both his musical creativity and his own sanity – even if in the process this meant sacrificing pop superstardom.

Devon Wilson's presence had already made an impact on Hendrix. After a night in the studio where Hendrix, Billy Cox, Wilson and a bevy of others got through no fewer than 45 takes of the Muddy Waters song 'Mannish Boy',

backing vocals. The albums constituted an ill-conceived attempt to release material that Hendrix had left unfinished but that was interesting in its own right. Their usefulness has since been removed because much of the relevant material has since been released in its original, fragmentary form. In 1992 Douglas talked openly about his methods. "I went into the library and listened to everything and decided to make some albums with the criteria that there was a Jimi Hendrix rhythm track, there was a Hendrix lead guitar track and there was a Hendrix solo vocal. And so consequently – Midnight Lightning aside for one moment – everything that is on Crash Landing was made from those three elements, or I didn't touch the tracks." On this basis, Douglas felt that Crash Landing had some integrity. "So I keep that in the catalogue. Midnight Lightning I took out of the catalogue because I had to stretch the material. I committed myself to deliver three albums and I would have liked it if they had been on one, frankly. Nine To The Universe [1980] is also very weak, but it's jamming and everybody knows it's jamming. *Midnight Lightning* I had my problems with – I had no choice at that point – but I have taken it off the market."[10]

The untreated takes of 'Crash Landing' that have surfaced on bootlegs reveal that Hendrix originally recorded the tune with drums, bass and organ, and that the original tempo was a touch slower. In a considered arrangement, the organ contributes effective chordal support while bass and drums concentrate on nailing their parts. It is a considerably more pre-planned composition than most that Hendrix was attempting around this time. The song's introduction and verse are underpinned by some effective, melodic slide-guitar playing (shades of Muddy Waters) followed by a riff not unlike that of 'Gypsy Eyes' but considerably simpler and more down-home. There is a sense of movement that gives the feeling of a story being told to a travelling companion – the imitation of trains, cars and planes in American popular song has a long and illustrious history – and the simple guitar riff provides a strong counterpoint to the bluesy but fragile melody line. On the bootleg versions there are no guitar overdubs, and this sparseness contributes to the rather desolate mood of the piece. The form is not quite right – there is an inconclusive and somewhat repetitive ending over a tumbling guitar and bass riff – but most of it holds up extremely well as Hendrix incorporates some judicious pauses and breaks and develops a very strong sense of narrative, pouring out his plaint to Devon Wilson. She is clearly the song's subject. Hendrix uses the image of a dagger, for example, one that would recur the following year in 'Dolly Dagger', which was specifically dedicated to her, although that song would be cast in a much more upbeat and humorous shape.

What Alan Douglas brought to this piece – apart from wiping the perfectly adequate backing tracks – was some white-hot guitar playing from Hendrix, especially during the flown-in solo, which is bursting with frustration, anger and despair, a perfect accompaniment to the desolation of the lyrics. Only the final "bang bang – shoot shoot" soul routine wears thin as the song comes to an end. Apart from that blemish, this is one of the more impressive of Hendrix's later songs, albeit one he never developed further, probably because he cannibalised it for a later composition, 'Freedom'. That same evening, April 24th, Hendrix pressed on with further attempts at an acceptable master for 'Bleeding Heart', plus a blues jam called 'Hey Country Boy', other jams that later picked up titles (including 'Drone Blues', which is no such thing), and an embryonic version of 'Night Bird Flying' (also known at this stage as 'Night Messenger') using the words from the still-incomplete ballad 'Ships Passing In The Night'.

All of this recording was done largely in the absence of Mitchell and Redding and from April 11th was fitted around the demands of the latest Experience tour of North America. This time the tour lasted just two months, with occasional days off, so the pace was not quite so killing as that of 1968. Supported by Redding's band Fat Mattress for the first ten days – Hendrix apparently referred to them dismissively as Thin Pillow[11] – the Experience enjoyed good receptions in Raleigh, North Carolina, and Philadelphia, PA, before spending a week in New York City for recording and rehearsals, the latter in an attempt to pull the act into sharper focus.

Around the same time Hendrix wrote a letter of apology to the two other members of the Experience. Redding was touched. "Though he often seemed aloof and spaced out, Jimi was, as the letter showed, acutely sensitive to what was going on around him," the bassist said later. "[He] felt strong affection for me and Mitch as fellow musicians, and lived for the music we made. ... Deep

inside he may have felt that as our lives became more and more fraught, the music had to be that much better to compensate. The pressure from outside was enormous, but maybe Jimi felt his own internal pressure most – pressure to innovate, to produce more and more brilliant music every time we went into the studio, to perfect everything we did. ... It's an old story; the agents, managers, promoters always want to preserve a successful format, while the artist needs to move on, fearing always that their creativity – the source of everything – will dry up."[12]

"A star, a soloist, gathers some guys around and they groove together. Maybe they exist for that one album, or go on for a year — but they don't stretch it out once it starts losing the sheer exuberance of jamming together."

Jimi Hendrix, thinking about jazz ideas in rock

This intuitive feeling for what Hendrix was experiencing is to some extent backed up by the guitarist's own statements in a series of interviews that spring, eventually published in one long article in *Beat Instrumental* in June 1969. "For three years," Hendrix claimed, "we've been working non-stop. That is a lot of physical and emotional strain. You go somewhere and the show is a bit under what it should be and you are told you are slipping ... but it is the strain. It is the strain of the moral obligation to keep going even when you don't feel that you can manage even one more show. Maybe I'll never get to take that break; all I know is that I'm thinking about it most of the time now, and that doesn't help create the right mood."

Hendrix was quick to reassure the magazine's readers that the Experience was holding up under this strain – in fact it wasn't – and that he was close to Mitchell and Redding. "It's like being married, with me and Mitch and Noel. Real happily married when we get our thing going without a single hang-up." Maybe the tag at the end of this sentence betrayed the truth of the matter, for the times when the trio got their "thing going without a single hang-up" were becoming exceedingly rare now. In the same interview he gave a clue about his current thinking on the functions of a group, comparing how he'd like to operate with the way jazz groups worked. "They get together for some jamming. That's great. No hang-ups. This has been happening on the jazz scene for years now. A star, a soloist, gathers some guys around and they groove together. Maybe the group only exists for that one album, maybe they go on for a year or so together – but they don't stretch it out once it has started losing the sheer exuberance of jamming together. Now it's happening on the pop side of things this can only be good."[13] All this is uncannily close to the career path Hendrix would take during the next nine months or so.

On-stage, the repertoire was still for the most part rooted in music from 1967 and 1968. Hendrix had even taken to playing 'Stone Free' live, perhaps because he was still thinking of making it the next single, though that idea evaporated over the summer. The only music not sourced from the first three albums and attendant singles was 'Getting My Heart Back Together'. This was a blues that hardly needed a translator for the audience in 1969, perhaps the peak year in America for the popularity of blues-derived pop music – from Creedence Clearwater Revival to Canned Heat.

On April 18th in Memphis, Tennessee, Hendrix met up again with Billy Cox: he'd asked the bassist to come over from Nashville to see him. During a private talk at Hendrix's hotel after the gig, Cox agreed to join Hendrix in whatever group he might be setting up. Cox went back to Nashville and waited for the call. With this private piece of business out of the way, Hendrix continued with the tour as the Experience played Houston and Dallas – despite difficult personal conditions they responded with some fiery group performances – before coming back to New York on April 21st. With Mitchell and Redding flying direct to Los Angeles for a short break prior to the LA Forum concert on the 26th, Hendrix went back into the Record Plant for the sessions already detailed. Cox, duly summoned, arrived in town the same day and immediately went to work with Hendrix, although nothing official was announced or arranged. Things were left casual and open during the three days of activity at the Record Plant.

Back in Los Angeles in time for the big show at the Forum, Hendrix and the Experience, now supported by Chicago and Cat Mother, were ready to make the maximum impression on an enthusiastic audience. As so often there was a troubled atmosphere in the arena reflecting the turmoil that continued to dominate America's social and political life: here it was exacerbated by the security personnel's reaction to provocation from unruly elements in the crowd. The entire 90-minute set was recorded in excellent sound; it has often appeared on bootlegs and (almost completely) on the official 1990 box-set *Lifelines*. A single track, 'I Don't Live Today', was on the 2000 *Jimi Hendrix Experience* box; it was this tune, the third item of a long set, that the band played immediately after the worst of the crowd trouble. It is predictably fierce and a little frayed around the edges, Hendrix pushing his guitar statement past sustain and feedback into occasionally blatant screeches of protest. The tapes of the concert also reveal Hendrix to be a consummate master when dealing with a difficult audience. Through verbal humour, cutting observations and common sense at the microphone, he repeatedly defuses a situation where more heavy-handed methods (like those tried by a clearly pissed-off Noel Redding) would only make things worse.

The Experience had opened with a 17-minute version of 'Tax Free' that included a long Mitchell drum solo: he was now well attuned to the double-bass-drum kit that had become his standard equipment since the end of the previous year. 'Tax Free' was followed by a happy-sounding but hardly inspired 'Foxy Lady'. In an effort to settle down the crowd once more and get the set back on balance, Hendrix called for 'Red House'. During an eleven-minute version he and the band maintain an iron grip on the crowd with a quietly spellbinding slow blues that builds inexorably to a fitting climax. The band had played the tune hundreds of times live in its three years of existence, and it was usually the tempo and mood that dictated whether it would be an exceptional or merely ordinary soul-drenching on any particular evening. On this evening the super-slow tempo gave the Experience the room to expand and relax into a masterful blues statement.

Even when Hendrix kicks in with his solo on the double-tempo section nothing is too hurried or too muddled: it all fits together precisely and with the utmost emotional impact. Hendrix's unaccompanied wah-wah guitar passage is a master-stroke, even more so when one considers that this entirely intimate instrumental statement was being made in front of thousands of people in a packed arena. His call-and-response patterns between voice and guitar in the final verse show just how remarkably independent his playing and vocalising could be – more impressively than virtually any other musician at the time. At no point is the fluidity and logic of his guitar playing interrupted by what he is singing, despite his occasional inability to remember his own lyrics. And it is difficult not to contrast Redding's excellent

and imaginatively varied bass playing here – including a deftly-played walking pattern towards the end of the long guitar solo – with the basic bottom-end playing that would be delivered later by Billy Cox on his accession to the trio.

Unfortunately the band do not sustain this high. A loose and rambling 'Spanish Castle Magic', overlong at more than 11 minutes, catches the guitarist in an off-hand mood. Hendrix delivers a long and relatively uneventful solo guitar passage that is an embryonic version of the set pieces he would successfully negotiate for concerts that summer and autumn, but at this point it has little shape or impetus. Part of the problem is pacing. The consequence of Hendrix's concern to keep up the momentum means that he gives himself too much to do at once, rather than finding a mood and developing it in a more organic way. 'Star Spangled Banner', a tune he played all through the tour, is delivered solo. He plays a verse largely unmodified before introducing the overtones and feedback that would create a larger context for the piece and soon make him one of the talking points of the year. Quite short compared to later versions, 'Banner' is segued into 'Purple Haze', which is played hard, with Mitchell launching an all-out attack to match Hendrix's own fire.

With the end now in sight, the group bludgeons through another 'Voodoo Child (Slight Return)' and 'Sunshine Of Your Love', giving a strong sense that they simply want to get off the stage in one piece before more trouble breaks out. Many commentators have suggested that this concert was well below par even for the standards of the 1969 tour, but it has its share of highlights and also reveals – in its complete form – just how professional the group could still be when they had to nurse their way through a show under duress. The following night, in Oakland, they played with a carefree attitude engendered by a happy crowd and indulged in some on-stage jamming with friends, including Jefferson Airplane's bassist Jack Casady.

"I didn't want to get into any of the politics. I had enough pressure on my mind just trying to play and remember all of this new music."

Billy Cox, bassist, ready to replace Noel Redding

The Experience were pleased to have escaped one potential disaster and moved into May with a night in Detroit on the 2nd, another engagement surrounded by tension and private angst. This time it was brought to the surface by Hendrix, who refused to fly to Detroit, insisting he would not play the gig and instead would stay in New York. Only the deft footwork of Bob Levine from Mike Jeffery's office ensured that Hendrix arrived in time to play the concert as planned. When Hendrix did at last turn up he found the mood on the ground to be deadly. As John McDermott described it, "His presence did little to improve the poisonous atmosphere backstage. Mitch, Noel and Jimi wouldn't talk to one another, not even to devise a set-list for the evening's performance."[14] Such unprofessional behaviour from Hendrix – for whatever reason he might give – was guaranteed to send Redding into a fury and kill the group's cohesion for the evening. It was this type of division, sparked by the willingness of Redding and Mitchell to fight their own corner at all times, that increasingly weighed down Hendrix as his own personal insecurities and needs intensified. Following the shambolic gig in Detroit, made worse for the musicians as the stoned audience thoroughly enjoyed it, they flew up to Canada the next day hoping that the worst was behind them. Unfortunately, the worst that this particular tour had to offer was just about to arrive. At Toronto airport the group were subjected to a customs search, a procedure with which they were by now all too familiar. Usually they managed to clear customs, because no matter how many drugs the entourage used from day to day and however careless or forgetful Hendrix was about such things, the tour managers always made sure that the group was clean when moving across borders. This time, however, Hendrix was found to be in possession of small stashes of marijuana and heroin, discovered along with other belongings in his flight bag.

This was something too hare-brained, even for Hendrix. His arrest, bail and the subsequent hearing on May 5th have all been related at length in previous Hendrix biographies, and a book about the music is not the place to pore over the fine detail of the entire incident. But many felt at the time and subsequently that the drugs were probably planted. Redding said as much in his book and Mitchell was equally sure that Hendrix did not try to smuggle drugs. "The Toronto bust didn't come as a big surprise," wrote Mitchell, "especially … as we felt that the thing had been set up by the Americans, for whatever reason."[15]

The incident plunged Hendrix into increased uncertainty. On top of all the other doubts and pressures of his life at this time, it was a major factor in determining his behaviour for the rest of the year. After the arraignment of May 5th Hendrix would have to wait until December that year before the case would come to trial and be dismissed. These were six months of real worry about his immediate personal future. Hendrix played the Toronto concert on bail with a police presence in the auditorium – and slipped admonitory lyrics from 'Crash Landing' into that night's rendition of 'Room Full Of Mirrors' – but at least this fulfilled the demands of his bail-bond and he was allowed to continue working. With occasional days off, the tour continued to zigzag across the US during May, including dates in North Carolina, Virginia, Alabama and Rhode Island.

"We remembered patterns, not notes. A lot of times we would come up with a pattern that was four bars long, eight bars or even sixteen bars."

Billy Cox, on new musical methods

Fortunately for his state of mind, during days off Hendrix could continue to record jams and workouts at the Record Plant in New York City. On May 6th he and Billy Cox worked through some new material and engaged in some low-key jamming. Among the unreleased rehearsals of new songs recorded that night were the first attempt at 'Straight Ahead' (at that point incomplete and called 'Hello My Friend'), 'Earth Blues' (now moving from under the shadow of 'Ships Passing In The Night') and a tune that remained undeveloped, 'Winter Blues'. Cox's position in the Hendrix set-up was still equivocal, to say the least. He had been brought in by Hendrix ostensibly to jam, just like the many other musicians Hendrix ushered into the studio. Privately, Cox was being lined up as Redding's replacement and was suddenly having to deal with high-power politics at the top end of the rock business. Cox said later that Hendrix told him not to hang out at Mike Jeffery's office in New York. "Honestly, I didn't want to get into any of the politics," Cox recalled to John McDermott. "I had enough pressure on my mind just trying to play and remember all of this new music. I wasn't doing any gigs. We would do some jamming at the Scene and a few other clubs, but that was it."[16]

"When I arrived in New York," Cox continued, "Jimi sat me down and admitted that his creativity had drawn dry. He just felt that he couldn't think of anything new. … I guess he thought of me, because even in the early days we had always been able to make up stuff. … Jimi must have felt that I could help him pull all the pieces of ideas that he had together into something as good as those three albums he had released."[17] The pair quickly established during Cox's first days in New York that they could still hit it off musically and work easily together. Their earlier friendship also allowed them to cut through all the formal business about 'star' and 'unknown' that might have rattled a stranger. For his entire professional life Hendrix was extremely sensitive towards the musicians he worked with, often absorbing their techniques and approaches unawares and re-using them to positive effect in another setting or a different way. Mitchell for example had had an enormous impact on him in 1966. The drummer's freedom and quick response to Hendrix's smallest musical nuance not only allowed him enormous flexibility in his choice of notes but also spurred him on to explore new areas of sound and rhythm. With Cox, Hendrix was looking for the anchor-like bass end that he felt he needed. He was happy to develop lines and patterns with Cox that the bassist could reiterate endlessly during long solos or extended workouts so that he and Mitchell might cut loose. This different angle quickly affected Hendrix's attitude to what he wanted out of a song and how he would shape a performance.

The change came most obviously in the way Hendrix visualised the character and development of a piece, especially its form and overall arrangement. With the original Experience, much of the excitement and innovation came from setting up contrasts and opposites that brought each element into sharp relief. On the Experience's most successful recordings – as opposed to the outstanding jams with an augmented band such as those on *Electric Ladyland* – Chas Chandler had helped shape the material, even if only by a process of editing and simplification. This was, after all, the key factor in Miles Davis's phenomenal success in the studio during 1969 and '70 when he and Teo Macero worked together to redefine what could be done with amplified instrumental music. Davis and Macero always isolated the most telling elements in a composition or a performance and highlighted them in ways that made them a revelation to the listener. Chandler, in his own way, had served a similar function for Hendrix until his departure from the team. Without him, Hendrix soon ran out of steam, not so much in his ideas for songs and lyrics but in the process needed to finish those ideas successfully and to a high level of perfection.

With Cox, Hendrix was looking for a new method of bringing his ideas to fruition. It would involve him in the extensive use of riffs and patterns at the expense of the chordal building-blocks that he'd used so successfully from 1966 to '68 but with which he was now disillusioned. As with most changes of process, there were gains and losses. "We played better with each other," Cox emphasised. "Not necessarily note for note, but pattern for pattern. We remembered patterns, not notes. A lot of times we would come up with a pattern that was four bars long, eight bars or even sixteen bars – all even. Other times, Jimi would come up with patterns which were seven bars, nine bars, or thirteen bars, which was weird."[18] This meant the music was driven largely by the marking of time and by following note patterns – known as 'parts' in compositional terms – rather than harmonically fleshing out a basic structure into a fully grown form. So much of Hendrix's later tunes was underpinned by a series of consecutive lines rather than a set of contrasting colours. In this way the music's character was changed fundamentally, although it is unlikely that anyone involved was aware of this before it happened. It was more instinctive than that. It was something the musicians just grew into. This is perhaps difficult to trace conclusively in Hendrix's music because, contrary to the normal perception of the way his muse waxed and waned, he had in fact by May 1969 outlined if not completed the composition of the majority of his most memorable songs. Many of the pieces he would spend months revising and polishing in the studio during 1970 had first been devised and at least given a try-out more than a year earlier.

The tunes conceived and brought to a performable completion after Cox's arrival and integration into Hendrix's working unit are strikingly different in character to those from before. Just as Hendrix's early Experience recordings delivered a new idea of what guitar-driven pop music could be, his attempt to find a new method to construct his ideas – incorporating the riff style of soul, the simplicity of R&B and blues, and the flexibility of form delivered by jazz – would open up a direction for countless other musicians, both black and white, who wanted to make fresh combinations and fusions of the elements of various musical genres. Sadly, Hendrix himself would not see this transitional phase of his music through to its end.

Meanwhile, there was jamming to do and a tour to finish. Just one day after the recorded rehearsal with Billy Cox, Hendrix pulled in a collection of stars from his usual hangout at the Scene club and took them to the Record Plant for a jam. This night it was the turn of Stephen Stills, Johnny Winter and Dallas Taylor, drummer with Crosby Stills Nash & Young. Hendrix and Stills had a mutual admiration for one another that went back a considerable time; Hendrix and Winter were familiar with each other from Scene jams dating back to the previous summer. Winter valued the new experience of jamming and recording with Hendrix. "I think he had time booked at the Record Plant every

In tune with himself? Jimi backstage at the Newport festival, Northridge, Los Angeles, June 20th 1969.

and he knew all those guys. That's what he was, really: a great electric blues player. He just stretched it out. He had more chords, he didn't stick to just a three-chord thing, but his playing was all blues. He had so much feeling, and he expanded it with electronics. ... I get all goofed up when I start using that stuff, but Jimi would hook up all these different things together and know how to work them."[21]

Winter was aware of the turmoil surrounding Hendrix at the time and saw him as a man under pressure – some of it unavoidable, some of it self-inflicted. "You see, black people often made Jimi feel strange – many of them felt that while he was playing with these young British musicians, he should have been devoting himself to Black Power and his people. ... He said I should stick with the blues, and not feel weird because I was white. He told me, 'You got it. You don't have to change anything; just keep doing what you're doing.' This was strange coming from Jimi, because if he'd taken his own advice, he'd have been so much better off. The white guys and managers would say, 'Don't play with these niggers, man; the 14-year-old kids can't relate to all that space stuff.' ... And the black guys would tell him he was selling out to whitey. Jimi was a sensitive person, plus he was pretty loaded all the time, and he didn't know what to do."[22]

In the absence of a clear sense of direction, Hendrix continued with the holding pattern he'd established. He waited for the latest tour to end so that he could take a break and do some solid thinking among friends. For most of his career he had instinctively shied away from business matters and looked for fulfilment mainly from his music. This was intensified now. "There was a time when I worried about the money," he told Beat Instrumental. "I was worried

damn night, and he'd get different people different nights: when the Scene would close down they'd go over to the Record Plant and put down jams. Then he'd listen to them the next day, when he'd be straighter, and hopefully get ideas from them. ... There was one Guitar Slim tune called 'The Things I Used To Do' where I played slide and Jimi played and sang. As far as I can remember that was the only song we did."[19] The musicians did indeed attempt four takes of Guitar Slim's old classic, two of them complete and featuring Winter on slide guitar. There was also a theme-less instrumental jam lasting some 12 minutes that at one point used the chords of 'Earth Blues' and at another the sequence from 'Driving South'. At the time of writing this material is only available on bootlegs, apart from one version of 'The Things I Used To Do' that turned up on the 1990 box-set Lifelines. Winter felt the jam was relaxed and friendly and thought their two styles meshed well. "Jimi really loved the blues, the real thing, though that wasn't what he wanted to play,"[20] he told one interviewer. Winter added, "He could play good straight blues,

about whether I was getting all I was entitled to and so on ... but money doesn't affect me right now. ... Music is what matters; I'd rather talk about that subject than any other. Well, nearly any other – 'cept I keep on saying that sex is the biggest motivating thing in the world and it's behind the music, too. I know I have enough money but if I had it all I'd still want to get music across to anybody who wanted to listen. I get my biggest kicks out of music; sometimes it is like a fantastic personal release."[23]

Jamming continued at the Record Plant for the next few nights with an array of musicians including pianist Sharon Lane, organist Larry Young and percussionist Juma Sultan along with Billy Cox. Cox claimed that Lane, a friend of his, was overawed by the occasion to the point where she did not do herself justice. The small amount of officially-released Hendrix material that features her piano playing supports this view. Some of the jams were released after Hendrix's death, mostly in edited form. One long one is based on an old blues riff first made famous in the 1930s by Duke Ellington in his tune 'Dooji

Wooji', although Ellington's musicians made a great deal more of the relative minor than do Hendrix's jamming colleagues. It was edited by various hands into two different pieces, 'Jam 292' (from the name assigned on the tape box) and 'Jelly 292'. None of it amounts to anything Hendrix would ever have wanted his public to hear, although the musicians mostly enjoy themselves. The problem with these jams is that the musicians are just waiting for Hendrix to lead, while he is hoping that they will grab the session by the scruff of its neck and make something happen for him to latch on to.

The best of these sessions is a jam with Larry Young, imaginatively titled 'Young/Hendrix' later by Alan Douglas, usually credited to May 14th but it could be from February 11th. The other two musicians, on bass and drums, for the most part keep out of the way, although the bassist is responsive to Hendrix's rhythmic ideas and is agile around his instrument, suggesting that it may be Billy Rich. Larry Young, a well-schooled musician from the jazz side of the fence, has no fear or awe of Hendrix and happily feeds him ideas during what is a fast jam on a single drone chord – very much de rigueur for the time. While it is a good deal more interesting than the bulk of Hendrix's mid-'69 jams with rock players, it's still more a record of a private event than anything being played for an intended audience.

A fascinating contrast to this largely directionless jamming came in the session Young cut with drummer Tony Williams and guitarist John McLaughlin at Olmstead studio just 12 days later. The date would provide the music for *Emergency!*, the first album from Williams's band Lifetime. The record is dedicated to the extensive improvisatory exploration of what can be achieved with a guitar-organ-drums power trio.

The pacing and adroit structures allow each musician in Williams's band to play out vast and impassioned dramas with great intensity and imagination. Given the state of Hendrix's life and his parlous musical position, Young stuck with Williams's band at the time. The music bears out his decision: Williams was leading the pack when it came to combining jazz techniques with rock ideas about sound and form – he was even ahead of Miles Davis and Hendrix himself. Meanwhile, another Hendrix jam from this period, once more with Stephen Stills and Dallas Taylor, consisted of some inconclusive fun that included tentative (and fragmentary) try-outs of some new Hendrix songs, 'Valleys Of Neptune' – a fast rocker with elements of 'Freedom' and 'Roomful Of Mirrors' – and the ballad 'Send My Love To Linda'.

The Experience tour continued through North America as May progressed, now with support bands Cat Mother and The Buddy Miles Express. No one in the band remembered the $100,000-grossing May 18th Madison Square Garden performance as a good one, partly because the arena was set up for boxing and wrestling matches. The performers had to survive a walk through the crowd to get to the central stage and the cavernous structure was an acoustic disaster. This was the only New York concert for the Experience on that spring tour and proved to be the end not only of the original band's ties to the city but also of Hendrix's increasingly long-distance relationship with Kathy Etchingham.

Etchingham was still staying in Hendrix's hotel suite but had seen him only sporadically as he moved between tour and recording commitments. Etchingham had travelled in the limousine with the band, but things went wrong once they arrived at the venue. The crowds had broken through the barriers outside and the security people were punchy. "I was hanging onto Mitch and Noel's arms for dear life, genuinely frightened by the numbers of people pressing in on us," she wrote later. "As we neared the gates the police charged forward and one of them hit me in the stomach with his baton, winding me and making me let go of Mitch and Noel who were then whisked inside, leaving me behind in the crowd as the gates slammed in my face."[24]

Fighting her way through, she caught a taxi back to the hotel. By the following evening she had moved out to stay with friends for a few days before catching a flight back over the Atlantic. She and Hendrix maintained contact by phone, but the break proved decisive.

In the four days left in New York before the Experience flew out to begin the West Coast section of their tour, Hendrix met some new people who would have a strong effect on the rest of his career and his subsequent legacy. Through Devon Wilson he met Stella Douglas at her New York clothes boutique. Once back in New York later in the year he met Stella's husband Alan, a man who soon became involved with Hendrix in the recording studio.

During these four days in New York Hendrix recorded another rather uninspired jam with Cox, Buddy Miles and Devon Wilson on the chords of 'Earth Blues' and 'Message To Love'. He also spent the entire evening of the 21st partying in the studio with Cox and Miles, ostensibly to advance the work on 'Earth Blues', 'Bleeding Heart' and 'Hear My Train A'Comin''. A loose version of 'Villanova Junction' was committed to tape but, along with the rest of the evening's music, was shelved and forgotten until after Hendrix's death.

Dave Ragno, the engineer that night, told John McDermott: "If Devon wasn't trying to drive him crazy, then someone else would come into the control room chugging a bottle of tequila and portioning out cocaine to anybody who wanted it. The session was just a big party. Some of the things that went down on tape were nice, but they weren't serious. They weren't the

"I think Hendrix had time booked at the Record Plant every damn night, and he'd get different people along different nights to jam."

Johnny Winter, guitarist

things he really wanted to do."[25] One wonders why Hendrix bothered hiring a recording studio at all for an evening like this rather than simply going down to a club and blowing all his blues away there. At least posterity would then have had less of a chance of catching up with him. As it was, the version of 'Bleeding Heart' was later issued on the 1994 compilation *Blues* and 'Hear My Train A'Comin'' turned up on bootlegs. This was the last gasp of the seemingly never-ending studio party that constituted Jimi Hendrix recording sessions at the time, a final session before the end of the US tour and the unacknowledged but effective disbandment of the original Jimi Hendrix Experience. The other two members had not made a session with their guitarist for six weeks.

The band proved they were still capable of good things on May 24th in San Diego at a concert professionally recorded for potential album release. They stuck to the staple concert fare: 'Hey Joe', 'Fire', 'I Don't Live Today', 'Spanish Castle Magic', 'Star Spangled Banner', 'Foxy Lady', 'Purple Haze', 'Red House' and 'Voodoo Child (Slight Return)'. But Hendrix, Redding and Mitchell filled the vast majority of the music with a fire and spirit that had become increasingly rare on this tour. Although the apparently unavoidable tuning problems affected some pieces and made them unsuitable for release at the time, there was a poised and passionate 'Red House' (released as early as 1972 on *Hendrix In The West*), a thundering 'Voodoo Child (Slight Return)' and a crazy, over-fast but very exciting 'I Don't Live Today'. Virtually the entire set was eventually released in 1991 on the four-CD set *Stages*, prepared by Alan Douglas. The band played a similarly upbeat set the following night in San José before flying off to Hawaii for three nights of concerts. According to most reports, the Hawaii concerts veered wildly from disastrous to the routine. Hendrix walked off stage on the first night complaining about too much amplifier noise, to the unconcealed disgust of Redding and Mitchell who were compelled to follow him off. By then the band were tired and in need of a break, from each other as much as from touring. They flew out of Hawaii on the second day of June – Redding and Mitchell to London via Los Angeles, Hendrix to LA for a week's rest – and looked forward to a break that would last until the 20th when they would reconvene for the Newport Pop Festival at the San Fernando Valley State College in Northridge, Los Angeles.

During his week off, Hendrix continued to hang out with friends and jam. Drummer Dallas Taylor recalled one session in early summer '69 at Stephen Stills's house. "I saw Hendrix sitting on one of Stephen's amps, playing his ass off, while Buddy Miles was literally pounding the shit out of my drums. It was very loud and hurt my ears. ... [Hendrix] always had a guitar in his hands – unless he was getting high or getting laid. Jimi stopped playing when we walked into the room. There was a big pile of cocaine on a mirror sitting on top of the B-3 organ and we all gathered around and took turns snorting from it. 'So, you guys gigging yet?' Jimi asked Stephen. *Snort.* 'Nah, we're still working shit out. We can't find a bass player,' Stephen said. *Sniff.* 'Yeah,' said Jimi, 'that's the story of my life. There's a definite shortage of bass players.' *Snort.* ... We played off and on that night. Mostly we attended to the coke on the B-3. But I do have tapes."[26]

During his stay in Los Angeles Hendrix also jammed in his hotel room with Taj Mahal, in front of the usual roomful of friends and hangers-on. Hendrix passed his own cassette recording of this event to Mitchell. Unfortunately, by his own admission Hendrix was stoned during the jam, saying to Taj Mahal: "I'm sorry I goofed up by taking all these fucking drugs."[27] Clearly it was a friendly but not earth-shattering meeting, providing a quiet footnote to whatever else was going down at the time.

For the first time since December 1968 Hendrix spent a month outside the recording studio, from early June to early July, although work was still being done on his music. In mid June engineer Eddie Kramer spent three days running through the accumulation of professionally recorded concerts from the winter and spring 1969 tour. He concentrated on three concerts in particular: the February 24th London Albert Hall date, the April 26th LA Forum, and May 24th San Diego Sports Arena. Kramer compiled rough mixes of an album's worth of material – including, strangely enough, the rushed and decidedly rough LA version of 'I Don't Live Today' – and delivered them to Mike Jeffery by June 15th for consideration as the long-planned live Experience LP. But again the option of releasing new material was allowed to slip. This live album was shelved in favour of Warner/Reprise's version of the *Smash Hits* compilation that Track Records had released in the UK in April 1968. It proved to be a bestseller. After Hendrix's death, Kramer's live LP selection was dusted down and, with alterations to include some 1970s performances (from Berkeley and the Isle of Wight), was released in 1972 as *Hendrix In The West*. It was regarded at the time as one of the better posthumous releases from the Hendrix tape archives.

Meanwhile, Hendrix talked in further interviews about his immediate plans for albums. In conversation with Richie Yorke for the *Toronto Globe & Mail* he claimed: "My next album, coming out in late summer, will be called *Shine On Earth, Shine On*, or maybe *Gypsy Sun*. There might also be a couple of other albums in between. A live album which we cut at the Royal Albert Hall in London, and a *Smash Hits* thing. But I have no control over those. All I know is that I'm working on my next album for summer release."[28] Indicative of his state of mind is the fact that the only album of those mentioned that would eventually be released was the *Smash Hits* package, the one over which he had no direct control.

The Newport Pop Festival should have been a highlight. Hendrix was appearing on a bill packed with talent, including Joe Cocker, Buddy Miles,

Taj Mahal, Eric Burdon, Albert King, and Tracy Nelson. The group had been apart for a couple of weeks and, having now spent a little relaxation time together and talked about the future, were more at ease with each other. Hendrix went so far as to tell Mitchell and Redding that, whatever other projects he might get involved in, the Experience would always come back together. Yet Redding, at least, was aware that no such promises could be offered: in Los Angeles he had seen more evidence of the wear and tear of Hendrix's lifestyle. "He was just this side of screaming, but he didn't have the

"They fed off his celebrity and he fed off the drugs they provided."

Noel Redding, on Jimi's circle of hangers-on

nerve to tell [the hangers-on] to fuck off. [They] cluttered up his living space and ran up bills on his room account. Mitch and I would occasionally clear them out, but the hordes soon regrouped. In a way, Jimi's ego fed off the attention, but in the end he was forced to become 'Jimi Hendrix', round-the-clock host to parasites. They fed off his celebrity and he fed off the drugs they provided."[29]

These were not the only people who were determined to capitalise on Hendrix's persona and position. At Newport, soon after arriving by helicopter, the band's mood was smashed by events in their caravan. Wandering around the site for a little, Redding returned to the caravan only to find Hendrix being intimidated by a group of "eight black heavies who dwarfed Jimi. He looked petrified and I was chilled to the bone by his appearance. I don't know what they were on about, but Jimi looked so relieved to see me it was pathetic. I told them to get the fuck out of our dressing room ... . Jimi wasn't politically active and would only question things he read about if he was stuck on a plane and there was nothing else to do. Probably saved himself a lot of aggravation. ... If the management didn't concern itself with Jimi's personal happiness, neither did those who hovered round him. They only worried that someone else was sucking his blood and they wouldn't get their cut."[30]

Needless to say, the Newport appearance suffered from the upset Hendrix had been forced to endure and he played a substandard set of around an hour in front of an unruly audience before walking off, though not before declaring 'Voodoo Child (Slight Return)' to be "a black militant song", no doubt pleasing the militants now in the audience who had intimidated him before the show. Mitchell regarded it as "a terrible performance. Absolutely awful. We were devastated, it was one of the worst gigs we ever played".[31] Once more the two embarrassed musicians had to leave the stage after their guitarist's rapid departure. Hendrix quickly regretted his actions and successfully pressed for a spot on the festival's programme two days later with a hastily convened scratch band, the other two members of the band having no heart for it any more. The situation was now beyond desperate.

The last show of the tour was in Denver on June 29th. Remarkably, given the Newport debacle, the Experience returned to form, but that was overshadowed by a ragingly enthusiastic crowd of thousands who came close to crushing the band members to death at the end of their set as they tried to leave a stadium choked by police tear gas.

This was the exact opposite of the reasons that Hendrix had for getting into the music business in the first place. It was great to be popular, for sure, but no one was listening and everyone seemed high on spectacle and nothing else. They were risking bodily harm simply to play, and if the only reason to keep on playing was to make money for someone else or be a rallying point for causes in which they had little or no involvement, why bother? Maybe it was time to call a halt and have a re-think. Trouble was, where, how and with whom? No one knew if it was possible for Hendrix in his current state of mind to get the right answers to these questions.

all systems stop

The Denver show of June 29th 1969 proved to be the last ever played by The Jimi Hendrix Experience. Noel Redding was incensed when a reporter asked why he was there, telling the bassist that Hendrix had announced to the press in a mid-June interview in Los Angeles that he was to be replaced by Billy Cox.[1] Redding was hurt by these tactics to replace him and flew back to London the next day, announcing that he was quitting the Experience to concentrate on his career with his own band, Fat Mattress.

Hendrix and Mitch Mitchell stayed on in the US for a while longer. Before anyone had time to re-think their lives, news broke that Brian Jones had been found dead in the swimming pool of his Sussex home. Hendrix and Jones had not seen much of each other for some time, but this dreadful event hit Hendrix hard. Jones's other close friends were shocked too; they'd all had a soft spot for this troubled but vulnerable, likeable man. There was nothing Hendrix could do for Jones now, but he could at least learn from what had happened and, in the process, try to pull his own life together. During the following months that is precisely what he attempted to do, but with little lasting success.

Hendrix fulfilled a commitment to appear on the *Johnny Carson* TV show and played 'Lover Man' with Billy Cox on bass and well-known jazz sessionman Ed Shaughnessy on drums. After that he was free to look for ways to expand the working band and accommodate his latest ideas about where he wanted to take his music. Mitchell was going back to London for a holiday and to catch up on his private life, so Hendrix started from scratch. He may have considered the recent example of Blind Faith, the so-called 'first supergroup' announced in May that featured Eric Clapton (ex-Cream), Steve Winwood (ex-Traffic), Rick Grech (ex-Family) and Ginger Baker (ex-Cream). But Hendrix was not looking for an all-star group. He wanted the space to explore his own musicianship and to lead from the front rather than have to surrender his own musical desires to the egos of others. Running a group was different to sitting in and jamming with friends. Unfortunately, while he had a firm grasp on one aspect of that vital difference, he thought that musicians with no significant challenge to offer could still somehow feed his inspiration and thus lighten the creative load. This meant that the idea he had

Gypsy Sun & Rainbows finally hit the stage at Woodstock; Hendrix is pictured with percussionists Jerry Velez (left) and Juma Sultan.

been nurturing for some months of forming a larger group of ever-flexible numbers that would provide a more supportive personal and musical environment was flawed from the beginning. And it would get worse.

Hendrix had tried out a number of keyboard players in Record Plant jams throughout the spring, perhaps because he felt that keyboards would mesh better with his extraordinary guitar playing than an extra guitar. For now he started by trying to find a drummer who would offer him the kind of steady musical support that he knew he could rely on from Buddy Miles. During mid July he auditioned drummers at the Café Au Go Go in New York City, but for one reason or another none was successful. He had also decided not to go for a keyboard player after all, instead opting for guitarist Larry Lee, another friend from his Nashville past. Thus he had twice broken Bob Dylan's golden rule: don't look back. He would get away with it in the case of Billy Cox, but with Lee he was not so fortunate. Unlike Cox, Lee was a musician with no 'listening ear' that would allow him to blend in with what was going on around him. He may have been personally close to Hendrix and provided a reminder of the old times, but his musical horizons had not changed since 1964. This would catch up on all the musicians involved in what Hendrix was now calling Gypsy Sun & Rainbows as rehearsals progressed. To help pull the band together, Hendrix and his management team decided to find a location outside the city where they could enjoy some peace and uninterrupted music-making. Michael Jeffery's team came up with a large house near the upstate New York hamlet of Shokan, about seven miles south-west of the town of Woodstock. It happened to be owned by Albert Grossman, Bob Dylan's manager.

"We were young and just banging away. I wish we had that opportunity today, now I'm really honing my craft as a player."

Jerry Velez, conga player, Gypsy Sun & Rainbows

There seems little chance that this was a coincidence. Hendrix would have been aware of Dylan's retreat to West Saugerties, also near Woodstock, in the second half of 1967, and of The Band renting the famous Big Pink house where the Basement Tapes were made and where The Band wrote all the material for their groundbreaking *Music From Big Pink* album of 1968. Hendrix must have thought that if a relocation had such a beneficial effect on one of his musical heroes – a hero who had been through similar over-exposure in the media and impossible expectations on every level – then it should work for him. Plans were made for Hendrix to spend a good deal of July and August at the Grossman house near Shokan. It was even arranged for engineer Eddie Kramer to drive up with a decent set of recording equipment so that anything Hendrix wanted to tape could be preserved for him to ponder. It took two weeks to set all of this up, during which time an agreement was signed to appear at the nearby Woodstock festival, envisaged as the new group's debut. Hendrix checked out musicians he thought likely to fit into his idea of an expanded band, and then flew out to Morocco for a week's holiday. His companions on this trip were Stella and Alan Douglas and Stella's sister, Colette Mimram, another friend of Hendrix's. This action, along with the shape and identity of the band Hendrix finally assembled in Shokan, soon had alarm bells ringing in Mike Jeffery's head.

Jeffery drove Hendrix up to the house near Shokan. The guitarist was still using his old haphazard methods of finding musicians for the group. Already there were Billy Cox, Larry Lee and a young Latin percussionist, Jerry Velez, whom Hendrix had seen playing in New York and invited along, as well as some other less permanent musicians, including Juma Sultan. Hendrix had met Sultan in New York back in his Blue Flames days, but the percussionist was now part of the musical community around Woodstock and introduced Hendrix to a number of local musicians. He liked what Sultan had to offer, both personally and musically, and invited him to become part of the Gypsy Sun & Rainbows band. In return, Sultan invited Hendrix down to the weekly Sunday jam session on August 10th at the Tinker Street cinema in Woodstock. This was just eight days away from the band's planned debut at the Woodstock festival. An amateur tape of the jam has circulated among collectors and, while it shows that there was a spirit of fun and community, little of any musical worth was played. The occasion is notable only as the first time Hendrix publicly tried out his new Uni-Vibe device, an effects unit that emulated a Hammond organ's rotating-speaker sounds.

Hendrix plunged into long jams and rehearsal sessions with his chosen musicians but quickly realised that it was difficult to hold the group together without a regular drummer. Mindful of the fruitless auditions a few weeks earlier, he called Mitch Mitchell back from England. Mitchell arrived a few days later. By this time Billy Cox was worried about the suitability of guitarist Larry Lee, however much his friendship had meant in the past. Lee had an unusual approach to rhythm and accompaniment. Cox tried to persuade Lee to change his attitude. "I preached to Larry about getting a different guitar but he preferred to play [his Gibson ES-335 guitar]," said Cox, "which was not compatible with where we were musically. Consequently, it did not blend properly. I would tell him that he needed a Stratocaster, but he just didn't listen."[2]

This was not the only problem. Hendrix wanted to teach the band some of his more recent material, hoping that it would emerge reborn in their hands. He also expected that playing with these new, eager players would stimulate his own creativity. Yet he found himself spending more time trying to straighten out basic problems in the ensemble than discovering any new kinds of inspiration. Mitchell turned up in the middle of all this. He'd already met Cox in New York, but the rest were new to him. Lee he recognised as "a guitarist who Jimi had known for years. ... Larry started putting a scarf round his head because he thought that's what hippies did – very strange. A nice man and a more than adequate guitar player, but did Hendrix need a rhythm guitarist? Also around were the two conga players, Jerry Velez ... and Juma Sultan, both good players in their own right but there's always a problem with two or more drummers or percussionists – either it works well or it gets competitive. It's all right having competition if you can count; if you can't you're fucked. They couldn't count. It was a shambles. Apparently they'd been working for about ten days when I got there, but you'd never have known".[3]

Conga player Jerry Velez had some sympathy for Mitchell's position when he spoke about the events years later. "I understand how from his point of view, he came into something, they had a great thing going, and Michael Jeffery wanted things to go along those lines. Jimi wanted to experiment and stretch out, and that's how we got involved. ... Michael is saying, 'Who the hell are these people? Who's this guy, Jerry Velez? I never heard of him.' And Jimi said, 'I like the way he plays and I want him in the band.' He brought in his Army buddy, Billy Cox, and Larry Lee. The musicianship level was not up to Jimi's level. [Mitchell] was walking into a situation with two percussionists, one on either side of him, and he's a busy player. I was young then and I didn't know my ass from a hole in the wall, and I played very busy and Juma was busy. From a musical standpoint, Mitch is probably saying, 'What the hell am I doing here?'"[4] Hendrix was keen to combine the Latin playing of Velez with Sultan's more African-inspired work, but even before Mitchell's arrival it had been too thick a stew, as Velez suggested. "Unfortunately, at that time, we were young and just banging away. I wish we had that opportunity today, now that I'm really honing my craft as a player."[5] Sultan was more circumspect when he recalled the rehearsals, though he did tell author Steven Roby that Hendrix "really didn't want to use Mitch"[6] and that he considered Hendrix's road crew phobic about having "too many blacks around" – surely an odd accusation to make of a road crew dedicated to serving and protecting Jimi Hendrix. Sultan claimed that the band wasn't rehearsed to have "every corner tight" because Hendrix didn't want that. "There was a certain looseness in the band, and a certain looseness was what he wanted."[7] Perhaps, but there is a difference between looseness and sloppiness.

Contrast this to what Santana was achieving at the same time and it suddenly becomes clear just how far this band was from achieving brilliance and sharpness. Too many times in the rehearsal tapes available among collectors the music is aimless and stodgily executed, whether in formal song structures or in jams. Hendrix leads, percussionists flail away and Mitchell tries valiantly to push everyone else along. There are moments of remarkable incompatibility between what Hendrix and Lee are doing with their guitars, moments when Lee seems incapable of reading the style and sound that his leader requires of him.

Alan Douglas knew Hendrix at this time and was soon to work with him in the studio. He felt that Hendrix was trying to strike a balance between broadening his musical base while creating a larger musical ensemble to express his ideas, and the specific need to sustain his popularity. It is a dilemma as old as popular music. "Jimi liked the people, he liked his audience," Douglas asserted. "He liked the feedback off the audience – that was the basic inspiration … and he was a virtuoso. I mean Jimi could do it with a song, could do it with a guitar, and he could do it with his appearance. But musically he needed bigger things; the trio format had run its course for him, I think. At that point he didn't quite know what to do with it or how to get out of it. He didn't know the musicians. He didn't know the business."[8]

So Hendrix prepared for the Woodstock festival with his chosen set of musicians in a house that was close to a large musical community, mostly consisting of ex-New York City musicians looking for a different way and with a huge range of skills across the musical spectrum. He met many other musicians in the area casually both before and after the festival. Some of these had good things to offer, some virtually nothing at all. He enjoyed meeting and hearing avant-garde jazz drummer Barry Altschul, a leading exponent of 'free time', but also came across players like pianist Mike Ephron, a moderate talent at best. Ephron, on electric harpsichord, noodled away one afternoon in September with Hendrix and Sultan: a private (and unauthorised) pressing of tapes from this jam called *This Flyer* appeared in early 1970, to Hendrix's dismay. Saga Records later released more of the same two years after Hendrix's death. The liner notes claimed they were recorded in 1964, to avoid copyright-infringement action. The records preserve for posterity the most arid and worthless musical venture that Hendrix ever had the misfortune to be involved in.

Back at the main event, Hendrix was struggling to get the ensemble up to scratch on repertoire that was unsuited to them. This music had been composed with a power trio in mind as much as three years previously. Congas on 'Foxy Lady' really didn't make a great deal of sense, and Hendrix should have directed his percussionists to sit out altogether on some tunes. But even on the new pieces that evolved to a state of completion at the house, discipline among the ensemble was occasional rather than constant, and proper shades and dynamics in the arrangements and their executions were at a premium. No wonder Mitchell was mostly in a bad mood. He was pretty sure that Hendrix was aware of the group's shortcomings, however much the guitarist wanted to believe in the project he'd started. "I got the feeling," Mitchell confided later in his book, "that Jimi realised it wasn't working and just wanted to get the gig over and start again. We rehearsed at the house …

for about a week or ten days. It was probably the only band I've ever been involved with that simply did not improve over that length of time."[9]

Whether it had improved or not, on August 18th the band still had to deliver the crowning set at the world's most overpopulated rock festival, "Three Days Of Peace And Music" at the Woodstock Music and Arts Fair. After all the politics, various weird scenes involving Mike Jeffery up at the house, and the difficult relationships within the band, Hendrix and his Gypsy Sun & Rainbows mounted the Bethel site's stage at dawn that Monday. They were about to deliver a set that would announce to the unsuspecting and largely exhausted crowd – and later to the world through the film of the event – that The Jimi Hendrix Experience was no more, and that a new Hendrix was imminent. The tired, wet, bedraggled crowd had waited long enough to see him, with many thousands in fact having already started the trek home. Those who stayed received a decidedly mixed and muffled message. The cinema-goers who saw him later in the film were delivered an entirely different message. How did that happen? Put it down to the power of the medium of film and its ability to tell an alternative story, as well as the media myth of Woodstock and the nurturing of the idea of 'the peace generation'. Graham Nash of Crosby Stills Nash & Young was aware of the distorting effect that the Woodstock legend had on their careers. Writing in 1992, he said: "In a way the music festival at Max Yasgur's farm became the sort of myth that was far greater in its impact than the real show was. Yes, hundreds of thousands of people had come to the farm, some interesting music had been made, some reputations had grown larger, but in reality it was miserably wet, muddy and tremendously exciting all at the same time."[10]

Even today, after something like three generations of commercial audio and visual releases of the Woodstock festival appearance by Hendrix, it is only on the bootlegs of the group's set that the entire picture is revealed. This is for a combination of reasons, mostly to do with the fashioning of an event for popular consumption and the preconceptions of what ought to be represented as the Hendrix legacy. So, for example, the two numbers sung by Larry Lee, 'Call Me Mastermind' and 'Gypsy Woman', have yet to appear on

"Musically Hendrix needed bigger things; the trio format had run its course for him."

Alan Douglas, producer

an official release. They were important to Hendrix as representatives of the kind of communal music-making he wanted to bring to the stage and present to his public, showing that he could deliver a satisfying set with different ensembles and under very different musical circumstances to those normally seen in concert. The absence of these songs from all official releases distorts what was being presented that morning. The other prime distortion – a technical problem that comes from recording live as much as anything else – is the balance between the instruments on the issued material. The percussionists tend to be buried in the mix and Larry Lee's guitar is recessed in favour of the band's backbone, Hendrix-Cox-Mitchell. This may have been done for good musical reasons – the trio was the most consistently professional unit in their presentation to the audience that day – but again it provides a false picture of what Hendrix was offering as his preferred music on the day.

Hendrix's own desires are indicated during his high-energy spoken welcome to the crowd and introduction of his band, an introduction that shows just how brilliant and charming an entertainer he could be when the mood took him. After an amusing member-by-member description of the band and the group's name – "call it Gypsy Sun & Rainbows. For short, it's nothing but a band of gypsies" – he gives his standard apology about tuning, rehearsed many times during Experience days, but adds some new thoughts as well. "Oh yeah, give us about a minute and a half to tune up, OK? Like, we only had about two rehearsals, so – uh – it was ... nothing but primary rhythm things, but, I mean, it's the first ray of the new rising sun anyway, so then the message starts from the earth, which is rhythm, right? Can you dig that?"

Hendrix's excited introduction was a jumble of thoughts that spilled all too eagerly from him, but what he said not only described the type of music he was now hoping to present to the still vast crowd, but also indicated the method by which he had attempted to get the band to work together. With the extra percussionists he was trying to bring a heavier emphasis to the crosscurrents of rhythm that had been a great feature of his music since he had met up with Mitchell. From the two extra players he wanted what today would be termed a more ethnic or roots-based foundation for the counter-rhythms and patterns. Not only would this bring a different sound to the rhythm, but it would change the texture and identity of his older music, those hits that he'd long tired of reiterating every night with the Experience. This in turn was a stepping stone, he hoped, to a new edition of Jimi Hendrix.

His references to the rising sun, harking back to last autumn's concept that had failed to materialise on record, would have seemed to him perfectly apt at this point. If Hendrix had been a little more adept at playing the music biz game, and – as Douglas suggested – had a wider and more resourceful pool of musicians from which to draw support and inspiration, then this plan may just have succeeded, and spectacularly. It would then have been possible to sort out the arrangements for each tune (new and old) and develop a formidable unit. As it was, Hendrix verbalised nothing. No one was told when to play and when not to play, with the inevitable result that plenty of inappropriate playing took place. This is especially noticeable in the case of the two percussionists. It is an old saw among musicians that percussionists without a precise brief will play through anything, regardless of how appropriate or inappropriate their contribution may be. They always think a few extra rhythms will help. The opposite is true. A constant thunder of uncoordinated percussion will dissipate the music's impact and prevent it from breathing properly, making it seem to drag along with heavy baggage rather than propelling the sound. A properly gradated percussion ensemble or section is a joy to hear and can add tremendous rhythmic vitality and excitement to a whole range of musical styles and ideas, whether Latin American, Cuban or African. With Hendrix's inability to define roles for his two percussion men, they had to fend for themselves, jockeying for a position in the music. This led to absurdities during the set, as on 'Foxy Lady' where Velez's heavy conga beats throw down a completely different and awkwardly executed rhythmic pulse to the rest of the band, simply because he couldn't think of anything else to do – and no one had told him not to play on that number.

Sometimes the inconsistencies and overlappings in the music are instructive. The long 'Hear My Train A'Comin' contains two burning guitar solos by Hendrix separated by a solo by Lee. Hendrix rarely failed to connect with this blues when playing live, and here he is fluently spectacular, stringing long, arching phrases together as the music pours out of him. (He also repeatedly uses a little guitar phrase when playing rhythm guitar that was soon to become the opening motif for 'Machine Gun'.) When Lee comes in for his relatively short solo – edited out of official releases – he tries very hard to match the emotional input of his leader. It is good blues guitar playing and carries things forward until Hendrix takes over once more with another couple of verses of soloing. Instantly one hears the difference between a good guitarist and a guitarist gifted with the ability to speak directly to his listeners through his instrument. Between Hendrix and us, there is simply no guitar in

the way. With Lee, however, the guitar is a tool that will always separate him from the listener.

The same is true of the other slow blues played that day, 'Red House'. Again, even when merely accompanying his vocals, Hendrix's guitar is like a voice, a commentary, an inspired fellow-traveller. His phrasing is so fleet, so natural and so rhythmically free that it is sometimes easy to forget just how advanced is his blues playing. With Lee contributing rhythm guitar behind him, the gap is evident between Hendrix and ordinary mortals, however talented. Lee's rhythm accompaniment is stodgy and unimaginative – something approaching what one would expect from a blues-band guitarist in a bar. Lee's solo is competent but wholly traditional, his tone classic electric blues, as is his phrasing. Hendrix's accompaniment of Lee is a revelation, because he coaxes, urges and cajoles Lee into playing harder and harder: Hendrix double-times, he plays lines parallel to Cox's bass, he chords and generally runs a commentary alongside his friend. This man really could do anything within the context of this tune and make it right.

By August 1969 Hendrix had for some time been stretching his blues vocabulary considerably beyond the usual pentatonic scales and blues patterns. He was using scales that he had picked up from a variety of sources over the past couple of years, in contrast to what Lee could offer on the same blues changes. Paul Caruso noted this aspect of his friend's developing blues improvisations. "Jimi was actually making up his own language, right on top

"In reality it was miserably wet, muddy and tremendously exciting all at the same time."

Graham Nash, singer, on Woodstock

of the blues. It's more than just the pentatonic scale. All twelve tones were explored within a key, and often in entirely unique ways."[11] This is largely true, but Hendrix's explorations of whatever key he was using in a blues were not systematic. He would employ any piece of musical information he'd picked up that he thought would fit. This meant that often the scales he used were not standard major or minor ones, but adopted modes or altered scales that he'd found would work in a particular blues modulation. He would use these scales more often than not in a melodic way, to construct an arresting new melodic shape rather than to explore any harmonic implications that a new scale offered him.

Hendrix was using the lessons he had absorbed from listening to Ravi Shankar and classical Indian music. Without stopping to learn the hundreds of modes that Indian musicians use, he plucked out the core of Shankar's message – a new and fresh approach to creating song or melody – and applied it to his own melodic sense. This liberated him from following the customary approach in any piece of music. As a supreme melodic inventor on his instrument, he could apply this gift to any musical situation in which he found himself. Caruso again: "He was totally intuitive, self-taught and ear-trained. I watched him practice and he was very physical and fluid in his approach to studying the instrument – if you could even call it studying, as it appeared to be a primitive process, following a code of his own. Yet Jimi was an amazingly sophisticated musician."[12] This sophistication just showed itself in different, unschooled ways. This is precisely why so many of the forward-thinking jazz musicians of the day, the progressives, found Hendrix so inspiring (the jazz conservatives could not get past the surface of the sound). His genius allowed him to escape the rules and still create inspired, fresh music. Perhaps the

Early morning August 18th 1969 (right) as Hendrix appears with his new band at the Woodstock festival.

most successful piece that the Hendrix ensemble played at Woodstock was Mitch Mitchell's 'Beginning', an instrumental in 12/8 time worked up and worked on extensively at the house – and one that had thus grown organically within the group that played it at the festival. The commercial releases of this performance have all been cut, and most are mixed so that all but the Hendrix-Cox-Mitchell trio are significantly below the level of these 'leaders'. Bootleg sources tend to offer a clearer picture, even when the sound quality itself is not so hot. They show, for example, a real and exciting dialogue between Hendrix and Lee both in the opening fast passage and riffs and the pounding second section, where the two really do strike sparks off each other.

There is a palpable air of excitement as the whole band takes off, emphasised by the long percussion interlude that follows, with Mitchell, Velez and Sultan whipping up an incredible storm of poly-rhythms across the slashing beat. Let loose on their own, all three manage a wild sort of discipline that really does seem to take flight. The reintroduction of the guitars and bass brings this instrumental to a heady and thrilling climax where even the poor tuning of Lee (and Cox's earlier mistake of playing the riff a semitone or half-step too high all the way through the first section) is forgotten in the excitement. In its unedited and properly mixed form, this is the finest musical moment from Gypsy Sun & Rainbows.

The two Larry Lee vocal performances 'Master Mind' and 'Gypsy Woman', regularly excluded from commercial releases but available on bootlegs, are fine R&B/soul ballads with sophisticated harmonic construction and presentable melodies, with Lee providing perfectly adequate and in-tune vocals. But the value of these renditions for Hendrix fans is in his accompaniment. As ever, his supporting guitar-playing is tasteful, brilliant and graceful. He was a complete rhythm guitarist, as his playing on these short but entirely presentable numbers proves beyond doubt. This is like a trip down memory lane for Hendrix, taking him back to his R&B days, and he revels in his role here. For this reason alone they should be made available as part of a complete Hendrix-at-Woodstock set.

"Give us about a minute and a half to tune up, OK? Like, we only had about two rehearsals."

Jimi Hendrix, to the crowd at Woodstock

Most discussions of Hendrix's Woodstock set centre on the closing sequence of 'Voodoo Child (Slight Return)', 'Stepping Stone', 'Star Spangled Banner', 'Purple Haze', an untitled instrumental, and 'Villanova Junction'. This is not necessarily due to the playing, which is indisputably great but hardly something new to Hendrix's concert audiences that year. He had been playing variations on this ending sequence since at least the Albert Hall shows in February. The main reason for the emphasis on this part of the Woodstock performance is because part of this sequence was shown in the resulting film. More than half of the pieces had not been released on record and would have been new to those who had not seen the Experience play live earlier in the year. As a result the collective impact of this 30-minute sequence was immense, raising Hendrix to another level of public appreciation. Yet the film version, released in June 1970, did not represent what had originally been played. Nor did the version on the Warner Bros three-LP set of music from Woodstock, released simultaneously with the film. Both were significantly edited in order to 'focus' the music. The film and LPs turned Woodstock into a media event rather than the reproduction of some music played in front of a live audience. While that media event is completely convincing, the unedited version has its own gripping story to tell.

Hendrix is making complex artistic and personal points within the sequence, not just the broadly recognised political and social points that made him every hippie's icon of the day. Hendrix announces 'Voodoo Child (Slight Return)' as "the new American anthem until we get another one together". For some time at concerts he had been regularly lengthening this song into a virtuoso piece, alternating it with 'Purple Haze' as the show-stopper for the past nine or more months. During 1969 he had embellished these tunes with 'Star Spangled Banner' in various guises. On this occasion Hendrix knew it would be the closing sequence and pulled out all the stops on 'Voodoo Child ('Slight Return')' even before starting the vocals, and then poured out an incendiary solo afterwards. He was taking a departure from his normal stagecraft to deliver a musical message that seemed stripped of its showmanship, instead substituting a window onto his soul. This was the image that Hendrix had been increasingly concerned to present – the musician-alchemist delivering his message to the world, not the louche entertainer unable to escape his guitar-biting routines of the past three years.

As if to underline this point, Hendrix gives Larry Lee yet another solo, this one about two-thirds of the way into 'Voodoo Child (Slight Return)'. The solo is beyond Lee. He tries to compete with the levels of intensity and eloquence that Hendrix has already reached but his ideas and technique are simply not in the same league. Yet Lee serves Hendrix's purpose, because he stops this from being a mere exhibition of guitar prowess and turns it into a communal affair. Twelve minutes into the piece Hendrix, after saying goodbye to the crowd, sings snatches of two different verses from 'Stepping Stone'. This is another bitter song about his testing relationship with Devon Wilson, and would later appear briefly as the A-side of his next single. He again says goodbye, adding: "You can leave if you want to, leave or clap." After some fourteen minutes 'Voodoo Child (Slight Return)' is thus brought to an end and Hendrix slips into his coda. This is the cue for 'Star Spangled Banner' / 'Last Post'. The performance is often described as a solo but it is not. Hendrix is turbulently accompanied throughout by Mitchell in his most Elvin Jones-like manner, and even Cox attempts for a short while to supply the root notes of the song's harmony before packing it in and watching. Must have brought back memories of the parade-ground for him. Hendrix's percussionists also throw themselves into the piece but their efforts are completely missing from the commercial mix and only occasionally audible on the bootlegs. The film occasionally shows them flailing away behind Hendrix.

The most striking quality of Hendrix's rendition of the famous theme – separate from the attention-catching bombs and planes that made for so much comment at the time – is its burning melodicism. Hendrix was not being ironic in his recasting of the song. He loved his country; he just didn't care for the way it could cause so much hate and division. Clearly inspired, just as he had been when he'd made that slashing, vehement performance of 'Red House' at TTG the previous autumn, and now similarly confounded by events and angered at the predicament in which he found himself, he launches into 'Purple Haze' and delivers perhaps the most devastating live version he'd ever played of the song.

He comes out of it flying, moving into yet another coda, this time unaccompanied, whipping through ideas and different guitar techniques by the second, employing styles that in part would perhaps have been more suited to an acoustic guitar. (Hendrix had seriously intended to play an acoustic instrument for part of the set and was only dissuaded by some next-to-last-minute hard talking from Mike Jeffery.[13] Whatever reason Jeffery may have had to stop Hendrix from doing this must have had little to do with music and everything to do with image.) This whole coda is a statement of intent from Hendrix, demarcating his live performances into pre-Woodstock and post-Woodstock: by playing this piece in such a place and on such an occasion, he was putting music first, showbiz second. Considering the nature and length of this section, it is no surprise that it was cut considerably when first released on record and on screen. This was something rock guitarists just didn't do. They did not drop below ear-splitting screams and move into entirely different styles, tones and feels, some of them associated with other genres of music altogether.

Ever the consummate performer, Hendrix knows that this is not the right way to complete the sequence, so he slips into 'Villanova Junction', played very slowly and sensuously, with great feel and considerable restraint. This sophisticated blues, with its slinky, beguiling melody reminiscent of jazz guitarist Wes Montgomery at his casual best, had first appeared as part of the 'Jimi/Jimmy' jam back in March. It is not inconceivable that it was written prior to that as an unspoken tribute to the immensely popular Montgomery, who had died of a heart attack in June 1968. Whatever its inspiration, 'Villanova Junction' is the perfect conclusion for the high-velocity playing that Hendrix had embarked upon, ever since kicking off 'Voodoo Child (Slight Return)' nearly half an hour earlier.

Even then, the stunned crowd demanded an encore. This was real life, after all, and a gig is a gig, however large. Hendrix gave them 'Hey Joe', both as a token of appreciation for their applause throughout a long and ragged set and as a way of cooling things out and finishing the festival on a quieter note. It worked. Gypsy Sun & Rainbows were off-stage and the show came to an end.

Hendrix was exhausted by the performance and the expectations it had placed upon him. He had also been suffering from a bout of food poisoning after drinking contaminated water during the hours he had waited to go on stage. He was completely drained. A much ballyhooed TV appearance on the *Dick Cavett Show* was blown out as Hendrix took some time to recover something like equilibrium. After close on a week of recuperation and reflection on the state of his career and his music, he returned to New York City and prepared for three nights of recording at the Hit Factory studio with Gypsy Sun & Rainbows, from August 28th to the 30th. They would concentrate mostly on the new material extensively rehearsed upstate prior to the festival. For those three nights Hendrix attempted to achieve useable masters for new material such as 'Message To Love' (at this point still called 'Message To The Universe'), 'Izabella', 'Machine Gun', 'Stepping Stone' and 'Beginning'. They also jammed on the new 'Burning Desire' in search of a suitable structure, and attempted an updated version of 'Lover Man', a tune that Hendrix had still not recorded in the studio to his satisfaction. The band also tried Larry Lee's vocal number 'Master Mind', plus a blues penned by Lee and a few other jams. Hendrix had pulled engineer Eddie Kramer from his task of developing Electric Lady studio to engineer most of these sessions.

Very little of the material recorded over those three nights has ever emerged into the world unscathed. 'Message To Love' / 'Message To The Universe' appeared on the *South Saturn Delta* CD of 1997, remixed to accentuate the Hendrix-Cox-Mitchell axis and relegating Lee, Velez and Sultan to the background. It is a relaxed take on the song, clearly some way short of full development and with no evolved ending. Instead there is an undignified scramble as Hendrix combines imitations of Eric Clapton and his own arabesques from *Electric Ladyland* days as the take comes to a rough conclusion. 'Beginning', the piece this same band had brought to such rousing completion at Woodstock, must have seemed a safe bet to lay down successfully in the studio, but it has never been released as originally recorded. Instead it appeared on 1975's *Midnight Lightning* with all the original parts aside from Hendrix's wiped and replaced with contemporary studio musicians – including some of the limpest lead guitar work ever heard on a Hendrix record when a player who shall remain nameless imitates Larry Lee's original melody statement on the second section. About the only thing producer Alan Douglas got right was to credit Mitch Mitchell as the song's

composer (most other 'Beginning' credits erroneously list Hendrix). Judged on Hendrix's own guitar playing on 'Beginning', it sounds as if the recording was a run-through rather than a concerted effort to achieve a master. The song was attempted on just one of the three nights of recording, indicating that Hendrix had only a lukewarm interest in taping it.

The first studio appearance of 'Izabella' is even more confused and unhappy. Although multiple attempts were made on every night to record it, nothing was completed. An August 29th take that was at least coherent and featured some pleasing interplay between Hendrix and Lee as they support the vocal line was kept in mind and overdubbed on September 23rd. (This

"He was totally intuitive, self-taught and ear-trained. Yet Jimi was an amazingly sophisticated musician."

Paul Caruso, friend

version, overdubbed and mixed on the latter date, was issued after further polishing on the four-CD *Jimi Hendrix Experience* box-set of 2000.) Izabella showed that, if only there had been strong direction coming from a session producer, this band could have provided a valid and exciting musical route for Hendrix to pursue, for when the interplay between all the different musicians clicked, it made for a fascinating tapestry. But there was no system to the sessions other than chance and routine, and no possibility of a working method emerging to sustain the fusion.

The only tangible result of all the work on 'Izabella' was the transplanting of a vocal line from the song to the opening of 'Machine Gun', a piece the band shifted to on August 29th. (The famous descending guitar riff of 'Machine Gun' bears a striking resemblance to the equally famous line in Cream's 'Sunshine Of Your Love' – a song Hendrix had been playing live for close to a year now; 'Machine Gun' too would become a fixture in his live sets during 1970.) Two takes were attempted of 'Machine Gun' on the 29th, though neither was anything more than a rough outline – Lee does most of the soloing on take two, Hendrix on the first – although some of the guitar work is spirited and Hendrix's vocals are impassioned. Both takes were plundered and combined, with studio musicians laid over the top, for Douglas's 1975 production *Midnight Lightning*. Neither performance came anywhere near the definitive live Band Of Gypsys recording that Hendrix would make at the end of the year. 'Stepping Stone', still known as 'Sky Blues Today', didn't even get to an acceptable finished take, while one of the jams, an instrumental given the title 'Easy Blues', was edited for release on the 1980 jam compilation *Nine To The Universe* and is one of the weaker tracks on that mediocre collection.

Hendrix must have left the studios after those three days feeling very downhearted. No matter how much effort he made, he couldn't pull the band into shape in the studio, and he was unsure if it was him, his material or the composition of the band itself that was at fault. In direct and ironic contrast, ten days earlier, across town in Columbia studios, Miles Davis had laid down the final tracks for what would become his best-selling fusion album, *Bitches' Brew*. Two of the mainstays of that record, Larry Young and John McLaughlin, had jammed in the studio with Hendrix during the course of the year but produced nothing of outstanding worth. On August 29th, McLaughlin was a guest star on another classic fusion album, Wayne Shorter's *Super Nova*, featuring Sonny Sharrock as a second guitarist, Chick Corea on drums and Airto on percussion, among other future fusion stars. The contrast with Hendrix's situation could hardly have been more stark. No doubt his own state of mind and body were fragile at this time. Always during this period the shadow of the Toronto court case hung over him, on top of any other worries, carrying the genuine threat of a gaol sentence. In a stand-off with his manager Mike Jeffery, who had organised a short but lucrative autumn tour of some 11 or so dates, Hendrix insisted that the tour be cancelled, saying not only that his band was nowhere near ready for such exposure, but that his health was at risk and he needed complete rest. Jeffery was severely exposed financially and put considerable pressure on Hendrix to honour the commitments. The manager was fronting the costs for the Electric Lady studio project at a time when money was being poured in to solve unforeseen problems and the probable completion date was slipping by the day. Income from records was temporarily in a lull and his major artist was spending, not earning, money. But Hendrix demurred. The tour had to be cancelled, at a considerable loss to all parties. Jeffery considered Hendrix's behaviour perverse and counter-

veiled audition for a new band, much against Hendrix's wishes. He showed his displeasure by barely involving himself for the whole show, which for the most part resembled an ambling jam session as musician after musician was tried out. This was the final appearance of Gypsy Sun & Rainbows, though it could hardly be termed a concert in the circumstances.

No new musicians were drafted into the band as a result of this public exhibition of confusion and chaos within the Hendrix camp. The guitarist quietly disbanded the group in the weeks after the gig, retaining only Cox, Mitchell and Sultan for his projected working group. Larry Lee, unhappy with the turmoil in which he was caught, left of his own accord a week after the Sheridan Square fiasco and returned to Nashville. Hendrix appeared with Cox, Mitchell and Sultan on the 9th on TV's *Dick Cavett Show*, where his elliptical conversation and sly humour continually evaded Cavett's conventional interview technique. The hippies loved him all the more for it, although the performance of 'Izabella' and 'Machine Gun', two of his most persuasive new tunes, was robbed of most of its impact thanks to inadequate sound systems and poor miking. This was the single live appearance of the shortlived quartet that emerged intact from the Gypsy Sun & Rainbows debacle, although they began sessions which spread over ten days late in September at the Record Plant in an effort to lay the foundations for a new album. This record became the fourth new studio album announced to the world for 1969. Mitchell told June Harris of the *New Musical Express*: "It's been about a year since

"After Woodstock, there was too much bullshit going down all around Jimi. I didn't think I was ever going to be involved with him again."

Billy Cox, bassist

productive. Hendrix saw it as basic to his survival as a human being and as a musician. Despite the evident failure of Gypsy Sun & Rainbows to turn into a tight working unit, he was still reluctant to dissolve the band. Indeed he spent two more evenings in early September trying once again to turn base musical metals into gold. He also fronted the band at two live appearances in New York City, on September 5th in Harlem and on the 10th in Greenwich Village. Nothing much came of these efforts.

In the studio the band attempted new material, this time 'Burning Desire', 'Master Mind', Valleys Of Neptune, 'Stepping Stone' (in a very early incarnation), 'Beginning' (part of a longer jam), a further series of blues jams, and one more despairing shot at 'Lover Man'. As with many other studio versions of this last number, Hendrix didn't get around to laying down a vocal track. None of this material has appeared commercially and the bootlegs that exist show why. The music is dispirited, messy and, in parts, unlistenable. The version of 'Beginning', for example, comes from a desultory jam where the rhythm section sound like a camel with a broken back.

The two New York engagements were undertaken in direct opposition to Jeffery's wishes and for intensely personal reasons. The September 5th appearance in Harlem had been organised by Hendrix's old friends the Allen brothers, and their local reputations were on the line. In addition, he was by then concerned that the trendsetters in the black community were not listening to or taking seriously either Hendrix himself or his music – a problem since his unheralded arrival in New York back in 1964. With Gypsy Sun & Rainbows, a band built around black musicians and with a decidedly more rootsy sound than the Experience, he must have felt as if he had a good chance of making the type of impression he craved.

At the Harlem event, he had to follow on-stage the great R&B shouter, Big Maybelle, a perennial Harlem favourite, and make a good impression in her wake. Being an old pro he knew what was expected, and delivered it. To his relief, the reviews in the following days were all positive, giving him credibility in that community at a time of maximum conflict in American life. Five days later, on the 10th, the band appeared once more, this time at The Salvation, in Sheridan Square, Greenwich Village. It was a shambolic event, largely because his management had insisted that the session be used as a

our last one and there's all this stuff lying around. After we've finished the album I'm going back to London and I'll do a few things of my own."[14] Hendrix said nothing. At this stage the pressure to complete an album had become more intense than ever; no new material had been released for a year. The US version of *Smash Hits* consisted entirely of old tracks, even if four of them had only been available in the UK until then, and the Ed Chalpin/PPX settlement had yet to be honoured.

What is both strange and telling in this quagmire of frustrated hopes, inadequate performances and financial overstretching is that Hendrix had more than enough material in the can for a new album to be prepared and released. *Electric Ladyland* outtakes alone could have supplied a new single LP. This would surely have taken some of the pressure from his shoulders, but he absolutely refused to allow it to happen. He was determined to produce something new that he felt was equal to his best efforts of the past. Equal, but different. But there was a serious gap between aspiration and reality. Each time he went into the studio, either with a bunch of new songs or a different collection of musicians, he was reinventing the wheel, relegating all the old recordings to the scrap-heap and starting from scratch.

What he seemed unable to grasp was that each new generation of The Next Album was of manifestly poorer quality and spirit compared to the last. Although there is copious testimony from friends and colleagues around him in late 1969 that he felt as if he was played out and thought his compositions merely covered old personal ground – true enough observations at that time, though not the whole story – he persisted with those songs and kept on recording. The Chalpin suit must have appeared particularly insoluble. The settlement allowed for PPX to be delivered an album of new material, but Hendrix was determined never to hand over to Chalpin a whole album of material that he passionately believed in and needed to control. For the moment the circle remained unsquared.

Recording was resumed with no fixed outcome in sight. One last, listless session with Lee and Velez on September 15th yielded no useable music and was good only for a couple of relaxed blues jams, neither of which have appeared officially. With the quartet of survivors assembled a week later, on the 23rd, the more recent material was once again attempted – 'Izabella',

'Valleys Of Neptune', 'Message To Love' and 'Beginning', plus a couple of incidental efforts. The atmosphere was no better than at the previous sessions and nothing of releasable standard was achieved. This session pushed Cox's patience too far. As he told John McDermott later, he'd originally come on board to help Hendrix get past Woodstock and to see what happened after that. Nothing good was happening. "After Woodstock, I hung around as long as I could, but there was just too much bullshit going down all around him," Cox recalled. "Jimi had gone down into this well. He said, 'Man, I just can't get it together. I've gotta rest my head.' I've gotta rest my head.' He told me that if he could, he was thinking of going off to Africa with Colette [Mimram]. I wished him Godspeed and told him I was glad I had been able to help him. That was it. I didn't think I was ever going to be involved with him again."[15]

Hendrix worked on without Cox: he and Mitchell had often recorded without a bassist present in the Experience days. Hendrix, Mitchell and Sultan reconvened the following day, the 24th, tentatively running through seven takes of 'Stepping Stone', 'Message To Love' and then multiple takes of an early incarnation of 'Power Of Soul', something of a twin in feel and lyric content to 'Message To Love', with Hendrix wearing his social commentator's hat. 'Stepping Stone' and 'Room Full Of Mirrors' were revisited the following day, but with Buddy Miles sitting in on drums instead of Mitchell. Nothing that was put down on tape that day proved to be salvageable.

After this last gasp, work effectively stopped on The Next Album. Hendrix and Mitchell attended a recording session for Alan Douglas's own Douglas label along with Stephen Stills, John Sebastian and Buddy Miles, where Hendrix played bass on some tracks (and Mitchell played drums on a few song demos with Stills after the main session). The music was later used as backing for some talks by Dr Timothy Leary, recorded on a separate occasion; due to contractual obligations, none of the musicians were named on the resulting album.

By this time Mitchell, like Cox and Lee before him, had seen enough to want a break from Hendrix. No progress was being made, the guitarist was recording the same songs over and over with no sign of completing any of them, and there was no longer a plan in place – apart from the apparent need to keep plugging away in the face of general

disintegration. There was not even a replacement bassist on the horizon. Mitchell flew back to London to take a break and see what else was going on in the world. Hendrix, having finally given up on the Woodstock house and the band that went with it, as well as the concomitant aspirations, withdrew from all active projects and brooded on the calamitous state of affairs surrounding him. There was no band, the Toronto court case now loomed in

Captured on film, the Woodstock festival was turned into an event with a symbolism that went far beyond some musicians playing in front of a large crowd.

early December, and Ed Chalpin/PPX were pressing for product. Surely there had to be a way out? Unfortunately Hendrix was too confused and wasted to know how to locate an escape route.

miles of trouble

For Hendrix, any form of musical upsurge remained tucked below the horizon in the first weeks of October 1969 as he kept to himself in New York, unsure which move to make. Roadie Gerry Stickells recalls him as "going through a period where he felt he couldn't write anything. Everything sounded the same as before. He was bored and directionless".[1] Hendrix was indecisive and unable to plan anything, making Mr. Micawber seem the epitome of method and industriousness. Later in the month there were a few hints of a new direction, but this proved shortlived and, as usual by this stage, unproductive.

Hendrix was seeing Alan Douglas regularly on a social level and spending a lot of time with Douglas's sister-in-law, Colette Mimram, after their mid-year holiday in Morocco together, as well as Douglas's wife, Stella, who was a long-term friend of Devon Wilson's. Given Hendrix's propensity for developing a relationship with whoever came along at any given time and Douglas's track record as a producer, it was hardly surprising that before the month was out Hendrix was asking him to come along and see what he could do about the guitarist's apparently perpetual problems in the studio.

Douglas's credentials were impressive. The producer had been working overseas for French record-company owner Eddie Barclay when Duke Ellington came to France to record the soundtrack for a United Artists movie, *Paris Blues*. In 1961, Douglas moved to United Artists in America. UA had already started up and closed one jazz venture, at one point in the late 1950s making two albums with pianist Cecil Taylor, both produced by Tom Wilson and one of them featuring John Coltrane. This second try at jazz by UA was equally shortlived, but while he was at the label Douglas recorded award-winning studio albums with Bill Evans (featuring Jim Hall), Duke Ellington (in a trio with Charles Mingus and Max Roach), Art Blakey (with The Jazz Messengers) and Ken McIntyre. The only artist Douglas signed to a deal was Mingus, who in turn led to Douglas leaving the label when Mingus's

And the jamming continued: Hendrix and bassist Billy Cox (opposite page) busy working out some more of their riffs and note patterns.

notorious *Town Hall Concert* big-band recording session of late 1962 spiralled out of control and produced virtually nothing that could be released at the time. "[Mingus] had these incredible concepts and got overwhelmed by the project. I probably gave him too much [money]," Douglas reflected in 1992, "because he began to indulge himself. We had to have all of Mingus's favourite players – that cost a lot of money. We required lots of arrangers, not just one arranger; there were three arrangers and many copyists and it all just overwhelmed him, I think, and me. Mingus spent more time screaming at the audience than playing music."[2]

Leaving UA, Douglas joined up with Monte Kay at FM Records, where he signed Eric Dolphy in 1963 for some of the saxophonist's most outstanding

Garcia with a jazz organist and tried to make that work – I guess it works, I'm not pledging myself yet – and did a lot of spoken voice. It was the beginning of the so-called counterculture."[3]

Douglas and his partner, Stefan Bright, had a vibrant little independent company making good records at a time when popular music was at another crossroads. Douglas was well aware of the electrification of jazz during 1969, keeping in touch through his cultural and political connections with rock, black music and the politically inspired art of the burgeoning counterculture. An intelligent and approachable man with excellent contacts, Douglas would have been attractive to Hendrix, who was facing only questions and had no answers of his own any more. Hendrix needed people he could trust in every

With Billy Cox, pictured at work in the studio. Hendrix's studio routines had become increasingly long-winded as he insisted on taping every moment of every jam – good, bad or indifferent.

sessions. While at FM, Douglas also released some of the earliest bossa-nova jazz albums before the style's massive wave of popularity hit the world. FM eventually went under and Douglas moved out of jazz. He then became involved in a wide range of projects, overseeing the Lenny Bruce legacy after the controversial comic died from an overdose, and guiding proto-rap band The Last Poets onto record. By 1969 he had set up his own independent label, Douglas Records, in New York City and was keen to combine the newly emerging fusion music with the most virulent and artistically challenging aspects of the counterculture revolution that pervaded the city at the time. As Douglas said in '92, "The roots of rap and the black oral culture are very African and spiritual in one sense, and very street in another. I got involved in that, and I accidentally did the first rap record. We didn't even know it was rap, we didn't call it rap at that point. Then I thought of diversifying a little more. I did an album for John McLaughlin and The Last Poets and I put Jerry

part of his life – some of the problem was that he had little or no facility for filtering out the users and the parasites – but he also wanted people around him whom he felt he really could trust. This was not necessarily the same thing. And by his reckoning, it did not include his current management team. They seemed extremely unsympathetic about his aspirations and dilemmas and only seemed to tell him how much money Electric Lady studio was costing and how a tour with a reformed Experience would restore everyone's finances. The implosion of Gypsy Sun & Rainbows had left him feeling he couldn't trust most of the musicians he'd been hanging out with. He wanted his friends around him, people whose motives were transparent.

So he got on the phone to Nashville in early October and started working on Billy Cox to come back. Cox had nothing urgent back in Nashville to attend to and returned to New York City with a promise from Hendrix that this time it would be different. For a start, Hendrix opened up about the difficulties he faced. "When I agreed to come back," Cox told John McDermott, "Jimi sat me down and explained what was going on."[4] For the first time in their relationship, Cox became proactive. He discussed the situation with Buddy Miles and both men agreed that it was time to help Hendrix through this particular rough patch. Miles had problems with his band, the Express, and was free to devote some time to a new project, while Cox was as available as Hendrix needed him to be. They did not bring up the subject of Mitch Mitchell, Juma Sultan and the others from the previous ensemble with Hendrix. The guitarist was clearly incapable of solving the problems associated with that band.

The three of them – Hendrix, Cox and Miles – had a jam at the Record Plant in mid October. Alan Douglas attended, on Hendrix's invitation. Douglas, like any other professional record producer used to budgets and deadlines, was appalled at Hendrix's working methods. "I never saw such disorganisation in all my life," he said. "No one in either the control room or the studio was taking care of business for him. The engineer just kept putting rolls of tape on the machine and pressing the record button. I was sitting there thinking, 'What the fuck is this?'"[5] Douglas, who had observed genius at work first-hand in the recording studio more than once in the jazz field, knew that the idea of spontaneous creation only took flight when some sort of blueprint had been agreed upon in advance. Even with jazz, which is an improviser's art, everyone knew the session leader's aims and the contours of each piece prior to the tape rolling.

This was patently not the case with Hendrix. As on most of his 1969 sessions, the trio simply jammed for hours with no particular goal in sight. Douglas left them to it. He knew this was not a satisfactory method. What he didn't yet know was that it was Hendrix's preferred way of working – and that he resented anyone interfering with what was nonetheless an incredibly wasteful process. Douglas found this out the very next night when he went down again and studied Hendrix at work with Cox and Miles. Within a short while he realised that the process was based on building up rhythm patterns – just as Cox has always said subsequently in many interviews – and that each pattern dictated the shape and character of the portion of a song in which it appeared. It was a method analogous to reinventing the wheel for every song, but it seemed the only way available, especially as neither Cox nor Miles, in particular, were exactly swift on the musical uptake. Hence the inordinate length of these sessions.

Soon after this, Miles took the opportunity while he and Hendrix were at the Douglas Records office to propose that they start a band together as a sort of project. The spur was that Bill Graham would welcome them with open arms at the Fillmore East, so they had an engagement to work towards. Oddly, there was immediate conflict over Billy Cox and whether he should be the bassist in what Hendrix and Miles quickly dubbed the Band Of Gypsys. Even though Cox had been instrumental in getting Miles involved in this new project, Miles and Douglas's partner, Stefan Bright, favoured bringing in the old Buddy Miles Express bassist Billy Rich. Rather than simply quashing this idea, Hendrix allowed them to contact Rich. He was unavailable. "I had moved to Denver," Rich told John McDermott, "and begun working on a project in San Francisco for Columbia Records when Alan Douglas called, asking if I wanted to do this album with Jimi Hendrix. At that time I just couldn't get away to do it."[6]

Bright in particular found it hard to reconcile himself to this loss. It made it easy for Hendrix to reinstate Cox in the absence of any other option, but it left Cox on a difficult footing with Bright and Douglas, especially as Bright made no pretence at welcoming Cox into the studio when the trio began studio rehearsals at Juggy studio in October and recording in November. Cox recalled: "I had words with Alan's partner, Stefan Bright. You couldn't create music under those circumstances. Those guys distracted my focus away from making music, and I couldn't get it together."[7] Cox also made it clear that he

didn't think Douglas or Bright were the right producers for Hendrix. As far as he was concerned, Hendrix could produce himself. From the evidence of the previous 12 months he was mistaken about that, whatever the pros and cons of the Douglas/Bright team.

It is unclear why Hendrix was not more forceful in demanding that Cox should be his bassist from the start of the project, but it doesn't reflect well on him. Perhaps he felt that this band belonged to Buddy Miles. Miles himself certainly thought so. Perhaps he was too distracted and too confused to take a stand. He was certainly unhappy and introverted and needed support to come his way. Few parts of his life were working happily and for the past 12 months he had seen dissolution rather than convergence.

For a time Cox once more stepped away from the project, leaving Hendrix and Miles to their own devices. This changeover seemed at one point as if it might affect every level of Hendrix's musical life, what with Alan Douglas's involvement in the studio, Mitch Mitchell's absence – however temporary – and the second walk-out by Billy Cox for very understandable reasons. It eventually became something of a watershed for Hendrix. It allowed him once again to set aside an unproductive few months where his own obsessive need for musical perfection – combined with his inability to verbalise his exact needs to his fellow musicians to inspire similar levels of input – had led to such a meagre output.

The sheer efficiency of the old Experience unit had masked this brewing crisis for the whole of 1969, and even perhaps for as much as a year. This is doubly ironic, because percussionist Juma Sultan claimed in one interview that what Hendrix had been looking for in Gypsy Sun & Rainbows was a band that could think for itself and create its own musical patina without the leader having to direct every move, suggesting that this was precisely what had been wrong with the Experience. "If he had a group of people that he didn't have to tell what to play it would have been another kind of band," Sultan said of the Gypsy Sun group, "and that was the kind of sound he was looking for. Somebody that was thinking for themselves. And that's the difference right now between the marketing of commercial music and music of true expression."[8] All the musical evidence points to the contrary, in the sense that all three musicians in the Experience did in fact think creatively for themselves and contribute to what was achieved in the recorded legacy of Jimi Hendrix. Each musician in Gypsy Sun & Rainbows could think as an individual, but too few of them could think past expressing themselves to embrace the complete sound that the band should or could be producing. Additionally, Hendrix could no longer consistently impose his will and pull

"Hendrix was fascinated by the studio and he was a perfectionist, and the result was he over-indulged there."

Alan Douglas, on Jimi's recording methods

the ensemble into shape. The task was beyond him in those months, for a combination of reasons. This meant that yet another generation of attempts at The Next Album were relegated to the back shelf.

In the wake of the Experience's dissolution, his working groups had attempted to achieve masters of the following tunes and jams, which would have been enough in ordinary circumstances for a single LP, if not a double: 'Power Of Soul', 'Ships Passing In The Night', 'Send My Love To Linda', 'Earth Blues', 'Bleeding Heart', 'Hear My Train A'Comin'', 'Villanova Junction', 'Message To Love', 'Lover Man', 'Izabella', 'Stepping Stone', 'Master Mind', 'Beginning', 'Burning Desire', 'Valleys Of Neptune', 'Machine Gun', 'Room Full Of Mirrors' and a number of jams, mostly blues. All were recorded prior to the formation of the Band Of Gypsys group and its inaugural recording session in October. Some of this material never got past a sketch, and none of it was brought to completion. Putting aside the supposed inadequacies of the groups he worked with, one has to ask whether Hendrix at this point was emotionally capable of completing a project. Perhaps his compulsion for perfection had temporarily become a disorder that went largely unrecognised in the general wash of frantic everyday activity.

Alan Douglas once noted in passing to an interviewer that "remixing something 15 times is not meticulous, that's over-indulgence. … [Hendrix] was fascinated by the studio and he was a perfectionist, and the result was he over-indulged there".[9] That Hendrix reached out to Douglas at this stage suggests that he knew he needed an outside agent to focus his energies and make decisions. That Douglas was the wrong person at that time – for a number of reasons, including the threat that Mike Jeffery decided he posed to Jeffery's managerial position – would quickly become apparent to all parties. Douglas would of his own volition eventually withdraw from active studio participation in order to preserve his friendship with Hendrix. For the time being, however, Hendrix and Buddy Miles decided it was time to begin intensive rehearsals to knock some material into shape and get an idea of what would and wouldn't work for the proposed group.

During early November the two of them spent a lot of time together in and out of studios, although not a great deal of new music was recorded. Both musicians were involved informally in a Last Poets session organised by Douglas on November 7th. On a rap track called 'Doriella du Fontaine' Hendrix and Miles contribute a funky guitar, drums and organ pattern to support the vocals by Lightning Rod. The story is something of a cliché, dealing with the exploits of a 'dolly dagger' type of woman who is evidently admired for dolly-dagger reasons, but it is excellently delivered and the music enhances the effect, even if it is somewhat monotonous. (The track was not released for many years but has recently become available on a CD single of the same name.) Also that evening Hendrix and Miles duetted on a range of Hendrix originals, with Douglas and Bright in the control room, but nothing from the session was ever used later and the recordings remain unreleased and unheard today. It was the same story three days later when the two again worked on 'Stepping Stone' (known then as 'Lonely Avenue', one of a series of working titles before its final name was adopted). On the 14th at the Record Plant studio the two jammed extensively on snippets of a whole range of Hendrix songs in an attempt to bed things down and work through possible combinations of ideas. Hendrix never revisited these tapes and they were quietly filed away.

On Monday 17th November Billy Cox was back on board and the Band Of Gypsys effectively came together as a functioning unit. As with all the other bands he'd worked with, Hendrix immediately took them into the studio to rehearse and work on the material he wanted to release. With Alan Douglas and Stefan Bright in the control room, there was a concerted effort that day to get down a useable master of 'Room Full Of Mirrors'. This was achieved, although the version recorded only produced a basic track that Hendrix would re-work in 1970 (it would finally be released after his death on the *Rainbow Bridge* 'soundtrack' album). This version was probably put aside until months later because the two producers were unfamiliar with Hendrix's working methods, especially his system for recording his master vocal (as opposed to the simple guide tracks that would be put down first for the benefit of the other musicians). All Hendrix's long-term studio partners – engineers, tape-ops and producers alike – knew how over-sensitive the guitarist was about recording his vocals. Bright confessed as much later. "I guess the other people who had worked with him knew this, but we didn't. When it came time to record his vocals, he instructed the engineer and the assistant engineer to set up baffles around him and turn all of the lights in the studio out. I said, 'What the fuck are you talking about your voice for? Your voice is unique, and

it's a part of your whole sound.' He said, 'I don't care what you say: this is the way I feel and this is what we're going to do.'"[10]

This exchange alone points to an early breakdown in communication between Hendrix's presumed producers and the musician himself. Such basic misunderstandings were not conducive to them developing a close creative partnership. This version of 'Room Full Of Mirrors' has recently appeared in the 1969 mix, on the 1997 CD *First Rays Of The New Rising Sun*, and betrays the tensions both in the studio and in Hendrix's life. Douglas later admitted: "You couldn't produce Jimi, you could only help him produce himself, really. I mean he knew what he wanted, I think, or he knew when he arrived at what he wanted. I recorded that 'Room Full Of Mirrors' with him, and a few other tracks, but only he knew what he wanted to do with all this stuff."[11]

The November 17th 'Room Full Of Mirrors' forces the tempo and pushes Hendrix's voice into an uncomfortable mixture of shouting and keening. This undermines the story being told in the lyrics, about someone who attempts to regain control over their own claustrophobic and self-deluding reality by smashing the confines and re-establishing some sort of freedom of action. As is often the case with Hendrix's lyrics, the character accomplishes this through his own spirit and the love of a partner whose identity remains unclear to both narrator and listener. In earlier studio and live versions of this song Hendrix had emphasised that the narrator was telling the story after the event rather than still being involved in it. But this version sounds as if the

"When I agreed to come back, Jimi sat me down and explained what was going on."

Billy Cox, told that this time it would be different

scene is taking place within the maelstrom, as slide-guitar parts fly around at a brisk tempo that finds the drums sounding forced and a little stiff. Miles could play at a number of tempos where he sounded completely in command and, as they say, in the pocket. This isn't one of them. There is also a rush of accompanying rhythm-guitar that gives the impression of a group of screaming harpies on his trail rather than the winds of freedom coursing through his hair.

Hendrix's recording career was normally one of profound musical achievement and unerring good judgement about how to present a tune to its best advantage. But this is one of the first instances of him simply getting it wrong. Stephen Stills, who saw Hendrix regularly around this time, remembered occasions when he and Hendrix were in the studio listening to a really good mix. "You could hear everything. Then Jimi would start fiddling and there was this wall of sound that hit you in the face. I would tell him, 'That sucked.' He would just look surprised and say, 'Oh really?'"[12] Hendrix remained ambivalent about 'Room Full Of Mirrors', as he indicated in a reply to a question from *Rolling Stone* the following February, saying he thought they'd never finish the track and then adding: "I hope not."[13]

Hendrix, Cox and Miles managed just two more organised recording sessions with Douglas and Bright, on November 20th and 21st, where material such as 'Them Changes', 'Burning Desire', 'Hear My Train A'Comin'', 'Lover Man' (yet again), 'Power Of Soul', 'Machine Gun' and 'Izabella' were all tried out. The session on the 20th has been labelled by some commentators as one of his most unproductive and uninspired, which must be something of a record given the dissipation of the previous 12 months. The second night was mostly devoted to attempting a decent master of 'Izabella'. This was

Hendrix in the studio (opposite page) with the tools of his trade: Strat, cans and microphone.

achieved, one take from the session being used for the shortlived 'Stepping Stone' / 'Izabella' single of early 1970, the first custom-made single consisting of new material since 'All Along The Watchtower' in 1968.

'Izabella' was written around the same time as 'Machine Gun' and also deals with Vietnam, a war that continued to polarise US domestic opinion. Hendrix had been growing closer to the idea of direct social comment in his lyrics throughout 1969, although the public knew nothing of this as none of his newer tunes was being issued on records. But he had only very recently made a concerted effort to talk directly to his listeners about some of the issues of the day that he cared about. 'Power Of Soul' and 'Message To Love' are also in this genre, although they deal with very different areas of social and personal existence. The two war songs both place their narrators in extreme situations. One is a soldier writing home from the front: "So keep those feelings comin' on strong / Soon I'll be holding you instead of this machine gun." The other is a civilian victim of the war, although it is not made clear if he is American or Vietnamese. Perhaps he's just a universal victim: "Machine gun / Tearing my body all apart."

'Izabella' is cast as an updated funk or soul tune, not far removed from the riffs and interplay that Sly & The Family Stone – a Hendrix favourite – were using on records and in concert around this time. It is put through Hendrix's unique musical filter, of course, and it illustrates the 'pattern' method that Billy Cox so often talked about, with each section of the tune built on the mood of the riff that underpins it. This method puts an undue emphasis on the strength of the melody and lyrics and the power of the guitar solo to render it memorable. The edge and excitement of the rhythm tracks in his earlier material are consciously avoided. Hendrix at this time was going for clean rhythm sounds on guitar and bass and relying on the groove provided by the rhythm section to deliver the power. Miles and Cox could certainly provide that when the circumstances were right, but it did mean that Hendrix's solos became more like set pieces rather than parts of the composition that arose out of the natural contrasts and development of the songs, as in the music he had made in his first couple of years in the spotlight. There are numerous testimonies by witnesses to the scores of attempts at solos that Hendrix would make on material such as 'Izabella' as he tried to lay down something fresh and arresting rather than a simple repetition of previous glories. On this particular track, he went for a full-frontal attack that at times approximated noise, so radical were the sounds he was using. But his choice of notes is very much in the blues and soul traditions.

"We've got enough material now for another two LPs. We are trying to decide what to release and at what time."

Jimi Hendrix

This November 21st session proved to be the last under the nominal production control of Alan Douglas and Stefan Bright, although no announcements to this effect were forthcoming until December. Douglas was an intelligent man with his own business to pursue: he had a record label to run and other projects underway, including preparation for the first Douglas Records session for John McLaughlin, featuring Larry Young, Billy Rich and Buddy Miles, which Bright would successfully produce. Douglas could see he

was getting nowhere fast in the studio with Hendrix. He reasoned that the guitarist clearly had other priorities – including the upcoming Toronto court case, now set for December 8th. But quite possibly the deciding factor in the timing of Douglas's withdrawal was the messy affair of the aborted album with Miles Davis and Tony Williams.

Since 1967 Miles Davis had been moving cautiously towards a blend that mixed strains of soul, funk and rock into his music, encouraged by his young drummer Tony Williams and also by the example of musicians like James Brown and Hendrix himself. Not a lot of listeners could have known this because many of Davis's earlier recordings reflecting this interest were left

"Hendrix was a real nice guy, quiet but intense, and was just the opposite of the wild and crazy image he presented on the stage."

Miles Davis, jazz musician

unissued at the time. During 1968 and '69 a number of musicians had demonstrated that crossover music could be commercially and artistically successful. The most impressive of these were Cannonball Adderley, with his string of instrumental hit singles (some penned by his pianist Joe Zawinul), Eddie Harris, who managed a million-selling soul-jazz single, 'Listen Here', and Herbie Mann, who had been looking to forge a new path between jazz and soul for some time. In August 1968 Mann had finally persuaded his record company, Atlantic, to allow him to make a record in Memphis with the Stax label's renowned studio musicians. "I'd been trying to do it for about two years," said Mann at the time. "Finally Tom Dowd said, 'OK, let's go down.' The first couple of days, it was just Larry Coryell and Roy Ayers and myself with their rhythm section. ... My basic idea was to do a rhythm-and-blues extended version of what Cream does, the long tracks; but those things to me primarily sound white. I don't really consider myself a white player."

Mann enthused about the Stax musicians and why they were so special. "We've got a one-minute version of 'Hold On, I'm Coming'. Those guys down there are fantastic. All they want to do is play rhythm and time. They don't want to do anything else. ... I will never attempt to do another R&B record or something aimed at the pop market anywhere but in Memphis. These New York musicians who do pop dates all think that they're doing you a big favour, because really, secretly, they're jazz players and just doing it for the money, and they don't like the idea."[14] The LP that resulted was *Memphis Underground*. It came out in April 1969 and became a million-seller, with the title single also charting. Miles Davis would not have missed this development. Davis already had *In A Silent Way* recorded and had early plans in place for the next studio album, which would become *Bitches' Brew*. Mann's record would have encouraged Davis to think radically about just what he should be playing, and with whom. A date with Hendrix, a musician he genuinely admired, would have seemed a perfect career move as well as something that had artistic and cultural validity. All parties – apart from Hendrix, who never had the opportunity to tell his side of the story –

attest to a burgeoning friendship between Hendrix and Davis throughout 1969. Hendrix had long been aware of Davis's music and the trumpeter was certainly very aware of Hendrix's impact in the past couple of years. He claimed in his autobiography that the woman he married in 1968, the young Betty Mabry, "turned me on to him". Their first personal contact came from Hendrix's "manager", who, said Davis, "wanted me to introduce him to the way I was playing and putting my music together".

This certainly does not sound like something Mike Jeffery would initiate. Jeffery would have instinctually headed in the opposite musical direction to what Davis had to offer, which he would have concluded to be commercially limiting and therefore of no interest or value. However, it is consistent with Alan Douglas's oft-repeated claim that he was leading a willing Hendrix in the direction of more jazz-based music. It also dovetails with Davis's claim that "Jimi liked what I had done on *Kind Of Blue* [his epochal album of 1959] and some other stuff and wanted to add more jazz elements to what he was doing. He liked the way Coltrane played with all those sheets of sound, and he played the guitar in a similar way".[15] Jeffery would not have been discussing the finer points of *Kind Of Blue* with his client, but Douglas certainly could and would. Douglas knew of Hendrix's interest in jamming with jazz musicians and was aware that if he could deliver Davis for a recording session he would be seen by Hendrix in the best possible light. Douglas himself said later that he had approached Davis about a record album with Hendrix, and that Davis was keen to participate.

In his book, Davis was being a little coy about his relations with Hendrix. Maybe he just didn't remember, or maybe it was because personal relations are by definition messy and hard to elucidate in

Only money stopped a recording session with Hendrix, Miles Davis (above) and drummer Tony Williams.

retrospect. But he and Hendrix were in relatively frequent contact during 1969 through the strange and exclusive world of the women they both knew. Carlos Santana has alluded to this on a number of occasions and Miles Davis's biographer Ian Carr dealt with it in passing. Santana once commented that in this period Hendrix "was, like, 'lady swapping', you know? And [Devon Wilson] would, you know, check the rounds and he knew that she was checking. ... I used to call her 'monitor' because she used to say everything about everybody ... but there was a family that we used to call The Cosmic Family. And it was the same family that hung out with Jimi Hendrix and Miles Davis – it was the same group of ladies. ... Like moons, they would just gravitate around certain things, you know?"[16]

Davis claimed that Hendrix would come around to his New York house and run through ideas with him. "He was a real nice guy, quiet but intense, and was nothing like people thought he was. He was just the opposite of the wild and crazy image he presented on the stage. When we started getting together and talking about music, I found out that he couldn't read music."[17] This suited Davis because it meant that he could assume the role of mentor, as he liked to do, even though he was absorbing as much from Hendrix as Hendrix was from him. Davis was right in the middle of the largest transition of his creative life. He was moving from the conventional acoustic jazz quintet he'd run up to that time to the proto-fusion bands of 1969 and into the 1970s. People like Hendrix, James Brown and Sly Stone were giving Davis the angles he needed to move from the abstract perfection of albums such as *Nefertiti*

and *Miles In The Sky* to *In A Silent Way* and *Bitches' Brew*, both recorded in 1969. But Hendrix was the key catalyst for Davis. Hendrix, the supreme natural improviser and sonic innovator, was a man who bridged black and white audiences. Davis was an astute individual who realised clearly that he too needed both those audiences, just like Hendrix, if he was to sustain and build his natural popular constituency. They had that need in common.

Both men were therefore interested in recording together. But the devil was always going to be in the detail and this is what eventually foiled Douglas. There had been talk of various studio collaborations for Davis and Hendrix with a mix of different backing musicians, but the project that got closest to lift-off was one that would involve Hendrix, Davis, an unspecified bassist, and Davis's ex-drummer Tony Williams. Williams, now the 23-year-old leader of Lifetime, was a big Beatles fan in 1964 and originally alerted Davis to the progressive side of rock. He was also a musician already known to Hendrix. According to Douglas, Davis suggested that such a record was a natural for the participants to make.

Douglas, with Hendrix's approval, proceeded to put in place the financial and contractual details. Clive Davis, the head of Miles Davis's label, Columbia, was keen because at the time Columbia were encouraging their jazz acts to look at ways to branch out into the burgeoning crossover territory between rock and jazz. Such a deal would have been the perfect illustration of what Clive Davis believed should be happening anyway, and could only boost Miles Davis's standing among the youth market. The record company would be Reprise, Hendrix's US label, with a complicated financial package to keep everyone sweet. There was also an agreement that Davis, Williams and Hendrix would contribute three compositions each, so that each man would generate the same income from royalties. According to Douglas, the studio time was booked and the day came, but the whole deal was scuppered at the eleventh hour by Davis. The trumpeter had his promoter/manager Jack Whittemore deliver a demand for an up-front $50,000 before he'd enter the studio. An astounded Douglas checked with the man himself, only to get a curt confirmation. Before he had time to run this past Hendrix and his team, Tony Williams's manager was on the phone as well. He'd heard what Davis had done and demanded equal up-front money. No one was going to out-rank him in this battle of egos. The record was dead by the time Douglas put the phone down. As Douglas told Michael Leonard, "Fuck it, that was Miles, man. It was not ... inconsistent with the man he was."[18]

This humiliation on top of the unproductive and unsettled sessions at the Record Plant led Douglas to send a formal letter on December 4th 1969 withdrawing from all business and production arrangements with Jimi Hendrix. They remained friends, continued to mix on the same social scene, and even talked about other projects, but did not enter a studio together again. The impact of Davis's venality – and Williams's inability to control his ego – must have been devastating for Hendrix, at this time desperately searching for a way forward musically and looking for whatever help he could get. These musicians were the best in their respective fields and could have done much to take him to the next stage. All they did, through their betrayal of his perhaps naïve trust, was to damage him even further. After all, if the musicians he respected and who he thought respected him could do such things and use him in such a naked way, then whom could he trust? Perhaps this was one of many things occupying his mind as he watched The Rolling Stones perform at Madison Square Garden on November 27th 1969, his 27th birthday – a gig the Stones recorded and later released as their live album, *Get Yer Ya Yas Out*.

What is so sad about this whole unedifying episode is that, whether Miles Davis was comfortable with the fact or not, he was deeply influenced by Hendrix at this time. For a man with an ego the size of Davis's, this may have proved hard for him to accept: hence the attempt to pull rank. Guitarist Jean-Paul Bourelly, who played with Davis in the late 1980s, observed later: "Hendrix absolutely influenced Miles. I think he influenced every player in jazz who did not block out funk and rock as possibilities to gain knowledge from. He's the reference for that, as Coltrane was the reference for improvisational jazz. Any jazz player who found funk and rock and even blues as a reference point to gain something from had ultimately to deal with Jimi. He's what Archie Shepp calls a transformational player."[19]

Not surprisingly, Hendrix turned back to tried and tested relationships, and not only those with Cox and Miles. There was the long-term trust and liking he had developed for promoter Bill Graham, and the strange, tortured, secretive but astute business and legal safety-net offered by Mike Jeffery and his management team. All these helped Hendrix get through a very difficult winter. One of the first steps he took was to hire a rehearsal room. Baggy's studio in New York City was an ordinary rehearsal building with basic recording facilities, hiring space and time at a fraction of the cost of a facility like the Record Plant. It enabled the new trio to rehearse with little or no regard to restrictions on time or budget, easing the economic burden that Hendrix had placed upon himself and his organisation in 1968 and '69 through profligate use of expensive studio time.

The simple 2-track recording gear at Baggy's allowed the band to check their progress on any item at any time without the pressure to deliver master-quality takes. Hendrix, Cox and Miles were in Baggy's regularly during November and December. Some of the material they worked on dated from the Gypsy Sun & Rainbows days – 'Message To Love', 'Machine Gun', 'Power of Soul', 'Earth Blues'. Some of it was old – 'Lover Man' – and some of it they pulled together as they rehearsed – 'Ezy Rider', 'Who Knows', 'Them Changes', 'Burning Desire' and 'We Gotta Live Together'.

Although the group also visited the Record Plant three times during December with a view to recording releasable versions of what they'd been rehearsing so intensively, the bulk of the hard work was done at Baggy's, and with one major aim. On December 4th Hendrix signed a contract with Bill Graham for the trio to appear at the Fillmore East in New York City for two nights, on new year's eve and new year's day. It's notable that Hendrix signed the contract: Buddy Miles has often claimed that he was the unspoken leader of this group and its driving force, yet while he may have been the dynamo that set the band running, it was Hendrix whose signature was required to make it all happen.

There was another decisive factor that made this appearance at the Fillmore attractive. Hendrix, his management and his record company, Warners, saw it as a way out of the nightmare of the settlement with PPX, to whom Hendrix still had to deliver an album of new material. Hendrix and his team planned to record the group at the Fillmore, which would surely result in a good quality album. It would mean they would not have to wait further months while Hendrix continued to fritter away studio time in pursuit of musical goals he could no longer clearly identify. Here was a finite and live occasion that had as good a chance as any of delivering the musical goods from Hendrix's most up-to-date ensemble. All of Hendrix's team were agreed, and plans were started to record the Band Of Gypsys at the Fillmore East.

Three days later, the 7th, Hendrix and his legal team flew to Toronto in readiness for the court case scheduled for the following day. The trial lasted

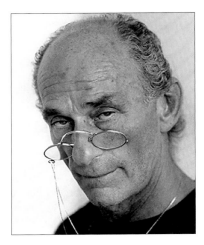

Alan Douglas, producer and album-compiler.

three days, during which time Hendrix and other witnesses were questioned and cross-examined. To the prosecution's dismay and the defendant's delight, Hendrix was acquitted of all charges on December 10th 1969 and allowed to leave the court a free man. This was a vital court victory for many reasons, not least in that it lifted the prospect of restrictions upon his passage through Canada, Britain, Japan and other countries.

He was free to play concerts, to tour or simply travel anywhere he chose without hindrance and with the minimum of harassment from customs and border officials. He could face the future with equanimity. On a more personal level, he was free of the threat of a possible gaol term, something he had been utterly dreading. Not only was it the best possible outcome, but the first really unequivocal sign all year of an upturn in his fortunes. The dissolution all around him was, for the moment, arrested.

While still in Toronto Hendrix granted a telephone interview to *Melody Maker*'s Bob Dawbarn. Although he absolutely would not talk about the court case, he discussed his musical plans freely. He presented himself as eager to re-form the Experience for a spring tour, portraying Redding and Mitchell as the ones who had to decide if it would happen. "I've been thinking about that for a long time," he said, adding that the tour "would certainly include Britain and I'd hope to be there around February, or maybe March, at the latest". He talked positively of "my new group" the Band Of Gypsys and said they had been recording. "I've been writing a whole lot of things. In fact we've got enough material now for another two LPs. We are trying to decide what to release and at what time." There seemed no conflict of interest in his mind about running the two groups, at least not in this interview. After suggesting that a single could be expected some time in January, he was drawn into a comparison of the drumming styles of Miles and Mitchell. His viewpoint was an unexpected one. "Buddy is more of a rock drummer. Mitch is more of a classic drummer – more of a funky, R&B type drummer."[20] Most people would perhaps have suggested Miles to be the funkier, more R&B type drummer of the two.

Hendrix returned to New York and plunged back into rehearsals with Cox and Miles with an increased relish and a new sense that there was after all a way out of all the blind alleys and conundrums of the past year. Buoyed by the prospect of new music with a new band, he also booked some official sessions at the Record Plant, on December 18th, 19th and 23rd. Although multiple takes of 'Bleeding Heart' and 'Message To Love' on the 18th once again produced nothing that could be termed a master, a number of takes of 'Ezy Rider' did finally resolve into a basic track. Hendrix was happy enough with the recording not only to deem it a master then, but to return to it the following year, overhauling and building on it for a final mix of the piece. On top of this, it is also likely that versions of 'Burning Desire' and 'Hoochie Coochie Man', made available after Hendrix's death on 1973's *Loose Ends*, were recorded this evening, even though some sources suggest Baggy's as the location, possibly at a different time on the same day.

'Ezy Rider' had emerged at least in part from the Noel Redding song 'Dance', first recorded by the Experience back in December 1967 but never completed to a level that made it a contender for release. The subject matter of 'Ezy Rider' marked a return to some of Hendrix's earlier concerns expressed in 'Stone Free', 'Highway Chile' and others. The character wanted to be free as the wind, but this time was searching for love down the metaphorical roads of life. What makes it something of a standout track (first released on *The Cry Of Love*, 1971) is the superior arrangement of the music, the edge to Hendrix's rhythm-guitar parts, and the sheer groove generated by the trio. As with 'Room Full Of Mirrors', this track is densely populated by guitar overdubs and the general emotional climate is shrill rather than excited. But the rhythmic raunch that makes it such a forceful track also helps alleviate the sense of desperation that blighted 'Mirrors', while the gradations and contrasts in the arrangement – from the quiet beginning through to the sustained, driving climax at the end – make for a much more integrated composition than Hendrix had managed for some time.

'Burning Desire', recorded the same day, was a lengthy new tune – over nine minutes – conceived in different and contrasting sections like a number of Hendrix ideas at this time. It is another of his songs concerned with the agonies and ecstasies of love and lust, as he sings: "You got my body drowning / In a sea of love / Burning desire / Hotter than an electric chair." It kicks off at medium tempo, with trademark Hendrix guitar chords and riff fragments that reach back to his R&B days, all over a rock-solid Buddy Miles beat. After the opening vocal there is a planned acceleration of tempo for the guitar solo, which moves through passages of common and triple time before a smart unison pattern leads to a dramatic drop in tempo, ushering in the second section of the song, a bluesy, dreamy melody with guitar and vocal lines moving together as a backdrop to the vocals.

This version of 'Burning Desire' recorded that night (and released on *Loose Ends* in 1973) has some painfully out-of-tune backing vocals from Miles and Cox during the second section, the only serious blemishes in the whole performance, which overall seems like a full-scale sketch of the piece. This section meanders a little as Hendrix noodles quietly with some blues phrases, but following a cue from the drums the song is returned to its opening mood for a quick recapitulation and then an accelerated-tempo climax, which generates a good head of steam. The piece shows Hendrix finding a workable balance between contemporary notions of blues, soul and R&B in an extended song. It marks a return to the inspired juxtapositions of his early compositions, where he took simple elements, combined them in exciting and novel ways, and set off his singing and guitar-playing to maximum advantage. This was in contrast to recent work where he had too often relied on the strength of his guitar solo or vocal to carry an otherwise mediocre new composition.

'Hoochie Coochie Man' and 'Burning Desire', first heard on *Loose Ends*, were not reissued on CD until they appeared as part of Dagger's 'official bootleg' *Baggy's Rehearsal Sessions* in 2002. The old Willie Dixon song is part of the same rehearsal as 'Burning Desire' and flows on directly from it: in fact, Buddy Miles asks over the microphone what time it is and, when he finds out, says, "We gotta stop." Hendrix, ignoring him, plays the 'Hoochie Coochie' riff, calls for Miles to play, and they fall into the song for six or so minutes of horsing around. It's fun for them; less so for anyone else listening in. This is the band enjoying themselves in much the same way as Eddie Kramer recalled from working with them at Electric Lady studio the following year. "Jimi would keep the sessions very light, always cracking jokes," said Kramer. "There were self-deprecating jokes as well: he'd take the piss out of himself, out of me, out of Billy and Buddy – anyone in the studio – just to keep things moving along."[21] Clowning with well known tunes was one of Hendrix's favourite ways of keeping the atmosphere positive in the studio, revealed by the number of parodies of such standards on tape. The shadow of the Toronto trial was beginning to recede and Hendrix was again enjoying making music with two good friends.

Recording on the following day, the 19th, produced more material eventually released than at any time in the studio for the past few months. The band got down a take of 'Message To Love' Hendrix deemed satisfactory after four months of aborted attempts at the song. In contrast to the strained and awkward recording of August 29th, this one has a settled rhythm, steered by Miles's commanding beat, over which the guitar and bass bubble happily in a series of riffs and patterns. The gospel-like "yeah"s and "ooh"s initiated by Miles and harmonised by Hendrix and Cox flesh out the verses in an entirely appropriate way, not heard since the Experience and their combinations of backing vocals developed in the studio and on-stage. This 'Message To Love' is kept deliberately simple, with just one rhythm-guitar track and a dropped-

in solo sufficient to give Hendrix the basic R&B feel he was looking for. The lyrics, although penned some months earlier, are in tune with the wider social and personal concerns of his more recent material, perhaps intended to fit into the loose theme Hendrix mentioned in interviews that he was toying with for a studio album at this time, to be called *People, Hell & Angels*. Like all the other proposed LP projects of 1969 it never saw the light of day.

'Earth Blues', another song that had so far eluded attempts to be captured effectively in the studio, was recorded to Hendrix's satisfaction on the 19th. He would return to this master twice in 1970, overdubbing and remixing for his next album and substituting an entirely new drum track by Mitch Mitchell. If one listens to this version with Buddy Miles on drums, released on the four-CD *Jimi Hendrix Experience* box-set, one can hear why Hendrix went for an alternative. There are a number of uncomfortable shifts in the rhythmic emphasis (especially on the bridge where The Ronettes repeatedly sing "everybody" in a gospel-style exchange with Hendrix's lead vocal) that find Miles sounding decidedly earthbound and just a little stiff. Such mid-song shifts were not ideal for Miles, whose forte was laying down a granite beat for the duration of a song, rather than interpreting how a song's feel should evolve and shift during a single performance. That, of course, was one of Mitchell's strengths.

The lyrics of 'Earth Blues' reflect Hendrix's increasing concern for themes and subjects reaching far beyond his own personal needs and desires. He sings: "Well I see hands and attesting faces / Reaching up but not quite

"He'd take the piss out of himself, out of me, out of Billy and Buddy, anyone, just to keep things moving along."

Eddie Kramer, engineer, on Jimi in the studio

touching the promised land / I see tears and a whole lot of precious years wasted / Saying, 'Lord, please give us a helping hand.'" Hendrix had witnessed the turmoil in America during 1969 and, under political pressure himself from all sides, he began increasingly to incorporate into his songs the idea that ultimately the troubles of the times could only be overcome through love. The music itself has that unbeatable Hendrix combination, a sophisticated compilation of simple elements. This time, however, the complexities are in the myriad guitar parts draped spectacularly over the simple construction, both during and after the vocals and punctuated as usual by breaks and stops that add to the song's dramatic effect. He builds up an entire tapestry of sounds to delight the listener, evoking an impression of a great sea of voices in a musical manifestation of the tide of humanity that his lyrics depict.

That same day, at Baggy's rehearsal studios, the band ran through some ideas about how to play 'Auld Lang Syne', 'Silent Night' and the old 1950s hit 'The Little Drummer Boy', realising that a combination of one or all of them would be demanded on new year's eve at the Fillmore. After appearances in the intervening years on many bootlegs and on a couple of briefly-available official vinyl singles produced by Alan Douglas, the medley finally came out intact on CD in 1999 when the Hendrix Estate issued an extended single. Apart from being an impressive demonstration of Hendrix's superb control of feedback, the sequence doesn't have much else to offer. A similar story can be told about a December 23rd Record Plant session where variations on 'Come Down Hard On Me' and 'Bleeding Heart' (called 'Honey Bed') were tried, along with a simple work-through of 'Night Bird Flying', before the session ended. With that, the new band were deemed ready for their two evenings at the Fillmore, now just days away.

burning bridges
DECEMBER 1969 TO MARCH 1970

Hendrix looked happier and more relaxed on-stage than at any time in the previous six months or more when Bill Graham introduced him alongside Billy Cox and Buddy Miles at their first Fillmore show on new year's eve, December 31st 1969.

Graham told the audience that the musicians were "some old friends with a brand new name – a Band of Gypsys". An observer from Down Beat, the distinguished writer and researcher Chris Albertson, was in the crowd that night. "It was in many ways a special evening," he wrote. "A new year was about to be rung in, a chaotic decade was coming to an end, and one of the star exponents of the music that so colored the decade was changing directions."[1] Hendrix's group was contracted to deliver two shows at the Fillmore on December 31st and two on January 1st. From these four recorded sets he and his management planned to extract material for the album that would settle the long-running dispute with PPX, who had already concluded a deal with Capitol to issue the resulting LP. PPX/Capitol had initially demanded a Jimi Hendrix Experience album, but eventually accepted that the group was not available as a working unit. The new band would play these four separate shows, in effect giving them four opportunities to come up with the goods. No two shows were exactly the same, although some songs were repeated in different sets.

The shows and songs were as follows, with * indicating all tracks on the *Live At The Fillmore East* two-CD set 1999, † indicating the few tracks only appearing (in various states) on the 1999 *Band Of Gypsys* DVD, ° indicating all tracks on the original 1970 *Band Of Gypsys* LP, and # indicating tracks only on *Band Of Gypsys 2* (1986).

December 31st 1969, first show: 'Power Of Soul', 'Lover Man', 'Hear My Train A'Comin''*#, 'Changes'*, 'Izabella'*, 'Machine Gun', 'Stop', 'Ezy Rider', 'Bleeding Heart', 'Earth Blues', 'Burning Desire'.

December 31st 1969, second show: 'Auld Lang Syne'*, 'Who Knows'*, 'Stepping Stone'†, 'Burning Desire', 'Fire' , 'Ezy Rider', 'Machine Gun'*, 'Power Of Soul', 'Stone Free', 'Changes', 'Message To Love', 'Stop', 'Foxy Lady', Voodoo Child (Slight Return)', 'Purple Haze'.

January 1st 1970, first show: 'Who Knows'°, 'Machine Gun'°, 'Changes', 'Power Of Soul'*, 'Stepping Stone'*, 'Foxy Lady' #, 'Stop'*#, 'Earth Blues', 'Burning Desire'*.

January 1st 1970, second show: 'Stone Free'*, 'Changes'°, 'Power Of Soul'°, 'Message To Love'°, 'Earth Blues'*, 'Izabella', 'Machine Gun'*, 'Voodoo Child (Slight Return)'*, 'We Gotta Live Together''*, 'Wild Thing'*, 'Hey Joe', 'Purple Haze'.

It was decided that the first set on the 31st should just be a warm-up to get the band settled and familiar with working live together in front of an audience. After that it was down to serious business. This went naturally with a new year's eve audience in the mood for celebration. As Albertson noted in his *Down Beat* review, "I braced myself as large figures appeared superimposed on the clock for the countdown of the last 10 seconds: 10-9-8-7-6-5-4-3-2-1. It was 1970 and the new decade was roared in by the playing of the awesome opening of Richard Strauss's *Also Sprach Zarathustra*. … With its playing, the screen was lifted, revealing the inner workings of the Joshua Light Show, which now projected its multicolored images on the cheering crowd. After a few thousand "Happy New Years" the screen slipped back into place, Joshua and his gang cast their imagination on it, and the star of the show, Jimi Hendrix, intoned a most unusual rendition of 'Auld Lang Syne', turning it into a bluesy thing of strange beauty." Albertson found the group's show to be built on blues-based repertoire and "promising" rather than fully delivered, "because Hendrix had not yet had time to fall into his new groove. … He still resorts to such crowd-pleasing tricks as playing his guitar with his teeth. There was less of this gimmickry than usual, however, and I suspect that he will eventually give it up".[2]

"One of the star exponents of the music that so colored the decade was changing directions."

Down Beat, on Hendrix at the Fillmore with the Band Of Gypsys

This contrasts with most of the limited amount of video footage where Hendrix often stands almost motionless for whole songs. But there were four shows, and what survives on video does not necessarily come from the shows that reviewers and other witnesses have commented upon. "There was one show," Billy Cox told an interviewer, "where Jimi just stood there. He put all the fire he could under the band. … And this one was the show that we were gonna give to the individuals that had reached the law suit and to kinda get him out from under that."[3] That show was neither of the new year's eve gigs.

Some comment has been made about Bill Graham telling Hendrix after one of the shows to stop clowning around on-stage and get down to some serious playing. According to Graham this took place after the first set on the 31st, and for the evening's second show Hendrix then gave "the most brilliant, emotional display of virtuoso electric guitar I have ever heard. I don't expect ever to hear such sustained brilliance in an hour and fifteen minutes. He just stood there, did nothing, just played and played".[4] But as Albertson reported in *Down Beat*, both shows on the 31st were crowd-pleasers, the band playing a mixture of material from the recent rehearsals and from Experience days amid plenty of Hendrix's usual stage routines. What seems more likely is that Graham in his memory of the events simply conflated the four shows across two evenings into two shows on one evening. He probably told Hendrix to get serious after both the 31st shows were over. That would fit with his idea of a chastened Hendrix delivering the goods on the first set the following day, as well as the guitarist's need to deliver a polished and convincing set of recordings for the PPX settlement. The devastating

guitar playing that Graham rightly remembered came on the first set of the second evening. Whatever the crowd then made of a largely stationary Hendrix, the aural evidence of some remarkable music being played is hard to dispute.

The first set on January 1st 1970 turned out to be considerably shorter than the second, but the two performances from it that appeared on the resulting *Band Of Gypsys* LP, 'Who Knows' and 'Machine Gun', would completely change the perception of Hendrix's capabilities as an improviser and musician. Looking at the repertoire recorded over the four sets and two evenings, the material released on the original LP skilfully blended past and present elements in its presentation of Hendrix's new group to his audience. There is a sizeable element of showmanship and crowd-pleasing in some of the music played, as well as a concerted effort to present fresh material. The new R&B and funk-influenced approach suggested in 'Message To Love' and 'Power Of Soul' would have been a surprise to the people attending the Fillmore, but both songs had been in preparation for some considerable time by Hendrix: he had opened his set at Woodstock the previous August with 'Message To Love'. The Buddy Miles features were his own 'Changes' and 'We Gotta Live Together', and the Ragavay/Shuman song 'Stop'. The drummer sang and played effectively, but these were pleasant distractions rather than anything more substantial. Of the previously untested material, only 'Burning Desire' and 'Machine Gun' had the gravitas to suggest that a fundamental shift might be occurring in Hendrix's music. 'Who Knows', a riff-based blues with lyrics borrowed from a number of sources, including variations on themes in 'Message to Love', is a jam that serves as a loosener, leaning heavily on old R&B styles for its structure, even if Hendrix's improvisation is a million miles removed from the instrumentals of Ike Turner and the like. Although often maligned, this easy groover contains some delightfully fresh guitar playing – economical, playful and intense by turns – with Hendrix allowing himself the space and time to craft something more than the usual flash and explosions from his guitar and its attendant electric devices.

In retrospect, the lasting impact of the Band Of Gypsys is as much driven by the media view of the Fillmore events as that of Woodstock. The one overwhelming performance from the four evenings is the version of 'Machine Gun' from the first set of the second night, which became the centrepiece of the LP selected by Hendrix from the concert tapes. Without those tapes and the resulting album, the band would not have been much more than a footnote in the short history of Hendrix's music and a golden memory for the people who attended the Fillmore East on those two evenings. The album and tapes represent only a fraction of what the band was presenting in concert at the time.

Hendrix had four Fillmore versions of 'Machine Gun' to choose from, and he unerringly chose the best, even if it suffers towards the end from some tuning problems that the guitarist himself complained about later. Why is this performance of 'Machine Gun' not only the best of the four but one of Hendrix's most towering achievements?

It has a lot to do with the inspiration of the moment, but ultimately what is so satisfying is the form that Hendrix devises for

The Fillmore audience gathers for new year's eve with the Band Of Gypsys, a festive tambourine on every seat.

the tale he has to tell. For a start, he performs the verses of this minor drone-blues up front, drenched in a Univibe-effect guitar commentary and with parallel guitar lines supporting his voice. He does this over a curt, precise accompaniment from bassist and drummer who stick to their allotted patterns and beats and hold such a firm grip on the time that it remains absolutely constant for the entire 12-plus minutes. This is what Miles and Cox do best and this is what is expected of them.

What is not expected – and Hendrix gives no hint of this on any previous version – is the staggering guitar solo that occupies the entire middle section of the performance, buttressed by machine-gun drum patterns and complementary bass lines. The first note is a screaming fourth (sounding as an A; Hendrix is tuned down by a tone) bent up a tone or whole-step to a perfect fifth (B), sustained almost beyond belief. From that moment, Hendrix is playing as if directly connected to some higher plane of creative inspiration. His ideas are not just fresh, they break new ground throughout. Even little patterns and motifs or devices he's used before – like the old-style blues minor-third trill, in Hendrix's case often played in tandem with swoops on the vibrato arm – he forces into new shapes and contexts, stretching the tortured contours beyond recognition into a new form of melody that not even he had touched on before he played this solo.

Beyond that, on his 'Machine Gun' solo Hendrix achieves supreme continuity through variation. He is not merely running through random sophisticated blues licks at a hectic rate here – he is coming up with a phrase, or a little motif, then working at it, changing its shape, rhythmically displacing it, and putting it into new and revealing contexts as he moves on. He does this with a number of ideas during different parts of the first solo – the major one – but most particularly in the sequence after he first returns to the 'machine gun' rhythm motif that Cox and Miles have stuck to. He then launches back into improvisation with a leap of over an octave to etch out an arching variation of the 'machine gun' motif, taking it through permutation after permutation in an astonishing variety of shapes and modifications as he inverts and extends it. At the same time he transforms his 'voice' for the solo's emotional message by applying his pedals and effects, just as other instrumentalists, especially wind players, use the different tonal characteristics of their instruments to express different approaches to each part of a song.

The solo is filled with extraordinary musical discoveries, mostly couched in the language of the blues but not to the exclusion of other sources. Some of his busy upward-sweeping melodic lines are of such emotional intensity and melodic inventiveness as to sound absolutely newly minted even now, over 30 years later. With this solo he is cutting the air in front of him for everyone else to follow, and it remains an object lesson in improvisational power and creativity. It is a weighty emotional statement on a par with anything made in the Western music of his time, in any genre or field.

When he brings the solo to a close – and realises that he has slipped considerably out of tune – he swaps to the tune's secondary riff and then plays some utterly heavenly guitar accompaniment to his second set of vocals, cajoling and nursing along his lyrics with a commentary at turns poignant and

December 1969 outside the Fillmore East: just another list of forthcoming talent.

raging. Bringing it down to a whisper and then resolving it with an unaccompanied depiction of a war scene, he completes a story told in music without bombast or sentimentality. This is not some 'programme music' that merely acts out the scenes sketched in the lyrics. The human and emotional landscape painted by Hendrix in 12:15 of inspired playing remains today a vast and infinitely moving picture, capable of speaking to every new generation of listeners who happen along. Kirk Hammett of Metallica spoke eloquently to *Rolling Stone* about the piece in 1999. "His music was so visual," said Hammett. "In the live 'Machine Gun' from *Band Of Gypsys* he goes into that whole thing where he's mimicking the bombers coming in, dropping bombs, the voices crying out. Hendrix had a way of saying something political without speaking outside his own language."[5]

In that sense this music has the depth and grandeur of John Coltrane at his most expansive. It overshadows everything else played in these concerts or selected for the original LP. Nothing else seems to matter after 'Machine Gun'. The four selections that made up side two of the original album were all taken from the second show of January 1st, but however engaging and intriguing, they sound like a sideshow entertainment in contrast. This is not to denigrate performances such as 'Power Of Soul' and 'Message To Love', but simply to underline the vast scope that Hendrix entertained with that live version of 'Machine Gun'. While he made other attempts at 'Machine Gun' in concert over the next nine months, playing it regularly through the spring and summer, there was never again a performance to touch this for its unity, emotional impact and improvisational freshness. But then, who needs two of a unique event? Only greedy people.

Buoyed by the music they played and the reaction to it, Hendrix, Cox and Miles planned a series of sessions at the Record Plant studio to lay down definitive versions of some of the newer material they'd been playing. At this point, with the tracks still to be selected and allotted to PPX/Capitol from the Fillmore East tapes, no one knew exactly what would be included on the live album and what they should prepare for a competing studio album. For that reason, on January 7th the trio worked on 'Stepping Stone', a song still in search of a definitive title and, on this occasion, misleadingly called 'I'm A Man'. After months of aborted efforts, a master take was managed on that night, with a great train-ride 8/8 rhythm pattern from Miles and some delicious vocal versifying from Hendrix.

'Stepping Stone' is a well-crafted song but some of its aspects did not bode well for the present or the immediate future in Hendrix's career. The lyrics continued the sequence of depression and desperation – even a sense of failing identity – that had been apparent in his new songs for over a year. This one includes the lines: "You're a woman / At least you say you are / You're a woman / At least you look like you are / You're a woman / At least you taste like you are / But you make it off in bed with my guitar." He also sings: "I'm a man / At least I'm trying to be." This is desperate stuff, hinting not too subtly at a meltdown of personal identity with no help offered or accepted for reconstruction. Musically, 'Stepping Stone' lacks a hook-line, although it does possess memorable vocal lines – a quite different attribute. All this makes it a very strange choice as the A-side of the band's first (and only) single, released eventually in April. Decidedly uncommercial, it is something of a throwback to the frenetic blues numbers Hendrix was attempting to pull together a year before with the Experience. A much more suitable choice for a single would have been 'Power Of Soul', with its perfect dance tempo, instantly catchy hook-line and sunny, optimistic lyrics. It was successfully attempted in the studio just a week later.

What prompted the choice? By the time the single's track selection was made by Hendrix, the band had split up. From January 14th-16th at Juggy studio Hendrix and Eddie Kramer had selected tracks and made provisional mixes for the *Band Of Gypsys* album, with 'Power Of Soul' included in a live version. The process of choosing and mixing the live album was not a pleasant one: Hendrix only fulfilled his legal obligation to PPX/Capitol under duress and with the greatest reluctance. Nevertheless, and as usual, he did choose the material with care. None of the selections was a re-hash of previously released compositions, some of the tunes were undoubtedly on a par with anything else he had available at the time, and in the case of 'Machine Gun' the performance chosen was the best of the four recorded over the two nights and stands today as one of his greatest musical achievements. Two songs lined up for the LP's second side, 'Power Of Soul' and 'Message To Love', could have been potential singles in new studio versions but Hendrix assigned live versions of them to Chalpin's company. It meant he was giving up a lot, especially as he'd released no new material since autumn 1968. Chalpin complained about both the 'live' quality of the material handed over to him and the fact that it wasn't an Experience album as stipulated in the settlement (though Capitol weren't so picky).[6] Not only was this insulting as far as Hendrix was concerned, but it adds to the considerable and continuing evidence that Chalpin's expertise lay in commercial exploitation rather than aesthetic judgement. The album reached the Top 10 on both sides of the Atlantic following its release in April.

Hendrix and his team completed final mixes of the live tracks on January 21st, after which the multitracks were filed in Mike Jeffery's office and forgotten. Hendrix then went over to the Record Plant and began a long session with Cox and Miles. While most of it remains unreleased even on bootleg – including two jams, and several takes of 'Burning Desire' and 'Send My Love To Linda' – some incomplete solo Hendrix workings on 'Linda' have been made available (though these are possibly from an earlier date) and progress was made on getting down an acceptable 'Power Of Soul'. 'Linda' was never advanced beyond this point in the studio, although Hendrix continued to think about the song. It shares the same chord sequence as 'Heaven Has No Sorrow', first sketched on a home tape-recorder back in September 1969, except that 'Heaven', while also never finished, at least had a hook-line with an accompanying musical progression.

Similarly fragmentary results were the only reward at a Band Of Gypsys session at the Record Plant two days earlier, where 'Burning Desire' failed yet again to come into focus. Following the early termination of this session Hendrix stayed on and experimented with backwards-running and varispeeded guitar tapes. The experiments have appeared on bootlegs and reveal Hendrix laying down a rhythm guitar track (in the normal tape direction) and then adding tracks, some speeded up and others reversed. These were simple experiments for private reference and did not represent an attempt to put together a new master. The overall effect is not unlike a shorthand version of his 1968-vintage backwards-guitar recordings such as 'New Rising Sun'.

January 20th was a good day in the studio for Hendrix. Mixing and overdubs were done for 'Earth Blues', 'Message To Love', 'Stepping Stone' and 'Ezy Rider', though only 'Stepping Stone' would be released in this incarnation. The following day the Hendrix-Miles-Cox trio laid down an invigorating early try at 'Astro Man', Hendrix singing the tongue-in-cheek lyrics with obvious relish, even starting off one take by exclaiming to the control room: "This is gonna be fun!" (This version is available on the four-

CD *Jimi Hendrix Experience* box-set.) The take has a very different feel to the version made with Cox and Mitch Mitchell in late June (which would be the first one released, on the posthumous collation *Cry Of Love*). The presence of Buddy Miles means that the tempo is more relaxed, the beat more funky, and with Hendrix in a good mood the vocal has an enjoyable facetiousness missing from the June take. Hendrix was considering this song, with its cartoon-character references and plotline, as a contender for a loose suite of tunes that he continued to work up through home demos and jottings over the months to come. He gave the collection the working title *Black Gold* in February. 'Astro Man' would be one of only two tracks from this suite – the other is 'Drifting' – that Hendrix would attempt to bring to perfection at Electric Lady studio in the last months of his life.

'Power Of Soul' was the other tune given a definitive reading on the 21st. It is one of the happiest combinations of the guitar-and-bass patterns so prevalent in the Band Of Gypsys, especially in the instrumental opening where each four-bar unit has a riff that is a variant of the one before, and they all relate back to the original that kicks off the song. Each of the variants is interesting in its own right, telling the listener a story they want to hear. When the verse arrives with its attendant underpinning riffs and the song grooving on Buddy Miles's unshiftable beat and the guitar-bass patterns, Hendrix's vocal seems to float effortlessly over the whole. The little stop-time patterns and cadences that he builds into the song reveal an attention to detail that genuinely adds a concerted musical commentary to the overall canvas. The lyric is again one of Hendrix's paeans to the value of working together towards valuable common aims – "With the power of soul / Anything is possible / With the power of you / Anything you wanna do" – sentiments that remain pertinent to today's self-improving America. This track, with overdubs from later in 1970, was being groomed by Hendrix in August 1970 for album release, and was briefly considered for the posthumous *Cry Of Love* LP where it would have been a welcome bonus. Instead, it had to wait decades for a release in its unaltered form on 1997's *South Saturn Delta* CD compilation.

> # "The most brilliant, emotional display of virtuoso electric guitar I have ever heard."
>
> Bill Graham, on Hendrix at his Fillmore East venue

An abortive mixing session on January 22nd for 'Izabella' and 'Stepping Stone' at least identified these as the two pieces chosen for the proposed single, with 'Izabella' initially planned as the A-side, but it would be a while yet before the songs were mixed to Hendrix's satisfaction. The following day the Band Of Gypsys made their final visit to the Record Plant. There were the usual jams, one of which, given the title 'Country Blues', has in part been officially released (on the *Jimi Hendrix Experience* four-CD box) but has also been extensively bootlegged in various incarnations. The jams contain snippets (and sometimes lyrics) of a whole string of Hendrix numbers, including 'Ezy Rider', 'Astro Man', 'Cherokee Mist', 'Villanova Junction' and 'Midnight Lightning'. Another jam was dedicated to fun workouts of 'Heartbreak Hotel' and 'Blue Suede Shoes'. The hard-driving guitar solo edited by John Jansen to appear in the pastiche he created called 'M.L.K.' (and released in 1975 on *Crash Landing* as 'Captain Coconut') comes from one of this day's jams. The ultra-slow blues 'Once I Had A Woman', featuring a shadowy harmonica player simply listed on all releases as 'Don', has been issued a number of times since the mid 1970s, with its latest and most faithful representation coming on the *Blues* CD of 1994.

All this enjoyable activity masked the fact that no progress was being

Warming up with the Gypsys at the Fillmore East. When Hendrix played 'Machine Gun' at the first of two shows there on January 1st 1970 he produced one of the most towering achievements of his entire career.

made on any of the current projects, but at least Hendrix seemed back on course and was having a good time in the studio again. Engineer Dave Ragno confirmed this to John McDermott. "Jimi cut back on the party crowd and was trying to focus on his work. He came in alone on a lot of nights, just wanting to do guitar overdubs or experiment with some mix ideas that he had. His creativity was on the upswing, because he didn't have all of these people around him. His own drug use, from what we could see, had diminished."[7] Such observations give the impression that Hendrix had pulled back from disaster with the help of his friends and musical colleagues, that he had regained balance and perspective and was ready to push forward once more. This was true, at least in part. What came as something of a shock soon after was the manner in which he moved forward. He had at least given hints at the beginning of January that he was looking beyond the current working trio with Cox and Miles for something else to fulfil his musical ambitions.

In an interview with the *New York Post* at the very start of the year Hendrix had hedged away from any firm commitment that the current line-up was a permanent one. He claimed: "We'll play anywhere, where we know it's gonna make some kind of penetration or some kind of impact. Anywhere! We can play at the Whiskey, and then we'll play at the Hollywood Bowl. We'll play at all the funky clubs. I mean, we could. We're gearing ourselves so we could play anywhere. I might not even be there all the time. Buddy might not even be there all the time." This appeared to leave Billy Cox as the only permanent and indispensable member of the group. Hendrix told the *Post*'s Al Aronowitz: "Musically we try to keep it together. That's why we have to change. That's why personnels in groups always change all the time, 'cause they're always constantly searching for that certain little thing. The fact of calling it Gypsys means it could even expand on personnel or so forth and so

on." He also mentioned that "we're waiting for Stevie Winwood. If I can get a hold of him and he agrees to it, that'll be another voice".[8]

This may have been wishful thinking or simply a red herring. Hendrix had admired Winwood for some time and told interviewers that he would welcome him into his band. Such overtures never turned into solid negotiations, either because Winwood had prior commitments or, when he was free, the timing wasn't right for Hendrix. Around then, Blind Faith had split and Winwood was working on *John Barleycorn Must Die*, an album that would eventually reunite sufficient members of the old Traffic for the group to re-form. Keyboardist and singer Winwood would have been a welcome member of what Hendrix conceived as a loose coalition of musicians intermittently working together towards common aims and on common projects. Hendrix may have considered Winwood in a similar light to Buddy Miles's position in the Band Of Gypsys: he knew Miles's track record as a leader of his own groups, that he was a man of ambitions and a singer in his own right, and that it was therefore only natural that Miles might want to want to dip in and out of other projects. What Hendrix couldn't plan for in all this was the rock and pop world's marked reluctance to countenance such loose arrangements. Most rock industry musicians – and their backers, such as managers and record companies – craved the security of permanent line-ups. As in so many other things, Hendrix was a rare exception.

Miles has said that the Band Of Gypsys was a working group terminated before its time. While it was originally pulled together to get his good friend out of a giant hole, it still had plenty of life in it, life that was stamped out by forces beyond his or Hendrix's control. Hendrix's management and record company usually get the biggest share of the blame. There was certainly continual pressure on Hendrix at the time. That Hendrix had a different idea to Miles about the nature of the trio is now hard to dispute. But to make it an issue of simple choice between the fatback grooves of Buddy Miles and the more flexible drumming of Mitch Mitchell is to ignore the diversity of Miles's experience and to falsify the position. At around the same time, Miles was playing very creditably in the studio with John McLaughlin and Larry Young, as McLaughlin's *Devotion* album testifies. He provided Hendrix with what he felt was appropriate to Hendrix's needs in each song, including vocals and the injection of the occasional composition. Hendrix had revealed in the *New York Post* interview that he was not entirely convinced about the long-term

"Jimi cut back on the party crowd and was trying to focus on his work."

Dave Ragno, engineer, on Hendrix in the studio

stability of the band. He was asked if the Experience might re-form. "With Mitch maybe, but not with Noel for sure,"[9] said Hendrix. The plain fact was that his working relationship with Mitchell had never been formally ended. Recently, Billy Cox remembered the beginning of the Band Of Gypsys as a more casual arrangement than Miles's recollections allow, although he agreed that it was pulled together quickly to help out Hendrix with the delivery of an album. "Since Mitch was out of the country," Cox said, "and Buddy was always hanging around the studio, we got it all together."[10]

Hendrix and Mitchell expected to work together again at some unspecified point and were still on very good personal terms, while the relationship with Redding had been strained beyond repair. Mitchell, an Englishman, had gone home for a time, and had hardly been idle. He'd joined a quartet with Jack Bruce and Larry Coryell called Jack Bruce & Friends, unfortunately undocumented on record but with a tantalising line-up. According to Mitchell, the band lasted a little less than four months: Bruce left to join Tony Williams's Lifetime, while Mitchell joined up with Hendrix once again.

There are a number of reports from Hendrix's friends and working circle suggesting occasional disagreements between Hendrix and Miles. Both men were accustomed to running their own band and getting their own way. Noel Redding once observed: "Buddy Miles was used to his own stardom; and there's one thing I know about Jimi – he liked being Top Cat."[11] Privately, Hendrix was also less than thrilled with the idea of Miles's singing, feeling that it diminished his role and was a distraction. Consequently, he gave low priority to the drummer's songs: in the three months of the band's existence they allotted studio time to a Miles song during just one session, recording six takes of 'Changes' and never returning to the song in the studio again.

The confused, messy ending to the Band Of Gypsys had everyone nursing their wounds and theorising about what really happened. In effect it was a logical consequence of Hendrix's already well established pattern of behaviour. Carol Shiroky had put her finger on it when she observed that as far back as 1966 Hendrix was adept at compartmentalising his relationships and keeping the different individuals not only separate but often unaware of one another's existence. Miles told John McDermott that the difference between the Band Of Gypsys and the Experience "was the communication between Jimi and Billy and myself. I think our greatest attribute was that we would work together with little or no effort. It's one thing when you have to explain music to people, it's another thing to [follow] a musician, especially if they're paving

the way".[12] This flies in the face of all that is known about the way the Hendrix-Redding-Mitchell trio worked: they built on minimal rehearsal, developed telepathic understanding of one another's patterns of play, and – until Redding's disaffection in 1969 – had a sympathetic rapport and loyalty between them. Again it comes back to the fact that the two bands had different working methods: as Miles states, he and Cox followed Hendrix. Redding – and Mitchell in particular – accompanied him. Miles could only have believed what he said if he'd been completely unaware of the closeness between the former group – regardless of its conflicts and the damage the members did latterly to each other.

It is a pity that the Band Of Gypsys disintegrated in such an undignified and damaging way, not only in full public view but in a series of rows and recriminations following a disastrous gig at New York's Madison Square Garden on January 28th. Without the knowledge of the rest of the band, Hendrix had already acceded to the idea of a reunion of the Experience, and although he was set against Redding's return, he allowed Jeffery to fly Redding over to New York for preliminary meetings about a planned spring tour. Hendrix was playing a deep game here. While he was happy to welcome Mitchell back and use the Experience name for what would be a relatively short tour, he was determined to have his own choice of bass player. But he kept his own counsel and allowed events to overtake everyone, including Mike Jeffery.

At the Madison Square Garden event, the *Winter Festival For Peace*, the Band Of Gypsys were part of a bill that included Harry Belafonte, Blood Sweat & Tears, Dave Brubeck, Judy Collins, Richie Havens, Mother Earth, Peter Paul & Mary, the cast of the hit musical *Hair*, and The Rascals. Reports suggest that Hendrix had for some time been looking forward to playing the show. The Fillmore concerts had been his first live work in months, and that was now nearly a month ago. Redding wrote in his autobiography that it had been agreed for him and Mitchell to come on "for a couple of numbers" towards the end of the Gypsys set.[13] Before the band even appeared on-stage, Hendrix's party knew things were wrong, but it was unclear if this was down to drugs, depression, or a combination of those and other still-unknown factors. After a period of relative drug abstinence, Hendrix had recently become more heavily involved again. Jim Marron, who was by then enmeshed in bringing Electric Lady studio into existence, was aware of the slide. "Drugs were not only screwing him up," said Marron, "they were destroying the environment he needed to create. With Electric Lady set to open, I didn't

"Personnels in groups always change all the time, 'cause they're always constantly searching for that certain little thing."

Jimi Hendrix

want to be the guy who procured drugs or women for him – I had seen Devon [Wilson] do that at the Scene. That wasn't my idea of personal management. Hendrix sat through many paternal lectures about his drug use from all of us, but I doubt it had any long-term effect on him."[14]

Backstage at the Garden, just prior to going on, Hendrix had sat in unmoving silence. Johnny Winter was there. "When I saw him, it gave me the chills," Winter recalled a few years later. "It was the most horrible thing I'd ever seen. He came in with this entourage of people, and it was like he was already dead. He just walked in – and even though Jimi and I weren't the greatest of friends, we always talked, always – and he came in with his head down, sat on the couch alone, and put his head in his hands. ... He really wanted to do the gig, but he never should have. It wasn't that it was bad, but his whole thing was inspiration, and there wasn't any. ... He was just so unhappy, there was no way that he could play the show."[15]

Buddy Miles was sure that he saw manager Mike Jeffery give Hendrix pills before the gig, and that this sent him insensible and unable to play properly. Jeffery may have been a ruthless money-maker, but he was not stupid, and would surely not have put in jeopardy this opportunity to make a vast amount of money in a very short space of time – something Hendrix had been conspicuously unable to do lately what with the lack of gigs and escalating recording costs, let alone the money being spent on Electric Lady. One of Jeffery's few direct personal contacts with Hendrix was through LSD, and Noel Redding claimed to have seen Hendrix accept a tab from Jeffery before going on-stage.[16] But it would have had to be bad to have such an immediate effect. Others have suggested that someone laced Hendrix's drink with LSD or something more savage.[17] The guitarist rarely got completely wrecked before a gig; he always wanted to put on a professional show. But there is evidence that he had a few drinks prior to this concert, which may have reacted badly with any drugs recently ingested. He had a

Not quite the new Experience, at a February 1970 interview. No one has yet told Redding he won't actually be in the band.

notoriously low tolerance for alcohol. It is perhaps more mundane but closer to the truth to conclude that Hendrix unintentionally wiped himself out, possibly due to the tension involved in anticipating the demise of the Band Of Gypsys, which he knew was very close to happening. In the event, it was closer than even he realised.

Hendrix made it through just two numbers on-stage before sitting on the drum riser and giving up. Jim Marron, at the front of the audience, was aghast. "I was given ringside seats for myself and my family and when I saw the state that Jimi [was in when he] entered the stage a half an hour late or maybe even an hour late I wanted to crawl under the seat and deny any association with him."[18] An embarrassed and angry Buddy Miles tried to cover for Hendrix, but after five minutes it was clear that nothing could be done. The band walked off, not to return. Backstage in the dressing rooms a furious Mike Jeffery fired Buddy Miles on the spot and called a halt to the Gypsys experiment. Hendrix stayed in his dressing room and let it all flow over his head. To this day Miles blames Jeffery. "I thought it was unfair. It really, really just kinda was tearin' at me because of the fact that, in and around the situation, that the management didn't want three brothers playing together, three blacks."[19]

To accept Miles's assertions is to take at face value Hendrix's unequivocal and ongoing concern to make closer contact with the brothers in Harlem and further afield in the US. It also once again makes Hendrix a pawn in someone else's game rather than a player in his own. There is no doubt that he was disturbed by the low interest shown in him by the black community, but he was hardly unknown to them. It was more to do with acceptance. In the

past few months before this concert he had wanted to be seen more positively by activists within the black rights movement and elsewhere. But he was only incidentally involved in politics: his philosophies were mostly concerned with hippie ideas of peace, love and living together in harmony, not with guns, violence and confrontation. He also had to consider that a close identification with activist politics of any kind might take away some of his existing audience. These were not financial concerns but more to do with his primary commitment to play music and be appreciated for it. Like Miles Davis, Hendrix paid little regard to where musicians came from, so long as they could play what he wanted them to play. Hendrix had needed the Band Of Gypsys to re-focus for a time and was now ready to broaden out again. As his friend Arthur Allen concluded about the whole Band Of Gypsys adventure, "We realised immediately that he had extracted everything that he needed from Band Of Gypsys and the Jimi Hendrix Experience to take him to the next stage of musical creativity."[20] What he'd 'extracted' may not have been only musical.

Mike Jeffery probably enjoyed being the executioner. It would have appealed to his self-image as a tough guy not fazed by anything or anybody. He was also probably furious at the debacle a few minutes earlier on-stage, and had struck while the blood was high. Jeffery's assistant, Trixie Sullivan, was adamant that Jeffery would never had acted unilaterally. "If you're talking specifically about Buddy Miles leaving the group and Mike Jeffery sacking him, it would have been *totally* on Jimi's instigation," she said later. "Under no circumstances would Mike come in and sack people without Jimi's permission [or] approval [or] in fact his instigation of the whole act."[21]

Billy Cox was once more sickened by the whole mess he'd been involuntarily involved in, and also suspicious like Miles that race had a part to play in the move to disbandment. Cox took himself off to Nashville, convinced that he no longer had a role to play. But he would be back. He'd reckoned without Hendrix's tenacious spirit and his need to have close friends around him. No matter how upset, guilty and depressed Hendrix had been by the debacle at Madison Square Garden, three days later he was jamming acoustically in his New York apartment with Mitch Mitchell. The drummer was back from his stint in England and feeling ready for the Hendrix experience once more. Hendrix had phoned him during January to tell him he was wanted, and Mitchell, appearing early that month at the Fillmore East with Jack Bruce & Friends, had spent most of his time in New York at Hendrix's Greenwich Village apartment. He quickly became aware that Hendrix wanted him back in his working group.

On February 1st Mitchell and Hendrix worked through a huge selection of material – some originals, some oldies – to familiarise themselves with each other's thoughts and also to bring Mitchell up to date with the material Hendrix had been writing since November. Noel Redding was already in New York and Hendrix, under pressure from Jeffery to pull together the old band in order to guarantee a major tour that was now firmly in place, even agreed to a group interview with John Burks for *Rolling Stone*, with photographer Baron Wolman in attendance. This publicity was intended to alert the world to the tour. Hendrix didn't want to talk about recent events with the Band Of

Gypsys. He said of its demise, "It was just something where the head changes, just going through changes. … I was very tired. You know, sometimes there's a lot of things that add up in your head about this and that. And they hit you at a very peculiar time, which happened to be at that peace rally, and here I am fighting the biggest war I've ever fought in my life – inside, you know? And like that wasn't the place to do it, so I just unmasked appearances."[22]

Hendrix admitted that there was a Gypsys single in the pipeline, but when asked if the Experience had a single coming he shied away from a direct

Unmasking appearances: Hendrix absorbed in a question at the *Rolling Stone* magazine interview, New York City, February 5th 1970.

answer. "We might have one from the other thing coming out soon; I don't know about the Experience though. All these record companies, they want singles, but you don't just sit there and say, 'Let's make a track, let's make a single,' or something. We're not going to do that. We don't do that." Asked if he'd given thought to touring with a group called the Experience that could vary in size, Hendrix demurred unconvincingly. "Maybe I'm the evil one, right," he laughed. "But there isn't any reason for it to be like that. I even want the name to be Experience anyway.… No, like about putting other groups on the tour, like our friends – I don't know about that right now, not at a stage like this, because we're in the process of getting our own thing together as far as a three-piece group. But eventually we have time on the side to play with friends. I'll probably be playing with Buddy and Billy – probably be recording, too, on the side, and they'll be doing the same."[23]

But he still couldn't reconcile himself to the idea of going back on the road with Redding, and voiced his misgivings to Mitchell that same evening. After they'd talked it through and Mitchell realised how set Hendrix was against Redding coming back, the drummer suggested Jack Casady as a potential bassist, but Hendrix came back to Billy Cox. Mitchell, who had got along well with Cox in the previous ensemble, agreed, and left the details for Hendrix to sort out. In typical fashion, nothing was sorted out apart from Cox being contacted by Mike Jeffery and invited to rejoin the fold. Redding flew back to London to await the call for

rehearsals to begin. With the situation hanging by a thread, Cox was also left waiting around for another month while other priorities were attended to. As Mitchell put it, "The unfortunate thing about Noel was that he wasn't told until he came back to America, expecting to rehearse for the tour. Basically nobody had the balls to do it."[24] Presumably Jeffery told Hendrix to do his own dirty work this time.

During February there was little going on musically apart from further retouching to the final mixes for the *Band Of Gypsys* album and the two tracks for that band's single, which were at last mixed to Hendrix's satisfaction on February 15th. On the following evening a jam without a bassist but with a drummer (who sounds like neither Buddy Miles nor Mitch Mitchell) and percussionist Juma Sultan produced some spirited playing on two originals – 'Gypsy Boy' was revived for the occasion and 'Freedom' was given an early reading – alongside some old rockers like 'Blue Suede Shoes', 'Summertime Blues' and 'Day Tripper', but nothing was intended for release and all but 'Freedom' remain in the can to this day. 'Freedom' is intriguing, partly because it has a relaxed, easy feel rather than the urgent, slightly desperate edge it would receive later, but also because it reveals its R&B and soul roots in this version. Hendrix plays the guitar riff in the manner of Curtis Mayfield rather than in any kind of rock style, while the drums mix sophistication with a very simple, driving beat. The track had to wait until 2000 and the *Jimi Hendrix Experience* four-CD set for its first release.

Redding arrived in New York on March 6th to give himself plenty of time to prepare for the rehearsals, scheduled to kick off later that month, and was invited by Jeffery's team to put together a group and make an album while he was waiting. As March dragged on, Redding saw no sign of Hendrix and was unable to reach him by phone. He made the album with some friends, including Family vocalist Roger Chapman. It was never released. Hendrix had in fact been in London during most of the time Redding was in New York waiting for him. Hendrix caught up with old friends, including Arthur Lee who was recording *False Start*, Love's new album, at Olympic studio. Of course he added some guitar to the sessions, ordinary by his standards, although of the three tracks he is supposed to have played on only 'The Everlasting First' appeared on the LP.

Hendrix also dropped in on Stephen Stills, recording his debut solo album at Island studio in London, and played on 'Old Times Good Times' as well as material that was not released, including 'White Nigger'. Although 'Old Times' is a fine song (on *Stephen Stills*, 1970) Hendrix plays nothing

"Just going through changes. I was very tired."

Jimi Hendrix, on the Band Of Gypsys split

remarkable and sounds like someone imitating his own earlier style. All this convivial recording, however, masked the real catalyst for Hendrix's sudden trip to London. He had been told that Kathy Etchingham had recently married, and phoned her on impulse to see if it was true. Finding out that it was, he flew over, in part to try to persuade her to turn back the clock. She, however, was sure that she'd found a different route in her life, and declined. "I was startled to see how completely devastated he was by the news," she wrote later. "I suddenly realised that he had pictured our relationship completely differently. He may have been sleeping around in America but he hadn't met anyone else he wanted as a permanent partner. He imagined I would be waiting for him, the good little woman keeping the home fires burning. ... I realised I had let him down just like his mum and dad had before me."[25] Hendrix retired to his room at the Londonderry Hotel – a room booked for him by Etchingham, who was now living with her new husband in the Brook Street flat and couldn't allow Jimi to stay there. While at the hotel he wrote the lyrics for some songs titled 'One Kiss Of Your Eyes', 'Suddenly November Morning', 'Love Is Trying', 'Pass It On' and 'Midnight Lightning'.[26] Many are intensely personal, dealing with love, pain, loss and personal identity, and some were drafted into his developing *Black Gold* suite.

Hendrix flew back to New York on March 19th and started pulling the revised Experience together for rehearsals. He phoned Cox in Nashville, who had already been alerted by Jeffery the month before, and talked him into re-joining. Years later Cox remembered: "I got a phone call from him saying, 'C'mon Bill, let's get it on!' I said, 'Hey man, you ain't gettin' nothin' on. I'm here in Nashville and I'm happy. I don't want to go through all that bullshit again.' [Hendrix] promised and promised that I would have no hassles, so, like a fool, I came back."[27] Rehearsals started as soon as Cox hit New York. Meanwhile Redding – still in the dark and waiting for a call – was finally told the truth when Mitchell's girlfriend unwittingly let it slip on the phone. Stunned, he limped around the New York scene until he'd finished his album, becoming progressively more depressed. "Jimi stopped by one night," Redding wrote in his autobiography, "sort of to say he was sorry, and had the grace to look embarrassed. He offered to play guitar [on the record] and gave me a snort of coke which was heavily laced with [heroin] and made me violently ill."[28] This seemed to be the inadvertent effect of Hendrix's influence on Redding's life from then on.

The last part of March was spent in rehearsal and preparations for the Hendrix-Mitchell-Cox tour. Two recording sessions at the Record Plant were used to produce a rough guide – just guitar and vocal – for developing 'Midnight Lightning', a blues that Hendrix (and Mitchell, who was not at the session) would return to more intensively later in the year. This version uses lyrics not found in other recordings, and may be the set that Hendrix had written shortly beforehand in London in the wake of the rebuff from Kathy Etchingham. The lyrics for this version are some of Hendrix's most striking, especially the images he evokes: "Midnight lightning flashing all around me / Lord, see it flashing all around the trees / See it flashing on my love and me. / Wake up, my sweet darling, and see the light on your eyes / Blue light flashing, shadows leap and church bells ring mad against the night / Hey my love, please stand up and watch [with] me right now... ." Certainly Hendrix paints a picture of what it is to be intensely alone. This bare and painfully honest rendering of a bleak emotional landscape is an object lesson in the way he could play and sing together so effectively, revealed here in all its naked simplicity. Guitarist Joe Beck, who had been familiar with Hendrix as a player since the Greenwich Village days in summer 1966, spoke later about this gift. "He had the ability to sing and play at the same time better than anybody I ever heard to this day," said Beck. "He could sing one song and play another. He just had this unique brain, is really what it was."[29] This may in part account for the emotional impact of Hendrix's singing, which he could focus on purely and directly regardless of what his fingers were doing on the guitar.

During February and March Mike Jeffery had been more than busy. He'd been making frantic attempts to keep the whole Hendrix bandwagon afloat in a sea of mounting debts for the studio, an absence of new releases, and a large gap in income. Eventually he'd turned to the record company, Warner Bros,

for an advance against future royalties on the keenly-anticipated Next Album. Jeffery secured around $300,000 in the process, thereby taking the pressure off as Electric Lady studio, still incomplete and the main financial drain, was brought up to scratch in advance of a grand opening planned for later in the year. After that it could start earning back the massive investment that both Jeffery and Hendrix had made. Unfortunately, Jeffery had also persuaded Warner Bros to take a large financial stake in a soundtrack album to a Hendrix film that did not even have a precise subject yet, let alone a story. It would become Jeffery's vanity project for the year as two young would-be film-

Despite the pressures, Hendrix's sense of humour was still never too far below the surface.

makers, Chuck Wein and Barry DePrendergast, flattered him into thinking that a career as a film producer and financier beckoned.

Hendrix, with most of his business associates looking the other way for the moment, could at least now prepare for the lucrative forthcoming tour in a less frenzied and pressured atmosphere. But how was he to mend his bleeding heart? Although he had Devon Wilson to alternately tend and torment him in New York, he already knew that ultimately she was not the axis around whom he wanted to revolve. He would keep looking until he found the elusive 'her'. Or until she found him.

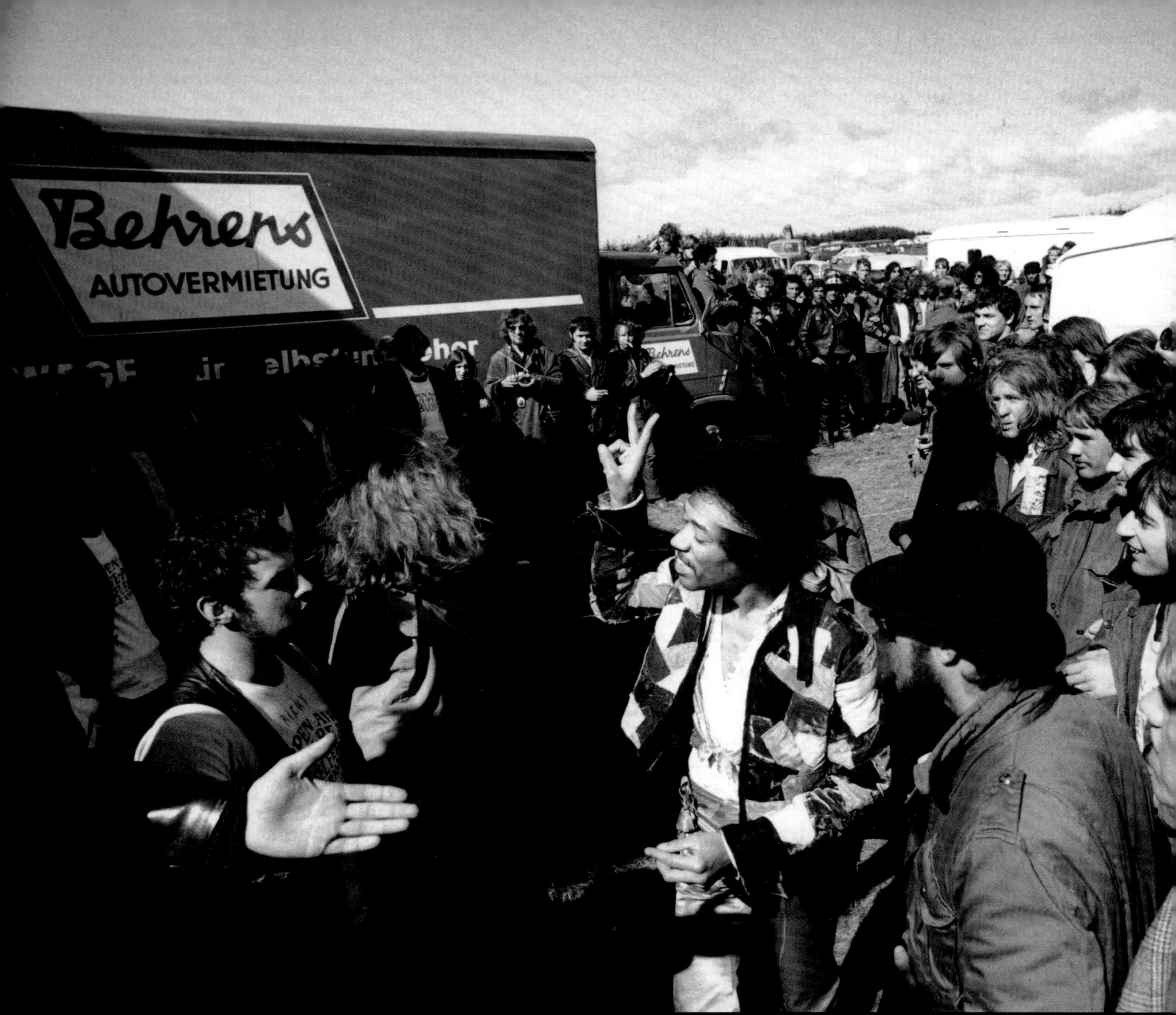
Behrens
AUTOVERMIETUNG

too much too late

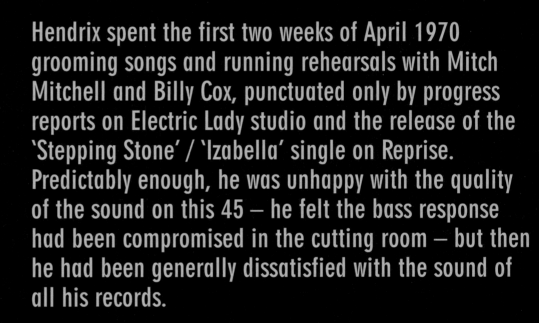

Hendrix spent the first two weeks of April 1970 grooming songs and running rehearsals with Mitch Mitchell and Billy Cox, punctuated only by progress reports on Electric Lady studio and the release of the 'Stepping Stone' / 'Izabella' single on Reprise. Predictably enough, he was unhappy with the quality of the sound on this 45 – he felt the bass response had been compromised in the cutting room – but then he had been generally dissatisfied with the sound of all his records.

T his time, Hendrix's twin obsessions – perfectionism and avoiding completion, two sides of the same coin – became retrospective. Hendrix complained to the record company and eventually had the 'Stepping Stone' single recalled for a second mastering. It was never reissued. This quick withdrawal ensured that it had no chance to chart on first release, making it not only the last but also the least successful Hendrix single issued during his lifetime.

Hendrix still resented the missed opportunity. During an interview with his old London friend Keith Altham in New York on April 13th, he said: "I don't know how good [the 'Stepping Stone' single] is – I can't tell any more. Some of the copies out there have no bass on them. I had to go out somewhere and told the guy to [re-cut] it but he didn't. Sure it matters – I'd like a hit single. It's nice to have people hearing your songs all over the world on the radio – nice to know. I wanted this out before people forgot about me."[1]

Hendrix talked to Altham about the upcoming tour and about new and old plans for records. He suggested that the current idea was to record the first few concerts by the Hendrix-Mitchell-Cox band and produce a live album. "I called the tour The Cry Of Love because that's what it's all about. The recording is really up to Mitch but I'd like to do it."[2] Looking ill and rundown, Hendrix admitted that the old LP project, now remembered as *The First Rays Of The New Rising Sun*, had been abandoned: he confirmed that he was now on to different studio projects, but declined to elaborate. He talked instead of the shortcomings of the *Band Of Gypsys* album – it was released in the US ten days after the interview – and of his ideas for making festivals more enjoyable for the audiences, perhaps by including side attractions. Hendrix certainly did have plans for future albums. Although he now had an enormous backlog of material by the various bands he'd fronted in the past 18 months, he was disinclined to work further on the vast majority of it. He was continually sketching new songs and was interested in recording these for an album with his new trio, but he was also investigating the idea of some special projects as a potential diversion from the main business of finalising the long-delayed studio album to follow up *Electric Ladyland*. One of these projects was the *Black Gold* suite he'd named after his fictional hero – a not even thinly disguised and often humorous idealisation of himself. By the time he went back out on tour in late April he had made a cassette tape as a personal aide-mémoire that collected apartment recordings of the complete *Black Gold* suite into a coherent whole. The concept was not one he talked about much to the media, probably because it was still at an early stage of development and there had been so many false starts in the past year or more, with announcements about new albums and singles coming virtually every month as his focus shifted. Even the choice of the latest Band Of Gypsys single had been publicly debated by Hendrix: he'd told *Melody Maker* in late December that it would either be 'Stepping Stone' (at that point still called 'Trying To Be') or 'Room Full Of Mirrors'. A month later he was dismissing 'Mirrors' as a thing of the past.

"I wish I could have learned how to write for instruments. I'm going to get into that next, I guess."

Jimi Hendrix

During the course of his February interview with *Rolling Stone*'s John Burks intended to herald the return of the Experience, he opened up a little and let slip some information about *Black Gold*. Hendrix answered a question about the Shokan house from the previous summer, saying no, he wasn't still living there with all the musicians. The reason? He wanted some quiet in order to write. Country living can get pretty hectic, it would seem. Asked what it was that he was writing, he replied: "I don't know. Mostly just cartoon material. Make up this one cat who's funny, who goes through all these scenes … you could put it to music, I guess. Just like you can put blues to music. … I want to get into what you'd probably call 'pieces'. Yeah – pieces, behind each other to make movements, or whatever you call it. I've been writing some of those." This line of thought provoked Hendrix to explain how he envisaged some music that was beyond what he could play on the guitar. "I can't play the guitar well enough to get all this music together, so I just lay around. I wish I could have learned how to write for instruments. I'm going to get into that next, I guess."[3]

This brought him right back to his feelings of two years ago, when he had first hit his head on the glass ceiling of frustration with his own formal musical limitations. Hendrix had continued to listen widely to all kinds of music and was even able to talk with enthusiasm about a limited amount of classical music he'd come across while living in London, including Handel's *Messiah*, Holst's *The Planets* and some Bach concertos. He constantly heard many other types of music and understood how that music was achieved. Some commentators have asserted that Hendrix would certainly have become musically literate within a short space of time had he lived, and would have moved on to write his own scores for larger ensembles. This seems unlikely. Other avenues were open to him. He could always hire good arrangers. He could realise more and more of his musical vision as recording studios grew more technically omnipotent: he was already working at the outer limits of the technology of the day and intended to push further. Electric Lady studio would presumably provide the facility of a permanent personal notebook where he could build up his sound pictures. He just needed the time to develop such ideas and allow them to mature.

This was also the case with *Black Gold*, a suite conceived using something like a cartoon technique in telling the story. He had talked in a December interview about the suite's oblique commentary on the contemporary world and his place in it. "Here was this cat come around called Black Gold, and there was this other cat came around called Captain Coconut. Other people came around. I was all these people. And finally when I went back home, all of a sudden I found myself being a little West Coast Seattle boy for a second. Then all of a sudden, when you're back on the road again, there he goes, he starts going back. That's my life until something else comes about."[4] Hendrix always maintained that his music, and especially the songs he wrote, were highly personal – often too much so for his own comfort – so it was natural that the suite he envisaged would be drawn at least in part from his personal observations and experiences. He had been a fan of comics since boyhood, was a radio and TV enthusiast in his youth, and was happy to use a comic-book and radio approach to storytelling and characterisation. This expansion of his musical work and lyric-writing fitted with his desire to investigate longer forms and larger structures in his music while retaining its essential characteristics, notably his intensely intimate communication with his listeners and strong sense of humour. Building up a suite on a picaresque story line with a hero not unlike himself seemed a sensible way forward.

Hendrix worked intensively on a small number of these songs later at Electric Lady. The other tunes would not be developed beyond home recordings during the short time left to him. Tony Brown, the late Hendrix expert and researcher, is the only person so far – other than Mitch Mitchell and the Hendrix Estate, which now owns the tape – to have heard the music on that home cassette. Brown made extensive notes on what he heard, and listed the suite's contents in order, as recorded on the cassette. Side 1: 'November Morning', 'Drifting', 'Captain Midnight' (aka 'Captain 1201'), 'Local Commotion', 'Local Commotion Pt.2', 'Here Comes Black Gold', 'Stepping Stone', 'Little Red Velvet Room'. Side 2: 'The Jungle Is Waiting', 'Send My Love To Joan Of Arc' (aka 'Send My Love To Linda' and 'Send My Love To Kathy'), 'God Bless The Day', 'Black Gold', 'Machine Gun', 'Here Comes Black Gold', 'Trash Man', 'Astro Man', 'Astro Man Pt.2', 'I've Got A Place To Go'.[5] Hendrix's working method on this occasion was to combine new material with suitable existing songs like 'Machine Gun' and 'Stepping Stone'. It is worth noting that 'Trash Man' bears no relation to the instrumental released by Alan Douglas in 1975 on *Midnight Lightning*, but instead is marked on Jimi's corresponding handwritten lyric-sheet notes as "slow blues with harmony". It has words unlike anything else he wrote, though it is consistent with the growth of his social concerns during 1969-70. For example: "I am your trashman / And don't forget I also want to live, not just survive / And we burn up all trash no later than 3.10 / I ain't your Black Slave / Just because I just might try to wash out your mind / It's up to you friend – so get up off your rusty behind."[6]

Brown reproduced lyrics for almost every song ('The Jungle Is Waiting' was an instrumental). They give the impression that the suite was a slice-of-life story about the character Black Gold as he experienced personal highs and lows, especially in 'November Morning', 'Send My Love To Joan Of Arc', 'Drifting' and 'Little Red Velvet Room', all of which have reflective, sensitive lyrics that often contain striking images. Hendrix reflected on the world as it was in those years, using the (often humorous) fantasies of 'Astro Man' and 'Black Gold' to tie together the threads of the suite. It's an intriguing concept and leaves a large question-mark over all his recording activity in 1970. Considering that Hendrix had assembled *Electric Ladyland*, an album with no narrative or theme, by fitting it all together in the best possible running order, and the existence of several lists compiled after the *Black Gold* cassette tape that detail tracks for The Next Album, it is unlikely that the suite would have appeared in exactly the form represented on the tape. Hendrix would probably have removed some of the tracks and replaced them with others, had he sustained the project. For example, in June he was recording a song called 'Captain Coconut', a name that crops up in an interview as he described the ideas for the suite, but it is not on this cassette version. What that recording does demonstrate is that Hendrix was at this stage not only capable of talking about ambitious plans, but was actually putting them into action.

All such far-reaching plans had to be put on hold, however, with the start of the spring tour of the US. This section was planned as the beginning of a staggered tour that would take the group not only through the United States but also to Europe and, for the first time, further afield. *Record Mirror* had reported in March that the intention was to tour the US for four to six weeks and then visit Japan and Europe, with a key date being the Isle Of Wight Festival in England in August, although it was not clear at that stage if the Japan dates would clash with the Isle Of Wight appearance. Although the Hendrix-Mitchell-Cox trio is often referred to as the Cry Of Love band, it was billed during the tour as the Jimi Hendrix Experience. The tour had been given *The Cry Of Love* as a theme and was publicised as such by Hendrix's management and promotions people, but the name was never used for the band (and was never in contention as a name for 'the next album' while Hendrix was alive).

On April 25th, the day after the release of the *Band Of Gypsys* live LP, the Hendrix-Mitchell-Cox Experience appeared at the LA Forum. Supporting were The Buddy Miles Express and a Seattle band, Ballin' Jack, that included on bass Luther Rabb, Hendrix's childhood friend and fellow member of school group The Velvetones. The concert is famous among Hendrix fans and collectors for a number of reasons, not least because bootleg tapes of the performance made in the audience were among the very first illicit Hendrix tapes to appear, just months later. There has never been anything officially released, nor at this point is there likely to be, for no soundboard recording has ever come to light. Another reason for the show's reputation is that it was a particularly good late example of Hendrix's live playing. He is fresh, this being his first tour date in months, the band is new and excited to be appearing together in front of their first audience, and at least part of the repertoire is new, even if some of the old favourites are trundled out again to please the crowd. The band have to manage as best they can with the usual problems of trying to keep in tune, but it's noticeable that after the long lay-off and a different bassist they play the older repertoire much closer to the tempos at which the songs were originally recorded. This is especially true of 'Foxy Lady', a tune Hendrix had grown tired of playing and would usually rush. Despite the poor-quality tape, on which Mitchell is virtually inaudible for large stretches and Cox mostly a suggestion rather than an identifiable presence on bass, flashes of imagination are identifiable in both old and new repertoire.

The version of 'Message To Love' has a surprising ascending guitar chord sequence against a static bass root-note that, although unorthodox, is resolved satisfyingly to the tonic chord. 'Ezy Rider' is sharp and punchy, with the band sounding as if they are in perfect sync. 'Machine Gun' features heavy use of the rich Uni-Vibe effect and some scorching, passionate guitar commentary on Hendrix's opening vocals. Mitchell has worked out a different series of drum patterns to those played by Miles at the Fillmore and uses a modified military beat, almost funereal in its effect. Hendrix had obviously been listening closely to the tapes for the *Band Of Gypsys* album released the previous day, because for his solo he models the entire opening chorus on some of the most memorable sections of his January 1st first-show solo. His second chorus, however, shows great daring, especially in one almost sub-musical noise he extracts from his amplifier and works with until it becomes an integral part of the piece's overall feel.

A fast version of 'Room Full Of Mirrors' is double-timed in the "Love plays tumble…" bridge, and the band race to a finish that segues into one of Hendrix's solo guitar improvisations. This one more than most harks back to the acoustic-guitar introductions found in Spanish flamenco music as, unaccompanied, Hendrix explores arabesques and altered scales before executing a shimmering gliss down the fingerboard, which itself introduces the minor-key chord sequence for 'Hey Baby (New Rising Sun)'. This is the song's first appearance in this guise, a re-working of '(Hey) Gypsy Boy'. The verse is partly based on 'All Along The Watchtower', but Hendrix's vocal melody is entirely his own, the words very personal and direct. This version at the LA Forum is among the slowest he ever played, and even the poor recording quality cannot mask what is an exquisite rendering, possibly the finest that has come to light. Hendrix finds some of his sweetest guitar melodies and the most beautiful touch while he solos, furthermore producing flighted minor-chord inversions to accompany the vocal that almost take one's breath away. A single listen is enough to reveal what the middle sections of 'Stairway To Heaven' were built upon. Hendrix's second solo, where he borrows the octave-doubling technique popularised by Wes Montgomery, is also very moving. One wishes the song could have been twice as long, but Hendrix is no doubt nervous about how it will be received – he had introduced it as merely a jam – and keeps it short, moving without fanfare into a brisk statement of the 'Villanova Junction' theme, itself the cue for a drum solo from Mitchell.

After the drum solo, Hendrix plays 'Freedom' for the first time in concert. The song would become one of the cornerstones of his live act for the rest of the year, and this debut is a lively version. After that, the concert follows the curve of his 1969 sets, with 'Star Spangled Banner' followed by 'Purple Haze' and the encore, 'Voodoo Child (Slight Return)'. This concluding troika became his standard closing for the 1970 concerts with only occasional variations. After a date in Sacramento the following evening came a five-day pause before ten days in early May where there was a concert virtually every night as the band moved from the West Coast to Oklahoma before plunging down to Texas. In San Antonio Hendrix experimented with the set-list, starting with the instrumental introduction to 'Hey Baby (New Rising Sun)' and then shifting neatly into 'Fire' followed by 'Foxy Lady' to reassure the audience. Clearly he was trying to present a balance of old and new and continued to do so for most of this spring tour. Later, in Baltimore, he kicked off the set with 'Pass It On', an early title for 'Straight Ahead'. Somehow, Hendrix managed to fit in a night in New York City on the way, meeting up with Johnny Winter and Noel Redding to drop in on a Timothy Leary benefit in the Village.

"I felt that I needed to take him home with me and save his life."

Steve Miller, rock musician, on seeing Hendrix in poor shape

Mitchell remembered this tour as being no less frantic than the previous one in the way it played havoc with personal lives. For the LA Forum gig they had stayed in Hendrix's favourite hotel in Los Angeles. "Talk about hangers-on," Mitchell complained. "I went up to see him once during the week we were there and stayed about two minutes. I thought, 'I don't want anything to do with this.'"[7] Mitchell found the tour too much of the same old grind, and he was less than inspired by the trio with Billy Cox, finding the music earthbound too much of the time. He also saw that, as before, Hendrix was not looking after himself, instead partying and indulging at every turn rather than pulling back and conserving energy. Many people who saw him during this last tour had the same opinion: Hendrix was ill, strung out, and in need not only of a complete rest but a great deal of help. He couldn't help himself. He was incapable of accepting help and there were few people around him apart from his road crew and fellow musicians who were willing or able to look out for him.

Johnny Winter was well aware of this syndrome. "See, once you've made it, everybody feels like they know you, and it can be very lonely. Jimi didn't have anybody who was just looking out after Jimi; that was one of the main problems. Everybody wanted something. It's too bad that Jimi wasn't looking out for Jimi either … but in those days drugs were thought of as something good, and Jimi and Janis were the king and queen of the drug culture."[8] Steve Miller saw Hendrix at much the same time when he shared the bill on May 16th with the Experience, The Grateful Dead and Cactus at Temple Stadium, Philadelphia. He told a *Crawdaddy* interviewer: "I was backstage … and his body stunk. He passed me and I said, 'Oh, man!'… They took him up on stage. He could hardly stand up he was so loaded. His band totally fell apart and nobody knew the difference. They tried opening with 'Sgt Pepper's Lonely Heart's Club Band' and Mitch Mitchell couldn't even keep time. The song just stopped."[9]

Years later, Miller made further observations about Hendrix's condition at the Philly concert. "I went out and watched [the Experience] and I remember it was really sad because there was this young girl and her mother, and the mother was going, 'Oh, yeah, [Hendrix] is really sexy. He is so cute.' But to me I was looking at him and I felt that I needed to take him home with me and save his life."[10] Miller, like Winter, knew that Hendrix was trapped, and felt sorry for him. "I travel a lot and people come up to me and go into my dressing room," Miller said. "And there's a group of people – they're there for all the performers, you know? They're not like groupies any more, they're just like hangers-on, scene-makers. These people think you just want to get as fucked up as possible after shows, 'cause that's groovy – it's Saturday night for them. But for you, it might be Tuesday night and you have to go out and do 25 more shows that month. And they want you to get as drunk as you can or as high on speed as you can or as down on smack as you can, or mix it all up, and it's real groovy. And you're supposed to look kind of pale and thin and unhealthy."[11] Sadly for Hendrix, he lived up to the expectations of such people. He had not been well since early spring, his body slow to recover from a number of minor ailments and continually hampered by his hard living. It is quite probable that his body "stunk", as Miller claimed: he was ill enough for the following three days of concerts to be cancelled.

During the two days before the Philadelphia concert he'd been in the studio with Cox and Mitchell to try out new songs and re-try some recent ones still not perfected. 'Come Down Hard On Me', 'Straight Ahead', 'Freedom', 'Valleys Of Neptune' and 'Hey Baby (New Rising Sun)' were all new to the studio, while 'Power Of Soul', 'Midnight Lightning' and 'Lover Man' had been tried before, some repeatedly. Two other brief selections arose from some horsing around in the studio, 'Theme From *Peter Gunn*' (one of the first things Hendrix had learned to play, back in Seattle) and 'Jealousy', with Hendrix substituting the word "catastrophe" and using sarcastic lyrics. Both somehow managed a commercial release on 1972's *War Heroes* LP; given the material that remained unreleased then, this was little short of incredible. Both songs might have been fun the first time through in the studio, but they were an embarrassment in 1972 and certainly do not bear repeated listenings. 'Peter Gunn', a loose jam that falls apart half way through, isn't even well played.

After Philadelphia the band did not re-group for another show until May 30th when they appeared at the Berkeley Community Center near San Francisco. Their appearance came at a time of tremendous tension across America with riots breaking out in some major cities, including the Bay Area of San Francisco. Mitchell remembered the time with little affection. "We'd

been through it in Chicago, looking out through the hotel window and seeing kids being beaten up really badly. It was really difficult to play that night. In Newark, New Jersey, there were tanks on the street and at Berkeley we arrived in the middle of mass confrontation and demonstrations."[12] A manifestation of this tension came during the between-songs chat in the second show when Hendrix referred to a security man who was becoming over-zealous in the crowd at the front: "You have to watch out for them – they're living in the past," he said over the PA, to loud applause.

The Berkeley show was professionally filmed in the hope that it would become a worldwide cinema release and remove from Hendrix some of the pressure on him to commit to long tours each year. In an odd coincidence, the film of Woodstock had its first batch of pre-premiere TV publicity in London just two days prior to this filmed concert (the UK premiere came on June

"We ended the film with Jimi Hendrix's music which is hard to listen to. The implication about it is that there is a lot wrong with America."

Michael Wadleigh, Woodstock film director

22nd). The *Woodstock* film launched the legend of the "perfect festival of peace" and the close association of Hendrix, along with Crosby Stills Nash & Young and Richie Havens, among others. The Atlantic/Cotillion three-LP set of music highlights from the festival was released at the same time. The Berkeley film – and the gig itself – was a much more straightforward presentation of a typical Hendrix concert. It included film of him being chauffeured around in the company of some hangers-on, smoking dope in the back of the limousine. In 1970, with Berkeley a centre of the counterculture and protest movement, openly smoking dope in front of a camera was as much a political stance as an in-group statement of intent, an endorsement of a way of life "they'll never understand". As Johnny Winter said, Hendrix was the king of drug-taking in the youth culture of the time, winning kudos from his fans for being open about his drug use. The world has changed so completely since then that this is hard to imagine now, but people took such matters very seriously in 1970, when drugs were still identified with personal searches for truth and individual spiritual values.

Hendrix did two sets at Berkeley on May 30th, duplicating around a third of the repertoire he used, including 'Machine Gun' and the closing sequence of 'Star Spangled Banner', 'Purple Haze' and 'Voodoo Child (Slight Return)'. The soundcheck was also recorded, and from this came Hendrix's light-hearted and rather limp version of 'Blue Suede Shoes', a track that would be issued a number of times, initially on the 1972 LP *Hendrix In The West*. The film of the event cuts between the two shows and the music is often edited to be considerably shorter than the actual performances. The audio, luckily, has been left alone, and at the time of writing the entire second set was being officially issued complete for the first time on CD.

The two most famous performances from the concert are 'Johnny B Goode' and 'Hear My Train A'Comin''. The Chuck Berry romp, full of fun, played fast and furious – perhaps a little too fast – became one of the star turns in the 1973 feature *A Film About Jimi Hendrix*. 'Hear My Train' from the first set was released on the *Rainbow Bridge* 'soundtrack' album in 1971. It's an intense performance where Hendrix solos with tremendous passion, a

strong contender for the best version of the song left to us by the guitarist. He even manages to maintain his tuning through close on ten minutes of live playing despite using his various soloing techniques to the full. He solos with a distinctive flavour, for the most part entirely melodic rather than the more usual fusion of chords, melody and outright sonic manipulation. As with every great improviser he had his own distinctive melodic shapes, and a lot of them crop up here. But he makes them fresh by placing them in new contexts, either by using different registers or one of his electronic effects (here wah-wah or Uni-Vibe) to alter the timbre and texture, or by re-ordering them to create different continuities of phrasing. Conversely, 'Red House', also from the first show, is uninspired. It's clean and well played, but Hendrix seems only partially engaged and fails to pull things together with the passion he usually conjured for this piece.

"We would spend up to ten or twelve hours at a time, recording take after take."

Eddie Kramer, engineer

Hendrix has a tendency to play his repertoire rather fast in this concert, especially during the first set. 'Ezy Rider', apart from its very out-of-tune guitar, is uncomfortably fast, and Hendrix has to rush the vocals, slurring the words and losing the groove that is the essence of this song. 'Stone Free' starts out fast and just about right, but soon accelerates – Hendrix is the one rushing – to the point of discomfort. 'Lover Man' suffers similarly in the second set, Hendrix missing half the notes in the preset semi-quavers (16th-notes) section of his solo. Surprisingly, the old chestnut 'Hey Joe' is given one of its most impressive workouts: the tempo is majestic, the guitar playing a perfect complement to the words that Hendrix sings with real feeling. That particular night he didn't want to "stop playing this rubbish" as he'd put it on the Lulu TV show 15 months earlier. 'Freedom' came from the other ends of the spectrum, now settling into its own funky groove and tempo and showing Billy Cox's contribution to the band in the best light. Cox would not usually vary his bassline spontaneously to add interest to long songs, especially the blues pieces, but here he moves between a series of lines and makes each one count. Unfortunately, tuning problems meant that the song was not issued at the time, and it only appeared eventually as part of a three-song bonus CD for the re-release of the film on video in 1991.

The first two weeks of June 1970 were taken up with the continuing tour, moving through the South and back up to Indiana and Maryland. Hendrix and his trio stuck quite closely to the mix of old and new that he'd begun in Los Angeles and at Berkeley. He may have been heartily sick of playing tunes like 'Foxy Lady', 'Hey Joe' and the others by this time – enough for him to gently berate the audience from time to time as they called out for them to be played – but he was at least partially to blame for this. One way to move along the audience's expectations is to continue to have hits. That way, even if you're playing the latest hit each night, it's at least something you weren't playing on the previous tour (and in the case of a good deal of Hendrix's repertoire, the tour before that and the tour before that). Hendrix had not had a hit single since 1968, and had only released one new single since then – all the rest after 'All Along The Watchtower' were taken from existing albums. The audiences had nothing new to embrace and so had to digest new, unheard repertoire on the spot. It is notoriously difficult to persuade an audience to do this, even when the majority of them are not stoned or tripping. Hendrix had to do it the hard way, every night. Of course, during this tour the *Band Of Gypsys* album was released and its songs began to percolate through his audiences as it sold its millions of copies, but the idea of 'touring the new album' that became de rigueur in the 1970s – and was prevalent with many bands by the late 1960s – was impossible in Hendrix's case.

Still, the Woodstock movie with its unblinking focus on Hendrix as the festival's highlight was at least helping to update his worldwide audience about the growth of his repertoire. Director Michael Wadleigh, talking in London at the time, made it clear why Hendrix was central to the movie. "We ended up with 120 hours of film but we had only eight hours of actual images when we had finished with using the split-screen techniques," Wadleigh explained. " Whoever we wanted in the film, Warner Brothers paid them. We just picked three or four numbers from those we selected. ... Some people I would have preferred to leave in we had to leave out because people, even top groups, cannot perform well all the time. The Band and Janis Joplin were both left out simply because they didn't perform well. ... We also had Jimi Hendrix doing the national anthem in a very un-nationalistic way. We didn't just include him because he did his own numbers. We really felt obliged to include as much of this kind of stuff as we could for political reasons. ... The film ends with Hendrix playing his national anthem and the film pans over all these incredible piles of rubbish that were left there when it was all over. It was Warner Brothers' idea to sell the film as a peace-and-happiness film but I don't think it was a peaceful film by any means. That's why we ended the film with Jimi Hendrix's music which is hard to listen to. The implication about it is that there is a lot wrong with America."[13]

Itching to work again on material for a Next Album that he would be able to tour later in the year, or by spring 1971 at the latest, Hendrix went back into the studio in mid June. But this wasn't just any studio – this at last, after all the money, problems and heartaches, was his own place, Electric Lady studio. It had been designed for his specific needs and was given a feel so far removed from the antiseptic atmosphere of most studios that Electric Lady quickly became Hendrix's home. It was still not complete – the official opening would come in August – but the main studio was sufficiently functional for Hendrix to begin work on his many unfinished tunes, starting on June 15th. The very first night of work involved a series of jams with Cox and Mitchell plus Steve Winwood and Chris Wood, his old friends from Traffic. Some were blues jams, others try-outs on original Hendrix themes. The only work that eventually proved constructive in the move towards The Next Album came with some vocal overdubs made to the existing multitrack version of 'Ezy Rider', with Buddy Miles on drums, which Hendrix had decided to refurbish.

For the rest of June in Electric Lady, Hendrix was working hard on a nucleus of new songs, trying to achieve perfect rhythm-track masters upon which to build. The new songs he recorded with Cox and Mitchell were 'Night Bird Flying', 'Straight Ahead' (initially called 'Have You Heard'), 'Freedom', 'Astro Man', 'Come Down Hard On Me', 'Just Came In' (later titled 'In From The Storm'), 'Drifting' and 'Heaven Has No Sorrow'. Older songs re-jigged, newly attempted, overdubbed or re-built in this period included 'Beginning', 'Cherokee Mist', 'Earth Blues', 'Stepping Stone' and 'Valleys Of Neptune'. Hendrix also recorded a handful of songs by other writers, of which the only one in contention for a place on any upcoming new album was Dylan's 'Drifter's Escape'.

Most of these tracks he would work on more intensively during sessions in July at Electric Lady, but 'Earth Blues' would receive no more attention as he felt he'd exhausted his ideas on the tune for now. He left it to consider later at his leisure. He had added new vocals during these late-June sessions, tried a completely different and more complementary mix, and put down a new lead-guitar track. This last addition was a special one. As in many of his 1970 recordings, Hendrix uses his lead guitar as a running commentary on the vocal lines throughout 'Earth Blues', as well as a powerful solo tool. (It was first released on the *Rainbow Bridge* LP and is on the *First Rays...* CD.) With his call-and-response vocal patterns, evocative of gospel music, as a fundamental theme in this music, the guitar comes along as another voice. At the end of the song the guitar takes over completely, its wailing melodies very carefully sculpted to imitate the human voice in full cry as Hendrix uses his electronic effects to an intensely human purpose. Using a classic Stratocaster sound, shooting off sparks of melodic fire, he finds some remarkable note patterns, especially one stuttering, climbing figure in the second verse of his solo (starting at 2:11) that for sheer inventiveness is alone enough to separate him from more or less any other electric guitarist of the time, in any genre.

Hendrix was doing all this intensive work at Electric Lady in tandem with Eddie Kramer, the engineer who masterminded the installation of the equipment into the studio and then tested it to bring it up to scratch in readiness for Hendrix's use. Kramer and Hendrix had not seen a great deal of each other over the past year because Kramer had been so deeply involved in the Electric Lady project and there had also been a certain cooling of the relationship between musician and technician. Kramer had made his feelings known about the circus-like atmosphere in the Record Plant back in 1968-69 and Hendrix had not appreciated it at the time. The engineer's sterling work at every stage of the building and launch of Electric Lady now gave them a new basis for a growth of trust as they put past frictions behind them. As the studio became functional, Hendrix was even prepared to allow Kramer at least a basic vetting system at the entrance to Electric Lady to screen out some of the unwanteds who had been so disruptive in the past. But this did not mean that the studio was bare of all but the musicians, engineer and tape-ops: Hendrix's close circle were present more often than not, including Devon Wilson who by this stage was functioning increasingly as Hendrix's general factotum rather than his demon lover.

Kramer was well aware that the studio had rekindled Hendrix's enthusiasm and imagination, not only because it was his very own place but because the facilities – and the sound they could produce – were manifestly better than anywhere else at the time. This was the cutting edge, and it was his to play with, making it the place he wanted to be in preference to anywhere else in the world. He could at last see the future again. "Jimi would arrive at sessions right on time – even early on occasion – something he rarely did," said Kramer. "We would spend up to ten or twelve hours at a time, recording take after take. … [He] came into Electric Lady with a distinctive idea as to how he wanted each track to sound. He would … work on his final lyrics right up until it was time to put his vocal on, sifting through pages and pages of handwritten lyrics, even lifting pieces from other songs, saying, 'Maybe that line would fit in here.'"[14]

By the last week of June 1970 Hendrix was beginning to formulate an emerging shape for The Next Album. He wrote a list in mid June headed "Songs for L.P. *Strate Ahead*". When the piece of paper with this list written on both sides came up for auction years later, the sale catalogue claimed its date of compilation as June 25th, but this does not correspond with the information on the list. Hendrix used a checking system to indicate how far he had progressed on each tune listed. 'Night Bird Flying', for which he had reached a master backing-track on June 16th, is for example noted on the list as a composition still to be tackled; the master of 'Drifter's Escape' was laid down on June 17th, but it is similarly devoid of the mark noting this. The list was more likely drawn up in the week before the studio opened, when Hendrix was out on tour and organising his thoughts for the task ahead. There were 25 pieces under consideration, numbered and in the following order: 'Ezy Rider', 'Room Full Of Mirrors', 'Earth Blues', 'Valleys Of Neptune', 'Have You Heard' ('Straight Ahead'), 'Cherokee Mist', 'Freedom', 'Stepping Stone', 'Izabella', 'Astro Man', 'Drifter's Escape', 'Angel', 'Bleeding Heart', 'Burning Desire', 'Night Bird Flying', 'Electric Lady', 'Getting My Heart Back Together' ('Hear My Train A'Comin'), 'Lover Man', 'Midnight Lightning', 'Heaven Has No Tomorrow' ('Heaven Has No Sorrow'), 'Sending My Love' ('Send My Love To Linda/Kathy/Joan Of Arc'), 'This Little Boy', 'Locomotion' ('Local Commotion'), 'Dolly Dagger', 'The New Rising Sun (Hey Baby)'.

For one reason or another 'Drifting', 'Beginning', 'In From The Storm', 'Belly Button Window' and 'Late Thursday Morning' are missing from this list, songs that he had already written or made home recordings of and that he would work on later this summer. But these selections more or less cover the real contenders for The Next Album, excluding any recorded jams that he may have wanted to organise and slip into the running order. 'Pali Gap', for example, may have become a contender for such a position when all the finished work was reviewed, although it was not considered during the later summer sessions. The combined list makes for 30 titles – excluding jams – under active consideration. That was enough for four LPs, or two doubles, when one considers that *Electric Ladyland* has 16 tracks. With Jeffery having signed Hendrix up to Reprise for an original soundtrack album for a film to be shot in July, the overflow would clearly be useful in planning what was to go where.

The continuing US tour, with concerts in places like Albuquerque, Ventura County, Denver and Boston, must have seemed a necessary evil to Hendrix. By this time he was fired up and full of thoughts of completing a recording project for the first time in close on two years. Maybe the summer would be kind to him and allow him time to finally pull it together. Or maybe he'd write further material that demanded to be recorded. Either way, Hendrix knew that Electric Lady would for the first time give him a true representation of the way he had always imagined his music to sound. The challenge – and the priority – was to convert his ideas into recorded reality. But as John Lennon was to note ten years later, life is what happens to you while you're busy making other plans.

Hendrix began July 1970 with a monumental session at Electric Lady studio, with Juma Sultan along to help Cox and Mitchell provide musical support. On the 1st they managed 19 takes of 'Dolly Dagger', the last of which proved to be good enough for a master. The song is harmonically varied, opening with an odd mixture of metres, as Hendrix then delivers a jubilant, tongue-in-cheek celebration of Devon Wilson's voracious carnal appetites: "Her love's so heavy, gonna make you stagger / Dolly Dagger / She ain't satisfied 'til she gets what she's after / She drinks the blood from a jagged edge / Better watch out baby, here comes your master."

Around this time Hendrix had asked for the multitracks of 1967's 'Highway Chile' to be recovered so that he could listen to them. No work was

"Electric Lady studio has only been open two weeks and we've had Joe Cocker there to record and Led Zeppelin."

Mike Jeffery, Hendrix's manager

ever done on a new version of the old song, in contrast to the abortive April 1969 remake of 'Stone Free', but the similarity of 'Highway Chile' to 'Dolly Dagger', in both form and detail, may be more than incidental. Both songs start with distinctive guitar fanfares, using rhythmically related descending phrases that usher in a vocal verse pattern shared between the two songs. The verse melody in both is simple and singsong-like with a catchy, repetitive shape that carries the vivid portraits of two very different characters. The guitar solo on both songs is introduced by a recapitulation of the opening riff – a simple, economical way to ensure continuity in the composition – while both songs fade on repeating riffs, sustaining the sense of narration or storytelling right to the last audible note. As with all good Hendrix, the complexity of the arrangement of 'Dolly Dagger' – which was proposed at this time as his next single – masks the essential simplicity of the conception, shared at least in part with one of his earliest and most popular B-sides.

Hendrix first attempted 'Here Comes The Sun' (aka 'Bolero') that same night. It was a piece he worked on a number of times during the summer at Electric Lady but never brought near completion. He also tried 'Midnight Lightning' and 'Hey Baby (New Rising Sun)', producing a good basic track for 'Hey Baby' which, though not designated a master and with no more than a live guide vocal attached, was later released on the 1971 *Rainbow Bridge* LP. For the concert performances of 'Hey Baby' that spring and summer he almost invariably prefaced the song with a solo guitar introduction of variable length, depending on his mood and how receptive the audience seemed. On an unspecified date that summer, Hendrix recorded a short version of this solo introduction at Electric Lady, probably intending it as a drop-in to be edited on to the studio master: both pieces begin and end in the same key and the tuning is almost identical, making an edit straightforward. Unfortunately the edit was never made, so that on its official release on *Rainbow Bridge* 'Hey Baby (New Rising Sun)' was deprived of its customary concert opening, consigning the studio guitar intro to obscurity. Its sole appearance to date was as the first part of the now-unavailable 'M.L.K.' compilation assembled by John Jansen in 1971 and issued in altered form on *Crash Landing* in 1975 as 'Captain Coconut'.

As if this were not enough for one evening, the band launched a new assault on Mitch Mitchell's instrumental, 'Beginning'. The master they produced was eventually released on *War Heroes* (1972) but is patently incomplete; it is not much more than a sketch of the tune's constituent parts, with only a single guitar track. It cannot begin to compete with the flawed but electrifying version recorded the previous August at Woodstock. The band also jammed on the old Spencer Davis Group hit 'Gimme Some Loving' leading straight on from the master take of 'Dolly Dagger': Cox can be heard falling into the bass riff as that song fades. At the conclusion of the jam ten minutes later, Hendrix emerges with a beautiful, spontaneous, meandering guitar improvisation over a simple and quiet riff pattern. He later capitalised on this by adding a second guitar line and solo, then left it in his pile of 'ongoing work'. Later it was edited for release and Mike Jeffery inserted it into the *Rainbow Bridge* 'soundtrack' LP as he cast around for studio material with which to fill that album. Although Hendrix made no indication of any plans to include it on the new album he certainly liked what he'd done here, and had earmarked it for placement in one of his many future projects. This is entirely understandable, for 'Pali Gap' is one of Hendrix's most charming and original creations of his final two years.

'Pali Gap' consists of two guitar tracks that intertwine with astonishing prescience and synchronicity, with Hendrix right inside his playing and anticipating his own phrasing, continually slipping apposite commentary into the spaces left by the guitar he'd first laid down. One of the overdubbed guitars solos first, at length, then allows room for a brief solo from the other, finally returning to make a concluding statement before the piece finds a natural, graceful end. There are technical errors in places – the type of thing Hendrix would never have left in a final mix – as for example where he fumbles with his articulation or simply plays a wrong note, but there are so many sublime little touches and felicities in the two guitar tracks to absorb and delight that these minor blemishes are a small price to pay for having the track available to enjoy. The two lines differ in sound but are completely compatible: Hendrix regularly changes the timbre and attack of one while keeping the other relatively constant in tone and volume.

Considering Hendrix's flexibility here and the imaginative way he uses these different guitar sounds for contrast and highlighting, it is difficult to think of another guitarist at the time who could have been so resourceful. The accompaniment from Mitchell, Sultan and Cox is also of a high calibre and extremely attentive. After such a remarkable night's work, the following evening was given over to overdubbing and mixing work on 'Ezy Rider' and

'Dolly Dagger' to keep the creative juices flowing. Meanwhile in the outside world, all the machinery for the summer's live appearances was continuing to run smoothly, although a row had broken out in the press between Mike Jeffery and Track Records, who had licensed the *Band Of Gypsys* LP for release in the UK. Not only had Track used a copy master rather than the original master from which to make their version, but in order to facilitate a speedy release the British record company had quickly thrown together a bizarre sleeve showing four puppets, one of which is Hendrix playing his guitar right-handed. At least this row did not interfere with summer tour plans: in England, *Record Mirror* dated July 4th carried a full-page advertisement for the coming Isle Of Wight Festival showing Joan Baez and Jimi Hendrix topping the bill.

For close on two weeks, the Experience went back out on the road in America to fulfil concert commitments. Some appearances went smoothly, with well-behaved and appreciative audiences. However, the summer festivals not only attracted large crowds but also seemed to act as a magnet for everyone with a radical cause – good, bad and indifferent – who felt that they could extract publicity, money or political credibility by creating disruption and discord at the events. This was beginning to make the festivals difficult and unpredictable for the artists playing them and at times traumatic for the headlining acts.

At the three-day Second Atlanta International Pop Festival, Hendrix's group appeared alongside such luminaries as Ginger Baker's Air Force, Captain Beefheart & His Magic Band, Gypsy, Mountain, Procol Harum, Jethro Tull (just making their first big impact in the US), Spirit, Ten Years After, Johnny Winter, The Allman Brothers, and B.B. King, among others. Hendrix's long set was warmly appreciated by his biggest live audience ever and witnessed by old band-mate Randy California, who visited the guitarist backstage. The group's set mixed old and new repertoire, kicking off with a vibrant version of 'Fire' and touching base with other staples such as 'Lover Man', 'Spanish Castle Magic', 'Hey Joe' and 'Stone Free'. In between these and the regular blues numbers that Hendrix always enjoyed playing, he tried out other less familiar tunes. These included an early arrangement of 'Straight Ahead' that revealed it to be still under construction at that date, with much of the studio version's lyrics missing and whole sections of the tune yet to be put in place. Being the 4th of July, a huge firework display on the site accompanied Hendrix on-stage, the two events merging spectacularly during 'Purple Haze', played mid-set.

One of the most interesting aspects of this appearance is the sheer sound of the group on this tour when they played the larger festivals: Hendrix's trio on this occasion sounded almost exactly as they would at the Isle Of Wight Festival in August. Playing in the open-air to these vast crowds necessitated such powerful on-stage amplification that Hendrix could drive his amps flat-out non-stop, with a consequent fattening and coarsening of his overall guitar tone, and still not feel that he was pushing things too hard. Yet the result was a massive, brutal soundscape that, though immensely exciting, hits the listener so hard between the ears as to occasionally overwhelm. Even in the annals of Hendrix's love-affair with amplified sound, this was something new – and something utterly different to the clarity and subtle variety he was trying to achieve at the same time in the studio.

Suitably serene at the end of the successful Atlanta gig, Hendrix concluded the set unusually with 'Hey Baby (New Rising Sun)' – a very mellow (if out-of-tune) way to bring the audience home. The band's appearance in Miami the next day saw another trouble-free if undistinguished concert, followed by similar dates in Louisville and Memphis on the 10th and 11th. The New York Pop Festival at the Downing Stadium on Randall's Island was another three-day affair, but this one was dogged by disruption and ill-feeling as two competing radical groups tried to face down the organisers for a share of the profits and an airing of their beliefs. Acts such as Grand Funk Railroad, John Sebastian, Steppenwolf and Jethro Tull had to cope with an excitable and at times aggressive crowd who were aware of the bad vibes and apprehensive about the possibility of an influx of non-paying 'freedom troops' looking for trouble. Many bands booked to play pulled out, worried by the brewing confrontations that had been splashed all over the local media. The Experience's set on Friday 17th was delivered in a sullen atmosphere and Hendrix soon adopted the mood, especially after his amplifiers started to pick up more or less continual interference from a local radio-station broadcast. Even 'Red House', which could usually be relied upon to demand his full attention, had Hendrix playing with much less than his usual warmth. After a more upbeat gig in San Diego on July 25th the group flew to Seattle for the last mainland United States concert of the tour. He arrived in the city to be greeted by his family, all of whom thought he looked tired and troubled.

During July, Hendrix's manager Mike Jeffery had, unusually, been doing press interviews himself to publicise some of the dates on the tour, and had also discussed some of their other plans. Talking to *Record Mirror* he explained Hendrix's long absence from UK concert appearances by mentioning the guitarist's commitment to New York City as a base, underlined by the building of Electric Lady studio. "The studio is in Greenwich Village and Jimi and I both have a half-share in it," Jeffery told the music paper. "It's only been open two weeks and we've had Joe Cocker there to record and Led Zeppelin."[15] Jeffery also took the very unusual step of speaking on behalf of Hendrix on a socio-political level. "Jimi is very sensitive to all the things around him. In America the atmosphere is electric. He feels he can help the situation with his music. ... You know instinctively what side of the fence people are on; there is increasing awareness. However right-wing the situation is, new values and new ideas will win through."[16] It is not known how Hendrix responded to being re-positioned in this way by Jeffery, who was

"Gil Evans told me that he and Jimi were going to get together, and that he wanted me to come down and participate. I told him that I would."

Miles Davis, jazz musician

probably influenced by the younger people he was now mixing with, but it certainly marked a departure for a manager who was normally very happy to remain the Svengali in the shadows. Jeffery also made the extraordinary claim that "with a person like Jimi, I never decide to do anything. If Jimi takes it up then I do it".[17]

By this stage in July 1970 Hendrix had put in some more long nights of recording at Electric Lady. His repeated attempts to achieve a master for the simple, stark medium-tempo blues 'Come Down Hard On Me' finally succeeded on the 15th, and overdubs were added. Hendrix also achieved an acceptable basic track for 'Lover Man' five days later, but this recording was then left incomplete and unmixed. More work was also done to try to straighten out 'Midnight Lightning'. According to Billy Cox, "It was a good song, but we were just bogged down with it. When we started touring, we got some new, refreshed ideas as to how to try and do it, but the process still wasn't complete."[18] Evidence for this temporary exhaustion includes Hendrix fitting the 'mother hubbard' nursery rhyme into part of a verse recorded on July 14th to enliven the proceedings. The song remained unfinished. Considering his past methods of working on tracks, and the mass of material abandoned at various points of completion and incompletion since the start of the *Electric Ladyland* sessions, it seems likely that this tune would have been put to one side by Hendrix when it came to finalising The Next Album.

The band also tried some more takes of 'Here Comes The Sun' ('Bolero') but cut nothing that reached the required level. This piece too seems then to

have been left on the shelf, for Hendrix didn't return to it after July 14th. One run at 'Last Thursday Morning' was committed to tape on the 20th, but this too was then left behind and the results remain unissued at the time of writing. Next, the band began intensive overdubbing and mixing work on songs that Hendrix considered to be the core of the planned LP: 'Night Bird Flying', 'Straight Ahead', 'Astro Man', 'Freedom', 'Dolly Dagger' and 'Drifter's Escape'. On July 21st and 23rd work on new songs was resumed: 'In From The Storm', 'Hear My Train A'Comin'', 'Drifting', 'Angel' and 'Belly Button Window'. ('Angel' of course dated back to 1967, and Hendrix had written the lyrics to 'Belly Button Window' at least 12 months earlier.)

After July 23rd Hendrix attempted no new recordings of previously unrehearsed or unrecorded songs. In effect he had completed basic recording of songs for The Next Album. What this would be called, or even its size, was still in the melting pot. Hendrix, as always, was pushing for more material to be issued, Jeffery for less. The guitarist at one point in mid summer was talking up the possibility of a three-LP set and certainly nothing less than two. Jeffery wanted a single-LP studio set, anticipating the need for tracks for the soundtrack album for the film he had been planning. Hendrix paid lip-service to the idea of this soundtrack album but had not given a second thought to writing the music. After all, it wasn't his project, it was Jeffery's. Hendrix had no interest in it; his focus was the new studio effort. Kathy Ebert, who was a member of Jeffery's staff but personally close to Hendrix, recalled the proposed triple-LP set. "*People, Hell And Angels* was going to be the title," she told John McDermott. "[Hendrix] couldn't settle on the songs or length of the album. In the early summer, *Straight Ahead* had emerged as a working title, and then later *First Rays Of The New Rising Sun* made a comeback of sorts. At the very least, he definitely wanted to release a two-record set."[19]

Hendrix was also interested in other recording projects. During 1970 he had kept on friendly terms with Alan Douglas and his circle and from time to time had talked with him about other possibilities; perhaps he could work with some top-flight musicians, arrangers and composers? There had been an abortive attempt the year before to record a track with arranger/producer Quincy Jones, but for whatever reason Hendrix had simply not showed up at the studio – the reverse of what had happened with Miles Davis. Hendrix was nervous of his lack of formal musical training and, intimidated by the idea, had perhaps simply avoided it. This time, Douglas was talking about bringing in Gil Evans, another self-taught genius and the mercurial, inspired arranger who had been Miles Davis's musical alter-ego for major projects between 1950 to 1968, the last (uncredited) collaboration being Davis's award-winning *Filles de Kilimanjaro* album of '68. Evans was a Hendrix fan. He was a sensitive and inspiring collaborator and had become very interested in the way that the electrification of contemporary music had opened up a new potential kaleidoscope of sound combinations. The Hendrix/Evans album already had a title: *The Voodoo Child Plays The Blues*.

Douglas felt that Evans could create ideal large-ensemble backdrops over which Hendrix would solo. Considering the obvious models – Wes Montgomery and Kenny Burrell – there was much to recommend the idea. Burrell had made *Guitar Forms* with Gil Evans back in 1965, produced by Creed Taylor. Montgomery had created a stream of big-selling albums by laying his distinctive playing over big-band arrangements that were more or less contemporary in style, especially on the two albums he made, *Down Here On The Ground* and *A Day In The Life*, prior to his untimely death. For Hendrix, the plan was for Evans to have already recorded his backdrops by the time the guitarist walked into the studio. Hendrix would then add the melody lines and his own unique improvisations along with other characteristic touches to create a work that would provide an intriguing and

entirely fresh angle on his talent. According to Evans, Douglas and others, this recording plan was well advanced, with an album-sleeve design already commissioned by late August and preliminary meetings scheduled for late September. At these Hendrix and Evans intended to discuss repertoire and approach. Miles Davis claimed in his autobiography that at a late stage he was asked to become involved in this project. "Gil Evans called and told me that he and Jimi were going to get together," wrote Davis, "and that he wanted me to come down and participate. I told him that I would."[20] This careful choice of words suggests that Davis had been asked to advise on the project, rather than to play. Davis planned to talk to Hendrix about the project in England after the Isle Of Wight Festival where they were both booked to play that August.

At the July 26th concert in Seattle attended by members of his family Hendrix played a diverse set of tunes: 'Fire', 'Message To Love', 'Lover Man', 'Machine Gun' ("dedicated to everybody here," Hendrix announced ambiguously), 'Star Spangled Banner' and 'Purple Haze'. Then came a truncated version of 'I Don't Live Today'. Hendrix left the stage while Mitchell played the distinctive drum intro and then came back on and changed the song to 'Hear My Train A'Comin''. The band, bringing the concert to a climactic end, launched into 'Voodoo Child (Slight Return)', 'Hey Baby (New Rising Sun)', 'Freedom' and 'Red House', finishing with 'Foxy Lady'. Local reaction was once again favourable, and the next day Hendrix decided to stay and spend a little time with his family: this would be his longest uninterrupted stay in Seattle since his Army furloughs in 1961. Family members and friends were concerned by Hendrix's physical and mental state.

After the concert, Hendrix visited Freddie Mae Gautier, who had nurtured Jimi as a baby. "It was after midnight when Jimmy got there," Gautier recalled to Mary Willix, "and he had never really done that before, so I felt something was bothering Jimmy."[21] Hendrix and Gautier had a long conversation about where his life

had got to and where it might be going, touching on many personal subjects, including his will, his family and whether he would ever marry and have children. Hendrix was non-committal with regard to his own life but was clearly concerned about trying to help his family and those close to him. He also talked about his lifestyle and about drugs. "Based on his conversation with me," Gautier continued, "he was definitely trying to get off [drugs]. ... He said to me, 'You know, it's important that young people and our kids not let drugs and things control them, because that's what it's all about. Controlling them.'"[22] This notion that unseen forces were somehow trying to

On-stage at the KB Hallen (left and above) in Copenhagen, Denmark, September 3rd 1970.

control freedom-seeking individuals was one commonly aired in the counterculture of the time. In many cases, such paranoia was justified – Watergate was not so far away and the people who perpetrated that event were already in place. Perhaps Hendrix's comment related directly to his feeling that he was being manipulated by his management and record company – something he complained about constantly in 1969 and '70 – or it was just a broader sense of a basic conflict within Western society. Subsequent events would invest his comments with more importance in hindsight than perhaps Hendrix could have known or meant at the time.

Hendrix's father Al wrote later that his son talked to him about dissatisfaction with his management and his desire to break free. But this could have just been family talk: Hendrix knew how deeply involved he was with Jeffery. Extricating himself from his current manager was not only a case of waiting until 1972 at the earliest for existing contracts to expire; it would additionally have taken years of financial and legal wrangles before all connections could be severed. Al recalled that Jimi came around to his house the day after the Seattle concert. "Jimi didn't feel too good the next day, so when the rest of the guys left, he stayed an extra day. Gerry Stickells, Jimi's road manager, stayed too. The last day Jimi was at home he talked to me about getting married, although he didn't mention a gal."[23] This is in direct contradiction to the conversation Hendrix had the previous night with Freddie Mae Gautier. Perhaps he'd been thinking about what she'd said. Perhaps it was just another example of his ability to compartmentalise his relationships and tell each person what he thought they wanted to hear. Stickells was aware of this aspect of Hendrix's character; it was one he saw virtually every day. He told Chris Welch: "I don't think [Hendrix] did have close friends. To everybody, he had a different side. I don't think anybody knew him. I knew one side of him. I don't believe anybody really knew where Jimi was at, or what he was thinking about at any point, although a lot of people profess they did."[24]

On July 28th Hendrix and his team flew from Seattle to Hawaii. He was supposed to play a concert in Honolulu on the first day of August, but before that was drafted to help Jeffery out of the hole the manager had dug himself for the film project that ultimately became *Rainbow Bridge*. As Mitch Mitchell commented later, "Jeffery was taking increasingly large amounts of acid and getting further into mysticism. Somehow he met these two film-makers who'd worked with Warhol, neither of whom could produce a piss-up in a brewery, and that's being kind."[25] Speaking to *Record Mirror* in July, Jeffery had been decidedly more sanguine about the prospects for the project. "Jimi will be working on music for the film. He's going out there with us for about six weeks, to Honolulu, and he'll sit back and compose. ... The idea of the film is a kind of space-age *Candid Camera*. We're going to place Pat [Hartley, the film's 'star'] in all kinds of real-life situations, and film what happens. We're going to shoot a lot of film and just see what comes out of it."[26] This sounds dangerously close to the see-what-happens approach that had led to the disappointments of The Beatles' 1967 TV film *Magical Mystery Tour*, although considered alongside *Rainbow Bridge* the *Mystery Tour* looks a masterpiece of cinematic planning.

Rainbow Bridge was a snafu of impressive dimensions even for the hippie generation. It quickly became evident to Jeffery that the project desperately

Hendrix's bassist Billy Cox lays down his solid groove at a concert in Denmark, September 1970.

needed the presence of Hendrix on-screen if it was to have any chance of commercial lift-off. Jeffery's office knew the film was a vanity project planned to provide him not only with another source of income but to give him credibility with a generation of fans younger than himself and – as the cliché goes – to allow him to get in touch with the child within himself. Plotless, scriptless and clueless, the film and its long-winded gestation is largely irrelevant to the purposes of this book. The project, once decanted from the weirder fringes of Los Angeles society onto the Hawaiian island of Maui, became so drug-addled, pseudo-mystical and stuffed with narcissistic, self-important onscreen hippies that the only hope of saving it was indeed to put Hendrix on celluloid. Sensibly, he stayed as far away from the camera as

possible, hanging out mostly with his band members, Pat Hartley and art director Melinda Merryweather – the only other people involved who did not take themselves too seriously.[27] It was Merryweather who eventually persuaded Hendrix to go in front of a camera long enough to join in with a stoned and directionless conversation about pseudo-metaphysical experiences, contributing his own oblique and tongue-in-cheek ramblings. Perhaps he didn't care to make any more sense, given the company.

Mike Jeffery, present on the island during the shooting and increasingly worried about his investment, made an executive decision that an impromptu Jimi Hendrix concert would be needed, up to this point an unplanned element of the film. He arranged with director Chuck Wein for a performance in Hawaii to be professionally shot and recorded. It was decided to hold the concert half way between two volcanic hills in a high windswept valley – an area that apparently produced electro-magnetic interference, later blamed for making half the recording equipment fail to work. The location on Kauai island was so far from mains electricity and the event so poorly prepared that the portable recording board had to be driven by the film-unit's generator. With a small crowd of some 300 enthusiastic hippie extras to cheer them on, the Experience played two sets on July 30th. The first, according to Merryweather, was prefaced by Hendrix apportioning a note representing a specific colour to match each sign of the zodiac, an allusion to the theme of the show, named The Rainbow Bridge Vibratory Color/Sound Experiment. The performance took place in an area called Rainbow Ridge; the extra letter was added to provide a suitably mystical dimension to the name.

The music from the two sets has been pirated and recycled many times since the early 1970s when it first appeared on vinyl bootlegs. There are a number of sources, from soundboard recordings to audience tapes and the film soundtrack itself. In 2002 soundboard tapes of both sets were commercially released, mastered from an incomplete source apparently from the archives of the Michael Jeffery Estate. They reveal the concert's set-lists. Set 1: 'Spanish Castle Magic', 'Lover Man', 'Hey Baby (New Rising Sun)', 'In From The Storm', 'Message To Love', 'Foxy Lady', 'Hear My Train A'Comin'', 'Voodoo Child (Slight Return)', 'Fire', 'Purple Haze'. Set 2: 'Dolly Dagger', 'Villanova Junction', Ezy Rider', 'Red House', 'Freedom', 'Beginning', 'Straight Ahead', 'Hey Baby (New Rising Sun)', 'Midnight Lightning', 'Stone Free', 'Hey Joe'. For the first set, Hendrix played his white Fender Stratocaster, as seen extensively in the movie footage of the concert. For at least part of the second set he played his (second) Gibson Flying V, seen in the only footage in the resulting film that comes from that set, the instrumental introduction to 'Hey Baby (New Rising Sun)'.

The issued performances reveal the band in good shape, with Hendrix sounding relaxed and outgoing, although it is difficult to evaluate the music fairly because of the myriad technical gremlins. Mitchell's drumming, for example, was only faintly recorded through overspill to other on-stage microphones and he had to overdub his parts in a studio at a later date in an attempt to make the tapes suitable for release. This results in the unfamiliar sense of Mitchell following the band rather than driving it; he is trying to emulate what he did at the concerts rather than engage in his usual dialogue with the other two musicians on-stage.

Yet there are worthy moments among what has been issued. The first set starts with a fiery and precise debut for 'In From The Storm', less than a week after the band had given the song its first complete run-throughs in the studio. Hendrix has some difficulty with his vocals throughout both sets, undoubtedly due to the primitive on-stage monitoring that gave him little chance to hear what he was doing. His guitar playing is busy, at times fresh, but largely unexceptional in the sense that Hendrix seems little concerned with laying down a live set to be used commercially and much more taken with the idea of having a good time and entertaining what for him was an intimate audience. One notable feature of both sets is his sustained use of the rich Uni-Vibe effect on his guitar in parts of the set that enables him to take a different slant on some of his tunes. In other numbers, such as 'Message To Love', the full guitar sound – with no Uni-Vibe this time – is not enough to rescue a song that still sounds studio-bound and lacking a strong arrangement suited to concert performance. 'Foxy Lady' is notably faster than the band had played it at the LA Forum in April, and much closer to what they would deliver at the Isle Of Wight Festival in a month's time. Yet it sounds like they were having fun.

The most striking music played (and preserved on the various official and unofficial sources) tends to come with the slower, more meditative pieces as well as the blues. Hendrix takes a solo on 'Hear My Train A'Comin'' that begins with a torrent of notes and some novel ideas – as well as others taken from many earlier performances – before falling away to the melancholy of the vocal lines. His short second solo verges on the brutal but he ends it gently, with his guitar very out of tune. 'Villanova Junction' is a slow and beautiful blues improvisation where Hendrix seems to have all the time in the world to make his point, and quite movingly. The other highlight is an exquisite instrumental introduction to 'Hey Baby (New Rising Sun)' from the second set. At the time of writing it has only appeared on audience-tape bootlegs, but perhaps one day it will be presented on CD in optimum sound quality. We can but dream.

The concert sequence in the *Rainbow Bridge* movie lasts around 20 minutes. It is very well shot and generally well edited, and indeed the whole film benefits from good camera work. Hendrix appears relaxed and healthy. The majority of the footage is in sync with the music heard on the soundtrack rather than visual 'filler' selected simply because it looks nice. There are some excellent long shots that detail his guitar technique, including a lingering view of his method for the sustained octave shrieks at the end of 'Purple Haze' where his right hand reaches over the top of the fingerboard rather than cradling it from behind. There are some good cut-ins of both Mitchell and Cox among the usual cutaways to the crowd looking stoned and happy. The sequence used in the film, taken entirely from the first set and not strictly in order, is: 'Hey Baby (New Rising Sun)', 'In From The Storm', 'Foxy Lady', 'Hear My Train A'Comin'', 'Voodoo Child (Slight Return)', 'Purple Haze', 'Hear My Train A'Comin''. That sequence bookended by the two versions of 'Hear My Train A'Comin'' consists of abrupt edits mid-song from one selection to the next, some better matched than others. The edit into 'Voodoo Child (Slight Return)' is badly matched, the one into 'Purple Haze' pretty good if one accepts that edits have to be made at all. None of this material ended up on the 'soundtrack' album due to a catalogue of errors and mishaps during and after the shoot. The on-location sound recordings suffered from grave technical failings. Some of them were also lost, as was a good quantity of the original film footage. (The 1971 *Rainbow Bridge* 'soundtrack' LP omitted 'Beginning', 'New Rising Sun', 'Bleeding Heart' and the Maui version of 'Ezy Rider' from the film's incidental music, substituted the Berkeley version of the live 'Hear My Train A'Comin'' for the Maui original, and ignored all the other tunes from the concert sequence, adding the studio 'Star Spangled Banner' – a song that does not appear anywhere in the film.)

For Hendrix and his group, the filmed concert was a diverting experience at the end of a spring and summer tour that, while not too onerous, had deflected Hendrix from his declared priority: to get into the studio and finish The Next Album. The 'soundtrack' album of the film Jeffery had committed him to was a long way down his list. A concert in Honolulu two days later, on

August 1st, brought the American leg of the tour to a close, with the group's short set of just eight numbers well received. The original tour plan had the group going to Japan after Hawaii – they were half way there from the American mainland, after all – but this idea had been allowed to slide as Hendrix's management gave priority to the work on the film.

Hendrix took advantage of this break in concert activity, with no confirmed bookings until the Isle Of Wight Festival on August 30th, to return to Maui for a rest in the seclusion of this relatively isolated community, away from the world and the usual hangers-on. Hendrix had been looking for somewhere to recharge his batteries and have time to do some uninterrupted thinking. He had talked to some of his family in Seattle about returning there in order to have a sustained period of quiet and calm, but the Seattle break never happened. That this came to nothing is probably connected with the statements Mike Jeffery was making to the media in mid July about trying to build some rest and relaxation time into the Hawaiian sojourn ("about six weeks" was his estimate to *Record Mirror*) specifically so that Hendrix could re-group and also write some new material in peaceful and isolated surroundings. Hendrix shared much of this extra time on Maui with Melinda Merryweather. At its end he gave her a cassette tape he'd recorded privately in his rented accommodation there. The tape was named *Scorpio Woman* in her honour, reflecting the zodiac themes of *Rainbow Bridge*. A patchwork of otherwise unheard new songs-in-progress and more complete compositions recognisable elsewhere, it was included on the Hendrix Estate's Dagger Records CD *Morning Symphony Ideas* released in 2000.

On August 13th Hendrix flew back to the mainland US and by the following evening had again taken up residence at Electric Lady. From then

"I don't believe anybody really knew where Jimi was at, or what he was thinking about at any point, although a lot of people profess they did."

Gerry Stickells, roadie

until the 24th he and his team worked regularly in Studio A on a group of songs with the aim of achieving final overdubs and proceeding to final mixes. During this ten-day period they gave serious attention to 'Dolly Dagger', 'Freedom', 'Room Full Of Mirrors', 'Straight Ahead', 'Ezy Rider', 'In From The Storm', 'Angel', 'Belly Button Window', 'Night Bird Flying', 'Astro Man' and 'Drifter's Escape'. The overdubs, as in July, were often done using 'direct injection' into the recording desk with the musician concerned sitting in the control room rather than out in the studio listening on headphones. Billy Cox explained, "Jimi and I were most comfortable doing our overdubs at the board. You didn't have the obstruction presented by those earphones. You could get right into it when you heard the music through those speakers. That was another benefit of working at Electric Lady. Eddie [Kramer] understood that this was our way of doing overdubs."[28]

During this last ten days of working on the new songs, Hendrix compiled another handwritten list of his latest thoughts on the songs that would best constitute The Next Album. Written on the back of a multitrack tape box that contained flanged parts for 'Ezy Rider', it showed the following. Side A: 1. 'Dolly Dagger'; 2. 'Night Bird Flying'; 3. 'Room Full Of Mirrors'; 4. 'Belly Button Window'; 5. 'Freedom'. Side B: 1. 'Ezy Rider'; 2. 'Astro Man'; 3. 'Drifting'; 4. 'Straight Ahead'. Side C: 1. 'Night Bird Flying'; 2. 'Drifter's Escape'; 3. 'Coming Down Hard On Me'; 4. 'Beginning'; 5. 'Cherokee Mist';

6. 'Angel'. Nothing was yet written next to side D. Note that 'Night Bird Flying' is down for both side A and side C, although the writing for the side A insertion is in bold and obviously a later re-think. Some of the tracks on side C have lines through them, as if Hendrix had changed his mind. And side D has no entries at all. The sides are quite uneven in length judging from the finished songs released on posthumous compilations. Side A makes 18:54, a perfect length for an LP side. Side B is a little short at just 15:31. Side C is too long at 20:36 and makes a rather awkward sequence with little variation in intensity or tempo. Finishing on 'Angel' seems particularly out of character for Hendrix, judging by the track-lists he had devised for his other LPs.

But this was much closer to a settled selection than the long list he'd made in mid June, which had been written largely in order of each song's state of completion. The songs he was working on diligently to bring to a finalised state in July and August would easily fill that empty last side: 'In From The Storm' (still provisionally called 'Just Came In'), 'Valleys Of Neptune', 'Hey Baby (New Rising Sun)', 'Stepping Stone' and 'Earth Blues'. Other titles on which he'd spent much time during the summer but which seem to have been set aside when it came to potential inclusion on The Next Album included 'Izabella', 'Lover Man', 'Bleeding Heart', 'Burning Desire', 'Heaven Has No Tomorrow' (aka 'Sorrow'), 'Hear My Train A'Comin'', 'Midnight Lightning' and 'Send My Love To Linda'. These could have filled a third disc, but the three-LP idea seems to have been quietly dropped, possibly as a compromise between Jeffery, who wanted a single album, and Hendrix, who thought three LPs was justifiable. Thus the outlines of the double-LP album Hendrix was aiming to complete that autumn seem clear, even if these lists were not entirely definitive. After all, Hendrix had left room for last-minute additions and deletions to both *Axis* and *Electric Ladyland*, so this could be described as his typical working method.

Treating his list (along with our assumptions about side D) as the last known form that Hendrix applied to his work in progress, we need now to examine the music not analysed so far. 'Night Bird Flying' has long been regarded as one of Hendrix's finest late achievements and an indication of the musical direction he was taking. It is a happy combination of simple elements and the guitar-drum dialogue that is always at the core of Hendrix's most winning compositions. As with tracks on *Axis* and *Electric Ladyland* there are many different rhythm patterns contained here within the same tempo, usually but not invariably divided into four-bar groups, each one bringing a change of mood and emphasis behind the vocal line. The breaks that Hendrix

work. Perhaps what Davis meant was western swing: certainly the beat and Hendrix's guitar phrasing here carry strong echoes of that musical style. The main disappointment on the track is the solo, which starts with a striking phrase but becomes a little too routined and heavy-handed, sounding like pre-rehearsed figures and ideas mostly derived from R&B rather than the light, skipping touches that the rest of the guitar commentary implies for the basic mood of the piece.

The other major issue concerning 'Night Bird Flying' is one that affects all the tracks intended to appear on The Next Album: the mixing. This was the first studio album that Hendrix was putting together completely under his own rules and with no supervision from elsewhere. Even *Electric Ladyland*, which had eventually been credited solely to Hendrix, had been started under Chas Chandler's direction and bears the shadow of Chandler's ideas on mixing and balance. For this new project, Hendrix used only his own instincts and perceptions, thereby shifting the basic guidelines. For example, he would now regularly mix his voice lower than it had been on earlier studio efforts, and certainly lower than on records by his contemporaries. This means that the accompanying guitars are often more dominant in the mix than they perhaps should be.

At the end of 'Night Bird Flying' there is a clear imbalance in the mix: one guitar is far too proud and does not blend properly with the others. But it was marked as a final mix, even though it might have benefited from another try. The same is true of the final mix of 'Room Full Of Mirrors' (as first released on the *Rainbow Bridge* LP of 1971). It suffers from two competing guitar-accompaniment tracks that are equally as prominent as the voice, making the piece sound over-busy and harsh, distracting the listener from what Hendrix is singing. The sound is ultimately too hard-driven for the subject matter. Hendrix had his own misgivings about this mix and the unduly prominent guitars, and was mulling over another attempt. There is also sometimes an imbalance in these mixes between the midrange instruments – guitars, mostly – and the bottom-end rhythm section – the bass and drums. The midrange is often congested and overbearing, giving a sense of little bottom-end presence. Tracks that have a more finely-judged relationship between voice and guitar include 'Dolly Dagger', 'Ezy Rider' and 'Freedom'.

A better balance between all the elements is found on 'Ezy Rider', one of the most intensively worked-on tracks of this whole project. Although once again Hendrix buries his voice a little too deep in the mix, it is at least double-tracked for extra presence, and the plethora of guitar overdubs are well blended, sitting down properly with the bass and drum parts rather than dominating them. The guitar obbligato for the voice generally enhances its commentary rather than distracting attention. The piece also benefits from the way Hendrix makes the tough verse riff the driving force as he sticks to the R&B principles on which he thrived. His arrangement is artfully considered, especially the build-up and release into the guitar solo where the rhythm section moves into a second bridge and the bass plays an alternating pattern of two notes an octave apart. Hendrix's guitar sustains the tension before the plunge into the verse structure and his screaming, white-hot,

"Hendrix looked tired and drawn, chewing throughout, but seemed determined to play, no matter what."

Brian Hinton, writer, on the Isle Of Wight Festival

and Mitchell always thrived on are spread liberally through the song, providing dramatic punctuations in natural cadences, especially at the ends of verses. Without this rich invention at the heart of the song's structure – the very stuff of good arranging – much of its charm would evaporate.

There are some pieces Hendrix recorded at this time which have such a plethora of guitar tracks, all with unique tonal qualities, that one longs to hear a wider range of textures from other instruments and backing voices. That is not the case on 'Night Bird Flying' where Hendrix's multiple overdubbed guitar lines create a supportive, colourful, harmonious context for his voice. The opening doubled-up guitar figure is one of his most vivid, immediately conjuring what Miles Davis called "hillbilly, country music played by them mountain white people"[29] – a strain that runs through much of Hendrix's

blues-laden solo.

'Freedom' was left in need of a few finishing touches from guitar overdubs and does not quite match the instrumental blend of 'Ezy Rider'. There are passages where something is clearly absent, especially in the transitions between verse and bridge (and vice versa). The main guitar accompaniment, which Hendrix has given extra echo and that chases the vocal shapes, again is often too dominant in the mix, distracting from the powerful surge generated by the basic guitar-bass-drums metre, which as the many live versions from this time demonstrate has its own urgency and excitement. Hendrix does have a noteworthy idea here: there is no featured guitar solo. He replaces it with a series of four-bar interjections from different guitar overdubs that keep the tune changing and provide a strong sense of an

Playing at the so-called Love & Peace Festival on Fehmarn island, Germany, September 6th 1970. This would turn out to be Hendrix's last ever concert appearance; he was dead less than two weeks later.

unfolding narrative, even during the instrumental passages. 'Freedom' also contains one of Hendrix's strongest sets of lyrics from this period. He patchworks together old and new lines, some stretching back a year or more, others still fresh, but offers a series of striking images and cleverly broadens the subject from the particular to the general. It could be about freedom in the wider world as much as it is a cry for freedom from two lovers at war with one another.

The edge and bite of those lyrics are unfortunately absent from the 1970 version of 'Angel'. Hendrix delivers a strangely self-pitying vocal performance that is devoid of any of the feelings of excited discovery and desire that had sustained his earlier demos of this ballad. One of the reasons for this is a drop in tempo here, making the song a dirge in comparison to the *Axis*-era versions. There is also none of the arrangement detail that made the 1967 work-outs of this tune so promising. Perhaps the detail would have come, given more time and work. It's clear that the track released on *The Cry Of Love* and all subsequent reissues is unfinished. Mitch Mitchell replaced his original drums after Hendrix's death in a bid to enliven the arrangement, and there is just a single guitar part all the way through. It is inconceivable

that Hendrix would not have laid down at least one additional guitar track, and probably more, while the vocal track sounds no more than a guide.

'Straight Ahead' has a strongly integrated and purposeful set of lyrics but unfortunately the structure and arrangement are less convincing. Given the evidence of the Atlanta performance in early July this tune was still being evolved and may well have changed further. The song, which shifts between a minor and major feel, has an imbalance between the lengths of the various verses and pre-choruses from which its incomplete arrangement cannot save it. This may be because it was put together from two different song ideas. The first idea (which in fact was the last to be added) is the 'Hello my friend...' verse section that starts with an E-minor-7 chord (with Hendrix as usual tuned down, here by a semitone or half-step), prefaced by an opening guitar dialogue. Without ceremony the song moves from the verse into major chords for a pre-chorus section (the second idea) more than twice as long as the verse, with little or no variation and a stilted verbal rhythm, plus a litany of vernacular verbal clichés of the period. The poor listener at this point wanders off in search of something more interesting among the relatively undeveloped backing music, longing for the beginning of the next section. But it is not here: Hendrix never had the chance to enhance the music sufficiently to compensate for the lack of substance in the lyrics, and so the periodic return to the E-minor-7 verse is like reaching an oasis in a musical desert. The musical backing for these sections is more fully developed, with interesting touches in the arrangement all through as little riffs appear, altering and disappearing, and well-controlled drum and bass punctuations highlight Hendrix's structuring. With a great deal more work he may have pulled this piece back on course; in its incomplete state we can but guess at what it might have become.

'Astro Man', originally designated as part of the *Black Gold* suite in the spring, was brought to a much higher degree of completion than 'Straight Ahead'. Perhaps the weakest link is Hendrix's vocal: he sounds strained and occasionally suffers from poor intonation. There are also moments where the arrangement seems temporarily to tread water, such as the concluding section in which Hendrix repeatedly sings "he's gonna foul up the rest of your life" while the accompaniment seems to be waiting for something else to happen. Nothing does happen, and the song, with nowhere else to go, ends in a fade. 'Astro Man' is a fun title, the lyrics are cleverly tongue-in-cheek, but it sits a little awkwardly with the general tenor of The Next Album, which is generally serious in its observations of the world and Hendrix's own experience. The deliberately cartoon-like images and absurdist humour would perhaps have fitted neatly into the suite for which 'Astro Man' was originally conceived, moving the story line forward and entertaining the listener, but nestled between 'Ezy Rider' and 'Drifting' on Hendrix's song-list it seems to be an interruption rather than a continuity, however deft its conception.

'Drifting', although incomplete, is generally regarded as one of Hendrix's most beautiful ballads. It is also something of a milestone in that it combines elements of his past styles, especially the dreamy lyricism of '1983' from *Electric Ladyland* or the TTG instrumental 'New Rising Sun', with the more conventional song structures of his later work. The two vocal verses paint a simple and effective picture of someone emotionally at sea and unable to locate a worthwhile direction. Hendrix sustains this picture musically with guitar eddies and waves lapping at the edges of his voice while Mitchell's drumming, here at its most sensitive, provides an impression of the deeper rhythms of the inner and outer landscapes sketched by the narrator. In the instrumental section after the vocals Hendrix opts for a series of overlapping and complementary guitar lines and counter-currents, some running backwards, some forwards, and all linking perfectly into the larger tapestry of the composition. Buzz Linhart's vibraphone was added after Hendrix's death; at the time Hendrix was undecided about adding another guitar or vibes to complete the instrumentation of the non-vocal parts. There is no doubt that the sonority of the vibes provides an exact match for everything else that is going on around them. The melancholy of this composition is universal, unlike the more personal and sentimental 'Angel', and shows Hendrix able to communicate basic truths about the human condition in a unique – and uniquely beautiful – way. Jazz writer Leroi Jones best described this particular gift: "That's one function of art, to reveal beauty, common or uncommon, uncommonly."[30]

The only other new composition that Hendrix came very close to finishing during his last mixing and overdubbing sessions in August at Electric Lady was 'In From The Storm', known to Hendrix as 'Just Came In' but given the better-known title after his death by Mitchell and Kramer. This is perhaps the closest Hendrix ever came to out-and-out heavy rock, with a thunderous drum rhythm, pounding guitar-bass unison riffs and declamatory vocals. It is not a huge step from this to Led Zeppelin, for whom Hendrix professed no great love when asked about the band in interviews that year. The final riff that carries 'In From The Storm' to its abrupt end is an exact copy of Jeff Beck's bludgeoning riff from 'Rice Pudding', an instrumental that closed his recently-released *Beck-Ola Cosa Nostra* album. Hendrix had long admired Beck and here publicly tipped his hat to the British guitarist. But the Beck influence on this track runs deeper. The entire sound-world of the piece is an evocation of the wall-of-sound acoustics of *Beck-Ola*, and one that is not generally found anywhere else in the late Hendrix studio recordings. There

are passages where Hendrix consciously imitates the guitar-generated quicksilver combinations of noise and sound on which Beck thrived. One such occurs in the stop-time instrumental section (2:20 to 2:35) where Hendrix scoops out some delightful explosions of noise à la Beck, and in a style quite different from the 'normal' gigantic legato sculptings he deployed in pieces like 'Machine Gun' and 'Star Spangled Banner'. Hendrix's impulse to make this kind of friendly tribute was not so unusual in itself. After all, the 1968 'Rainy Day' session had come about because he'd wanted to see what happened when he played a Jimmy Smith-Kenny Burrell type shuffle.

Another song that came within an ace of completion was his Dylan cover, 'Drifter's Escape'. This has been unjustly neglected, mostly because it suffered the misfortune to be overlooked for release until *Loose Ends* in 1973, a mostly lame and underweight collection of sub-par performances and rehearsals that nonetheless contained one or two gems (the LP was so scorned at the time that Reprise US didn't even bother to pick up their option for a release). This poor treatment meant that neither Alan Douglas nor the Hendrix Estate saw fit to include 'Drifter's Escape' on *Voodoo Soup* (1995) or *First Rays...* (1997), their versions of What The Last Album Was Meant To Contain, thereby contradicting Hendrix's own list.

Hendrix re-cast 'Drifter's Escape' from Dylan's original *John Wesley Harding* performance, most obviously and significantly through the removal of its major-chord tonality. Dylan plays the entire song over one G-major chord and leaves the melodic shape intact for its duration. Hendrix disturbs the melody line and constructs riffs that imply a minor tonality without completely removing the harmonic ambiguity, giving himself great interpretative freedom in the process. Once again he gives undue prominence in the mix to the multiple guitar overdubs, making for an over-busy and at times slightly hysterical atmosphere that overshadows his keening vocal. Seesawing riffs carried in unison by the guitar and bass keep up the pressure and the general sense of unease as Hendrix unfolds the miracle-play story of Dylan's lyrics. As so often in his music, Hendrix's accompanying guitar lines act almost as a sort of impromptu Greek Chorus commenting on the vocals, reaching their brilliant apogee as he recreates the flash of lightning used by Dylan as the moment of divine intervention and liberation that precipitates the drifter's escape. One can imagine how keenly Hendrix empathised with that moment.

The other items Hendrix and his team worked on during those overdub and mixing sessions in August 1970 were left much less complete. 'Belly Button Window' is a warmly good-humoured song about the baby Mitch Mitchell and his wife were expecting (she arrived during the September tour). Hendrix, Mitchell and Cox worked on it as a group performance but never completed the recording; the version that has been in circulation since its release on *The Cry Of Love* LP in 1971 is a relaxed 4-track demo Hendrix recorded spontaneously on August 22nd. Pleased with the result, he then overdubbed an extra guitar part. This notebook version would never have been his choice to represent the song on an album. 'Come Down Hard On Me' is a modified 12-bar blues that owes something to 'Bleeding Heart' for its melodic shape and draws from contemporary R&B for its feel. Hendrix achieved a basic rhythm master, made a reasonable vocal and a single guitar overdub, but the piece was still far from completion. 'Valleys Of Neptune' is a narrative song at a bright tempo with a note of optimism in the lyrics, but it never progressed past early attempts at a master take, some with guide vocals, some just instrumental. 'Cherokee Mist' was at an even cruder stage of redevelopment, with no single version ever completed, although it was occasionally used as a basis for studio jams. None of the other tunes Hendrix had been preparing for recording during 1970 even reached that stage during these last months of session work.

On August 26th Hendrix reluctantly attended the official opening party of Electric Lady studio, succumbing to pressure from Jim Marron. As the operating manager, Marron pointed out to him that the absence of the celebrity co-owner of the studio would be about as bad as it could get in adverse publicity. After a short time at the event, Hendrix left the studio with friends. The next day he flew to London in the company of road manager Eric

Barrett to begin preparations for a short European tour and his headlining appearance at the 1970 Isle Of Wight Festival.

By late August, although he had taken a fortnight's holiday in Maui and had not played a concert in over three weeks, Hendrix was in poor shape. Kathy Etchingham wrote later in her autobiography that some friends called her to his suite at the Londonderry Hotel in Park Lane: he was out of control and she was the only person they could think of who might be able to calm him down. "I went through to the bedroom," said Etchingham. "The first thing that hit me was the heat. It was a blazing hot day outside but all the windows were shut and a blow-heater was going full blast, making the air feel dry and uncomfortable. Jimi was lying in bed under a pile of blankets, shivering uncontrollably. There was an empty bottle of Jack Daniels and some glasses on the bedside table. ... I sat on the edge of the bed and put a cool flannel on his forehead to try to bring his temperature down. He seemed to be dangerously feverish and kept sniffing and complaining that he had a cold. He was thin and grey and looked really ill. I assumed he had a bad case of flu. In retrospect it is obvious that he was suffering from some kind of withdrawal symptoms."[31]

Somehow he got what he needed, and got it quite quickly, because later that day and for the next two he gave a series of interviews to European publications. The conversations reflected his thinking about the future and his music. He talked to *Record Mirror*'s Bob Partridge about his health, among other things, saying: "We've been getting some mental rest. After you've done something like three [US] tours you feel completely mentally exhausted. I wanted to record some new things, but in that sort of state we couldn't make it." He went on to mention his plans for new albums, including the continuing dialogue concerning the shape and size of The Next Album. He told Partridge that it would be released in Britain "next month", in other words September 1970. "I was doing some recording before I came here," Hendrix continued. "I flipped out after two days because much of the stuff was recorded in the gap, you know, between the time the Experience broke up and the Band Of Gypsys. So that stuff's another age. I'm losing time with myself. Then, after the next album there'll be a double-album, though don't ask me when that'll be out."[32] This seems to indicate that he may have been bending to Mike Jeffery's idea of putting out a single album in time for Christmas, which would

"After you've done something like three US tours you feel completely mentally exhausted."

Jimi Hendrix

buy him time for a more considered double-album the following year. The tunes that he'd been mixing and finishing so intensively during August would have comfortably filled the two sides of a single LP, leaving plenty of choice cuts to help start off a follow-up double.

That same day he met Danish model and actress Kirsten Nefer through a mutual friend and they spent much of the next two weeks together. During that time she saw some wild mood-swings from Hendrix, possibly the result of drug dependency that he still did not have under control. "He changed all the time," Nefer told interviewer Karsten Laybourn. "He was also unbearable at times. He was so jealous that it was on the verge of insanity. ... He was incredibly insecure and did not rely on anybody. And very suspicious also because he was surrounded by nothing but 'yes people', so he had difficulties figuring out who meant him good and the ones who didn't. ... His mood changed a lot."[33] Two days later, on Sunday August 30th, Hendrix travelled to the Isle of Wight and arranged for Nefer and her friend Karen Davis to meet

him at his hotel there. He was due to appear at the Isle Of Wight Festival late that same evening, but the usual festival-type delays and knock-ons meant that the Experience didn't hit the stage until the early hours of Monday morning. Nefer recalled the atmosphere at the Festival as "terrible". She said, "There were people everywhere, and there were rumours that bikers had surrounded the festival area and they had been fighting. Jimi went on-stage at two or three in the morning and there was a strange atmosphere."[34]

The Festival itself had started the previous Thursday, the 27th, and had slowly built to its climax on the Sunday, with something in the region of 600,000 people in attendance over the weekend. Acts playing on the first two days included Supertramp (then an unknown band), Hawkwind, Taste, Tony Joe White, Chicago, Family, and Procol Harum. By Saturday, the tension and suppressed violence affecting parts of the crowd had been whipped up by various groups and come to the surface. Many performers had to tread carefully in order to keep things calm. The performer who seemed to manage this best was John Sebastian of Lovin' Spoonful fame. He started off the Saturday with a relaxed and popular set, inspired enough for some to call him the hit of the festival that year. Acts that followed included Joni Mitchell, Tiny Tim, Miles Davis, Ten Years After, Emerson Lake & Palmer (there was talk at the time that Hendrix planned to link up with them for some concerts later the same year), The Doors, The Who, Melanie, and Sly & The Family Stone. Joni Mitchell was forced to endure a nightmare scene when someone in the VIP box needed treatment for a bad acid trip during her second song. An American with some sort of message then grabbed her microphone and was briefly allowed to rant to the audience unchecked. Mitchell was reduced to tears. One reviewer noted, "As the stage-crew were hauling him away the crowd started screaming, 'Let him speak! Let him speak!' Joni was trembling: 'Last week I visited a Hopi Indian reservation and some of the tourists were getting into it like Indians and some were getting into it like tourists. You're getting into it like tourists. Give us some respect!' They did."[35]

The festival was continually disturbed by violence and trouble-makers. The same reviewer described the scene. "A group of French rabble-rousers made daily sieges on the site, battering down fences, destroying catering equipment, and looting food. Thousands and thousands of less violently inclined anti-capitalists merely ignored admission fees by camping out on an ill-placed hill overlooking the stage. ... As more and more damage was incurred and more and more people listened for free, [the Festival compère] stopped pleading for 'peace and love' and began screaming and cursing the people who had destroyed this festival."[36] Nevertheless, the performers who delivered good music and a hip stage act received a fair hearing, including Miles Davis and, later on, The Who, whose performance was later released on a two-CD set that gives some credence to the claim that this was one of their best shows ever. The Doors contributed a dark, ominous set in which Jim Morrison stood out, the troubled star still in the throes of a legal nightmare, having been charged in the US of indecent exposure on-stage and under threat of a gaol sentence if found guilty.

The line-up on Sunday included sets by Free (one of their best), Donovan, Pentangle, The Moody Blues, and Jethro Tull before Hendrix and his group took the stage. After Hendrix's set, Joan Baez, Leonard Cohen and, finally, Richie Havens would bring the festival to its climax and close. Jethro Tull and their leader Ian Anderson gave one of the standout performances of the weekend, and everyone was keyed up for Hendrix's return to the UK stage. But there was an unaccountable 90-minute delay before the Experience came on. Various explanations for the delay have been made since, but according to the festival's biographer, Brian Hinton, folk performer Ralph McTell overheard a telling conversation. "McTell had earlier heard a roadie saying that Hendrix was 'very out of it' in someone's garden, and they were worried that he would not be up to playing." They had good cause. The long set delivered by the band was very uneven and included some utterly uninspired and listless playing from Hendrix, especially on the more familiar numbers. Hinton wrote: "Hendrix was pencil thin and barely filled his multi-coloured smock – mainly in pink – apparently run up by a hallucinating tailor. With his newly-trimmed Afro hairstyle, he looked tired and drawn, chewing … throughout, but seemed determined to play, no matter what."[37]

Hinton's apparently flippant criticism of Hendrix's attire is in fact an important one. During 1970, Hendrix's stage outfits sometimes slipped from the challenging or iconoclastic into plain bad taste. There are pictures of him from this time in costumes that are only a small step away from the high kitsch of the later Elvis Presley stage gear. Hendrix now lacked the dazzling contrasts and arresting new combinations of elements that had previously set his clothing apart, and the outfits he wore for some of his 1970 shows unhappily presage elements of the more tasteless excesses of Britain's 'glam' rock, then only a year or so away.

The Isle of Wight set was indifferently received, after a rousing response to the band's introduction and Hendrix's twisted attempt at 'God Save The Queen'. Hinton thought that "the uncertainty [on-stage] spread to the audience. At the end of one number there was no applause at all: some 600,000 souls sat in the darkness in total silence. Perhaps they had all fallen asleep. I know I almost did. The trio, no longer an Experience, were obviously under-rehearsed and relying on magic and miracles, which seemed in short supply".[38] Mitchell later confirmed this impression, saying that it had been a mistake to play such a gig after a month's layoff. There was also the difficulty – for both the band and the crowd – of being inspired in the yawning chill of 3.00am. But there was more to it than that, as Nefer hinted. Hendrix's indisposition prior to coming on-stage, which had delayed proceedings for so long, lingered on through the first part of the set.

The band certainly do sound under-rehearsed, but the first few numbers are ragged in a gripping way, as if the three men are doing battle with some phantastical dark beast. Hendrix's guitar tone is often ugly, his music reflecting his mood, while Mitchell's drumming is unusually heavy as he constantly resorts to his double bass-drum in a bid to push the whole thing along. There are times when the listener forgets Billy Cox is even on-stage as his metronomic lines and self-effacing tone seem to belong to another performance entirely. The drama of the Hendrix set at this festival has always been compelling, right from when the music first appeared on bootlegs within months of it being played, through its official release on a single LP the following year, and on through its various incarnations, up to and including the first complete release, in 2002, on 2CDs and a DVD.

Hendrix had demons to vanquish beyond the music, just as Joni Mitchell had the previous day, but his took a quite different shape. He recovered during the time he was on-stage from whatever it was that had wiped him out beforehand. But he also had to contend with a barrage of intermittent interference reproduced over the amplifiers and PA system from the festival's security walkie-talkies, operating on a frequency that meant they were picked up and broadcast to the enormous crowd, often mid-solo or mid-vocal. Hendrix reacted to this in different ways during the set, sometimes mimicking the security chat on his guitar to the amusement of the audience, at others showing anger. His dark mood is reflected in many of the songs, but especially the 25-minute version of 'Machine Gun'. It contains a brutal, angry opening solo constructed from broad, blunt melodic shapes rather than the beautifully conceived and flowing blues lines he usually delivered. After a long drum solo from Mitchell – not his greatest recorded moments – Hendrix plays an angular riff and launches into a second solo. It is more coherent and not quite so broodingly dark, but the music still sounds like a fight to the death against titanic odds. When the second riff is introduced, it is as if a new chapter of a terrifying book is starting. With the second set of lyrics, Hendrix

once more demonstrates his uncanny ability to sing one line and play an independent guitar line simultaneously, as if in conversation with himself. But then the monsters rise up once more and he returns to his deadly battle, using a whole range of effects as weapons, including the riff from 'Race With The Devil'. Quite appropriate. Like the brooding and slightly crazed set The Doors had performed the night before, this transfixes with its raw ugliness. It is utterly unlike the message Hendrix had delivered with 'Machine Gun' at the Fillmore East just eight months earlier.

The crowd seemed stunned by the onslaught. After a fast and sloppy 'Lover Man' Hendrix announced, "OK, I think we're gonna start all over again: Hello England, glad to see ya." If this was his way of attempting to wipe out the previous 40 minutes or so of hard work, it didn't really come off. The next song is 'Freedom', and initially it seems to take off rhythmically, but Hendrix is still dropping notes in unaccustomed confusion. For the most part impassive and only occasionally checking in on the audience, this was the Jimi Hendrix who desperately wanted to be a musician first and foremost to his fans, not a performing seal. No wonder in interviews straight afterwards he would say he wanted once again to try a larger group to take some of the weight of expectation from his shoulders.

Hendrix plays 'Red House' next and, like a break in the storm, it provides its usual balanced contrasts. The song gives him time to regroup as he leans into his old-time guitar licks. He sounds relaxed for the first time that night. After a disastrously sloppy 'Dolly Dagger' he reverts back to slow blues with a version of 'Midnight Lightning' that is low-down, dirty and moving, especially as he sings: "My head is dizzy and shakin' / Lord, my whole soul is so tired and achin' / Feel like I got run over / By public opinion in the past." He sure did. This performance is linked to the next song, 'Foxy

> # "Hendrix is now so avant-garde that he plays above most pop fans."
>
> Newspaper report, Sweden

Lady', by a long, sustained feedback guitar note that screeches and tears at the audience's ears while Hendrix talks to them, finally dedicating the song – as he usually did on tour that year – to particular people present at the gig. This time he named "Linda", "the cat right there with the silver face" (Hawkwind's Nick Turner), "Kirsten" (Nefer), "Karen" (Davis) and an unidentified four-year-old who missed the dedication as she stood side-stage. The version of 'Foxy Lady' that follows is one of the most brutal and punishing performances of the song Hendrix ever gave. At one point he leaves the stage while his guitar speaker keeps the music flowing, and at another, during the solo, he seems to be making the guitar and amplifier violently sick. This is not about rock'n'roll any more: we are once more back to the titanic struggles of earlier in the set. It is enthralling and horrifying at the same time.

A truly ghastly 'Message To Love' is best forgotten, the ugly sounds of this performance entirely unsuited to the song's message. The unaccompanied intro to 'Hey Baby (New Rising Sun)' is full of frustration and violence rather than beauty, and the rest of this usually serene, melancholy ballad is marred by poor guitar tuning, although Hendrix still manages a few arresting, mercurial phrases to accompany his vocal. For the rest of the set he is back to slaying dinosaurs; after 'Ezy Rider', with the end in sight, the hits are tossed into the air and gored on the trio's electric amplified horns – 'Hey Joe', 'Purple Haze', 'Voodoo Child (Slight Return)'. In order to be sure the beast is quite dead, the group powers into 'In From The Storm', Mitchell leading the way with a bludgeoning attack on his double bass-drums, snares and cymbals. Everything is wrong with it, from out-of-tune vocals and guitar, forgotten

Hendrix's last band, with Billy Cox and Mitch Mitchell, at the Fehmarn festival site, September 6th 1970.

lyrics, rhythmic gaps like yawning chasms between all three players, and overplaying from Hendrix and Mitchell. Nonetheless, it is so overwhelming in its desperation and the sheer amount of effort they put into the music that one cannot but sit in awe as the band grinds to the end of the set, especially given the sheer noise that Hendrix concocts on his guitar after completely ruining the last verse of vocals.

A number of witnesses claim that Hendrix collapsed backstage after throwing down his guitar and walking off. At the same time a small fire broke out in the stage area when a firework was set alight among some canvas, shifting back poor Joan Baez's set even further into the early morning. It had been a long, long night – and after Baez there were still two more acts to go. By then Hendrix was gone, whisked away in a helicopter to his hotel on the island. Some indication of what Hendrix was thinking that morning may be found in Richie Havens's report of his conversation with the exhausted guitarist at the festival, prior to their appearances. "He was terribly unhappy," said Havens, "extremely depressed, and he asked for my help. 'I'm having a real bad time with my managers and lawyers; they're killing me; everything is wired against me and it's getting so bad I can't eat or sleep. … You've been doing this longer than me, man, I need to talk to a lawyer, man. You must know somebody.' I told him I knew a very good lawyer. … I told Jimi I would be glad to introduce him and that I would be in London for four days after the festival and would be going directly back to New York. I told him to come by and see me when he left the Isle of Wight. He never showed up."[39] Hendrix only returned to London some time after Havens had left. He would never go back to New York.

The next day Hendrix flew to Stockholm to begin the final appearances of this European mini-tour. Concerts there that night and the next were well received by the audiences but uninspired. A local paper reported: "One hour too late, Jimi Hendrix started his show … but instead he played twice the time scheduled – more than an hour and a half as opposed to the 45 minutes scheduled. … The first hour of the concert was boring. Hendrix seemed tired, uninspired and in bad shape. … A few times [he] showed glimpses of his greatness."[40] Another report of the concert said that "many left before the show had ended. … Hendrix is now so avant-garde that he plays above most pop fans. It was hard to follow when the sound came cascading from the guitar and the improvisations went where only Jimi knew. … Unfortunately, Jimi Hendrix is boring at such length."[41]

This entire tour, from August 31st to September 6th, seems now like a sped-up microcosm of the cycle of depression and elation that Hendrix had been experiencing for virtually the whole of the year so far. One or two of the concerts were good and the audiences appreciative; others were nothing short of disastrous. The September 2nd concert in Århus was probably a low in Hendrix's career only equalled by the Band Of Gypsys fiasco at Madison Square Garden in January. Some reports suggest Hendrix was unwell before he arrived in Århus and that his illness took hold there, but Kirsten Nefer said that he was acting strangely in the hours before the show and, just before he travelled to the concert hall, had swallowed some Mandrax (or Quaalude) tablets. The effect of this barbiturate-like sedative is to make one generally spaced out, incapable of co-ordinated movement and liable to crash into things. That's how Hendrix was backstage.

On-stage it was worse. The audience knew immediately. Hendrix had often hit the stage high, but would not normally take anything that seriously affected his capacity to perform. By this point his standards had fallen so far – or his desperation had increased so dramatically – that such considerations seemed no longer to be a constraint. A Danish newspaper reporter witnessed the fiasco. "'Do you feel all right?' Hendrix asked when he finally walked on-stage. It was obvious to everyone who had eyes to see that Hendrix did not. … He threw himself into the first song. The notes that came from his guitar were surprisingly powerful … but as the song continued it got weaker and

thinner: no verve, no sweat, no strength, nothing. No one felt much like applauding at the world-famous musician just because he was world-famous. The song was miserable. … Hendrix's face revealed clearly that he was aware of the situation. … His performance was simply not good enough."[42] The band tried one more number but Hendrix stopped playing and Mitchell covered with a drum solo. Before that came to an end Hendrix had slipped off-stage and did not return. The other two band members followed, leaving a very unhappy audience and a dismayed promoter.

The next day the local press ran a post-mortem on the calamity. One reporter wrote, "When he arrived at Århus he seemed to be in bad shape, a member of the reception committee at [Århus airport] tells us. He was trembling and sweating a lot. Hendrix is simply too tired and you can't say much about that, his road manager Gerry Stickells says. His programme is demanding."[43] This parallels the state in which Kathy Etchingham had found him just a few days earlier in London. His conversations with friends during these weeks continually circled around the same obsessive subjects. His alienation from the people around him, his exhaustion, his commitment to music – all became a litany of issues for him. He told a reporter in Denmark, "I'm tired of lying down and I feel mentally hollowed. … I've been looking for a place, far away from this mechanical world where cities and hotel rooms merge into each other. I've found it, inside myself. Now I want to spread it. My music needs love and understanding. Through music you get more religion than through anything else."[44]

Hendrix moved on to Copenhagen, staying with Kirsten Nefer at her mother's house where he claimed he had his first good sleep since he'd left New York. The benefit was obvious in the improved performance he gave that night at the KB Hallen. The reviewer for *Information* wrote: "In connection with the aborted Århus concert Jimi Hendrix is reported to have said, 'I've been dead for a long time.' If this report is correct [it remains unsubstantiated] I would suggest that the concert two days later in Copenhagen was a rising from the dead. Such liveliness I have rarely experienced. It lasted one and a

"My music needs love and understanding. Through music you get more religion than through anything else."

Jimi Hendrix

half hours and left me like a rag. It was hard to bear – one does not usually experience something like this. I have to think all the way back to John Coltrane's first visit, nine years ago. There is such supple grace in every movement during his playing."[45]

This peak was followed by another trough. Billy Cox, tempted at an after-gig party to drop some acid for the first time in his life, entered the beginnings of what became a protracted nervous breakdown. (It would necessitate his eventual removal back to the United States on September 9th, with the last handful of shows of the tour cancelled as a result.) Hendrix's cycles of extreme highs and lows continued. He told Danish interviewer Anne Bjorndal that he felt exhausted by his responsibilities. "I am the bus driver and you're my passengers," he quipped before getting down to detail. "Music is my life," he said, while discussing with her the likelihood of starting a record company with The Rolling Stones. "You have to be honest with it. It's about emotions and feelings and you must take your time for it like any other occupation. In my case I sacrifice a part of my soul every time I play. There are also certain moments when I feel I have got to write, especially before I go off to sleep when all my thoughts run through my brain. My guitar is my medium and I want everybody to get into it. I want to turn the world on. Music – and soundwaves – are cosmic when they vibrate from one side to the other. I'm not sure I will live to be 28 years old. I mean, the moment I feel I have just got nothing more to give musically, I will not be around on this planet any more, unless I have a wife and children, otherwise I've got nothing to live for."[46]

It is perhaps simplistic to offer this interview as evidence for his increasingly desperate attempts to find a stable relationship during his relatively brief European sojourn. But other evidence is available. Kirsten Nefer said he asked her to marry him, and although she didn't take it too seriously – they'd met less than a week previously – she could see that he was sincere at least for the moment he said it. It is a sad indication of just how

"I sacrifice a part of my soul every time I play."

Jimi Hendrix

loose was Hendrix's grip on everyday realities. Nefer was aware of this part of his character and his by now almost uncontrollable insecurity. To her it was "why he asked so many girls if they wanted to marry him. That's what he wanted but he couldn't find out how to handle it, he didn't trust anybody. He didn't even realise how big and famous he was. I don't think he knew how many fans he had".[47]

This loss of perspective also applied to his creativity. As 1970 progressed he increasingly lost the ability to identify the nature and worth of his own unique musical contribution. Many of his guitar-playing colleagues, in the US and Britain, have recalled that during 1970 they would no longer see him with guitar in hand everywhere he went, that he seemed for the moment to have fallen out of love with the guitar. For someone like Hendrix, who had lived by the guitar for the previous decade, this was a fundamental change. The instrument was a close part of his own identity: if he was no longer able to see it in this way, what could take its place in someone so insecure and so vulnerable? The answer in the short term seemed to be people – or young women, at least. But Hendrix had never exactly been careful about his selection process, and when he ended up in a good relationship it seemed to be more by luck than judgement. He also had a taste for – to put it at its simplest – strange relationships. As Kathy Etchingham wrote, "Jimi had picked up some pretty weird women when he was away from home. It seemed to be almost a compulsion with him. Every night he had to have someone new and, according to the others who were on tour with him, he would often choose the worst possible dogs or crazies, take them back to his hotel room, have sex with them and then become agitated with them and ask them to leave."[48]

Given that perspective, Nefer was a stroke of good fortune, and their relationship genuinely blossomed, albeit briefly. It survived Hendrix's departure for two dates in Germany: a concert in Berlin – which started with some whistling from the audience but settled into one of the better recitals of the repertoire on this tour – and the so-called Love And Peace Festival on Fehmarn island. The festival was sabotaged by days of non-stop rain and unruly elements in the crowd intent on violence, including various biker gangs. Drummer Jon Hiseman was on the bill with Colosseum and he remembers a miserable affair characterised by interminable waiting around – and mud. "I remember getting off the bus with Mitch," says Hiseman, "and then waiting for something to happen. But it didn't. The water was pouring down, everything was waterlogged. The day had to be abandoned – you couldn't see anything, it was just a sea of mud. Worst experience I've ever had. I remember Jimi, Mitch and all of us on this bus, waiting for the rain to

stop, and it never did. Jimi was very quiet, very withdrawn. He was sick, and looked very tired. Mitch was twitchy. They were in what I would consider as poor shape. I didn't hang out with them in their dressing rooms, so I can't say what happened later. I just remember them as we waited in vain for the rain to cease."[49] The concert was poor and the festival itself a disaster. Someone hit Gerry Stickells in the head with a plank of wood that had six-inch nails sticking out of it. Hendrix eventually delivered as near a complete set as he could muster amid the rain, the chaos and the squalling, uneasy crowd. Then the whole entourage grabbed a flight out of the site in a helicopter laid on for the performers, flying direct to Hamburg and transferring to flights that took them on to London.

Hendrix met up with Nefer once more in London, spending time and unwinding with her between September 8th and 11th. He saw Billy Cox on to a plane back to the US on the 9th. Some of his New York friends, including Alan Douglas and Devon Wilson, had followed him across the Atlantic, apparently against his wishes. On Friday 11th he gave what turned out to be his final interview, to Keith Altham. He was due back at Electric Lady in New York ten days later, on Monday 21st, to work on his album. During the interview Hendrix disguised his lack of direction and centre, talking of future plans and making judgements about what would be good for him musically. "I'd like to have a small group, and a large one, and maybe go touring with one of them," said Hendrix. "We're trying to get another tour of England together, and that's definitely a new bass player. Billy Cox has split."[50] The finality of his comment about Cox was confirmed later by Mitchell, who said that he and Hendrix had already discussed possible replacements in the days following Cox's return to the US. There were, after all, recording sessions waiting for them on their return, let alone more concerts.

The reference Hendrix made to two bands, small and large, may have been an oblique one to the project with Gil Evans and his ensemble. There may well have been promptings to tour the proposed album, an idea Evans would have embraced. Hendrix admitted to Altham that he needed more diversity in his music, a better balance of elements, and wanted to develop his talents more fully. "I'm still trying to get my writing together. All I write is what I feel, that's all. And I don't really round it off too good, it's almost naked. And the words are so bland that nobody can get into them … [but] I'm trying to do too many things at the same time, which is my nature. I just hate to be in one corner, I hate to be put as only a guitar player, or only a songwriter, or only a tap dancer! I like to move around."[51] Altham, who had known him since 1966, got him to look back over the past few years – a rarity in a Hendrix interview. He admitted that he felt much changed from the person who had written and recorded Are You Experienced. He had also moved past the stage of seeing music as a force for change in the world. "It's a reflection," he asserted, and said he was no longer political. "Not really. I was ready to get into all that, but everybody goes through those stages, too. It all comes out in the music."[52] That view was confirmed later from a different angle by Eric Burdon. "Well, we all have our business problems, we all sign our lives away at the beginning of our careers and regret it somewhat later," said Burdon. "But no, I don't think that was at the bottom of his problems. Everything an artist does is reflected in his real life. You can talk about going on-stage and becoming another person, but I don't buy that. We are what we project. An actor can turn it on and turn it off 'cause that's what he's supposed to do, but rock'n'rollers are a different breed. What Jimi came up against in a creative sense he would eventually have to come up against on a spiritual level. He was a very complex person; there were many facets to him. He had a lot of things to work out."[53]

Unfortunately for Hendrix, he was handicapped by an inability to help himself. In the past two years he'd hardly been short of good advice from friends and colleagues, but he'd turned a deaf ear to most of it. Instead he kept himself going by looking for flattery from the very sycophants, groupies and hangers-on he ultimately distrusted, creating a vicious circle he no longer had effective weapons of his own to defeat. Since leaving home he had relied on his own instincts, however wayward, to get him through life, but his world had changed so much that this was no longer enough. In this situation one has to adapt and grow to survive or one doesn't survive. Hendrix, unwilling to change but desperate for help, thus found himself in an untenable position, isolated and very vulnerable. This again parallels the career of Elvis Presley, whose failure to rise above his fears and insecurities in his private life left him reliant on an inner circle of acquaintances who were as much a part of the problem as the solution. Presley and Hendrix, both perennially in pursuit of the perfect female companion, equally found it impossible – for different reasons – to build a long-term relationship based on such fundamental tenets as compromise and mutual support. They were latterly locked into a cycle of desperate embrace and quick rejection. There was also the shared problem of drug use, which in Presley's case was a long-term dependency, while Hendrix simply didn't get the time to work that one out.

Many musicians of Hendrix's generation faced the same despair, terror and stark choices. Some survived, some didn't. Some had help at the right moment, some got the timing wrong. Eric Clapton felt that Hendrix's case was one of the most extreme, precisely because of his genius. "I think that that is probably the curse of genius, you know, that you are alone. … Nobody can understand the depths that you go to when you reach down inside yourself to play or to express – you can't take anyone with you to these places, and sometimes you find things that are very scary. And I think you have to survive that on your own, and that is a very lonely experience and it's not something you choose. It's not something you would necessarily go after, it's something you inherit with your gift and [Hendrix] had it in aces."[54]

On Monday September 14th Kirsten Nefer had to report for work on actor George Lazenby's latest film, *Universal Soldier*, on location in England. Before she left, an unsettled Hendrix repeatedly asked her to phone him, but predictably was never at his hotel to return the calls. Considering her departure for work and her career as a rejection of him and his needs, he pushed her into the background and looked for other women who might boost

Not only did Jimi Hendrix's music outlive its creator, but it will outlive all the rest of us.

his flagging spirits. It was hardly the first time he had reacted in this way. One woman he certainly saw again after Nefer left was his old sparring partner Devon Wilson, then staying with Alan and Stella Douglas not far from his hotel. By this time, though, the heady rush of their early affair was long gone, their relationship closer to that of old friends. He now had just a handful of days left in London before his return to New York, and much to do if he was to meet his planned business commitments as well as enjoy himself. Nefer made a sustained attempt to contact Hendrix by phone for three days, but she did not drop everything to come back to London and seek him out. She was aware that life went on; she knew that certain things work out and others don't. The next woman to whom Hendrix turned his attentions would not share such views.

He spent Monday 14th to Thursday 17th seeing friends and colleagues, attending parties, jamming and shopping. Meetings were scheduled with a range of business and personal contacts, including Ed Chalpin and Track Records, but few were kept. He looked

"I'm trying to do too many things at the same time, which is my nature. I just hate to be in one corner."

Jimi Hendrix

up Chas Chandler and spent an evening at his old producer's London flat. Chandler remembered this happening on Wednesday 16th[55] but that seems unlikely, for that evening Hendrix went down to Ronnie Scott's club to jam with Eric Burdon and his band War; Ronnie's did not close until 2.00am and Hendrix stayed jamming until the end. It's more likely that Chandler met up with Hendrix on the Monday night, especially as he recalls Hendrix sitting playing with Chandler's baby son on his knee; hardly a thing to be doing in the early hours. Alan Douglas claimed two different dates in two interviews[56] for when he and Hendrix talked all night, but it seems likely this happened on the Wednesday. Hendrix knew Douglas was always ready for a chat, whatever the hour. According to Douglas, Hendrix had arrived alone and stayed the night alone. Then the following morning, Thursday 17th, Hendrix joined Douglas in his taxi to Heathrow airport where Douglas was due to catch a flight to New York.

Both Chandler and Douglas claimed that Hendrix asked them to step in and take charge of his affairs in one capacity or another. Douglas felt that Hendrix was looking for ways to break from Mike Jeffery and that he was being lined up to help Hendrix negotiate one-off projects, such as the Gil Evans recording, once he'd cut free. According to Douglas, Hendrix specifically cited the ongoing debate about whether The Next Album should be a single or a double. Douglas also recalled them talking extensively about plans for future music and how his career should develop. If that was so, then it may be that Hendrix felt he was simply talking things through with a friend rather than commissioning him to act on his behalf.

Chandler had more prosaic aims, and was sure Hendrix did too. Chandler, like Mitch Mitchell, had just become a father, and Hendrix dropped in to congratulate the new parents. He also came to talk business. "We sat talking until two or three in the morning," Chandler recalled on a TV documentary many years later. "[Hendrix] said that he felt he wasn't satisfied with what he'd been recording in the 15 months since we'd parted company. And he couldn't really see what he'd done."[57] This is plausible, given that there was virtually no vinyl output to show for Hendrix's seemingly endless hours in the studio since he'd stopped working with Chandler. Even with enough material in progress and near completion back in New York to fill three vinyl LPs, he still had not been able to settle on a release that would satisfy his ambitions and creative criteria. He was testing Chandler to see if he could receive the type of guidance he needed from a person he knew understood his music and with whom he had been successful in the past.

Chandler felt that he had come to an understanding with Hendrix that evening about what was to be done. "I said, 'Well, I'm going back to Newcastle on Friday, you're going back to New York … . Bring all your tapes back to London and we'll go into the studio and start sifting through them, find out what's on there."[58] Chandler's recollection was supported by Eddie Kramer who said he had a phone conversation with Hendrix soon after where Hendrix asked him to fly from New York to London with all the tapes they'd been working on.[59] Kramer demurred, reminding Hendrix that he was due back in the studio in a few days himself and they could talk it through then. After some thought, Hendrix agreed to this.

Meanwhile, Hendrix attended to other things. In between all the activity during the three days since Nefer had gone off to her film set – including meetings, chats, socialising and the Ronnie Scott's jam – Hendrix had taken up with Monika Dannemann, a woman he'd met briefly in Germany 18 months earlier. When she heard that Hendrix was on tour in Europe she had come to London and made contact with him. They met up late in the afternoon of Tuesday 15th and she claimed that Hendrix took her that evening to see Eric Burdon's band at Ronnie Scott's club, though other witnesses suggest he was there solely with Devon Wilson and Alan and Stella Douglas. While at the club, Hendrix had made arrangements to sit in with Burdon's band the following evening.

Hendrix and Dannemann also spent time together during a very busy Wednesday and she claimed to have accompanied him back to Ronnie Scott's

that night. Hendrix had been due to meet Mitch Mitchell, Eric Clapton and others to see Sly & The Family Stone at The Lyceum and then jam with Sly at the Speakeasy club that Wednesday night. Sly had flown into Heathrow the same day and was excited about the prospect: Mitchell had confirmed the arrangements with Hendrix around 7.00pm that evening. Clapton said he saw Hendrix at the Lyceum, but afterwards Hendrix seems to have chosen the previously agreed jam with Burdon and War at Ronnie's. After leaving Scott's club, he turned up alone to see Alan Douglas and spent the rest of the night talking with him. Dannemann claimed to have spent all day Thursday with Hendrix, but Douglas remembered him sharing the taxi out to Heathrow late that morning; others (including Kathy Etchingham) recalled encountering

"He had a lot of things to work out."

Eric Burdon, singer, on Hendrix

Hendrix around London and that he was by himself. He had met up again with Dannemann by early evening. Once more he was keeping the various strands of his life quite separate.

On the evening of Thursday 17th Hendrix went to a party at Stella Douglas's flat, apparently getting Dannemann to drop him there. For the second night running he had left her and visited the flat where Devon Wilson and the Douglases were staying. Within a short time Dannemann was back to insist on picking him up; Hendrix, perhaps already with an eye to ending the relationship, asked people at the party to help put her off. After repeated badgering from Dannemann over the flat's intercom, Hendrix left the party at around 3.00am and returned to Dannemann's basement room in the Samarkand Hotel, a converted Victorian terraced house in Ladbroke Grove, west London.

What happened there only Hendrix and Dannemann knew for certain, but some time early in the morning of Friday September 18th Hendrix died. According to the post-mortem and inquest his death was the result of kidney failure and inhalation of vomit brought about by a fatal combination of barbiturates (probably sleeping tablets given him by Dannemann), wine and whatever else was floating around in Hendrix's system.

One of Hendrix's habitual jottings of lyrics or verses was found in the room after his death: for years he had been writing down such things on scraps of hotel paper or anything else that came to hand. These three pages were as usual undated, with notes on both sides. They could have been composed earlier, or that night, or both. They start as if words for a song: the tempo indication "slow" is written in brackets at the beginning. The last two sides include the words "the story – of life is quicker / Than the wink of an eye. / The story of love – [is] hello and goodbye – until we meet again". Hendrix said in many interviews that his lyrics were very personal, sometimes embarrassingly so for him. It is possible that what Hendrix wrote here constituted a goodbye note to Dannemann, who by then was quite probably wearing out her welcome, judging by Hendrix's reluctance to be with her over the past 24 hours. Hendrix may have been planning to jettison her upon his return to New York that weekend. Perhaps she knew that. If so, she never said so subsequently.

Jimi Hendrix was in the middle of trying to set his career in order and to sort out where he was headed. Instead his life was snatched from him in obscure circumstances. However that came about, there is no doubt that this pointless waste of life is the greatest cause for regret, and for that Hendrix must take as much responsibility as anyone else involved. We may rely on other people to solve for us the most difficult and intractable of our problems, but at the last moment, no one else can guarantee that our heart keeps pumping and our blood still courses through our body.

The fact that this untimely death still matters today, decades after the event, is a testament to Hendrix's unique and enduring artistry. Any time you feel like testing that claim, just listen to the music.

hendrix gear

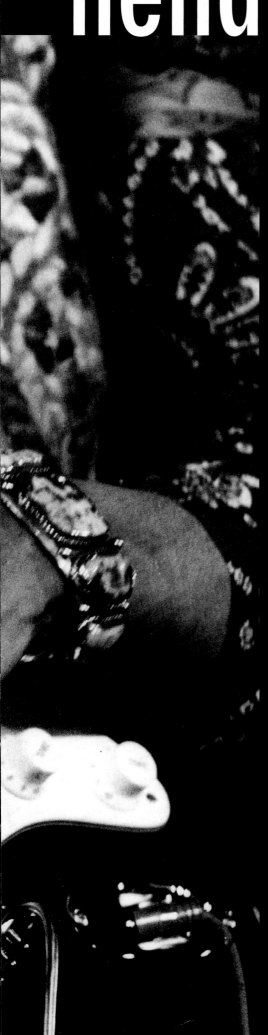

Now that we have finished the story of Jimi Hendrix's music, it's time to examine in brief the tools of his trade – the guitars, amplifiers and effects-units that he used in order to create that remarkable music.

The guitar with which Jimi Hendrix is most associated is the Fender Stratocaster. He got his first one early in 1966, probably a white-finish model that he seems to have acquired at Manny's music store in New York City.[1] Later in the year, after that was stolen, he got a '64 sunburst-finish Strat with rosewood fingerboard, and it may have been this guitar that he took with him to England – and fame – in September 1966.[2] Fender's Stratocaster had first appeared in 1954, a revolutionary three-pickup solidbody electric guitar, with vibrato bridge. In the early 1960s the young Hendrix would surely have noticed his hero Curtis Mayfield playing a Strat, and had also probably spotted guitarists like bluesman Buddy Guy and left-handed surf king Dick Dale wielding the futuristically-styled Fender. The Stratocaster was an excellent instrument, and one to aspire to. In 1966 a new sunburst Strat with vibrato cost $281.

Hendrix was in part attracted by the model's playability and its sonic versatility. "The Stratocaster is the best all-around guitar for the stuff we're doing," he said in summer 1967. "You can get the very bright trebles and the deep bass sound."[3] Strats would remain Hendrix's main choice for recording and performing live throughout the rest of his career, and he used quite a number. His manager Chas Chandler said in spring 1967: "Jimi always uses Fenders and is hoping for a tie-up with them. He's been through six already – two stolen, two others fogged up on him. Always has two with him on dates."[4] As for colour, Hendrix favoured Stratocasters finished in sunburst, white, or black-finish models at various times, and was even pictured playing the occasional red-finish Strat. (He selected a red Strat for conflagration at Monterey.)

He loved to visit music stores to find out about new guitars and effects, regularly buying items he liked. He enjoyed trying new things – he'd pick up fellow players' instruments out of curiosity, too – and during his career would sometimes be photographed with instruments he used for only a short time. Some he would give away, as Henry Goldrich of Manny's recalled. "I'd see kids come in the store with guitars I'd sold Jimi the week before. If he liked a kid, he'd give him his guitar, brand new."[5]

Towards the end of his career Hendrix favoured his 1968 black-finish Stratocaster (serial number 222625). He used this maple-fingerboard guitar between October 1968 and his death in September 1970. Significant dates with it included the famous Lulu television show on January 4th 1969, the Royal Albert Hall gigs in February 1969, the Band Of Gypsys concerts on December 31st 1969 and January 1st 1970 (seen in the *Band Of Gypsys* video), the Atlanta Pop Festival on July 4th 1970 (*Jimi Hendrix At The Atlanta Pop Festival* video), the Isle Of Wight festival on August 30th 1970 (*Jimi Hendrix At The Isle Of Wight* video), and most of the concerts on his last tour from August 31st to September 6th 1970. After Hendrix's death on September 18th 1970, Monika Dannemann took possession of the black Strat until she died in 1996. It's not known what's happened to it since. When the guitar was examined in 1993 the body's back plate was missing.[6] This plate on Strats covers a cavity for the vibrato system's springs and the 'sustain block' with its string-end retainers. Hendrix rarely left the plate in place on his Strats, presumably to allow easier access when changing strings or adjusting the vibrato. He would occasionally 'pluck' the revealed springs of the vibrato system for sound effects, as heard at 11:31 in 'Machine Gun' (recorded first show, January 1st 1970) from *Band Of Gypsys*. The black Strat in its 1993 state had five springs in the vibrato cavity, which is how Hendrix usually set up his Strat vibrato systems. This meant that, like many players, Hendrix could use the vibrato arm only to lower the pitch of notes, not raise them. Unusually, however, in that same performance of 'Machine Gun' he is heard (4:57 to 5:15) making striking use of the vibrato arm to raise the pitch of the notes (and one can see him doing so in the *Band Of Gypsys* video), so the vibrato bridge of the black Strat must have allowed this, at least for this concert. Hendrix would bend and manipulate pitch using the vibrato system, often to extreme effect. Listen for example to 'Third Stone From The Sun' (January and April 1967) from *Are You Experienced* and hear how he uses the vibrato to lower the pitch of the notes, often radically, from 2:27 to the end of the track.

The other Stratocaster most associated with Hendrix is his white-finish 1968 maple-fingerboard model (serial number 240981), which he used from October 1968 until his death, including notable dates such as the Woodstock festival in August 1969 and the 1970 European tour, though he appears to have played it less frequently than the black Strat. After Hendrix's death, Experience drummer Mitch Mitchell sold it to Italian TV chat-show host Gabriele Ansaloni at Sotheby's in 1990 for £198,000 (then about $375,000). It was subsequently sold in 1993 and currently forms a major part of the displays at the Experience Music Project museum in Seattle, Washington, which opened in 2000.

Strats: early sunburst (top); a later white one (above) with Fender amps.

Hendrix was left-handed. Most left-handers use their right hand to fret notes and chords on a guitar's fingerboard, and the left to pick and strum the strings – the reverse, naturally, of a right-hander's style. The majority of Hendrix's guitars were regular right-handed models that he had to convert for left-handed playing. Chas Chandler once reported: "Funny thing about Jimi, he's a left-handed guitarist, but he just won't use a left-handed specially-built instrument. Says they can't be as good because there aren't so many made."[7] Hendrix would flip a regular guitar around so that the neck was to his right. The main conversion work then necessary was to re-string the guitar so that the strings would still be in the regular pattern: lowest-pitched string nearest the player, down to the highest-pitched string furthest away. Another left-hander – and a big influence on Hendrix – was Albert King, but he didn't bother to re-string after turning the guitar around. And a few left-handers simply play right-handed guitars in regular right-handed fashion.

Turning a regular Stratocaster around for left-hand use means that the guitar's vibrato arm and its controls – master volume and two tone rotaries,

plus pickup selector switch – are now on the upper part of the guitar's body. Some guitarists would find that these get in the way of their plucking hand, but Hendrix took advantage of their proximity in order to make quick changes in tone and volume, and to quickly grab the vibrato arm. A good example of this can be seen in the intro to the live June 1967 Monterey version of 'Wild Thing' on the *Jimi Plays Monterey* video. Flipping a Strat around also means that the body's deepest cutaway, which gives good access to the upper frets for a right-handed player, is less useful, but Hendrix's long fingers helped him overcome any disadvantages in that area.

The sonic differences that resulted from Hendrix flipping his Strat have been the subject of intense debate among guitarists ever since. Technically, it's possible that reversing the 'staggered' polepiece arrangement on the pickups – the different-height magnets that 'balance' the sound of a regular set of strings – caused small changes to the way the strings were sensed. Maybe there was drop-out on different bass notes compared to a regular right-hander playing a right-handed Strat, and perhaps the second and third strings were louder. Arguably, the arrangement of the strings might also have assisted string-bending. But with Hendrix playing at high volume, and with his natural dexterity and playing skill, any differences would have been minimal.

One problem associated with Hendrix's conversion is worth a brief explanation. When a right-handed guitar is flipped and re-strung for a left-hander, the slots in the guitar's nut (the small guide bar over which the strings pass from neck to headstock) will now be in the 'wrong' places, with thin strings sitting in wide slots and thick strings failing to fit in the narrowest slots. There are a couple of solutions, and Hendrix seems to have tried both. Depending on the type of nut, it's possible simply to do some minor filing of what had been the thinnest string-slots in order to accommodate the thickest strings and hold them in place. On his '68 black Strat and '67 Flying V, and probably other guitars, Hendrix simply filed some of the thinnest slots to accommodate the lowest-pitched strings, leaving the rest as they were. The alternative is, where possible, to remove the nut (tricky, as some are rigidly glued in place) and either reverse it or replace it with another suitable nut. The nut of his '68 white Strat had been reversed in this way. Again, though, it's debatable if any of this made much impression on his sound, especially given the sheer volume at which he played.

With the Experience, Hendrix started off by generally tuning his guitars to regular 'concert' pitch (E A D G B E, lowest to highest-pitch string) but increasingly he came to favour tuning down by a semitone (half-step) – Eb Ab Db Gb Bb Eb – and sometimes down a whole tone (whole-step) to D G C F A D. He did this so there would be less strain on his voice, since he would be singing in a slightly lower register. Also, the lower-pitched strings would be slightly slacker, making it easier for Hendrix to 'bend' strings, a technique he habitually used for musical effect. Of the eleven tracks recorded for *Are You Experienced* (between November 1966 and April 1967) five have the guitar at concert pitch, and six are tuned down by a semitone. On all 13 tracks on the second album, *Axis: Bold As Love* (recorded May and October 1967), Hendrix tunes down by a semitone, and of the 15 tracks featuring guitar on *Electric*

Ladyland (made between December 1967 and August 1968) two are at concert pitch, 12 have the guitar tuned down a semitone, and 'Voodoo Chile' is tuned down by a whole tone. On the live *Band Of Gypsys* (recorded live, December 31st 1969 and January 1st 1970) four of the six tracks have Hendrix tuned down a semitone, while on 'Machine Gun' and 'Who Knows' he is tuned down a whole tone.

Hendrix described the set-up on his Strat around 1967 as "Fender light-gauge strings, using a regular E-string for a B and sometimes a tenor A-string for a [high] E to get my kind of sound on the Stratocaster. [I] put the strings on [with a] slightly higher [action], so they can ring longer".[8] This particular string-swapping routine was a popular modification at the time. It resulted in a set of strings as light as possible, aiding not only string-bending but also finger-vibrato. On a later guitar, his black Strat, the surviving strings indicate he preferred 'light' gauges (relative thicknesses) .009″ to .038″.

In the late 1960s a player would select the Strat's three pickups individually by setting the guitar's pickup switch to one of three fixed positions. Hendrix often (but certainly not exclusively) favoured the neck pickup's full tone. 'Machine Gun' on the original *Band Of Gypsys* album offers the chance to hear him deploying each of the three pickup sounds in close proximity. At 6:47 he selects the bridge pickup: the subsequent high-register phrase has the distinctly sharp, piercing, trebly sound of this setting. At 6:54 he changes to the middle pickup and a split second later activates the Octavia effects unit – but despite the sound colouring from the effect, one can hear a distinct change as the middle pickup's more neutral tone is engaged, neither particularly trebly nor particularly bassy. At 7:00 Hendrix switches to the neck pickup, albeit with the tone rolled slightly down and still with the Octavia on, and delivers some serious note cramming with this pickup's full, bassy sound, until 7:06 when he returns to the middle pickup.

To achieve two further pickup sounds, Hendrix, like many players, would lodge the selector switch between two of its fixed positions, giving a 'hollow' or 'honking' tone (what some players erroneously call 'out-of-phase'). He can be heard using the trick on 'Little Wing' (October 1967) from *Axis: Bold As Love*, for example, where he has the switch lodged between neck and middle-pickup positions throughout the song for the rhythm guitar part – though it's most strikingly heard during the song's introduction, until 0:23.

Long before his fame, the young Hendrix's first electric guitar way back in 1959 had been a cheap white-finish Supro Ozark 1560S solidbody bought for him in a Seattle music store. This was stolen in 1960 and his father replaced it with another relatively cheap guitar, a Danelectro Model 3012 semi-solidbody with bronze-coloured top, which Hendrix soon painted red. Around summer 1963, while in Nashville, Hendrix acquired a better electric guitar, a solidbody cherry-finish Epiphone Wilshire SB432, probably trading in his Danelectro for it. He got the Fender bug around the time he joined The Isley Brothers in

1964, using his first Fender, a humble blond (white-finish) Duo-Sonic model to which a non-standard Epiphone vibrato was fitted. Around early 1965 he acquired a much better Fender solidbody, a sunburst Jazzmaster model, which he used during his time with Little Richard, the Isleys again, and Joey Dee. A little later he used another Duo-Sonic, this time a sunburst model, which early in 1966 he probably traded it in at Manny's music store in New York City for his first Fender Stratocaster.

As we've seen, Hendrix certainly favoured the Stratocaster for live and

"He's been through six Stratocasters already — two stolen, two others fogged up on him. Always has two with him on dates."

Chas Chandler, Jimi's manager, 1967

studio work, and more than any other 1960s guitarist he opened up the tonal potential of that model. Consequently his sound is strongly associated with that guitar, but he didn't play a Strat exclusively in his classic period. In live shows he would often use a Gibson instrument for blues numbers in the set, to get a 'thicker' sound. From around June 1967 to January 1969 he played live blues on a right-handed dark-brown-finish 1967 Gibson Flying V (serial number 000256), which he re-strung left-handed and painted with coloured patterns. Years later this V, its decorations gone, came into the possession of ex-Kane Gang guitarist Dave Brewis, who carefully restored Hendrix's paint job. Hendrix was also seen at least twice (in May 1968) playing a black 1955 Gibson Les Paul Custom (serial number 5 6043, now in the possession of the Experience Music Project).

He gave the '67 Flying V to Eire Apparent guitarist Mick Cox in January 1969, but by October 1968 already had a new guitar for in-concert blues, a 1968 white-finish Gibson SG Custom (serial number 899617; today it's owned by the Hard Rock Café). Hendrix then replaced the white SG, which he used until about September 1969, with a circa 1970 left-handed black-finish Gibson Flying V (serial number 849976) again for live blues numbers. This V, with an unusual non-standard fingerboard inlay, was one of the very few true left-handed guitars that Hendrix played. It later went to Experience roadie Eric Barrett, who subsequently sold it to the Hard Rock Café. A note of Hendrix's guitars early in 1968 documents him owning another Gibson instrument (an unusual double-neck six-string/12-string guitar) as well as a Rickenbacker bass and two Hagstrom eight-string basses "sometimes played by Noel on sessions".[9]

Hendrix's very first childhood guitar had been a cheap acoustic, but he acquired some better flat-tops later on. A

A favourite black Stratocaster, pictured here at the Isle Of Wight Festival amid Marshall amps and WEM PA gear.

unique occasion captured on film shows Hendrix accompanying himself solo on an acoustic for the blues 'Hear My Train A'Comin'' (aka 'Getting My Heart Back Together Again') for the *Experience* TV movie (the audio is included on the 1994 Hendrix *Blues* compilation CD). For this performance at a London photography studio in December 1967, Hendrix borrowed a Zemaitis 12-string flat-top acoustic guitar from the film's director, Peter Neal, who in turn had borrowed it from a friend. The Zemaitis was a right-handed model, restrung for Hendrix. It was tuned down two whole tones (whole-steps), with the lowest E-string now sounding C, and probably done to emulate the style of the revered 12-string blues player Leadbelly.

Hendrix owned a '68 Martin D-45 flat-top acoustic guitar (serial 239387) that he played in his New York apartment around 1968. It later came into the possession of Experience drummer Mitch Mitchell, who sold it at Sotheby's to Dave Brewis as the guitar "bought, owned and used by Jimi Hendrix". Brewis later sold the guitar to the Experience Music Project in Seattle. This D-45 is a right-handed instrument (a left-hand version was not generally available from Martin at the time Hendrix acquired it). Another acoustic that Hendrix apparently used to knock around with at home was an Epiphone Cortez flat-top, reportedly broken at some point by his girlfriend Kathy Etchingham.

A significant part of Hendrix's individual sound came from his choice of amplifiers and the way he used them. At the start of his career in the early 1960s he used whatever he could get, including a cheap Silvertone amp with 2x12 cabinet (meaning two 12″ loudspeakers mounted in a single cabinet).[10] He would often borrow gear from other guitarists or club owners. Later, Hendrix became most associated with Marshall amplification. His choice of that brand was at least in part influenced by Pete Townshend, who when asked by Hendrix for a recommendation said he was in the process of moving from Marshall to Sound City and was using both.[11] Experience drummer Mitch Mitchell introduced Hendrix to Jim Marshall, founder of the Marshall amplification company. Mitchell had worked a Saturday job at Marshall's music store. "I think Jimi bought, as far as I can remember, four stage set-ups," Marshall said later, "which he [would store] in strategic places so that they didn't have to transport [them] around." Marshall's recollection was that Hendrix used standard 100-watt amplifier heads and standard model-1960 4x12 cabinets.[12]

Jimi tried a psychedelic gift-paper look when he hand-painted his '67 Flying V.

The Marshall stack – a powerful amplifier head 'stacked' on top of and connected to two 4x12 loudspeaker cabinets – quickly became a popular choice for rock guitarists. Pete Townshend was already using this kind of rig. Eric Clapton recorded John Mayall's *Blues Breakers* album (April 1966) with a Marshall model-1962 'combo' (combination amp-and-speaker in one box) but changed to Marshall stacks just before joining Cream in summer 1966. Jeff Beck shifted to Marshall around May 1967 after using Vox with The Yardbirds, and Jimmy Page moved to Marshall stacks at the time of *Led Zeppelin II* (1969). Hendrix experimented with different combinations of Marshall stacks, ranging from one 100-watt head feeding two 4x12 cabinets to three 100-watt amps with six 4x12 cabinets. Partly this was curiosity, to see how different mixtures altered the sound, and partly to gain greater volume when playing bigger venues. The PA or public address equipment intended to project the band's overall sound – but primarily at this time the vocals – was still in its infancy during the second half of the 1960s, and guitarists had to provide most or all of their volume from their personal amplification rig, unlike today when the sound is usually boosted and refined through the PA.

Presumably influenced by Townshend, Hendrix started using a Sound City stack of one 100-watt head and two 4x12 cabinets for live performances in November 1967, in addition to his Marshall stacks, but he used this combination only until January 1968. Hendrix also used Sunn speakers and amplifiers on-stage briefly from February 1968. Electronics man Roger Mayer, who was on tour with Hendrix in the US at the time, says: "Quite frankly the Sunn amps didn't stand up to the travelling. The transformers were falling off, and they were not very good."[13] Consequently Hendrix soon dropped Sunn equipment from his live guitar set-up.

In the studio Hendrix would sometimes use an 85-watt Fender Twin Reverb combo, providing where necessary a cleaner sound for recording, either as well as or instead of Marshall(s). He had used a similar amp since his days with King Curtis early in 1966. During 1968 he used Fender amplifiers on-stage, too, usually three Dual Showman stacks in various configurations, each stack comprising an 85-watt head with a variety of big Fender cabinets, each fitted with two JBL 15-inch speakers. He had employed a Showman amp in the studio as early as summer 1967, for 'Burning Of The Midnight Lamp'.

Hendrix generally used his Marshall amps on what became known as 'the Hendrix setting' – all the controls turned up full to the number 10 setting. This gave him a distorted sound with the notes sustaining well. Roadie Eric Barrett recalled what this would sound like in untrained hands. "If I tried to test his equipment, all I got was feedback. Jimi could control it all with his fingers, and I still don't understand to this day how he did it. It was all part of his genius."[14] With his amp full-on, Hendrix would where necessary adjust the volume control on his guitar to achieve varying dynamic levels. Turning the guitar volume down would also significantly cut the distortion level, allowing for a relatively cleaner tone. Barrett reported that the Hendrix setting took its toll on

Rare 1969 Jimi-plays-Fender ad (left); a Gibson SG (above) for live blues.

Searching for the Hendrix setting: Jimi fiddles with the controls on a Marshall and a Sound City stack during a soundcheck at London's Royal Albert Hall.

equipment. "I have to change speakers after every show," he said in 1969. "Jimi destroys at least two whenever he plays. I have 16 spare speakers. When he smashes them, I put in the spares and send the broken ones back to New York to get them re-coned…. He ruins a lot of [vibrato arms] too. Very often his guitar has to be stripped down and built up again…. Jimi also burns up a lot of [amplifier] tubes because of the great volume. When a tube burns out, the volume starts to drop."[15] Henry Goldrich at Manny's claimed that the Marshall factory would fit Hendrix's amps with sturdier tubes to withstand the extremes of volume.[16]

Hendrix started experimenting with feedback in the summer of 1966, and possibly earlier. Feedback is an electronic howling and squealing caused by the sound from an amplifier 'feeding back' into the pickups of the guitar and then continuing round on itself to create more and more noise. Until the mid 1960s it had usually been considered a technical nuisance to be avoided, but players like The Who's Pete Townshend were turning it into a new part of the rock guitarist's sonic arsenal. Hendrix made the distortion, sustain and feedback that came from playing at high volume his own. "I started using feedback first of all in [Greenwich] Village," Hendrix claimed. "It made the weirdest sounds."[17] He would continue to use feedback to great effect, especially live, and examples can be heard on some of the concert recordings. He makes extensive use of it in the introduction to the October 1968 Winterland version of 'Are You Experienced?' from *The Jimi Hendrix Concerts*, and employs it rather more subtly in 'The Star Spangled Banner' from *Woodstock* (August 1969) as he controls the feedback, allowing it to catch hold of sustained notes at, for example, 0:06, 0:10 and 0:13.

As Hendrix learned to control feedback, using volume level and the position of the guitar relative to the loudspeakers, he made it part of his

sound. This meant playing at high volume in the studio when the effect was required. Listen to the striking introduction of 'Foxy Lady' (December 1966 and February 1967) on *Are You Experienced?*. Hendrix starts a vibrato'd note with the volume control on the guitar turned down to zero, then gradually turns up the control, and as the vibrato'd note rises in volume, feedback takes hold of it. Hendrix's preference for playing at high volume in the studio led to problems, as manager and producer Chas Chandler recalled. "Jimi threw a tantrum because I wouldn't let him play his guitar loud enough in the studio. It was a stupid argument over sheer volume. He was playing through a Marshall twin stack, and it was so loud in the studio that we were picking up various rattles and noises."[18] Eric Clapton had experienced similar objections to playing at loud volumes when recording John Mayall's *Blues Breakers* album in 1966.

Hendrix would often use his live set-up for recording, and the engineer would customarily place a microphone near a speaker cabinet to capture the sound. Hendrix's high volume placed a strain on the studio equipment. One of the studios that Hendrix used regularly was Olympic in London, and boss Keith Grant would order the expensive microphones to be locked away in case Hendrix damaged them.[19] A later exception to the habit of miking a cabinet came with 'Dolly Dagger' (recorded July and August 1970), later released on *Rainbow Bridge*, which includes a guitar part recorded by direct injection. This is where a guitar signal is fed directly into the mixing desk, bypassing any microphones, with the intention of capturing a cleaner, more 'pure' sound. But engineers have recalled that when it came to recording Hendrix there was no single formula. Hendrix's frustration as studios failed to realise his expectations would in part prompt him to build his own recording facility, Electric Lady, in New York City.

Hendrix's constant search for new sounds meant that he soon expanded on the tonal possibilities of a Fender Stratocaster through a Marshall stack by using effects units – boxes and 'pedals' that are plugged between guitar and amp to add a variety of sonic treatments. He used a fuzz box and a wah-wah widely, and occasionally the Octavia frequency doubler and a rotating-speaker simulator, the Uni-Vibe. Roger Mayer says Hendrix always wanted the newest sounds. "He'd say, 'That sound was great on that record, but what have you got up your sleeves for tomorrow?' He tried never to use the same sound twice – because there was no reason to. He'd say something like: I want

Another Albert Hall soundcheck, another white Strat. At his feet, a Fuzz Face fuzz-box and (bottom right) a Vox wah-wah pedal.

a guitar that comes screaming out of the sky and it's got to make the people wince like they've been burnt. Oh. Right. Let's see what we can do."[20] Hendrix's girlfriend Kathy Etchingham remembered that he was "on the same wavelength" with Mayer. She said they would often talk "about the sorts of sounds, feedback and distortion Jimi wanted to achieve and adapting all sorts of electronic equipment to make the guitar sound different. I had to stand for hours with my foot on the pedal while they fiddled about with knobs and switches".[21]

Hendrix was by no means the first guitarist to use a fuzz box, a unit that adds distortion to the guitar's sound. Keith Richards of The Rolling Stones had famously used a Gibson Maestro Fuzz-Tone fuzz box for the riff of '(I Can't Get No) Satisfaction' (recorded May 1965). It was blatant, gratuitous and certainly not subtle. Hendrix would use fuzz much more as part of his overall sound, and the unit he used most was a Fuzz Face. Earlier in his career he'd used an unspecified fuzz box, built for him by a member of The Fugs, that he used with Curtis Knight in late 1965 and into 1966 and heard for example on '(I'm A) Fool For You Baby'. Mike Bloomfield recalled seeing Hendrix using a Maestro fuzz box in New York's Greenwich Village in the summer of 1966.[22] The earliest known photograph of Hendrix using a Fuzz Face was taken at the London Marquee club in January 1967. He continued to use the Fuzz Face live and in the studio for the rest of his career.

The British-produced Arbiter Fuzz Face was first made in late 1966 (a few years later it was renamed the Dallas Arbiter Fuzz Face). It came in a round case with two simple controls, for Volume and Fuzz, and an on/off footswitch. Roger Mayer sometimes modified Hendrix's effects, and says that Fuzz Faces varied in sound quality, depending on what kind of transistor was fitted. Hendrix can be heard using a Fuzz Face in the intro to 'Purple Haze' (recorded January and February 1967) where he uses the effect in a relatively restrained way to colour an already distorted guitar tone. The Fuzz Face effect can also be heard in 'Bold As Love' (October 1967) from *Axis: Bold As Love* at the beginning of Hendrix's guitar solo. A clear contrast in tone is evident between the relatively clean-toned run that leads into the start of the solo and the Fuzz Face'd guitar that takes over the solo at 1:50.

As we've learned, Hendrix played with his amps on 10 so they would produce a distorted tone if the guitar's volume was also on full, and this can make it difficult for anyone keen to know if any 'fuzz' on Hendrix's guitar is due to a Fuzz Face or a cranked-up guitar and amp. Often it's a combination of the two. Roadie Eric Barrett explained in 1969 that Hendrix would run his Fuzz Face and wah-wah through the on-stage amplifiers, and that when he switched on either effect it acted like a pre-amp, boosting the power tremendously. "That's how he gets really high feedback," said Barrett at the time. "When he wants feedback, he turns the guitar up and presses down on the wah-wah pedal and the fuzz."[23] For example, listen to Hendrix switching on the Fuzz Face at 1:42 in the live October 1968 Winterland version of 'Fire' released on *The Jimi Hendrix Concerts* album, provoking a burst of feedback before he brings the sound under control.

The wah-wah pedal was invented by Vox in 1967, and was first advertised in the UK by late April. The earliest well-known record to feature its distinctive onomatopoeic sound was Cream's 'Tales Of Brave Ulysses' (May 1967), B-side of the 'Strange Brew' single. In effect, a wah-wah is a tone-booster control built into and operated by a pedal that incorporates an on/off footswitch. The pedal can be lodged in one position to add a particular tone colour, or rapidly depressed and raised for articulated shaping of the sound as the internal tone control boosts high and then low frequencies. Hendrix had employed a slow wah-wah-like sound – presumably before he'd even heard one – on 'I Don't Live Today' (recorded February 1967) from *Are You Experienced* for example from 0:35 to 0:45, and in the solo. He probably did this by manipulating the tone controls on the studio's mixing desk – but soon he got his own wah-wah pedal. Hendrix probably acquired a wah-wah in New York City on July 7th 1967 after seeing Frank Zappa using one, and used it the same evening for recording 'The Burning Of The Midnight Lamp'. He can clearly be heard using it at various points in the released mix, especially on the main riff at the beginning. Hendrix favoured Vox wah-wah pedals.

Electronics ace Roger Mayer says he would doctor the wah-wah circuits to suit Hendrix's taste. Maybe only one in four units would be any good,

"Very often his guitar had to be stripped down and built up again."

Eric Barrett, roadie, reviewing the regular wear-and-tear

largely because of cheap components used by manufacturers. "When Jimi said that a particular wah-wah was a great one, I'd say let me take it away and find out why. That way I could classify what it was that made it good, and then when Jimi got another one we'd know what to modify."[24] Other notable recordings where Hendrix uses a wah-wah include the chording throughout and the two solos on 'Up From The Skies' (recorded October 1967) from *Axis*; the beginning of 'Voodoo Child (Slight Return)' (May 1968) on *Electric Ladyland* where from 0:00 to 0:10 he uses the pedal to articulate the rhythm on damped (partially muted) strings and then from 0:10 to 0:32 to colour the intro's middle-register riff; and 'Rainy Day Dream Away' (June 1968), also from *Ladyland*, where he uses the wah-wah to imitate speech from 3:12 to the fade. Hendrix certainly wasn't the only musician to make the wah-wah pedal an important part of his sound, but he explored the tonal possibilities and practical applications of the unit more than any other guitarist of the era.

Roger Mayer built the Octavia specially for Hendrix. When music-fan Mayer met Hendrix early in 1967 he was working for the Royal Naval Scientific Service in Teddington, Middlesex as an Assistant Experimental Officer carrying out vibrational and acoustical analysis on boats, torpedoes and so on. Mayer had already built early fuzz boxes for his friend Jimmy Page. He showed Hendrix his latest gadget, the Octavia. Mayer designed it to double the frequency of a guitar an octave up, to make a two-guitars-at-once sound. In practice it produced a more complex sound. The result would alter according to the way the guitarist played. Mayer describes it, on reflection, as an adaptive circuit that changes with the signal put into it. Not only is the main note doubled, but all the harmonics swirling around are doubled too, creating a pleasing, organic sound. Hendrix said of the effect: "It comes through a whole octave higher so that

Jamming anywhere, any time, with anyone's instrument – even a right-hander flipped around.

when [I play] high notes it sounds like a whistle or a flute."[25] He first used one for the solo and ringing outro of 'Purple Haze' (recorded February 1967), achieving an exotic-sounding but melodic lead for the solo with a sitar-like, Eastern feel. Mayer claims that Hendrix used a borrowed Telecaster for this session after damaging his Stratocaster at a gig earlier the same evening.

The Octavia also turned up on *Axis*, for example on 'One Rainy Wish', most clearly heard in the flourishes from 2:11 to 2:35, and 'Little Miss Lover', in the solo from 1:19 to 1:37. Later, Mayer was called on for a new Octavia for the *Band Of Gypsys* live album, recorded over the 1969/70 new year. Hendrix used it in conjunction with a clean sound in 'Who Knows', from 6:28 to the end, producing a peculiar, artificial sound not unlike a primitive synthesiser. Starting at 8:07 he adds in the wah-wah to the Octavia for some highly distinctive and effective 'honking' sounds. Because the Octavia was custom-built for Hendrix, it's impossible to compare his use with the way other players applied it at the time. In recent years a revitalised Octavia has

become commercially available; Robin Trower, Frank Marino, Jeff Healey and the late Stevie Ray Vaughan all tried it. But no one has made it such a part of their sonic vocabulary as Hendrix.

The Uni-Vibe unit that Hendrix occasionally used was designed by the Uni-Vox company of Long Island, New York, for use with electronic organs as a portable, electronic alternative to the popular Leslie organ cabinet. It was first marketed in early 1969 by Merson Musical Products of New York. (The Leslie, originally designed for use with the Hammond organ, is a heavy wooden cabinet inside which are speakers and horns in individually rotating drums that can be controlled to create swirling tremolo and chorale effects.) The Uni-Vibe has been described as a four-stage swept filter, similar to the kind of filter later used in phaser effects units. The Uni-Vibe had two inputs, one output, a rotary Volume control for the output signal, a rotary Intensity control for the level of the effect, a two-way switch for selecting either Chorus or Vibrato mode, and a five-pin socket to connect to a wah-wah-type pedal for controlling the speed of the 'rotating' element of the effect.

Hendrix had used a proper Leslie cabinet in the studio for 'Little Wing' (recorded October 1967) from *Axis: Bold As Love* where the rotating speaker's ethereal effect can be heard at the end of the rhythm-guitar intro from 0:23 to 0:32. But once he acquired a Uni-Vibe in August 1969 he was able to create similar effects more easily (and in a more portable form). He can be heard bringing in the chorus mode of the effect from about 0:12 at the beginning of 'Hey Baby (New Rising Sun)' (July 1970) released on *Rainbow Bridge*, and on 'Machine Gun' (January 1970) from the *Band Of Gypsys* album where he uses it to thicken the sound of the muted-string machine-gunfire noises at various points in the song, and to add a 'warbling' effect to the long sustained notes that begin at 4:00. Hendrix used a Uni-Vibe throughout most of the instrumental on 'Star Spangled Banner' (August 1969) at Woodstock, notably on sustained notes when it adds a 'warbling' effect, as on the sustained open B-string at 0:04 to 0:07 and on the string-bend from 0:45 to 0:48. Contrast this with the sound of the sustained notes in the 'bugle call' passage from 2:33 to 2:42 where Hendrix is not using the Uni-Vibe (he switches it off at 2:33). When plugged in as part of the signal-chain between guitar and amplifier but not switched on, the Uni-Vibe still seemed to have an effect on the sound, making it slightly more bassy and mellow.

Inevitably, any survey of Hendrix's tools – the guitars, amplifiers and effects that he employed to create his music – tell only a small part of the story. Many players have since tried to chip off a little of the Hendrix magic by borrowing some of his ideas and specs, but they never quite manage to conjure the unique blend that was Hendrix in full flow. Of course there was more to it than mere strings and tubes and wires. Hendrix had a radical, even revolutionary, effect on the sound of the electric guitar. No one else at the time could match what he did with pickups, feedback, effects and amplifiers. He made the instrument sound different, not least through his ability to meld disparate styles, and his passion for the sheer joy of sound for sound's sake. He took the guitar to unknown, uncharted places. But no matter what guitar or amp he used in order to get there, he always sounded like Jimi Hendrix.

endnotes

Pages 8-11 (Seattle, the place and the music)
1 James Allen Hendrix with Jas Obrecht *My Son Jimi* p.35 (AlJas Enterprises 1999), **2** Paul de Barros *Jackson Street After Hours – The Roots of Jazz in Seattle* p. vii (Sasquatch 1994), **3** de Barros p.2, **4** de Barros p.40, **5** de Barros p.37, **6** de Barros p.60, **7** de Barros p.60, **8** de Barros p.76, **9** de Barros p.78, **10** de Barros p.153, **11** de Barros p.154

Pages 12-17 (A Seattle boy)
1 James Allen Hendrix with Jas Obrecht *My Son Jimi* p.21 (AlJas Enterprises 1999), **2** Hendrix p.48
3 Hendrix p.87, 4 Mary Willix *Voices From Home* p.13 (Creative Forces Publishing 1995), **5** *Record Mirror* February 25th 1967, **6** *Record Mirror* September 19th 1970, **7** Willix p.55, **8** *Fabulous 208* November 4th 1967, **9** *Melody Maker* February 22nd 1969, **10** Hendrix p.82, **11** Hendrix p.79 , **12** Willix p.137, **13** Willix p.28 , **14** Hendrix p.82, **15** Willix p.51, **16** Hendrix p.113, **17** *Melody Maker* February 22nd 1969, **18** *Melody Maker* October 28th 1967, **19** Willix p.56/57, **20** Hendrix p.113, **21** Radio interview with Hans Karl Schmidt, Frankfurt, Germany, May 17th 1967, **22** Radio interview with Hans Karl Schmidt, Frankfurt, Germany, May 17th 1967, **23** Hendrix p.112

Pages 18-25 (Music in the air)
1 Lionel Hampton *Hamp – An Autobiography* p.75 (Warner Books 1989), **2** Hampton p.81, **3** Hampton p.91, 4 Arnold Shaw *Honkers And Shouters* p.79 (Collier 1978), **5** Leonard Feather's 1969 interview in booklet notes to *Complete Louis Jordan On Decca* (Bear Family Records 1990), **6** CD insert notes by Peter Grendysa to *Let The Good Times Roll* (Bear Family 1992), **7** Shaw p.259, **8** Champion Jack Dupree, lyrics to 'Old Time Rock & Roll', Vik single X/4X-0279B, **9** John Hammond with Irving Townsend *John Hammond On Record* p.224 (Penguin 1981), **10** Hampton p.69, **11** Hampton p.70, **12** Helen Oakley Dance *Stormy Monday: The T-Bone Walker Story* (Louisiana State University 1987), **13** Dance, **14** Dance, **15** Alan Govenar *Meeting The Blues* (Taylor 1988), **16** Dance, **17** Shaw p.114, **18** Shaw p.142/143, **19** CD booklet notes by Chris Strachwitz to *Lightning Hopkins – The Gold Star Sessions* (Arhoolie 1990), **20** Shaw p.143, **21** Shaw p.180/183, **22** Shaw p.183, **23** Shaw p.261

Pages 26-35 (Strike up the band; 1957 to May 1961)
1 Mary Willix *Voices From Home* p.58-59 (Creative Forces Publishing 1995), **2** Willix p.55, **3** Willix p.59, **4** Willix p.58-59, **5** James Allen Hendrix with Jas Obrecht *My Son Jimi* p.126 (AlJas Enterprises 1999), **6** Willix p.12, **7** Willix p.13, **8** Willix p.16, **9** *Hitparader* January 1968 p.19, **10** Booklet notes to *Ray Charles: The Complete R&B Recordings 1952-59* (Rhino/Atlantic 1991), **11** Willix p.29, **12** Willix p.14/p.13, **13** Willix p.30, **14** Willix p.57, **15** Willix p.69, **16** Willix p.45, **17** Paul de Barros *Jackson Street After Hours – The Roots of Jazz in Seattle* p.204 (Sasquatch 1994), **18** Willix p.46, **19** Willix p.46, **20** de Barros p.172, **21** de Barros p.204, **22** Willix p.68, **23** de Barros p.206, **24** Willix p.58, **25** de Barros p.205-206., **26** Willix p.67/8, **27** *Melody Maker* February 22nd 1969, **28** Willix p.15-16, **29** Willix p.65, **30** *Beat Instrumental* March 1967, **31** Willix p.100, **32** Johnny Black *Eyewitness: Jimi Hendrix* (Carlton 1999), **33** Willix p.75, **34** Willix p.90, **35** *Melody Maker* February 22nd 1969, **36** Willix p.86, **37** Willix p.77, **38** Tony Brown *Jimi Hendrix In His Own Words* (Omnibus 1994), **39** Willix p.77, **40** Willix p.74/p.75, **41** Tony Brown *Jimi Hendrix In His Own Words* (Omnibus 1994), **42** Willix p.91-92, **43** Hendrix p.113, **44** Willix p.96, **45** Willix p.77-78, **46** Willix p.100-101, **47** Unknown Danish publication 1970, **48** Willix p.151, **49** Willix p.149, **50** Willix p.157, **51** Interviewed by Heather MacIntosh May 2000 www.historylink.org, **52** Willix p.164-5, **53** Willix p.159, **54** Willix p.159, **55** Willix p.65-66, **56** Willix p.81, **57** Hendrix p.122-123, **58** Willix p.50, **59** Willix p.85, **60** Hendrix p.123, **61** Willix p.159-160, **62** Kathy Etchingham *Through Gypsy Eyes* p.66 (Gollancz 1998), **63** Hendrix p.124, **64** Willix p.161, **65** Willix p.161, **66** Tony Brown *Jimi Hendrix In His Own Words* (Omnibus 1994), **67** Willix p.153, **68** Willix p.153, **69** Willix p.153, **70** *Melody Maker* February 22nd 1969, **71** Hendrix p.129

Pages 36-45 (The last train to Clarksville; June 1961 to autumn 1963)
1 James Allen Hendrix with Jas Obrecht *My Son Jimi* p.132 (AlJas Enterprises 1999), **2** Letter dated 12th September 1961, *Jimpress* 30, **3** Letter dated 1st November 1961, *Jimpress* 32, **4** Letter dated 13th November 1961, Tony Brown *Jimi Hendrix: A Visual Documentary* p.24 (Omnibus 1992), **5** Letter dated 1st November 1961, *Jimpress* 32, **6** *Melody Maker* 22nd February 1969, **7** *Melody Maker* 22nd February 1969, **8** *Guitar Player* September 1995, **9** *A Film About Jimi Hendrix* (1973), **10** *Guitar Player* September 1995, **11** *Guitar Player* December 1968, **12** Letter dated January 17th 1962, *Jimpress* 34, **13** Hendrix with Jas Obrecht *My Son Jimi* p.136 (AlJas Enterprises 1999), **14** *Guitar Player* September 1987, **15** *A Film About Jimi Hendrix* (1973), **16** *Vi Unge* August 31st 1967 translation by Claus Rasmussen and Karsten Laybourn, **17** CD insert notes to James Nixon *No End To The Blues* (Black Magic 2001), **18** *A Film About Jimi Hendrix* (1973), **19** *Rave* June 1967, **20** *Melody Maker* February 22nd 1969, **21** *Melody Maker* February 22nd 1969, **22** Vi Unge August 31st 1967 translation by Claus Rasmussen and Karsten Laybourn, **23** *Vi Unge* August 31st 1967 translation by Claus Rasmussen and Karsten Laybourn, **24** *Rave* June 1967, **25** *Rave* June 1967, **26** *Beat Instrumental* March 1967, **27** *Guitar Player* September 1995, **28** *Juke Blues* 44, 1999, p.28, **29** *Guitar Player* September 1995, **30** *Guitar Player* September 1995, **31** *Guitar Player* September 1987, **32** *Guitar Player* September 1995, **33** *A Film About Jimi Hendrix* (1973), **34** *Beat Instrumental* March 1967, **35** Tony Brown *Jimi Hendrix In His Own Words* p.17 (Omnibus 1994), **36** *The Tennessean* 1992, **37** Interview on August 25th 1967 for *Los Angeles Free Press*, **38** Brown *Own Words* p.17, **39** *Juke Blues* No.44, **40** Steven Roby *Black Gold: The Lost Archives of Jimi Hendrix* p.19 (Billboard 2002), **41** www.earlyhendrix.com, **42** www.earlyhendrix.com, **43** *The Kitchener Waterloo Record* July 4th 1997, **44** Harry Shapiro & Caesar Glebbeek *Jimi Hendrix: Electric Gypsy* p.64 (Heinemann 1990), **45** Shapiro p.65, **46** *Experience Hendrix* 602, **47** *Melody Maker* February 22nd 1969, **48** Brown *Own Words* p.17, **49** *Guitar Player* September 1987, **50** Peter Guralnik *Sweet Soul Music* p.45 (Harper & Row 1986), **51** *Melody Maker* February 22nd 1969

Pages 46-57 (Highways to hell and back; November 1963 to April 1965)
1 Tony Brown *Jimi Hendrix Concert Files* p.17 (Omnibus 1999), **2** Harry Shapiro & Caesar Glebbeek *Jimi Hendrix: Electric Gypsy* p.72 (Heinemann 1990), **3** Richie Havens *They Can't Hide Us Anymore* p.30 (HarperCollins 1999), **4** Robert Shelton *No Direction Home* p.93 (Beech Tree 1986), **5** Haves p.33, **6** Shelton p.93, **7** Havens p.32, **8** Peter Guralnik *Sweet Soul Music* p.46 (Harper & Row 1986), **9** LP sleevenotes to Baby Face Willette *Stop And Listen* (Blue Note 1961), **10** Ted Fox *Showtime At The Apollo* p.109 (Quartet 1983), **11** *Guitar World* September 1985, **12** *The Independent* (US) letter November 2002, **13** *Washington Journal* November 2002, **14** *Washington Journal* November 2002, **15** News Channel 5, November 2002., **16** www.historylink.org May 2000, **17** www.bluesrevue.com 2002, **18** Fox p.26, **19** *Guitar World* September 1985., **20** *A Film About Jimi Hendrix* (1973), **21** *Guitar World* September 1985, **22** Steven Roby *Black Gold: The Lost Archives Of Jimi Hendrix* p.32 (Billboard 2002), **23** *Juke Blues* No.47 2000, **24** *Juke Blues* No.47 2000, **25** Roby p.34, **26** *Juke Blues* No.47 2000, **27** Guralnik p.273, **28** *Guitar Player* September 1985, **29** Letter dated September 28th 1964, Tony Brown *Jimi Hendrix Concert Files* p.19 (Omnibus 1999), **30** *Guitar Player* September 1975, **31** *Guitar Player* September 1985, **32** Letter dated October 8th 1964 Tony Brown *Jimi Hendrix Concert Files* p.19 (Omnibus 1999), **33** Guralnik p.14, **34** Letter dated January 25th 1965, Tony Brown *Jimi Hendrix Concert Files* p.23 (Omnibus 1999), **35** Tony Brown *Jimi Hendrix Concert Files* p.23 (Omnibus 1999), **36** *South Bank Show: Jimi Hendrix* ITV October 1st 1989, **37** Tony Brown *Jimi Hendrix: A Visual Documentary* p.32 (Omnibus 1992), **38** Author's interview November 2002, **39** Charles White *The Life & Times Of Little Richard* p.123-124 (Pan 1985), **40** White p.122, **41** White p.124-125, **42** *Rare & Unreleased* radio programme, disc 1 track 3, **43** White p.126-127, **44** *A Film About Jimi Hendrix* (1973), **45** Tony Brown *Jimi Hendrix Concert Files* p.24 (Omnibus 1999), **46** *Melody Maker* March 16th 1968, **47** Letter May/June 1965, Tony Brown *Jimi Hendrix Concert Files* p.24 (Omnibus 1999), **48** White p.129

Pages 58-73 (Do the New York scuffle; May 1965 to June 1966)
1 *Gallery* September 1982, **2** *Gallery* September 1982, **3** *Gallery* September 1982, **4** *A Film About Jimi Hendrix* (1973), **5** *A Film About Jimi Hendrix* (1973), **6** *A Film About Jimi Hendrix* (1973), **7** *Gallery* September 1982, **8** *A Film About Jimi Hendrix* (1973), **9** *UniVibes* 38, April 2000, p.33, **10** Letter dated August 8th 1965, Tony Brown *Jimi Hendrix Concert Files* p.24 (Omnibus 1999), **11** *A Film About Jimi Hendrix* (1973), **12** *Guitar World* September 1985 p.71, **13** *Guitar World* September 1985 p.71, **14** *Guitar World* September 1985 p.71, **15** *Guitar World* September 1985 p.72, **16** *Experience Hendrix* #602, **17** *Rolling Stone* March 19th 1970, **18** *Jimpress* No.39 p.27, **19** *Guitar Player* September 1975 p.22, **20** *UniVibes* No.43 December 2002 pp.6/7, **21** *UniVibes* No.43 December 2002 pp.6/7, **22** *Jimpress* 39, June 1995 p.11-12, **23** www.earlyhendrix.com, **24** *Jimpress* 39, June 1995 p.12, **25** *UniVibes* 38, April 2000, p.34, **26** *Jimpress* 39, June 1995 p.13/14, **27** *Jimpress* 39, June 1995 p.23, **28** *UniVibes* 38, April 2000, p.34, **29** *UniVibes* 38, April 2000, p.34, **30** *Jimpress* 69, October 2000, **31** *UniVibes* 38, April 2000, p.34, **32** *Jimpress* 39, June 1995 p.14, **33** *UniVibes* 38, April 2000, p.34-35, **34** *Jimpress* 26 p.16, **35** Postcard dated November 23rd 1965, Tony Brown *Jimi Hendrix: A Visual Documentary* p.35 (Omnibus 1992), **36** www.earlyhendrix.com, **37** www.earlyhendrix.com, **38** *Jimpress* 39, June 1995 pp.22-27, **39** mywebpages.comcast.net, **40** www.earlyhendrix.com, **41** www.earlyhendrix.com, **42** *Guitar World* September 1985 p.72, **43** Tony Brown *Jimi Hendrix: A Visual Documentary* p.38 (Omnibus 1992), **44** Letter dated January 13th 1966, Tony Brown *Jimi Hendrix: A Visual Documentary* p.38 (Omnibus 1992), **45** Jimpress 39, June 1995 p.17, **46** *Juke Blues* No.29 p.9, **47** www.earlyhendrix.com, **48** www.earlyhendrix.com, **49** *UniVibes* 38, April 2000, p.35, **50** *UniVibes* 38, April 2000, p.35, **51** www.earlyhendrix.com, **52** mywebpages.comcast.net, **53** mywebpages. comcast.net, **54** mywebpages.comcast.net, **55** Booklet notes to Lonnie Youngblood Featuring Jimi Hendrix *Two Great Experiences* (Empire Musicwerks 2003), **56** mywebpages.comcast.net, **57** Booklet notes to Lonnie Youngblood Featuring Jimi Hendrix *Two Great Experiences* (Empire Musicwerks 2003), **58** *Guitar Player* September 1975 p.57, **59** *Jimpress* 39, June 1995 p.28, **60** *Experience Hendrix* 502, **61** *Jimpress* 69, p.13, **62** Nat Shapiro & Nat Hentoff *Hear Me Talkin' To Ya* p.379 (Souvenir 1992), **63** Shapiro & Hentoff p.379, **64** Richie Havens *They Can't Hide Us Anymore* p.102 (HarperCollins 1999), **65** *Guitar World* September 1985 p.36, **66** Havens p.102-103, **67** Brown *Visual Documentary* p.39, **68** Brown *Visual Documentary* p.39, **69** Brown *Visual Documentary* p.39, **70** Havens p.103, **71** *Melody Maker* 16th March 1968 p.9

Pages 74-85 (The birth of Jimi Hendrix; June to October 1966)
1 *Hitparader* January 1968 p.19, **2** *A Film About Jimi Hendrix* (1973), **3** *Jimpress* 69, October 1999, p.15, **4** *UniVibes* 21, February 1996, p.31, **5** *UniVibes* 21, February 1996, p.31, **6** *A Film About Jimi Hendrix* (1973), **7** *Jimpress* 69 October 1999 p.10, **8** *Debris* January 1987, **9** *Guitar World* September 1985 p.82, **10** *Straight Ahead* October/November 1994, **11** *Guitar World* September 1985 p.82, **12** Steven Roby *Black Gold: The Lost Archives Of Jimi Hendrix* p.52 (Billboard 2002), **13** *Straight Ahead* October/November 1994, **14** *Jimpress* 39, June 1995, p.26-27, **15** *Guitar* September 1995 p.76, **16** *Guitar* September 1995 p.76, **17** *A Film About Jimi Hendrix* (1973), **18** *A Film About Jimi Hendrix* (1973), **19** *A Film About Jimi Hendrix* (1973), **20** John McDermott & Eddie Kramer *Setting The Record Straight* p.8 (Little Brown 1992), **21** McDermott *Record Straight* p.9, **22** McDermott *Record Straight* p.9, **23** *Jimpress* 69, October 1999, p.15, **24** Roby p.53, **25** Jan Mark Wolkin & Bill Keenom *Michael Bloomfield: If You Love These Blues* p.132-133 (Miller Freeman 2000), **26** *Guitar Player* September 1975 p.22, **27** *Guitar Player* September 1975 p.22, **28** *A Film About Jimi Hendrix* (1973), **29** Sean Egan *Not Necessarily Stoned, But Beautiful* p.25 (Unanimous Press 2002), **30** Egan p.30-31, **31** *A Film About Jimi Hendrix* (1973), **32** *A Film About Jimi Hendrix* (1973), **33** *Guitar Player* September 1975 p.20, **34** *Guitar Player* September 1975 p.20, **35** *Hitparader* January 1968 p.19, **36** *Guitar World* September 1985 p.17, **37** *Guitar World* September 1985 p.17, **38** *Guitar Player* September 1975 p.20, **39** *Guitar World* September 1985 p.17., **40** www.canadianblues.ca, **41** *Hitparader* January 1968 p.19, **42** www.canadianblues.ca, **43** McDermott *Record Straight* p.18, **44** *UniVibes* 38, April 2000, p.33, **45** *Hitparader* January 1968 p.19, **46** Mitch Mitchell & John Platt *The Hendrix Experience* p.18 (Hamlyn 1990), **47** *UniVibes* 38, April 2000, p.33, **48** Simon Napier-Bell *You Don't Have To Say You Love Me* (New English Library 1983), **49** Kathy Etchingham *Through Gypsy Eyes* p.67-68 (Gollancz 1998), **50** *South Bank Show: Jimi Hendrix* ITV October 1st 1989, **51** Tony Brown *Jimi Hendrix: A Visual Documentary* p.42 (Omnibus 1992), **52** Noel Redding & Carol Appleby *Are You Experienced?* p.18 (Fourth Estate/Picador 1990), **53** Redding p.23, **54** Redding p.23, **55** Redding p.23, **56** Author's interview November 2002, **57** *Record Mirror* August 13th 1966, **58** Brown *Visual Documentary* p., **59** Geoffrey Giuliano *Jimi Hendrix: If Six Was Nine* Audio Book Laserlight (Durkin Hayes 1997), **60** *Record Mirror* June 24th 1967, **61** Brown *Visual Documentary* p.43, **62** *South Bank Show: Jimi Hendrix* ITV October 1st 1989, **63** Author's interview December 2002, **64** Mitchell p.15, **65** Mitchell p.15, **66** Etchingham p.80, **67** Redding p.26, **68** Mitchell p.16-17, **69** Etchingham p.80, **70** Mitchell p.17, **71** Redding p.26, **72** Author's interview November 2002

Pages 86-93 (Live in Paris and London; October to December 1966)
1 Mitch Mitchell & John Platt *The Hendrix Experience* p.21 (Hamlyn 1990), **2** Tony Brown *Jimi Hendrix: A Visual Documentary* p.43 (Omnibus 1992), **3** Mitchell p.23, **4** Noel Redding & Carol Appleby *Are You Experienced?* p.33 (Fourth Estate/Picador 1990), **5** Mitchell p.24, **6** Brown *Visual Documentary* p.44, **7** Brown *Visual Documentary* p.44, **8** Kathy Etchingham *Through Gypsy Eyes* p.76 (Gollancz 1998), **9** Brown *Visual Documentary* p.44, **10** Author's interview June 2003, **11** *Hitparader* January 1968, **12** *Rolling Stone* April 1st 1999, **13** Author's interview November 2002, **14** *A Film About Jimi Hendrix* (1973), **15** Etchingham p.77, **16** *Record Mirror* December 10th 1966 p.2, **17** *Record Mirror* December 10th 1966 p.2, **18** *Record Mirror* December 10th 1966 p.2, **19** *Record Mirror* December 10th 1966 p.10, **20** Keith Altham *The PR Strikes Back* p.286-287 (Blake 2001), **21** *Guitar World* September 1985 p.67, **22** *Guitar Player* September 1975 p.58, **23** *Guitar Player* September 1975 p.57, **24** *Guitar World* September 1985, p.67, **25** Redding p.34, **26** *Melody Maker* January 14th 1967 p.7, **27** *Record Mirror* December 24th 1966

Pages 94-107 (Get experienced; January to April 1967)
1 *Record Mirror* January 14th 1967, **2** Mitch Mitchell & John Platt *The Hendrix Experience* p.24 (Hamlyn 1990), **3** *Melody Maker* January 14th 1967 p.7, **4** Mitchell p.24, **5** *Jazz Times* August 2001 p.45, **6** Kathy Etchingham *Through Gypsy Eyes* p.88-89 (Gollancz 1998), **7** Steven Roby *Black Gold: The Lost Archives Of Jimi Hendrix* (Billboard 2002), **8** Mitchell p.24, **9** *South Bank Show: Jimi Hendrix* ITV October 1st 1989, **10** Mitchell p.26, **11** Mitchell p.30, **12** Mitchell p.26, **13** Author's interview December 2002, **14** *Beat Instrumental* April 1967, **15** Mitchell p.49, **16** Author's interview December 2002, **17** Author's interview December 2002, **18** Noel Redding & Carol Appleby *Are You Experienced?* p.33 (Fourth Estate/Picador 1990), **19** Redding p.35, **20** Redding p.37, **21** Mitchell p.32, **22** Etchingham p.127, **23** Interview with Tony Bacon July 10th 2003, **24** John Scofield interviewed by Bill Milkowski, Jazz Times August 2001 p.45, **25** *Melody Maker* January 28th 1967, **26** *Hitparader* January 1968 p.19, **27** *Melody Maker*, **28** *Record Mirror* February 25th 1967, **29** *Beat Instrumental* March 1967, **30** Tony Brown *Jimi Hendrix: A Visual Documentary* (Omnibus 1992), **31** *Melody Maker* March 18th 1967, **32** *Melody Maker* February 25th 1967 p.13, **33** Mitchell p.47, **34** *Melody Maker* March 4th 1967 p.5, **35** *Record Mirror* March 25th 1967, **36** *Melody Maker* March 18th 1967 p.5, **37** Mitchell p.41, **38** Keith Altham *The PR Strikes Back* p.262 (Blake 2001), **39** *Melody Maker*, **40** Mitchell p.49, **41** *Melody Maker* April 15th 1967

Pages 108-121 (From Marylebone to Monterey; May to September 1967)
1 *South Bank Show: Jimi Hendrix* ITV October 1st 1989, **2** *Record Mirror* June 24th 1967, **3** Kathy Etchingham *Through Gypsy Eyes* p.107 (Gollancz 1998), **4** *Nya Wermlands-Tidningen* May 22nd 1967 translation by Claus Rasmussen and Karsten Laybourn, **5** *Melody Maker* June 10th 1967, **6** *Melody Maker* 10th June 1967 p.8, **7** Mitch Mitchell & John Platt *The Hendrix Experience* p.63 (Hamlyn 1990), **8** Jan Mark Wolkin & Bill Keenan *If You Love These Blues – Michael Bloomfield, An Oral History* p.144-145 (Miller Freeman Books 2000), **9** Joel Selvin *Monterey Pop* p.86 (Chronicle 1992), **10** *Melody Maker* June 24th 1967 p.9, **11** *Down Beat* August 10th 1967 p.24, **12** *South Bank Show: Jimi Hendrix* ITV October 1st 1989, **13** Mitchell p.61, **14** *Live And Unreleased* (Westwood One Radio 1988), **15** *South Bank Show: Jimi Hendrix* ITV October 1st 1989, **16** *Guitar World* March 1988 p.36, **17** *Guitar World* March 1988 p.36, **18** *Melody Maker* July 22nd 1967 p.7, **19** Mitchell p.67, **20** *Guitar World* March 1988 p.36, **21** Noel Redding & Carol Appleby *Are You Experienced?* p.58 (Fourth Estate/Picador 1990), **22** *New Musical Express* July 29th 1967, **23** *Record Mirror* September 9th 1967 p.3, **24** *Guitar Player* September 1975 p.20, **25** *Melody Maker* February 10th 1968, **26** Mitchell p.68-69, **27** Redding p.58, **28** *Melody Maker* September 9th 1967., **29** www.earlyhendrix.com, **30** Redding p.59, **31** Redding p.60-61, **32** *Melody Maker* September 9th 1967, **33** *Record Mirror* August 26th 1967, **34** Author's interview December 2002

Pages 122-133 (Turning on the Axis; October to December 1967)
1 *Guitar World* September 1985 p.66, **2** *Jazz Times* August 2001 p.45, **3** *Guitar Player* September 1975 p.50, **4** Noel Redding & Carol Appleby *Are You Experienced?* p.65-66 (Fourth Estate/Picador 1990), **5** *Melody Maker* October 14th 1967 p.4, **6** *Melody Maker* 16th September 1967 front page, **7** Mitch Mitchell & John Platt *The Hendrix Experience* p.76 (Hamlyn 1990), **8** *Guitar Player* September 1975 p.22/56, **9** *Guitar World* September 1985 p.66-67, **10** *Guitar World* September 1985 p.22/66, **11** Mitchell p.78, **12** Kathy Etchingham *Through Gypsy Eyes* p.97 (Gollancz 1998), **13** *Melody Maker* December 9th 1967 p.5, **14** *Down Beat* December 28th 1967 p.18, **15** John Kruth *Bright Moments: The Life & Legacy of Rahsaan Roland Kirk* p.221 (Welcome Rain 2000), **16** Kruth p.221, **17** Chris Welch, Melody Maker Caught In The Act, 25th November 1967., **18** Mitchell p.83, **19** *Melody Maker* December 23rd 1967 p.14, **20** Author's interview July 2002, **21** Author's interview July 2002

Pages 134-149 (The Road to Electric Landlady; January to April 1968)
1 *Kritikernekalder* January 4th 1968 translation by Claus Rasmussen and Karsten Laybourn, **2** Noel Redding & Carol Appleby *Are You Experienced?* p.71 (Fourth Estate/Picador 1990), **3** Redding p.73, **4** Mitch Mitchell & John Platt *The Hendrix Experience* p.86 (Hamlyn 1990), **5** Kathy Etchingham *Through Gypsy Eyes* p.95 (Gollancz 1998), **6** *Expressen* January 8th 1968 translation by Claus Rasmussen and Karsten Laybourn, **7** *Expressen* January 8th 1968 translation by Claus Rasmussen and Karsten Laybourn, **8** *Ekstra Bladet* January 8th 1968 translation by Claus Rasmussen and Karsten Laybourn, **9** *Politiken* January 14th 1968 translation by Claus Rasmussen and Karsten Laybourn, **10** *Politiken* January 14th 1968 translation by Claus Rasmussen and Karsten Laybourn, **11** Etchingham p.110, **12** Etchingham p.110, **13** Author's interview November 2002, **14** Author's interview November 2002, **15** Author's interview November 2002, **16** Author's interview November 2002, **17** Redding p.76, **18** Mitchell p.88, **19** Author's interview November 2002, **20** Redding p.77, **21** Author's interview November 2002, **22** Author's interview December 2002, **23** *Guitar World* September 1985 p.18, **24** Author's interview November 2002, **25** Redding p.79, **26** *Rolling Stone* December 15th 1994, **27** Karen O'Brien *Shadows And Light: Joni Mitchell* (Virgin 2001), **28** *Melody Maker* March 16th 1968, **29** Redding p.84, **30** *Hendrix – Reputations* (BBC) and Tony Brown *Jimi Hendrix: A Visual Documentary* (Omnibus 1992), **31** *Guitar World* September 1985 p.71, **32** *Purple Haze: The Story Of Jimi Hendrix* BBC Radio-2, January 2002, **33** *Melody Maker* April 20th 1968 p.15, **34** *Beat Instrumental* May 1968, **35** *Beat Instrumental* May 1968, **36** Etchingham p.107, **37** Mitchell p.114, **38** Etchingham p.118, **39** *Jimpress* 45, February 1996, p.21, **40** Redding p.86, **41** *Guitar World* September 1985 p.71, **42** Etchingham p.118, **43** Etchingham p.118, **44** John McDermott et al *Jimi Hendrix Sessions: The Complete Recording Sessions 1963-70* p.57 (Little Brown 1995), **45** *Beat Instrumental* May 1968, **46** CD insert notes to *Damned Damned Damned* (Castle 2002)

Pages 150-157 (America calling; May to August 1968)
1 Noel Redding & Carol Appleby *Are You Experienced?* p.87 (Fourth Estate/Picador 1990), **2** Mitch Mitchell & John Platt *The Hendrix Experience* p.107 (Hamlyn 1990), **3** Mitchell p.108, **4** Redding p.87, **5** Kathy Etchingham *Through Gypsy Eyes* p.117-118 (Gollancz 1998), **6** John McDermott et al *Jimi Hendrix Sessions: The Complete Recording Sessions 1963-70* p.63 (Little, Brown 1995), **7** John McDermott & Eddie Kramer *Setting The Record Straight* p.161 (Little Brown 1992), **8** *Melody Maker* July 9th 1968 p.3, **9** *Melody Maker* July 20th 1968 p.5, **10** Redding p.99-100, **11** *Jimpress* 69, October 2000, p.9, **12** Author's interview November 2002

Pages 158-167 (The sun ain't rising; September to December 1968)
1 Author's interview November 2002, **2** Noel Redding & Carol Appleby *Are You Experienced?* p.104 (Fourth Estate/Picador 1990), **3** Mitch Mitchell & John Platt *The Hendrix Experience* p.118 (Hamlyn 1990), **4** *Circus* interview unknown publication date reproduced in David Henderson *'Scuse Me While I Kiss The Sky* pp.222-225 (Omnibus 1993), **5** *Guitar Player* December 1968, **6** *Guitar World* September 1985 p.73, **7** *Guitar World* September 1985 p.73, **8** *Jimpress* 69, October 2000, p.11, **9** *Jimpress* 69, October 2000, p11, **10** Redding p.105, **11** CD insert notes to *Blues* (Polydor 1994), **12** *Beat Instrumental* December 1968, **13** Author's interview November 2002, **14** *Melody Maker* November 16th 1968, **15** *The Observer* November 10th 1968, **16** *Beat Instrumental* December 1968, **17** Redding p.108, **18** Mitchell, p.118, **19** Redding p.110, **20** *Hitparader* January 1969 p.60

Pages 168-179 (Playing with the massed Alberts; January to March 1969)
1 Kathy Etchingham *Through Gypsy Eyes* p.121 (Gollancz 1998), **2** *Melody Maker* January 11th 1969 p.5, **3** *Melody Maker* January 11th 1969 p.5, **4** *The Daily Mirror* January 11th 1969, **5** *Melody Maker* January 11th 1969 p.3, **6** *SuperLove* March 1st 1969 translation by Claus Rasmussen and Karsten Laybourn, **7** *Hej!* March 2nd 1969 translation by Claus Rasmussen and Karsten Laybourn, **8** John McDermott et al *Jimi Hendrix Sessions: The Complete Recording Sessions 1963-70* p.93 (Little, Brown 1995), **9** *Jimpress* 45, February 1996, p.20, **10** Interview with Meatball Fulton, December 1967, **11** *International Times* March 28th 1969, **12** Harry Shapiro & Caesar Glebbeek *Jimi Hendrix: Electric Gypsy* p.345-346 (Heinemann 1990), **13** *Melody Maker* January 11th

1969 p.5, **14** John McDermott & Eddie Kramer *Setting The Record Straight* p.215 (Little Brown 1992), **15** Mitch Mitchell & John Platt *The Hendrix Experience* p.128 (Hamlyn 1990), **16** Noel Redding & Carol Appleby *Are You Experienced?* p.116 (Fourth Estate/Picador 1990), **17** McDermott *Record Straight* p.217, **18** Etchingham p.128-129, **19** Author's interview November 2002, **20** Redding p.116, **21** *New Musical Express* March 15th 1969, **22** Etchingham p.121, **23** *Melody Maker* March 1st 1969 p.14-15, **24** *Down Beat* May 29th 1969 p.31, **25** John Kruth *Bright Moments: The Life & Legacy of Rahsaan Roland Kirk* p.221 (Welcome Rain 2000), **26** Author's interview November 2002, **27** Etchingham p.138, **28** *Jimpress* 45, February 1996, p.22, **29** Los Angeles radio station KDAY, March 1969

Pages 180-189 (Jam today, no experience needed; April to June 1969)
1 *Guitar World* September 1985 p.45, **2** *Guitar World* September 1985 p.74, **3** *Guitar Player* September 1975 p.14, **4** *Jazz Times* August 2001 p.50, **5** *Guitar World* September 1985 p.74, **6** *Jazzwise* December 2002/January 2003 p.25, **7** Author's interview March 1992, **8** *Guitar Player* September 1975, **9** Author's interview March 1992, **10** Author's interview March 1992, **11** Noel Redding & Carol Appleby *Are You Experienced?* p.128 (Fourth Estate/Picador 1990), **12** Redding p.121, **13** *Beat Instrumental* June 1969, **14** John McDermott & Eddie Kramer *Setting The Record Straight* p.237 (Little Brown 1992), **15** Mitch Mitchell & John Platt *The Hendrix Experience* p.132 (Hamlyn 1990), **16** John McDermott et al *Jimi Hendrix Sessions: The Complete Recording Sessions 1963-70* p.104 (Little Brown 1995), **17** McDermott *Sessions* p.103, **18** McDermott *Sessions* p.103, **19** Johnny Winter, How Do White Men Play The Blues?, Guitar World September 1985 p.68, interviewed by Gene Santoro., **20** *Guitar Player* September 1975 p.16, **21** *Guitar Player* September 1975 p.16, **22** *Guitar Player* September 1975 p.16, **23** *Beat Instrumental* June 1969, **24** Kathy Etchingham *Through Gypsy Eyes* p.137 (Gollancz 1998), **25** McDermott *Sessions* p.108, **26** Dallas Taylor *Prisoner Of Woodstock* p.34-35 (Thunder's Mouth 1995), **27** Steven Roby *Black Gold: The Lost Archives Of Jimi Hendrix* p.201 (Billboard 2002), **28** *Toronto Globe & Star* June 1969; *Los Angeles. Times* July 9th 1969, **29** Redding p.128, **30** Redding p.130, **31** Mitchell p.136

Pages 190-199 (All systems stop; July to September 1969)
1 *Rolling Stone* July 12th 1969, **2** John McDermott et al *Jimi Hendrix Sessions: The Complete Recording Sessions 1963-70* p.110 (Little Brown 1995), **3** Mitch Mitchell & John Platt *The Hendrix Experience* p.140 (Hamlyn 1990), **4** *Jimpress* 65, October 1999, p.23, **5** *Jimpress* 65, October 1999, p.24, **6** Steven Roby *Black Gold: The Lost Archives Of Jimi Hendrix* p.131-132 (Billboard 2002), **7** *Jimpress* 66, December 1999, p.22, **8** Author's interview March 1992, **9** Mitchell p.142, **10** Dallas Taylor *Prisoner Of Woodstock* introduction (Thunder's Mouth 1995), **11** *Jimpress* 69, October 2000, p.7, **12** *Jimpress* 69, October 2000, p.7, **13** *Jimpress* 66, December 1999, **14** *New Musical Express* October 25th 1969, **15** McDermott *Sessions* p.123

Pages 200-209 (Miles of trouble; October to December 1969)
1 John McDermott & Eddie Kramer *Setting The Record Straight* p.288 (Little Brown 1992), **2** Author's interview March 1992, **3** Author's interview March 1992, **4** John McDermott et al *Jimi Hendrix Sessions: The Complete Recording Sessions 1963-70* p.123 (Little Brown 1995), **5** McDermott *Record Straight* p.295, **6** McDermott *Sessions* p.125, **7** McDermott *Sessions* p.125, **8** *A Film About Jimi Hendrix* (1973), **9** *The Guitar Magazine* April 1995 p.36, **10** McDermott *Sessions* p.126, **11** Author's interview March 1992, **12** *The Guitar Magazine* April 1995 p.35-36, **13** *Rolling Stone* February 4th 1970 / *Guitar Player* September 1975, **14** *Down Beat* November 28th 1968 p.17, **15** Miles Davis with Quincy Toupe *The Autobiography* p.282 (Macmillan 1990), **16** *UniVibes* 17, February 1995, **17** Davis *Autobiography* p.282, **18** *The Guitar Magazine* April 1995 p.36, **19** *Jazz Times* August 2001 p.51, **20** *Melody Maker* December 20th 1969 p.5, **21** *Band Of Gypsys* DVD 1999

Pages 210-219 (Burning bridges; January to March 1970)
1 *Down Beat* March 5th 1970 p.32, **2** *Down Beat* March 5th 1970 p.32, **3** DVD notes to *Band Of Gypsys* (MCA/Experience Hendrix, 1999), **4** Harry Shapiro & Caesar Glebbeek *Jimi Hendrix: Electric Gypsy* p.407 (Heinemann 1990), **5** *Rolling Stone* April 1st 1999, **6** John McDermott & Eddie Kramer *Setting The Record Straight* p.326 (Little Brown 1992) / Harry Shapiro & Caesar Glebbeek *Jimi Hendrix: Electric Gypsy* p.410 (Heinemann 1990), **7** John McDermott et al *Jimi Hendrix Sessions: The Complete Recording Sessions 1963-70* p.134 (Little Brown 1995), **8** *New York Post* January 2nd 1970, **9** *New York Post* January 2nd 1970, **10** *Jimpress* 64, August 1999, p.37, **11** Noel Redding & Carol Appleby *Are You Experienced?* p.130 (Fourth Estate/Picador 1990), **12** CD insert notes by John McDermott to *The Jimi Hendrix Experience* four-CD box-set (MCA/Experience Hendrix 2002), **13** Redding p.142, **14** McDermott *Record Straight* p.315, **15** *Guitar Player* September 1975 p.16, **16** Redding p.142, **17** Shapiro p.413, **18** DVD *Band Of Gypsys* (MCA/Experience Hendrix, 1999), **19** DVD *Band Of Gypsys* (MCA/Experience Hendrix, 1999), **20** DVD *Band Of Gypsys* (MCA/Experience Hendrix, 1999), **21** DVD *Band Of Gypsys* (MCA/Experience Hendrix, 1999), **22** *Guitar Player* September 1975, **23** *Rolling Stone* February 4th 1970 / *Guitar Player* September 1975, **24** Mitch Mitchell & John Platt *The Hendrix Experience* p.146-147 (Hamlyn 1990), **25** Kathy Etchingham *Through Gypsy Eyes* p.145 (Gollancz 1998), **26** *Jimpress* 31, September 1994, **27** McDermott *Sessions* p.139, **28** Noel Redding & Carol Appleby *Are You Experienced?* p.140 (Fourth Estate/Picador 1990), **29** *Jazz Times* August 2001 p.45

Pages 220-243 (Too much too late; April to September 1970)
1 *Melody Maker* May 9th 1970, **2** *Melody Maker* May 9th 1970, **3** *Rolling Stone* February 4th 1970 / *Guitar Player* September 1975, **4** D.K. Hall & Sue C. Clarke *Superstars – In Their Own Words* (Music Sales 1970)., **5** *Jimpress* 31, September 1994, **6** *Jimpress* 31, September 1994, p.18-19, **7** Mitch Mitchell & John Platt *The Hendrix Experience* p.148 (Hamlyn 1990), **8** *Guitar World* September 1985 p.68, **9** *Crawdaddy* February 1975 p.52, **10** Belmo & Steve Loveless *Jimi Hendrix – Experience The Music* p.19 (Collector's Guide 1998), **11** *Crawdaddy* February 1975 p.52, **12** Mitchell, p.149, **13** *Melody Maker* July 4th 1970, **14** John McDermott & Eddie Kramer *Setting The Record Straight* p.330-331 (Little Brown 1992), **15** *Record Mirror* July 11th 1970, **16** *Record Mirror* July 11th 1970, **17** *Record Mirror* July 11th 1970, **18** John McDermott et al *Jimi Hendrix Sessions: The Complete Recording Sessions 1963-70* p.XX (Little Brown 1995) p.160, **19** McDermott *Record Straight* p.337, **20** Miles Davis with Quincy Toupe *The Autobiography* p.308 (Macmillan 1990), **21** Mary Willix *Voices From Home* p.142 (Creative Forces Publishing 1995), **22** Willix p.142, **23** James Allen Hendrix with Jas Obrecht *My Son Jimi* p.168 (AlJas Enterprises 1999), **24** Chris Welch *Hendrix: A Biography* p.65-66 (Ocean Books 1972), **25** Mitch Mitchell & John Platt *The Hendrix Experience* p.149 (Hamlyn 1990), **26** *Record Mirror* July 11th 1970, **27** Steven Roby *Black Gold: The Lost Archives Of Jimi Hendrix* p.176 (Billboard 2002), **28** McDermott *Sessions* p.167, **29** Davis *Autobiography* p.283, **30** LP sleevenotes by Leroi Jones to John Coltrane *Live At Birdland* (Impulse! 1963), **31** Kathy Etchingham *Through Gypsy Eyes* p.148 (Gollancz 1998)., **32** *Record Mirror* September 19th 1970, **33** *UniVibes* 19, p.19, **34** *UniVibes* 19, p.20, **35** *Jazz & Pop* December 1970 p.27, **36** *Jazz & Pop* December 1970 p.26-27, **37** Brian Hinton *Message To Love: The Isle Of Wight Festival 1968, 1969, 1970* p.159 (Castle Communications 1995), **38** Hinton p.159, **39** Richie Havens *They Can't Hide Us Anymore* p.105 (HarperCollins 1999), **40** *Aftonbladet* September 1st 1970 translation by Claus Rasmussen and Karsten Laybourn, **41** Unknown publication Tröttsam, Sweden September 1970 translation by Claus Rasmussen and Karsten Laybourn, **42** *Stiftstidende* September 1970 translation by Claus Rasmussen and Karsten Laybourn, **43** *Stiftstidende* September 1970 translation by Claus Rasmussen and Karsten Laybourn, **44** *Stiftstidende* September 1970 translation by Claus Rasmussen and Karsten Laybourn, **45** *Information* September 1970 translation by Claus Rasmussen and Karsten Laybourn, **46** *Morgen Posten* September 6th 1970 translation by Claus Rasmussen and Karsten Laybourn, **47** *UniVibes* 19, p.24, **48** Etchingham p.148, **49** Author's interview December 2002, **50** *Record Mirror* October 10th 1970, **51** *Record Mirror* October 10th 1970, **52** *Record Mirror* October 10th 1970, **53** *Guitar World* September 1985 p.70, **54** *South Bank Show: Jimi Hendrix* ITV October 1st 1989, **55** *South Bank Show: Jimi Hendrix* ITV October 1st 1989, **56** Harry Shapiro & Caesar Glebbeek *Jimi Hendrix: Electric Gypsy* p.468 (Heinemann 1990) / John McDermott & Eddie Kramer *Setting The Record Straight* p.355-356 (Little Brown 1992), **57** *South Bank Show: Jimi Hendrix* ITV October 1st 1989, **58** *South Bank Show: Jimi Hendrix* ITV October 1st 1989, **59** McDermott *Record Straight* p.355-356

Pages 244-251 (Hendrix gear)
1 Tony Brown *Jimi Hendrix: A Visual Documentary* p.39 (Omnibus 1992), **2** Harry Shapiro & Caesar Glebbeek *Jimi Hendrix: Electric Gypsy* (Heinemann 1990), **3** *Los Angeles Free Press* August 25th 1967, **4** *Beat Instrumental* May 1967 p.22, **5** *Guitar Player* September 1975 p.11, **6** *UniVibes* 12, **7** *Beat Instrumental* May 1967 p.22, **8** *Disc & Music Echo* date unknown, circa 1967, **9** *Melody Maker* February 24th 1968, **10** *Beat Instrumental* March 1967, **11** *Guitar World* September 2002, **12** Shapiro, **13** Interview with Tony Bacon, July 10th 2003, **14** Shapiro, **15** *Hitparader* July 1969, **16** *Guitar Shop* Fall 1994, **17** *Guitar Shop* Fall 1994, **18** John McDermott et al *Jimi Hendrix Sessions: The Complete Studio Recording Sessions, 1963-70* (Little Brown 1995), **19** Shapiro, **20** Interview with Tony Bacon, July 10th 2003, **21** Kathy Etchingham *Through Gypsy Eyes* p.127 (Gollancz 1998), **22** *Guitar Player* September 1975 p.22, **23** *Hitparader* July 1969, **24** Interview with Tony Bacon, July 10th 2003, **25** *Music Maker* February 1968

selected recordings

OFFICIAL COMMERCIAL RELEASES 1964-2003

This selected discography begins with a look at Hendrix's pre-Experience releases, and then moves on to the Experience period and afterwards. No albums of material featuring Hendrix as a sideman were released prior to his years of fame, making it more likely that session tapes could have been altered, either to re-shape the performance or sonically boost Hendrix's role. That means either hunting down the limited numbers of singles involving the pre-Experience Hendrix as a sideman – records released with no motivation for pro-Hendrix tampering – or acquiring more recent CDs. While by no means perfect, the CDs at least tend to have reasonable sound and some info attached. The following selective list omits pointlessly bizarre stuff such as Jayne Mansfield's London-label single 'As The Clouds Drift By' / 'Suey', recorded by Ed Chalpin in late 1965.

PRE-EXPERIENCE 45RPM SINGLES

(Initial release label and catalogue number, year)
The Isley Brothers Testify Pts 1 & 2 (T-Neck 501, 1964); The Last Girl/Looking For A Love (Atlantic 2263, 1964); Move Over And Let Me Dance/Have You Ever Been Disappointed (Atlantic 2303, 1965).
Don Covay Mercy Mercy (Rosemart 801, 1964).
Rosa Lee Brooks My Diary/Utee (Revis 1013, 1965).
Little Richard I Don't Know What You've Got Pts 1 & 2 (Vee Jay VJ-698, Fontana TF 652, 1965).
Curtis Knight How Would You Feel/Welcome Home (RSVP 1120, 1966).
Curtis Knight & The Squires Hornet's Nest/Knock Yourself Out (RSVP 1124, 1966).
Billy LaMont Sweet Thang/Please Don't Leave (20th Century-Fox 45-6707, 1968).
The Icemen (My Girl) She's A Fox/(I Wonder) What It Takes (Samar S-111, 1966).
Jimmy Norman You're Only Hurting Yourself/ That Little Old Groovemaker (Samar S-112, 1966).
Ray Sharpe Help Me (Get The Feeling) Pts 1 & 2 (Atco 45-6402, 1966).
Lonnie Youngblood Go Go Shoes/Go Go Place (Fairmount F-1002, 1966?); Soul Food/Goodbye Bessie Mae (Fairmount F-1022, 1966?).
Jimi Hendrix No Such Animal Pts 1 & 2 (Audio Fidelity AF167, 1971).

PRE-EXPERIENCE HENDRIX ON CD

The Isley Brothers *Story Vol.1: Rockin' Soul* (Rhino R2 70908) Provides four of the six sides Hendrix cut with the Isleys; two B-sides are missing.
Little Richard *The Second Coming* (Charly CPCD 8244-2 two-CD set) Currently the best-remastered reissue of the Richard material, including alternative takes of both parts of 'I Don't Know What You've Got'. But five tracks of interest across a two-CD set means lots of Richard for not much Hendrix.
Jimi (sic) **Hendrix** *Knock Yourself Out* (Jungle 068) A single-CD issue concentrating on the 1965/66 Curtis Knight/Squires recordings and including versions of the material on the issued RSVP singles.
Curtis Knight/Jimi (sic) **Hendrix** *The Complete PPX Sessions* volumes 1-7 (SPV 088-20802) Not for the faint-hearted, this is a relatively comprehensive reissue of the Knight-Squires-Hendrix material of 1965/66/67 in its various edits and remixes, little of it in any useful order, either by recording date or original release dates.
Lonnie Youngblood/Jimi (sic) **Hendrix** *Two Experiences Together* (Empire Meisterwerke/BMG 80269-39063-2) The latest reissue of this material still ignores its original performers and shies away from issuing the original 45rpm single versions. But it's better than nothing.

ORIGINAL SINGLES, EXPERIENCE AND AFTER, 1967-1973

Hey Joe/Stone Free (Polydor 56139, 1966)
Purple Haze/51st Anniversary (Track 604001, 1967)
The Wind Cries Mary/Highway Chile (Track 604004, 1967)
Hey Joe/51st Anniversary (Reprise 0572, 1967)
Purple Haze/The Wind Cries Mary (Reprise 0597, 1967)
The Burning Of The Midnight Lamp/The Stars That Play With Laughing Sam's Dice (Track 604007, 1967)
Foxy Lady/Hey Joe (Reprise 0641, 1967)
Up From The Skies/One Rainy Wish (Reprise 0665, 1968)
All Along The Watchtower/Long Hot Summer Night (Track 604025, 1968)
All Along The Watchtower/The Burning Of The Midnight Lamp (Reprise 0607, 1968)
Crosstown Traffic/Gypsy Eyes (Reprise 0792, 1968; Track 604029, 1969)
Stepping Stone/Izabella (Reprise 0905, 1970)
Voodoo Child (Slight Return)/Hey Joe/All Along The Watchtower (Track 2095, 1970)
Freedom/Angel (Reprise 1000, 1971)
Dolly Dagger/Star Spangled Banner (Reprise 1044, 1971)
Johnny B. Goode/Little Wing (Polydor 2001-277, 1972)
Hear My Train A'Comin'/Rock Me Baby (Reprise K14286, 1973)

ORIGINAL VINYL ALBUMS 1967-1970

ARE YOU EXPERIENCED (UK version: Track 604004, 1967) ***SIDE A:*** Foxy Lady, Manic Depression, Red House, Can You See Me, Love Or Confusion, I Don't Live Today. ***SIDE B:*** May This Be Love, Fire, Third Stone From The Sun, Remember, Are You Experienced?.
ARE YOU EXPERIENCED (US version: Reprise 6261, 1967) ***SIDE A:*** Purple Haze, Manic Depression, Hey Joe, Love Or Confusion, May This Be Love, I Don't Live Today. ***SIDE B:*** The Wind Cries Mary, Fire, Third Stone From The Sun, Foxy Lady, Are You Experienced?.
AXIS: BOLD AS LOVE (Track 613003, Reprise RS 6281, 1967) ***SIDE A:*** EXP, Up From The Skies, Spanish Castle Magic, Wait Until Tomorrow, Ain't No Telling, Little Wing, If 6 Was 9. ***SIDE B:*** You Got Me Floatin', Castles Made Of Sand, She's So Fine, One Rainy Wish, Little Miss Lover, Bold As Love.
ELECTRIC LADYLAND (Reprise 2RS 6307, Track 613 008/9, 1968) ***SIDE A:*** …And the Gods Made Love, Have You Ever Been (To Electric Ladyland), Crosstown Traffic, Voodoo Chile. ***SIDE B:*** Little Miss Strange, Long Hot Summer Night, Come On (Part One), Gypsy Eyes, Burning Of The Midnight Lamp. ***SIDE C:*** Rainy Day Dream Away, 1983 (A Merman I Should Turn To Be), Moon Turn The Tides … Gently Gently Away. ***SIDE D:*** Still Raining Still Dreaming, House Burning Down, All Along The Watchtower, Voodoo Child (Slight Return).
SMASH HITS (UK version: Track 613004, 1968) ***SIDE A:*** Purple Haze, Fire, The Wind Cries Mary, Can You See Me, 51st Anniversary, Hey Joe. ***SIDE B:*** Stone Free, The Stars That Play With Laughing Sam's Dice, Manic Depression, Highway Chile, The Burning Of The Midnight Lamp, Foxy Lady.
SMASH HITS (US version: Reprise MS 2025, 1969) ***SIDE A:*** Purple Haze, Fire, The Wind Cries Mary, Can You See Me, Hey Joe, All Along The Watchtower. ***SIDE B:*** Stone Free, Crosstown Traffic, Manic Depression, Remember, Red House, Foxy Lady.
BAND OF GYPSYS (Capitol STAO-472, Track 2406 002, 1970) ***SIDE A:*** Who Knows, Machine Gun. ***SIDE B:*** Changes, Power Of Soul, Message To Love, We Gotta Live Together.
VARIOUS ARTISTS **WOODSTOCK** (Cotillon SD3500, three-LP set, 1970) Hendrix material ***SIDE F:*** Voodoo Child (Slight Return), The Star Spangled Banner, Purple Haze, Villanova Junction.
HISTORIC PERFORMANCES RECORDED AT THE MONTEREY INTERNATIONAL POP FESTIVAL (Reprise MS 2029, 1970) ***SIDE A:*** Like A Rolling Stone, Rock Me Baby, Can You See Me, Wild Thing. (Side B is Otis Redding performances.)

POSTHUMOUS VINYL LPS 1970-1989

THE CRY OF LOVE (Reprise MS 2034, Track 2408 101, 1971) First posthumous aggregation of tracks that Hendrix was preparing for The Next Album prior to his death. A fair stab, apart from the inclusion of obvious ringers like My Friend from 1968.
VARIOUS ARTISTS **WOODSTOCK 2** (Cotillon SD 2400, 1971) A whole LP side given over to Hendrix's set, including the first appearance of Mitchell's 'Beginning', called here 'Jam Back At The House'.
EXPERIENCE (Ember 5057, 1971) First appearance of some of the music from the February 24th 1969 Albert Hall concert.
RAINBOW BRIDGE (Reprise MS 2040 [US], K44159 [UK], 1971) So-called 'soundtrack' album for the film of the same name. Mixes tracks Hendrix was compiling for The Next Album with studio and live performances 1968-1970.
ISLE OF WIGHT (Polydor 2302 016, 1971) Single-LP first issue of August 1970 appearance. Brilliant sound but eccentric track choice.
VARIOUS ARTISTS **ISLE OF WIGHT/ATLANTA** (Columbia G3X 30805, CBS 66311, 1971) Uneven selection of previously unissued material from both festival sets, interwoven with music from many other artists.
HENDRIX IN THE WEST (Polydor 2302 018, Reprise MS 2049, 1972) Uneven but entertaining selection from various 1969-1970 tour dates, ranging from the disposable ('God Save The Queen') to the essential ('Hear My Train A'Comin'').
MORE EXPERIENCE (Ember NR 5061, 1972) Strange further stirrings of the pot from the soundtrack to the Albert Hall concert stew.
WAR HEROES (Polydor 2302 020, Reprise MS 2103, 1972) A Mike Jeffery-inspired combination of studio offerings 1968-1970, from the sublime ('Tax Free', 'Izabella') to the ridiculous ('Peter Gunn Catastrophe').
A FILM ABOUT JIMI HENDRIX original soundtrack (Reprise K 64017 [UK], 2RS 6481 [US], 1973) Useful collation of live cuts and interviews telling the story of the film.
LOOSE ENDS (Polydor 2310 301, 1973) Weak last-gasp Jeffery compilation of studio material that still has its moments, including the first release of 'Drifter's Escape'.
CRASH LANDING (Reprise MS 2204, Polydor 2310 398, 1975) First of the Alan Douglas reconstitution jobs. Interesting.
MIDNIGHT LIGHTNING (Reprise MS 2229, Polydor 2310 415, 1975) Second of the Alan Douglas reconstitution jobs. Not so interesting.
ESSENTIAL JIMI HENDRIX VOLUME 1 (Reprise 2RS 2245, Polydor 2612 034, 1978) *Essential Jimi Hendrix Volume 2* (Reprise 2RS 2293, Polydor 2311 014, 1979) These were the first attempts since Hendrix's death to repackage his chart-topping material and combine it with some of the lesser-known album tracks.
NINE TO THE UNIVERSE (Reprise HS 2299, Polydor 2344 155, 1980) Specialist-only album's worth of instrumental jams, mainly from spring 1969.
THE JIMI HENDRIX CONCERTS (Reprise 2306, CBS 88592, 1982) First fresh dip into the live material since 1973 resulted in this musical smorgasbord covering dates from Winterland 1968 to Randall's Island 1970.
THE SINGLES ALBUM (Polydor PODV 6, 1983) A further attempt at and update of the *Smash Hits* concept.
BAND OF GYPSYS 2 (Capitol SJ 12416 [US], 064 26 1174 [UK], 1986) Grisly revisiting of Fillmore East concerts in less than optimum sound, fleshed out with tracks from Atlanta and Berkeley 1970.
JOHNNY B. GOODE (Capitol MLP 15022 [US], FA 2160 [UK], 1986) More scrapings from Atlanta and Berkeley 1970, in no particular order.
JIMI PLAYS MONTEREY (Reprise 25358, Polydor 827 990-2, 1986) First issue of the complete Hendrix set from the 1967 Monterey Pop festival.
LIVE AT WINTERLAND (Rykodisc RCD 20038, Polydor 833 004-2, 1987) Selection of tracks from a variety of October 1968 Winterland sets.
RADIO ONE (Rykodisc RAPL 0078-2 [US], Castle CCSLP 212 [UK], 1988) Incomplete first shot at releasing the BBC cache of Hendrix recordings.
LIVE & UNRELEASED (Castle Communications HBCD/LP 100, three-CD or five-LP set, 1989) Frustrating compilation of rare Hendrix, presented in snippets and combined with tedious if well-meaning radio programme.

CD-LED FIRST RELEASES, 1989-2003

RED HOUSE: VARIATIONS ON A THEME (Hal Leonard HL006600400, 1989) Specialist compilation of six different Hendrix 'Red House' performances, with a John Lee Hooker version added for good luck.
LIFELINES (Reprise 26435-2, four-CD set, 1990) Another long and well-meaning radio programme, this time with an add-on CD of selections from the April 1969 LA Forum gig.
STAGES (Reprise 28732-2, Polydor 511 783-2,

four-CD set, 1991) Good idea, shame about the execution. Four-CD set of Hendrix live, one concert each from the years 1967 to 1970. Poor sound mix, even on the later, well-recorded material, and no sign of the 1966 Paris material even though the 1967 disc is nowhere near full.
CALLING LONG DISTANCE (UniVibes UV-1001, 1992) First *UniVibes* magazine subscriber-only release: a collection of studio out-takes, TV and live performances, 1967-70, plus a December '67 Tony Hall interview.
BLUES (MCA 11060, Polydor 521 037-2, 1994) Alan Douglas's take on Hendrix as a blues musician. Worthy if uneven effort; copiously annotated, too.
EXP OVER SWEDEN (UniVibes UV-1002, 1994) Second *UniVibes* release concentrating on live Experience performances in Sweden, 1967-69.
WOODSTOCK (MCA 11063, Polydor 523 384-2, 1994) This is Douglas's view of the August 1969 Woodstock performance. Very personal sound mix and edit, with somewhere around half the concert represented.
VOODOO SOUP (MCA MCAD 11236, 1995) Alan Douglas's last Hendrix project, his elliptical version of The Last Album.
JIMI IN DENMARK (UniVibes UV-1003, 1995) Third *UniVibes* release, a collation of music and interviews taken from successive Hendrix tours of Denmark, 1967-70.
FIRST RAYS OF THE NEW RISING SUN (MCA/Experience Hendrix MCD 11599, 1997) The Hendrix Estate's version of The Last Album. Not really any closer to Hendrix's intentions than Douglas was on *Voodoo Soup*, judging by the lists he left behind at his death.
SOUTH SATURN DELTA (MCA/Experience Hendrix MCD 11684, 1997) Hendrix Estate's CD of leftovers from *First Rays* (see above), plus other studio odds and ends.
THE BBC SESSIONS (MCA/Experience Hendrix MCD 1742, two-CD set, 1998) (Almost) complete issue of the Hendrix BBC archive and an important release, marking not only the availability of this treasure-trove but a welcome change in issue policy towards complete (or near-complete) projects.
LIVE AT THE OAKLAND COLISEUM (Dagger DBRD2-11743, two-CD set, 1998) April 1969 concert, the first issue on Hendrix Estate's specialist label, Dagger. Mail-order only, direct from Experience Hendrix.
LIVE AT WOODSTOCK (MCA/Experience Hendrix MCD 11987, two-CD set, 1999) This second shot at getting Woodstock right still falls short of the mark: both of the Larry Lee features are missing and there are some questionable edits. At least the sound is better than before.
LIVE AT FILLMORE EAST (MCA/Experience Hendrix 111 931-2, two-CD set, 1999) A messy couple of CDs' worth of extra material from the 1969/70 new year's eve/day concerts at the Fillmore East. Maybe one day all four sets will be released in order of performance.
MERRY XMAS & HAPPY NEW YEAR (Experience Hendrix 088 155 651-2, 1999) The Band of Gypsys Christmas non-single issued as an extended CD single.
LIVE AT CLARK UNIVERSITY (Dagger DBRD 12033, 1999) Second Dagger release of live material, taken from a good sound source of this March 1968 concert.
MORNING SYMPHONY IDEAS (Dagger 088 112 353-2, 2000) Fascinating but extremely disparate collection of previously-unheard private tapes of Hendrix working out ideas and tunes. For specialists only.
THE JIMI HENDRIX EXPERIENCE (MCA/Experience Hendrix 112 316-2, four-CD set, 2000) Close, but no cigar. This interesting collation of outtakes, early versions, remixes and previously unissued songs from 1966-1970 misses some of the obvious material still floating around out there in bootleg-land.
LIVE IN OTTAWA (Dagger 088 112 737-2, 2001) Another Dagger release of live material from a March 1968 concert.
ALBERT HALL EXPERIENCE (Charly 822, two-CD set, 2001)A further shot at pulling together the complete February 24th 1969 Albert Hall concert. Sound quality still poor, concert still incomplete – despite what the liner-notes say.
THE SUMMER OF LOVE SESSIONS (Jungle 067, 2001)A single CD that focuses on the 1967 PPX material and at least spots the wood among the trees.
THE BAGGY'S REHEARSALS SESSIONS (Dagger 088 112956-2, 2002) Twelve tracks from the Band Of Gypsys studio rehearsals of late 1969.
THE RAINBOW BRIDGE CONCERT (Haze 001, two-CD set, 2002) Poor sound-quality issue of the two July 1970 Hawaii concerts.
WILD BLUE ANGEL: COMPLETE ISLE OF WIGHT 1970 (MCA/Experience Hendrix 113 082-2, two-CD set, 2002) First complete issue of the August 1970 Hendrix set. Only one niggle in an otherwise perfect release: why split the two CDs between two tracks that are tied together by Hendrix's guitar feedback and announcements?
JIMI HENDRIX EXPERIENCE: PARIS 1967/SAN FRANCISCO 1968 (Dagger CATF-0506-2, 2003) For specialists only: first full commercial issue of the Paris concert; first commercial release of amateur tapes of February 1968 Fillmore dates. Includes a version of Traffic's 'Dear Mr Fantasy'.
JIMI HENDRIX: LIVE AT BERKELEY (THE SECOND SET) (MCA/Experience Hendrix 986 075-2, 2003) First complete commercial issue of second May 1970 Berkeley set. Contains twelve selections, in concert order.

THE ALBUMS THAT MIGHT HAVE BEEN...

Hendrix's recorded output over just four years was phenomenal and he laid down much more material – studio and live – than appeared on albums and singles released at the time. He and his management also planned many more albums than appeared in his few years of fame. Here then is a speculative look at what could be made out of Hendrix's recorded legacy, given the will and a smidgen of tangential thinking. It's completely subjective, of course, being solely this author's perspective, is not meant to be definitive, but might just encourage others to try putting together new and intriguing collations of Hendrix's uncollected recording legacy. Some of the tracks listed are below Hendrix's normal studio standards and some are incomplete. Such tracks could never become part of the permanent Hendrix edition, especially on the albums he personally controlled. But perhaps Experience Hendrix would consider a limited-availability collectors-edition series of albums along these lines.

STUDIO ALBUMS

Standard albums 1967-1968
The three classic studio albums could each be released in expanded sets to encompass material recorded at the time but for various reasons not originally included.
ARE YOU EXPERIENCED (1967)
Laudably, Experience Hendrix has released a CD of this album that at last incorporates all the tracks put out on singles during the same period but not included on the album. However, there is more, including – potentially Beatles-*Anthology* style – the sensational cumulative takes of two of the album's best-known tracks.
Potential extra tracks: Lover Man, First Look Around The Corner, Midnight Lightning, Gypsy Blood, La Poupee Qui Fait Non, Teddy Bears Live Forever, Title B, Go My Own Way, Hound Dog. *Outtakes:* Red House, I Don't Live Today.
AXIS: BOLD AS LOVE (1967)
Potential extra tracks: Mr Bad Luck, Angel, Taking Care Of No Business, Cat Talking To Me, The Dragon From Carlisle.
ELECTRIC LADYLAND (1968)
Potential extra tracks: Dream, Dance, Little One (Mushy Name), Angel/Sweet Angel, South Saturn Delta, Tax Free, My Friend, Somewhere, Three Little Bears, Cherokee Mist, Room Full Of Mirrors (with Paul Caruso).

Proposed albums 1968-1970
Now for the albums that never happened. Some of these Hendrix and his circle talked about repeatedly in contemporary interviews; others stayed as projects that never even got that far.
FIRST WAVE OF THE NEW RISING SUN (1968/9) Look Over Yonder, Electric Church Red House, Calling All Devil's Children, Peace In Mississippi, New Rising Sun, Messenger, Izabella, Gypsy Blood, Room Full Of Mirrors, Shame Shame Shame/It's Too Bad, Lover Man, and four (untitled) jams.
SHINE ON, EARTH, SHINE ON (aka GYPSY SUN) (1969) Star Spangled Banner, Gypsy Boy, Midnight, Bleeding Heart, Trashman, Stone Free (Again), Hear My Train A'Comin', Ships Passing In The Night, Midnight Lightning (Devon Wilson/Paul Caruso version), Room Full Of Mirrors, Crash Landing, Valleys Of Neptune, Mannish Boy, Driving South, various jams including sessions with Larry Young, Stephen Stills, Johnny Winter, Jim McCarty.
GYPSY SUN & RAINBOWS (1969) Message To Love, Izabella, Beginning, Machine Gun, Jungle Jam/Captain Coconut, Burning Desire, Valleys Of Neptune, Lover Man, Blues For Me And You, Power Of Soul.
PEOPLE, HELL & ANGELS (BAND OF GYPSYS) (1969/70) Room Full Of Mirrors, Ezy Rider, Earth Blues, Stepping Stone, Izabella, Power Of Soul, Them Changes, Astro Man, Burning Desire, Message To Love, Send My Love To Linda, Country Blues, Midnight Lightning (unaccompanied version).
STRAIGHT AHEAD (1970) Hendrix's own (incomplete) list for a double vinyl LP was: ***SIDE A:*** Dolly Dagger, Night Bird Flying, Room Full Of Mirrors, Belly Button Window, Freedom. ***SIDE B:*** Ezy Rider, Astro Man, Drifting, Straight Ahead. ***SIDE C:*** Night Bird Flying, Drifter's Escape, Coming Down Hard On Me, Beginning, Cherokee Mist, Angel. ***SIDE D*** he left blank.

The songs Hendrix was working on diligently to bring to a final state during July and August 1970 would easily fill that last side D – as well as the gap on side three caused when he moved 'Night Bird Flying' from Side C to Side A.

So we can construct a version of Side D: Just Came In (In From The Storm), Valleys Of Neptune, Hey Baby (New Rising Sun), Stepping Stone, Earth Blues.

Other titles Hendrix spent much time developing during the summer but seems to have excluded from the immediate album in prospect include 'Izabella', 'Lover Man', 'Bleeding Heart', 'Burning Desire', 'Heaven Has No Sorrow', 'Hear My Train A'Comin'', 'Midnight Lightning' and 'Send My Love To Linda'. A live version of 'Hear My Train A'Comin'' plus a handful from Hendrix's list for his album would end up on the 'soundtrack' album for *Rainbow Bridge*, placed there by Mike Jeffery and his team after Hendrix's death. Cross-referencing to what was included in the film results in our next entry.
RAINBOW BRIDGE SOUNDTRACK (MOSTLY 1970) Earth Blues, Dolly Dagger, Bleeding Heart, Pali Gap, Hey Baby (New Rising Sun), Beginning, Look Over Yonder, New Rising Sun, Room Full Of Mirrors. Plus concert audio.

As far as studio albums go, that should more or less have been it, but the release listings above tell a markedly different story. Hendrix's death not only left important tracks incomplete but also removed his intentions from the equation. His premature death also left his management of the time with pressing considerations and commitments that had to be dealt with. All these contingencies resulted in the decisions that gave us the posthumous vinyl legacy we all know so well. These speculative lists suggest possible alternatives that are available to us today.

LIVE ALBUMS

WINTERLAND, SAN FRANCISCO, OCTOBER 10th-12th 1968 The original idea was to produce a single live LP from the Winterland engagement. The Experience played two sets on each of three consecutive evenings, October 10th, 11th, and 12th 1968. While it is now impossible to know the shape of the live album that Hendrix and his management may have been planning from these concerts, a special edition of the entire three days' playing would now make a fascinating addition to Hendrix's official recorded legacy. As it is, more than two CDs worth of material have been officially released in no particular order (mostly by Alan Douglas). Complete set-lists are: **October 10th, first show** Are You Experienced, Voodoo Child (Slight Return), Red House, Foxy Lady, Like A Rolling Stone, Star Spangled Banner, Purple Haze, Sunshine Of Your Love. **October 10th, second show** (* = Jack Casady on bass) Tax Free, Lover Man, Sunshine Of Your Love, Hear My Train A'Comin', Killing Floor*, Hey Joe*, jam, Star Spangled Banner, Purple Haze. **October 11th, first show** (* - Virgil Gonsalves on flute) Are You Experienced, jam*, Voodoo Child (Slight Return), Red House, Foxy Lady, jam, Star Spangled Banner, Purple Haze. **October 11th, second show** (* = Herbie Rich on organ) Tax Free, Spanish Castle Magic, Like A Rolling Stone*, Lover Man, Hey Joe, Fire, Foxy Lady, Purple Haze. **October 12th, first show** Fire, Lover Man, Like A Rolling Stone, Foxy Lady, Mitchell/Redding jam leading into Tax Free, Hey Joe, Purple Haze, Wild Thing. **October 12th, second show** Foxy Lady, Manic Depression, Sunshine Of Your Love, Little Wing, Spanish Castle Magic, Red House, Voodoo Child (Slight Return), Star Spangled Banner, Purple Haze.
ALBERT HALL, LONDON, FEBRUARY 24th 1969
All of the so-called 'complete' releases of this material issued so far seem to have been sourced from the sound mix of the film footage shot at the concert. Hendrix worked on multitrack mixes of some of the Albert Hall performances in early 1970 but nothing was concluded. Some tracks released on various Hendrix albums stem from the superior multitrack audio recordings made at the same time as the film track, but no complete concert release has yet appeared from this source. There is speculation that this is planned by the Hendrix Estate's Experience Hendrix label.
Set-list (* = Rocky Dijon on congas; ** = Rocky Dijon on congas, Chris Wood on flute, Dave Mason on guitar) Lover Man, Stone Free, Hear My Train A'Comin', I Dont Live Today, Red House, Foxy Lady, Sunshine Of Your Love, Bleeding Heart, Fire, Little Wing, Voodoo Chile (Slight Return)*, Room Full Of Mirrors**, Purple Haze (encore), Wild Thing (encore), Star Spangled Banner/ Smashing Of Amps.
LA FORUM APRIL 26th 1969
This concert was professionally recorded with the intention that its highlights – combined with those of others from the same US tour – would form the long-anticipated Experience live album. In fact nothing from the show was officially released until its appearance (incomplete) as a special 'extra' disc with the *Lifelines* package (see above) released in 1990 by Alan Douglas. During the long period between, the complete concert appeared many times, in excellent sound, on a range of bootlegs, usually across two CDs. **Set-list** Tax Free, Foxy Lady, I Don't Live Today, Red House, Spanish Castle Magic, Star Spangled Banner, Purple Haze, Voodoo Child (Slight Return), drum solo, Sunshine Of Your Love, Voodoo Child (Slight Return) reprise.
SAN DIEGO MAY 24th 1969
Alan Douglas released this concert on CD as part of the *Stages* set in 1991. The show was specifically recorded to use as one of the sources for a 1969 live album but this never appeared during Hendrix's lifetime and was superseded by *Hendrix In The West* after his death. **Set-list** Fire, Hey Joe, Spanish Castle Magic/Sunshine of Your Love, Red House, I Dont Live Today, Star Spangled Banner, Foxy Lady, Purple Haze, Voodoo Child (Slight Return).
LIVE EXPERIENCE (LA FORUM / SAN DIEGO)
This was the 1969 live album contemplated by Hendrix and his management for delivery to PPX/Capitol as part of the settlement with Ed Chalpin. But it was overtaken by events – including the break-up of the Experience and formation of Gypsy Sun & Rainbows. Although mixing and provisional track-selection took place that summer, the album was dropped before a complete definitive track order was established. Some tracks from the 1969 dates eventually appeared on the posthumous *Hendrix In The West*.
LIVE AT BERKELEY 1970 MAY 30th 1970
This appearance was filmed and recorded as part of the plan by Hendrix and Mike Jeffery to release live concerts so that Hendrix would not have to tour so extensively, but the project was allowed to slide. Some of the concert recordings were used on later posthumous releases guided by Jeffery. A CD of the second set from this concert was released in September 2003 by the Hendrix Estate's Experience Hendrix label, in conjunction with MCA, just as this book went to press. **Soundcheck** Message To Love, Blue Suede Shoes, Hey Baby (New Rising Sun), Earth Blues, Room Full Of Mirrors, Villanova Junction, Keep On Grooving (Midnight Lightning), Freedom, Paper Airplanes (Power Of Soul), Machine Gun. **First show set-list** Fire, Johnny B Goode, Hear My Train A'Comin', Foxy Lady, Machine Gun, Freedom, Red House, Message To Love, Ezy Rider, Star Spangled Banner, Purple Haze, Voodoo Child (Slight Return). **Second show set-list** Pass It On (Straight Ahead), Hey Baby (New Rising Sun), Lover Man, Stone Free, Hey Joe, I Don't Live Today, Machine Gun, Foxy Lady, Star Spangled Banner, Purple Haze, Voodoo Child (Slight Return).

key to photographs

After the relevant page number we list the illustration, followed by the photographer and/or agency. In a few instances, despite diligent efforts, we could not trace the owner of an image; we would welcome any further information so that we can provide the correct credit in future editions.

Jacket front Elliott Landy/Redfern's. **Jacket front flap** Baron Wolman. **Jacket rear** Baron Wolman. **Endpapers** Amalie Rothschild. **2/3** Michael Ochs/Redfern's. **6** Amalie Rothschild. **7** Baron Wolman. **8/9** University Of Washington Libraries. **10** Al Smith. **12/13** Michael Ochs/Redfern's. **14** UniVibes Collection. **15** UniVibes Collection. **17** UniVibes Collection. **18/19** Michael Ochs/Redfern's. **20** William Gottlieb/Redfern's. **21** Michael Ochs/Redfern's. **22** Michael Ochs/Redfern's. **24** Michael Ochs/Redfern's. **26/27** UniVibes Collection. **31** UniVibes Collection. **32** Michael Ochs/Redfern's. **36/37** Hulton Archive. **43** Davis Pearcy Collection. **46/47** UniVibes Collection. **50/51** all Sylvia Pitcher. **58/59** Sal Manzi. **61** Michael Ochs/Redfern's. **67** UniVibes Collection. **73** UniVibes Collection. **74/75** Ivan Keeman/Redfern's. **79** Jason Laure. **86/87** Jean-Pierre Leloir. **88** Robert John/UniVibes Collection. **89** Balafon Image Bank. **90** Pictorial Press. **91** London Features International. **93** Pictorial Press. **94/95** Rex Features. **97** Gunter Zint/Redfern's. **99** Rex Features. **100** Jan Olofsson/Redfern's. **102** Retna. **103** Petra Niemeier/Redfern's. **105** Rex Features. **107** both Pictorial Press. **108/109** Rex Features. **111** both Jan Persson. **113** Jan Persson. **115** Rex Features. **116** Ray Avery/Colin Beard. **119** Rex Features. **120** Michael Ochs/Redfern's. **121** Michael Ochs/Redfern's. **122/123** Pictorial Press. **124** Miki Slingsby. **126** London Features International. **127** both Mick Gold/Redfern's. **129** Val Wilmer. **130** Bruce Fleming/Rex. **131** Bruce Fleming/Rex. **132** Bruce Fleming/Rex. **134/135** Baron Wolman. **136** both Baron Wolman. **137** Baron Wolman. **141** Baron Wolman. **143** both Baron Wolman. **147** Roger Mayer. **150/151** Elliott Landy/Redfern's. **154** London Features International. **155** Elliott Landy/Redfern's. **158/159** Michael Ochs/Redfern's. **161** Michael Ochs/Redfern's. **162** Michael Ochs/Redfern's. **163** Michael Ochs/Redfern's. **165** Sal Manzi. **168/169** London Features International. **171** Rex Features. **174** Jan Persson. **175** Jan Persson. **176** Mirrorpix. **177** Mirrorpix. **178** David Redfern/Redfern's. **179** David Redfern/Redfern's. **180** Jan Persson. **187** Rex Features. **190/191** Allan Koss. **195** Allan Koss. **199** Allan Koss. **200/201** Experience Music Project. **202** Experience Music Project. **205** Experience Music Project. **207** David Redfern/Redfern's. **208** John Livzey. **210/211** Amalie Rothschild. **212** Amalie Rothschild. **213** Amalie Rothschild. **215** Amalie Rothschild. **217** Baron Wolman. **218** Baron Wolman. **219** Baron Wolman. **220/221** Michael Ochs/Redfern's. **225** Peter Sanders. **230** Jan Persson. **231** Jan Persson. **232** Jan Persson. **235** Michael Ochs/Redfern's. **239** K&K/Good Times/Redfern's. **242** Jan Persson. **244/245** Jan Persson. **246** Rex Features (top); Baron Wolman (below). **247** Peter Sanders. **248** Fender (left); Tom Copi/Frank Driggs Collection (top); Jan Persson (below). **249** Val Wilmer. **250** London Features International. **251** London Features International.

index

bibliography

NEWSPAPERS, JOURNALS AND PERIODICALS
The following publications proved valuable as sources for information on Jimi Hendrix: Beat Instrumental, Crawdaddy, The Daily Mirror, The Daily Telegraph, Down Beat, Guitar Player, Guitar World, Jazz & Pop, LA Free Press, Hitparader, Jimpress, Melody Maker, New Musical Express, The New York Times, The Observer, Record Mirror, Rolling Stone, Straight Ahead, UniVibes, The Village Voice.

BOOKS
Andy Aledort et al Jimi Hendrix: Band Of Gypsys: Transcribed Scores (Experience Hendrix/Hal Leonard undated)
Andy Aledort & Jesse Gress Jimi Hendrix: First Rays Of The New Rising Sun: Recorded Guitar Versions (Experience Hendrix/Hal Leonard undated)
Keith Altham The PR Strikes Back (Blake 2001)
Tony Bacon 50 Years Of Fender (Balafon/Miller Freeman 2000)
Tony Bacon (ed) Fuzz & Feedback: Classic Guitar Music Of The 60s (Balafon/Miller Freeman 2000)
Tony Bacon London Live (Balafon/Miller Freeman 1999)
Belmo/Steve Loveless Jimi Hendrix – Experience The Music (Collectors' Guide 1998)
Johnny Black Eyewitness: Jimi Hendrix (Carlton 1999)
Tony Brown Jimi Hendrix: A Visual Documentary – His Life, Loves and Music (Omnibus 1992)
Tony Brown Jimi Hendrix Concert Files (Omnibus 1999)
Tony Brown Jimi Hendrix In His Own Words (Omnibus 1994)
Tony Brown et al The Complete Book Of The British Charts (Omnibus 2000)
Ian Carr Miles Davis – A Critical Biography (Quartet 1982)
Martin Celmins Peter Green, Founder Of Fleetwood Mac (Sanctuary 1995)
Alan Clayson The Yardbirds (Balafon 2002)
Miles Davis with Quincy Troupe The Autobiography (Macmillan 1989)
Paul de Barros Jackson Street After Hours – The Roots Of Jazz In Seattle (Sasquatch 1993)
Sean Egan Not Necessarily Stoned, But Beautiful – The Making Of Are You Experienced (Unanimous 2002)
Kathy Etchingham & Andrew Crofts Through Gypsy Eyes – My Life, The Sixties and Jimi Hendrix (Gollancz 1998)
Ted Fox Showtime At The Apollo (Quartet 1983)
Gary Geldeart Look Over Yonder – A Comprehensive Guide To The Visual Archives Of Jimi Hendrix (Jimpress 1997)
Gary Geldeart & Steve Rodham Jimi Hendrix – The Studio Log (Jimpress 1996 and update 2000)
Gary Geldeart & Steve Rodham From The Benjamin Franklin Studios: A Complete Guide To

The Available Recordings Of Jimi Hendrix And Complete Bootleg Discography (Jimpress 1998 and updates)
Peter Guralnik Sweet Soul Music – Rhythm & Blues And The Southern Dream Of Freedom (Harper & Row)
John Hammond & Irving Townsend John Hammond On Record – An Autobiography (Penguin 1981)
Richie Havens & Steve Davidowitz They Can't Hide Us Anymore (HarperCollins 1999)
Lionel Hampton & James Haskins Hamp – An Autobiography (Warner 1989)
David Henderson 'Scuse Me While I Kiss The Sky – The Life Of Jimi Hendrix (Omnibus 2002)
James Allen Hendrix with Jas Obrecht My Son Jimi (AlJas Enterprises 1999)
The Jimi Hendrix Experience: Axis: Bold As Love: Transcribed Scores (Experience Hendrix/Hal Leonard undated)
Brian Hinton Message To Love – The Isle Of Wight Festival 1968/1969/1970 (Castle 1995)
John Kruth Bright Moments – The Life & Legacy Of Rahsaan Roland Kirk (Welcome Rain 2000)
Colin Larkin (ed) The Guinness Encyclopedia Of Popular Music (Guinness 1992)
Mike Leadbitter et al Blues Records 1943-1970 (Record Information Services 1994)
John McDermott & Eddie Kramer Setting The Record Straight (Little Brown 1992)
John McDermott et al Jimi Hendrix Sessions: The Complete Recording Sessions 1963-70 (Little Brown 1995)
Mitch Mitchell & John Platt The Hendrix Experience (Hamlyn 1990)
Charles Shaar Murray Crosstown Traffic – Jimi Hendrix And Post-war Pop (Faber 1989)
Bill Nitopi Cherokee Mist – The Lost Writings (Harper Collins 1993)

Noel Redding & Carol Appleby Are You Experienced? – The Inside Story Of The Jimi Hendrix Experience (Picador 1990)
Steven Roby Black Gold – The Lost Archives Of Jimi Hendrix (Billboard 2002)
Michel Ruppli Atlantic Records – A Discography (Greenwood 1979)
Michel Ruppli The Chess Labels – A Discography (Greenwood 1983)
Michel Ruppli The King Labels – A Discography (Greenwood 1985)
Michel Ruppli The Mercury Labels – A Discography (Greenwood 1993)
Joel Selvin Monterey Pop (Chronicle 1992)
Harry Shapiro & Caesar Glebbeek Jimi Hendrix: Electric Gypsy (Heinemann 1990)
Arnold Shaw Honkers And Shouters – The Golden Age Of Rhythm & Blues (Collier 1978)
Wes Smith The Pied Pipers Of Rock 'n' Roll – Radio Deejays Of The 50s and 60s (Longstreet 1989)
Dallas Taylor Prisoner Of Woodstock (Thunder's Mouth 1994)
Chris Welch Hendrix – A Biography (Ocean 1972)
Chris Welch Cream – The Legendary Sixties Supergroup (Balafon 2000)
Joel Whitburn The Billboard Book of USA Top Hits Fifth Edition (Billboard 1992)
Joel Whitburn Top R&B Singles 1942-1999 Billboard (Record Research 2000)
Charles White The Life & Times Of Little Richard, The Quasar Of Rock (Pan 1985)
Dave Whitehill The Jimi Hendrix Experience: Electric Ladyland: Transcribed Scores (Experience Hendrix/Hal Leonard undated)
Dave Whitehill & Andy Aledort The Jimi Hendrix Experience: Are You Experienced: Transcribed Scores (Experience Hendrix/Hal Leonard undated)
Mary Willix Jimi Hendrix: Voices From Home (Creative Forces Publishing 1995)

acknowledgements

The publisher, Backbeat UK, would like to thank: Bill Allerton, Andy Babiuk, Keith Badman, Niko Bauer (earlyhendrix.com), Don Bernstine (Hard Rock Cafe), Johnny Black, Joel J. Brattin, Dave Brewis, Walter Carter (Gibson), Doug Chandler, Paul Cooper, Paul Day, Kees de Lange, Simon Edwards (Universal), Tony Gale (Pictorial Press), Caesar Glebbeek (UniVibes), Dave Gregory, Douglas Hinman, Dave Hunter, Allan Koss, Jason Laure, Sal Manzi, Roger Mayer, Joe McMichael, John Morrish, David Nathan (National Jazz Archive), Andy Neill, Bill Nitopi, Douglas J. Noble, Jan Persson, Martin Pittaway (Mirrorpix), Greg Prevost, Claus Rasmussen, Julian Ridgeway (Redfern's), Steve Rodham (Jimpress), Alan Rogan, Janette Beserbrook (Experience Music Project), Amalie Rothschild, Harry Shapiro, Rich Siegel (Fender), Kim Simmonds, Miki Slingsby, Brad Smith (Hal Leonard), Jake Steele (Experience Music Project), Peter Symes, Andrew Thompson (Experience Music Project), Chris Welch, Jon Wilton (Redfern's), Baron Wolman.

The author, Keith Shadwick, has included his acknowledgements in the introduction at the start of the book.

Douglas J. Noble, author of the Hendrix Gear appendix, would like to thank Caesar Glebbeek.

"For as yet I did not understand fame, that public destruction of one in the process of becoming, into whose building-ground the mob breaks, displacing his stones."
RAINER MARIA RILKE THE NOTEBOOK OF MALTE LAURIDS BRIGGE (HOGARTH PRESS 1930) TRANSLATED BY JOHN LINTON

BLT 5/04

Shadwick, Keith,
1951-

Jimi Hendrix.

DATE			